Preface

Many manufacturers are using computer-aided solid modeling to help create new product designs and revise existing ones. Drawing a solid model of a product has advantages over using standard two-dimensional drawings:

- Once the solid model is drawn, different viewpoints of the model provide any standard two-dimensional drawings.
- Three-dimensional drawings from any viewpoint can be made.
- Different materials can be assigned to the model so that engineering information that influences the design can be obtained.
- Once the solid model is drawn, other engineering documentation, such as volume, area, weight, and center of gravity, can be obtained.

AutoDesk's Designer Program and AutoCAD SOLIDS commands do all of the above and also provide a means of rendering the solid model to obtain a shaded image of the model in color.

Engineering Drawings and Models Using AutoCAD Solid Modeling and Designer leads the student through the basics of AutoCAD two-dimensional drawing and into the three-dimensional environment of solid modeling using the commands found on the SOLIDS Menu and AutoCAD Designer. Tutorial exercises in each drawing chapter are used to teach new topics that are introduced. A Prompt/Response format leads the reader through each new AutoCAD command to avoid confusion and frustration. No previous AutoCAD experience is necessary to use this book.

The text is divided into four parts:

I The AutoCAD Program
II Two-Dimensional Drawing
III Solid Modeling
IV The AutoCAD Designer Program

The text includes many features designed to help the reader master the AutoCAD and Designer Programs:

- An overview of what solid modeling is, how it is used, and what hardware and software is necessary to run the program efficiently.
- Menus located in the margins help the user to locate AutoCAD commands within the AutoCAD menus and submenus for both DOS and Windows.
- Over 400 figures support the text and reinforce the material.
- Tutorial exercises give the student the necessary AutoCAD two-dimensional background for effectively using solid modeling.
- Tutorial exercises lead the student through drawing basic solid shapes, creating complex models, making changes to solid models, and using advanced Designer commands.
- Region modeling, which allows you to make three-dimensional models from two-dimensional drawings, is described.
- Learning objectives and review questions in every chapter reinforce the learning process.
- Practice exercises in every chapter review the topics learned.
- An *Instructor's Manual* is available to support the text.

This text is designed to give engineering students the necessary AutoCAD two-dimensional background for using solid modeling. It then teaches solid modeling in detail to give the student a complete engineering graphics package.

For computer-aided design students, this text provides a review of two-dimensional AutoCAD. It then uses tutorial exercises to provide an extensive solid modeling learning package based on real-world applications for manufacturing industries.

Engineering Drawings and Models Using AutoCAD® Solid Modeling and Designer

JAMES M. KIRKPA
Eastfield College

Prentice Hall
Upper Saddle River, New Jersey *Columbus, Ohio*

Library of Congress Cataloging-in-Publication Data

Kirkpatrick, James M.
Engineering drawings and models using AutoCAD solid modeling and designer / James M. Kirkpatrick.
p. cm.
Includes index.
ISBN 0-02-364463-X
1. Mechanical drawing. 2. Engineering models. 3. AutoCAD (Computer file) 4. AutoCAD Designer. 5. Computer-aided design.
I. Title.
T353.K57 1997
604.2′0285′5369—dc20 96-15282
CIP

Editor: Stephen Helba
Production Editor: Stephen C. Robb
Design Coordinator: Julia Zonneveld Van Hook
Cover Designer: Proof Positive/Farrowlyne Associates
Production Manager: Deidra M. Schwartz
Production Supervision: Karen Fortgang, bookworks
Marketing Manager: Danny Hoyt

This book was set in Times Roman and Folio by Clarinda Company and was printed and bound by Quebecor Printing/Semline. The cover was printed by Phoenix Color Corp.

Printed in the United States of America

10 9 8 7 6 5 4 3 2 1

ISBN: 0-02-364463-X

Prentice-Hall International (UK) Limited, *London*
Prentice-Hall of Australia Pty. Limited, *Sydney*
Prentice-Hall Canada Inc., *Toronto*
Prentice-Hall Hispanoamericana, S. A., *Mexico*
Prentice-Hall of India Private Limited, *New Delhi*
Prentice-Hall of Japan, Inc., *Tokyo*
Simon & Schuster Asia Pte. Ltd., *Singapore*
Editora Prentice-Hall do Brasil, Ltda., *Rio de Janeiro*

Contents

PART I THE AUTOCAD PROGRAM

1 Introduction

OBJECTIVES

When you have completed this chapter, you will be able to:

□ Describe the purpose of this book.
□ Identify the types of models and drawings to be drawn using this textbook.
□ Describe how the textbook is organized.

INTRODUCTION

Computer-aided solid modeling is currently being used by many manufacturers to help create new product designs and revise existing ones. Drawing a solid model of a product has the following advantages over using standard two-dimensional (2-D) drawings:

□ Once the solid model is drawn, different viewpoints of the model can provide any standard 2-D drawings.
□ Three-dimensional drawings can be made from any viewpoint.
□ Different materials can be assigned to the model to provide engineering information that influences the design.
□ Once the solid model is drawn, other engineering documentation, such as volume, area, weight, and center of gravity can be obtained.

AutoDesk's Designer Program and AutoCAD SOLIDS commands perform all the tasks listed and also provide a means of rendering the solid model to obtain a shaded color image of the model.

PURPOSE

The purpose of this book is to present information so that you can learn solid modeling by actually drawing with the AutoCAD and Designer programs. A minimum number of pages is devoted to subjects that do not involve hands-on use of AutoCAD and Designer commands.

The book is written for both DOS and Windows versions of AutoCAD Release 13 and AutoCAD Designer Release 1.2. Although many of the commands used in this book exist in earlier versions of AutoCAD, the new SOLIDS Menu and the commands on that menu are new to Release 13. The Advanced Modeling Extension (AME) used in earlier versions has been replaced by the SOLIDS commands on the SOLIDS menu found in Release 13.

The text leads you through the basics of AutoCAD 2-D drawing and into the 3-D environment of solid modeling using the commands found on the SOLIDS menu and AutoCAD Designer. Tutorial exercises in each drawing chapter are used to teach new topics that are introduced. A Prompt/Response format leads you through each new AutoCAD command to prevent confusion and frustration. No previous AutoCAD experience is necessary to use this book.

Types of Drawings and Models

The following are the types of drawings and models that you will produce while completing this book:

Two-dimensional geometric constructions
Two-dimensional manufacturing drawings
Sectional drawings
Three-dimensional solid geometric constructions
Complex solid models
Dimensioned drawings
Two-dimensional drawings from 3-D models
Exploded views
Rendered illustrations in color
Parametric models

These drawings are described briefly in the following paragraphs. Later chapters describe them in greater detail.

Two-Dimensional Geometric Constructions

Two-dimensional geometric constructions are the building blocks of all types of drawings. Terms such as *parallel, perpendicular, horizontal, vertical,* and *tangent* are defined, and the concepts are used to create these constructions. The term *geometric* may sound as if higher-level math will be required; this is not the case in computer-aided design as presented in this book. If you can add, subtract, multiply, and divide on a calculator, you can make all the drawings and models in this book. Figure 1–1 shows the geometric constructions covered in Chapter 6. These constructions are often difficult to draw manually, but

FIGURE 1–1
Geometric Constructions

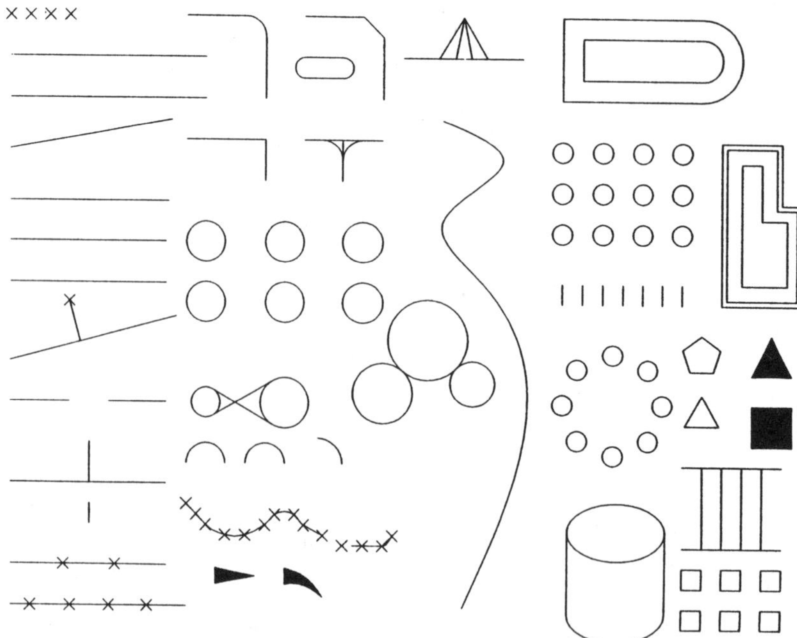

are easy to do with the computer. If the correct commands are used to draw them, the constructions can be extremely accurate and beautifully drawn.

Two-Dimensional Manufacturing Drawings

Two-dimensional, or orthographic, drawings are the universal language of technical drawing. Only two dimensions are seen in any one view. Those dimensions may be height and width, height and depth, or width and depth. Figure 1–2 shows some examples of orthographic drawings. The top drawing shows three views of a single object. The middle drawing is a two-view drawing of a design for an acoustical guitar. The bottom drawing is a floor plan showing a single view of a structure. Further details are presented in a later chapter.

Sectional Drawings

Sectional drawings are used in many different industries to clarify internal or hidden external construction. AutoCAD allows the spacing of shading lines to be very accurate and eliminates the tedious task of drawing those lines. The drawing on the left in Figure 1–3 could have been created by establishing a construction plane through a solid object and using the Section: command.

Three-Dimensional Solid Geometric Constructions

The solid geometric constructions shown in Figure 1–4 are described in Chapter 10. These are the building blocks used for complex solid models in later chapters.

Complex Solid Models

Figure 1–5 shows several complex models created with SOLIDS commands in AutoCAD. Each model is a composite of geometric shapes that have been welded together using the Union: command and holes that have been subtracted from the composite with the Subtract: command. These models can now be used to create 2-D drawings and can be rendered in color.

Dimensioned Drawings

A dimensioned drawing is a type of orthographic drawing that gives the size and location of features. AutoCAD is very useful in dimensioning because it can become almost automatic when drawings are made full size. The top two illustrations of Figure 1–6 show two drawings that have been drawn full size and dimensioned using AutoCAD. The bottom illustration of Figure 1–6 shows a drawing that has been dimensioned using geometric tolerances. All drawings used to build parts have tolerances (limits) that are placed on all dimensions. For example, a tolerance of ±.005 on a 3.000″ dimension means that the part, when inspected, must measure between 3.005″ and 2.995″ to pass. AutoCAD allows parts to be drawn and dimensioned with extreme accuracy.

Two-Dimensional Drawings from Three-Dimensional Models

AutoCAD and Designer give you ways to create 2-D drawings automatically from 3-D models. These drawings may then be dimensioned and annotated as if they had originally been drawn in two dimensions. Figure 1–7 shows an example of a 2-D drawing that was created automatically from a 3-D model.

Exploded Views

Exploded views are often used in manuals that are used to build, assemble, install, and repair equipment. Figure 1–8 shows an exploded view. Many of you have used exploded views to assemble a bicycle, fix a car, or hook up a VCR.

Rendered Illustrations in Color

Figure 1–9 shows a black-and-white rendering done with the Shade: command. Shaded renderings can also be done in color. The Render: command is used to produce more realistic renderings. AutoVision and 3D Studio (not part of the standard package) can be used to produce very realistic renderings of AutoCAD models and animate them.

FIGURE 1–2
Orthographic Drawings

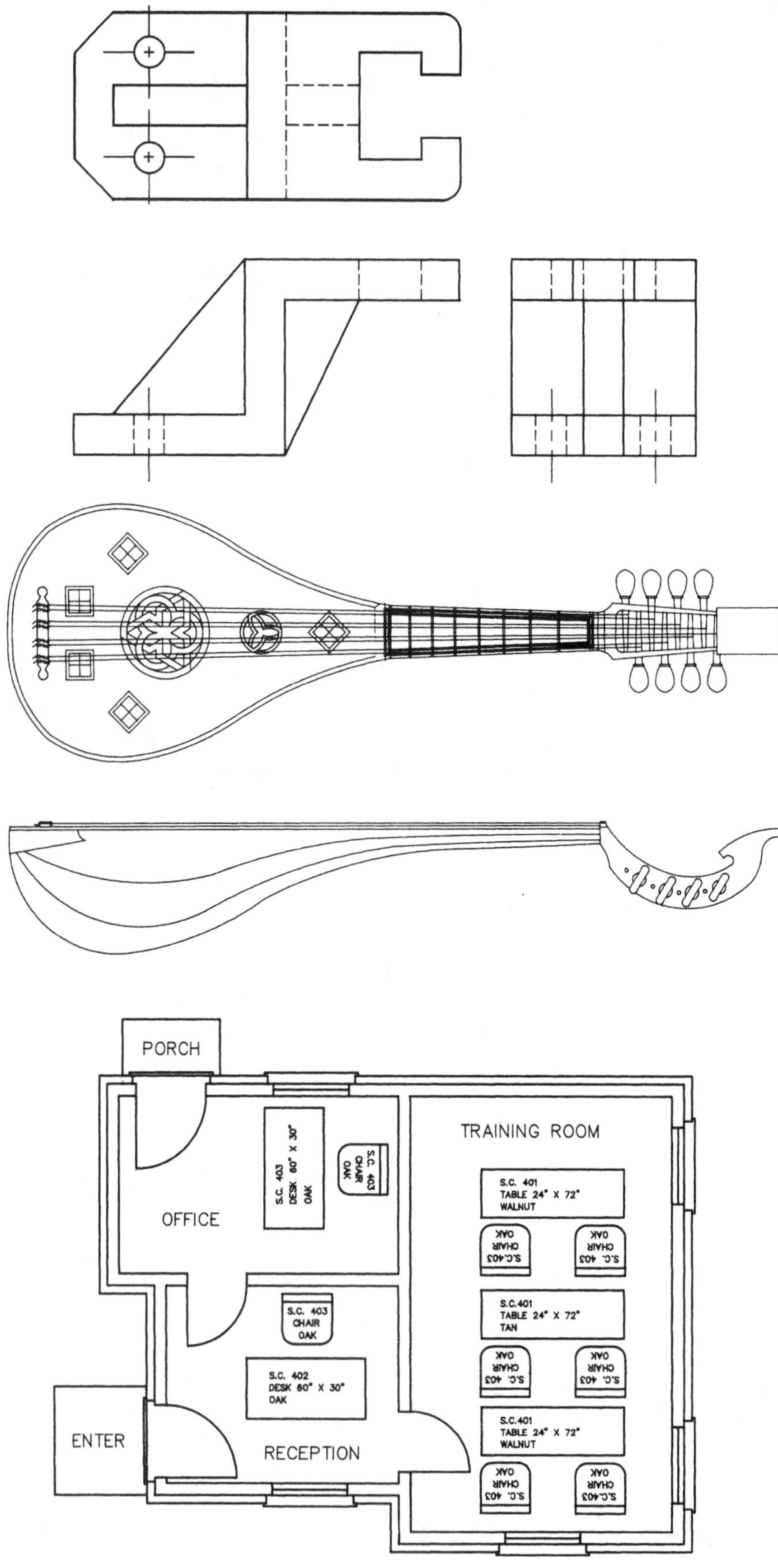

FIGURE 1–3
Sectional Drawings

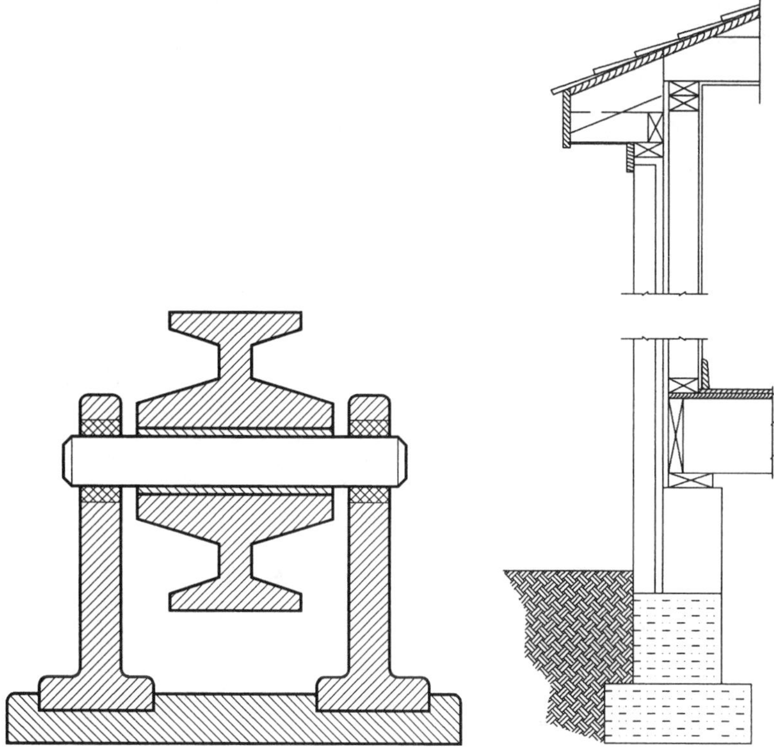

Parametric Models

AutoCAD Designer allows you to create parametric models. You can think of parameters as the measurements of the part. When you apply parametrics to modeling parts, the parameters define the size and shape of the part. You make design changes by changing the parameters and let AutoCAD Designer redraw the part. The part shown in Figure 1–10 was changed from the shape on the left side to the shape on the right side by typing a different number for the parameters defining the length and height of the part and using other Designer commands to change the sizes of and to delete other features. Designer reshaped the part. Designer also automatically made the drawings in Figure 1–7 from the solid model in Figure 1–10.

FIGURE 1–4
3-D Solid Geometric Constructions

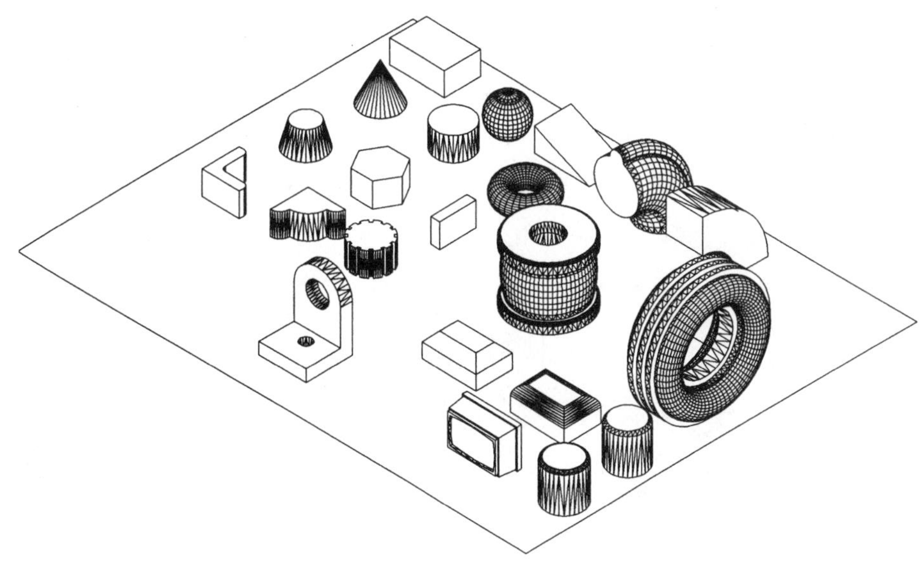

FIGURE 1–5
Complex Solid Models

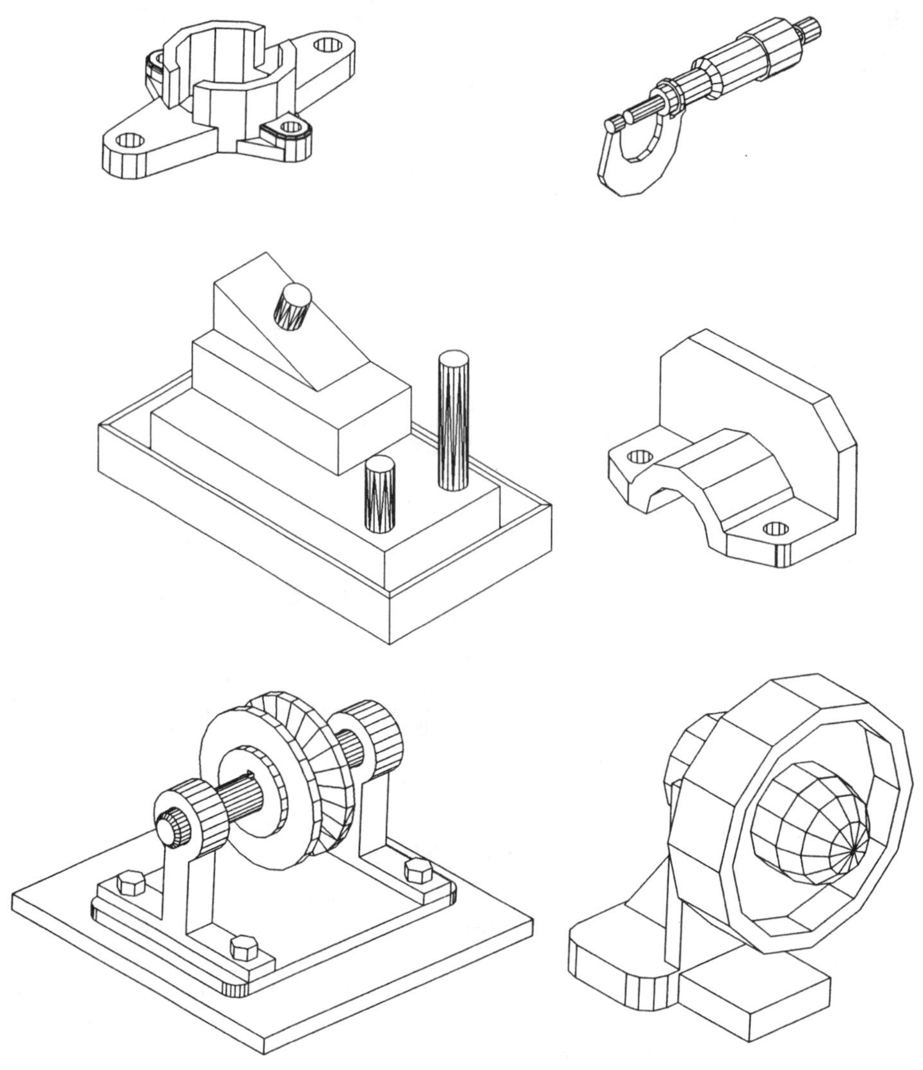

FIGURE 1–6
Dimensioned Drawings

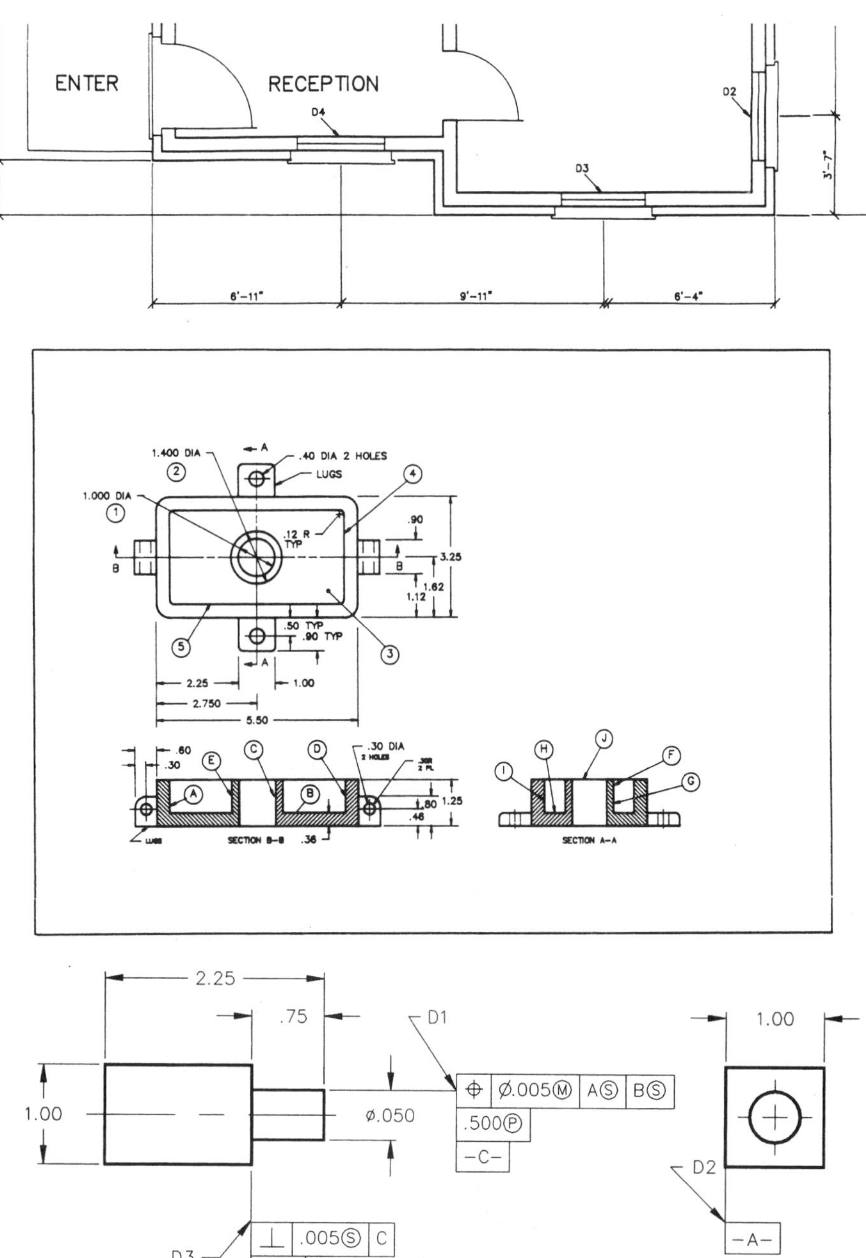

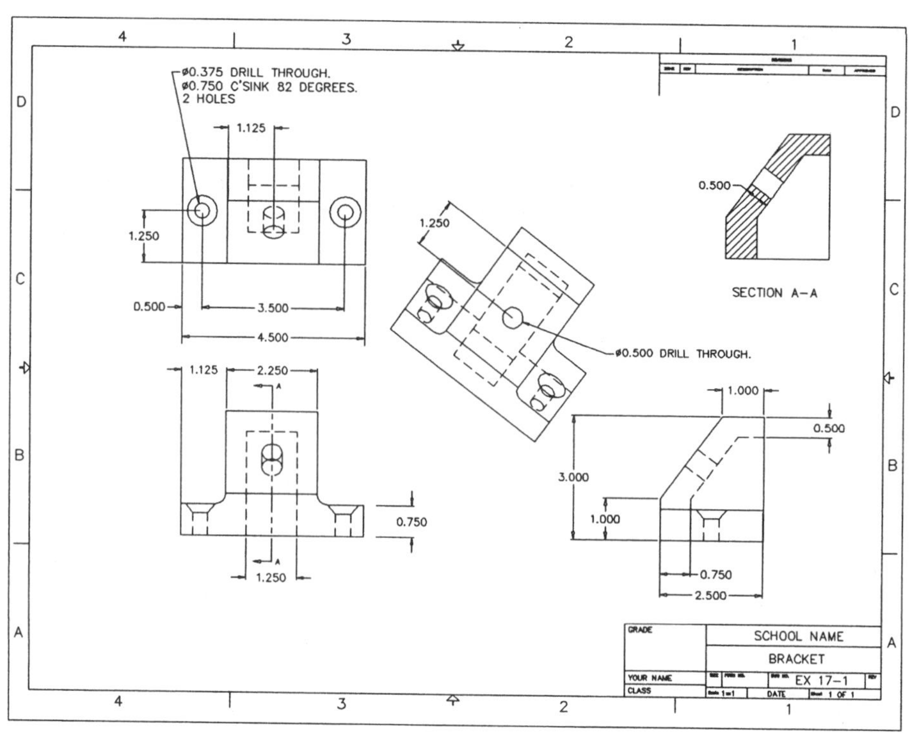

FIGURE 1–7
2-D Drawings from a 3-D Model

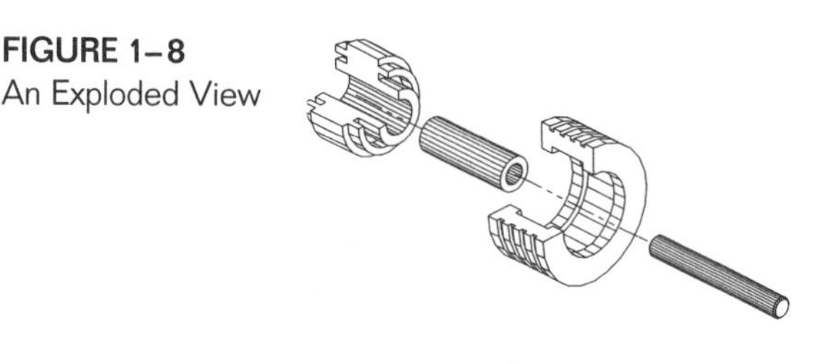

FIGURE 1–8
An Exploded View

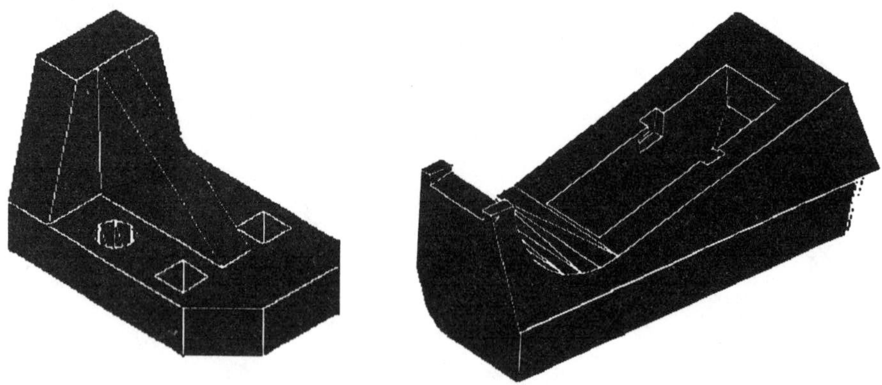

FIGURE 1–9
Solid Models Rendered with the Shade Command

FIGURE 1–10
Parametric Models

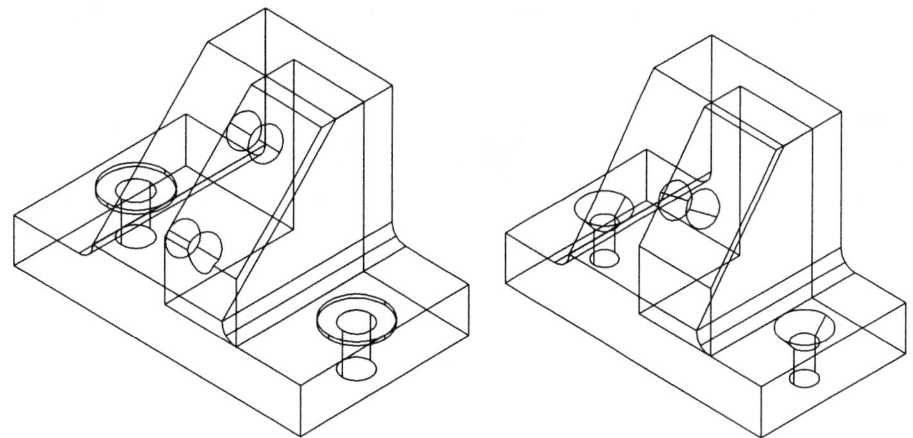

REVIEW QUESTIONS

1. What is the purpose of this book?

   ____

   ____

2. List the menu that contains the commands that replaced the Advanced Modeling Extension (AME) of earlier versions of AutoCAD.

   ____

3. List 10 types of drawings and models described in this book.

   ____

   ____

   ____

   ____

   ____

   ____

   ____

   ____

   ____

   ____

4. Define the following:

   Two-dimensional drawing ____________________

   ____

   Sectional drawing ____________________

   ____

   Solid model ____________________

   ____

   Parametric model ____________________

   ____

5. List two programs that are not part of AutoCAD that can be used to render and animate solid models.

   ____________________ ____________________

2 The AutoCAD Program for DOS

OBJECTIVES

When you have completed this chapter, you will be able to:

- □ Start the AutoCAD Program for DOS.
- □ Describe the AutoCAD for DOS screen, and begin using parts of the screen.
- □ Describe the AutoCAD Tablet menu.

EXERCISE 2–1
ACTIVATING THE AUTOCAD PROGRAM FOR DOS AND DESCRIBING THE PARTS OF THE AUTOCAD FOR DOS SCREEN

Start the AutoCAD Program for DOS

Step 1. Turn on the computer and start AutoCAD for DOS.

AutoCAD for DOS may be activated in one of two ways:

1. In many situations, once the computer has been turned on, the screen will display a menu of programs and functions loaded in the computer. Pick the letter or number corresponding to AutoCAD for DOS to begin AutoCAD.

or

2. If the computer you are working with displays a Root directory prompt such as C:\, you must make sure you are in the AutoCAD directory. The AutoCAD directory is often named ACADR13. Type CD\ACADR13 from the keyboard and then press the enter key to access the AutoCAD directory. Then type ACAD and press the enter key to start the AutoCAD program. If the system is configured so that you need to type ACAD13 or some other variation to start the AutoCAD program, you need to learn the proper command to use.

Also, if the system is configured so that the AutoCAD program can be started directly from the Root directory prompt, you need to know that to use it. For instance, if the system is configured so that typing and entering **A** to the Root directory prompt starts the AutoCAD program, it is quicker to use that response.

When AutoCAD R13 for DOS is started, the AutoCAD for DOS screen appears (Figure 2–1). It provides the display area for drawing and the commands used to create, modify, view, and plot drawings. You can begin by naming the new drawing, or you may immediately begin drawing without naming the drawing. When you are ready to end the drawing session, you must save the drawing using Save: or Save As:, at which time you must name the drawing. Details of how to start new drawings or call up existing ones are included in Chapter 4.

AutoCAD communicates with you on various parts of the screen. A brief introduction to each part of the screen (Figure 2–1) follows.

FIGURE 2–1
AutoCAD for DOS Screen

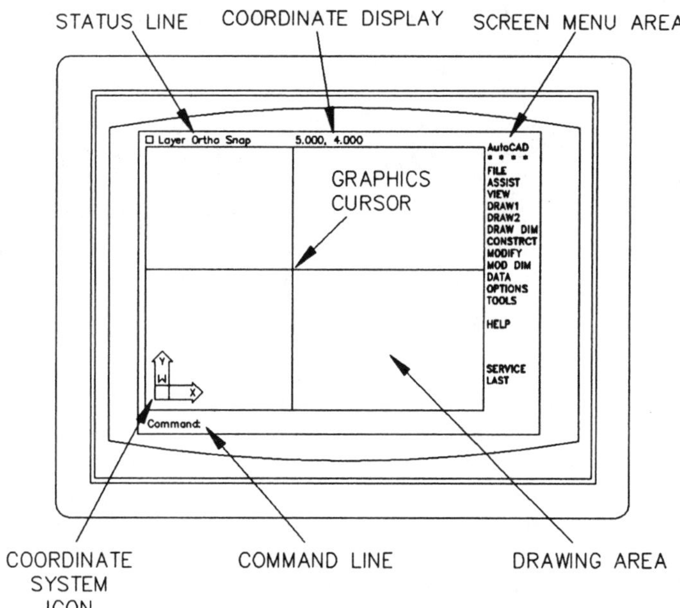

The AutoCAD for DOS Screen

Step 2. Learn the various parts of the AutoCAD for DOS screen.

Drawing Area and Graphics Cursor

The drawing area is where your drawing is displayed. The graphics cursor (or cross hairs) follows the movement of a mouse or puck when points of a drawing are entered or a command is selected.

Command Line

The command line area is where AutoCAD communicates with you once a command is activated. AutoCAD prompts you to enter specific information to further define a command and then responds with action on the screen or additional prompts. Always watch the command line to make sure you and AutoCAD are communicating.

Coordinate System Icon

The coordinate system icon shows the orientation of the X, Y, and Z axes of the current coordinate system. When AutoCAD is started, you are in the World Coordinate System (WCS), as indicated by the W in the coordinate system icon.

Coordinate Display

In an X and Y axis coordinate system, the coordinate display numbers tell you where the cursor or cross hairs on the screen are located in relation to point 0,0 (the lower left corner).

Status Line

The status line keeps you informed about your drawing by displaying the current drawing layer and the status of modes that affect your drawing.

Screen Menus

FIGURE 2–2
Screen Root Menu

The screen root menu (Figure 2–2) on the right side of the AutoCAD for DOS screen contains the complete AutoCAD command set. Items on the screen root menu when highlighted and clicked (press the left mouse button once) take you to a detailed menu of related commands. Many of the commands are used and described in the following chapters; however, the brief description of the screen menu items on the following pages provides an introduction.

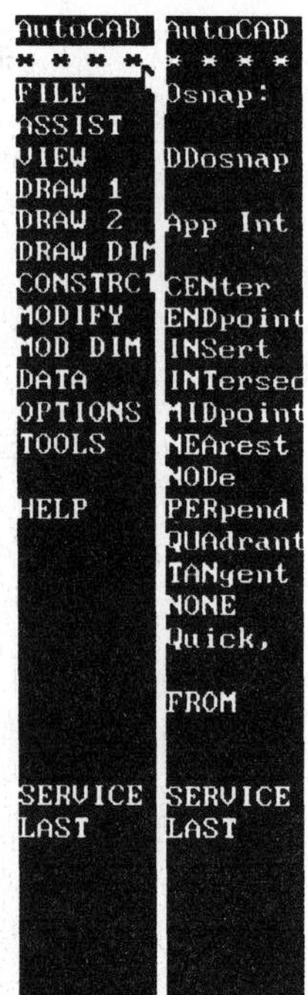

FIGURE 2–3
Osnap Menu

Step 3. Pick each screen root menu item and view the command menus.

AutoCAD This item remains constant and appears on the screen root menu and all command menus. When you are in a command menu, picking AutoCAD returns you to the screen menu.

******** (Figure 2–3) This item leads you to a menu of features called object snap (Osnap). Osnap features help you to draw very accurately. Some of the features are CENter, ENDpoint, and INTersection. The capital letters indicate what must be typed to activate the Osnap mode from the keyboard.

Pick AutoCAD at the top of the menu to return to the screen menu.

FILE (Figure 2–4) This menu contains the commands needed to start a new drawing, open an existing one, save a drawing, print a drawing, import and export data, manage files, and exit from the AutoCAD program. It also contains commands related to external references. An external reference is attached to a primary drawing. Any changes made to the external reference drawing are reflected in the primary drawing each time the primary drawing is loaded in AutoCAD.

ASSIST (Figure 2–5) This menu contains the Undo: command (allows you to undo or reverse the most recent command) and the Redo: command (will redo one undo). You can also set the Grid (a visible pattern of dots for your drawing) and Snap (an invisible pattern of dots to which your cross hairs snap). Ortho can be turned off and on; when Ortho is on, you can draw lines perfectly horizontal and vertical.

The Select:, Filter:, Group:, and PikStyl: commands on this menu are used to group drawing entities (such as circles, lines, and arcs) for editing. The Select: command allows you to preselect items to be edited. Then the option Previous in the SERVICE menu can be picked to refer to the selection set. Filter: allows you to define a list of properties and select items that have those properties. Group: is a command that allows you to preselect items so they may be selected as a group by name. PICKSTYLE is a system variable.

When picked, INQUIRY leads you to a menu of commands used to obtain information about the drawing. The List: command gives you information about drawing entities, such as the length of lines, the sizes of circles and arcs, the location of entities, and the names of blocks and the layers on which they reside. The ID: command displays and identifies the coordinates of a designated point in the drawing for a one-time use in the following command. The Dist: command gives you the distance between two selected points. The Area: command calculates the area and perimeter that are enclosed by points you enter, and MassPro: calculates and displays the mass properties of regions or solids.

The Cancel: command cancels a command.

FIGURE 2–4
File Menu

VIEW (Figure 2–6) The View menu contains all the commands that control the appearance of your drawing display. When Redraw: is picked, AutoCAD redraws and cleans up your drawing. Any blips (small crosses caused by picking points or selecting objects) disappear, and drawing entities affected by editing other objects are redrawn. RedrwAl: is used when more than one viewport is on the screen. (The screen may be divided into areas each of which contains the same or different views of the drawing. These areas are called *viewports*.)

The Zoom: commands control the magnification of any part of the display. Pan: allows you to move to another part of the display at the same magnification.

DDview uses a dialog box to name, save, and restore selected views of your drawing. Plan:, Vpoint:, Dview, and several other commands are used in 3-D display.

The remaining commands on the VIEW menu are varied and can be used to create multiple viewports, change to paper space (a presentation mode) from model space (where you draw your drawing), and change the location of the coordinate system.

DRAW 1 (Figure 2–7) The DRAW 1 menu contains commands used to draw lines, arcs, circles, donuts, ellipses, rectangles, polygons, and 2-D solid areas.

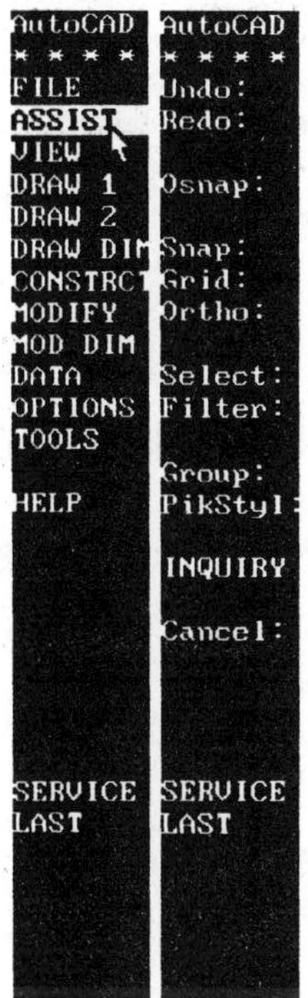

FIGURE 2–5
ASSIST Menu

FIGURE 2–6
VIEW Menu

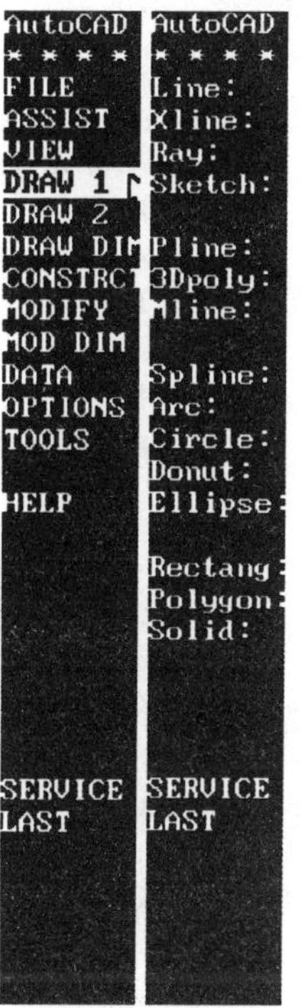

FIGURE 2–7
DRAW 1 Menu

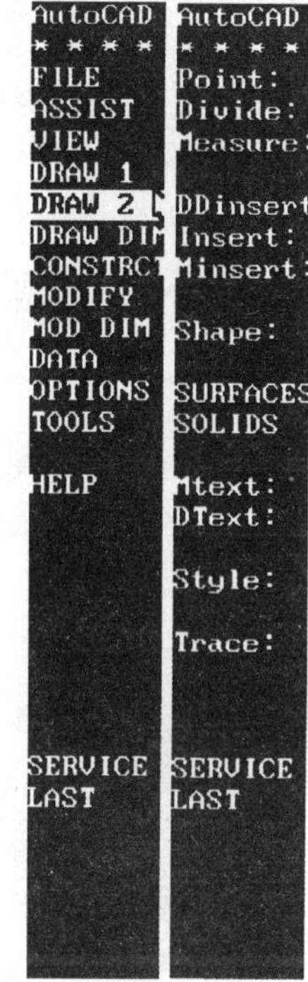

FIGURE 2–8
DRAW 2 Menu

DRAW 2 (Figure 2–8) The DRAW 2 menu contains commands used to draw points (used as markers), divide drawing entities into equal parts, measure a specified distance along an entity, insert blocks and shapes, insert drawings into other drawings, create a text style, and place text on drawings.

The SURFACES menu is used to draw 3-D surface models. The SOLIDS menu is used to draw 3-D solid models.

DRAW DIM (Figure 2–9) The DRAW DIM menu contains all the commands necessary to place dimensions and tolerances on drawings.

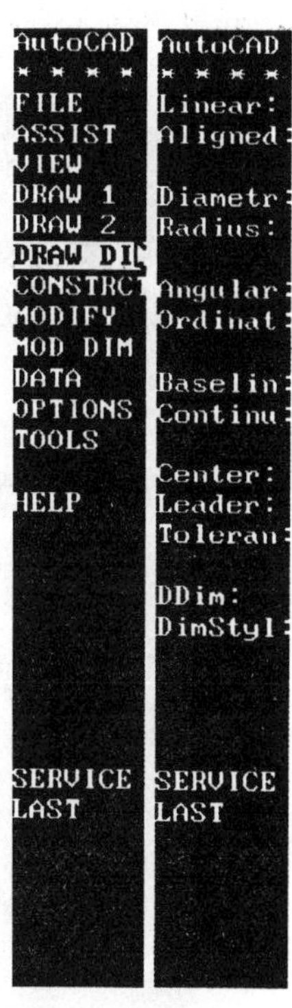

FIGURE 2–9
DRAW DIM Menu

CONSTRCT (Figure 2–10) The CONSTRCT menu contains commands used to create objects from existing objects. These commands include Copy:, Offset:, Mirror:, Array:, Chamfer:, and Fillet:.

Commands used for cross hatching are Bhatch: (boundary hatch) and Boundary: (creates the boundary). PSfill: (PostScript fill) is used to shade areas. The Region: command is used in 2-D to create an enclosed area that can be analyzed, and in the creation of solid 3-D models.

The DDatDef: command allows you to add information text to a block.

The attribute information can be extracted from the drawing using the Attext: command.

3Darray:, Mirro3D:, and Rotat3D: are all used to create objects from existing objects in 3-D.

MODIFY (Figure 2–11) The MODIFY menu contains commands that are used to change existing drawing entities. The Modify:, Change:, and Ddchpro: (dynamic dialog change properties) all change entity properties such as layer, color, and linetype. Other commands allow you to Move:, Rotate:, Align:, Stretch:, Scale:, Lengthn:, Trim:, Extend:, and Break: existing entities. There is a group of edit commands that edit polylines, multilines, splines, text, hatching, and attributes. The Erase: command on the MODIFY menu erases entities, and the Oops: command will restore everything erased by the last Erase: command.

MOD DIM (Figure 2–12) The MOD DIM menu contains commands used to save and restore a dimensioning style and to edit existing dimensions.

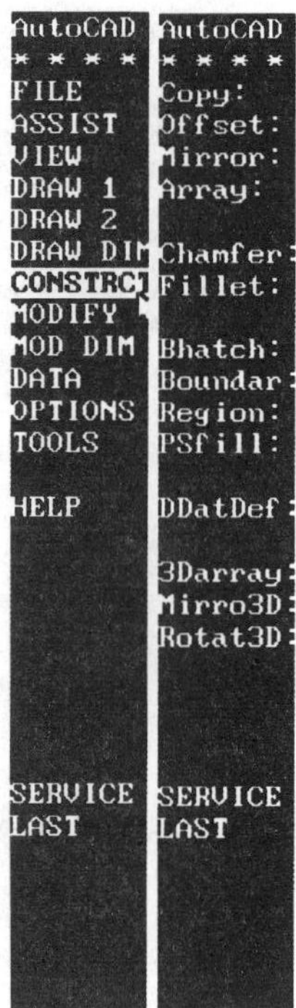

FIGURE 2–10
CONSTRCT Menu

DATA (Figure 2–13) The DATA menu contains commands that help you set up the drawing environment and prepare to draw with AutoCAD. The DDlmode: (layer control) and VPlayer: (viewport layer control) commands create and control the layers on which you are drawing. DDemode (object creation modes) creates and controls layers as well as other entity properties.

Every drawing entity (such as an arc, line, or circle) will have a color and linetype. The Color: and DDltype: (select linetype dialog box) commands are used to set color and linetype. MLstyle: creates and sets multiline styles, Style: creates and sets the style for text, and DDim: creates and sets a dimensioning style.

The Units: command establishes the drawing units. For example, an inch is a drawing unit. The Limits: command sets the page size you draw on. Time: gives you the time spent on the drawing, and Status: gives you the current status of the drawing, displaying drawing statistics, modes, and extents.

The Rename: command allows you to rename Blocks, Layers, Viewports, etc., and the Purge: command allows you to get rid of any items no longer needed, such as Blocks, Layers, or Styles.

OPTIONS (Figure 2–14) The DDrmode: command of the OPTIONS menu leads you to a dialog box that sets a Grid and Snap. The DDosnap (Running Object Snap) dialog box sets a running snap mode that helps you draw very accurately. The Coords: setting variable turns the coordinate display on and off. DDselec: leads you to a dialog box that has various modes you can set to control how drawing entities are picked. *Grips* are small squares that appear at specific points on a drawing entity, such as the endpoint or midpoint of a line. These squares can be used to edit entities. The DDgrips (Grips) dialog box allow you to enable grips, set their color and size. The UCS commands control the visibility of the coordinate system icon. DISPLAY commands allow you to select how you want solids, attributes, points, and text displayed, and the scale for linetypes, such as hidden and center lines. Viewres:, Regenmo:, and Dragmod: allow you to change the view resolution, regeneration, and drag modes. Config: and Dlgcolr: are used to configure the AutoCAD Program features. Tablet allows you to

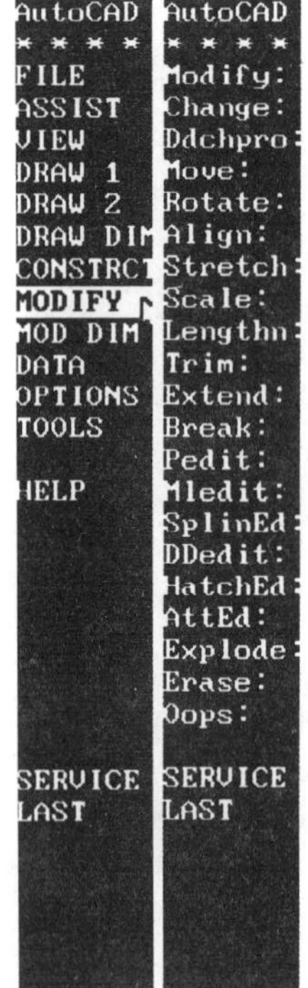

FIGURE 2–11
MODIFY Menu

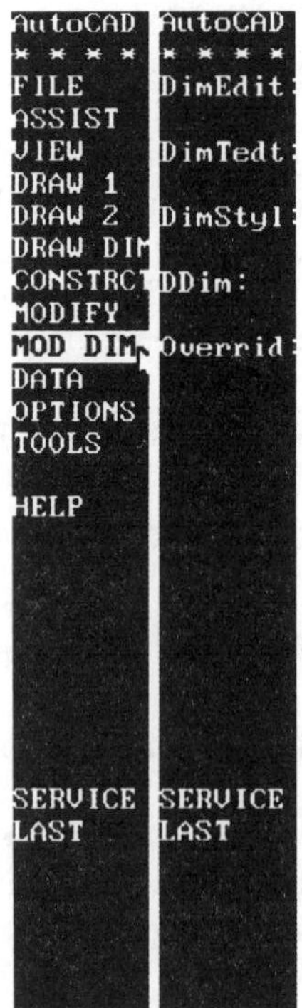

FIGURE 2–12
MOD DIM Menu

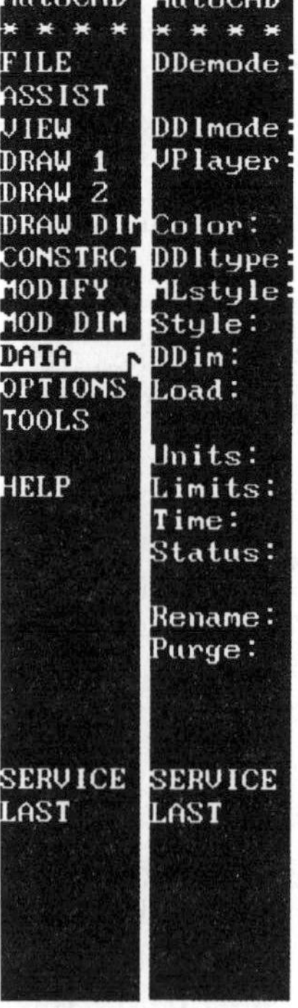

FIGURE 2–13
DATA Menu

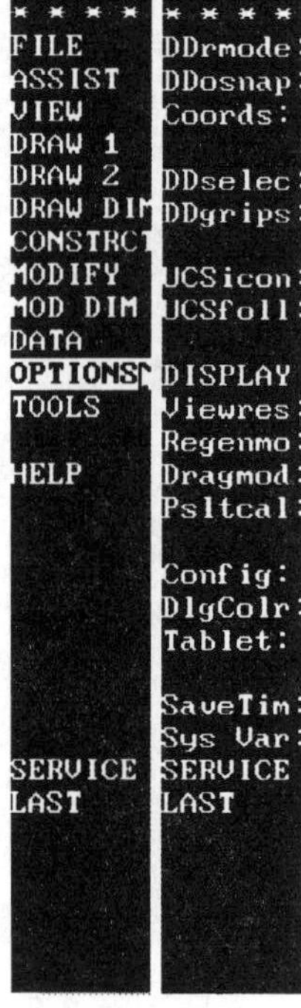

FIGURE 2–14
OPTIONS Menu

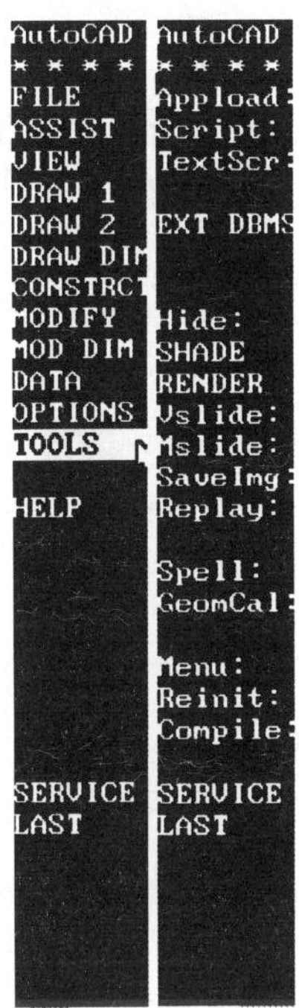

FIGURE 2–15
TOOLS Menu

configure and use a tablet menu. SaveTim: sets the time interval between automatic saves. The Sys Var: command allows you to access and set system variables (sizes, modes, and limits).

TOOLS (Figure 2–15) Appload: has a dialog box that will load Autolisp routines (custom routines similar to AutoCAD commands) and other applications that are not automatically loaded when the AutoCAD program is activated. The Script: dialog box runs script files. TextScr: flips your screen display to the text screen.

EXT DBMS contains the commands used to manage data that are part of an AutoCAD drawing (attributes), using an external database management system (such as dBASE). Hide:, SHADE, and RENDER are used on 3-D models.

The Mslide: command makes a slide file of a drawing while it is active on the display screen; it is a file containing a "snapshot" of the display on the screen. Vslide: is used to view the slide. SaveImg: saves a rendered image, and Replay: displays the image.

From the TOOLS menu you can also spell check your drawing; access a calculator; load a menu file; reinitialize ports, digitizer display, and program parameters files; and compile a shape or font file.

HELP The Help: command allows you to get information about any AutoCAD command. Pick HELP (from the root menu, then pick Help. The AutoCAD Help dialog box, Figure 2–16, appears with instructions on how to use Help. It is a very useful tool for any AutoCAD user.

SERVICE (Figure 2–17) This menu contains various options for selecting drawing entities for editing, such as Last, Previous, ALL, CPolygon (Crossing Polygon), WPolygon (Window Polygon), Fence, Group, Add, and Remove.

Filters relate to the X, Y, and Z coordinates of a point. They allow you to avoid drawing unnecessary construction lines and save time when used effectively.

The Osnap:, Draw Aid:, Entity:, Layer:, and Group: commands take you to dialog boxes that are included in other menus. They are the Running Osnap dialog box, the Drawing Aids dialog box, the Object Creation Modes dialog box, Layer Control dialog box, and the Object Grouping dialog box.

LAST When LAST is picked, the previous menu selected appears.

Menu Bar

The menu bar is located in the status line area (Figure 2–18). As the pointer is moved across the top of the display screen, in the status line area, the menu bar appears and the status line goes away. You can open a menu item on the menu bar by holding the pointer on the menu name and picking it. Use the Esc key or the Ctrl and C keys simultaneously to close the menu or to cancel any command activated.

FIGURE 2–16
AutoCAD Help Dialog Box

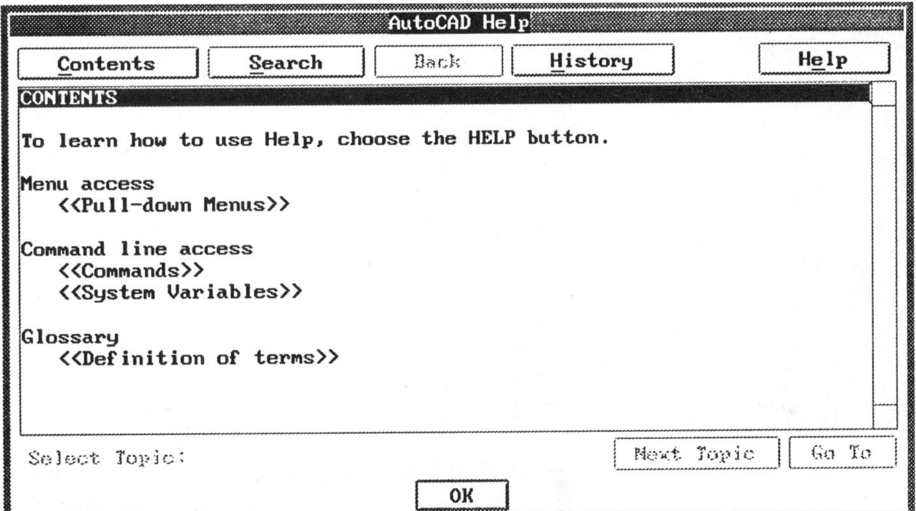

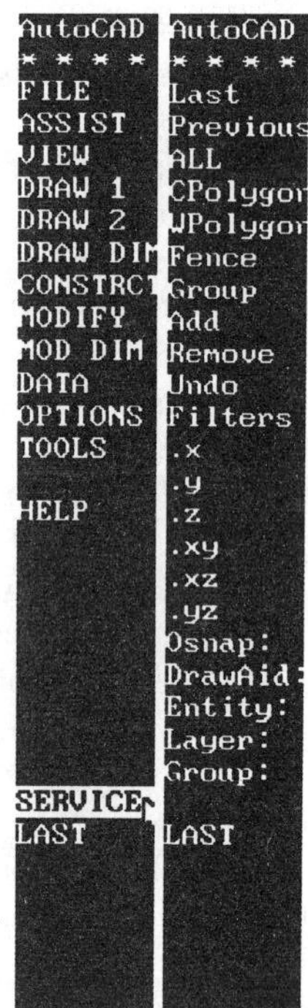

FIGURE 2–17
SERVICE Menu

A pull-down menu will appear for each item on the menu bar when the item is picked (Figures 2–19 through 2–28). Pull-down menus provide access to many of the same commands that are included in the screen menu items. The commands followed by ellipsis points (. . .) display a dialog box when picked. Use the Esc key or pick the Cancel button in the dialog box to cancel it. Those pull-down menu items with an arrow symbol to the right have a cascading menu. Many of the menu bar commands are used in the following chapters; however, the following brief description of the general content of the menu bar provides an introduction.

Step 4. Pick each menu bar item and view the pull-down menus.

File (Figure 2–19) This menu bar item contains many of the same commands that the screen menu item FILE leads you to.

Assist (Figure 2–20) This menu bar item contains many of the same commands that the screen menu item ASSIST leads you to, in a slightly different order.

View (Figure 2–21) This menu contains most of the same commands as in VIEW on the screen menu. The command Floating Model Space does not appear on the root menu, and the command Paper Space operates in a slightly different manner, as you will experience in later chapters.

Draw (Figure 2–22) This menu and its submenus contain most of the same commands that are in DRAW 1, DRAW 2, and DRAW DIM on the screen menu. Examine all the cascading menus of this item so you will know where everything is. For example, the submenu under Polygon contains Rectangle, Polygon, and 2D Solid.

Construct (Figure 2–23) This menu bar item contains most of the same commands as CONSTRCT on the screen menu with a few exceptions. Union, Subtract, and Intersection on this menu are found on the SOLIDS menu under DRAW 2 on the screen menu. Bhatch: and PSfill: on the screen CONSTRCT menu are found when Hatch under Draw in the menu bar is picked.

Modify (Figure 2–24) This menu contains many of the commands that the screen menu item MODIFY leads you to.

Data (Figure 2–25) This menu contains many of the commands that the screen menu item DATA leads you to. The command Viewport Layer Controls (VPlayer: on the DATA screen menu) is grayed out, meaning that it is not available for use until another setting is made.

FIGURE 2–18
Menu Bar

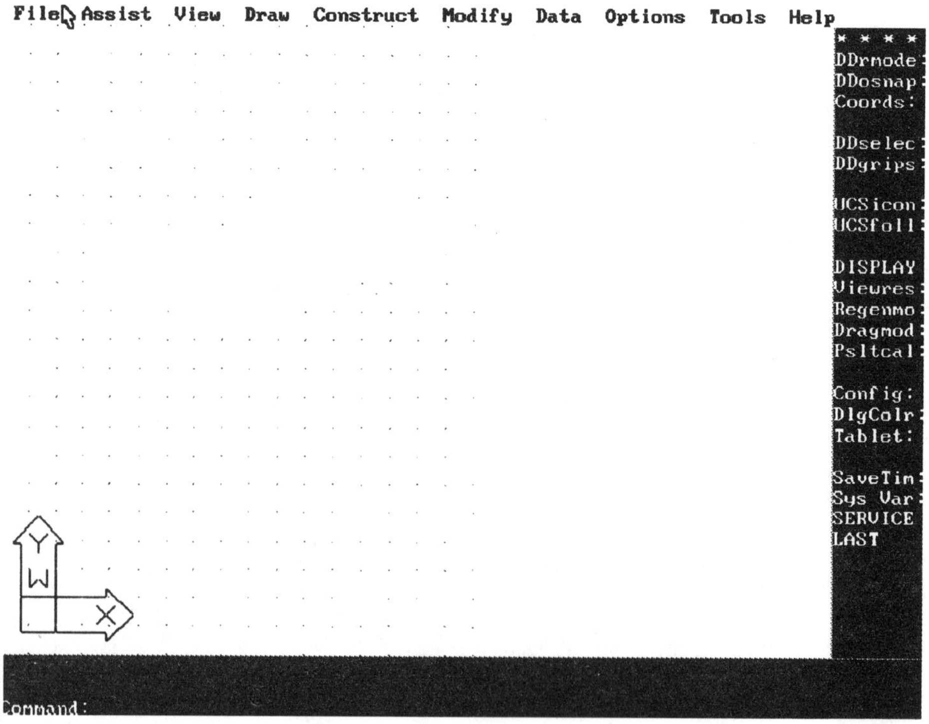

File Assist View Draw Construct Modify Data Options Tools Help

* * * *
DDrmode:
DDosnap:
Coords:
DDselec:
DDgrips:
UCSicon:
UCSfoll:
DISPLAY
Viewres:
Regenmo:
Dragmod:
Psltcal:
Config:
DlgColr:
Tablet:
SaveTim:
Sys Var:
SERVICE
LAST

Command:

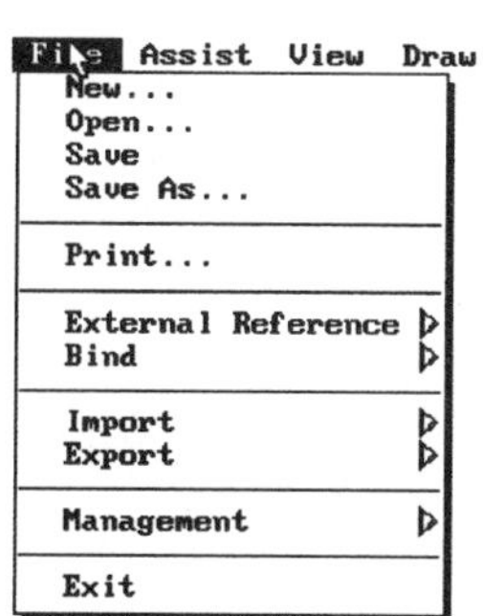

FIGURE 2–19
File Pull-Down Menu

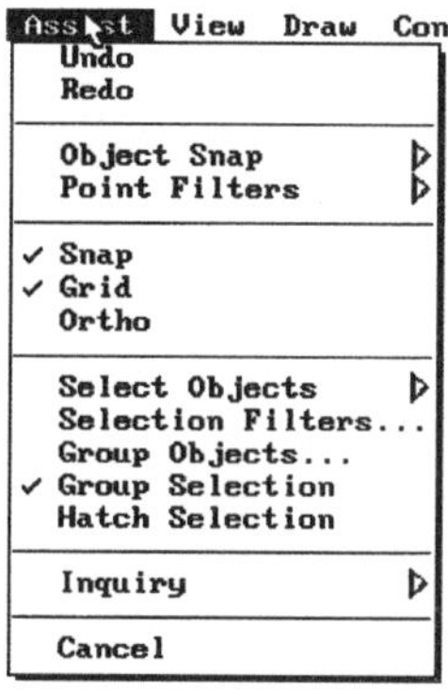

Assist View Draw Construct
Undo
Redo
Object Snap
Point Filters
✓ Snap
✓ Grid
Ortho
Select Objects
Selection Filters...
Group Objects...
✓ Group Selection
Hatch Selection
Inquiry
Cancel

FIGURE 2–20
Assist Pull-Down Menu

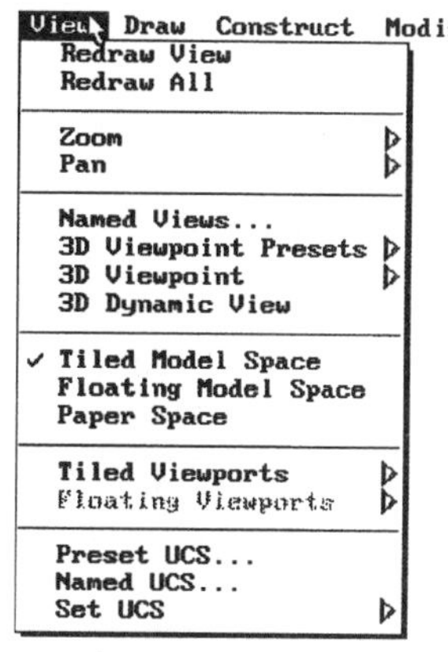

FIGURE 2–21
View Pull-Down Menu

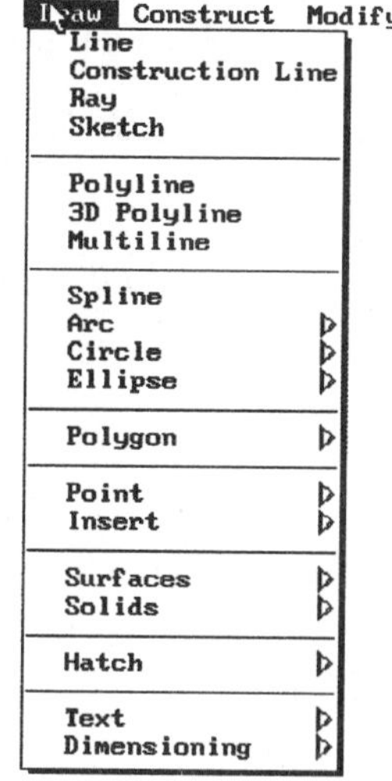

FIGURE 2–22
Draw Pull-Down Menu

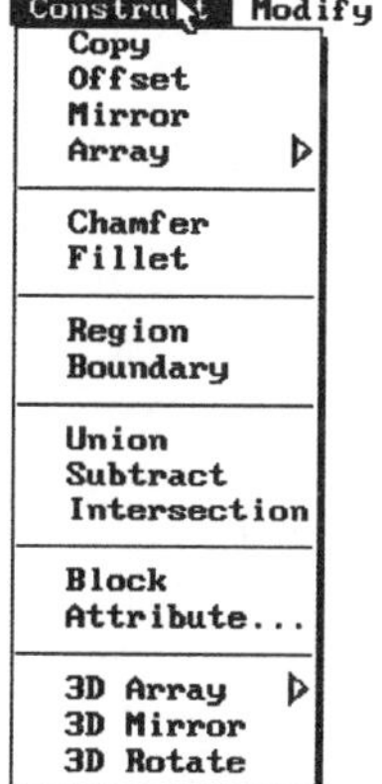

FIGURE 2–23
Construct Pull-Down Menu

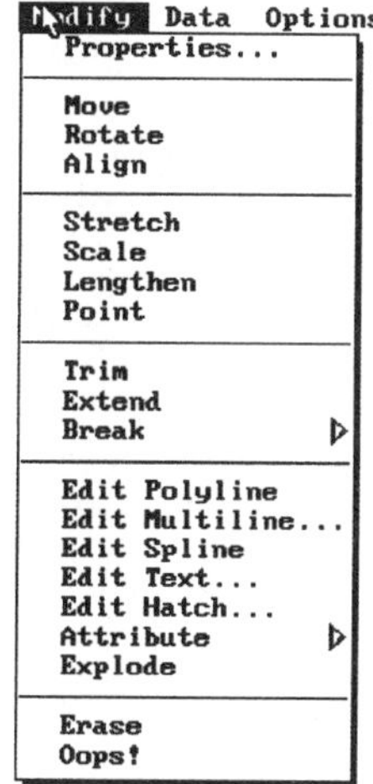

FIGURE 2–24
Modify Pull-Down Menu

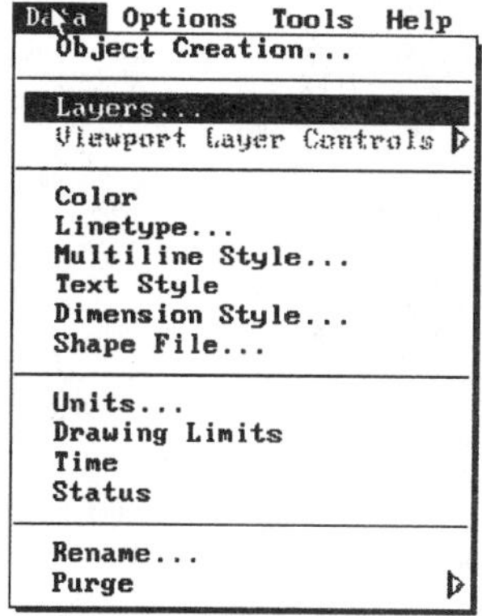

FIGURE 2–25
Data Pull-Down Menu

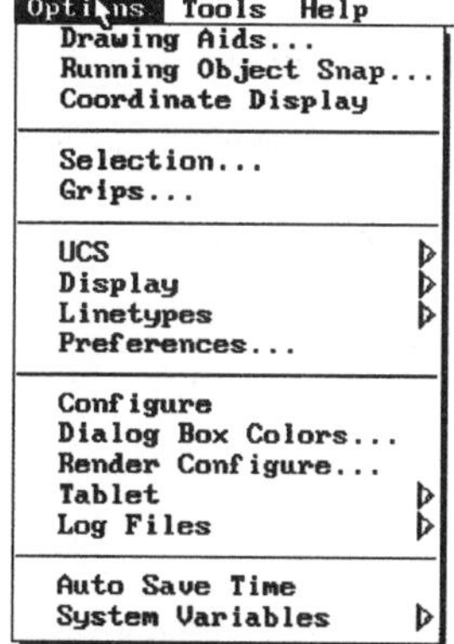

FIGURE 2–26
Options Pull-Down Menu

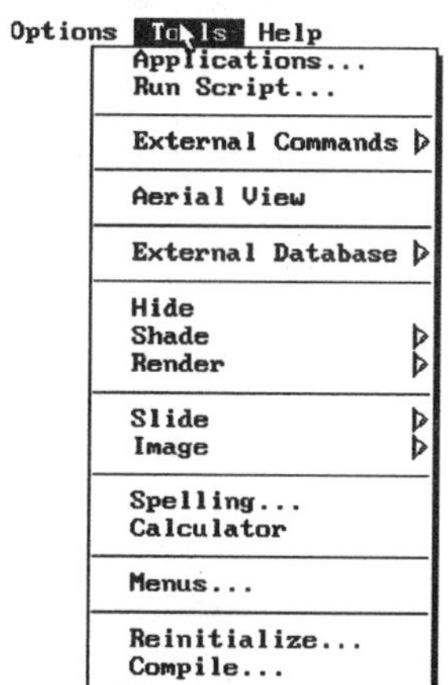

FIGURE 2–27
Tools Pull-Down Menu

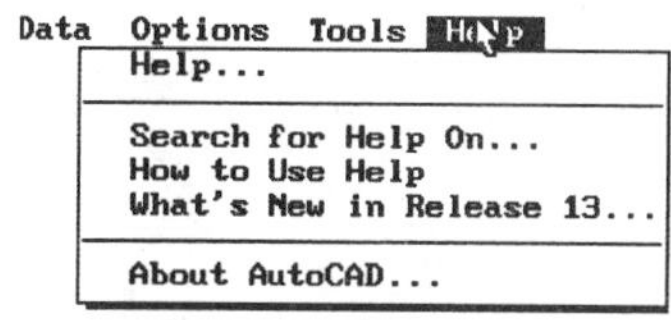

FIGURE 2–28
Help Pull-Down Menu

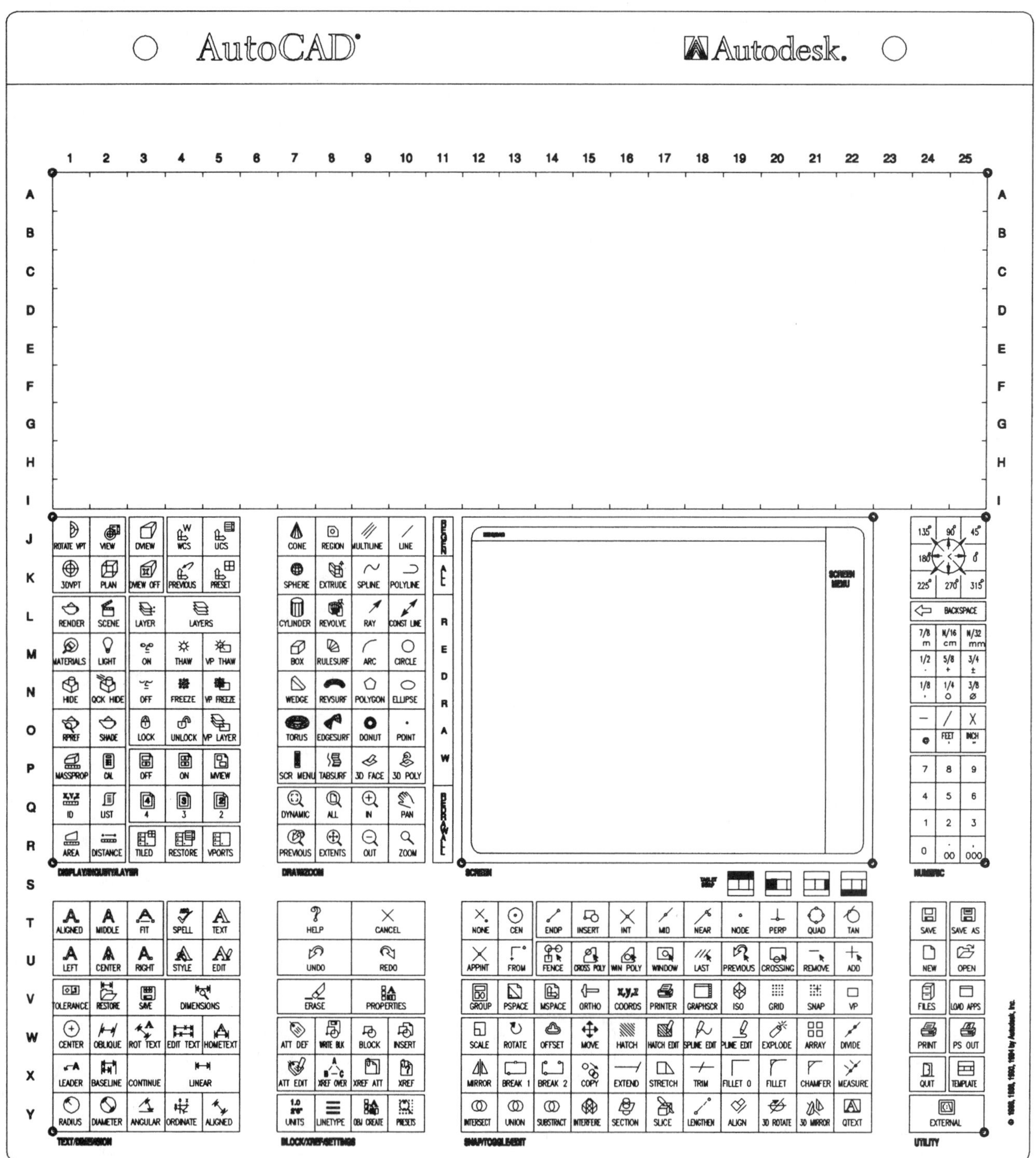

FIGURE 2–29
AutoCAD Tablet Menu

Options (Figure 2–26) This menu contains many of the same commands that the screen menu item OPTIONS leads you to.

Tools (Figure 2–27) This menu contains most of the commands that are in TOOLS on the screen menu.

Help (Figure 2–28) Help is similar to the screen menu HELP. Pick **Help. . .** to access the AutoCAD Help dialog box.

THE AUTOCAD TABLET MENU

The tablet menu (Figure 2–29) allows you to select commands without going through the hierarchy of the screen menu. It provides major categories of commands. Although every command does not appear on the tablet Menu, the tablet and screen menus are integrated and work together so that you can access the screen menu to display and use the remaining commands.

REVIEW QUESTIONS

1. What part of the AutoCAD for DOS screen keeps you informed about your drawing by displaying the current drawing layer and other status modes?
   a. Command line
   b. Status line
   c. Coordinate system icon
   d. Coordinate display
   e. Drawing area
2. Which of the following screen menus contains all the commands that control the appearance of your drawing display?
   a. DRAW 1
   b. DRAW 2
   c. FILE
   d. VIEW
   e. ASSIST
3. Which of the following screen menus contains a command used to start a new drawing or open an existing drawing?
   a. FILE
   b. ASSIST
   c. VIEW
   d. AutoCAD
   e. CONSTRCT
4. Which of the following commands sets the page size on which you will draw?
   a. Limits:
   b. Units:
   c. DDrmode:
   d. CONSTRCT
   e. Snap:
5. What screen menu item remains constant on all command menus and is picked to return you to the screen root menu?
   a. FILE
   b. ASSIST
   c. VIEW
   d. AutoCAD
   e. CONSTRCT
6. Describe the purpose of the command line.

   ____

   ____

7. Describe how to locate the AutoCAD Help dialog box.

   ____

   ____

8. List the 17 AutoCAD screen root menu items.

   ____________________ ____________________
   ____________________ ____________________
   ____________________ ____________________
   ____________________ ____________________
   ____________________ ____________________
   ____________________ ____________________
   ____________________ ____________________
   ____________________ ____________________
   ____

9. List the 11 AutoCAD menu bar items.

   ____________________ ____________________
   ____________________ ____________________
   ____________________ ____________________
   ____________________ ____________________
   ____________________ ____________________
   ____

10. What single key and what combination of keys may be used to close a pull-down menu or cancel a command?

    Single key: ______________________________

    Combination of ______________ and ______________

3 The AutoCAD Program for Windows

OBJECTIVES

When you have completed this chapter, you will be able to:

- □ Start the Microsoft Windows operating system and begin using the system.
- □ Start the AutoCAD Program for Windows.
- □ Describe the AutoCAD for Windows screen and begin using parts of the screen.
- □ Activate, hide, dock, float, reshape, and resize toolbars.
- □ Change the right side of the AutoCAD for Windows screen to show a DOS screen menu.

EXERCISE 3–1
ACTIVATING THE MICROSOFT WINDOWS OPERATING SYSTEM AND RUNNING THE WINDOWS TUTORIAL

Start the Microsoft Windows Operating System

Step 1. Turn on the computer and start Microsoft Windows (Figure 3–1).

Microsoft Windows may be activated in one of two ways:

1. You may have a menu that allows you to pick a picture or type a number or letter to activate Microsoft Windows.

   or

2. You may activate it from the C: prompt (if your hard drive containing the Microsoft Windows program is identified as C:):

Prompt	Response
C:\>	*Type:* **WIN** ↵

When the Microsoft Windows program is started, the Program Manager window appears on the screen. Figure 3–1 shows a typical display of the Program Manager window.

The Program Manager window has a variety of group icons on it. A group icon represents a collection of similar applications that are grouped together. When the group icon is opened, it enlarges and is displayed on the screen as a group window. Hold the mouse pointer on the group icon and double click (press the left mouse button quickly twice) to choose or open a group icon, as follows.

Step 2. Open the AutoCAD R13 group icon (Figures 3–1 and 3–2).

Prompt	Response
The Program Manager window is displayed:	*Double click:* **AutoCAD R13 group icon** (shown highlighted in Figure 3–1)
The AutoCAD R13 group window is displayed.	

FIGURE 3–1
Program Manager

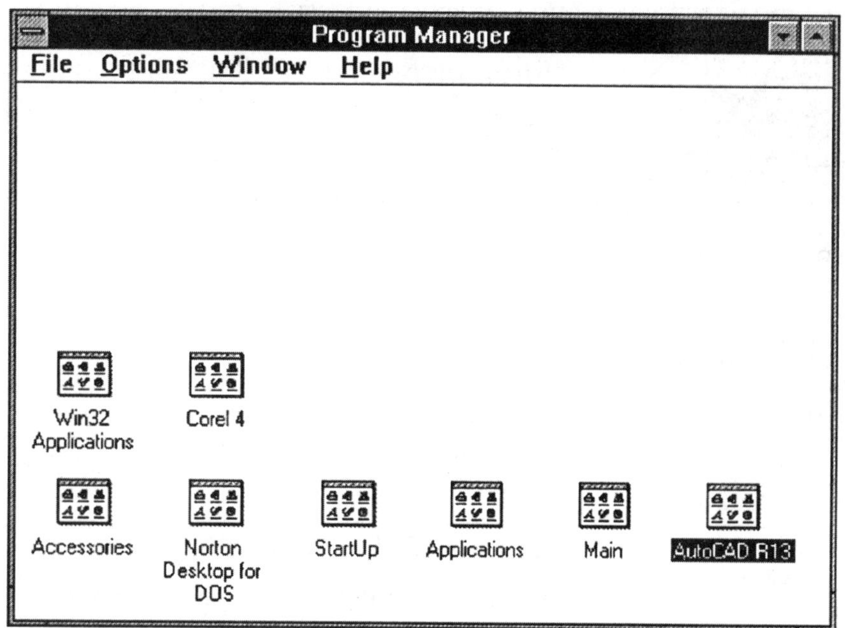

The AutoCAD group window is shown in Figure 3–2. Each icon in the window represents an application. Choosing the AutoCAD R13 for Windows icon (Figure 3–3) would activate the AutoCAD Program for Windows now.

Before entering the AutoCAD R13 Program, take the time to use the Windows Tutorial to become familiar with how the operating system works, as follows.

Step 3. Close the AutoCAD R13 group icon.

Prompt	Response
The AutoCAD R13 group window is displayed:	*Double click:* **the bar in the upper left corner of the AutoCAD R13 group window.**
The Program Manager is displayed.	

FIGURE 3–2
AutoCAD R13 Group Window

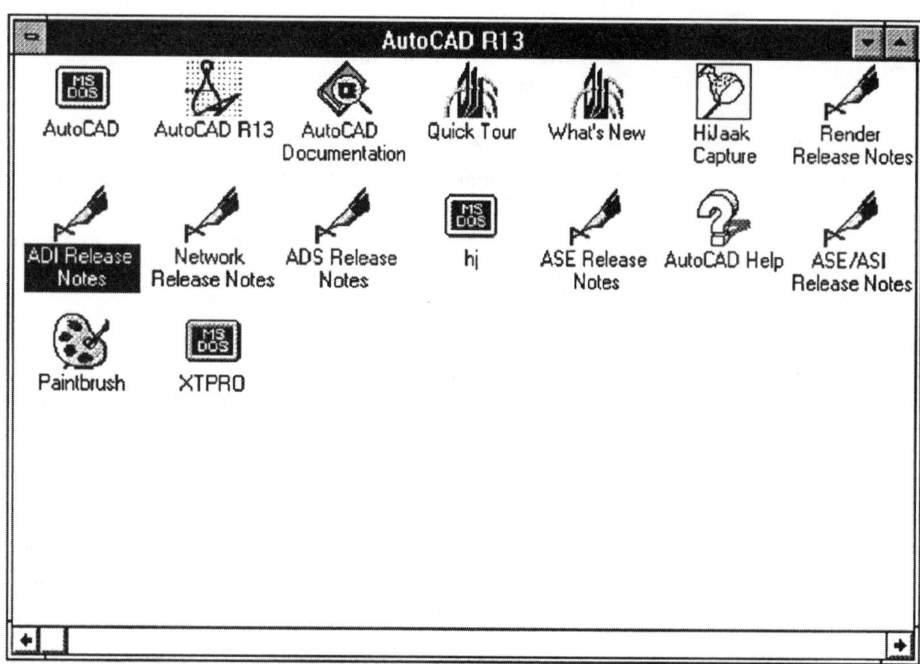

FIGURE 3–3
AutoCAD R13 for Windows Icon

Note: Windows 95 operates in a similar manner to earlier Windows versions. If you have Windows 95, pick START and then pick the Programs icon to find AutoCAD and run it.

Run the Windows Tutorial

Step 4. Open the Windows Tutorial, and run the tutorial lessons.

Prompt	Response
The Program Manager is displayed:	*Pick:* **Help** (from the menu bar)
A cascading menu is displayed:	*Pick:* **Windows Tutorial**
Follow the Windows Tutorial lessons.	

Practice with the tutorial until you feel comfortable with the basic functions of Microsoft Windows.

EXERCISE 3–2
DESCRIBING THE PARTS OF THE AUTOCAD FOR WINDOWS SCREEN

Start AutoCAD R13 for Windows

Step 1. Start AutoCAD R13 for Windows as follows:

1. Turn on the computer and start Microsoft Windows.
2. Open the AutoCAD R13 for Windows group icon.
3. Double click the AutoCAD R13 for Windows icon to start AutoCAD R13 for Windows.

When AutoCAD R13 for Windows is started, the AutoCAD for Windows screen appears. It provides the display area for drawing and the commands used to create, modify, view, and plot drawings. You can begin by naming the new drawing, or you may immediately begin drawing without naming the drawing. When you are ready to end the drawing session, you must save the drawing using Save or Save As . . . , at which time you must name the drawing. Details of how to start new drawings or call up existing ones are included in Chapter 4. AutoCAD communicates with you on various parts of the screen. You may have a slightly different appearing screen, depending on the preferences selected. A brief introduction to each part of the screen (Figure 3–4) follows.

The AutoCAD for Windows Screen

Drawing Window & Graphics Cursor

The drawing window is where your drawing is displayed. The graphics cursor (or cross hairs) follows the movement of a mouse or puck when points of a drawing are entered or a command is selected.

Command Window

The command window (which you may move and resize) is where AutoCAD communicates with you once a command is activated. AutoCAD prompts you to enter specific information to further define a command and then responds with action on the screen or additional prompts. Always watch the command window to make sure you and AutoCAD are communicating.

Coordinate System Icon

The coordinate system icon shows the orientation of the X, Y, and Z axes of the current coordinate system. When AutoCAD is started you are in the World Coordinate System (WCS), as indicated by the W in the coordinate system icon.

Coordinate Display

In an X and Y axis coordinate system, the coordinate display numbers tell you where the cursor or cross hairs on the screen are located in relation to point 0,0 (the lower left corner).

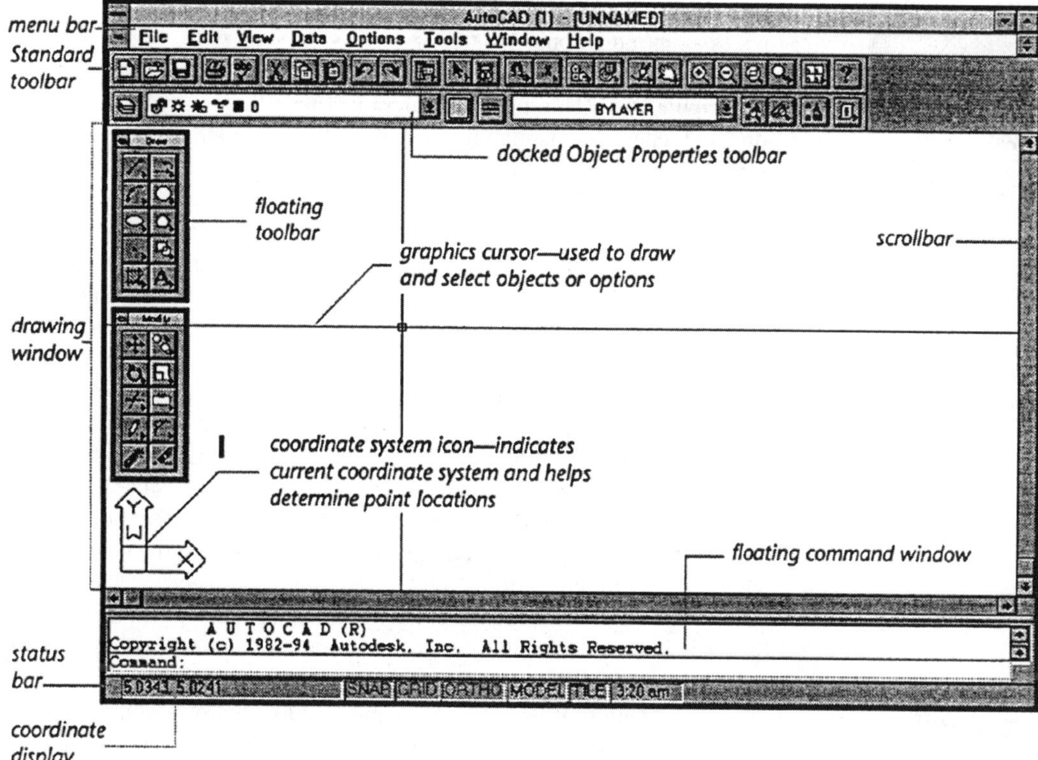

FIGURE 3–4
The AutoCAD for Windows Screen

Status Bar

The status bar keeps you informed about your drawing by displaying the status of modes that affect your drawing: SNAP, GRID, ORTHO, MODEL, and TILE. These modes can be turned on and off by double clicking on the mode name with the pick button of your mouse. The time is also displayed.

Scroll Bar

The scroll bar on the bottom and right side of the screen area allows you to move the drawing display at the same magnification, up and down, left and right. The scroll bars can be turned on and off, using the Preferences. . . dialog box under Options in the menu bar, which is described next.

Menu Bar

Step 2. Practice using the menu bar.

You can open a menu item on the menu bar by holding the pointer on the menu name and picking it; pick the menu item again to close the menu, or use the Esc key to cancel any command activated. A pull-down menu will appear for each item on the menu bar when the item is picked (Figures 3–5 through 3–11). Pull-down menus provide access to many of the same commands that are included on the tool bars. The commands followed by ellipsis points (. . .) display a dialog box when picked. Use the Esc key or pick the Cancel button in the dialog box to cancel it. Those pull-down menu items with an arrow symbol to the right have a cascading menu.

When you hold your finger steady on the click button of your mouse and highlight each menu bar item, pull-down menu command, or cascading menu command, a text string at the bottom of the display screen (in the coordinate display and status bar area) gives a brief description of the commands. Many of the menu bar commands are used in the following

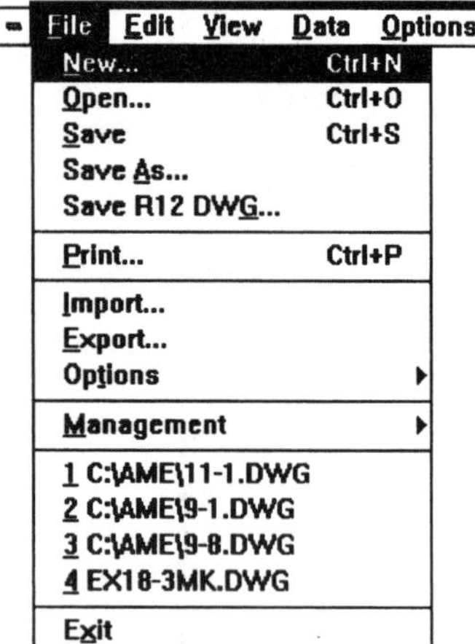

FIGURE 3–5
The File Pull-Down Menu

chapters; however, the following brief description of the general content of the menu bar provides an introduction:

File (Figure 3–5) This menu bar item contains the commands needed to start a new drawing, open an existing one, save drawings, print a drawing, import and export data, manage files, and exit from AutoCAD.

Edit (Figure 3–6) This item contains the Undo command (allows you to undo or reverse the most recent command) and the Redo command (will redo one undo). It also contains the commands related to the Windows Clipboard: Cut, Copy, Copy View, Paste, and Paste Special. . . . Drawings or text from other applications (such as WordPerfect or Paintbrush) can be cut or copied onto the Windows clipboard and then pasted from the clipboard into an AutoCAD drawing. The reverse is also possible; AutoCAD drawings can be pasted into other applications. The Properties. . . command allows you to modify drawing entities (such as a line, circle, or arc). The Links. . . command is a Windows feature that allows you to link or unlink an AutoCAD drawing and another application's object (document or drawing). When a drawing is copied and placed in a document in another program such as Paintbrush or WordPerfect and then linked, editing it updates the information in both the original drawing and the new document. The Insert Object. . . command allows you to insert a linked object.

Edit View Data Options
Undo Ctrl+Z
Redo
Cut Ctrl+X
Copy Ctrl+C
Copy View
Paste Ctrl+V
Paste Special...
Properties...
Links...
Insert Object...

FIGURE 3–6
Edit Pull-Down Menu

View (Figure 3–7) This menu contains commands that control the display of your drawing. The Redraw View and Redraw All commands redraw the display screen to remove blips and redraw any part of the drawing that is missing. The Zoom commands control the magnification of the drawing display, and Pan allows you to move the drawing up and down, left and right. The Named Views. . . command provides a dialog box that allows you to name drawing views, save them, and restore them as needed. There are some 3-D commands on the pull-down menu as well as commands for model space (where your drawing is created) and paper space (where a presentation is created). There are also commands that allow you to change the orientation of the coordinate system icon to create a user coordinate system.

Data (Figure 3–8) This menu bar item contains commands that help you set up your drawing environment and prepare to draw with AutoCAD. The Layers. . . command creates layers on which different parts of a drawing can be placed. Every drawing entity (such as an arc, line, or circle) will have a Color and Linetype. . . . You will learn in later chapters to create a Text Style and Dimension Style. . . so you can add text and dimensions to your drawing. The Units. . . command establishes the drawing units. For example, an inch is a drawing unit. The Drawing Limits command sets the page size you draw on. The Rename. . . command allows you to rename layers, text styles, dimension styles, and more. Purge allows you to purge unused parts of your drawing, such as an extra layer, text style, or dimension style that you do not use.

View Data Options Tools
Redraw View
Redraw All
Zoom
Pan
Named Views...
3D Viewpoint Presets
3D Viewpoint
3D Dynamic View
✓Tiled Model Space
Floating Model Space
Paper Space
Tiled Viewports
Floating Viewports
Preset UCS...
Named UCS...
Set UCS

FIGURE 3–7
View Pull-Down Menu

Options (Figure 3–9) The Drawing Aids. . . command leads you to a dialog box that sets a Grid (a visible pattern of dots for your drawing) and Snap (an invisible pattern of dots your cross hairs snap to). The Running Object Snap. . . dialog box sets a running snap mode that helps you draw very accurately. Coordinate Display turns the coordinate display on and off. The Selection. . . dialog box has various modes you can set to control how drawing entities are picked. Grips are small squares that appear at specific points on a drawing entity, such as the endpoint or midpoint of a line. These squares can be used to edit entities. The Grips. . . dialog box allows you to enable grips and set their color and size. The UCS commands control the visibility of the coordinate system icon. Display allows you to select how you want solids, attributes, points, and text displayed. Linetypes allows you to set the scale for linetypes such as hidden and center lines. The Preferences. . . dialog box allows you to customize various AutoCAD settings. Configure and Render Configure. . . are used to configure the AutoCAD Program and Render features. Tablet allows you to configure and use a tablet menu. Auto Save Time sets the time interval between automatic saves. The System Variables commands allow you to access and set system variables (sizes, modes, and limits).

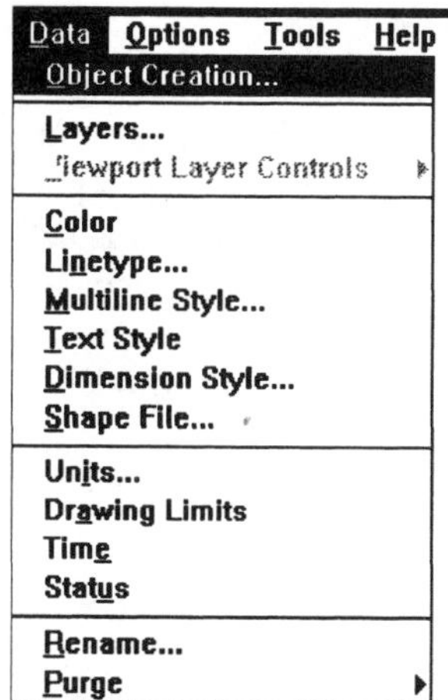

FIGURE 3–8
Data Pull-Down Menu

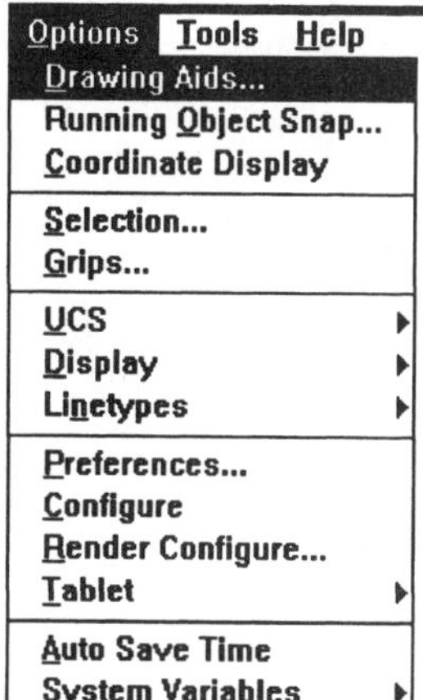

FIGURE 3–9
Options Pull-Down Menu

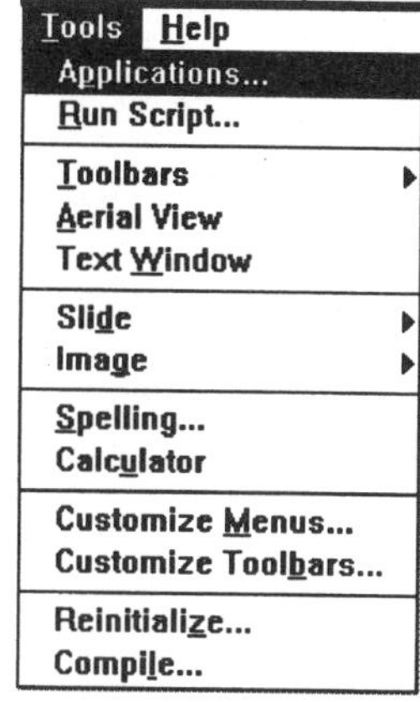

FIGURE 3–10
Tools Pull-Down Menu

Tools (Figure 3–10) The Applications. . . command loads Autolisp routines (custom routines similar to AutoCAD commands) and other applications that are not automatically loaded when the AutoCAD program is activated. The Run Script. . . command runs a script file that is used to display the slides in the correct order and with an appropriate amount of delay between slides. When Toolbars is picked, it leads you to a pull-down menu that displays a list of *top level toolbars*. When a toolbar name is picked, that toolbar is displayed in the drawing window. Aerial View allows you to simultaneously see a reduced view of your drawing as well as one that has been magnified. Text Window flips your screen display to text. The Slide command makes a slide file of a drawing while it is active on the display screen; it is a file containing a "snapshot" of the display on the screen. From the Tools menu you can also spell check your drawing, access a calculator, and customize menus and toolbars.

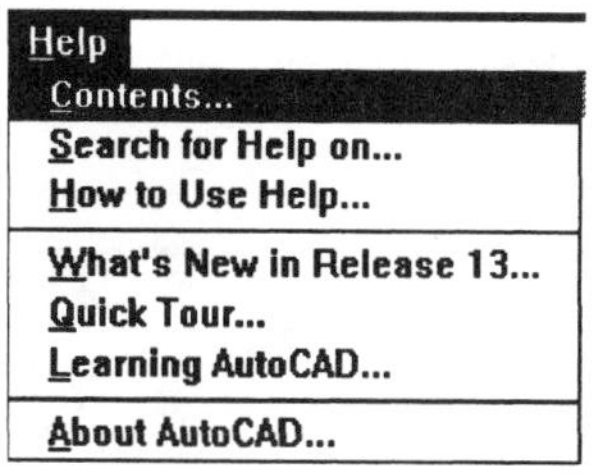

Help
Contents...
Search for Help on...
How to Use Help...
What's New in Release 13...
Quick Tour...
Learning AutoCAD...
About AutoCAD...

FIGURE 3–11
Help Pull-Down Menu

Help (Figure 3–11) This menu bar item has commands that teach you how to use the Help command. The Help command provides information about how to use AutoCAD commands. It is a very helpful tool for any AutoCAD user. Other commands in this menu item provide information about AutoCAD 13.

Top Level Toolbars

The AutoCAD screen shown in Figure 3–4 has four top level toolbars displayed: a docked Standard toolbar, a docked Object Properties toolbar, a floating Draw toolbar, and a floating Modify toolbar. You can turn the visibility of toolbars off and on, move, resize, reshape, or customize them. There are 18 top level toolbars that represent categories of AutoCAD commands, settings, and modes. The Standard toolbar (Figure 3–12) is visible by default. The Standard toolbar contains tools that represent frequently used commands.

Step 3. Activate the Standard toolbar's tooltips (Figure 3–12).

As you hold the mouse pointer steady (do not click) on each tool of the Standard toolbar, tooltips will display the name of the command, as shown in Figure 3–12. A text string at the bottom of the display screen (in the coordinate display and status bar area) gives a brief description of the command.

FIGURE 3–12
Standard Toolbar with Tooltip Showing

Step 4. Activate the Standard toolbar's flyouts (Figure 3–13).

Tools with a small black triangle in the lower right corner have flyouts. A *flyout* is a group of icons nested under a single icon in the toolbar. Hold the pointer on the tool, press and hold the pick button, and the flyout will appear, as shown in Figure 3–13. When you position the pointer on a tool in the flyout and release the pick button, the command is activated: a dialog box appears, or a command sequence begins. The most recently activated tool icon replaces the top icon that was previously visible in the Standard toolbar; the location of the icon changes to reflect the most recently used command. Use the Esc key to cancel any command.

Step 5. Locate the names of the top level toolbars (Figure 3–14).

Prompt	Response
Command:	*Pick:* **Tools** (from the menu bar)
A pull-down menu appears:	*Pick:* **Toolbars**
A list of the top level toolbars appears.	

Many of the toolbars are used in the following chapters; however, a brief description of the top level toolbar's commands provides an introduction.

Step 6. Activate and look at each toolbar.

To activate each toolbar, highlight and pick the toolbar name from the list. After studying each toolbar, you can close it by clicking the box in the upper left corner of the toolbar.

Draw (Figure 3–15) This toolbar has tools used to draw objects and to place lettering on the drawing. Every tool on the Draw toolbar has a small black triangle on it, so a flyout will appear for each tool. As shown in Figure 3–15, from left to right, the Draw toolbar flyout icons are Line, Polyline, Arc, Circle, Ellipse, Polygon, Point, Block, Hatch, and Text.

Modify (Figure 3–16) This toolbar contains some very powerful commands. The Copy command, for example, can be used to make multiple copies of drawing entities such as

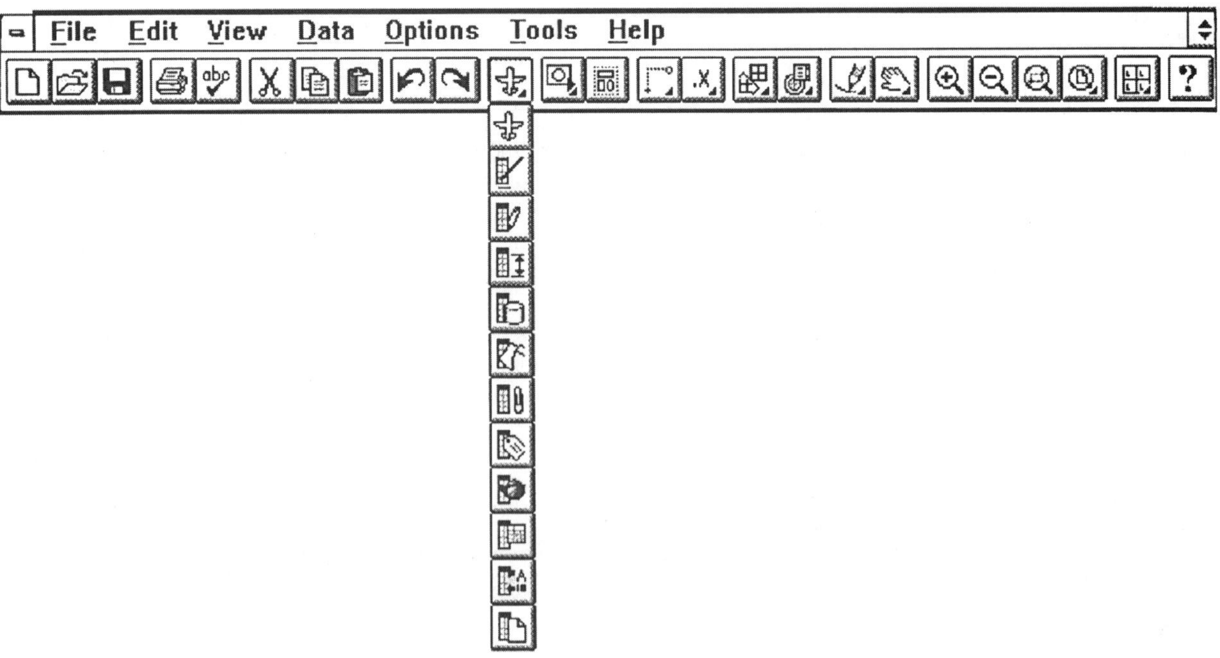

FIGURE 3–13
Standard Toolbar with Flyout Showing

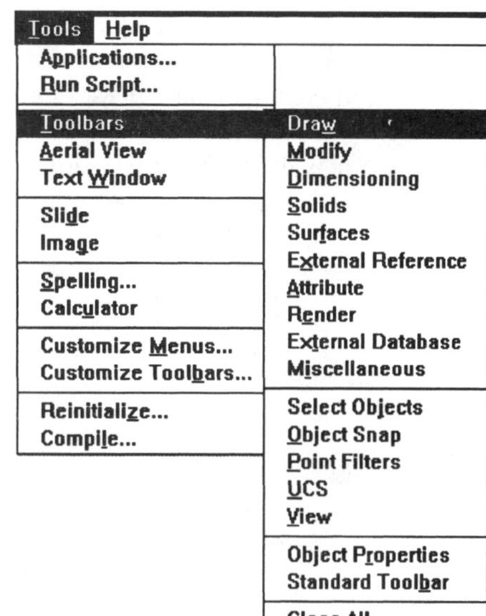

FIGURE 3–14
Top Level Toolbars

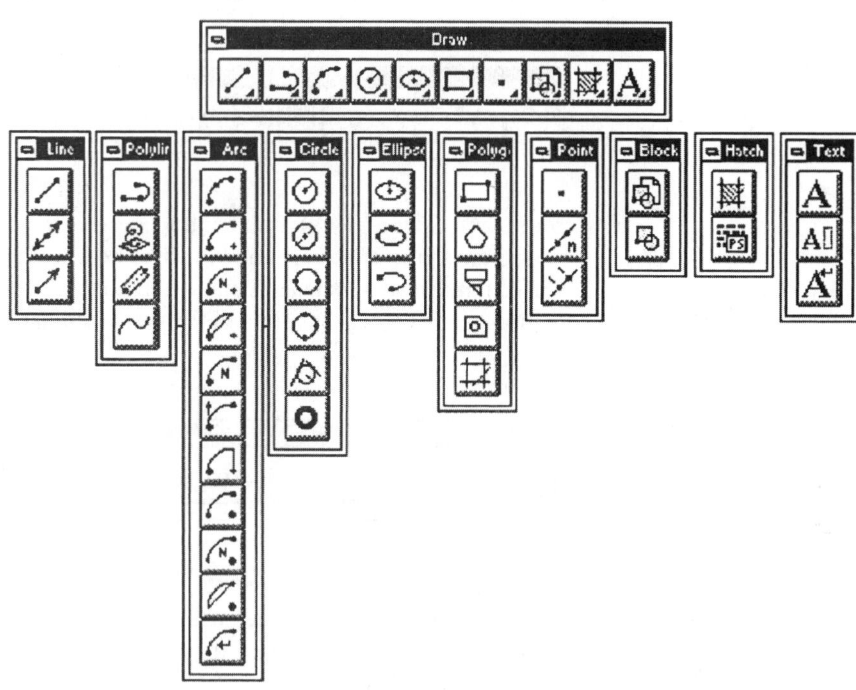

FIGURE 3–15
Draw Toolbar and Flyouts

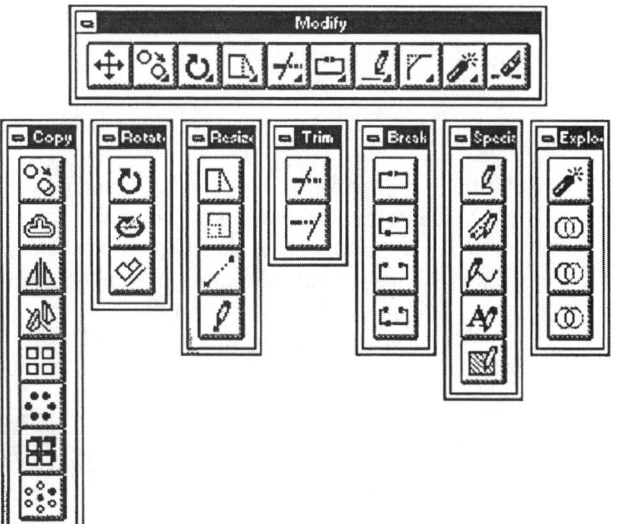

FIGURE 3–16
Modify Toolbar and Flyouts

circles, lines, and other shapes. Other commands allow you to make a mirror image of an object, to rotate objects, erase, extend, and trim objects. From left to right, the Modify toolbar icons are Move (no flyout), Copy, Rotate, Resize, Trim, Break, Special Edit, Chamfer (no individual toolbar), Explode, and Erase (no flyout). (Some of the tooltips may differ on your Modify toolbar.)

The flyouts for the Draw and Modify toolbars are shown in Figures 3–15 and 3–16 to help you understand that each individual flyout has a separate toolbar. The flyouts are not shown in the figures for the other toolbars. To view the other toolbar flyouts, hold your pointer on the tool, press and hold the pick button, and the flyout will appear.

Dimensioning (Figure 3–17) This toolbar is used to dimension drawings.

FIGURE 3–17
Dimensioning Toolbar

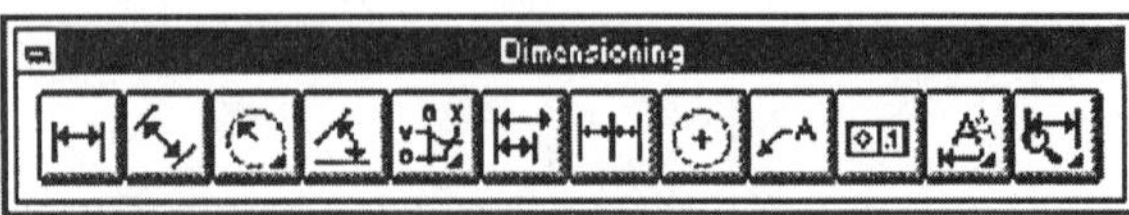

Solids (Figure 3–18) This toolbar contains the commands used to make AutoCAD solid models. AutoCAD solid modeling is described in Part III.

FIGURE 3–18
Solids Toolbar

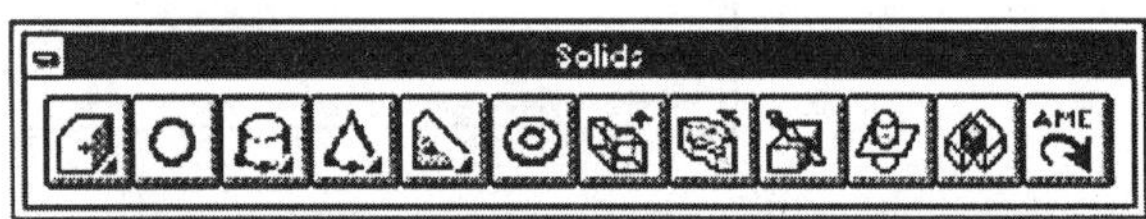

Surfaces (Figure 3–19) This toolbar contains the commands used to draw 3-D objects that are shown as surfaces only, such as box, wedge, pyramid, cone, sphere, dome, dish, and torus. It also contains commands used to create surfaces on 3-D wire frames. A wire frame is an object consisting of lines only, similar to the wires of a bird cage. This technique is called *surface modeling*.

FIGURE 3–19
Surfaces Toolbar

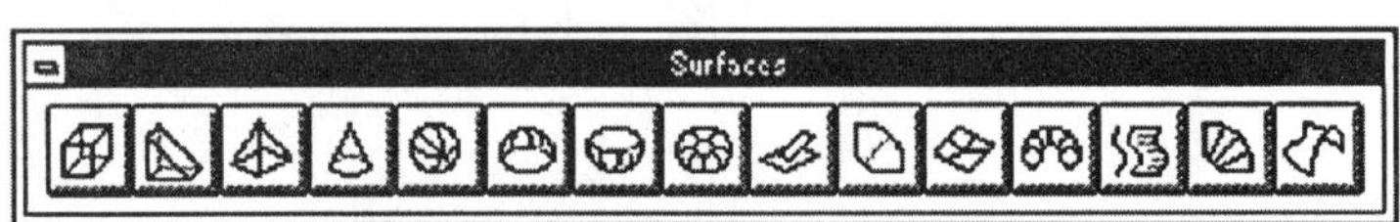

External reference (Figure 3–20) This toolbar contains commands related to external references. An external reference is attached to a primary drawing. Any changes made to the external reference drawing are reflected in the primary drawing each time the primary drawing is loaded in AutoCAD.

FIGURE 3–20
External References Toolbar

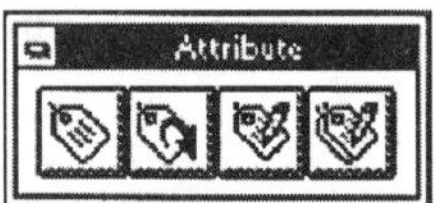

FIGURE 3–21
Attribute Toolbar

Attribute (Figure 3–21) This toolbar contains commands related to Attributes. An attribute is information, such as part number, color, or price that is attached to a drawing symbol. This information can then be extracted from the drawing using an external database management system (such as dBASE) in a form such as a parts list.

Render (Figure 3–22) This toolbar contains the commands used to create a shaded image of a 3-D surface model or solid model.

FIGURE 3–22
Render Toolbar

FIGURE 3–23
External Database Toolbar

External database (Figure 3–23) This toolbar contains the commands used to manage data that are part of an AutoCAD drawing (attributes), using an external database management system (such as dBASE).

FIGURE 3–24
Miscellaneous Toolbar

Miscellaneous (Figure 3–24) This toolbar contains miscellaneous commands that are seldom used. Other commands in AutoCAD perform the same tasks, are easier to use, and are more versatile.

Select objects (Figure 3–25) Many of the AutoCAD Modify commands start with the Command: prompt "Select Objects." This toolbar contains the selection options used to select the item or group of items to be modified. The selection options are window, crossing window, group, previous, last, all, polygon, crossing polygon, fence, add, remove, and selection filters.

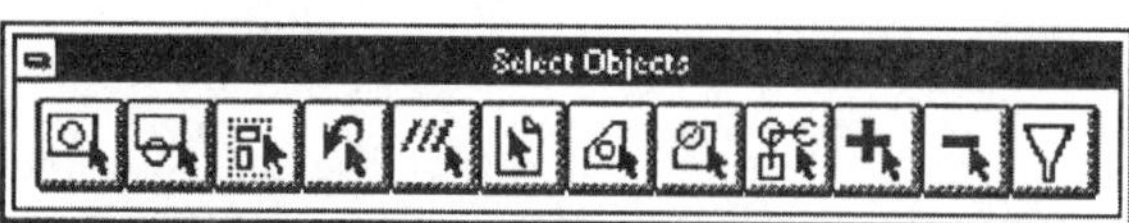

FIGURE 3–25
Select Objects Toolbar

Object snap (Figure 3–26) This toolbar contains a list of command modifiers called OSNAP or Object Snap. Object Snap features help you draw very accurately. Some of the Object Snap modifiers are center (of a circle or arc), endpoint (of a line or arc), and intersection. This toolbar also contains the calculator command.

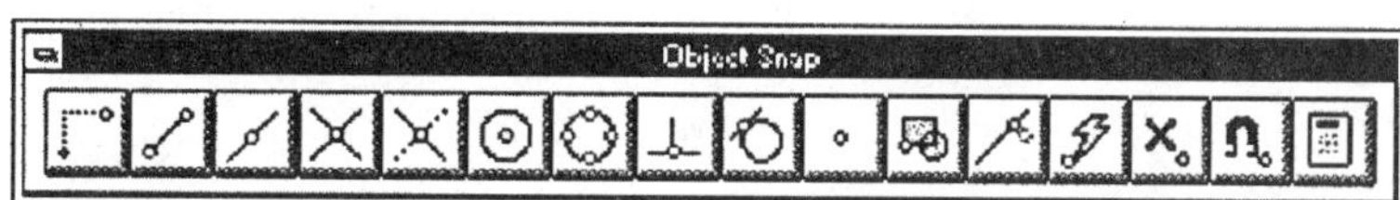

FIGURE 3–26
Object Snap Toolbar

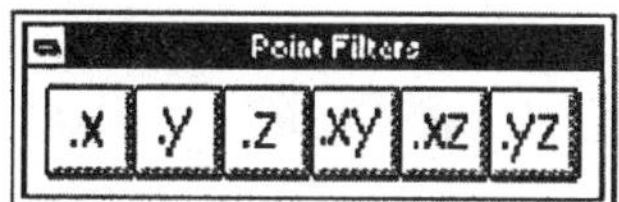

FIGURE 3–27
Point Filters Toolbar

Point filters (Figure 3–27) Filters relate to the X, Y, and Z coordinates of a point. They allow you to avoid drawing unnecessary construction lines and save considerable time when used effectively.

UCS (Figure 3–28) AutoCAD starts up in the World Coordinate System (WCS), as indicated by the W in the coordinate system icon. The coordinate system icon shows the orientation of the X, Y, and Z axes of the current coordinate system. This toolbar contains the commands used to create a user-defined coordinate system (UCS).

FIGURE 3–28
UCS Toolbar

View (Figure 3–29) This toolbar contains the commands used to view a 3-D model.

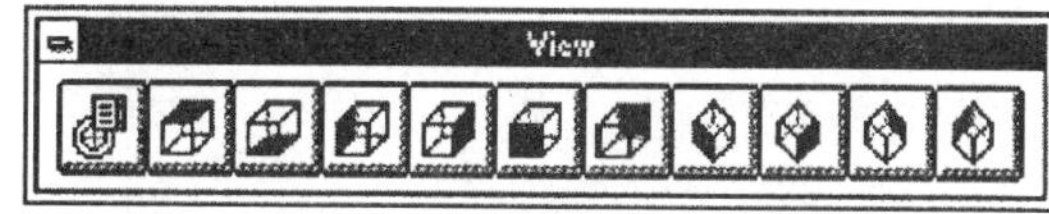

FIGURE 3–29
View Toolbar

Object properties (Figure 3–30) Every drawing entity (line, arc, circle, etc.) is drawn on a layer and can inherit the properties of that layer. This toolbar contains the Layer Control dialog box, which is used to create layers and assign properties such as color and linetype. It also contains the commands for setting color, linetype, defining multiline styles, modifying drawing entities, and listing information about an entity.

FIGURE 3–30
Object Properties Toolbar

Standard toolbar (Figure 3–12) As described earlier in this chapter, the Standard toolbar is visible by default. The Standard toolbar contains tools that represent frequently used commands.

Close all This command closes (or hides) all toolbars.

Floating Toolbars

A floating toolbar floats or lies on any part of the AutoCAD for Windows screen. A floating toolbar can be moved to another part of the screen and can be reshaped and resized. Any of the top level toolbars can be displayed and will float on the screen as follows.

Step 7. Display the Draw toolbar.

Prompt	Response
Command:	*Pick:* **Tools** (from the menu bar)
The pull-down menu appears:	*Pick:* **Toolbars**
The cascading menu appears:	*Pick:* **Draw**

The Draw toolbar appears on the screen.

Step 8. Display the Modify toolbar.

Use the same steps to display the Modify toolbar as you used to display the Draw toolbar.

To hide any toolbar you do not want visible, click on the bar in the upper left corner of the toolbar.

Step 9. Reshape and move the Draw and Modify toolbars (Figure 3–31).

Change the shape of the toolbars to match those shown in Figure 3–31, by changing the width and height. Slowly move the pointer over the borders of each toolbar until you get the double-arrow pointer that allows you to resize it. Refer to the Windows Tutorial if needed.

Move the Draw and Modify toolbars to the same position as shown in Figure 3–31 by picking the title bar of each toolbar and dragging it to the new location.

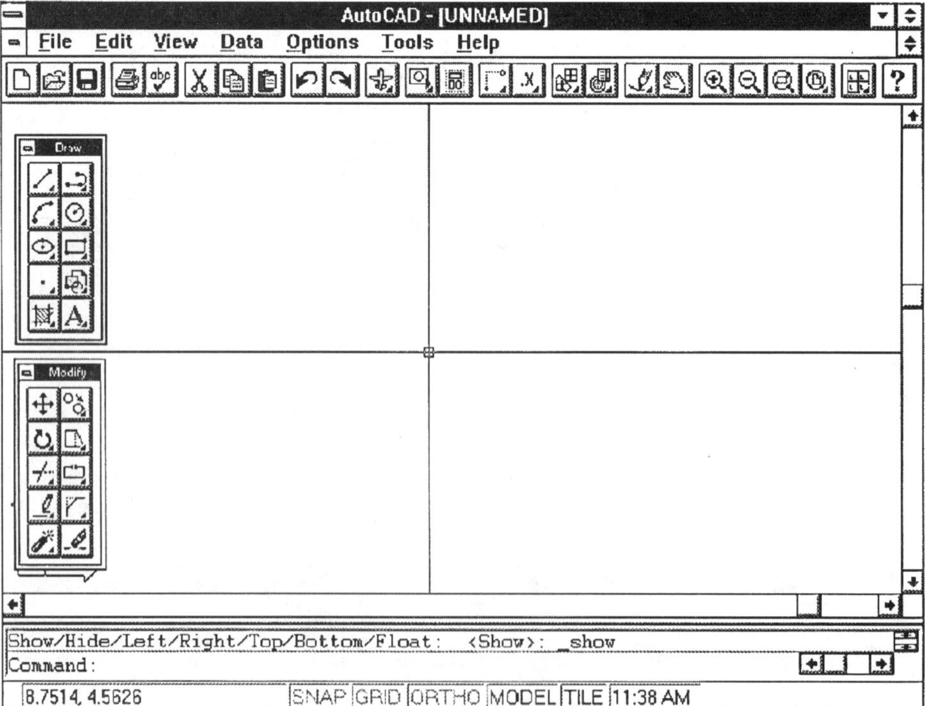

FIGURE 3–31
Reshaping and Moving the Draw and Modify Toolbars

Step 10. Change the size of the toolbars (Figure 3–32).

Prompt	Response
Command:	*Pick:* **Tools** (from the menu bar)
The pull-down menu appears:	*Pick:* **Customize Toolbars. . .**
The Toolbars dialog box appears (Figure 3–32):	*Pick:* **Large Buttons** (the check box, to put an X in the box; turning it on)
An X appears in the Large Buttons check box:	*Pick:* **Close** (to exit)
All the toolbars are larger.	

Use the same steps to change the toolbars back to the smaller size.

Docked Toolbars

Step 11. Display the Object Properties toolbar.

Prompt	Response
Command:	*Pick:* **Tools** (from the menu bar)
Command:	*Pick:* **Toolbars** (from the pull-down menu)
Command:	*Pick:* **Object Properties**

The Object Properties toolbar appears on the screen.

Step 12. Dock the Object Properties toolbar.

A toolbar can be *docked,* which means it attaches to any edge of the drawing window. Once docked, the toolbar does not lie on any part of the drawing area; it also cannot be reshaped. One way to dock a toolbar is to pick on the name of the toolbar and drag it to an edge. When you see an outline of the toolbar along an edge (showing you how the toolbar will look in the docking area), release the pick button on the mouse to dock the toolbar.

To undock the toolbar, pick in any part of the gray area (grab region) around the tools, and drag the toolbar away from the edge.

Pick on the name of the Object Properties toolbar and drag it to the top edge of the drawing area and dock it as shown in Figure 3–34.

FIGURE 3–32
Toolbars Dialog Box

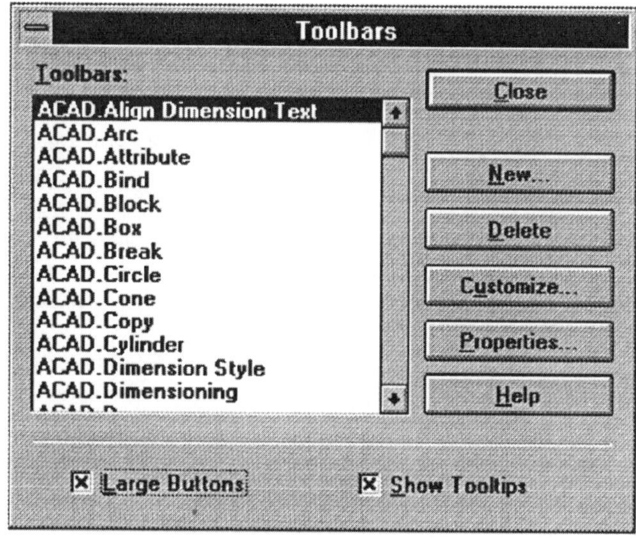

Toolbar Command

Step 13. Use the Toolbar command to dock the Modify toolbar on the right side of the drawing area.

Prompt	Response
Command:	*Type:* **TOOLBAR** ↵
Toolbar name (or ALL):	*Type:* **MODIFY** ↵
Show/Hide/Left/Right/Top/Bottom/ Float: <Show>:	*Type:* **R** ↵
Position <0,0>:	↵
The Modify toolbar is docked on the right side of the drawing area.	

The other options of the Toolbar command, when activated, allow you to dock a toolbar on the left, top, or bottom of the drawing area, float a docked toolbar, show a not visible toolbar, or hide a visible toolbar. You can use the ALL option to make all the toolbars visible or hide all the toolbars.

Customizing Toolbars

You can customize toolbars using the Customize Toolbars dialog box under Tools in the menu bar. Using this dialog box, you can add, delete, move, or copy existing tools, or create a new toolbar using existing or new tools.

Activating a Screen Menu in the AutoCAD for Windows Screen

If you are used to using the AutoCAD screen menu for DOS, you can change the right side of the AutoCAD for Windows screen so that it shows the AutoCAD screen menu and use that instead of toolbars to activate commands.

Step 14. Use the Preferences dialog box to change the AutoCAD screen (Figures 3–33 and 3–34).

Prompt	Response
Command:	*Pick:* **Options** (from the menu bar)
The pull-down menu appears:	*Pick:* **Preferences. . .**
The Preferences dialog box appears (Figure 3–33):	*Pick:* **Screen Menu** (the check box, to put an X in the box, turning it on)
An X appears in the screen menu check box	*Pick:* **OK** (to exit)
The AutoCAD screen menu appears on the screen (Figure 3–34).	

Using the System tab of the Preferences dialog box, you may also change the font used for the screen menu, the colors used in the graphics window, the time interval for automatic save, turn automatic save on or off; turn scroll bars on or off; and make other settings that may be more to your liking than the standard AutoCAD screen.

Using AutoCAD for Windows with Other Programs

All commands related to the Windows Clipboard, such as Cut, Copy, Paste, and Insert Object, are available only in AutoCAD for Windows. Drawings or text from other applications (such as WordPerfect or Paintbrush) can be cut or copied onto the Windows Clipboard and then pasted from the Clipboard into an AutoCAD drawing. The reverse is also possible; AutoCAD drawings can be pasted into other applications.

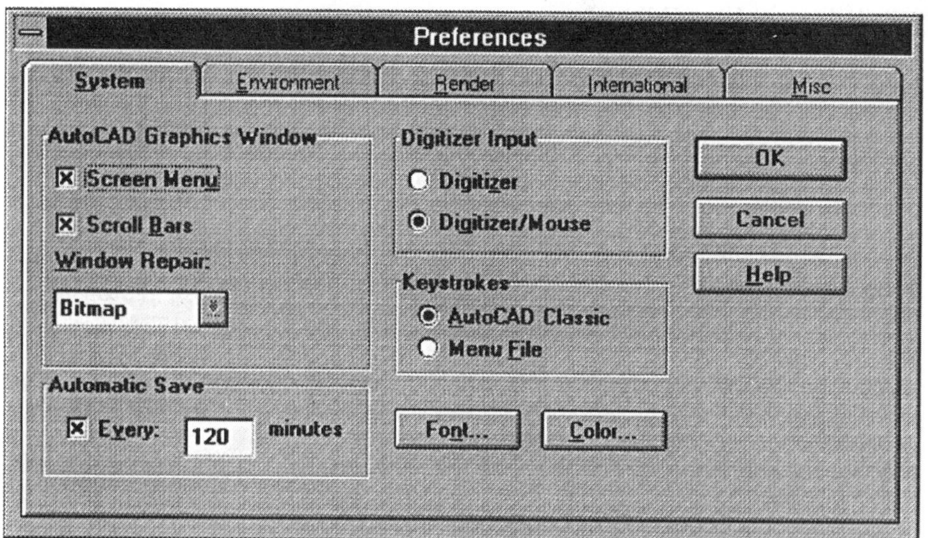

FIGURE 3–33
Preferences Dialog Box

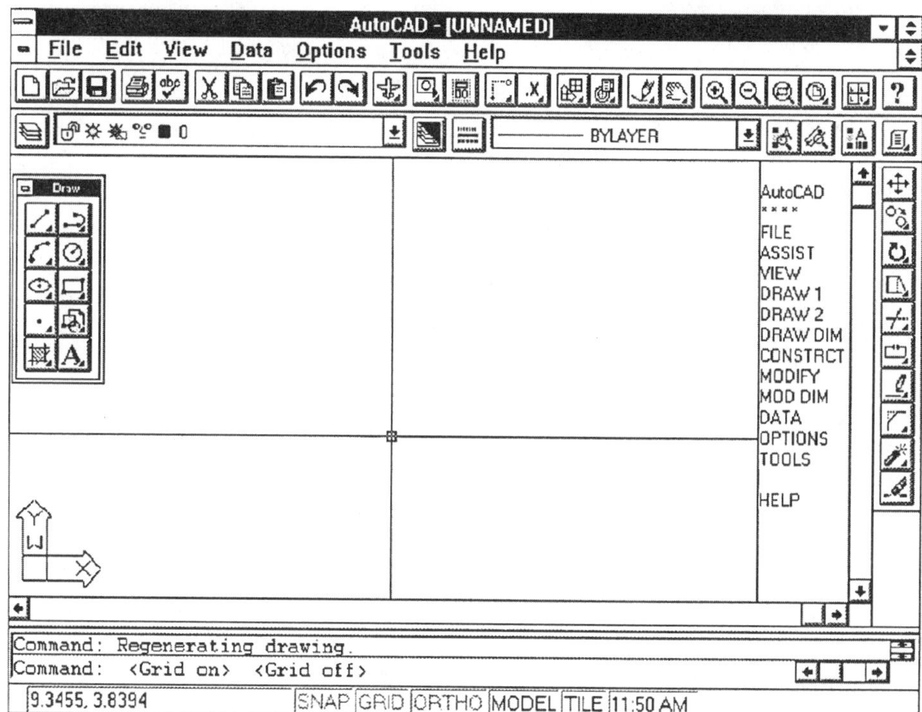

FIGURE 3–34
AutoCAD for Windows Screen with Screen Menu

REVIEW QUESTIONS

1. Which is the correct response to activate Microsoft Windows from the C: prompt?
   a. *Type:* **WINSTART**
   b. *Type:* **WINDOW** ↵
   c. *Type:* **WIN**
   d. *Type:* **WIN** ↵
   e. *Press:* ↵
2. What do you do to open a group application that is shown on the Program Manager as an icon?
   a. *Type:* **Open** ↵
   b. Double click on the icon
   c. Pick above the icon
   d. Hold the pointer on the icon and press enter
   e. *Type:* **Enter** ↵
3. Double clicking the bar in the upper left corner of the AutoCAD R13 group window:
   a. Closes the AutoCAD R13 group window and displays the Program Manager.
   b. Closes the Program Manager and displays the Exit Windows dialog box.
   c. Enters the AutoCAD R13 Program.
   d. Opens the AutoCAD R13 group window.
   e. Resizes the AutoCAD R13 group window.
4. To maximize the AutoCAD R13 group window:
   a. Pick the arrow on the bottom right of the group window.
   b. Pick the arrow on the bottom left of the group window.
   c. Pick the arrow pointing up in the upper right corner of the group window.
   d. Pick the arrow pointing down in the upper right corner of the group window.
   e. Pick on the bar in the upper left corner of the group window.
5. Which menu on the AutoCAD menu bar contains the command needed to start a new drawing?
   a. File
   b. Edit
   c. Tools
   d. Data
   e. Options
6. Which menu on the AutoCAD menu bar contains the commands related to the Windows Clipboard?
   a. File
   b. Edit
   c. Tools
   d. Data
   e. Options
7. Which menu on the AutoCAD menu bar allows you to make and set layers, select drawing units, and set drawing limits.
   a. File
   b. Edit
   c. Tools
   d. Data
   e. Options
8. Which menu on the AutoCAD menu bar contains a list of the top level toolbars?
   a. File
   b. Edit
   c. Tools
   d. Data
   e. Options
9. Which toolbar is usually on by default?
   a. Modify
   b. External Reference
   c. Standard toolbar
   d. Draw
   e. Select Objects
10. Double clicking GRID in the status bar when it is grayed out does which of the following?
    a. Turns the GRID off.
    b. Displays the GRID and turns SNAP on.
    c. Displays the GRID and turns SNAP off.
    d. Displays the GRID.
    e. Has no effect on the display screen.
11. List the five modes displayed on the status bar.

    ____________ ____________ ____________

    ____________ ____________
12. Write the first sentence displayed on the Help Basics window when you double click "How to Use Help" on the Help menu and then pick "Help Basics."

    ____
13. Describe the purpose of the Command window.

    ____

    ____

    ____
14. Name the four top level toolbars shown in Figure 3–4.

    ____

    ____

    ____
15. Describe how to open or activate a toolbar.

    ____

    ____
16. Describe how to close or hide a toolbar.

    ____

    ____
17. Describe how to undock a toolbar.

    ____

    ____
18. Describe how to change the AutoCAD for Windows screen so that the screen menu is displayed on the right side of it.

    ____

    ____
19. Describe the function of the scroll bars on the bottom and right side of the AutoCAD for Windows screen.

    ____

    ____
20. Describe how to activate a toolbar's tooltips and flyouts:

    Tooltips: ______________________________

    Flyouts: ______________________________

PART II THE AUTOCAD PROGRAM: TWO-DIMENSIONAL DRAWING

4 Preparing to Draw with AutoCAD

OBJECTIVES

When you have completed this chapter, you will be able to:

- □ Identify the types of floppy disks and their features.
- □ Begin a new AutoCAD drawing.
- □ Edit an existing AutoCAD drawing.
- □ Use all parts of any dialog box.
- □ Use function keys F1 (flip screen), F7 (grid), and F9 (snap) to control the display screen, grid, and snap as required.
- □ Correctly set drawing units, limits, grid, and snap.
- □ Correctly use seven commands—Save:, Qsave, SaveAs:, Exit:, QUIT, End, and SAVEASR12—so that you can save your work in the desired drive and directory and exit AutoCAD after you have saved your work.
- □ Create drawing layers.
- □ Describe .DWG and .BAK file types.
- □ Correctly reboot the computer.

FLOPPY DISKS

Although you may save the drawings done with AutoCAD on the hard disk, it is very important to save your work on a floppy disk also. A variety of accidents can happen that cause the loss of saved drawings; for example, someone could erase your drawing from the hard disk. It is very discouraging to lose any work that you have completed. Saving your work in at least two places (the hard disk and one or two floppy disks) helps prevent this problem.

5-1/4″ Floppy Disk

Two Types of 5-1/4″ Floppy Disks

1. *Double density:* Stores approximately 360K (360,000) bytes of information. This disk is used in a double-density drive.
2. *High density:* Stores approximately 1.2 megabytes (1,200,000 bytes) of information. This disk is used in a high-density drive.

Features of a 5-1/4″ Floppy Disk

The 5-1/4″ floppy disk (Figure 4–1) is protected by a nonremovable protective envelope. The *drive spindle hole* in the center of the disk fits on the disk drive spindle and allows the disk to be rotated within the envelope. The exposed area called the *head slot* is where the disk drive's magnetic head touches the surface of the disk and reads information from or writes information to the disk. The *write-protect notch* can be covered with a write-protect tab to prevent accidental erasure and overrecording. When the notch is covered, the drive can read information from but cannot write information to the disk. When the tab is removed, information can be written to the disk.

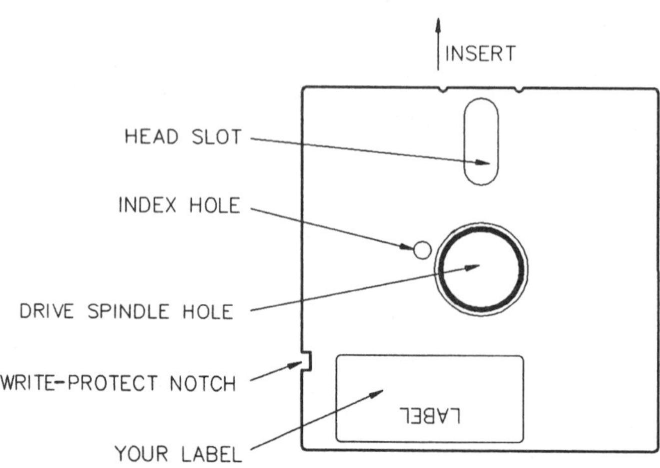

FIGURE 4–1
5-1/4″ Floppy Disk

The 5-1/4″ double density floppy disk can be distinguished from the 5-1/4″ high density floppy disk by the ring on the area around the drive spindle hole, as shown in Figure 4–1. The high density floppy disk does not have the ring.

Disks are divided into concentric circles called *tracks*. Each track is partitioned into smaller parts called *sectors*. The small *index hole* in the jacket and in the disk itself helps the disk drive determine the orientation of the disk and where information is stored on the disk.

Inserting a 5-1/4″ Floppy Disk into the Disk Drive

To insert the disk into the disk drive, hold the disk with your thumb on the label and the write-protect notch facing left. Slide the disk into the drive and turn the drive handle to close the drive.

3-1/2″ Floppy Disk

Two Types of 3-1/2″ Floppy Disks

1. *Double density:* Stores approximately 720K (720,000) bytes of information. This disk is used in a double density drive.
2. *High density:* Stores approximately 1.44 megabytes (1,440,000 bytes) of information. This disk is used in a high density drive.

Features of a 3-1/2″ Floppy Disk

The principle of operation of the 3-1/2″ floppy disk (Figure 4–2) is similar to that of the 5-1/4″ disk. It is protected by a hard plastic shell. The head slot is covered by an *automatic head-slot shutter* when the disk is removed from the drive. The *write-protect window* in the corner has a sliding tab. When the window is open, the disk is write protected. When the window is covered, information can be recorded or erased.

Inserting a 3-1/2″ Floppy Disk into the Disk Drive

Insert the disk with the *insertion arrow* on the upper left-hand side pointing toward the drive. The disk is automatically locked into place.

FIGURE 4–2
3-1/2″ Floppy Disk

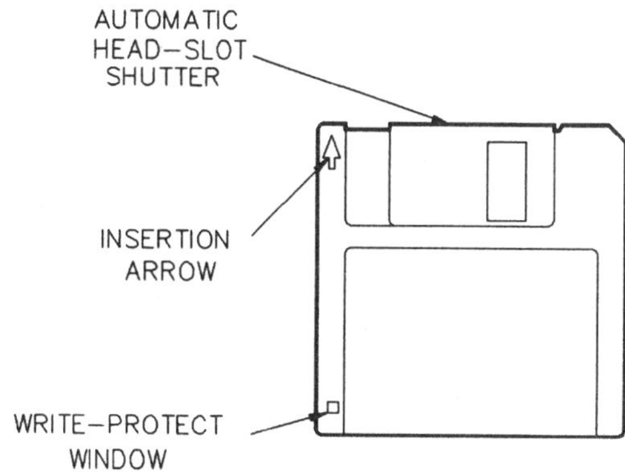

Handling Floppy Disks

The 5-1/4″ floppy disk is fragile and can be damaged easily. Be especially careful not to touch the head-slot area. Always handle the disk carefully by its edges. Store it in a protective sleeve and in a box when you are not using it. Be careful to keep it from extreme temperatures and magnetized items. Use only a felt tip pen to write on the disk label.

With its hard plastic shell and automatic head-slot shutter, the 3-1/2″ disk is much less fragile than the 5-1/4″ floppy disk. There is less danger of damaging the 3-1/2″ disk.

A small light on the disk drive tells you when the drive is active. Never remove or insert a disk in the drive or turn the computer off when the light is on.

Formatting a Floppy Disk

You can purchase either unformatted floppy disks or ones that have already been formatted. If the new floppy disk has not been formatted, it must be formatted before a drawing can be saved on it. Formatting prepares the disk so it can be used, and needs to be done only once. Formatting also deletes all information that is stored on the disk. The information cannot be retrieved. *Be very careful when formatting a floppy disk from a DOS prompt. You may accidentally format the hard disk. If the hard disk is formatted, all programs and data stored on it are completely gone—forever!* In the classroom you may have a menu from which the floppy disk can be formatted. Have someone familiar with the system you are working on help you format a disk for the first time.

EXERCISE 4–1
BEGINNING AN AUTOCAD DRAWING; USING DIALOG BOXES; SETTING UNITS, LIMITS, GRID, AND SNAP; SAVING YOUR WORK AND EXITING AUTOCAD

When starting a new drawing with AutoCAD, you must make four major settings before you begin to draw. These settings are UNITS, LIMITS, GRID, and SNAP. This exercise provides a hands-on, step-by-step description for establishing and savings those settings for the drawing you will complete in Exercise 5–1 (Chapter 5).

To begin, turn on the computer, and start AutoCAD. Because the AutoCAD screen appears immediately, you could make settings and begin your drawing right away, before naming it. But . . . *do not* make any settings or begin your drawing before using the New: command, as the following section describes.

New:

Step 1. Begin a drawing named 5-1(your initials) on the hard drive (Figure 4–3).

Prompt	Response
Command:	**New:**
The Create New Drawing dialog box appears:	*Type:* **5-1(your initials)** ↵

FIGURE 4–3
Create New Drawing Dialog Box

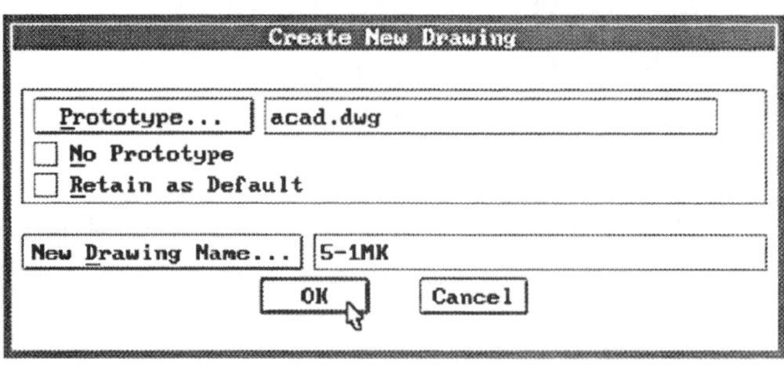

The new drawing name can be as long as your operating system permits, usually eight characters. It can include only letters, numbers, and three special characters: $ (dollar sign), - (hyphen), and __ (underscore). Each drawing is a file. The name you enter becomes the file name under which a drawing is stored when it is saved. AutoCAD stores it under ".DWG" file type. Do not add .DWG to your drawing name; AutoCAD adds it automatically. The letters DWG following the period are called an *extension.*

Because a path was not specified with the name, the drawing, by default, will start on the hard drive in the current directory. Always work on the hard drive. Never work on a floppy disk in the floppy drive, because you may lose some of your work. AutoCAD updates a database for a drawing after any command is used that changes the drawing. Recent versions of AutoCAD recommend that space equal to four times the drawing size be available on the disk. When the floppy disk is full, the program will crash and you may lose the most recently completed work (the work completed since the last SAVE).

Using the Create Drawing File Dialog Box

When the New Drawing Name. . . button of the Create New Drawing dialog box is picked, a Create Drawing File dialog box (Figure 4–4) appears. (The gray box in Figure 4–4 is the dialog box for Windows.)

FIGURE 4–4
Create Drawing File Dialog Box

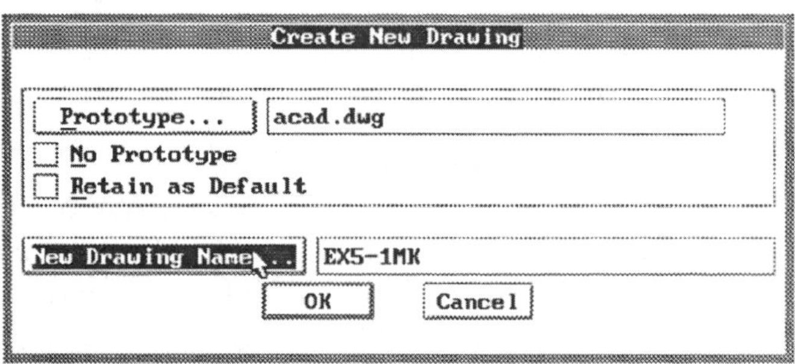

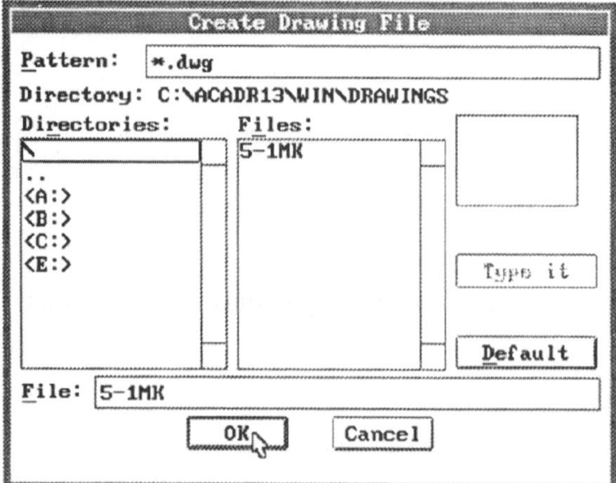

Step 2. Use the Create Drawing File dialog box (Figure 4–4).

Prompt	Response
COMMAND:	**New:**
The Create New Drawing dialog box appears:	Move the cursor (now an arrow) over the "New Drawing Name. . ." words, and pick.
The Create Drawing File dialog box appears.	

Note: The hard disk and floppy disks may use directories to separate files into groups. The AutoCAD program files are usually located in a directory called ACAD, on the hard disk.

The Create Drawing File dialog box allows you to look through the lists of file names in different directories. This allows you to verify existing file names before determining a new drawing name or to replace an existing file with a new drawing by picking an existing name.

All dialog boxes have some basic components. The following list describes the components that appear in the Create Drawing File dialog box (Figure 4–4).

1. *Cross hairs:* Change to an arrow.
2. *OK button:* Pick this button to complete the command, leave the dialog box, and return to the drawing. If any changes have been made, they will remain as changes. Pressing the enter key has the same effect. Note that the OK button has a heavy border, denoting that it is the default selection. Pressing the enter key automatically selects any default button.
3. *Cancel button:* Pick this button to cancel the command, leave the dialog box, and return to the drawing. If any changes have been made, they will be canceled, and the original settings will return. Pressing the Ctrl-C keys or the Esc key on the keyboard has the same effect.
4. *Grayed-out button* (DOS version only): This means the button is disabled. Different commands use the same dialog boxes; the name of the dialog box (at the top of the dialog box) is changed, but the basic function remains the same. In this case, this is a standard file dialog box, which you will see for any command that requires a list of files. The grayed-out button functions when the same dialog box is used with a different setting or different command.
5. *File: (File Name:) edit box:* An edit box has two parts, its name and the area where information is entered. With the File: (File Name:) edit box, a file name can be highlighted and picked from the list of Files and entered into the File: edit box, or a file name can be typed and entered into the File: edit box.

   The following editing keys can be used to edit the text in an edit box:

   Backspace key: Deletes characters to the left of the text cursor one at a time as it is pressed.
   Delete key: Deletes characters to the right of the text cursor one at a time as it is pressed.
   Left arrow: Moves the text cursor to the left, without changing the existing text.
   Right arrow: Moves the text cursor to the right, without changing the existing text.
   Home key: Moves the cursor to the beginning of the characters.

6. *List box and scroll bar:* Two list boxes (Directories: and Files:) and two scroll bars appear in the Create Drawing File dialog box. You may use the scroll bar to move through and view the complete list of directories and files. The arrow in the scroll bar that points down, when picked, will scroll down one item. The arrow that points up will scroll up one item. The slider box in the scroll bar shows the relative position of the directories and files visible in the whole list. When the box is at the top, the first page is listed. When the box is at the bottom, the last page is listed. Pick the slider box to activate it, drag it to the position you want, and release the pick.

   To list files in other directories, double click the individual directory. Double click \ or . . to return to the original list of directories and files.

7. *Preview window:* When a file name is highlighted and picked from the list of Files: and entered into the File: edit box, the preview window allows you to view the drawing that is stored under that file name. You can then pick the Cancel button to cancel the operation, or pick the OK button to replace the existing drawing shown in the preview window with a new drawing.
8. *Moving dialog boxes around the screen:* Pick the name area (dark strip across the top) of the dialog box, and hold the pick button of your mouse down, to move the dialog box around the screen. Release the pick button to reposition the dialog box.
9. *AutoCAD message:* When an existing drawing name is selected from the Files: list, and the OK button is picked, an AutoCAD Message dialog box appears (Figure 4–5). It says, "That drawing file exists. Replace it with the new drawing? When the No button is picked, AutoCAD returns to the Create Drawing File dialog box, and you may start the selection again. If a Y or Yes response is entered, the new drawing will replace the existing drawing (.DWG file). When one dialog box appears in front of another (as shown in Figure 4–4) the action in the top dialog box must be completed before you can work on the underlying dialog box.

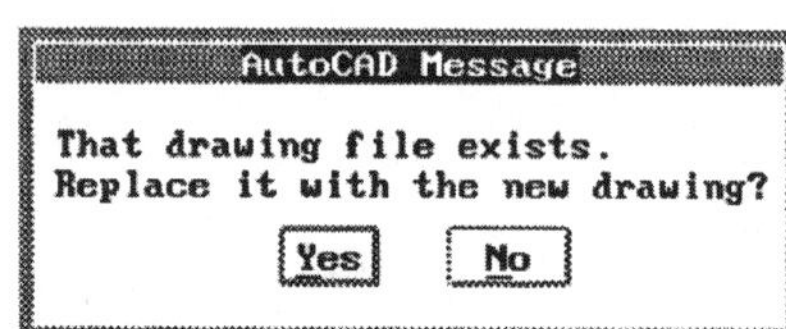

FIGURE 4–5
AutoCAD Message Dialog Box

Step 3. On Your Own:

While in the Create Drawing File dialog box, experiment with the different areas of the dialog box. Use the Cancel button to cancel any changes, leave the dialog box, and return to the drawing.

Starting a Drawing, Then Using the NEW. . . Command

When the AutoCAD Program is started, and the AutoCAD screen appears, you may immediately begin drawing without using the New: command to name your drawing. If you begin drawing, you are working in an unnamed drawing. When the New: command is used *after starting a drawing,* a Drawing Modification dialog box (Figure 4–6) will appear:

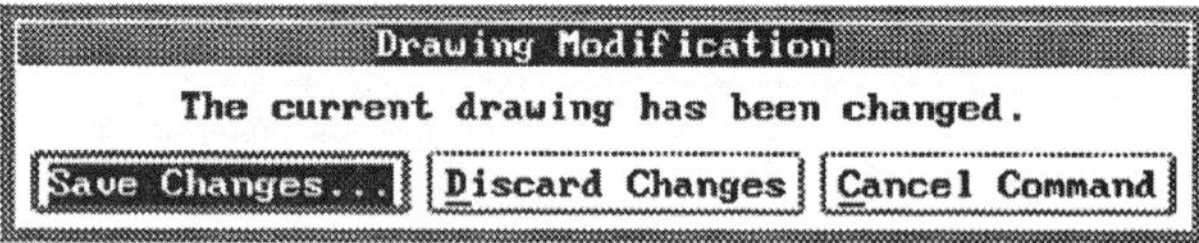

FIGURE 4–6
Drawing Modification Dialog Box

1. If the **Save Changes. . .** button is picked, a Save Drawing As dialog box (Figure 4–7; the gray box is the dialog box for Windows) appears for you to name the current drawing, and then a Create New Drawing dialog box (Figure 4–3) appears in which to name and start a new drawing.
2. If the **Discard Changes** button is picked, the existing drawing is discarded, and a Create New Drawing dialog box appears in which to name and start a new drawing.
3. Picking the **Cancel Command** button cancels the command.

If you start your AutoCAD drawing before naming the drawing, use the Save: command to name and save the drawing. When Save: from the FILE menu is selected, the Save Drawing As dialog box (Figure 4–8) appears. You can enter the drawing name, save the drawing, then continue drawing, or exit from AutoCAD. Saving your drawing and exiting from AutoCAD is described at the end of this exercise.

FIGURE 4–7
Save Drawing As Dialog Box

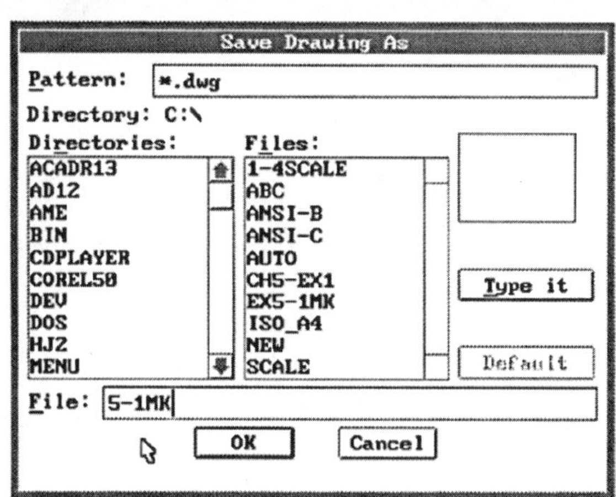

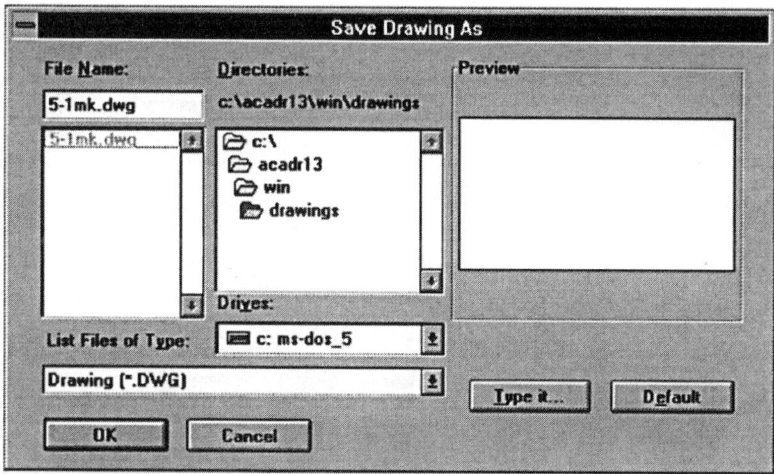

FIGURE 4–8
Save Drawing Dialog Box

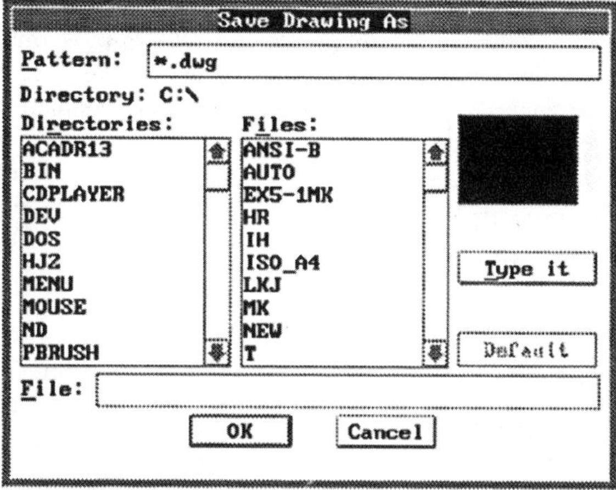

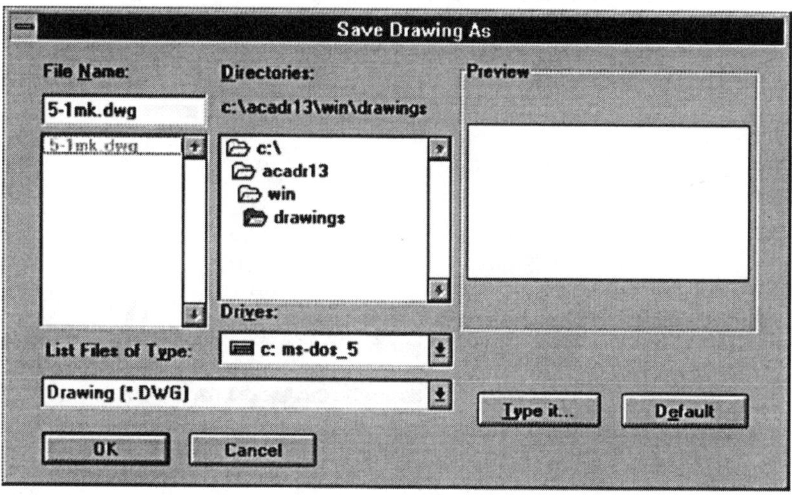

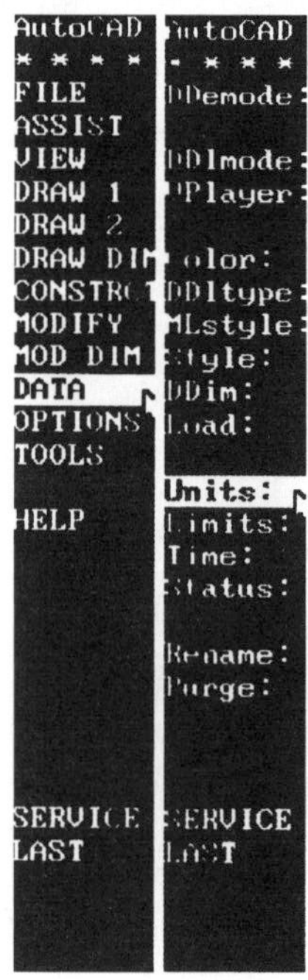

Units:

Units: refers to drawing units. For example, an inch is a drawing unit. Most manufacturers use decimal units, and that is what is used in this exercise. The following describes AutoCAD's text screen response when UNITS is typed and entered from the keyboard. (When UNITS is typed and entered, AutoCAD flips automatically from the graphics screen to the text screen.)

Step 4. Set drawing UNITS.

Prompt	Response
Command:	*Type:* **UNITS** ↵
Report formats:	(Examples)
1. Scientific	1.55E+01
2. Decimal	15.50
3. Engineering	1′-3.50″
4. Architectural	1′-3 1/2″
5. Fractional	15 1/2

With the exception of Engineering and Architectural formats, these formats can be used with any basic unit of measurement. For example, Decimal mode is perfect for metric units as well as for decimal English units.

Note: A default value is usually the most recent setting entered for a command. It is shown in angle brackets (< >) in the prompt area. Press the enter key to use a default value.

Prompt	Response
Enter choice, 1 to 5 <default>:	*Type:* **2** ↵
Enter choice, 1 to 5 <2>: 2	
Number of digits to right of decimal point (0 to 8) <default>:	*Type:* **4** ↵

The remaining settings under Units: are for measuring angles. There is no reason to change these settings. By using the enter key, AutoCAD's default values, which measure angles using decimal degrees in the counterclockwise direction, are accepted as follows:

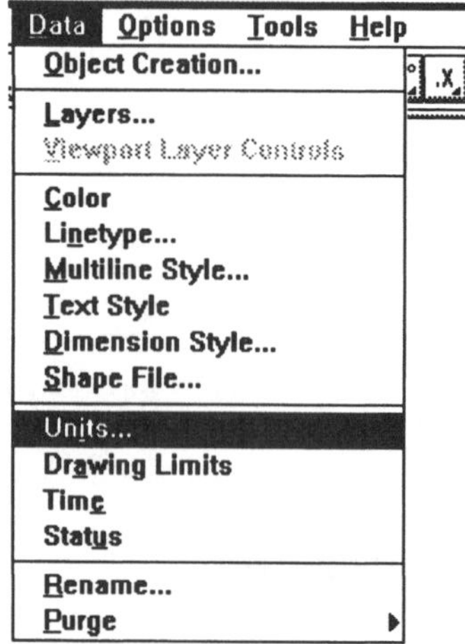

Prompt	Response
Systems of angle measure:	(Examples)
1. Decimal degrees	45.0000
2. Degrees/minutes/seconds	45d0′0″
3. Grads	50.0000g
4. Radians	0.784r
5. Surveyor's units	N 45d0′0″ E
Enter choice, 1 to 5 <1>:	↵
Enter choice, 1 to 5 <1>: Number of fractional places for display of angles (0 to 8) <0>:	↵
Direction for angle 0: East 3 o'clock = 0 North 12 o'clock = 90 West 9 o'clock = 180 South 6 o'clock = 270	
Enter direction for angle 0 <0>:	↵
Do you want angles measured clockwise? <N>	↵

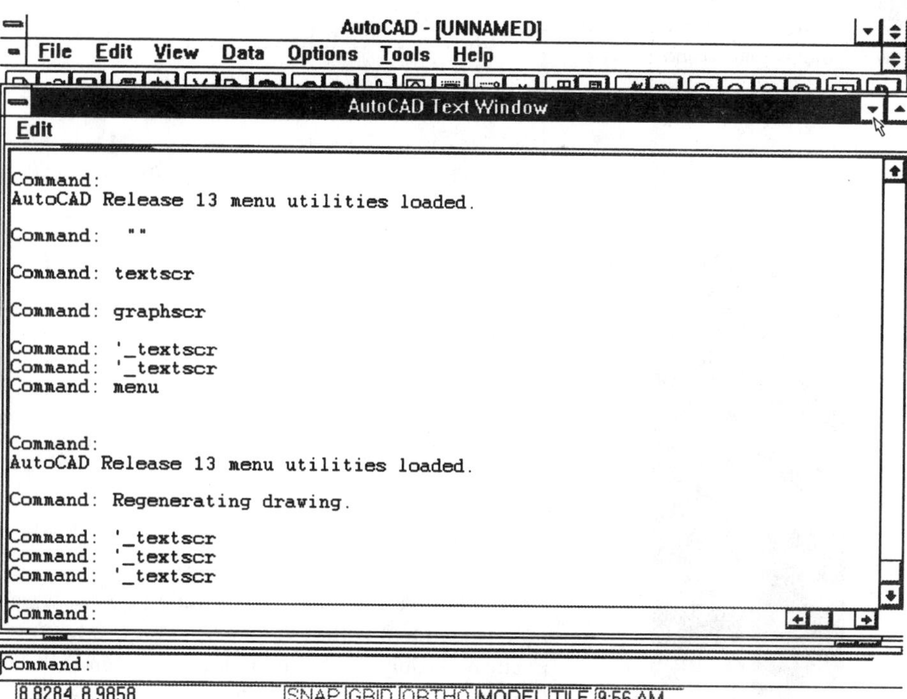

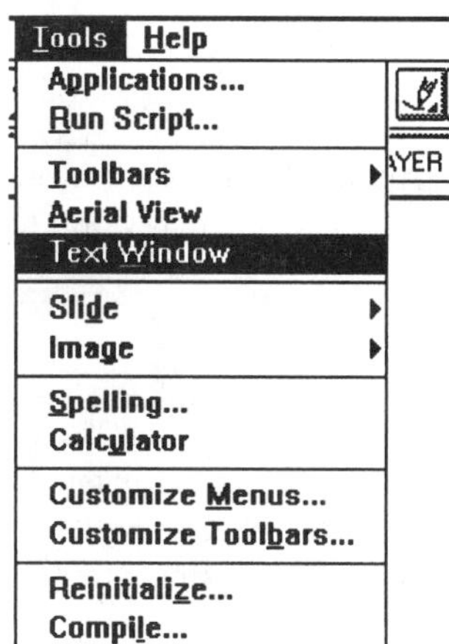

Command:

Press: **F1** (for DOS, to flip from the text screen to the graphics screen and vice versa).

Pick: **the down arrow in the upper right corner** (for Windows, to flip from the text screen to the graphics screen) or *Press:* **F2**

Pick: **Text Window** (on the Tools menu on the menu bar to flip from the graphics screen to the text screen).

Units Control Dialog Box

Units may also be set using the Units Control dialog box.

To locate the Units Control dialog box, move the pointer across the top of the display screen, in the status line area, and highlight Data on the menu bar that appears. Pick Data, and a pull-down menu appears under the Data title. Move your pointer to highlight Units. . . , then pick it. The Units Control dialog box (Figure 4–9) now appears on your screen. Picking Units: on the Data menu will also access the Units Control dialog box. As you can see, all items described in the preceding list can be selected from this dialog box.

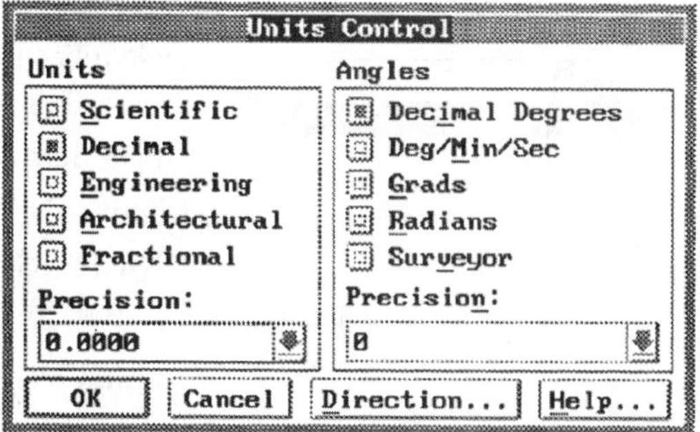

FIGURE 4–9
Units Control Dialog Box

FIGURE 4–10
Drawing Limits with X and Y Axes Shown

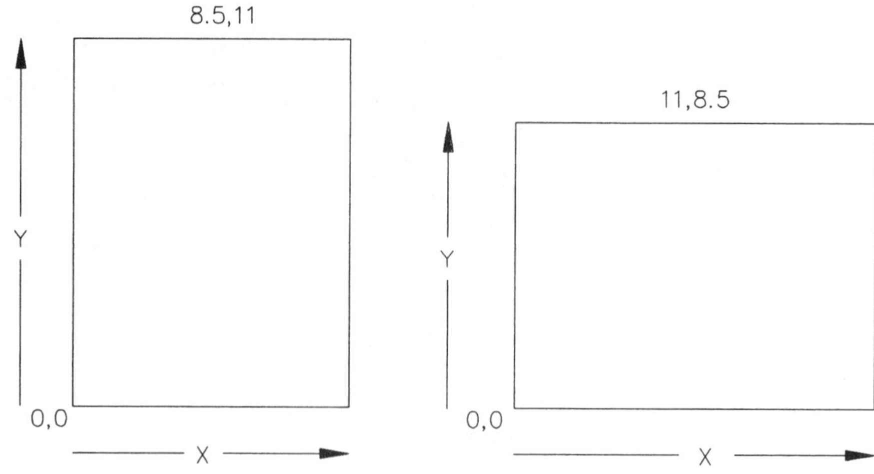

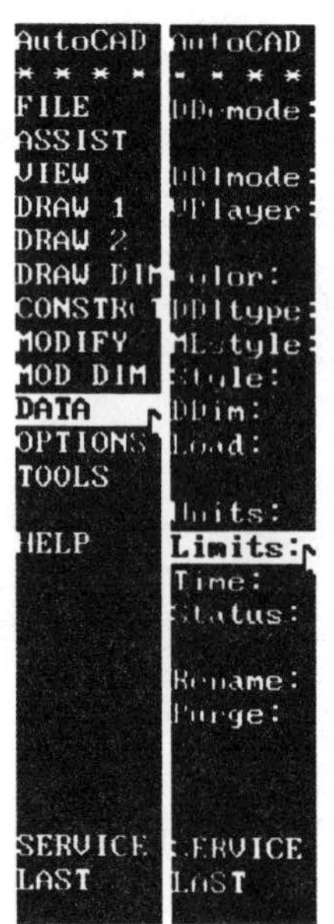

Note: Pick AutoCAD from the top of any DOS menu to return to the AutoCAD root menu.

Another basic component of dialog boxes, which appears in the Units Control dialog box, is the radio button. A *radio button* is a button that is part of a group that is mutually exclusive—only one button in the group can be picked. The five radio buttons in the Units Control dialog box used to select units are Scientific, Decimal, Engineering, Architectural, and Fractional. Only one can be selected at a time; when the button is selected, a black box appears inside the square button.

Drawing Scale

A drawing scale factor does not need to be set. While using AutoCAD to make drawings for the exercises in this book you will automatically draw full scale, using real-world feet and inches. Full-scale drawings can be plotted in any scale.

Limits:

Think of drawing limits as the sheet (paper) size or sheet (paper) boundaries. 8-1/2″ × 11″ will be set as the drawing limits. In AutoCAD decimal units that setting is entered as 8.5,11. A comma (with no space) is used to separate the X and Y axes (Figure 4–10). The inch symbol is not required. The X axis is first (8.5) and measures drawing limits from left to right. The Y axis is second (11) and measures drawing limits from bottom to top. You will be drawing in a vertical 8.5″ × 11″ area.

The lower left corner of the drawing boundaries is 0,0. The upper right corner is 8.5,11 (Figure 4–10). To turn the 8.5″ × 11″ area horizontally, the limits would be entered as 11,8.5 (Figure 4–10).

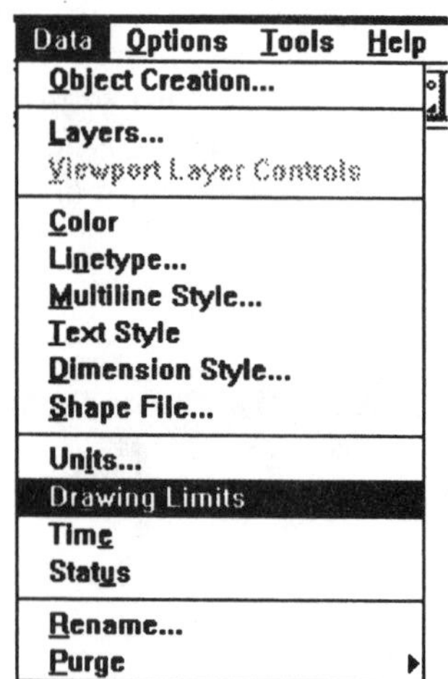

Step 5. Set limits.

Prompt	Response
Command:	*Press:* **F7** (to turn the grid on)
Command: <Grid on>:	**Limits:**
ON/OFF/<Lower left corner> <0′-0″,0′-0″>:	↵
Upper right corner <default>:	*Type:* **8.5,11** ↵
Command:	↵
ON/OFF/<Lower left corner> <0′-0″,0′-0″>:	*Type:* **ON** ↵

Tip: Press the ↵ key to repeat the last command prompt.

LimChk: (a limits checking system variable) can be on or off. When the ON (1) mode is activated, AutoCAD prevents you from drawing outside the drawing limits and provides the error message in the "** Outside limits" prompt line when a point is selected outside the limits. Some drawing elements, such as a circle, may be started inside the limits and completed outside the limits without causing this prompt to appear. The OFF (0) mode, when activated, allows you to draw outside the drawing limits.

If the drawing limits need to be changed, you may do so at any time by entering new limits to the "Upper right corner <default>:" prompt. Changing the drawing limits will automatically change the grid pattern to fit the new limits.

Grid:

The grid is a visible pattern of dots on the display screen. The grid size will be set at .25 for drawing 5-1(your initials). With a setting of .25, each grid dot will be spaced .25″ vertically and horizontally. The grid is not part of the drawing but helps provide a sense of the size and relationship of the drawing elements. It does not plot.

Step 6. Set the grid spacing.

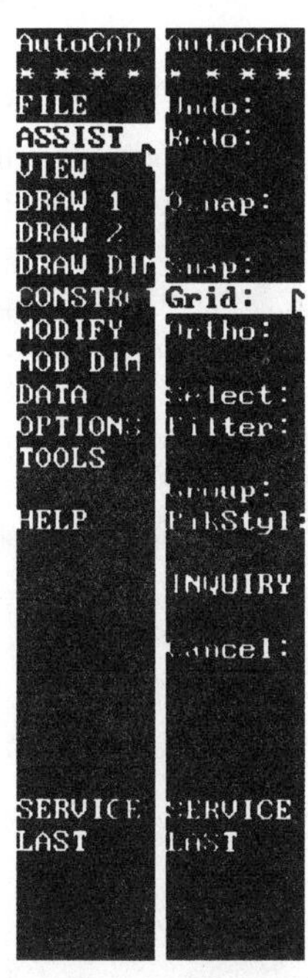

Prompt	Response
Command:	*Type:* **GRID** ↵
Grid spacing (X) or ON/OFF/Snap/ Aspect <0.000>:	*Type:* **.25** ↵

A brief explanation of the other Grid: prompt options follows.

Grid Spacing (X)

The grid can be set as a multiple of snap (see Snap: in the next section). When you type and enter a number followed by X in response to the prompt "Grid spacing (X) or ON/OFF/Snap/Aspect <default>:", the grid will be set at every snap point indicated by the number. For instance, entering **4X** will set the grid at every fourth snap point.

ON/OFF

Function key F7 turns the grid on or off. You can also turn the grid on or off by selecting either option in response to the prompt "Grid spacing (X) or ON/OFF/Snap/Aspect <default>:".

Snap

If the grid is set at 0, the spacing will automatically be the same spacing as the snap spacing (see Snap:, following). If S or SNAP is typed as a grid setting option and entered, or if grid-snap is picked from the side menu, the grid is set at 0 and will be the same spacing as the snap spacing.

Aspect

If Aspect is picked from the side menu in response to the Grid: prompt, AutoCAD will respond with prompts allowing you to set the grid with differing X and Y (horizontal and vertical) axis spacing.

Snap:

Step 7. Set the snap spacing.

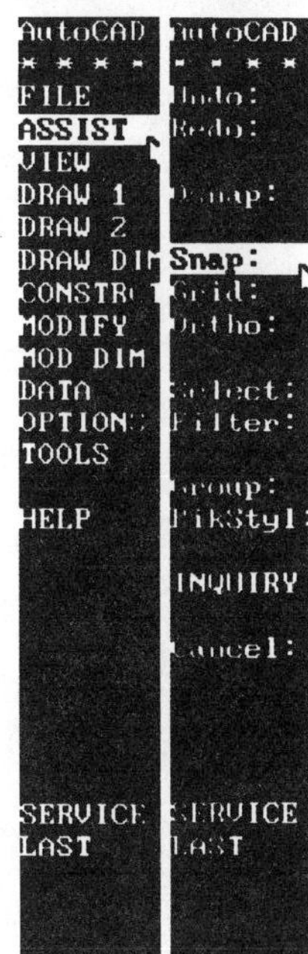

Prompt	Response
Command:	*Type:* **SNAP** ↵
Snap spacing or ON/OFF/Aspect/ Rotate/Style <default>:	*Type:* **.125** ↵

You have set .125 as the snap spacing. Snap is an invisible pattern of dots on the display screen. As you move the pointer across the screen the cross hairs will snap or lock to an invisible snap grid when snap is on. With a setting of .125, each snap point is spaced .125″ horizontally and vertically. Drawing with Snap on, helps you draw accurately. A brief explanation of the other Snap: prompt options follows.

ON/OFF

The function key F9 turns snap on or off. Snap can also be turned ON or OFF by selecting either option in response to the prompt "Snap spacing or ON/OFF/Aspect/Rotate/Style <default>:".

Aspect

If Aspect is picked from the side menu in response to the Snap: prompt, AutoCAD will respond with prompts allowing you to set the snap with differing X and Y axis spacing.

Rotate

Rotate allows you to select a base point and rotate the snap and grid around a base point at any angle.

Style

The Style snap option allows you to select an isometric snap grid.

Drawing Aids Dialog Box

The grid and snap spacing may also be set using the Drawing Aids dialog box.

To locate the Drawing Aids dialog box, move the pointer across the top of the display screen, in the status line area, and highlight and pick Options on the menu bar that appears (Figure 4–11). A pull-down menu appears under the Options title. Move your pointer to highlight Drawing Aids. . . , and pick it. The Drawing Aids dialog box (Figure 4–11) now appears on your screen. Picking DDrmode: at the top of the DOS OPTIONS menu or on the Grid: and Snap: menus will also access the Drawing Aids dialog box.

Another basic component of dialog boxes, which appears in the Drawing Aids dialog box, is the *check box*. If the box is checked (an X is showing), it is on. You can toggle the Snap and Grid modes on and off as well as the additional modes (such as Ortho and Blips) that you will learn about in later chapters.

FIGURE 4–11
Drawing Aids Dialog Box

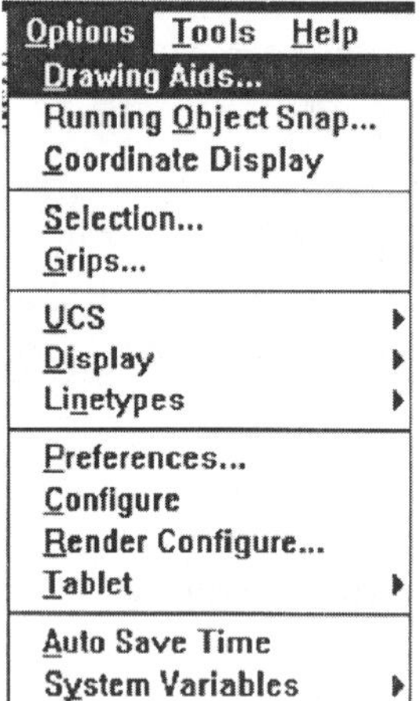

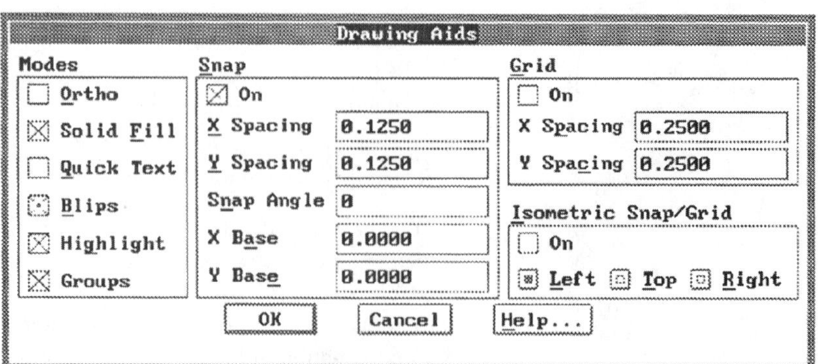

Step 8. On Your Own: (Figure 4–11):

While in the Drawing Aids dialog box experiment with the different editing keys to become familiar with their functions. The dialog box is a handy tool for quickly setting the snap and grid spacing. After experimenting, be sure to return the grid spacing to .25 and the snap to .125 to have the correct settings for Exercise 5–1. You can use the Cancel button to cancel any changes, leave the dialog box, and return to the drawing.

Saving Your Work and Exiting AutoCAD

Seven commands—Save:, Qsave, SaveAs:, Exit:, QUIT, End, and SAVEASR12—and their uses must be understood so that you can save your work in the desired drive and directory and exit AutoCAD after you have saved your work. The following part of this exercise will describe these commands. It will provide step-by-step instructions for saving drawing 5-1 (your initials) with the settings (units, limits, grid, and snap) to the hard drive, and to a floppy disk, and exiting AutoCAD.

Save:

In AutoCAD Release 13, when the SAVE command is typed and entered, a Save Drawing As dialog box (Figure 4–12) appears. This is the same standard file dialog box we saw earlier in this exercise, with a different name. AutoCAD provides several different options to select from to save your drawing using this dialog box.

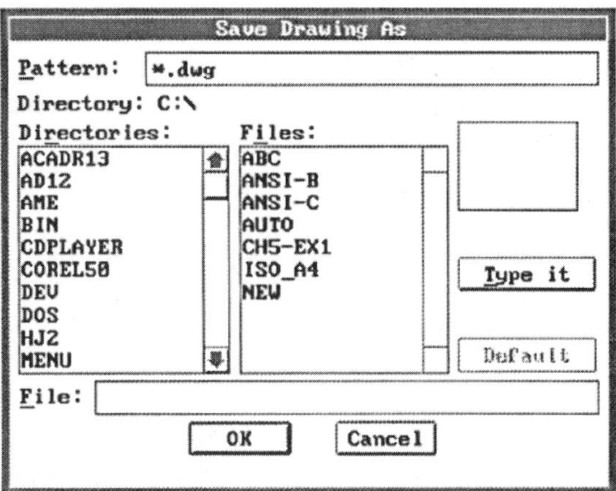

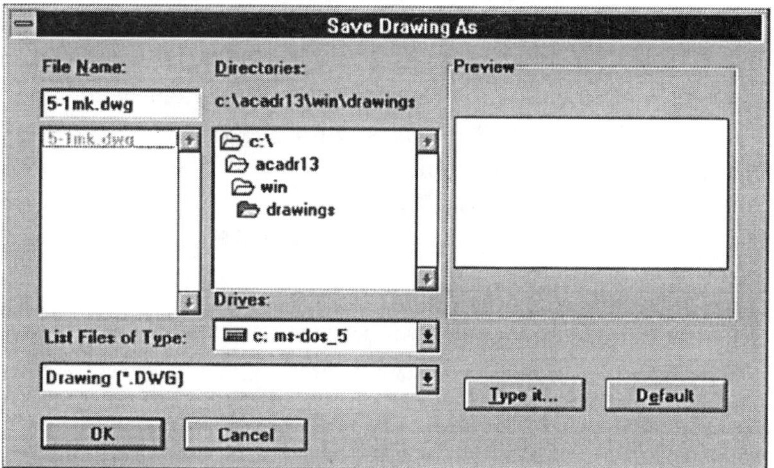

FIGURE 4–12
Save Drawing As Dialog Box

Step 9. Save drawing file 5-1(your initials).

Note: Save. . . and SaveAs. . . are located in a pull-down menu under File in the menu bar.

Prompt	Response
Command:	*Type:* **SAVE** ↵
The Save Drawing As dialog box appears.	

Save Drawing As Dialog Box

The parts and functions of the Save Drawing As dialog box (Figure 4–12) are as follows:

1. *Pattern: edit box (List Files of Type: for Windows):* Shows the file type (extension) under which the file will be stored. The pattern (extension) may be changed to list and search for other files with a different extension. In DOS systems, enter *.* to list all files.
2. *Directory: label line:* This is a label that shows your current drive and directory path. It changes as you double click other directories in the Directories: list box to search through directories. It also changes when you pick other directories to save the drawing in. When you are working on a drawing, make sure this line shows the hard drive (C:) so you know you are working on the hard drive and not on a floppy disk drive.
3. *Directories: list box (Directories: and Drives: are separated for Windows.):* You may double click any of these directories or drives to get a listing of the files in them. The drives are listed in brackets (<A:>). The files will be of the type shown in the Pattern: edit box. You may also get a listing of other files by changing the pattern (extension) in the Pattern: edit box. If you pick one of the floppy drives (A: or B:), be sure to have a floppy disk in the drive, or an error message will appear.

   You can double click a different directory or drive to save your drawing in; it will appear in the directory label. Pick the OK button, and the drawing will be saved in the directory or drive you have selected.
4. *Files: list box:* Lists the files contained in the drive, directory, and drawing pattern (extension) shown in the dialog box.
5. *File: edit box (File Name: for Windows):* The file name under which the drawing will be saved appears here. You may change the drawing name under which the drawing will be saved by erasing the name and typing in a new name, or you may pick a name from the Files: list box.

   You may also type a different drive or directory in front of the file name to save it in a different drive or directory. When you save to a floppy disk, the drawing name is set to include that drive. When this occurs, you are working on the floppy disk in that drive. Do not work on a floppy disk, or you may lose some of your work. If you want to continue working on the drawing, save to the hard drive to reset the drawing name so that you are working on the hard drive.
6. *OK button:* When picked, will execute the SAVE command.
7. *Cancel button:* When picked, will cancel the command. Ctrl-C and the Esc keys have the same effect.
8. *Type it button:* When picked, will allow you to type the drive, directory, and name to which you want the file saved from the command line.
9. *Default button:* When picked, will return information in the dialog box to the original information.
10. *Preview (Windows only):* Shows a picture of the previous version of the drawing if the drawing is picked from the File Name: list box.

Step 10. On Your Own:

1. Pick the **Type it** button.
2. Select one or both of the following drives to save your drawing files.
3. Save your file in at least two places.

To save drawing file 5–1(your initials) to a floppy disk in the A drive:

Prompt	Response
SAVE drawing as <C:5-1 (your initials)>:	*Type:* **A:5-1(your initials)** ↵
Current drawing name set to A:5-1 (your initials).	

If you had pressed enter to the prompt "SAVE drawing as <C:5-1(your initials)>:", the drawing would have been saved to the hard drive.

Change the floppy drive name (for example, **B:**) if you want to save to a different floppy drive. Remove the first floppy disk and insert a second one, then repeat the SAVE command to save the drawing file to a second floppy disk.

When you save to a floppy disk, the drawing name is set to include that drive. When this occurs, you are working on the floppy disk in that drive. Do not work on a floppy disk; you may lose some of your work. If you want to continue working on the drawing, save to the hard drive to reset the drawing name so that you are working on the hard drive, as described in the following:

To save drawing file 5-1(your initials) to the hard drive in the directory in which you are working after you have saved to a floppy disk in drive A: (or B:):

Prompt	Response
Command:	*Type:* **SAVE** ↵
The Save Drawing As dialog box appears:	*Pick:* a spot in front of the drawing name to move the flashing cursor in front of the name. *Type:* **C:** *Pick:* **OK button**
Current drawing name set to C:\5-1 (your initials)	

You are now logged onto the hard drive and can continue working on the drawing.

The SAVE command can be activated in three different ways: **SAVE** can be typed and entered, as you just did. When **Save:** is picked from the screen FILE menu, or when **Save** is picked from the pull-down menu under File in the Menu Bar, AutoCAD (in most instances) behaves like the command Qsave.

Qsave

Qsave is the quick save command. When the drawing is named, this command saves the current drawing without asking for a file name. If the drawing is unnamed, and Save: is picked from the screen FILE menu or from the pull-down menu under File in the menu bar, or if QSAVE is typed and entered at the Command: prompt, a Save Drawing As dialog box (Figure 4–12) appears. By now you are familiar with this dialog box. Enter the drawing name, select a drive or directory if you want to save it in a different drive or directory, and pick enter to save your drawing.

SaveAs:

Whether the drawing has been named or is unnamed, when SaveAs: is picked, the Save Drawing As dialog box (Figure 4–12) appears and can be used as described previously.

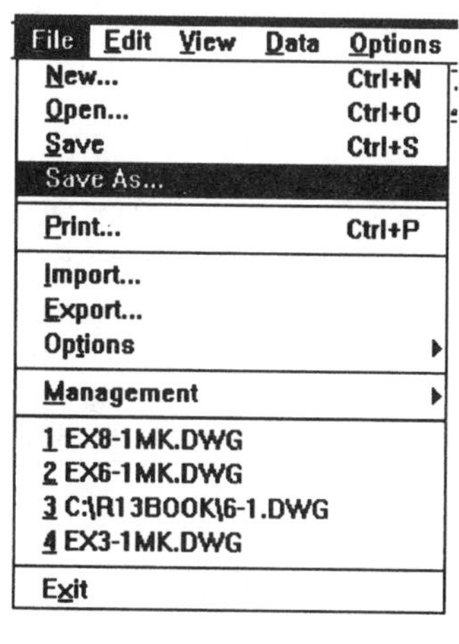

Features of the Save:, Qsave, and SaveAs: commands

When working on a drawing, it is best to use the Save:, Qsave, or SaveAs: commands to save your drawing periodically (every hour or so; less time if you prefer) to guard against losing more than an hour's work to an unexpected mishap such as a power interruption. As mentioned earlier, when the Save: or SaveAs: commands are used to save to a floppy disk, the drawing name is set to include that drive. When this occurs, you are working on the floppy disk in that drive. Do not work on a floppy disk, or you may lose some of your work. If you want to continue working on the drawing, save to the hard drive to reset the drawing name so that you are working on the hard drive, as described in the following.

Some additional features of these commands:

1. A drawing file can be saved and you may continue to work, because with the Save:, Qsave, and SaveAs: commands, the AutoCAD Program is not exited.

2. When the drawing is saved to the default drive (the drive on which you are working), and is reentered, edited, and saved again, a .DWG and a .BAK file are created. The .BAK file is a copy of the drawing as it was when it was first reentered.
3. To change the name of the drawing, you may type and enter the SAVE command, or pick the SaveAs: command to save the drawing under a new name. Type a new name to the prompt (when the Type it button is picked), or change the name in the File: edit box.
4. A drawing may be saved to as many floppy disks or to as many directories on the hard drive as you wish. You should save your drawing in two places as insurance against catastrophe.

Exit and QUIT

The Exit and QUIT commands exit the AutoCAD Program if there are no unsaved changes. You have just saved your drawing, so to immediately exit AutoCAD, use the Exit command.

Step 11. Exit AutoCAD.

Prompt	Response
Command:	**Exit**

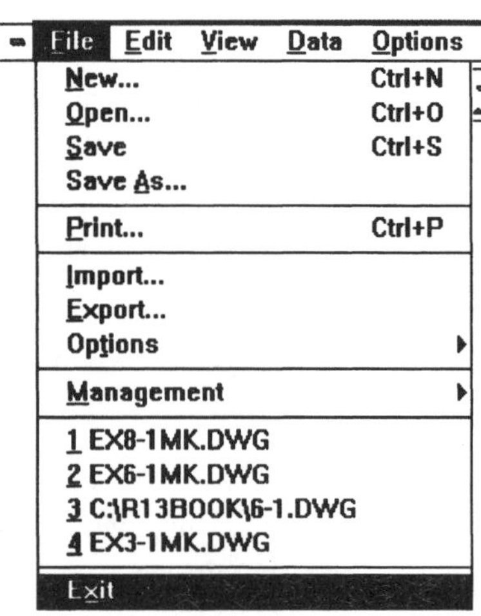

Note: The Exit AutoCAD command located in a pull-down menu under File in the menu bar acts like the QUIT command.

QUIT works the same as Exit, but QUIT (not available on a menu) is typed and entered at the Command: prompt. When either Exit or QUIT is used, and you have named your drawing but have not saved it, or if you started a drawing but have not named it, a Drawing Modification dialog box (Figure 4–13) appears.

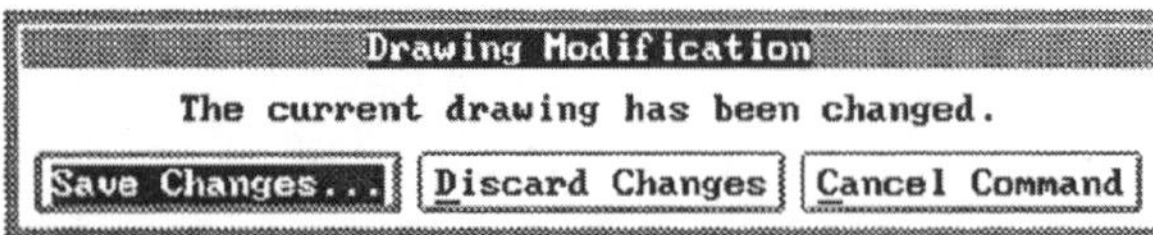

FIGURE 4–13
Drawing Modification Dialog Box

1. If the Save Changes. . . button is picked, the drawing is saved and AutoCAD is exited. A Create Drawing File dialog box appears to name your drawing, if it needs to be named, before the drawing is saved and AutoCAD is exited.
2. If the Discard Changes button is picked, the existing changes are discarded, and AutoCAD is exited.
3. Picking the Cancel Command button cancels the command.

If you have just entered a drawing, have made a lot of mistakes, and just want to get rid of the work you have done since entering, you can use the Exit or QUIT command. If you reenter an existing drawing, use the Exit or QUIT command, and pick Discard Changes, the stored .DWG file and .BAK files are preserved unchanged.

END

If you are storing your drawing file to the hard drive, the END command may be used. It automatically saves your drawing (whether there are changes or not) and exits AutoCAD. If you type and enter END, a new drawing will be saved in a .DWG file in the drive and directory in which you are working. For an existing drawing, a .DWG file and a .BAK file are created when END is used. END differs from SAVE in the following respects:

1. AutoCAD is exited.
2. A different output file cannot be specified.
3. The name of the drawing file cannot be changed.

SAVEASR12

When you want to use a Release 13 drawing in a Release 12 AutoCAD Program, use the SAVEASR12 command. When SAVEASR12 is typed and entered at the Command: prompt, a Save Release 12 Drawing As dialog box (Figure 4–14) appears. This is the same standard file dialog box we saw earlier in this exercise, with a different name. This dialog box works just like the Save Drawing As dialog box.

FIGURE 4–14
Save Release 12 Drawing As Dialog Box

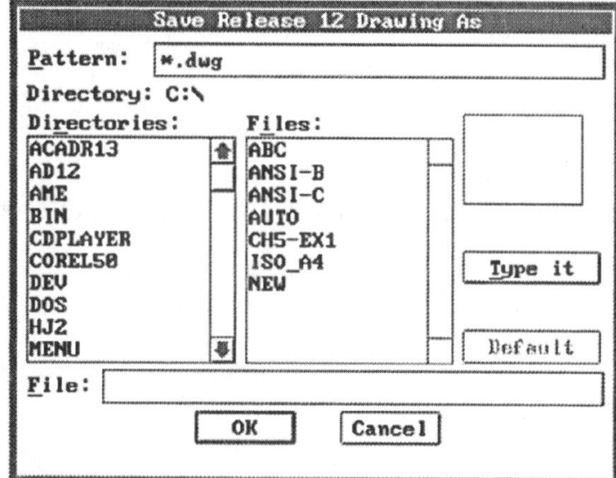

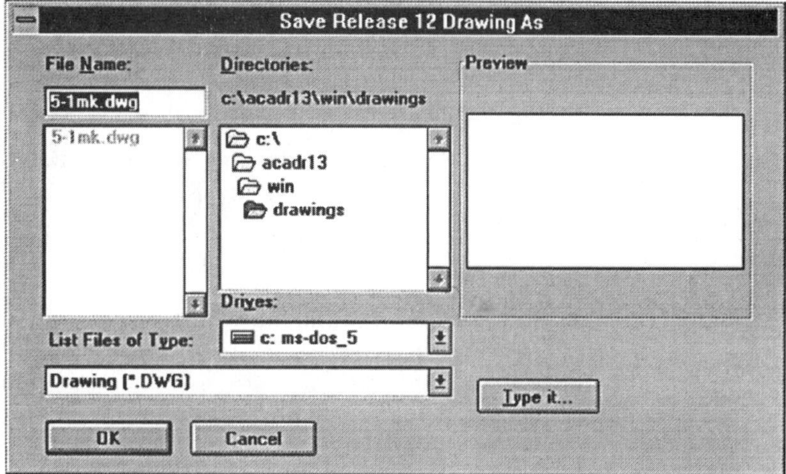

.DWG and .BAK File Types

While you are making a new drawing AutoCAD is creating a .DWG (drawing) file for your drawing. There is no .BAK (drawing file backup) file for a new drawing.

When an existing drawing is reentered, edited, and then saved on the drive on which you are working (the hard drive), the previously saved .DWG file is renamed as a .BAK file, and the most recent drawing is saved as a .DWG file. A .BAK file is not created when a drawing is saved to a drive other than the one on which you are working. When an existing drawing is reentered, edited, and then the END command is used, a .DWG and a .BAK file are created.

Each time an existing drawing file is reentered for editing, the original drawing file (.DWG) becomes the drawing file backup (.BAK) when Save: and END are used on the drive on which you are working. The new edited version of the drawing becomes the .DWG file. Thus there is a copy of the drawing file as it was originally (.BAK) and a copy of the new edited version (.DWG).

Rebooting the System

To *boot* means to start the computer and the operating system program. Avoid *rebooting* (turning the machine off and back on) when you are in the AutoCAD Program. This practice creates scattered bits of information on the hard disk, which slows the response time of the computer. Always exit the AutoCAD Program before turning the computer off.

Rebooting or restarting is sometimes necessary when the computer is locked up or AutoCAD ceases to function. If you are working on a drawing and have to reboot, bits of information will be scattered on the hard disk (or the disk you are working on) and you will lose the work completed since entering AutoCAD. Save drawings often to protect against losing work.

To reboot the system when the computer is locked up, hold down the Ctrl, Alt, and Del keys at the same time. This is known as a *warm boot*. If this does not work, turn off the computer and wait for the drives to come to a stop. Then turn the computer back on. This is known as a *cold boot*. Some computers are equipped with a reset switch. If your computer is equipped with one, use it instead of Ctrl-Alt-Del or turning the machine off.

EXERCISE 4–2
REENTERING AN EXISTING DRAWING AND CREATING LAYERS

While drawing with AutoCAD it is very easy to save your drawing and then bring it back again. In Exercise 4–1 you established the settings for drawing 5-1(your initials). In this exercise you will reenter saved drawing 5-1(your initials) and create layers. After you have learned about creating layers in this exercise, you will be ready to start drawing with AutoCAD in Chapter 5.

To begin Exercise 4–2, turn on your computer and start AutoCAD.

Begin an Existing Drawing On the Hard Drive

If drawing 5-1(your initials) is stored on a floppy disk, proceed with the following. If drawing 5-1(your initials) is stored on the hard disk, skip to "To begin existing drawing 5-1(your initials) on the hard drive when it is stored on the hard disk."

Step 1. Begin existing drawing 5-1(your initials) on the hard drive when it is stored on a floppy disk that has no directories (Figure 4–15).

Prompt	Response
Command:	**New:**
The Create New Drawing dialog box appears:	*Type:* **5-1(your initials) = A:5-1 (your initials)** ↵

The drawing appears with grid and snap set.

FIGURE 4–15
Create New Drawing Dialog Box

The Create New Drawing dialog box (Figure 4–15) allows you to specify a prototype drawing. By using the equal (=) sign you have instructed AutoCAD to start a drawing on the hard drive by copying the drawing you have on the floppy disk in drive A as the prototype drawing. AutoCAD recognizes the equal sign but as a separation between the name of the drawing and the prototype drawing, not as part of a drawing name. The drawing starts on the hard drive. Do not work on a floppy disk; always work on the hard drive.

If you use a drawing on a floppy or hard disk as a prototype drawing but want to change the name of the new drawing, you can use a new name. For example, to name the drawing "CHAPT4," you would type and enter CHAPT4=A:4-1MK. 4-1MK remains stored on the floppy disk.

Before starting the new drawing, AutoCAD checks to see if a drawing with the name entered exists on the hard drive. When an existing drawing name is used, an AutoCAD Message dialog box appears with the message, "The drawing file exists. Replace it with the new drawing?"

The default prototype drawing is usually acad.dwg, and that name appears in the Prototype. . . edit box. The acad prototype drawing's environment (settings, layers, etc.) can be tailored to suit your particular needs. Then when a new drawing is started, all settings in the acad prototype drawing appear on the screen.

When the Prototype. . . button of the Create New Drawing dialog box is picked, a Prototype Drawing File dialog box (Figure 4–16) appears. It allows you to look through the lists of file names in different drives and directories and specify a prototype drawing by double clicking a new drive, directory, or file name. That name then appears in the Prototype. . . edit box of the Create New Drawing dialog box (Figure 4–17). You could have done this earlier instead of typing 5-1(your initials) = A:5-1(your initials). The prototype drawing can be on any drive. After the prototype is selected, type the New Drawing Name. . . in that edit box (Figure 4–17) and click the OK button to start the drawing on the hard drive.

FIGURE 4–16
Prototype Drawing File Dialog Box

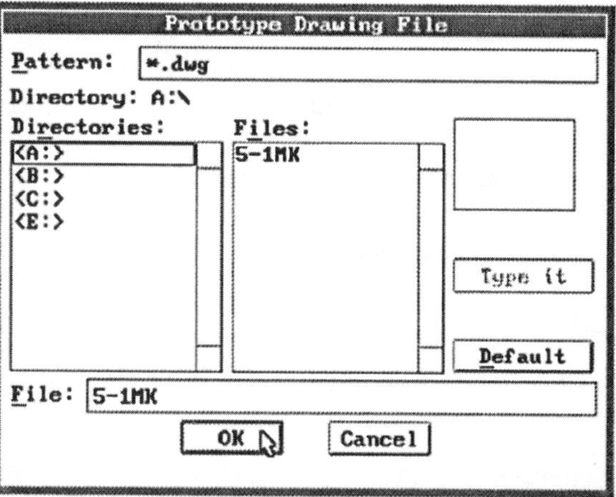

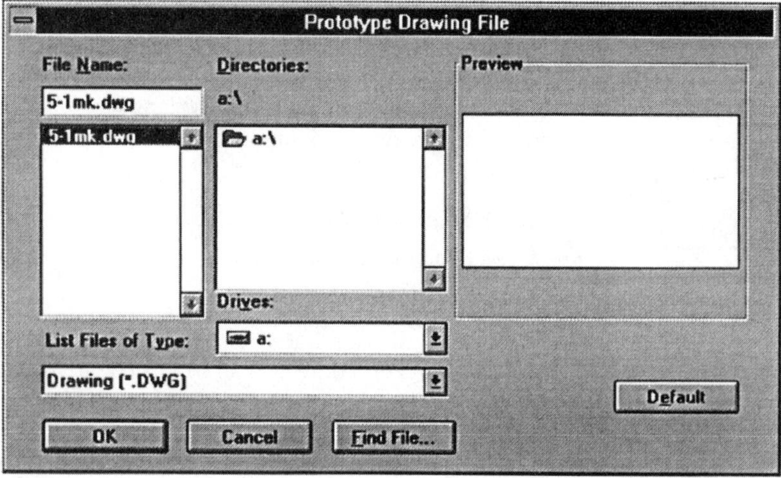

FIGURE 4–17
Create New Drawing Dialog Box

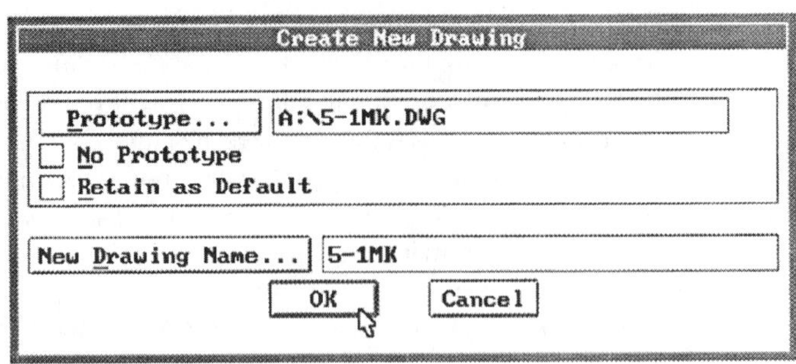

When the No Prototype check box is checked, all settings for the New drawing are cleared to a default setting. Retain as Default check box retains any prototype drawing name shown in the Prototype. . . edit box as the default prototype drawing for subsequent drawings, until it is changed.

Step 1. (alternate) Begin existing drawing 5-1(your initials) on the hard drive when it is stored on the hard disk (Figure 4–15).

Note: Open. . . is also located in a pull-down menu under File in the Menu Bar.

Prompt	Response
Command:	**Open:**
The Open Drawing dialog box appears (DOS): *or* the Select File dialog box appears (Windows):	*Type:* **4-1(your initials) and Pick: OK or double click the drawing name from the Files: list box.**

The drawing appears with grid and snap set.

Two new check boxes appear in the Open Drawing dialog box (Figure 4–18). The AutoCAD VIEW command allows you to name and save different views of a drawing. For example, you may want to name and save a portion of a drawing (a portion that is changed often) so that you can recall that view (or portion) easily. The Select Initial View check box provides a subdialog box that allows you to recall the view when you first enter the drawing. Check the Read Only Mode check box if you want to open a drawing file and protect it from being changed at all.

Zoom:

Step 2. Use Zoom: All to view the entire drawing area.

Prompt	Response
Command:	**Zoom:**
All/Center/Dynamic/Extents/Left/Previous/Vmax/Window/<Scale(X/XP)>:	**All**

The Zoom: All command lets you view the entire drawing area. Use it after setting up or entering a drawing so that you are familiar with the size and shape of your limits and grid. Otherwise you may be viewing only a small part of the drawing limits and not realize it.

Step 3. On Your Own:

Use F7 to turn the grid on, if it is not already on.

Layer

Different parts of a drawing can be placed on separate layers. The object lines may be on one layer, hidden lines on another, text on another layer, and so on. There is no limit to the number of layers you may use in a drawing. Each is perfectly aligned with all the others. Each layer may be viewed on the display screen separately or in combination with one or

FIGURE 4–18
Open Drawing and Select File Dialog Boxes

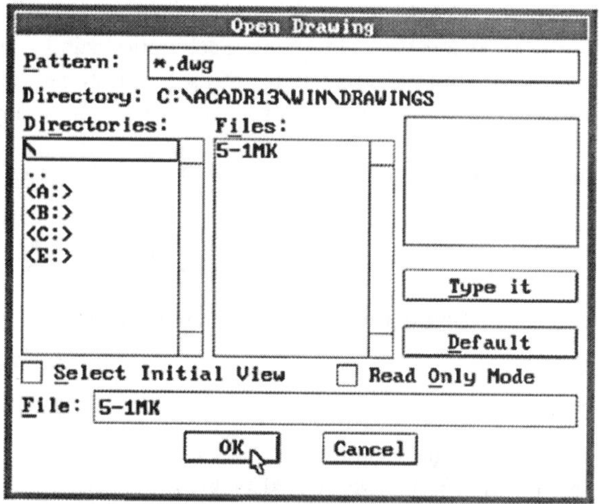

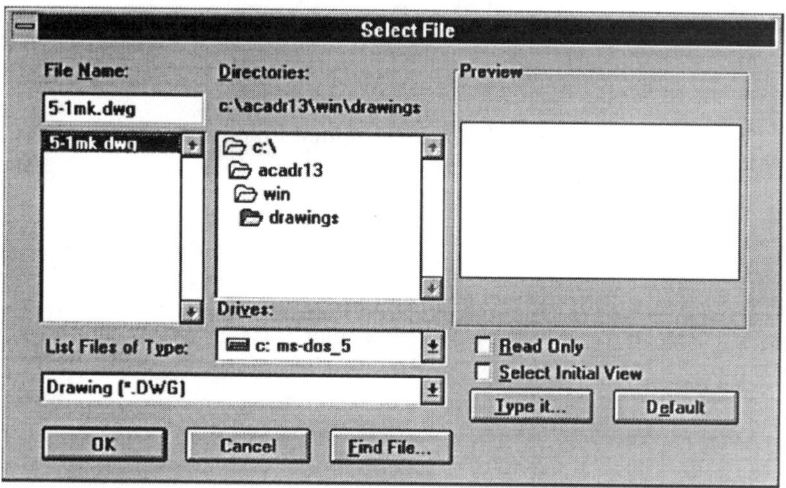

more layers, or all layers may be viewed together. Each layer may also be plotted separately or in combination with other layers, or all layers may be plotted at the same time.

To make layers, you can use either the Layer Control dialog box (Figure 4–19), or you may use the Command: prompt line. First, we will examine all the LAYER command options using the Command: prompt line. Second, we will examine the Layer Control dialog box.

FIGURE 4–19
Layer Control Dialog Box

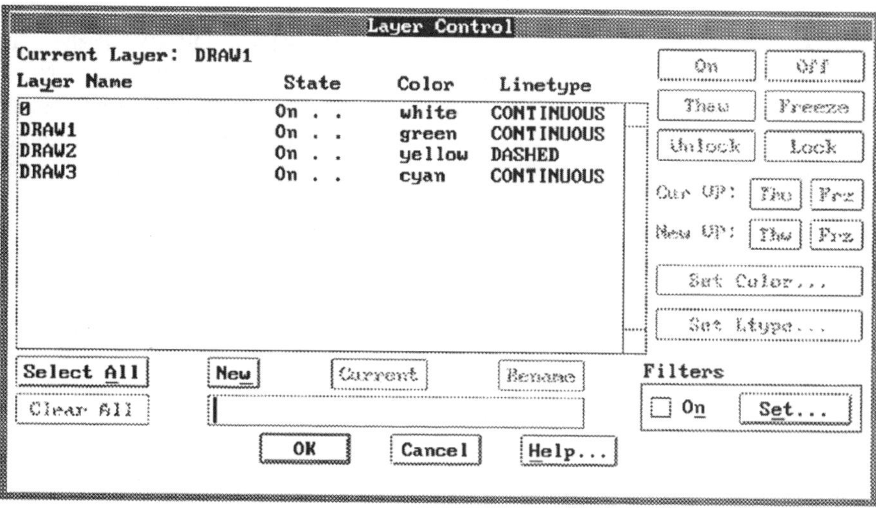

The LAYER: prompt "?/Make/Set/New/ON/OFF/Color/Ltype/Freeze/Thaw/LOck/Unlock:" offers you 12 options. Each option can be selected from the LAYER side menu, or the capital letter (or letters) of each option can be typed and entered to select it. The following examines the LAYER command prompt options:

Make and Color

Note: AutoCAD for DOS: Pressing two keys—Ctrl and C—at the same time cancels the command selection process and returns AutoCAD to the Command: prompt. Use Ctrl-C if you get stuck in a command.
AutoCAD for Windows: Press the Esc key to cancel a command.

The option Make allows you to create one new layer. The option Color allows you to assign a color to a layer.

Step 4. Use the option Make to create a layer named DRAW1.

Prompt	Response
Command:	*Type:* **LA** ↵ (Do not pick Layer:)
LAYER ?/Make/Set/New/ON/OFF/Color/Ltype/Freeze/Thaw/LOck/Unlock:	**Make** (or *Type:* **M** ↵)
New current layer <0>:	*Type:* **DRAW1** ↵

Step 5. Use the option Color to assign a color to layer DRAW1.

Prompt	Response
?/Make/Set/New/ON/OFF/Color/Ltype/Freeze/Thaw/LOck/Unlock:	**Color** (or *Type:* **C** ↵)
Color:	*Type:* **G** ↵
Layer name(s) for color 3 (green) <DRAW1>:	↵
?/Make/Set/New/ON/OFF/Color/Ltype/Freeze/Thaw/LOck/Unlock:	↵

With the option Make from the LAYER: prompt you have just created a layer named DRAW1. Upper- or lowercase letters may be entered for the name. AutoCAD converts all layer names to uppercase. The name may be as short as 1 character and as long as 31 characters, including numbers and letters. It may include only letters, numbers, and three special characters: $ (dollar sign), - (hyphen) and __ (underscore).

Note that the prompt is for "New current layer <0>". When you use the option Make, one new layer is created and automatically set as the current layer on which you will draw. The new layer name appears in the status line on the display screen as the current layer on which you will be working.

Using the option Color from the LAYER: prompt allows you to choose a color from seven standard colors and assign it to a layer in response to the prompt "Layer name(s) for color 3 (green) <DRAW1>:". DRAW1 is the default, so the enter key is used. If the option Color is not used, the layer will default to the color white.

If your display screen has a dark background, color number 7 is white. If your display screen has a light background, color number 7 is black instead of white. The seven standard colors that may also be assigned by entering the number of the color are:

1. Red
2. Yellow
3. Green
4. Cyan
5. Blue
6. Magenta
7. Black (or White)

Depending on your display, you may be able to assign additional colors. Colors other than the standard ones are assigned by number. To see which colors (and the color number) are available on your display, proceed with the following:

View available colors:

Prompt	Response
Command:	**Color:** (from the DATA menu)
New object color <BYLAYER>:	**Chroma**

The AutoCAD Chroma Slide appears on the screen (Figure 4–20). The numbers 10,20,30, . . . , in the middle of the two color groupings are added to the side numbers, 0,2,4,6,8, and 1,3,5,7,9 to determine the number of the colors that appear. The visible colors are the colors that your display has available for layer colors.

The option Ltype was not used, so the linetype for layer DRAW1 will default to a continuous linetype. Continuous is a solid line.

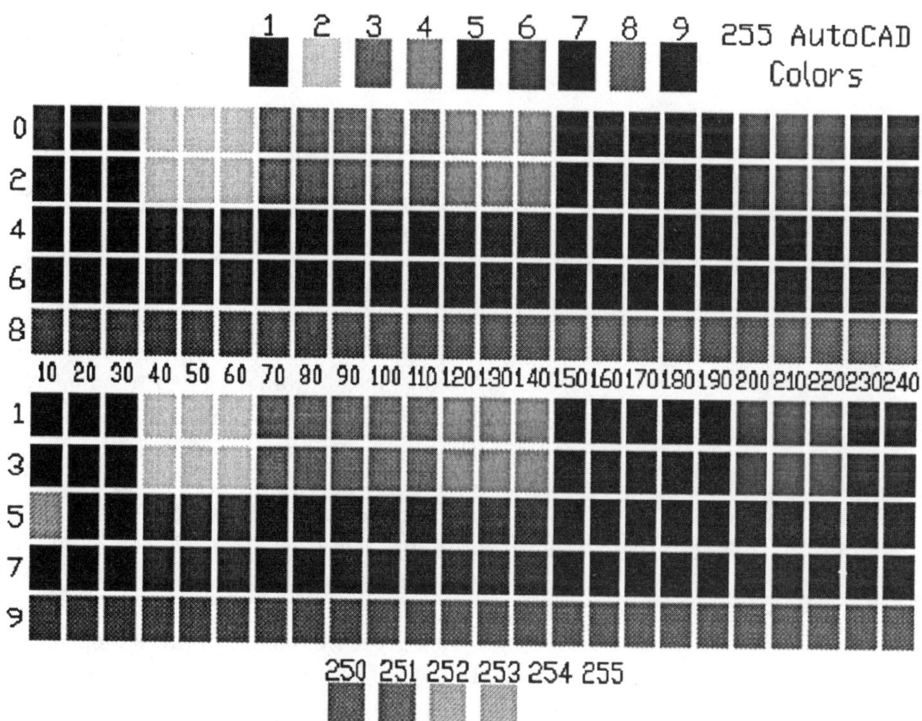

FIGURE 4–20
AutoCAD Chroma Slide

Step 6. On Your Own:

To return to the display screen, type R ↵ (for redraw).

New, Color, and Ltype

The option New allows you to create more than one new layer. The option Ltype allows you to assign a linetype to a layer.

Step 7. Use the option New to create two layers, named DRAW2 and DRAW3.

Prompt	Response
Command:	*Type:* **LA** ↵
LAYER ?/Make/Set/New/ON/OFF/ Color/Ltype/Freeze/Thaw/LOck/Unlock:	**New** (or *Type:* **N** ↵)
New layer name(s):	*Type:* **DRAW2, DRAW3** ↵

Step 8. Use the option Color to assign a color to layer DRAW2.

Prompt	Response
?/Make/Set/New/ON/OFF/Color/ Ltype/Freeze/Thaw/LOck/Unlock:	**Color**
Color:	*Type:* **Y** ↵
Layer name(s) for color 2 (yellow) <DRAW1>:	*Type:* **DRAW2** ↵

Step 9. Use the option Ltype to assign a linetype to layer DRAW3.

Prompt	Response
?/Make/Set/New/ON/OFF/Color/ Ltype/Freeze/Thaw/LOck/Unlock:	**Ltype**
Linetype (or?) <CONTINUOUS>:	*Type:* **DASHED** ↵
Layer name(s) for linetype DASHED <DRAW1>:	*Type:* **DRAW3** ↵

Step 10. Use the option Color to assign a color to layer DRAW3.

Prompt	Response
?/Make/Set/New/ON/OFF/Color/ Ltype/Freeze/Thaw/LOck/Unlock:	**Color**
Color:	*Type:* **C** ↵
Layer name(s) for color 5 (cyan) <DRAW2>:	*Type:* **DRAW3** ↵
?/Make/Set/New/ON/OFF/Color/ Ltype/Freeze/Thaw/LOck/Unlock:	↵

With the option New from the LAYER: prompt you have just created two layers named DRAW2 and DRAW3. The prompt is for "New layer name(s):". One or more layers may be created at the same time. Enter the layer names, separated by a comma. Do not use spaces.

Using the option Color from the LAYER: prompt, you first selected the color yellow and then assigned it to layer DRAW2. You could have used the option Color again immediately to select and assign the color cyan to the layer DRAW3, but instead you went on to the option Ltype and returned to Color later.

The option Ltype from the LAYER: prompt allows you to choose a linetype from nine standard linetypes and assign it to a layer. Nine standard linetypes may be assigned: continuous, dashed, hidden, center, phantom, dot, dashdot, border, and divide. In response to the prompt "Layer name(s) for linetype DASHED <DRAW1>:", DRAW3 was typed and entered to assign linetype DASHED to layer DRAW3. A linetype was not assigned to layer DRAW2, so it will default to a continuous linetype.

One or more layers may be created with the option New, but unlike the option Make, none of the new layers is made current. The current layer is not affected when you use the option New to create new layers.

Set

The option Set from the LAYER: prompt allows you to set an existing layer current.

Step 11. Use the option Set to make layer DRAW3 current.

Prompt	Response
Command:	*Type:* **LA** ↵
LAYER ?/Make/Set/New/ON/OFF/ Color/Ltype/Freeze/Thaw/LOck/ Unlock:	**Set** (or *Type:* **S** ↵)

New current layer <DRAW1>:	*Type:* **DRAW3** ↵
?/Make/Set/New/ON/OFF/Color/ Ltype/Freeze/Thaw/LOck/Unlock:	↵

When you respond to the prompt "New current layer <default>:" with an existing layer name, any existing layer may be made the current layer on which you will draw. The new layer name will appear in the status line on the upper left of the display screen.

Unlike Make and New, the option Set does not *create* layers. The layer must already exist to use the Set option.

?

The option ? from the LAYER: prompt provides a checklist of the layers created, showing their names, colors, and linetypes as well as which layer is current.

Step 12. Use the option "?" to view a list of the layers created.

Prompt	Response
Command:	*Type:* **LA** ↵
LAYER ?/Make/Set/New/ON/OFF/ Color/Ltype/Freeze/Thaw/LOck/Unlock:	**List?**

The following appears on the display screen:

Layer Name	State	Color	Linetype
0	On	7 (white)	CONTINUOUS
DRAW1	On	3 (green)	CONTINUOUS
DRAW2	On	2 (yellow)	CONTINUOUS
DRAW3	On	4 (cyan)	DASHED

Current layer: DRAW3

Note the "0" layer, color white, with a continuous linetype. Layer "0" is created automatically by AutoCAD. It has some special properties that we will use in later chapters.

Step 13. On Your Own:

Press: F1 for DOS, F2 for Windows (flip screen) to return to the display screen.

Note: Some commands require AutoCAD to regenerate an entire drawing. During regeneration, AutoCAD recomputes the screen coordinates for all parts or entities of the drawing. Regeneration can be time-consuming if a drawing is complex. Release 13 performs many operations without regenerating the drawing.

ON or OFF; FREEZE or THAW

The options ON and OFF pertain to the visibility of layers. When a layer is turned OFF, it is still part of the drawing, but any entity drawn on that layer is not visible on the screen and cannot be plotted. One or more layers can be turned OFF and ON as required to get the combination of layers needed.

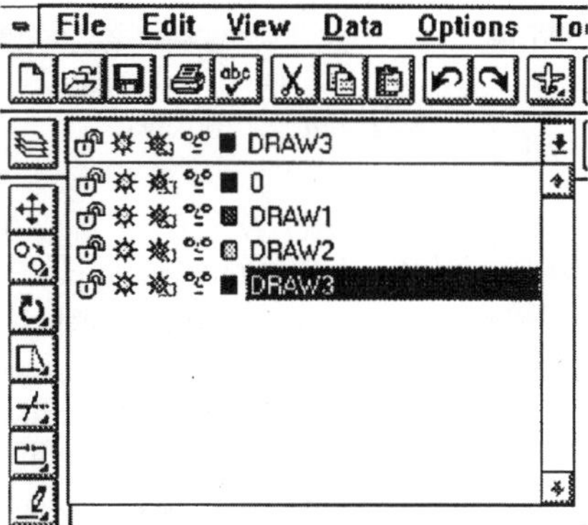

The options Freeze and Thaw also pertain to the visibility of layers. The difference between ON/OFF and Freeze/Thaw is a matter of how quickly the drawing regenerates on the display screen. If a layer is frozen, it is not visible, cannot be plotted, and AutoCAD spends no time regenerating it. A layer that is turned OFF is not visible and cannot be plotted, but AutoCAD does regenerate it.

On some computers, regeneration of a layer takes time. If you are switching between layers, and doing some editing on each of the layers, it is best to use ON and OFF. If, while you are editing layers, there are layers that you do not need to edit or see, it is best to Freeze those layers to avoid their regeneration.

When a layer is created, it is automatically turned ON and is thawed.

Lock or Unlock

When a layer is locked, it is visible, and you can draw on it. You cannot use any commands to edit any of the drawing entities on the layer. You can use other commands to add entities to the locked layer but you cannot accidentally change any entity that is already drawn.

Layer Control Dialog Box

You have just created layers using options from the LAYER: prompt at the Command: prompt line. Layers can also be created using a dialog box. To access the Layer Control dialog box (Figure 4–21), pick Layer: from the SERVICE menu, or DDlmode: from the DATA menu, or Layers. . . from the pull-down menu under Data in the menu bar.

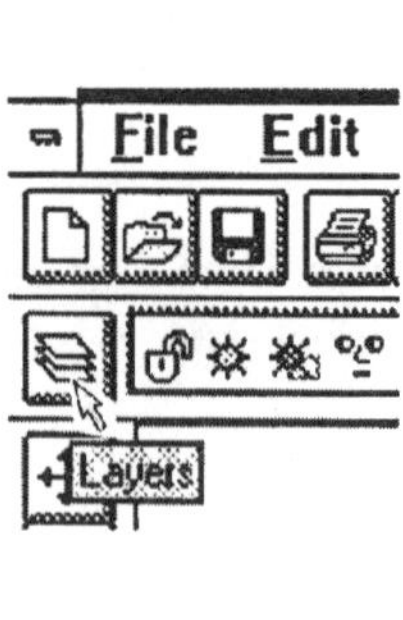

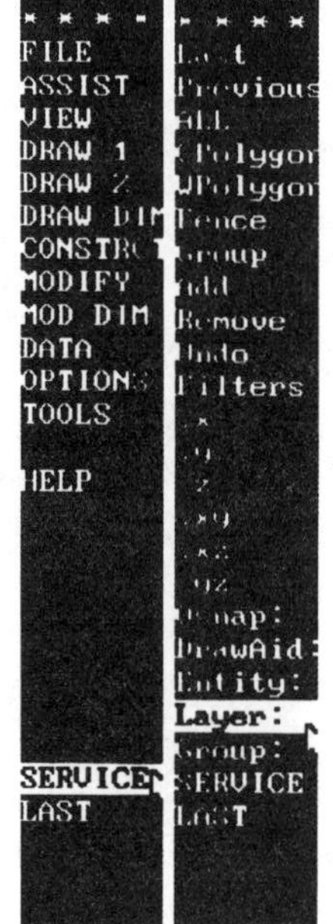

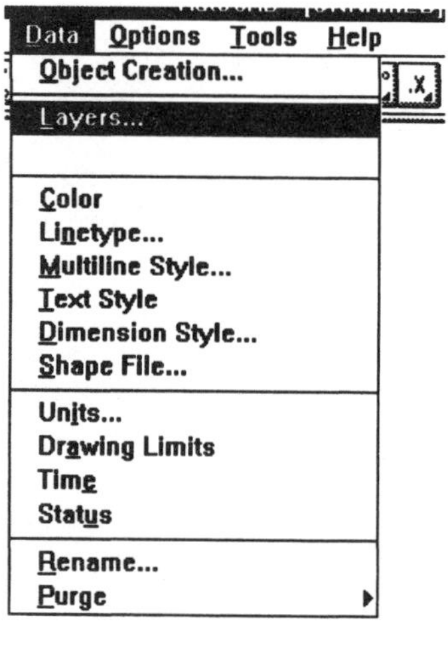

Like the other dialog boxes you have already used, the Layer Control dialog box has an OK, a Cancel, and a Help. . . button. The parts of the Layer Control dialog box (Figure 4–21) are as follows:

1. *Layer Name list box:* The name of all existing layers and their properties (State, Color, and Linetype) are listed in the Layer Name list box. If the name of an existing layer is picked from the list box, it will be highlighted in the list box and will appear in the Layer Name edit box. Pick the layer name a second time, or pick the Clear All button, to cancel the selection and clear the name from the Layer Name edit box. When a layer name is highlighted in the Layer Name list box, the grayed out buttons On, Off, Thaw, Freeze, Unlock, Lock, Set Color. . . , Set Ltype. . . , Current, Rename, and Clear All become active.
2. *Layer Name edit box:* A new layer is created (when the cursor is flashing) by typing the new layer name from the keyboard. When the new layer name appears in the Layer Name edit box, pick the New button, and the new layer name will move to

FIGURE 4–21
Layer Control Dialog Box

Layer Control

Current Layer: DRAW1

Layer Name	State	Color	Linetype
0	On . .	white	CONTINUOUS
DRAW1	On . .	green	CONTINUOUS
DRAW2	On . .	yellow	CONTINUOUS
DRAW3	On . .	cyan	DASHED

On | Off | Thaw | Freeze | Unlock | Lock
Cur VP: Thw | Frz
New VP: Thw | Frz
Set Color... | Set Ltype...
Select All | Clear All | New | Current | Rename
Filters: On | Set...
OK | Cancel | Help...

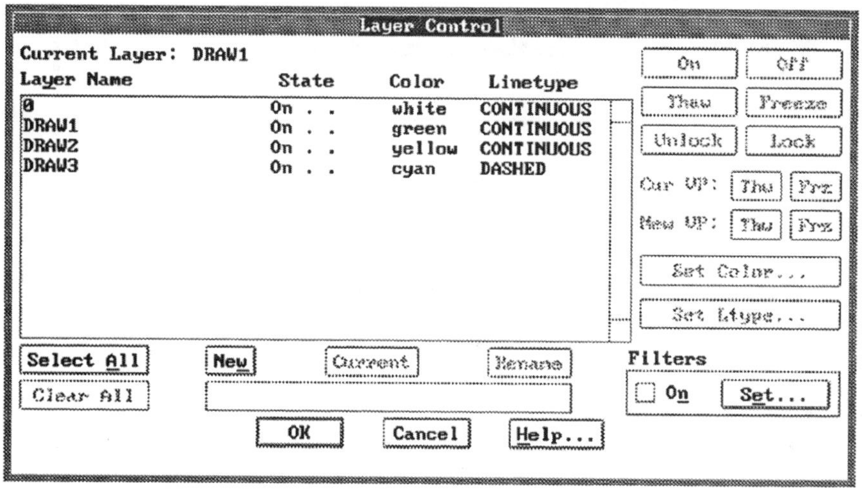

the Layer Name list box. One or more layers may be created at the same time. Enter the layer names, separated by a comma. Do not use spaces. Then pick the New button.

The layer name that appears in the Layer Name edit box is the selected layer that is acted on by the other buttons in the Layer Control dialog box.

3. *New button:* A new layer is created when its name is typed into the Layer Name edit box, the New button is picked, and the new layer name moves to the Layer Name list box.
4. *Current button:* The Current button is active when one layer name is picked from the Layer Name list box and appears in the Layer Name edit box. That layer is made current when the Current button is picked.
5. *Rename button:* The Rename button is active when one layer name is picked from the Layer Name list box and appears in the Layer Name edit box. While the layer name is in the Layer Name edit box change the name, then pick the Rename button to complete the rename of the layer in the Layer Name list box.
6. *Select All button:* When picked, selects and highlights all the layer names listed in the Layer Name list box.
7. *Clear All button:* Pick to clear one or more layer names that are highlighted in the Layer Name list box.
8. *On/Off buttons:* When the layer name is in the Layer Name edit box, it can be toggled on or off by picking these buttons.
9. *Thaw/Freeze buttons:* When the layer name is in the Layer Name edit box, it can be frozen or thawed by picking these buttons.
10. *Unlock/Lock buttons:* When the layer name is in the Layer Name edit box, it can be locked or unlocked by picking these buttons.
11. *Cur VP: and New VP: buttons:* These buttons concern freezing layers in selected viewports. Freezing layers in separate viewports is used in a later chapter.
12. *Filters check box, and Set Layer Filters dialog box:* When the Filters Set. . . button is picked, the Set Layer Filters dialog box (Figure 4–22) appears. This allows you to show layer names in the Layer Name list box based on properties specified in the Set Layer Filters dialog box. The properties are On/Off, Freeze/Thaw, Lock/Unlock, Current Vport, New Vports, Layer Names, Colors, and Ltypes. Those buttons allow you to select the property of the layers you want to see.

    When you want to cancel layer filtering, so that all layer names will be visible in the Layer Name list box, pick the Filters check box to toggle filters off.

FIGURE 4–22
Set Layer Filters Dialog Box

Set Layer Filters

On/Off:	Both
Freeze/Thaw:	Both
Lock/Unlock:	Both
Current Vport:	Both
New Vports:	Both
Layer Names:	*
Colors:	*
Ltypes:	*

Reset

OK Cancel Help...

13. *Set Color. . . button:* When the layer name is in the Layer Name edit box, the color for a new layer may be selected, or if the layer is existing, the color may be changed by picking the Set Color. . . button. When the button is picked, a Select Color dialog box appears (Figure 4–23) with check buttons for nine standard colors and an input button for entering color numbers. Pick or enter the desired color, and pick the OK button to exit. The new color is set.

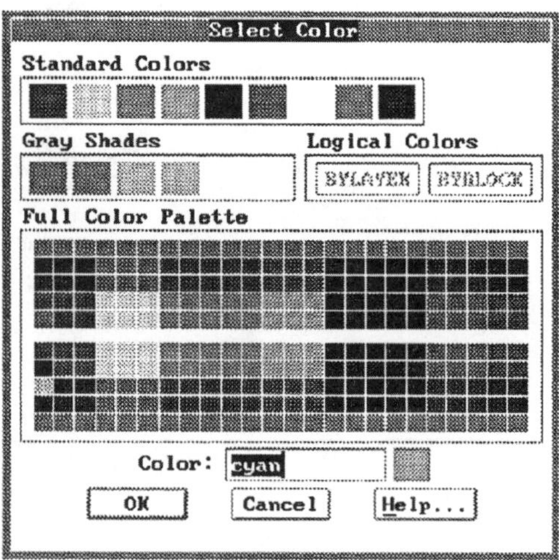

FIGURE 4–23
Select Color Dialog Box

14. *Set Ltype. . . button:* When the layer name is in the Layer Name edit box and one or more layer names are highlighted, the linetype may be changed by picking the Set Ltype. . . button. *The linetype has to be loaded first.*

Step 14. Load all linetypes.

Prompt	Response
With the Layer Control dialog box visible:	*Pick:* **DRAW1** (from the list box)
Layer DRAW1 is highlighted:	*Pick:* **Set Ltype. . .**
Select Linetype dialog box appears (Figure 4–24):	*Pick:* **Load. . .**

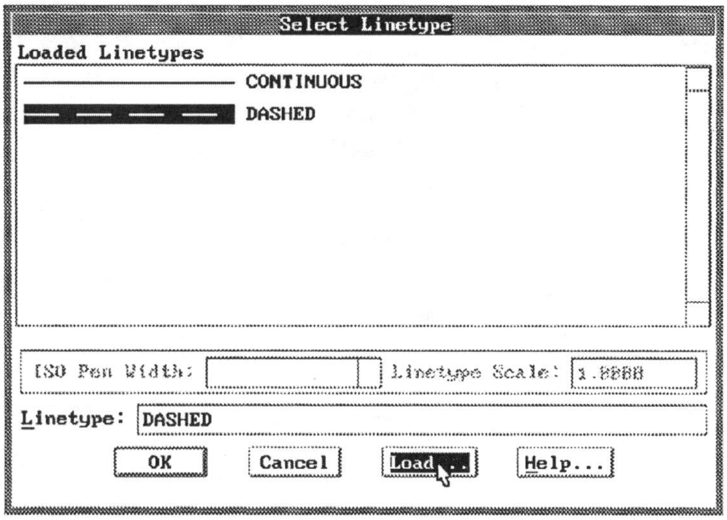

FIGURE 4–24
Select Linetype Dialog Box

Load or Reload Linetypes dialog box appears (Figure 4–25): *Pick:* **Select All**

Load or Reload Linetypes dialog box *Pick:* **OK**

Select Linetype dialog box reappears with all the linetypes loaded and visible. Now any linetype can be selected from the Select Linetype dialog box.

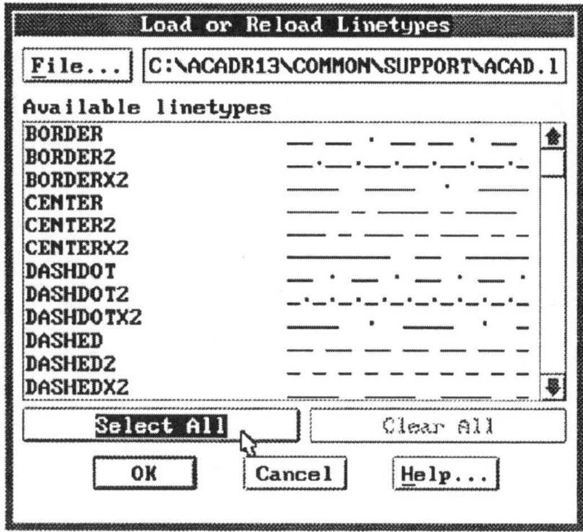

FIGURE 4–25
Load or Reload Linetypes Dialog Box

After the linetypes are loaded, when the Set Ltype. . . button is picked, the Select Linetype dialog box appears (Figure 4–26) with the AutoCAD library of standard linetypes. The AutoCAD library of standard linetypes (Figure 4–27) provides you with three different sizes of each standard linetype other than continuous. For example, the dashed line has the standard size called DASHED, a linetype half the standard size called DASHED2, and a linetype twice the standard size called DASHEDX2.

Pick on the linetype desired, and pick the OK button to exit. The new linetype is set.

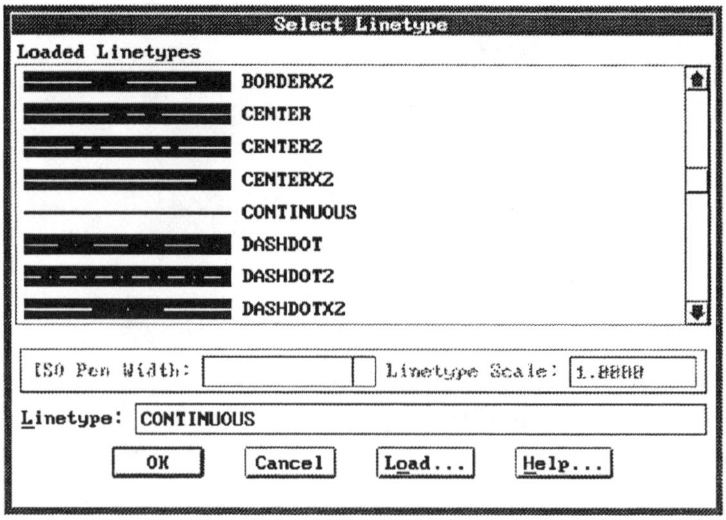

FIGURE 4–26
Select Linetype Dialog Box

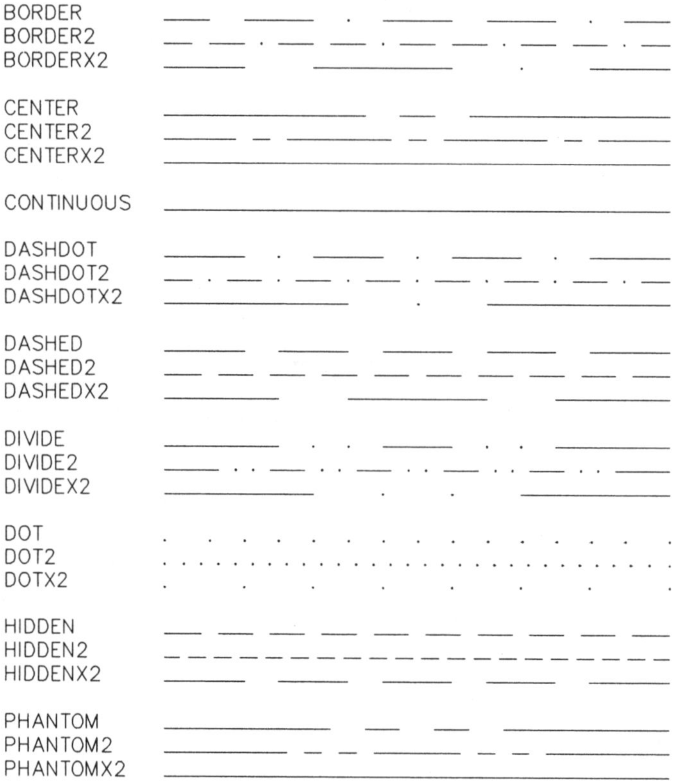

Select Linetype

Loaded Linetypes

BORDERX2
CENTER
CENTER2
CENTERX2
CONTINUOUS
DASHDOT
DASHDOT2
DASHDOTX2

ISO Pen Width: Linetype Scale: 1.0000

Linetype: CONTINUOUS

OK | Cancel | Load... | Help...

FIGURE 4–27
AutoCAD Library of Standard Linetypes

BORDER
BORDER2
BORDERX2

CENTER
CENTER2
CENTERX2

CONTINUOUS

DASHDOT
DASHDOT2
DASHDOTX2

DASHED
DASHED2
DASHEDX2

DIVIDE
DIVIDE2
DIVIDEX2

DOT
DOT2
DOTX2

HIDDEN
HIDDEN2
HIDDENX2

PHANTOM
PHANTOM2
PHANTOMX2

Step 15. On Your Own:

1. Experiment with all parts of the Layer Control dialog box. If you create some layers that you do not need and cannot delete, simply don't use them in Exercise 5–1. Be sure the following layers, colors, and linetypes are set for Exercise 5–1, and ignore any extra layers you may have created.

Layer Name	State	Color	Linetype
0	On	7 (white)	CONTINUOUS
DRAW1	On	3 (green)	CONTINUOUS
DRAW2	On	2 (yellow)	CONTINUOUS
DRAW3	On	4 (cyan)	DASHED

Current layer: DRAW1

2. Save your drawing, quit, and exit AutoCAD

When you have completed creating the layers for drawing 5-1(your initials), save your work in at least two places. When you save the drawing to a floppy disk (or any drive/directory other than the one in which you are working), because the drawing was previously saved, AutoCAD will print the message "A drawing with this name already exists. Do you want to replace it?" <N>

You want to update the old 5-1(your initials) drawing file and replace it with the new 5-1(your initials) drawing file (with setting and layers created), so the answer is to type Y ↵ to the prompt.

After saving your drawing in two places, type and enter QUIT to exit AutoCAD.

REVIEW QUESTIONS

1. The units used in a drawing may be set using a dialog box.
   a. True b. False
2. Entering 11,8.5 as the upper right corner drawing limits provides the following sheet size:
   a. 11′ × 8.5′
   b. 11″ × 8.5″
   c. 8.5′ × 11′
   d. 8.5″ × 11″
   e. None of the above
3. Function key F7 does which of the following?
   a. Provides a check list of the layers created.
   b. Turns Snap on or off.
   c. Flips the screen from the text display to the graphics display.
   d. Turns Grid ON or OFF.
4. Units:, Limits:, Grid: and Snap: can all be found under the Data menu on the menu bar.
   a. True b. False
5. Which of the following options from the LAYER: prompt creates a new layer and sets it current?
   a. Make
   b. Set
   c. New
   d. ON
   e. OFF
6. Which of the following options from the LAYER: prompt creates a new layer but does not set the layer current?
   a. Make
   b. Set
   c. New
   d. ON
   e. OFF
7. Which of the following function keys is used to turn Snap on and off?
   a. F7
   b. F9
   c. F1
   d. F8
8. When a layer is off, it will regenerate but is not visible.
   a. True b. False
9. When the grid is set at 0, it will automatically be the same spacing as the snap spacing.
   a. True b. False
10. The name of a drawing can include a . (dot) or an * (asterisk).
    a. True b. False
11. Name the two keys that when pressed at the same time cancel the command selection process and return AutoCAD to the Command: prompt in DOS.

    ____
12. If you are working in the hard drive and want to save a drawing named DATA to a floppy disk in drive A, what response is entered to the prompt "SAVE current changes as <DATA>:"?

    ____
13. An invisible grid to which the cross hairs will lock is called:

    ____
14. How many layers may be used in a drawing?

    ____
15. Describe what .DWG and .BAK files are.

    .DWG ______________________________

    ____

    .BAK ______________________________

    ____
16. How can you tell if a disk drive is active?

    ____
17. What must be done first before a linetype is selected or changed in the Layer Control dialog box?

    ____

    ____
18. What disaster may occur to your work if you work in a floppy drive?

    ____

    ____
19. What does the QUIT command do when used by itself?

    ____

    ____

    ____
20. What is the process called that prepares a new floppy disk so that a drawing may be saved on it?

    ____

5 Placing Text on Drawings

OBJECTIVES

When you have completed this chapter, you will be able to:

- □ Use different fonts on the same drawing.
- □ Place text on several different parts of the drawing with a single command.
- □ Use the modifiers Center, Align, Fit, Middle, Right, Top, and Style.
- □ Use the Style: setting to create condensed, expanded, rotated, backward, inclined, and upside-down text.
- □ Use the Style: setting to change any style on the drawing to a different font.
- □ Use standard codes to draw special characters such as the degree symbol, the diameter symbol, the plus-minus symbol, and underscored and overscored text.
- □ Use Mtext: to create paragraph text.
- □ Spell check your drawing.

When a project that is to be manually drafted is started, decisions are made about the number of drawings required, the appropriate text size, and font. Similar decisions are made when preparing to draw with AutoCAD. This chapter provides exercises in using DText: and Mtext: and their settings to place text on a drawing.

PLACING LETTERING ON DRAWINGS

Before you begin drawing with AutoCAD, you need to know how lettering is placed on the drawing. AutoCAD uses DText: for short, simple lines, and Mtext: for paragraphs with internal formatting. DText: is a powerful command that is a vast improvement over the TEXT command used in earlier versions of AutoCAD. The following list describes several of the features of DText:.

Different fonts may be used on the same drawing.

DText: may be used to place text on several different parts of the drawing with a single command.

DText: modifiers—Center, Align, Fit, Middle, Right, Top, and Style—may be used to locate text around a picked point.

The Style: setting may be used to create condensed, expanded, rotated, backward, inclined, and upside-down text.

The Style: setting may be used to change any style on the drawing to a different font.

Standard codes may be used to draw special characters such as the degree symbol, the diameter symbol, the plus-and-minus symbol, and underscored and overscored text.

So that you may experience how these features work, call up the drawing you have just saved.

EXERCISE 5–1
PLACING TEXT ON A DRAWING

In Chapter 4 you made the settings and layers for drawing 5-1 (your initials). You will use that setup in Exercise 5–1 to complete your first drawing exercise. When you have completed Exercise 5–1, your drawing will look similar to the one in Figure 5–1.

To begin Exercise 5–1, turn on the computer and start AutoCAD.

FIGURE 5–1

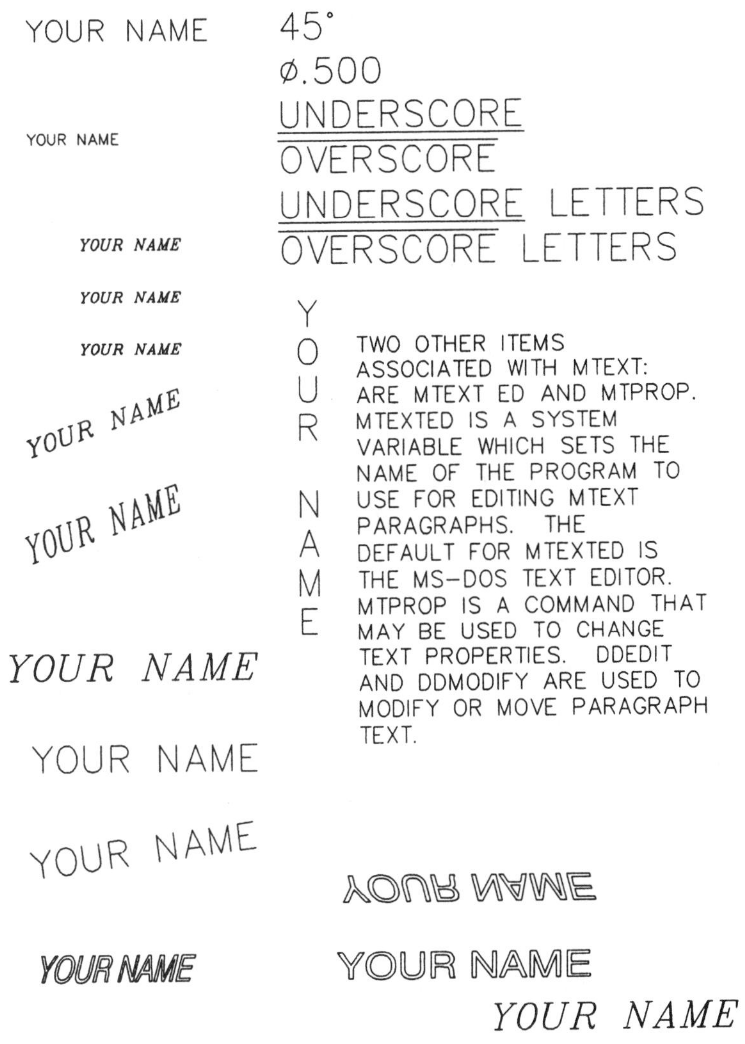

YOUR NAME
45°
Ø.500
UNDERSCORE
YOUR NAME
OVERSCORE
UNDERSCORE LETTERS
YOUR NAME
OVERSCORE LETTERS
YOUR NAME
YOUR NAME
YOUR NAME
YOUR NAME
Y O U R N A M E
TWO OTHER ITEMS ASSOCIATED WITH MTEXT: ARE MTEXT ED AND MTPROP. MTEXTED IS A SYSTEM VARIABLE WHICH SETS THE NAME OF THE PROGRAM TO USE FOR EDITING MTEXT PARAGRAPHS. THE DEFAULT FOR MTEXTED IS THE MS–DOS TEXT EDITOR. MTPROP IS A COMMAND THAT MAY BE USED TO CHANGE TEXT PROPERTIES. DDEDIT AND DDMODIFY ARE USED TO MODIFY OR MOVE PARAGRAPH TEXT.
YOUR NAME
YOUR NAME
YOUR NAME
YOUR NAME
YOUR NAME
YOUR NAME
YOUR NAME

Begin an Existing Drawing on the Hard Drive

If your drawing 5-1 (your initials) is stored on a floppy disk, proceed with the following. If your drawing 5–1 (your initials) is stored on the hard disk, skip to the section "To begin existing drawing 5-1 (your initials) on the hard drive when it is stored on the hard disk."

To begin existing drawing 5-1 (your initials) on the hard drive when it is stored on a floppy disk that has no directories:

Prompt	Response
Command:	**New:**
The Create New Drawing dialog box appears:	*Type:* **5-1 (your initials)=A:5-1 (your initials)** ↵
Drawing 5-1 (your initials) appears with the settings and layers.	

To begin existing drawing 5–1 (your initials) on the hard drive when it is stored on the hard disk:

Prompt	Response
Command:	**Open:**
The Open Drawing dialog box appears: *or* the Select File dialog box appears:	*Type:* **5-1 (your initials)** ↵ or double click the drawing name from the Files: list box.
Drawing 5-1 (your initials) appears with the settings and layers.	

Zoom:

Use Zoom: All to view the entire drawing area:

Prompt	Response
Command:	**Zoom:**
All/Center/Dynamic/Extents/Left/ Previous/Vmax/Window/<Scale(X/XP)>:	**All**

The Zoom: All command lets you view the entire drawing area. Use it after setting up or entering a drawing so that you are familiar with the size and shape of your limits and grid. Otherwise you may be viewing only a small part of the drawing limits and not realize it.

Grid

The grid is visible when it is on. Press the F7 function key to turn the grid off and on. Turn the grid off and on to clean up any blips that appear on the screen while you are drawing.

Step 1. On Your Own:

Dos and Windows: press function key F7 to turn the grid on.
Windows: Pick GRID at the bottom of the screen.

1. Turn the grid on.

Ortho

DOS and Windows: Press function key F8 to turn ortho on and off.
Windows: Pick ORTHO at the bottom of the screen.

2. Turn ortho on.

Ortho mode, when on, helps you draw lines perfectly horizontally and vertically. It does not allow you to draw at an angle, so turn Ortho off and on as needed.

Snap

DOS and Windows: Press function key F9 to turn snap on and off.
Windows: Pick SNAP at the bottom of the screen.

Snap helps you draw accurately; it is desirable to draw with snap on most of the time. If you need to turn snap off to draw or to edit a drawing entity, remember to turn it back on as soon as possible.

3. Turn snap on.
4. Set layer DRAW1 current.

USING DIFFERENT FONTS ON THE SAME DRAWING

Let's begin by taking a look at a drawing, Figure 5–2, that contains two different text fonts. The names in the boxes are one font (ITALIC). The titles and the names outside the boxes

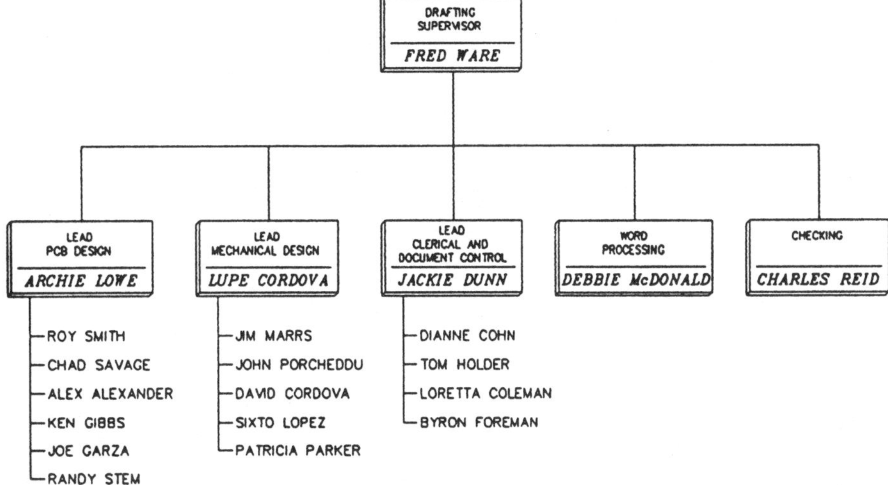

FIGURE 5–2
An Organizational Diagram or Chart

are different sizes of the same font (SIMPLEX). Using different fonts on the same drawing is made possible by the Style: setting of the DText: command. For example, suppose that you wanted the first style setting to be simplex. This setting was obtained as follows:

Note: The style name is a means of keeping the fonts separate. The style name "TITLE" could be assigned the simplex font. The style name "NAMES" could be assigned the ITALIC font. Only one style may be active at a time. The style name can be any letters or numbers you wish to use to keep the fonts separate on the drawing. You may choose to use the same name for the style as used for the font, or you may wish to use a single number or letter for the style name to reduce the amount of typing necessary when you want to change styles.

Step 2. Draw your name in all capital letters, .2 high, with the SIMPLEX font.

Prompt	Response
Command:	**Style:**
Text style name (or ?)<STANDARD> (This is the default.)	*Type:* **TITLE** ↵ (Name it anything you like; the default, STANDARD, is all right.)

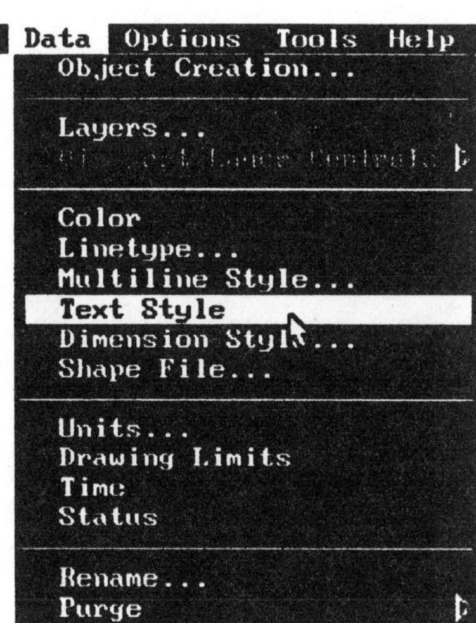

Prompt	Response
The Select Font File dialog box appears with TXT in the File: button. (This is the default. It was never meant to be used on drawings. TXT regenerates faster than other fonts. This is useful on drawings with slow regenerating fonts such as ROMAN, but all lettering with the TXT font should be changed before the drawing is plotted or printed.)	*Type:* **SIMPLEX** (in the File: button or select from the Files: box. Use the slider bar to move to the SIMPLEX font.) *Pick:* **OK**
Height <0.0000>:	↵ (Accepting the default of 0 will allow you to draw different heights of the same letter style.)
Width factor <1.0000>:	↵ (Accept the default of 1 unless you wish to condense or expand the letter. You will see an example of that later.)
Obliquing angle <0>:	↵ (Accept the default of 0 unless you want slanted letters. You will see an example of this also.)
Backwards? <N>	↵
Upside-down? <N>	↵
Vertical? <N>	↵
TITLE is now the current text style.	

Any typing done on the drawing now will be in the SIMPLEX font. Whenever the DText: command is used, the height prompt will appear, with the default being the last height used. If you want a different size, enter the new size at the height prompt. The new size then becomes the default height.

Let's see how this works.

Prompt	Response
Command:	**DText:**
Command: __dtext Justify/Style/<Start point>:	Pick a point on the drawing 1″ to the right and 1″ down from the upper left corner or *Type:* **1,10.**
Height <0.2000>:	↵
Rotation angle <0>:	↵
Text:	*Type:* **(YOUR NAME)** (in all capital letters—press CAPS LOCK to turn it on) ↵
Text:	↵

Step 3. Draw your name in all caps with the SIMPLEX font, .1 high.

Prompt	Response
Command:	**DText:** (If you press return to repeat the last command, AutoCAD assumes you want to use the same letter height again. Pressing ↵ again places the DText cursor beneath the previously drawn text. Selecting DText: again will allow you to choose a different height.)

Command: __ dtext Justify/Style/<Start point>:	Pick a point 1″ down from the previous DText (or *Type:* **1,9.**
Height <0.2000>:	*Type:* **.1** ↵
Rotation angle: <0>:	↵
Text:	*Type:* **(YOUR NAME)** (all caps) ↵ ↵

Now that you have drawn all the SIMPLEX lettering you want, return to the Style: setting to create a new Style: category for the ITALIC font.

Step 4. Set a new style with the Italic font.

Prompt	Response
Command:	**Style:**
Text style name (or ?) <TITLE>	*Type:* **NAMES** ↵ (The name is your choice.)
The Select Font File dialog box appears:	*Type:* **ITALIC** in the File: button (or select from the list in the File Name box.) *Pick:* **OK**
Height <0.0000>:	↵
Width factor <1.00>:	↵

Continue to respond with ↵ to accept the default for the remaining prompts until you get to the prompt "NAMES is now the current text style." Any number of fonts may be used on the same drawing by using the Style: setting in this manner.

USING DText: TO PLACE TEXT ON SEVERAL DIFFERENT PARTS OF THE DRAWING WITH A SINGLE COMMAND

The DText: box that appears when the DText: command is selected displays the starting point for the command, the letter height, and the angle at which the lettering will be drawn. Figure 5–3 shows the cursor cross hairs, D1 (the picked point for a line of centered text), the displayed text before centering occurs, and the DText: box that is displayed after one line of centered text has been entered. The box may now be moved to any other location on the drawing to create another line of centered text by picking the new location, D2, shown in Figure 5–4. This procedure may be continued until all centered text of the current style has been entered on the entire drawing. Two returns complete the command, and all the lines that have been entered will be displayed in their centered position (Figure 5–5). Draw your name three more times using centered DText:.

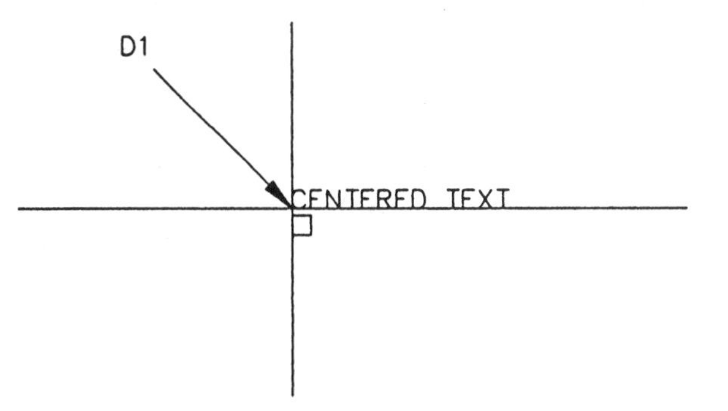

FIGURE 5–3
Centered Text

FIGURE 5–4
Second Line of Centered Text

FIGURE 5–5
Centered Text after Return

Step 5. Draw your name three more times using centered DText:.

Prompt	Response
Command:	**DText:**
__dtext Justify/Style/<Start point>:	*Type:* **C** ↵
Center point:	Pick a point 1″ down and 1″ to the right of the previous DText (or *Type:* **2,8** ↵.)
Height <0.1000>:	↵
Rotation angle <0>:	↵
Text:	*Type:* **(YOUR NAME)** ↵
Text:	Pick a point two grid marks down from the last DText.
Text:	*Type:* **(YOUR NAME)** ↵
Text:	Pick a point two more grid marks down.
Text:	*Type:* **(YOUR NAME)** ↵
Text:	↵

USING THE DText: MODIFIERS: CENTER, ALIGN, FIT, MIDDLE, RIGHT, TOP, AND STYLE

Center

Center draws the text so that the bottom of the line of lettering is centered on the picked point. Centering is not displayed until the second return is pressed, as described previously. You may also choose the top or the middle of the line of lettering by selecting Top Cent or Mid Cent options.

Align

Align draws the text between two picked points. It does not condense or expand the font but instead adjusts the letter height so that the text fits between the two points. Figure 5–6

FIGURE 5–6
Aligned Text

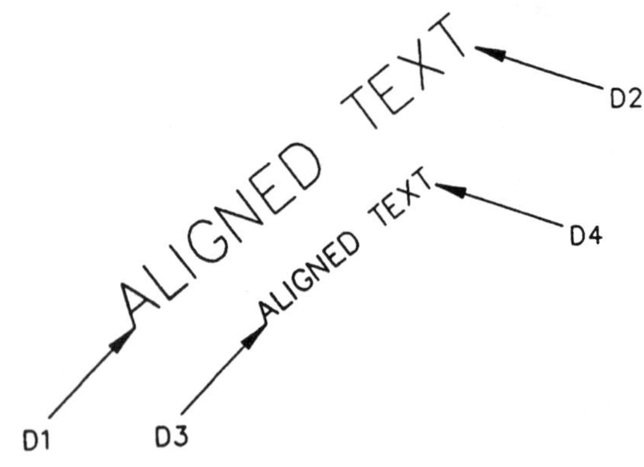

shows the results of two different sets of points. The text between points D1 and D2 is more than twice the height of the text between points D3 and D4. Use DText-Align and draw your name between two points.

Step 6. Draw your name using aligned DText:.

Prompt	Response
Command:	**DText:**
__dtext Justify/Style/<Start point>:	*Type:* **A** ↵
First text line point:	Pick a point 1″ down from the last DText and 1″ from the right side of the drawing (or *Type:* **1,6** ↵.)
Second text line point:	Pick a point six grids to the right and two grids up from the first point.
Text:	*Type:* **(YOUR NAME)** ↵
Text:	↵

Fit

Fit draws the text between two picked points, as the align modifier does, but instead of changing the letter height, Fit condenses or expands the font to fit between the points. Figure 5–7 shows a .25-high font that DText: squeezed to fit between points D1 and D2. Use DText-Fit to draw your name between two picked points.

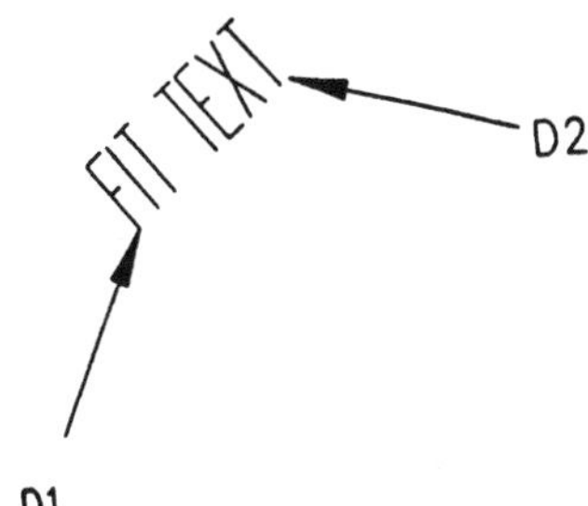

FIGURE 5–7
Fit Text

Step 7. Draw your name using fit DText:.

Prompt	Response
Command:	**DText:**
__dtext Justify/Style/<Start point>:	*Type:* **F** ↵
First text line point:	Pick a point 1″ down from the last DText and 1″ from the right side of the drawing (or *Type:* **1,5** ↵.)
Second text line point:	Pick a point six grids to the right and two grids up from the first point.
Height <0.1000>:	*Type:* **.25** ↵
Text:	*Type:* **(YOUR NAME)** ↵
Text:	↵

Middle

Middle draws the text so that the middle of the line of lettering is centered around a picked point. This is very useful when a single line of lettering must be centered in an area such as the box shown in Figure 5–8. Use DText-Middle-Centered to draw your name once again.

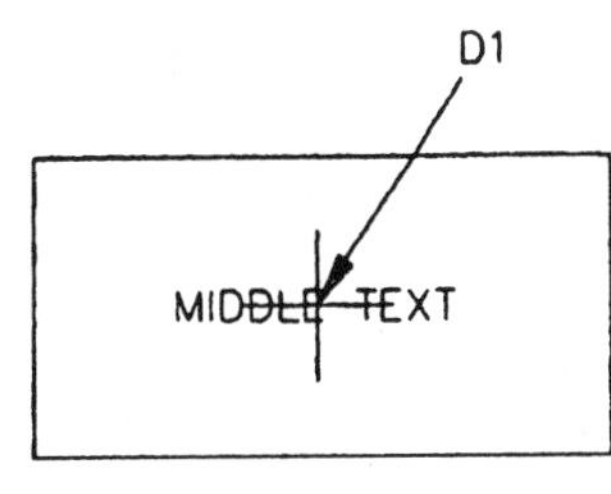

FIGURE 5–8
Middle Text

Step 8. Draw your name using middle centered DText:.

Prompt	Response
Command:	↵
__dtext Justify/Style/<Start point>:	*Type:* **MC** ↵
Middle point:	Pick a point 1″ down from the last DText and 2″ from the right side of the drawing (or *Type:* **2,4** ↵.)
Height <0.2500>:	↵
Rotation angle <0>:	↵
Text:	*Type:* **(YOUR NAME)** ↵
Text:	↵

Right

Right draws the text so that each line of text is right-justified (ends at the same right margin). The text above the cursor cross hairs shows the display before the second return is struck. The text below the cursor cross hairs shows the text in its right-justified position. Use this modifier to draw your name in the lower right corner .5″ to the left and .5″ up from the lower right corner (Figure 5–9).

FIGURE 5–9
Right-Justified Text

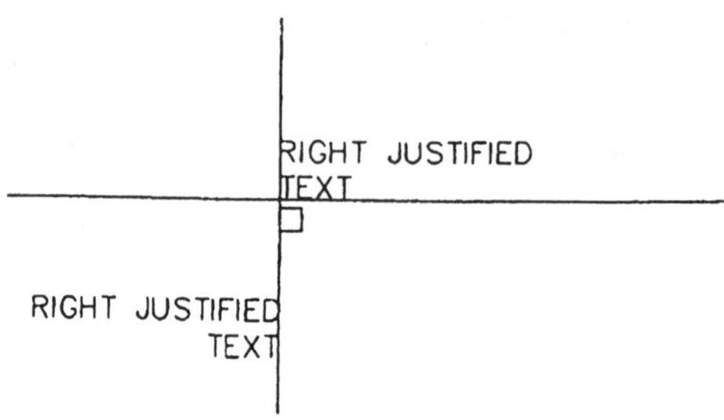

Step 9. Draw your name using right-justified DText:.

Prompt	**Response**
Command:	↵
__dtext Justify/Style/<Start point>:	*Type:* **R** ↵
End point:	Pick a point .5″ to the left and .5″ up from the lower right corner of the drawing (or *Type:* **8,.5** ↵.)
Height <0.2500>:	↵
Rotation angle <0>:	↵
Text:	*Type:* **(YOUR NAME)** ↵
Text:	↵

Top, Middle, Bottom

The Justify Option from the DText: prompt allows you to select the TOP, MIDDLE, or BOTTOM of a line of text to be centered or left- or right-justified.

Prompt	**Response**
Command:	**DText:**
Justify/Style/<Start point>:	*Type:* **J** ↵
Align/Fit/Center/Middle/Right/TL/TC/TR/ML/MC/MR/BL/BC/BR:	*Type:* **MR** ↵ (to select middle right justification)
Middle/rightpoint:	Pick a convenient point for right justification.
Height <0.2500>:	↵
Rotation angle <0>:	↵
Text:	*Press:* **Esc** (to cancel the command)

Note: Letters such as TL, TC, and TR on the Justify prompt have the following meanings:

TL	Top of the line, left-justified
TC	Top of the line, centered
TR	Top of the line, right-justified
ML	Middle, left-justified
MC	Middle, centered
MR	Middle, right-justified
BL	Bottom, left-justified
BC	Bottom, centered
BR	Bottom, right-justified

Type the two letters indicating your choice at the Justify prompt, as shown in the example, or bypass the Justify prompt and type the two letters at the first DText: prompt.

Style:

Style: allows you to select a new style for the text you are about to draw. In the example of Figure 5–2, the new style TITLE can be selected after all the NAMES style lettering has been done without exiting from the DText: command. The following shows this procedure:

Step 10. Draw your name using another style.

Prompt	Response
Command:	↵
__dtext Justify/Style/<Start point>:	*Type:* **S** ↵
Style name (or ?): <NAMES>:	*Type:* **TITLE** ↵
Justify/Style/<Start point>:	Pick a point 1″ down from the last DText and 1″ from the left side of the drawing (or *Type:* **1,3** ↵.)
Height <0.1000>:	*Type:* .25 ↵
Rotation angle <0>:	↵
Text:	*Type:* **(YOUR NAME)** ↵
Text:	↵

If the situation demands that a line of text be placed at an undetermined angle, two points may be picked to show DText: the direction the line should take (Figure 5–10). The procedure is as follows.

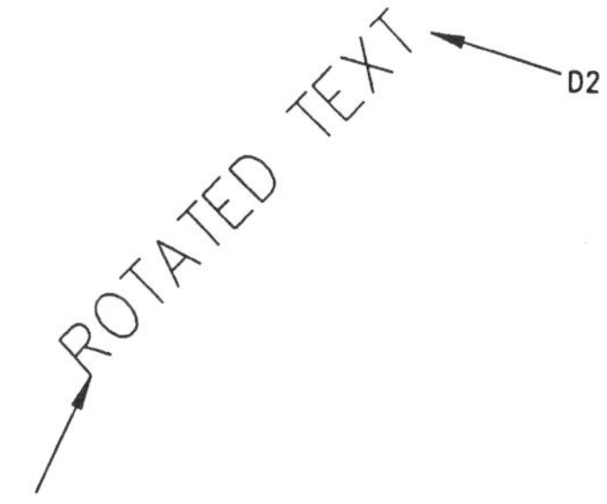

FIGURE 5–10
Rotated Text

Step 11. Draw your name with rotated text.

Prompt	Response
Command:	↵
__dtext Justify/Style/<Start point>:	Pick D1 1″ down from the last DText (Figure 5–10) (or *Type:* **1,2** ↵.)
Height <0.2500>:	↵
Rotation angle <0>:	Pick D2 (Figure 5–10) eight grids to the right and one grid up.
Text:	*Type:* **(YOUR NAME)** ↵
Text:	↵

USING THE STYLE: SETTING TO CREATE CONDENSED, EXPANDED, ROTATED, BACKWARD, INCLINED, AND UPSIDE-DOWN TEXT

The Style: setting may be used to create condensed, expanded, rotated, backward, inclined, and upside-down text. Figures 5–11 through 5–13 show examples of some of these Style settings. The condensed form of Figure 5–11 was drawn using a width setting of .75 and an obliquing angle of 10°. An expanded form could be drawn by using a width setting of 1.25 or larger.

FIGURE 5–11
Inclined and Condensed Text

FIGURE 5–12
Backward Text

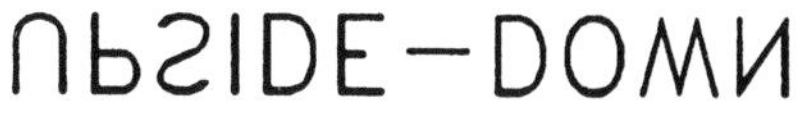

FIGURE 5–13
Upside-Down Text

Step 12. On Your Own:

1. Set a style using the Style: command.

Name it:	SWISSCOND
Font:	SWISS (*Select:* .ttf in the List Files of Type list box when the select Font File dialog box appears.)
Height:	0.0000
Width factor:	.75
Obliquing angle:	15

2. Draw your name in the SWISSCOND style, .25 high, 1″ to the right and 1″ up from the lower left corner of the page (type 1,1 for start point). Make sure your rotation angle is 0.

Step 13. On Your Own:

1. Set a style using the Style: command.

Name it:	SWISSEXPAND
Font:	SWISS.ttf
Height:	0.0000
Width factor:	1.25
Obliquing angle:	0

2. Draw your name in the SWISSEXPAND style, .25 high, 4″ to the right and 1″ up from the lower left corner of the page (type 4,1 for start point). Make sure your rotation angle is 0.

Step 14. On Your Own:

1. Set a style using the Style: command.

Name it:	SWISSUPSIDEDOWN
Font:	SWISS
Height:	0.0000
Width factor:	1.25
Obliquing angle:	15
Upside down?	Y

2. Draw your name in the SWISSUPSIDEDOWN style, .25 high, 4″ to the right and 2″ up from the lower left corner of the page (type 4,2 for start point). Make sure your rotation angle is 0.

Step 15. On Your Own:

1. Set a style using the Style: command.

Name it:	VERTICAL
Font:	SIMPLEX
Height:	0.0000
Width factor:	1.0000
Obliquing angle:	0
Vertical?	Y

2. Draw your name in the VERTICAL style, .25 high (type 3.75,7.25 for start point). Make sure your rotation angle is 270. You should have a vertical line of text as shown in Figure 5–1.

USING THE STYLE: SETTING TO CHANGE A STYLE ON THE DRAWING TO A DIFFERENT FONT

If a drawing has been completed with a font that is not acceptable to the customer, that font can easily be replaced by making a single change to the Style: setting. Let's say, for example, that your customer did not like the ITALIC font. The ITALIC font was typed with the name NAMES. The style NAMES can be changed to a different font, and all the text that was drawn with the NAMES style is changed instantly. The procedure is as follows.

Step 16. Use Style: to change a style to a different font.

Prompt	Response
Command:	**Style:**
Text style name (or ?) <whatever the current style is>	*Type:* **NAMES** ↵
The Select Font File dialogue box appears (Figure 5–14):	*Type:* **SCRIPTS** (in the File: button) ↵ (or select from the dialogue box and *Pick:* **OK**)
Height <0.0000>:	

FIGURE 5–14
Select Font File Dialog Box

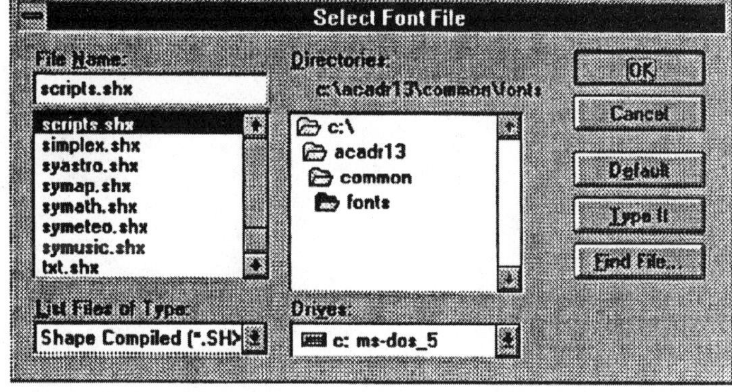

Accept the default for all other prompts to change the NAMES style from the ITALIC font to the SCRIPTS font, as shown in Figure 5–15.

FIGURE 5–15
Changing an Existing Font

YOUR NAME

YOUR NAME

your name

your name

your name

your name

your name

your name

YOUR NAME

YOUR NAME

YOUR NAME

YOUR NAME

YOUR NAME

your name

45%%D

45°

FIGURE 5–16
Degree Symbol Code

Figures 5–16 through 5–20 show the use of codes to obtain several of the commonly used symbols, such as the degree symbol, the diameter symbol, the plus-minus symbol, and underscored and overscored text. The top line of Figure 5–16 shows the code that must be inserted to obtain the degree symbol following the number 45. The top line is displayed until ↵ is pressed to obtain the degree symbol shown on the bottom line. Two percent symbols followed by the letter D produce the degree symbol.

%%C.500

∅.500

FIGURE 5–17
Diameter Symbol Code

Figure 5–17 illustrates that two percent symbols followed by the letter C produce the diameter symbol. Any text following the symbol must be inserted immediately following the code.

Figure 5–18 shows the code for the plus-minus symbol.

Figure 5–19 shows the code for underscore: two percent symbols followed by the letter U. Notice that the first line contains only one code. The second line contains two codes: one to start the underline and one to stop it.

%%P.005

±.005

FIGURE 5–18
Plus-Minus Symbol Code

FIGURE 5–19
Underscore Code

%%UUNDERSCORE

UNDERSCORE

%%UUNDERSCORE%%U LETTERS

UNDERSCORE LETTERS

Figure 5–20 shows the code for overscored text. The same code sequence for starting and stopping the overscore applies.

FIGURE 5–20
Overscore Code

%%OOVERSCORE

OVERSCORE

%%OOVERSCORE%%O LETTERS

OVERSCORE LETTERS

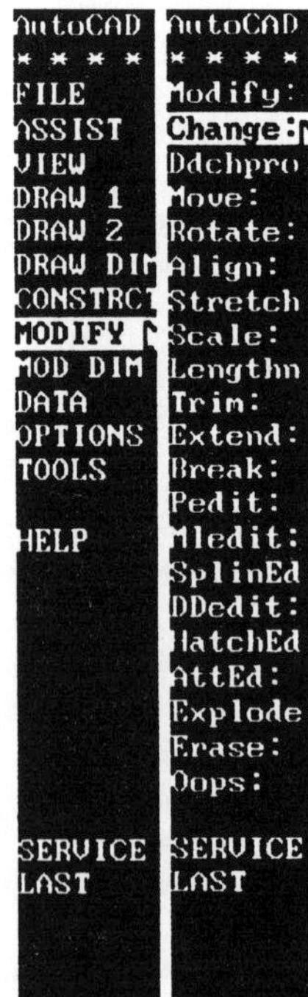

Let's test these standard codes:

Step 17. Use standard codes to draw special characters.

Prompt	**Response**
Command:	**DText:**
__dtext Justify/Style/<Start point>:	*Type:* **S** ↵
Style name (or ?) <NAMES>:	*Type:* **TITLE** ↵ (The SIMPLEX font will demonstrate these codes well.)
Justify/Style/<Start point>:	*Type:* **3.5,10** ↵
Height <0.2500>:	↵
Rotation angle <0>:	↵
Text:	*Type:* **45%%D** ↵
Text:	*Type:* **%%C.500** ↵
Text:	*Type:* **%%P.500** ↵
Text:	*Type:* **%%UUNDERSCORE** ↵
Text:	*Type:* **%%OOVERSCORE** ↵

Text:	*Type:* **%%UUNDERSCORE%%U LETTERS** ↵
Text:	*Type:* **%%OOVERSCORE%%O LETTERS** ↵
Text:	↵

Step 18. Use the Style: setting to change the NAMES style back to the ITALIC font.

Let's say that your customer has decided that the ITALIC font looks better on his drawing than the SCRIPTS font.

Step 19. On Your Own: Use the Style: command to change the NAMES style from the SCRIPTS font to the ITALIC font.

All the text you have done to this point is called *line text.* You will also make a paragraph of paragraph text with the Mtext: command. Before you do that, however, let's see how to change line text that you already have on your drawing, which you will often have to do.

AutoCAD gives you three commands to do that: Change:, DDedit: (Edit Text. . . on the Modify menu on the menu bar), and Modify: (Properties. . . on the Modify menu on the menu bar).

CHANGING TEXT

Change:

The Change: command is an all-purpose command that can be used to change the endpoint of a line, the radius of a circle, text, and the properties of an entity. Let's use it once here to change some text.

Step 20. Use the Change: command to remove the underscore and change the text height of UNDERSCORE.

Prompt	Response
Command:	**Change:**
Select objects:	*Pick:* UNDERSCORE
Select objects:	↵
Properties/<Change point>:	↵
Enter text insertion point:	(We don't want to change the location of the text, so ↵.)
New style or RETURN for no change:	(This style is OK, so ↵.)
New height <0.2500>:	*Type:* **.2** ↵ (To change the text height)
New rotation angle <0>:	↵
New text <%%UUNDERSCORE>:	*Type:* **UNDERSCORE** ↵

DDedit: (Edit Text. . . on the Modify Menu on the Menu Bar)

DDedit: allows you to change the text (or attribute) contents and that is all. If that is all you want to change, this is the command to use.

Step 21. Use DDedit: to change UNDERSCORE to UNDERSCORE.

Prompt	Response
Command:	**DDedit:**
<Select a TEXT or ATTDEF object>/ Undo:	*Pick:* **UNDERSCORE**
The Edit Text dialog box appears:	Pick to the left of the U (between U and the box outline). *Type:* **%%U**

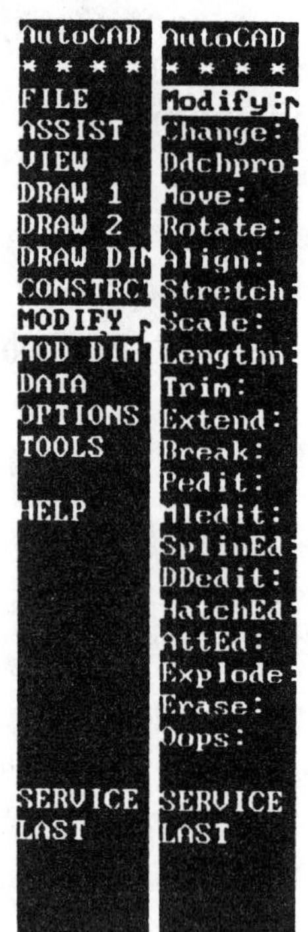

Prompt	Response
	Pick between the R and S. *Type:* **%%U** *Pick:* **OK** (or ↵)
<Select a TEXT or ATTDEF object>/ Undo:	↵

Modify: (Properties. . . on the Modify Menu on the Menu Bar)

Modify: is an all-purpose command that can be used to change almost anything. When text is selected, Modify: can be used to change any of that text's characteristics.

Step 22. Use Modify: to change UNDERSCORE to UNDERSCORE, change the text height, and the layer it is on.

Prompt	Response
Command:	**Modify:** (or Properties. . . on the menu bar)
Select object to modify:	*Pick:* **UNDERSCORE** ↵
The Modify Text dialog box appears:	Pick to the left of SCORE and backspace over %%U. Pick the Height: button (between 2 and 0), and change the height to 0.2500. Pick the Layer. . . button.
The Select Layer dialog box appears:	*Pick:* **DRAW2** *Pick:* **OK** or ↵
The Modify Text dialog box, Figure 5–21, appears:	*Pick:* **OK**

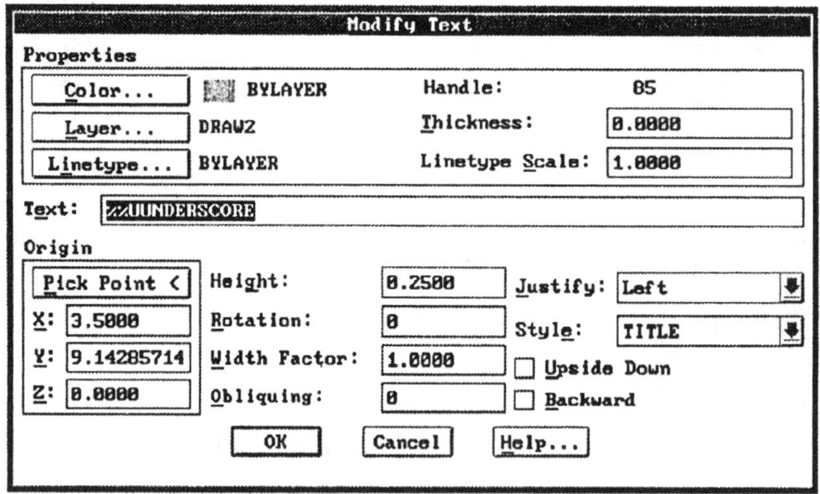

FIGURE 5–21
Modify Text Dialog Box

Now let's create a paragraph of text using the Mtext: command.

MAKING PARAGRAPHS OF TEXT

Mtext:

The Mtext: command creates paragraphs that fit inside a boundary. The text boundary specifies the width and alignment of the paragraph. Each paragraph is a single text object. Mtext: options are:

Attach

Controls which part of the text boundary aligns at the insertion point. The option you select determines text justification (left, right, or centered) and text spill (how excess text flows out of the text boundary). TL is Top Left, TC is Top Center, etc.

Rotation

Specifies the rotation angle of the text boundary.

Style

Specifies the text style to use for paragraph text.

Height

Specifies the height of uppercase text.

Direction

Specifies the direction (horizontal or vertical) of the paragraph.

Stack

Allows you to type vertical fractions.

Step 23. Set Layer DRAW3 current, and use Mtext: to create a text paragraph.

Prompt	Response
Command:	*Type:* **LA** ↵
?/Make/Set/New/ON/OFF/Color/Ltype/ Freeze/Thaw/LOck/Unlock:	*Type:* **S** ↵
New current layer <DRAW1>:	*Type:* **DRAW3** ↵
Command:	**Mtext:**
Attach/Rotation/Style/Height/Direction/ <Insertion point>:	*Type:* **A** ↵
TL/TC/TR/ML/MC/MR/BL/BC/BR:	*Type:* **BL** ↵ (to specify bottom left)
Attach/Rotation/Style/Height/Direction/ <Insertion point>:	*Type:* **S** ↵
Style name (or ?) <NAMES>:	*Type:* **TITLE** ↵ (if you get an error message in Windows, select the Arial font and pick OK.)
Attach/Rotation/Style/Height/Direction/ <Insertion point>:	*Type:* **H** ↵
Height <0.2500>:	*Type:* **.15** ↵
Attach/Rotation/Style/Height/Direction/ <Insertion point>:	*Type:* **4.25,7** ↵
Attach/Rotation/Style/Height/Direction/ Width/2Points/<Other corner>:	*Type:* **7.75,3** ↵
In AutoCAD for DOS the MS-DOS Editor appears:	Type the following paragraph in all caps. Deliberately misspell the word SYSTEM.
In AutoCAD for Windows the Edit MText dialog box appears:	Type the following paragraph in all caps. Deliberately misspell the word SYSTEM.

TWO OTHER ITEMS ASSOCIATED WITH MTEXT: ARE MTEXTED AND MTPROP. MTEXTED IS A SOSTEM VARIABLE WHICH SETS THE NAME OF THE PROGRAM TO USE FOR EDITING MTEXT PARAGRAPHS. THE DEFAULT FOR MTEXTED IS THE MS-DOS TEXT EDITOR. MTPROP IS

A COMMAND THAT MAY BE USED TO CHANGE TEXT PROPERTIES. DDEDIT AND DDMODIFY ARE USED TO MODIFY OR MOVE PARAGRAPH TEXT.

In AutoCAD for DOS, after you have typed the paragraph, pick: File, then Save, then Exit.

In AutoCAD for Windows, after you have typed the paragraph, pick OK. Now spell check the drawing.

Spell:

The Spell: command checks the spelling of words AutoCAD considers dubious. You have the options of adding these words to the dictionary, changing them to the suggested word, or ignoring the word and moving on to the next dubious word.

Step 24. Spell check the text paragraph.

Prompt	Response
Command:	**Spell:**
Select objects:	Pick any point on the text paragraph.
The Check Spelling dialog box, Figure 5–22, appears with MTEXT: in the Current word button and TEXT: in the Suggestions: button:	Pick the Ignore All button (to ignore MTEXT: every time it is encountered.)

Do the same for all other words that are not misspelled. When you come to SOSTEM, and the suggested word is SYSTEM,

Pick: **SYSTEM**

Pick: the **Change button**

Continue with spell check until you get the AutoCAD alert indicating that spelling check is complete. Pick OK.

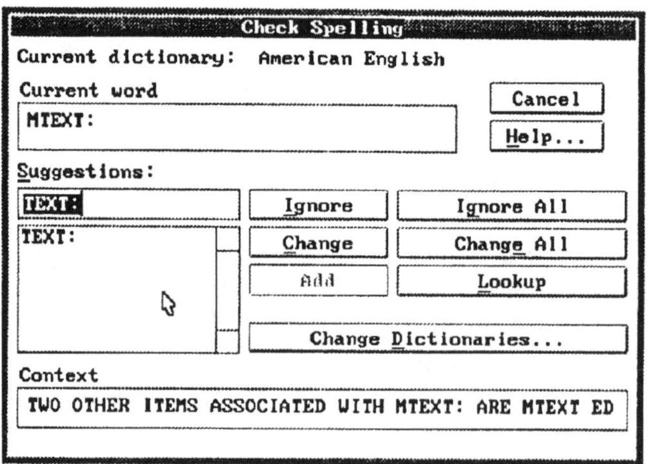

FIGURE 5–22
Check Spelling Dialog Box

Your misspelled word is now changed and the exercise is complete.

Step 25. Print your drawing on an 8.5″ × 11″ sheet. (See Chapter 6 for printing instructions.)

Step 26. Save your drawing in two places and exit from AutoCAD.

REVIEW QUESTIONS

1. The command used in this chapter to place line text on drawings is
   a. DText: d. DDedit:
   b. TXT: e. MS-DOS Text Editor
   c. Mtext:
2. The command used in this chapter to place paragraph text on drawings is
   a. DText: d. DDedit:
   b. TXT: e. MS-DOS Text Editor
   c. Mtext:
3. Which of the following could be used as a Style: name?
   a. SIMPLEX d. A
   b. TITLE e. All the above
   c. NAMES
4. Which of the following is a font name?
   a. SIMPLEX d. A
   b. TITLE e. All the above
   c. NAMES
5. You can change from one text style to another from within the DText: command.
   a. True b. False
6. When you set the text style, which of the following text height settings will allow you to draw different heights of the same text style?
   a. 0.2500 d. 10000
   b. 0.0000 e. On
   c. 1
7. Which of the following DText: modifiers draws text between two picked points and adjusts the text height so that it fits between the two points?
   a. Fit d. Middle
   b. Align e. Style
   c. Justify
8. Which of the following DText: modifiers draws text between two picked points and condenses or expands the text to fit between the two points but does not change the text height?
   a. Fit d. Middle
   b. Align e. Style
   c. Justify
9. The justification letters MR stand for
   a. Middle, Right-justified
   b. Margin, Right-justified
   c. Midpoint, Left-justified
   d. Bottom, Right-justified
   e. Margin Release
10. Which of the following modifiers should be selected if you want the bottom of the line of text to end .5 above and .5 to the left of the lower right corner of the drawing limits?
    a. TL d. TR
    b. BR e. MR
    c. BL
11. List three commands that can be used to edit text.

    ______________ ______________ ______________
12. List the command that allows you to change only the text contents.

    ____
13. List the command that allows you to change text height, contents, properties, justification, style, and origin.

    ____
14. List the command used to create a paragraph of text.

    ____
15. List the command that will spell check any line or paragraph of text you select.

    ____
16. Describe the difference between text style name and font name.

    ____

    ____

    ____
17. List the setting for Style: height that must be used for AutoCAD to prompt you for height when DText: is used.

    ____
18. Write the description for the abbreviations TL, ML, BR.

    ____

    ____
19. Describe how to change quickly all the text on a drawing done in the STANDARD style, TXT font, to the SIMPLEX font.

    ____

    ____

    ____
20. List the standard codes for the following.
    a. Degree symbol ______________________
    b. Plus-minus symbol ______________________
    c. Diameter symbol ______________________
    d. Underscore ______________________
    e. Overscore ______________________

6 Printing and Plotting

OBJECTIVES

When you have completed this chapter, you will be able to:

- □ Print drawings on dot-matrix or laser printers to scale or to fit on standard sheets.
- □ Print drawings at various scales using pen or laser plotters using two or more different-size pens on standard sheets.

In Release 13, a single Plot Configuration dialog box is used for obtaining hard copies of your work. This chapter describes the parts of the Plot Configuration dialog box that are used to print on either a printer or a plotter. If for some reason the dialog boxes are disabled (CMDDIA set to 0), prompts are issued that describe the parts of the Plot Configuration dialog box and can be answered in the same manner, as described next.

PRINTING ON A PRINTER

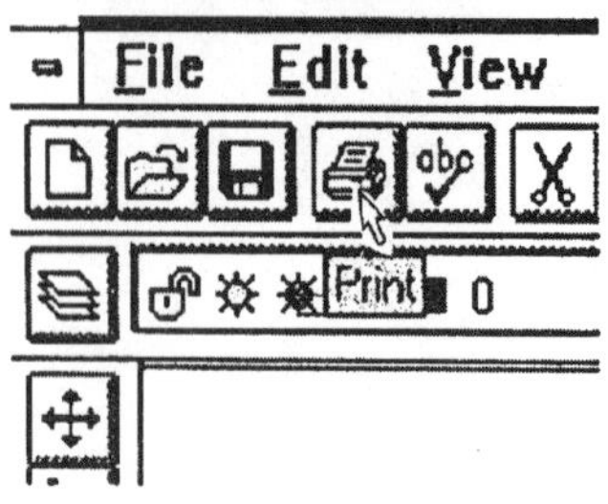

EXERCISE 6–1
MAKING A PRINTER PLOT OF DRAWING 5–1 (YOUR INITIALS)

The following is a hands-on, step-by-step procedure for making a printer plot of drawing 5-1 (your initials). To begin, turn on the computer and start the AutoCAD program.

Step 1. On Your Own:

1. Start drawing 5-1 (your initials) on the hard drive so it is displayed on the screen. Remember, if your drawing has been saved on a floppy disk in the A drive, select New. . . and type 5–1 (your initials) = A:5–1 (your initials) in the New Drawing Name button, or pick the Prototype. . . button and select 5-1 on the A drive as the prototype.
2. Pick the Print: command from the root menu, or pick Print. . . under File on the menu bar, or type PLOT ↵ to access the Plot Configuration dialog box (Figure 6–1).

Device and Default Information Area

The text line in the Device and Default Information area shows the current plot device. When the Device and Default Selection. . . button is picked, a Device and Default Selection dialog box (Figure 6–2) appears. It has a list box that shows all the plot devices that are configured to your computer. The device in the list box that is highlighted is the current plot device. You can select the printing or plotting device that you want to use. Each time you select a different device, the settings of the parameters change to the default for that device.

You can save the plot parameter settings to a file and retrieve the saved file using the File Defaults buttons. The Device Specific Configuration buttons allow you to view additional configuration requirements or to change them.

Step 2. Select the printer.

If the text line does not show the correct printer, use the Device and Default Selection dialog box to select the printer that you will use to print your drawing 5-1 (your initials). If

FIGURE 6–1
Plot Configuration Dialog Box

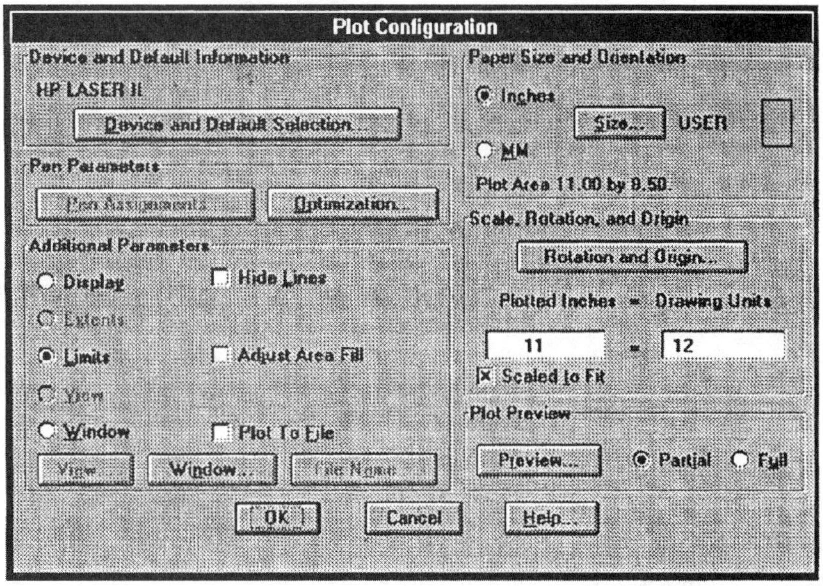

the correct printer is not shown in the Device and Default Selection list, cancel the plot and configure AutoCAD for the correct printer. (Type CONFIG ↵, then 5 ↵ to configure the plotter, then 1 ↵ to add a plotter configuration, then respond to the prompts.) Select the correct printer, and pick OK.

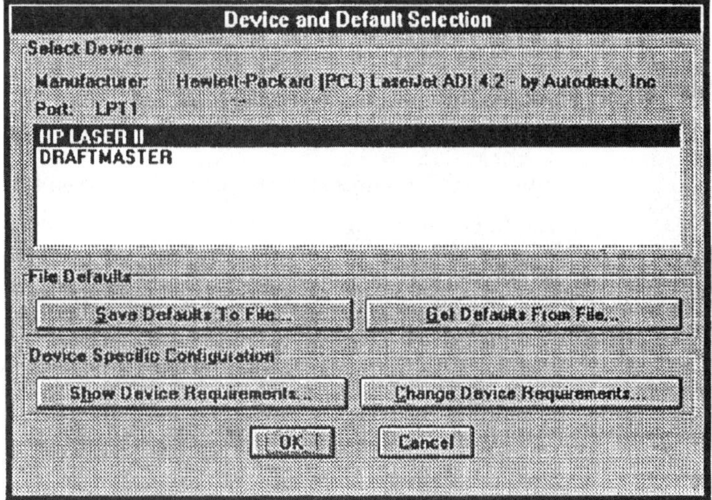

FIGURE 6–2
Device and Default Selection Dialog Box

Pen Parameters Area

We will use pens in Exercise 6–2, when the step-by-step procedure for printing on a plotter is described. Notice that the Pen Assignments. . . button, Figure 6–3, is grayed out, indicating that pens cannot be assigned to the current device; they are available only on plotters, not on printers.

Additional Parameters Area: Specify the Part of the Drawing That Is to Be Plotted

A dialog box *radio button* is a button that is part of a group that is mutually exclusive—only one button in the group can be picked. The five radio buttons in the Additional Parameters area—Display, Extents, Limits, View, and Window—specify the part of the drawing that is to be printed, and only one can be selected at a time. When the button is selected, a black dot appears inside the button.

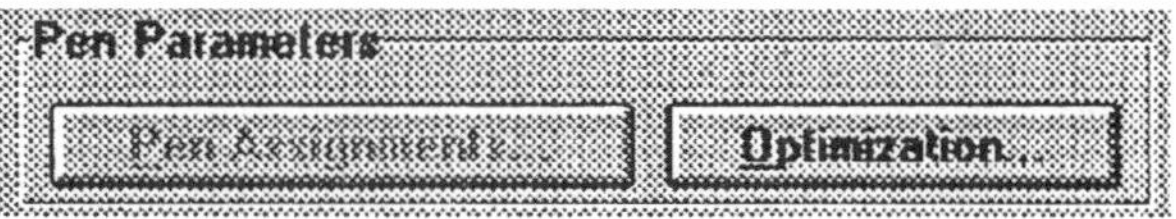

FIGURE 6–3
Pen Assignments Grayed Out

Step 3. **Pick the Limits radio button to select Limits as the part of the drawing that is to be printed.**

Limits This option plots the part of the drawing that lies within the drawing limits. The limits for drawing 5–1 (your initials) are 8½,11.

Display This option plots the part of a drawing that is displayed on the screen at the time the plot is made.

Extents This option plots the drawing extents. The drawing extents are whatever graphics are actually drawn, including any graphics that lie outside the limits of the drawing area.

View This selection plots any view that has been saved and named as a result of using the View: command. It is grayed out because no view was saved and named for drawing 5–1 (your initials). If you have saved a view, pick the View. . . button (below the Window check button) to use the View Name dialog box to select the named view.

Window This selection allows you to pick two corners of a window and plot only the part of the drawing that is within the window. When the Window. . . button (below the Plot to File check button) is picked, it displays a Window Selection dialog box (Figure 6–4). Selecting the Pick button clears the dialog boxes so you can view your drawing and use your mouse to pick the two corners of a window. AutoCAD will then return to the Plot Configuration dialog box.

FIGURE 6–4
Window Selection Dialog Box

Additional Parameters Area: The Hide Lines Check Button

The Hide Lines check button refers to 3-D objects only. When you use the Hide: command, AutoCAD hides any surface on the screen that is behind another surface in 3-D space. If you want to do the same on your plot, you must pick the Hide Lines check button to select it (an X will appear in the middle). (If you are printing viewports in paper space, this button has no effect. The Hideplot option of the Mview: command must be used to hide viewports in paper space.)

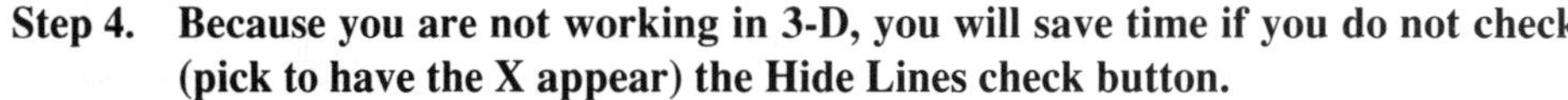

Step 4. **Because you are not working in 3-D, you will save time if you do not check (pick to have the X appear) the Hide Lines check button.**

Additional Parameters Area: The Adjust Area Fill Check Button

The Adjust Area Fill check button is used in conjunction with the pen width. For example, if you check the button, all filled areas, such as solids, arrowheads, donuts, and wide polylines, will be drawn ½ pen width smaller all around (with a 0.010 wide pen, that is .005). For most plotting applications this is not appropriate.

Step 5. **Do not check the Adjust Area Fill check button.**

Additional Parameters Area: The Plot to File Check Button

If you do not check the Plot to File button, AutoCAD plots directly from your computer. If there is a cable leading from your computer to the printer or plotter, do not check the Plot to File button.

If you do check the Plot to File button, a file is created with the extension .PLT. Pick the File Name. . . button (below the Plot to File check button) to see the Create Plot File dialog box (Figure 6–5) with the plot file name. The plot file may be copied onto a floppy

FIGURE 6–5
Create Plot File Dialog Box

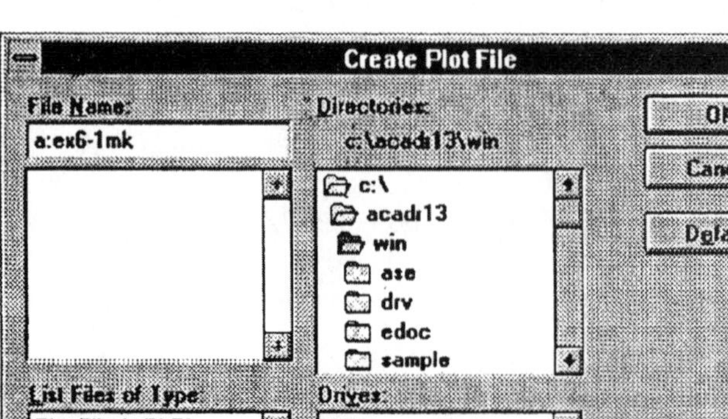

disk or created on the floppy disk (add the drive information in front of the file name in the File Name: edit box) and carried to a plot station, where the plot is performed with a plotting software package. The plot station is often faster and more convenient and requires less expensive equipment than a computer dedicated to plotting .DWG drawing files. The plot file may also be created on the hard drive and sent via a network to the plot station.

Step 6. If you need to create a plot file, check the Plot to File button.

Paper Size and Orientation Area

The radio buttons Inches and MM allow you to select either inches or millimeters for specifying the paper size.

The text line below the MM button lists the current paper size selected. When the Size . . . button is picked, the Paper Size dialog box (Figure 6–6) appears. It lists the paper

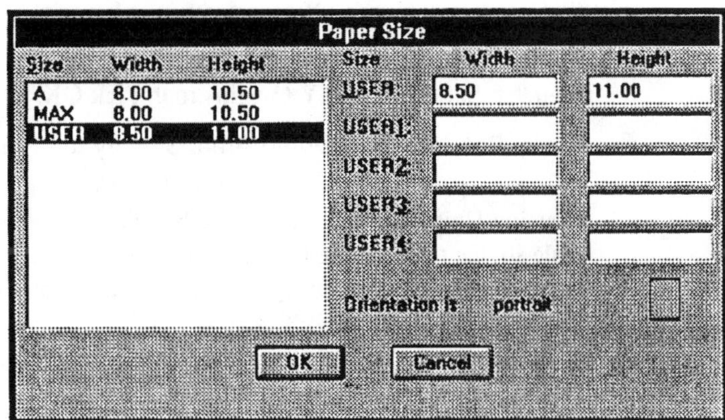

FIGURE 6–6
Paper Size Dialog Box

sizes the printer can accommodate; the current size is highlighted. The MAX size is the maximum size the printer can print. An A or B displayed beside the size indicates a standard American National Standards Institute (ANSI) size area. You can enter a USER plotting size by entering the Width and Height in the USER: input boxes. The size then appears in the list box labeled USER.

If your printer naturally accepts an 8½″ × 11″ sheet of paper in the vertical position, that is a portrait orientation (not landscape); enter the paper size as 8.5 Width and 11 Height. If the size is entered as 11 Width and 8.5 Height, the printer cuts off the drawing graphics at 8½″ on the 11″ height. You may specify a plotting size that is smaller than the actual paper size and then trim the paper.

Step 7. Select the Inches radio button and enter 8.5″ Width × 11″ Height as the paper size. Pick OK.

Scale, Rotation, and Origin Area: Determine the Plot Rotation

When the Rotation and Origin. . . button of the Plot Configuration dialog box is picked, the Plot Rotation and Origin dialog box (Figure 6–7) appears. AutoCAD allows you to rotate the drawing to change its orientation within the specified paper size. Drawing 5-1 (your initials) does not need to be rotated because it has the same orientation as the

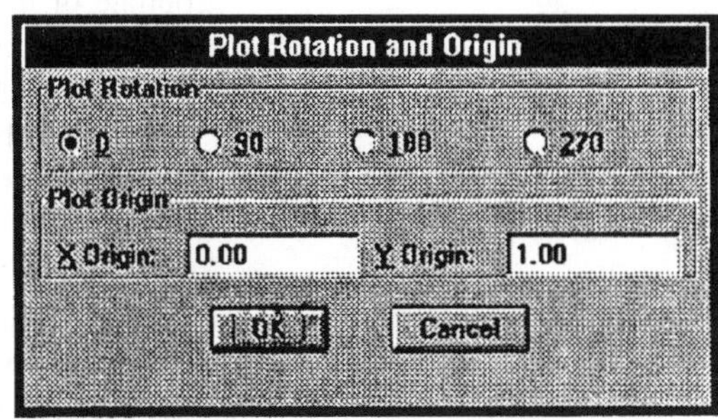

FIGURE 6–7
Plot Rotation and Origin Dialog Box

8.5″ × 11″ paper size entered in Step 8. If drawing 5-1 (your initials) had limits of 11,8.5, it would be rotated 90°, to fit within the 8.5,11 specified paper size.

Step 8. Set the plot rotation at 0.

Scale, Rotation, and Origin Area: Determine the Plot Origin

For a printer, the Plot Origin (0,0) is often located in the upper left corner of the printer paper. If the drawing is not plotted in the desired location, changing the X Origin: by ½″ (for example, from 0.00 to 0.50), or more if needed, moves the plot to the right. Changing the Y Origin: from 0.00 to 0.50 moves the plot ½″ down from the upper left corner of the paper.

To verify the location of 0,0 and how the printer moves the origin of the plot, plot a simple drawing such as a border only. First, plot the drawing with a plot origin of 0,0. Second, change only the X Origin by ½″ (.5,0) and replot. Third, change only the Y Origin by ½″ (0,.5) and replot again. Your printer may have its origin in the lower left corner so that changing the Y origin to .5 will move the plot up ½″.

Step 9. Set the X and Y Origins to 0. Pick OK.

Scale, Rotation, and Origin Area: Specify the Plotting Scale

You can specify a plot drawing scale by entering the scale in the Plotted Inches = Drawing Units input buttons. Some basic calculations can help you determine the correct scale so that the drawing fits within the specified paper size. To be able to measure a plotted drawing accurately using a scale, you must enter a specific plotting scale, such as the following:

Plotted Inches	=	Drawing Units	
1	=	1	(Full size)
.5	=	1′	(½″ = 1′)
.25	=	1′	(¼″ = 1′)
.125	=	1′	(⅛″ = 1′)
.5	=	1	(Half size)
.75	=	1	(¾ size)
1	=	4	(¼ size)
2	=	1	(Twice size)

You can enter fractions in Architectural units, but AutoCAD shows the fraction in decimal units (Example: ½ = 12 defaults to .5 = 1′).

You may respond by checking the Scaled to Fit check box instead of entering a specific scale. When you check this box, AutoCAD scales the drawing as large as possible to fit the specified paper size.

Step 10. Type .9 (Plotted Inches) 5 1 (Drawing Units) for plotting your drawing 5–1 (your initials).

Plot Preview Area

When you pick the Partial radio button and the Preview. . . button, the Preview Effective Plotting Area dialog box (Figure 6–8) appears. This allows you to preview the plot and, if any warnings appear, change the plotting parameters. A *Partial* preview shows only an outline of the effective plotting area of the drawing, while the *Full* preview shows the entire drawing.

The effective plotting area, measured from the plot origin, is the actual size of the graphics to be plotted on the paper. If the maximum size for the printer is exceeded, AutoCAD prompts in the Warnings: area, "Plotting area truncated to maximum." If this warning appears, or if the effective plotting area appears too small, cancel the plot and recheck the drawing limits, or extents, and any layers that are off or frozen, and see how they relate to the plot status parameters. Review the plot status parameters that include the plot origin, paper size, plot rotation, and scale, and change them accordingly to get a successful plot.

FIGURE 6–8
Preview Effective Plotting Area Dialog Box

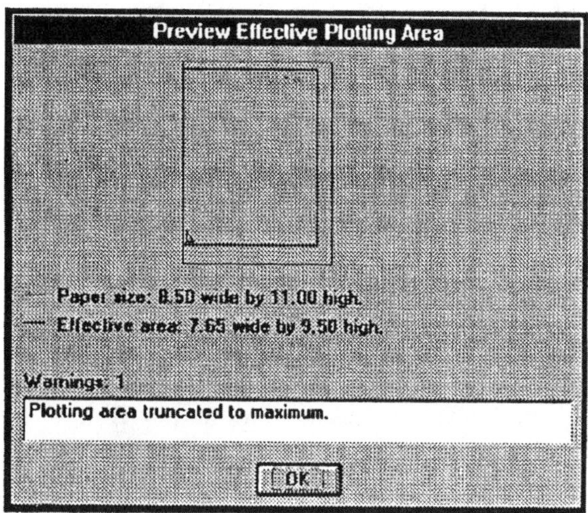

Step 11. Preview your plot.

Pick the Full preview radio button and preview your plot for 5-1 (your initials). It should look similar to Figure 6–9. If there is something wrong with the plot, pick End Preview and make the necessary adjustments. If the preview looks OK, pick End Preview.

FIGURE 6–9
Full Plot Preview

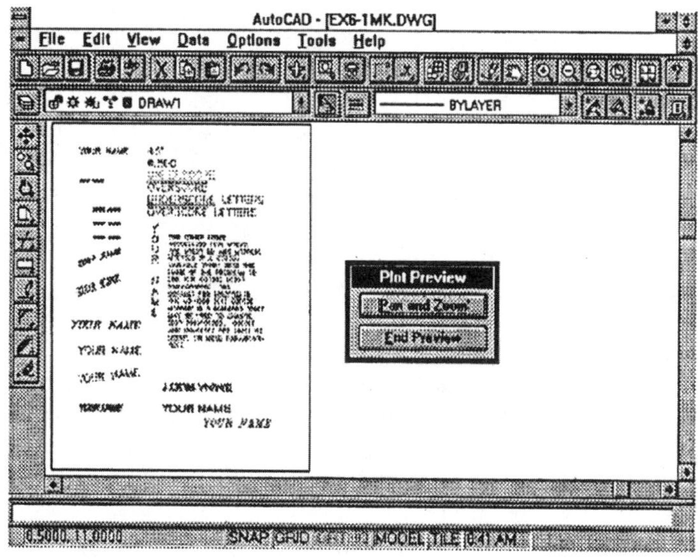

Note: To cancel a plot after it has started, Press: Esc.

Step 12. Print your plot.

The printer plot proceeds from this point. Pick the OK button of the Plot Configuration dialog box. If you have not created a plot file, remove the completed plot from the printer and exit AutoCAD if you are finished with this session. If you have created a .PLT file, take your floppy disk to the plot station or send your plot via a network.

PRINTING ON A PLOTTER

EXERCISE 6–2
MAKING A PLOTTER PLOT OF DRAWING 5–1 (YOUR INITIALS)

The following is a hands-on, step-by-step procedure to make a plotter plot of Drawing 5–1 (your initials).

Step 1. On Your Own:

1. Turn on the computer, and start the AutoCAD program. Start drawing 5-1 (your initials) on the hard drive so it is displayed on the screen.
2. Type: CHPROP ↵. Pick the UNDERSCORE and OVERSCORE text (there are four of them), and change them to the DRAW3 layer. You need to have the entities on two layers (in two colors) to demonstrate the use of multiple pens.
3. Pick the Print: command from the root menu, or pick Print. . . under File on the menu bar, or type PLOT ↵ from the keyboard to access the Plot Configuration dialog box.

Device and Default Information Area

Step 2. Select the plotter.

If the text line does not show the plotter device, use the Device and Default Selection dialog box to select the plotter that you will use to plot your drawing 5-1 (your initials).

Pen Parameters Area

When the Pen Assignments. . . button is picked, if your plotter supports multiple pens, a Pen Assignments dialog box (Figure 6–10) appears. Let's examine the meaning of the items in the dialog box and then select pens for plotting drawing 5–1 (your initials).

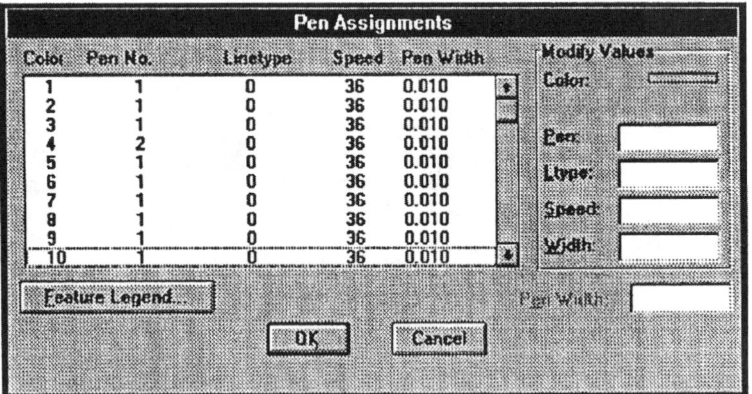

FIGURE 6–10
Pen Assignments Dialog Box

Color The list box lists as many colors as your system supports. Each drawing entity has a color associated with it (such as the color associated with a layer). The Color portion in the list box cannot be changed. Each entity color may be plotted with a different pen number, plotter linetype, pen speed, and pen width, and those parameters can be changed.

Pen No. This is the number of the slot on the plotter's pen carousel. A pen of any color or width may be inserted into the slot. Any pen number may be used for any entity color. The following examples further describe how a pen is selected to draw an entity color.

Example 1. Place a thin black pen in slot 1 of the plotter's pen carousel. Change the pen numbers in the list box to read as shown below. (To change Pen No.s digitize all the lines you want to change, then digitize the Pen: Edit box and change the Pen No. to 1, Press: ↵.)

Entity Color	Pen No.
1 (red)	1
2 (yellow)	1
3 (green)	1
4 (cyan)	1
5 (blue)	1
6 (magenta)	1
7 (white)	1

Result. All the red, yellow, green, cyan, blue, magenta, and white lines on the drawing are plotted as thin black lines.

Example 2. Place a thin black pen in slot 1 of the plotter's pen carousel and a thick black pen in slot 2. Change the pen numbers in the list box to read as follows:

Entity Color	Pen No.
1 (red)	1
2 (yellow)	1
3 (green)	1
4 (cyan)	2
5 (blue)	1
6 (magenta)	1
7 (white)	1

Result. The cyan lines of your drawing are plotted as thick black lines. All red, yellow, green, blue, magenta, and white lines are drawn as thin black lines.

If you have a laser plotter, some of the information, such as placing pens in a carousel, does not apply.

Plotter Linetype Although most users do not change linetypes during plotting, this option allows you to do that. The plotter linetypes are shown as 0 through 6 when you pick the Feature Legend. . . button. Do not combine entity linetypes (such as those associated with a layer) and plotter linetypes. Use a plotter linetype only if the entity linetype is CONTINUOUS. If the entity linetype is any linetype other than CONTINUOUS, use the plotter's continuous linetype, number 0.

Pen Speed Pen speed varies with the pen used and the paper or film on which the drawing is plotted. AutoCAD normally starts with the fastest pen speed. You will need to test the speed for your situation. If the pen skips or moves too quickly, you can slow the pen speed.

Pen Width The pen width setting generally is a concern when you are plotting extremely accurate art work. The pen width setting governs how often the plotter pen must be raised and lowered to fill solids and polylines. If the pen setting is wider than the actual pen width, AutoCAD may fail to raise and lower the pen between closely spaced lines. Be sure to convert a metric measurement on any pen to an inches measurement before setting the pen width when you are using the inch unit. It is unlikely that you will need to change this setting from the AutoCAD default.

Modify Values Area Pick and highlight the item or items you want to change from the list box. Use the edit boxes in the Modify Values area to change the values of the pen number, linetype, pen speed, or pen width.

Step 3. Install pens and make pen settings

For drawing 5–1 (your initials), the following layers were used: (Other layers were created but only two were used.)

Layer Name	Color	Linetype
DRAW1	Green	CONTINUOUS
DRAW3	Cyan	CONTINUOUS

Determine the pens you have available and select two slots in the plotter's carousel (Examples: 1 and 2). Insert two different colors or widths of pens in the two slots. Set the two different pen numbers for Color 3 (green) (Example Pen No. 1) and Color 4 (cyan) (Example Pen No. 2). Keep Linetype set at 0, continuous line for both colors.

Pen Parameters Area: Optimization. . . Button

When this button is picked, the Optimizing Pen Motion dialog box appears (Figure 6–11). The check boxes show different levels of optimizing pen motion (minimizing wasted pen motion) and reducing plotting time.

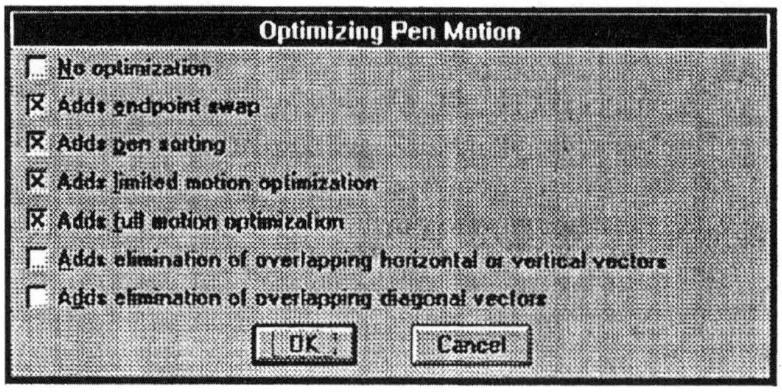

FIGURE 6–11
Optimizing Pen Motion Dialog Box

Optimizing Pen Motion

- [ ] No optimization
- [x] Adds endpoint swap
- [x] Adds pen sorting
- [x] Adds limited motion optimization
- [x] Adds full motion optimization
- [ ] Adds elimination of overlapping horizontal or vertical vectors
- [ ] Adds elimination of overlapping diagonal vectors

OK Cancel

Step 4. Do not change any of the Optimizing Pen Motion check boxes.

Additional Parameters Area: Specify the Part of the Drawing That is to be Plotted

Step 5. Select the Extents radio button to specify the extents as the part of the drawing that is to be plotted.

Additional Parameters Area: The Hide Lines Check Button

Step 6. Do not check the Hide Lines check button. This check button refers to 3-D objects only.

Additional Parameters Area: The Adjust Area Fill Check Button

Step 7. Do not check the Adjust Area Fill check button.

Additional Parameters Area: The Plot to File Check Button

Step 8. If you have a plot station, check the Plot to File check button. Change the file name or write the file to another disk if you need to.

Paper Size and Orientation Area

Step 9. Select the Inches radio button.

Step 10. Pick the Size. . . button, and enter 11″ Width × 8.5″ Height USER paper size in the Paper Size dialog box.

The list box in the Paper Size dialog box lists the paper sizes the plotter can accommodate and highlights the current selection. When these sizes match the ANSI standard size paper, the size is shown as A, B, C, or D. The MAX size is the maximum size the plotter can plot. When a plotting size is entered that is different from the MAX or standard ANSI plotting sizes for your plotter, it will appear in the list box labeled USER.

The ANSI standard sheet sizes for paper are as follows:

Size	Width	Height
A	11	8.5
B	17	11
C	22	17
D	34	22
E	44	34

The sheet sizes listed in the list box may reflect the standard ANSI sheet sizes, reduced by ¼″ to ½″. This is because the rollers that grip the plotter paper use this space and reduce the plotting size accordingly.

Many users specify a plotting size that is larger than the actual plotting size the drawing requires. That allows a drawing with an effective plotting area that is touching the boundaries of the smaller paper size to be plotted without interference from the rollers that grip the plotter paper. The paper is then trimmed to the smaller standard sheet size.

If you are using a standard architectural paper size, you must enter that size in the USER edit boxes. Standard architectural sheet sizes are as follows:

Size	Width	Height
A	12	9
B	18	12
C	24	18
D	36	24
E	48	36

A new plotting size is usually entered using the landscape paper orientation. If your plotter allows you to insert the paper in the plotter in only the vertical orientation, test the 0,0 location to verify that the plotter automatically changes the X-Y direction and the 0,0 location accordingly.

Scale, Rotation, and Origin Area: Determine the Plot Rotation

Step 11. Pick the Rotation and Origin. . . button to access the Plot and Rotation and Origin dialog box. Set the Plot Rotation radio button to 90.

To determine plot rotation, look at the drawing before beginning the plot routine, and decide the best orientation of the drawing with the specified plotting size.

Scale, Rotation, and Origin Area: Determine the Plot Origin

Step 12. Set the X Origin and Y Origin to 0.

For a plotter plot, the plot origin (0,0) is normally located in the lower left corner of the paper, assuming a horizontal paper orientation (for example, 22,17). Changing the X Origin by 1″ moves the plot 1″ to the right. Changing the Y Origin by 1″ moves the plot 1″ up from the home position.

Scale, Rotation, and Origin Area: Specify the Plotting Scale

Step 13. Set the Plotted Inches = Drawing Units to 1 = 1.

Plot Preview Area

Step 14. Preview your plot.

Check the plot preview for drawing 5–1 (your initials); if it looks like Figure 6–12, the origin needs to be changed. Pick End Preview and pick the Rotation and Origin button.

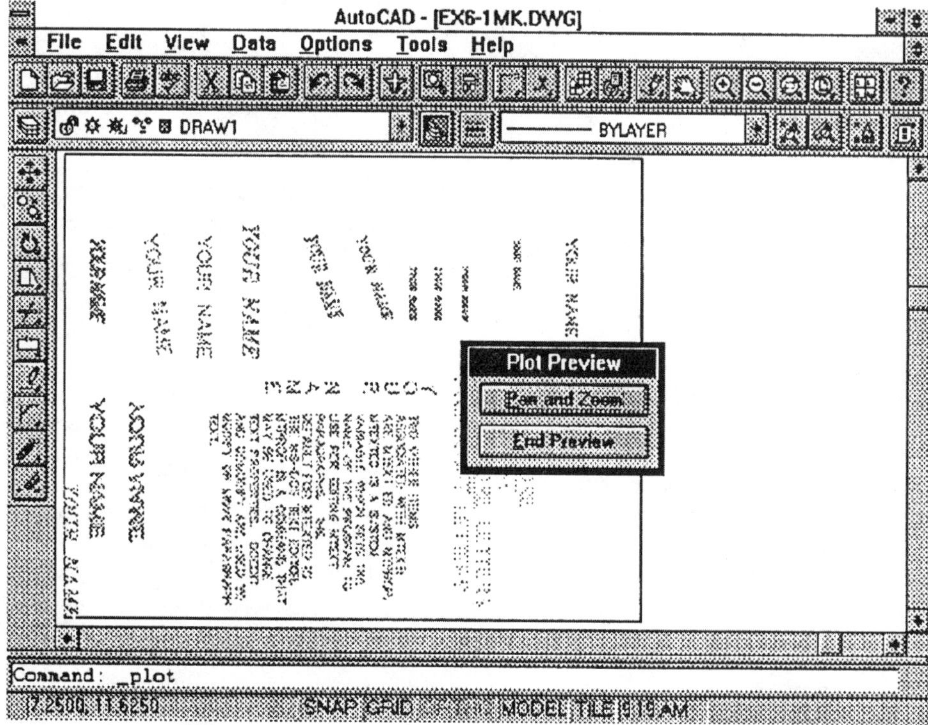

FIGURE 6–12
Plot Preview Shows Drawing Is off the Sheet

Change the X Origin: to 0.50 and the Y Origin: to 0.50 (Figure 6–13), pick OK, and check the full plot preview again. It should look like Figure 6–14.

Step 15. Plot your plot.

Pick the OK button of the Plot Configuration dialog box. The plotter plot proceeds from this point. If you have not created a plot file, remove the completed plot from the plotter and exit AutoCAD if you are finished with this session. If you have created a .PLT file, take your floppy disk to the plot station or send your plot via a network.

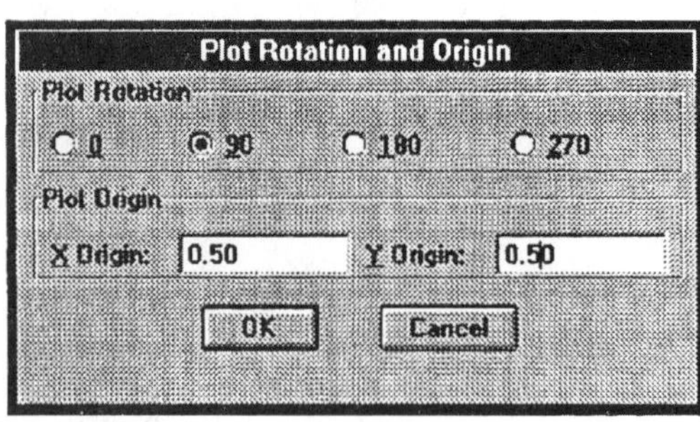

FIGURE 6–13
Change Plot Origin to .5, .5

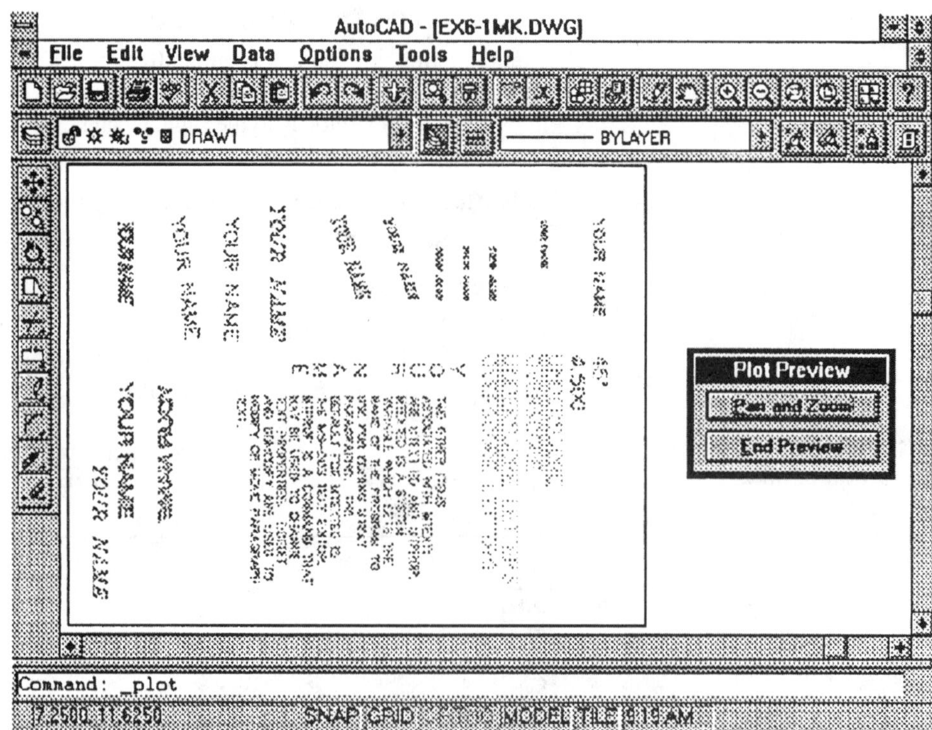

FIGURE 6–14
Good Plot Preview

REVIEW QUESTIONS

Circle the correct answer.

1. A printer plot may not be performed while the drawing is active (displayed on the screen).
   a. True b. False
2. Which of the following pull-down menus contains the Print . . . command?
   a. File d. Tools
   b. Data e. Service
   c. Options
3. Which of the following will produce a plot of the screen area only?
   a. Display d. View
   b. Extents e. Window
   c. Limits
4. Which of the following will produce a plot of the entire drawing, even if part of it is outside the limits?
   a. Display d. View
   b. Extents e. Window
   c. Limits

5. A plot file has which of the following extensions?
   a. .BAK
   b. .DWG
   c. .PLT
   d. .CFK
   e. .PWD
6. A plot that shows only half of what should have been plotted could probably be corrected by doing which of the following?
   a. Moving the origin .5
   b. Selecting VIEW instead of EXTENTS
   c. Rotating the plot 90°
   d. Writing the plot to a file
   e. Selecting a smaller page size
7. The question "remove hidden lines?" on the plot routine refers to which of the following?
   a. 3-D objects
   b. Isometric drawings
   c. Hidden linetypes
   d. 2-D objects
   e. Slide files
8. A drawing that is to be plotted so that it fits on a particular size sheet without regard to the scale requires which scale response?
   a. 1 = 1
   b. Full
   c. 1 = 2
   d. FIT
   e. MAX
9. A drawing that is to be plotted at a scale of ¼″ = 1′ should use which scale response?
   a. Full
   b. FIT
   c. 48 = 1
   d. 1 = 48
   e. ¼ = 1
10. Which message indicates that the plot is proceeding as planned?
    a. Plot proceeding
    b. Printing
    c. Processing vectors
    d. Response O.K.
    e. PLOT RETURNED
11. List three items that must be checked on a plotter plot that are not answered on a printer plot.

    a. ______________________________

    b. ______________________________

    c. ______________________________
12. If a pen plotter has a thick pen in slot 2 and a thin pen in slot 1, which pen numbers should be selected for each of the drawing lines shown? Write 1 or 2 in the pen-number blank.

Color	Width	Pen No.
Red	Thick	______
Blue	Thin	______
Yellow	Thick	______
Cyan	Thin	______

13. If red lines on the drawing should be plotted red, blue lines plotted blue, and white lines plotted black, which pens should be placed in the plotter slots? Fill in red, blue, or black in the correct plotter pen slots.

Color	Pen No.	Plotter Slot
Red	1	1 ______
Blue	2	2 ______
White	3	3 ______

14. Give the response that cancels a plot.

    ____
15. Which area must be selected to make sure you plot the entire drawing even if part of it is outside the drawing limits?

    ____
16. Give the plotting scale needed to plot a drawing twice the size it was drawn.

Plotted Inches	=	Drawing Units
______		______

17. Give the plotting scale needed to plot a drawing at ½ size.

Plotted Inches	=	Drawing Units
______		______

18. Give the plotting scale needed to plot a drawing at a scale of ⅛″ = 1′.

Plotted Inches	=	Drawing Units
______		______

19. Describe the major function of the Device and Default Selection button.

    ____

    ____
20. Describe how "Pen width in inches" and "Adjust area-fill boundaries for pen width" are related.

    ____

    ____

    ____

    ____

7 Using 2-D Commands to Draw Geometric Constructions

OBJECTIVES

When you have completed this chapter, you will be able to:

- □ Draw and edit points, lines, circles, arcs, ellipses, solids, and polygons and use them in common geometric constructions.
- □ Answer review questions regarding the following commands and settings:

Aperture:	Divide:	Measure:	Redraw:
Arc:	Dsviewer:	New:	Redrawall:
Array:	Ellipse:	Offset:	Regen:
Break:	Extend:	Osnap:	Regenall:
Chamfer:	Fill:	Pan:	Rotate:
Change:	Fillet:	Pedit:	Solid:
Chprop:	Group:	Pickbox	Spline:
Circle:	Lengthen:	Point:	Stretch:
Copy:	Line:	Polygon:	Trim:
DDchprop:	Mledit:	Polyline:	Undo:
DDosnap:	Mline:	Ray:	Viewres:
DDDtype:	Mlstyle:	Redo:	Zoom:

Before beginning to make production drawings that can be used to build or assemble products, a chapter containing many of the drawing constructions is needed. Familiarity with geometric constructions shown in this chapter will allow later drawings to be done much faster. At least one method is shown for each of the constructions presented. You will discover other methods; you may even find faster methods.

TYPES OF CONSTRUCTIONS

The following geometric constructions of this chapter are shown in Figure 7–1.

- □ Lines and points
- □ Parallel lines
- □ Perpendicular lines
- □ Breaking lines
- □ Dividing lines into equal parts
- □ Fillets
- □ Chamfers
- □ Circles
- □ Tangents
- □ Arcs
- □ Curves through points
- □ Breaking a polyline
- □ Similar shapes
- □ Arrays of circles and lines
- □ Polygons
- □ Solid shapes
- □ Ellipses and tangents to them
- □ Extending lines
- □ Trimming lines
- □ Changing line length
- □ Stretching lines

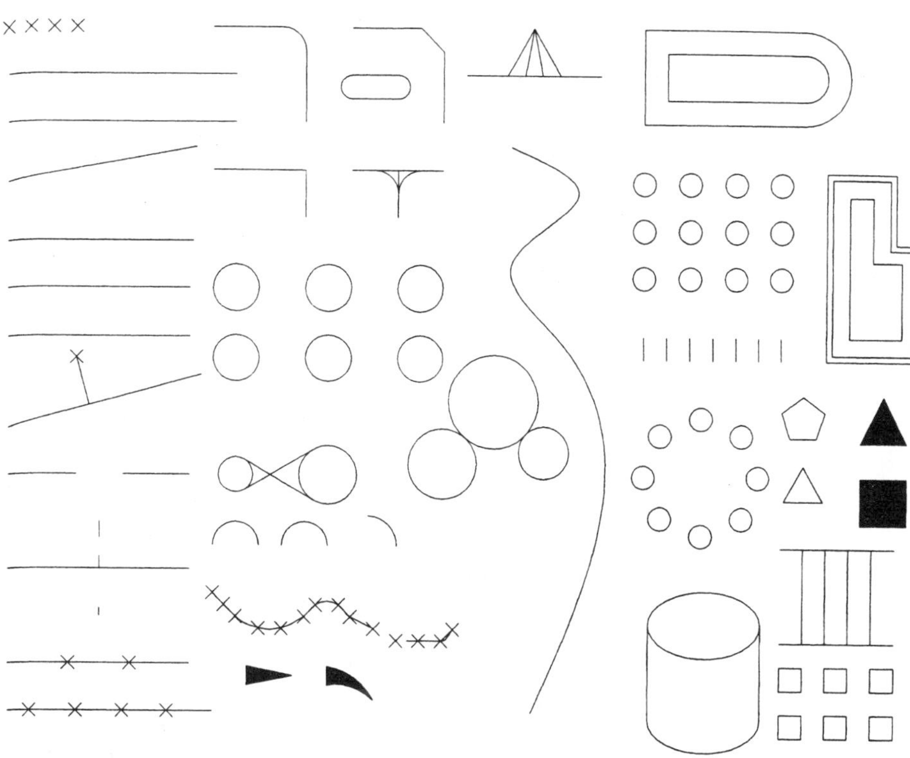

FIGURE 7–1
Geometric Constructions

EXERCISE 7–1 GEOMETRIC CONSTRUCTIONS

Set Up the Drawing

Step 1. On Your Own:

1. Pick New. . . from the menu bar file menu. Name the drawing: 7–1 (your initials).
2. Make the following settings:

Tip: The snap and grid settings may also be made from the pull-down OPTIONS menu.

Note: Do not be afraid to try any command. You can always return to where you were before the command was issued by using UNDO (type U on the keyboard). You can also REDO one UNDO by typing REDO or selecting it from the menu. Also, if you get into the middle of a command sequence and you do not want to finish it, press Esc to cancel.

UNITS: Decimal; 3 digits to the right of the decimal point
LIMITS: Lower left corner: 0,0
Upper right corner: 11, 8.5
GRID: .25
SNAP: .125
STYLE: STANDARD; FONT—SIMPLEX; HEIGHT: 0
Create the following layers:

LAYER NAME	COLOR	LINETYPE
Y	YELLOW	CONTINUOUS
R	RED	CONTINUOUS
G	GREEN	CONTINUOUS

Set layer Y current.

You should now have displayed at the upper left of your drawing (Windows users: bottom of the screen) the following:

Note: Ortho allows you to draw lines, copy, move, etc vertically or horizontally so that the row or column is perfectly straight. You have to turn ortho off to construct anything at an angle.

Layer Y Ortho Snap (If this is not what you find, you may need to use the function keys to turn on snap, grid, coordinates, and ortho.)
F6 COORDINATES
F7 GRID FUNCTION
F8 ORTHO FUNCTION
F9 SNAP FUNCTION

Using Object Snap

*** * * * (Osnap:)**

It is very important to become familiar with and use Object Snap modes while drawing. If an existing drawing entity is not drawn on a snap point, it is nearly impossible to snap a line or other drawing entity exactly to it. You may try, and think that the two points are connected, but a close examination will reveal they are not. Object Snap modes can be used to snap exactly to specific points of existing objects in a drawing. Object Snap modes need to be used constantly for complete accuracy while drawing.

Onsnap: commands can be activated in five different ways: by picking * * * * from the root menu, by picking Osnap: from the ASSIST menu on the menu bar or the screen menu, by pressing the Osnap: button on your mouse, by picking the snap from icon on the standard tool bar, or by typing the first three letters of the desired osnap mode from the keyboard.

Running Osnap: Modes

You may select individual modes while in another command by picking them directly from the Osnap: menu or typing them when AutoCAD prompts for a point. You may also set a "running" Osnap: mode to be constantly in effect while drawing, until it is disabled. A running Osnap: mode may include one or more modes. When Osnap: is typed and entered at the Command: prompt, or Osnap: <mode> is picked from the pull-down menu, the prompt is "Object snap modes:". If you respond to the prompt by typing two or three modes, separated by a comma or commas, and pressing the enter key, all the modes can be used while drawing. For instance if "INT,MID,NOD" is typed and entered, all three modes will be in effect. When one or more modes are entered this way, they become the running object snap modes. Running Osnap: modes may also be set from the Running Object Mode dialog box, which is activated by selecting DDosnap from the Osnap: menu or picking Running Object Snap from Options on the menu bar. The running mode can be disabled by responding to the prompt "Object snap modes:" by typing or picking None and pressing the enter key or by digitizing the existing X next to the Osnap: Mode on the Running Object Snap dialog box. You can also override the running mode for a single point by selecting another mode not included in the running mode. The running mode set by the Osnap: command returns after the single override.

When Osnap: is activated, a *target symbol* or small box is added to the screen cross hairs. This small box shows the area within which AutoCAD will search for Object Snap candidates. The size of the box is controlled by the APERTUR: command.

Osnap: Modes That Snap to Individual Drawing Features

Apparent Intersection: Snaps to the apparent intersection of two entities even if one is below the other (helpful in 3-D drawing).

CENter: Snaps to the center of an Arc or Circle. (You must point to a visible part of the circumference to designate the Arc or Circle. If this mode is combined with others, you may have trouble with another object snap point being closer than the center).

ENDpoint: Snaps to the closest endpoint of a Line or Arc.

FROM: The From object snap differs from the other Osnap: modes in that it establishes a temporary reference point from which a point may be specified. For example, if you need to start a line 2″ in the X direction and 4″ in the Y direction from the endpoint of a line, the following sequence of steps would do that:

Prompt	Response
Command:	**Line:**
From point:	**FROM** (from the Osnap menu)
Base point:	**ENDpoint**
of	Pick the end of the line.
<Offset>	*Type:* **@2,4** ↵
To point:	

INSert: Snaps to the insertion point of Text, Attribute, Attribute Definition, or Block entity. (You have already learned about Text; the other entities, Attribute, Attribute Definition, and Block are described in later chapters.)

INTersec: Snaps to the intersection of two Lines, a Line with an Arc or Circle, or two Circles and/or Arcs. For this Object Snap mode, both objects must cross the target on the screen.

MIDpoint: Snaps to the midpoint of a Line or Arc.

NEArest: Snaps to the point on a Line, Arc, or Circle that is visually closest to the position of the cross hairs, or snaps to the Point entity that is visually closest to the cross hairs.

NODe: Snaps to a Point entity. Points may be placed on locations in a Block definition and thus function as "snap nodes" after the Block has been inserted.

QUAdrant: Snaps to the closest quadrant point of an Arc, Circle, or Ellipse. These are the 0°, 90°, 180°, and 270° points on an Arc, Circle, or Ellipse (only the visible quadrants of an Arc may be selected).

Osnap: Modes That Snap to Features with Respect to the Last Point Entered

PERpend: Snaps to the point on a Line, Circle, or Arc that forms a 90° angle from that object to the last point.

TANgent: Snaps to the point on a Circle or Arc that, when connected to the last point, forms a line tangent to that object.

For the Line command, you can use the Tangent and Perpendicular Object Snap modes when specifying the first point of the line. In this case, the last point is not used in the calculation. Rather, this special case allows you to construct a line tangent to, or perpendicular to, an existing object. However, the rubber-band line normally drawn to help you select the next point will not be drawn.

Osnap: QUICK

The Osnap: QUICK mode stops searching as soon as it finds one object with at least one point of the specified type. Object Snap normally searches for all objects crossing the target and selects the closest potential snap point of the specified type(s). When many entities are visible on the screen, this search can result in a noticeable delay. In such a situation, you can use Quick mode along with your other Object Snap modes.

If two or more objects with candidate object-snap points cross the target, Quick mode chooses the first one it sees. Since it is difficult to predict which object will be seen first, it is recommended that you have just one such object in the target when using Quick Object Snap mode.

If intersection is one of the specified Object Snap modes, a full search is performed regardless of the presence of Quick mode.

APERTUR:

The APERTUR: command can be used to change the size of the Osnap: target symbol, or small box that is added to the cross hairs when Osnap: is activated.

The PICKBOX: command that is on the Object Selection Settings dialog box can be used to change the size of the *object selection target,* or small box that replaces the screen cross hairs when using the MODIFY commands.

Complete the following exercise to change the size of each.

Step 2. Use APERTUR: to change the size of the Osnap: target symbol.

Prompt	Response
Command:	*Pick:* **Running Object Snap. . .** (from the Options menu on the menu bar).
The Running Object Snap dialog box appears:	Pick the Max arrow on the Aperture Size button to increase the size of the Aperture, or pick the Min arrow to decrease the size of the Aperture. When the size is what you want, *Pick:* **OK.**

Help: If you make a mistake, you can erase it by using the *Erase:* command. Just pick, Erase: then select objects by picking them. Press ↵ when you are finished. Erase: can also be used with a window or a crossing window. *Window* selects everything entirely enclosed by the window. *Crossing window* selects everything within or crossed by the window. To use these, select Erase: and then type W ↵ for *window* or C ↵ for *crossing.* Then pick two points to form a box that selects objects to be erased. The selection window may also be activated by picking any point that does not contain an entity (such as a line or arc) and dragging to the right. The crossing window may be activated in a similar manner and dragging to the left. Windows can also be used with other commands, such as Copy: and Move:.

Step 3. Use PICKBOX: to change the size of the MODIFY object selection target.

Prompt	Response
Command:	*Pick:* **Selection. . .** (from the Options menu on the menu bar.)
The Object Selection Settings dialog box appears:	Pick the Max arrow on the Pickbox Size button to increase the size of the Pickbox, or pick the Min arrow to decrease the size of the Pickbox. When the size is what you want, *Pick:* **OK.**

HELP:

If you have forgotten the name of a command or the options that are available for a specific command, the HELP: command is available to refresh your memory. The HELP: command provides a list of the AutoCAD commands, and it also provides information regarding specific commands.

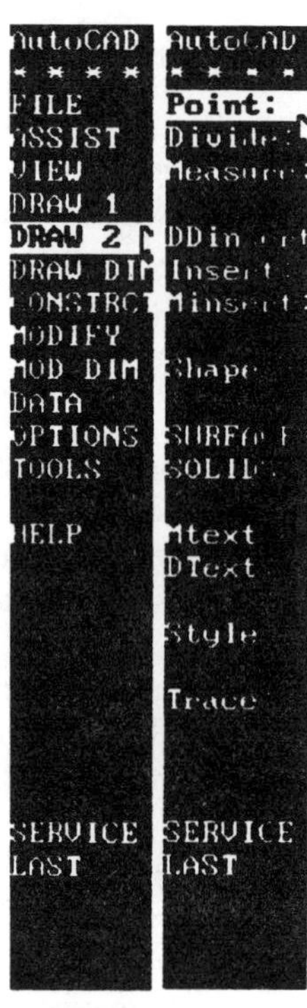

Step 4. Use HELP: to obtain a list of AutoCAD commands.

Prompt	Response
Command:	*Type:* **HELP** ↵ (or *Select:* **Help** from the menu bar)
The AutoCAD Help dialog box appears:	*Pick:* **Help** Instructions on how to use Help appear. Read these instructions and use Help when you need it. *Pick:* **OK** to exit from Help.

Dont' forget that the HELP: command is available. Use it to refresh your memory when needed. You can use the HELP: command also while in the middle of a command. Type "'help" in response to any prompt that is not asking for a text string, and information is supplied about the current command. The information is sometimes specific to the current prompt.

Lines and Points

With the coordinates, grid, ortho, and snap on, it is very easy to draw points or lines in increments of ¼″, or whatever your snap setting is. To do this, select the DRAW 2 Menu from the root menu, select Point: and follow the given sequence. Before using Point: SET Pdmode AND Pdsize:

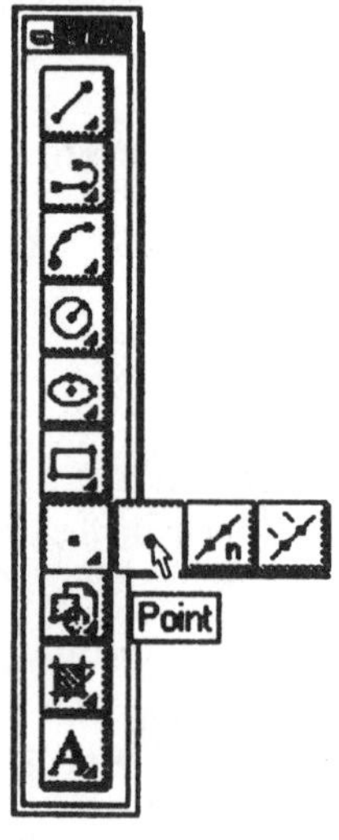

Step 5. Set Pdmode and Pdsize.

Prompt	Response
Command:	**Point** (on the DRAW 2 menu)
POINT Point:	**DDPtype:**
The Point Style dialog box appears:	**X** (■ Set size in Absolute units Point Size: 0.1.) **OK**

Pdmode and Pdsize are set and you may now proceed with the Point: command.

Windows users: Set PDMODE by typing PDMODE ↵ and give it the value 3. PDSIZE may be set by typing PDSIZE ↵ and giving it the value .1.

FIGURE 7–2
Points

Tip: If you cannot get out of the *Point:* command, press Esc.

Remember: To remove picked blips on the screen (those marks you make when you pick points), use REDRAW from the DISPLAY menu (or type R↵) or press the F7 (grid) key twice to refresh the screen.

Step 6. Draw points on a grid (Figure 7–2): (Start the first point at ½″ from the left boundary and ½″ from the top—coordinates should read .500,8.000.).

Prompt	Response
Command:	**Point:**
_point Point:	(Pick four points; place points ¼″ apart.)
_point Point:	↵

Step 7. Draw a horizontal line 2″ long .500″ below the first point you drew (Figure 7–3).

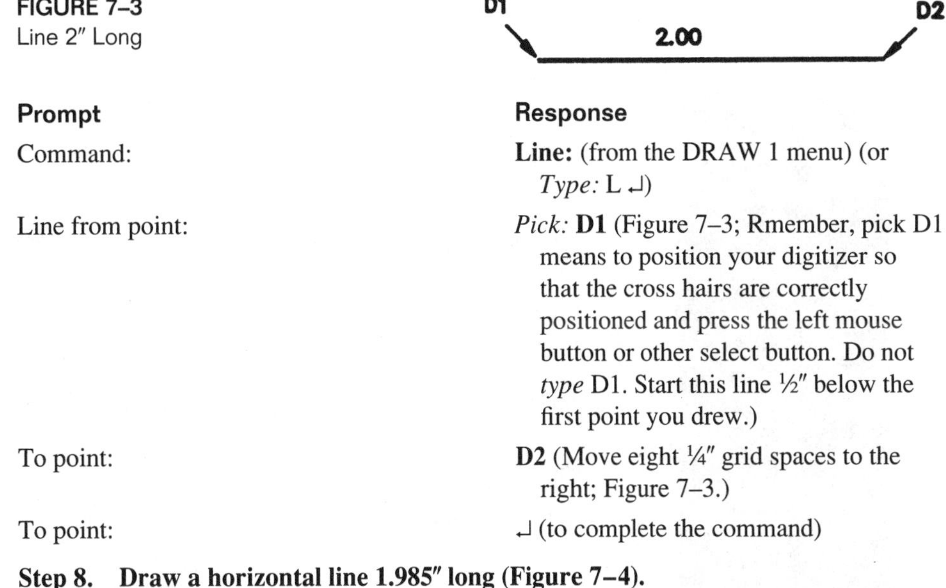

FIGURE 7–3
Line 2″ Long

Prompt	Response
Command:	**Line:** (from the DRAW 1 menu) (or *Type:* L ↵)
Line from point:	*Pick:* **D1** (Figure 7–3; Rmember, pick D1 means to position your digitizer so that the cross hairs are correctly positioned and press the left mouse button or other select button. Do not *type* D1. Start this line ½″ below the first point you drew.)
To point:	**D2** (Move eight ¼″ grid spaces to the right; Figure 7–3.)
To point:	↵ (to complete the command)

Step 8. Draw a horizontal line 1.985″ long (Figure 7–4).

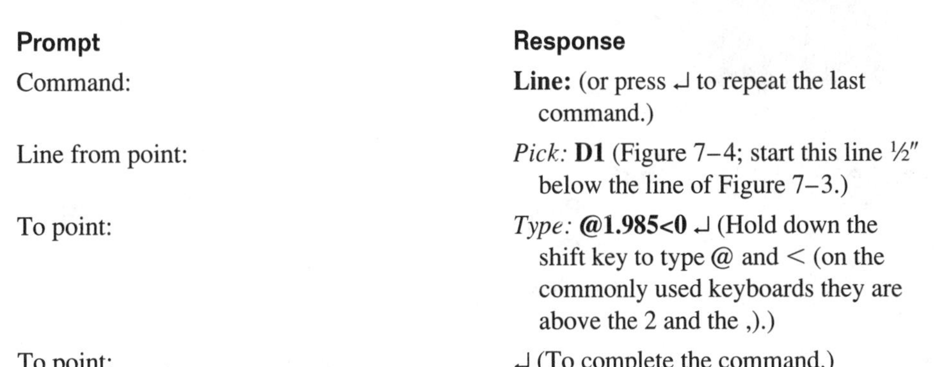

FIGURE 7–4
Horizontal Line 1.985″ Long

Prompt	Response
Command:	**Line:** (or press ↵ to repeat the last command.)
Line from point:	*Pick:* **D1** (Figure 7–4; start this line ½″ below the line of Figure 7–3.)
To point:	*Type:* **@1.985<0** ↵ (Hold down the shift key to type @ and < (on the commonly used keyboards they are above the 2 and the ,).)
To point:	↵ (To complete the command.)

You have told AutoCAD to draw a line 1.985″ long in the 0 direction. Figure 7–5 shows the direction for all lines.

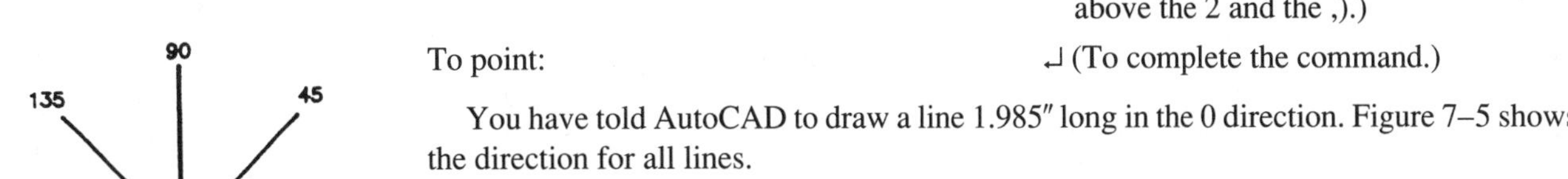

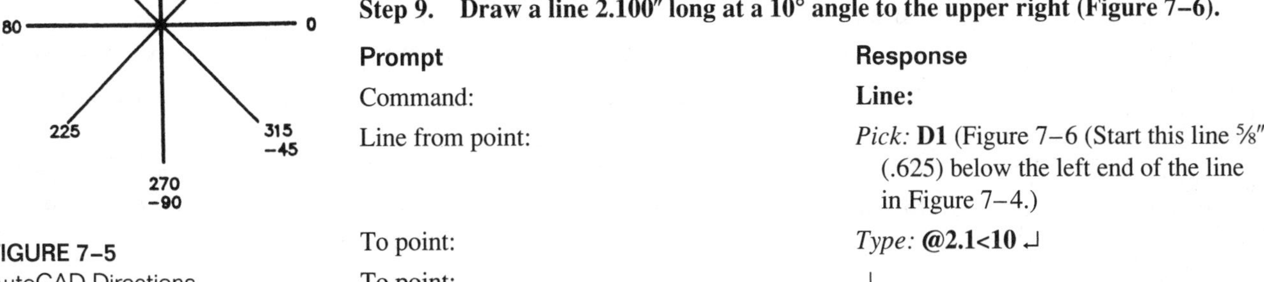

FIGURE 7–5
AutoCAD Directions

Step 9. Draw a line 2.100″ long at a 10° angle to the upper right (Figure 7–6).

Prompt	Response
Command:	**Line:**
Line from point:	*Pick:* **D1** (Figure 7–6 (Start this line ⅝″ (.625) below the left end of the line in Figure 7–4.)
To point:	*Type:* **@2.1<10** ↵
To point:	↵

FIGURE 7–6
Line 2.100″ Long, 10° Angle

Step 10. Draw a line from one location to another location (Figure 7–7).

FIGURE 7–7
Line, Start One Location, End Another Location

START LINE AT ONE LOCATION

END AT ANOTHER LOCATION

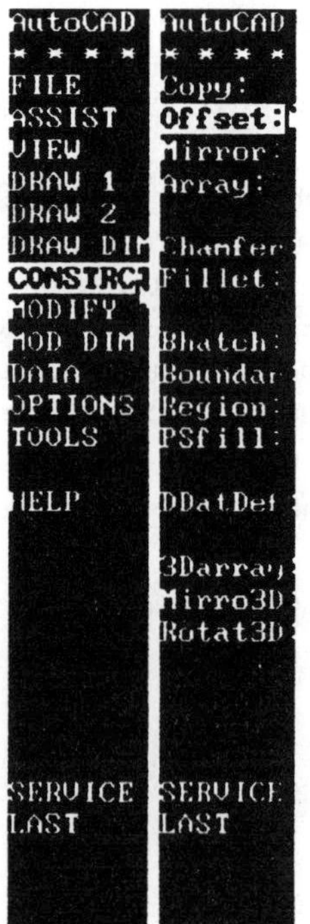

Start the line ½″ from the left side of the page and 5¾″ from the bottom of the page. End it 2.532″ from the left side and 5¾″ from the bottom.

Prompt	Response
Command:	**Line:**
Line from point:	*Type:* **.5,5.75** ↵
To point:	*Type:* **2.532,5.75** ↵
To point:	↵

Parallel Lines

Step 11. Draw 2″ lines parallel to each other, .517″ apart (Figure 7–8).

FIGURE 7–8
Parallel Lines, .517″ Apart

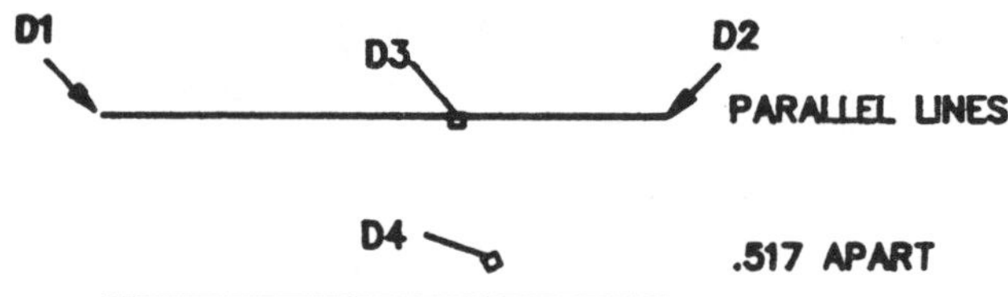

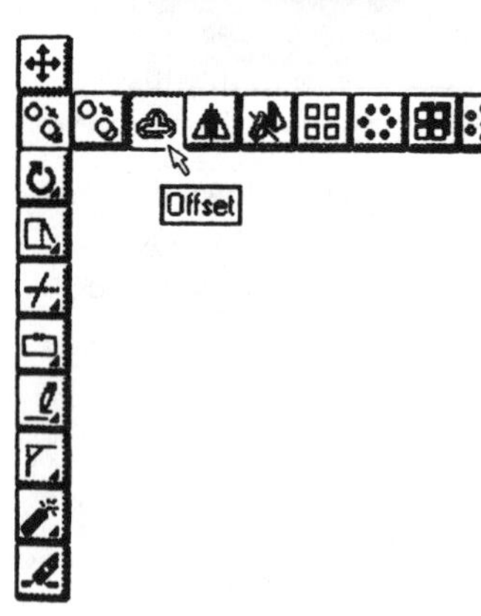

Prompt	Response
Command:	**Line:**
Line from point:	*Pick:* **D1** (Start this line ½″ below the left end of the line you drew in Figure 7–7.)
To point:	*Pick:* **D2** (2″ to the right of D1; use the grid spaces for reference (snap and ortho must be on).)
To point:	↵
Command:	**Offset:** (from the CONSTRCT menu)
Offset distance or Through <Through>:	*Type:* **.517** ↵ (the distance that the lines are apart)
Select object to offset:	*Pick:* **D3** (Select the line anywhere on it.)
Side to offset?	*Pick:* **D4** (anywhere on the side you want the other line to appear)
Select object to offset:	↵

Help: If you draw something in the wrong location, use the *Move:* command to move the object to the correct location. Select Move:, then select the object by digitizing it or by using a window. The base point is the point on the object that is to be moved, such as the endpoint of a line. The second point of displacement is the point to which you want to move the base point.

Perpendicular Lines

Step 12. Draw a line perpendicular to another line through a point (Figure 7–9).

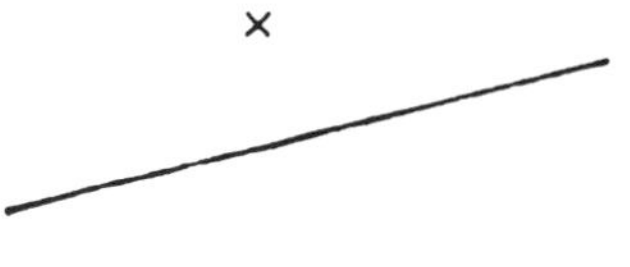

FIGURE 7–9
Line, Perpendicular through a Point

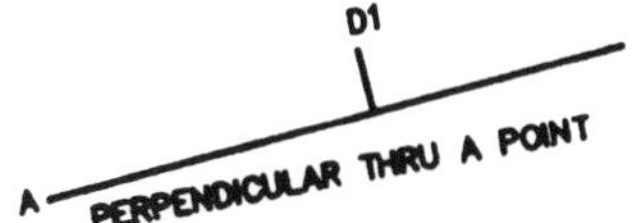

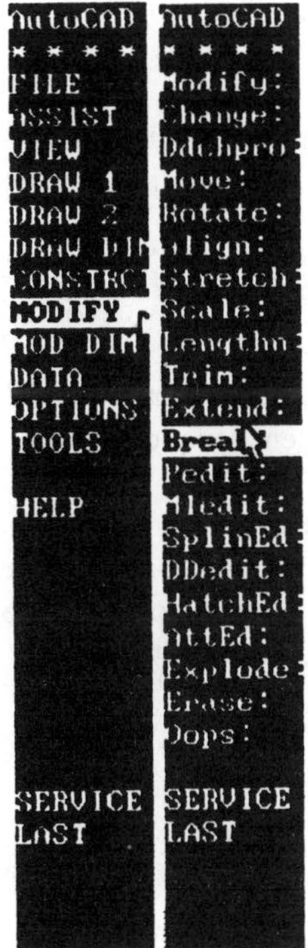

Before you start, draw a line 2.200" long at a 15° angle to the upper right and 1" below the lines you drew in Figure 7–8. Draw a point approximately ½" above this line near the center. After you have drawn this line and point, proceed as follows.

Prompt	Response
Command:	**Line:**
Line from point:	**Node** (From the Osnap menu) (press the Osnap button on the mouse for the Osnap menu or **** on the main menu or Assist—Object Snap on the pull-downs); then *pick:* the
of:	point D1.)
To point:	**Perpendicular** (from the Osnap menu)
_per to	(Pick any point on the line AB.)
To point:	↵

Breaking Lines

Step 13. Break a line AB with no interference from other lines (Figure 7–10).

FIGURE 7–10
Simple Line Break

A B GIVEN
A D2 D1 B

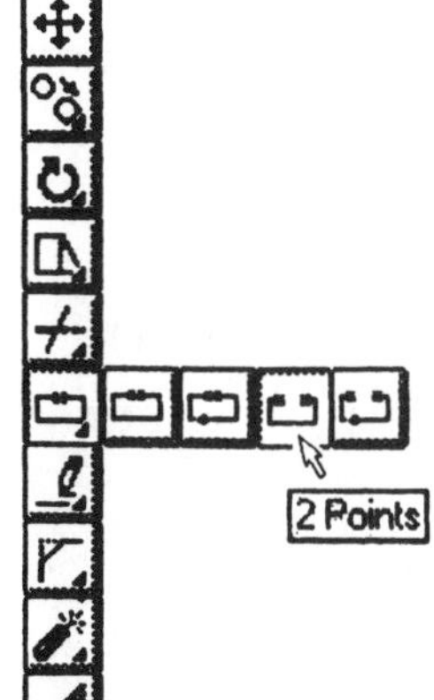

Before you start, draw a 2" horizontal line ½" below the line you drew in Figure 7–9.

Prompt	Response
Command:	**Break:**
Select object:	(Select the line by picking at one end of where the break will be made.) *Pick:* **D1** ↵
Enter second point (or F for first point):	(Pick the second point—the other end of the break.) *Pick:* **D2** ↵

Step 14. Break a line at an intersection with another line (Figure 7–11).

FIGURE 7–11
Complex Break

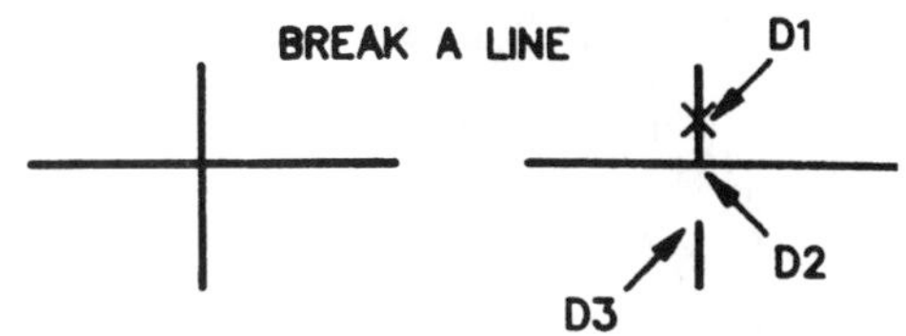

Tip: Use *Zoom: Window* from the pull-down display menu to enlarge the display of the part of the drawing on which you are working. The prompts "first corner" and "other corner" allow you to pick two points in a diagonal direction to describe the area you wish to enlarge. Use *Zoom: All* to display the entire drawing. Other display commands are described later. You will find Zoom: Window helpful for many of the exercises in this chapter.

Before you start; draw a 2″ horizontal line 1″ below the line described in Figure 7–10. Draw a 1″ vertical line through the center of the horizontal line.

Prompt	Response
Command:	**Break:**
Select object:	(Select line to be broken.) *Pick:* **D1**
Enter second point (or F for first point):	*Type:* **F** ↵ (from keyboard)
Enter first point:	**Intersection** (from the Osnap menu and pick the intersection the two lines.) *Pick:* **D2** ↵
Enter second point:	(Pick the end of the break.) *Pick:* **D3** (approximately ¼″ below D2)

The Break: command offers the following four other options:

Sel Pt (labeled "1 Point" on the MODIFY menu on the menu bar or the Modify toolbar)—This option allows you to pick a single point on the line (or other entity) to be broken. The line is broken into two pieces at that point.

Sel, 2Pts (labeled "2 Points Select" on the MODIFY menu on the menu bar or the Modify toolbar)—This option allows you to select the object and then pick two points on the object to create the break.

Sel, 1st (labeled "1 Point Select" on the MODIFY menu on the menu bar or the Modify toolbar)—This option allows you to select the line to be broken then pick a single point where the line will be broken into two pieces.

Sel, 2nd (labeled "2 Points" on the MODIFY menu on the menu bar or the Modify toolbar)—This option allows you to select the line to be broken. This point becomes the first point of the break. The option then allows you to pick the second point of the break.

Experiment with these options until you feel comfortable with them. You will find uses for all break options.

Dividing Lines into Equal Parts

Step 15. Divide a given line into three equal parts (Figure 7–12).

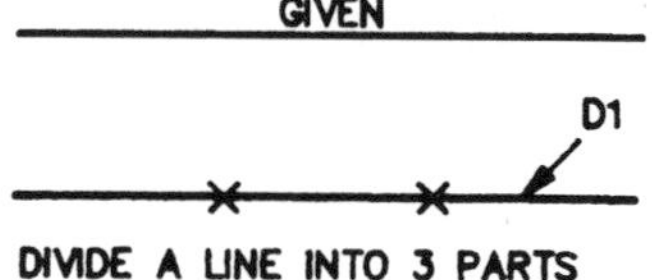

FIGURE 7–12
Dividing a Line into Equal Parts

Note: The line has not been broken into three parts; a node, or point, has been placed at the proper interval so further construction can be done at those points.

Before you start, draw a 2″ horizontal line ½″ below the vertical line you drew in Figure 7–11.

Prompt	Response
Command:	**Divide:**
Select object to divide:	*Pick:* **D1** (anywhere on the line)
<Number of segments>/Block:	*Type:* **3** ↵

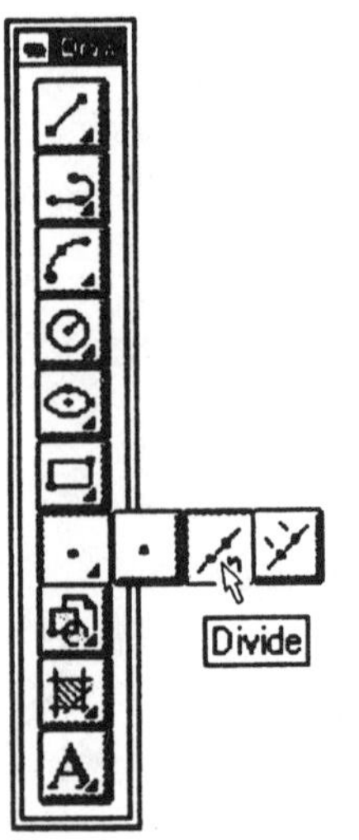

Step 16. Divide a line into certain-size parts (Figure 7–13).

FIGURE 7–13
Dividing a Line into Certain-Size Parts

D1
DIVIDE A 2 1/4" LINE INTO 1/2" PARTS

Before you start, draw a 2¼″ horizontal line ½″ below the horizontal line you drew in Figure 7–12.

Note: The divisions start from the end of the line closest to the picked point. The ¼″ left over appears on the left because the ½″ parts were measured beginning from the right end of the line.

Prompt	Response
Command:	**Measure** (from the DRAW 2 menu)
Select object to measure:	*Pick:* **D1** (Figure 7–13)
<Segment length>/block:	*Type:* **.5** ↵

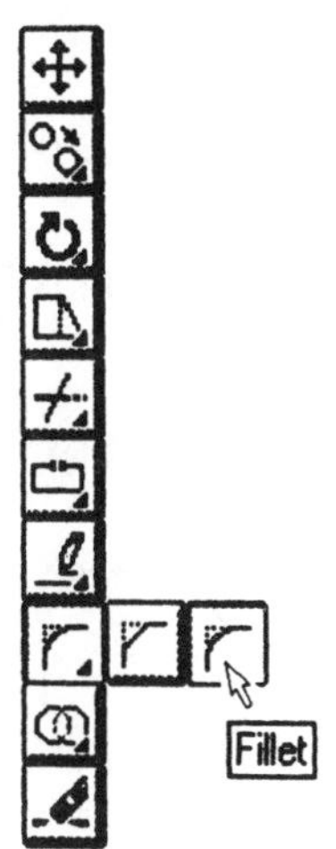

Fillets

Step 17. Make a fillet (a radius of a specific size) at the junction of two lines (Figure 7–14).

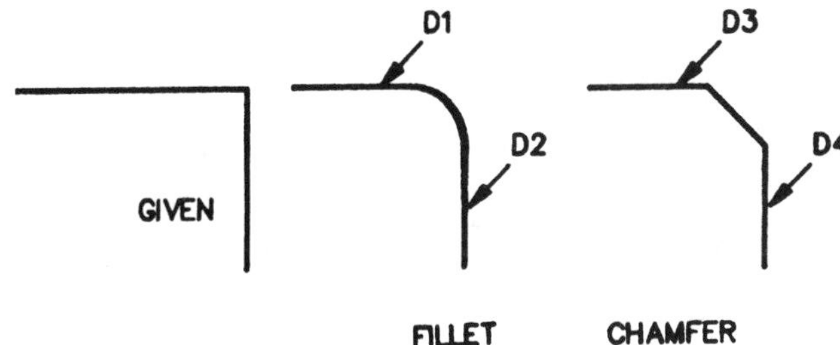

FIGURE 7–14
Fillet and Chamfer

Before you start, draw a 1″ horizontal line from coordinates 2.75,8 to 3.75,8. Draw a 1″ vertical line perpendicular to the right end of the horizontal line.

Prompt	Response
Command:	**Fillet:**
(TRIM Mode) Current Fillet radius=0.000	
Fillet Polyline/Radius/Trim/<Select first object>:	**Radius** (or *Type:* **R** ↵)
Enter fillet radius (0.000):	*Type:* **.25**
Command:	↵
<Select first object>:	*Pick:* **D1** (Figure 7–14)
Select second object:	*Pick:* **D2**

Chamfers

Step 18. Make a chamfer (an angle of a specific size) at the junction of two lines (Figure 7–14).

Before you start, draw 1″ horizontal and vertical lines as you did for Figure 7–14, FILLET. Locate these lines ½″ to the right of the fillet.

Prompt	Response
Command:	**Chamfer:**
(TRIM mode) Current Chamfer Dist1 =0.000, Dist2=0.000	
Chamfer Polyline/Distance/Angle/Trim/Method/<Select first line>:	**Distance** (or *Type:* **D** ↵)
Enter first chamfer distance: <0.000>	*Type:* **.25** ↵
Enter second chamfer distance <0.250>:	↵ (to make a 45° chamfer)
Command:	↵
<Select first line>:	*Pick:* **D3**
Select second line:	*Pick:* **D4**

Suggestion: Try another chamfer, giving different measurements for each leg of the chamfer.

Zero-Radius Fillet or Chamfer

Step 19. Make a zero-radius fillet or chamfer (Figure 7–15).

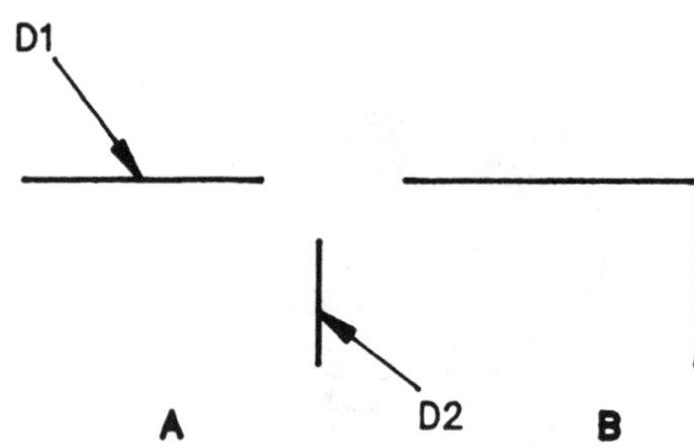

FIGURE 7–15
Zero-Radius Fillet

Tip: A zero-radius *fillet* or *chamfer* may also be used to connect lines that are not perpendicular. They may even be used to connect some curves with other curves or straight lines. This is a good command with which to experiment.

You will often find it necessary to join lines that do not intersect. A zero-radius fillet or zero-distance chamfer does this easily. *Before you start, draw a ¾" horizontal line ½" below the fillet of Figure 7–14. Draw a ¼" vertical line ¼" to the right and ¼" below the right end of the ¾" horizontal line (Figure 7–15A). Your final drawing after the fillet will appear as in Figure 7–15B.*

Prompt	Response
Command:	**Fillet**
(TRIM mode) Current fillet radius = 0.250	
Polyline/Radius/Trim/<Select first object>:	**Radius 0** (or *Type:* **0↵**)
Command:	↵
(TRIM mode) Current fillet radius = 0.000	
Polyline/Radius/Trim/<Select first object>:	*Pick:* **D1** (Figure 7–15)
Select second object:	*Pick:* **D2** (Figure 7–15).

Step 20. Use the No Trim option of the Fillet: and Chamfer: commands (Figure 7–16).

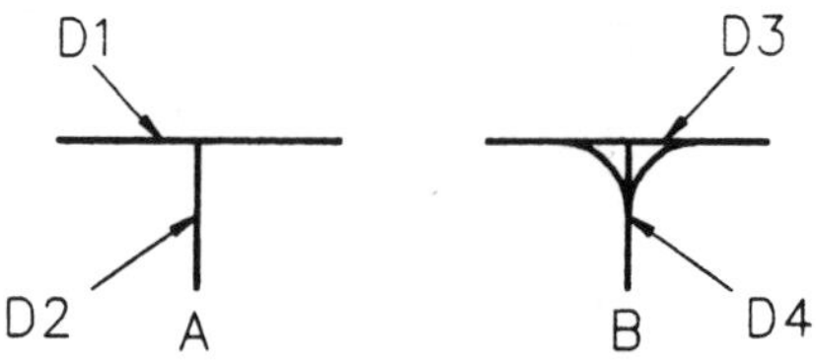

FIGURE 7–16
Using the NOTRIM Option of Fillet:

The No Trim option is often helpful when two fillets or chamfers from a single line are needed.

Before you start, draw a 1" horizontal line ½" to the right of the zero-radius fillet and a ½" vertical line downward from the midpoint of the 1" horizontal line (Figure 7–16A). Your final drawing after the fillet will appear as in Figure 7–16B.

Prompt	Response
Command:	**Fillet:**
(TRIM mode) Current fillet radius = 0.000	
Polyline/Radius/Trim/<Select first object>:	**Trim** (or *Type:* **T** ↵)

Trim/No trim <Trim>:	**No Trim** (or *Type:* **N** ↵)
Polyline/Radius/Trim/<Select first object>:	**Radius** (or *Type:* **R** ↵)
Enter fillet radius <0.000>:	*Type:* **.25** ↵
Command:	↵
(NOTRIM mode) Current fillet radius = 0.250	
Polyline/Radius/Trim/<Select first object>:	*Pick:* **D1** (Figure 7–16A)
Select second object:	*Pick:* **D2** (Figure 7–16A)
Command:	↵
(NOTRIM mode) Current fillet radius = 0.250	
Polyline/Radius/Trim/<Select first object>:	*Pick:* **D3** (Figure 7–16B)
Select second object:	*Pick:* **D4** (Figure 7–16B)

Step 21. Use the Fillet: command to make a fillet between two parallel lines, Figure 7–17.

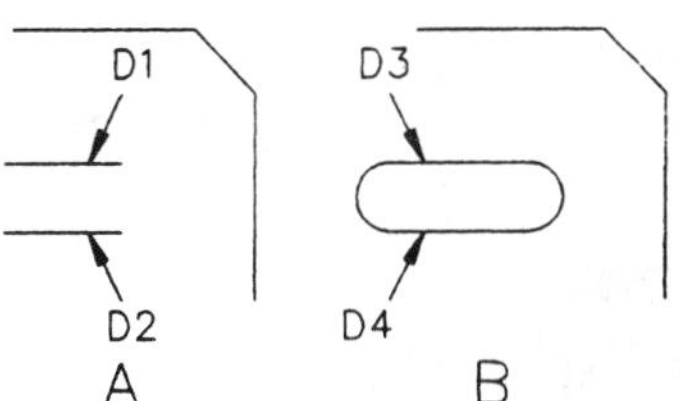

FIGURE 7–17
Fillet to Two Parallel Lines

Before you start, draw two ½″ horizontal lines ¼″ apart inside the chamfered lines as shown in Figure 7–17.

Prompt	**Response**
Command:	**Fillet:**
Polyline/Radius/Trim/<Select first object>:	**Radius** (or *Type:* **R** ↵)
Enter fillet radius <default>:	*Type:* **.125** ↵
Command:	↵
Polyline/Radius/Trim/<Select first object>:	*Pick:* **D1** (Figure 7–17A)
Select second object:	*Pick:* **D2** (Figure 7–17A)
Command:	↵
Polyline/Radius/Trim/<Select first object>:	*Pick:* **D3** (Figure 7–17B)
Select second object:	*Pick:* **D4** (Figure 7–17B)

Circles

Step 22. Draw circles of a specific size at a specific location (Figure 7–18).

Draw six ½″-diameter circles, 1″ between centers, horizontally, ¾″ vertically, in 2 rows of 3 each.

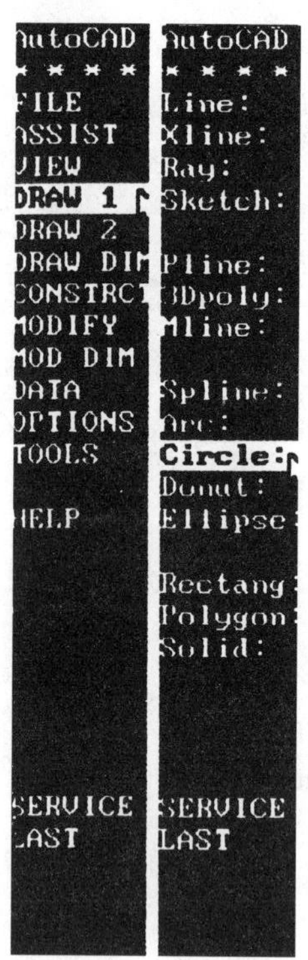

FIGURE 7–18
Methods of Drawing Circles

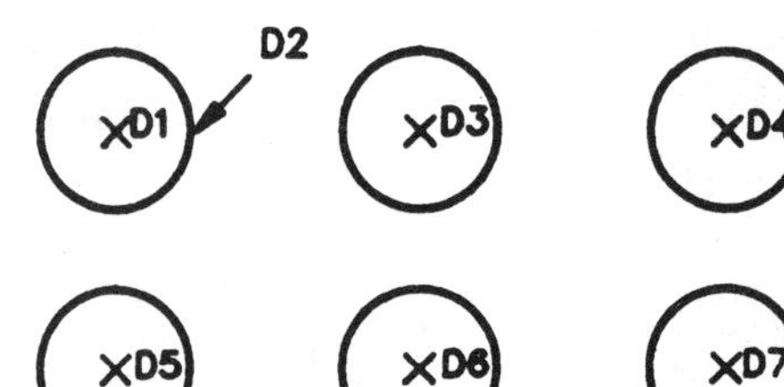

Prompt	Response
Command:	**Circle-Cen Rad**
Circle 3P/2P/TTR/<Center Point>:	*Pick:* **D1** (with snap on, 1¼″ below the left end of the zero-radius fillet and ¼″ to the right)
Diameter/<Radius>:	*Type:* **.25** ↵ (Because radius is in the default brackets, .25 is the radius for this circle.) or *Pick:* **D2** (The picked point will specify the radius) or *Type:* **D** ↵ (to tell AutoCAD you want to specify a diameter.)
Diameter:	*Type:* **.5** ↵

Help: Be sure ortho (F8) is off and snap is on when you start the Copy: command.

Draw five more circles of the same size on 1″ centers.

Prompt	Response
Command:	**Copy:** (from the CONSTRCT menu) (or *Type:* **CP** ↵)
Select object:	*Pick:* **D2** (Pick anywhere on the circle circumference.)
Select objects:	↵
<Base point or displacement>/Multiple:	**Multiple** (from the screen menu, or *Type:* **M** ↵)
Multiple base point:	*Pick:* **D1** (the center of the first circle)
Second point of displacement:	*Pick:* **D3, D4, D5, D6, D7** ↵

Circle Center Radius

Step 23. Draw a circle by locating the two endpoints of its diameter (Figure 7–19).

FIGURE 7–19
Tangents to Circles

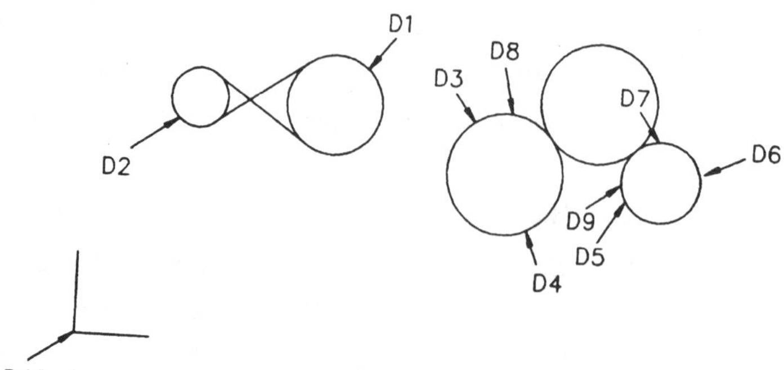

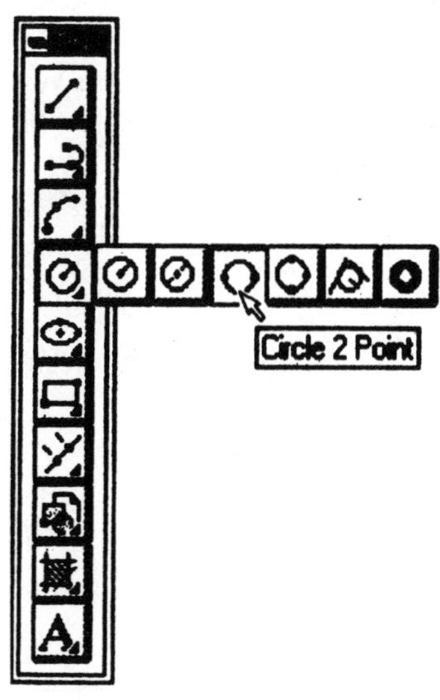

Prompt	Response
Command:	*Type:* **C** ↵
_Circle 3P/2P/TTR/<Center Point>:	*Type:* **2P** ↵
2P First point on diameter:	*Pick:* **D3** (approximately ¾″ below the right quadrant of the last circle copied)
Second point on diameter:	*Pick:* **D4** (move 3 grid spaces downward)

Step 24. Draw a circle by picking three points on its circumference.

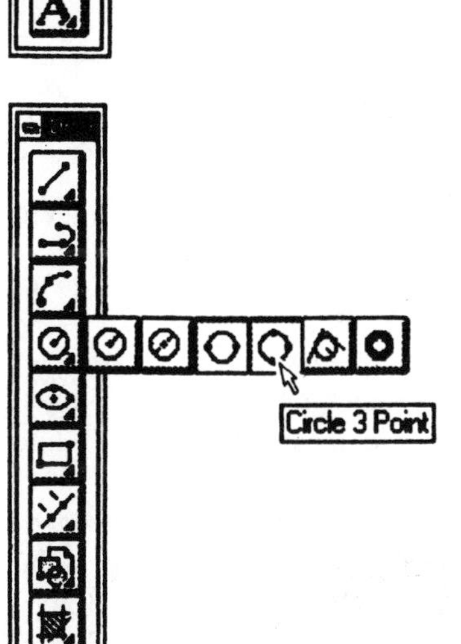

Prompt	Response
Command:	↵
<Center point>:	*Type:* **3P** ↵
3P First point:	*Pick:* **D5** (approximately ½″ to the right of the other circle)
Second point:	*Pick:* **D6** (2 grid spaces to the right)
Third point:	*Pick:* **D7** (1 grid space up)

You just learned four different methods of drawing circles. Experiment with different-size circles and the different methods until you become comfortable with them.

The next option on the circle command is TTR. This stands for tangent, tangent, and radius. Tangent means to touch at a single point. To see how TTR is used, draw the following.

Step 25. Draw a circle with a ½″ radius tangent to two other circles (Figure 7–19).

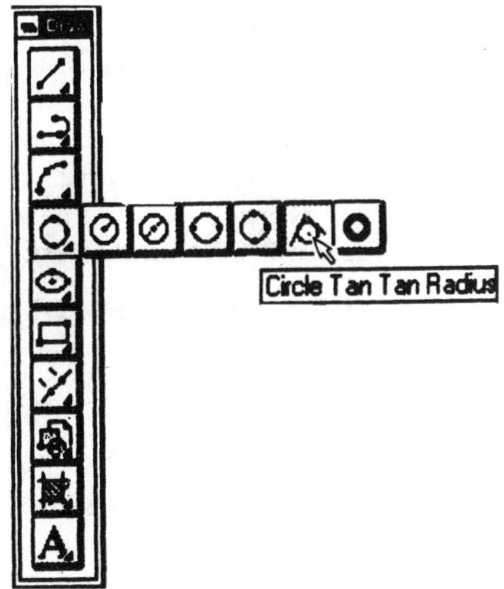

Prompt	Response
Command:	*Type:* **C** ↵
_Circle 3P/2P/TTR/<Center point>:	*Type:* **TTR** ↵
Enter Tangent spec:	*Pick:* **D8**
Enter second Tangent spec:	*Pick:* **D9**
Radius <default>:	*Type:* **.5** ↵

Experiment with different-size circles. The location of the tangent circle will change with different radius sizes.

Tangent, Tangent, Tangent Option

The last option for constructing circles is the TaTaTan: which is the tangent, tangent, tangent option. This method may be used to draw a circle tangent to three other entities.

Copy Radius Command

The final item on the Circle: menu is the Copy Rad command. This command allows you to digitize any circle and have the radius of that circle copied as the default radius for the next circle you draw.

Tangents

Step 26. Draw a line tangent to a circle (Figure 7–19).

Tip: Use *QUAdrant* from OSNAP menu to draw lines or arcs to specific parts of a circle.

Note: The half of the circle that is digitized is the half where the tangent occurs. The other line tangents were drawn in the same manner.

Before you start, draw a .375"-diameter circle and a .625"-diameter circle, 1" from center to center. Locate these centers 1" below the six circles of Figure 7–18.

Prompt	Response
Command:	**Line:**
LINE from point:	**Tangent** (from the OSNAP menu)
Tangent to:	*Pick:* **D1**
To point:	**Tangent**
Tangent to:	*Pick:* **D2**
To point:	↵

On Your Own: Draw another line tangent to these two circles, as shown in Figure 7–19.

ZOOM:

The different Zoom: commands (All, Center, Dynamic, Extents, Left, Previous, Vmax, Window, and Scale) control how you view the drawing area on the display screen. While drawing the lines and circles for this chapter you have been able to view the entire 8½" × 11" drawing limits on the screen. The Zoom: All command was used earlier to assure that view.

The following exercise uses the Zoom: Window command to look more closely at the tangent circles on the drawing. The Zoom: Window command allows you to pick two opposite corners of a rectangular window on the screen. The cross hairs of the pointer change to form a rubber band that shows the size of the window on the screen. The size of the window is controlled by the movement of the pointer. The part of the drawing inside the windowed area is magnified to fill the screen when the second corner of the window is picked.

Step 27. Use ZOOM: Window.

Prompt	Response
Command:	**Zoom:** (or *Type:* **Z** ↵)
All/Center/Dynamic/Extents/Left/ Previous/Vmax/Window/<Scale (X/XP)>:	**Window** (You do not have to *Select:* Window; you can just pick 2 points.)
First corner:	*Pick:* **D10** (lower left corner of the window; Figure 7–19)
Other corner:	*Pick:* **D11** (upper right corner of the window)
Command:	*Type:* **REGEN** ↵

The area that was windowed is now displayed to fill the screen. The two corners of the window may also be entered by typing and entering coordinate points.

When the magnification of the circles was enlarged with the Zoom: Window command, to save regeneration time, AutoCAD did not regenerate the drawing. Only the part of the drawing that was windowed and magnified was redrawn. That is why the circles may not look like they are touching each other. Small line segments called *vectors* make up a circle. When the entire page is displayed, fewer line segments are used to make up the smaller circles. By zooming in and not regenerating, the small number of vectors became obvious. By typing and entering REGEN, you issued a regeneration of the drawing. AutoCAD regenerated the circles with the optimal number of line segments (making the circle smoother) for the larger magnification.

Now that you have a windowed area of the drawing, how do you view the entire drawing again? Use Zoom: All in the following exercise to view the entire drawing area.

Step 28. Use Zoom: All.

Prompt	**Response**
Command:	**Zoom:** (or *Type:* **Z** ↵)
All/Center/Dynamic/Extents/Left/ Previous/Vmax/Window/<Scale (X/XP)>:	**All** (or *Type:* **A** ↵)
All Regenerating drawing.	

The prompt tells you that AutoCAD regenerated the drawing. AutoCAD always performs a regeneration of a drawing when the Zoom: All command is used. Regeneration involves converting a floating-point database to screen coordinates for every entity in the drawing. If the drawing is large and complex, regeneration can take a lot of time.

To view the tangent circles again without using Zoom: Window, use Zoom: Previous in the next exercise.

Step 29. Use Zoom: Previous.

Prompt	**Response**
Command:	↵
All/Center/Dynamic/Extents/Left/ Previous/Vmax/Window/<Scale (X/XP)>:	**Previous** (or *Type:* **P** ↵)

Zoom: Previous is a very convenient feature. AutoCAD remembers previous views. This is especially helpful and time-saving if you are working on a complicated drawing.

To see how Zoom: Vmax works, complete the following exercise.

Step 30. Use ZOOM: Vmax.

Prompt	**Response**
Command:	↵
All/Center/Dynamic/Extents/Left/ Previous/Vmax/Window/<Scale (X/XP)>:	**Vmax** (or *Type:* **V** ↵)
Command:	*Type:* **Z** ↵
All/Center/Dynamic/Extents/Left/ Previous/Vmax/Window/<Scale (X/XP)>:	*Type:* **P** ↵

To save regeneration time, AutoCAD maintains a virtual screen, separate from the display screen drawing. The virtual screen contains the drawing already generated. The Zoom: Vmax command allows you to zoom out to the AutoCAD virtual screen without forcing a complete regeneration of the drawing. With Vmax, only a redraw, which requires much less time, is required to change the virtual screen to the display screen that you view.

Another Zoom: command that saves regeneration time is Zoom: Dynamic. To understand Zoom: Dynamic, first Zoom: Window the tangent circles in your drawing again or do a Zoom: Previous to bring a windowed area of the tangent circles to the display screen. Then complete the following exercise.

Step 31. Use Zoom: Dynamic.

Prompt	**Response**
Command:	↵
All/Center/Dynamic/Extents/Left/ Previous/Vmax/Window/<Scale (X/XP)>:	**Dynamic** (or *Type:* **D** ↵)

There are now three areas that you see on the screen:

1. The green (or, on some displays, magenta) box is the tangent circle area and previously windowed.
2. The black (or, on some displays, white) box shows the drawing limits or the drawing extents, whichever is larger.
3. The white (or, on some displays, black) box is the same size as the window that you just made when you windowed the circles. This window can be moved. It follows the movement of your pointer. Experiment by moving it around the screen.

The size of the window can also be changed. Change the size of the window by pushing the pick button on the pointer. The X inside changes to an arrow when you push the pick button. When the arrow is in the window, the movement of the pointer changes the size of the window. Experiment with changing the size of the window. Push the pick button on the pointer to return the X to the center of the window. With the X in the center of the window, the size remains constant and you may move the window to the area of the drawing that you want to window or zoom in on next.

When you have decided on the area of the drawing to view next and have the size of white box (or window) needed, with an X in the center, place the white box on the area to be enlarged. By pushing the enter button on the pointer, the area inside the white box will appear enlarged on the screen.

When you have completed the Zoom: Dynamic exercise, use the Zoom: Extents command to view the drawing, as follows:

Step 32. Use Zoom: Extents.

Prompt	**Response**
Command:	**Zoom:**
All/Center/Extents/Left/Previous/Vmax/ Window/<Scale(X/XP)>:	**Extents**
Extents Regenerating drawing.	

Zoom: Extents always performs a regeneration of the drawing. The Zoom: Extents command allows you to view the extents of a drawing. To understand Zoom: Extents, the difference between drawing limits and drawing extents needs to be understood. The limits of a drawing are the size of the page set with the Limits: command. The extents of a drawing are what are actually drawn on the page. If only half the page is full, the extents are half the page. Sometimes a drawing entity is drawn outside the limits; this, too, is considered the drawing extents. The Zoom: Extents command will provide a view of all drawing entities on the page that is as large as possible and fills the screen. The Zoom: All command will display the entire drawing limits or extents, whichever is larger. The extents are larger than the limits when a drawing entity is drawn outside of the set limits.

The remaining Zoom: commands are Scale, Center, and Left. A brief explanation of each follows.

Zoom: Scale

In the Zoom: command prompt, the default is Zoom: Scale. It is stated within the angle brackets as <Scale(X/XP)>. The Scale feature allows you to increase or decrease the magnification of the objects on the screen when you are viewing the entire page or a windowed view. If, while viewing the entire page or limits of the drawing, 2 is typed and entered to the command prompt, the new displayed view will have a magnification twice as large as the full view. If .25 is typed and entered, the view will be decreased to ¼ of the full view. To view the entire drawing as displayed within the set limits, enter 1 to the Zoom: prompt.

While in a windowed view, with an object already zoomed in on, enter 2 followed by an X (2X) to increase the magnification of the windowed view by 2. A number followed by an X increases or decreases the object *currently* displayed. If, while in the windowed area, the number 2 is entered but not followed by an X, the full view or entire drawing area (not the windowed area) will be magnified by 2 and displayed.

Zoom: Center

When Center is picked in response to the Zoom: prompt, AutoCAD asks you for a center point of a window. After you have picked the center point of the window on the drawing, the prompt asks for "Magnification or Height <current height>:". The current height (11″ on your current drawing) is shown in default brackets. If 2 is typed and entered, a view of 2″ of the current drawing is enlarged to fill the screen. A height larger than the current height (such as 15) decreases the magnification by changing the height of the displayed view to 15″ instead of 11″.

If 2X is entered to the prompt "Magnification or Height <current height>:", the current drawing display is magnified by 2.

The "XP" in the Scale part of the Zoom: command prompt refers to paper space, which is discussed in a later chapter.

Zoom: Left

Zoom: Left is identical to Zoom: Center, except AutoCAD asks for the "Lower left corner point:" of a window instead of the center point.

Pan:

The Pan: command lets you stay in a windowed view and see parts of the drawing that are off the screen and not originally visible in the view. It allows you to move the drawing in any direction while still looking at the windowed view. Pan: does not change the magnification of the view. To use Pan:, first window a portion of the drawing and then complete the following exercise:

Step 33. Use Pan:.

Prompt	Responses
Command:	**Pan:**
'_pan Displacement:	Pick the middle of the windowed view.
Second point:	Pick a point 2 grid marks to the right of the first point.

The 'PAN Displacement (the direction of the drawing movement) may also be entered using relative coordinates. For instance, typing and entering @−.5,0 or @−½,0 to the first prompt "'PAN Displacement:" and pushing the enter key for the "Second point:" prompt will move the drawing ½″ to the left. Windows users may also use the bottom and left slider bars to PAN.

Redraw: and Redrawall:

Digitizing Redraw: (or typing R ↵) from the VIEW command menu will cause AutoCAD to redraw and clean up your drawing in the current active viewport. Any marker blips on the screen will disappear and drawing entities affected by editing of other objects will be redrawn. Pushing function key F7 twice will turn the grid OFF and ON and will also redraw the screen. Redrawall: redraws the screen in all viewports.

Viewres:

Digitizing Viewres: from the OPTIONS command menu causes AutoCAD to prompt: "Do you want fast zooms? <Y>." If you respond *yes,* AutoCAD will maintain the virtual screen and perform redraws when possible. If the response is *no,* AutoCAD will always regenerate the drawing when the view is changed. Press ↵ to accept yes.

The next prompt from Viewres: is "Enter circle zoom percent (1–20000) <100>:". Remember the line segments or vectors discussed earlier that make up circles and arcs? The circle zoom percent affects the number of vectors that make up circles, arcs, and linetypes. The AutoCAD default of 100 tells AutoCAD to use its internal computation to set the number of vectors. If you enter a number less than 100, the circles and arcs may not look as smooth, but the drawing will regenerate more quickly. If you enter a number higher than 100, the circles and arcs will appear very smooth as you zoom in, but regeneration time will be increased. Viewres: affects only the display screen; it does not affect how the circles, arcs, and linetypes plot. (A Viewres: value of 500 is a good working setting.) Type 500 ↵ and Zoom: All.

Now we continue with the drawing constructions.

Dsviewer

This command is available only in AutoCAD for Windows. It allows you to see the entire drawing and zoom in on an area at the same time.

Regen: and Regenall:

Picking Regen: regenerates the drawing in the active viewport and smooths curves on the display. Regenall: regenerates the drawing in all viewports.

Arcs

Note: These are two different methods for the same arc.

Step 34. Draw arcs of a specific size or angle (Figure 7–20).

Draw these arcs approximately ½″ below the tangents.

FIGURE 7–20
Methods of Drawing Arcs

Method using three-point selection on Arc menu:

Prompt	Response
Command:	**Arc:**
ARC center/<start point>:	*Pick:* **D1** (since default is the start point)
Center/End/<Second Point>:	*Type:* **C** ↵
Center:	*Pick:* **D2** (¼″ to the left of D1)
Angle/Length of Chord/<End Point>:	*Pick:* **D3** (¼″ to the left of D2)

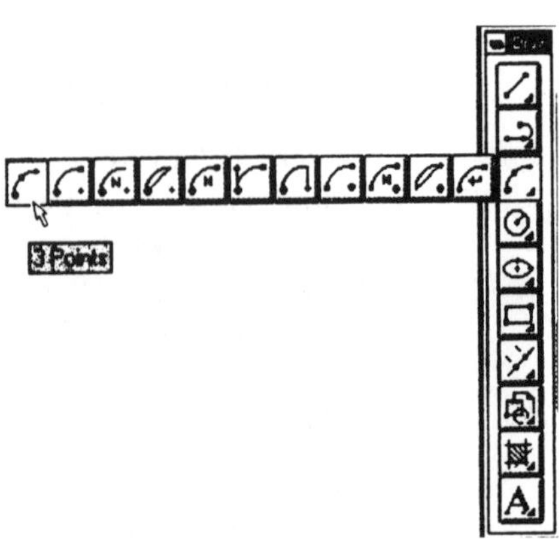

Method using St, C, End on the ARC menu:

Prompt	Response
Command:	**Arc:** then St, C, End
ARC Center/<Start Point>:	*Pick:* **D4**
C Center:	*Pick:* **D5**
Angle/Length of Chord/<End Point>:	*Pick:* **D6**

Now that you have drawn two arcs of the same size and shape, consider the choices you have in making an arc. First, look at the definitions given for the elements of an arc, Figure 7–21.

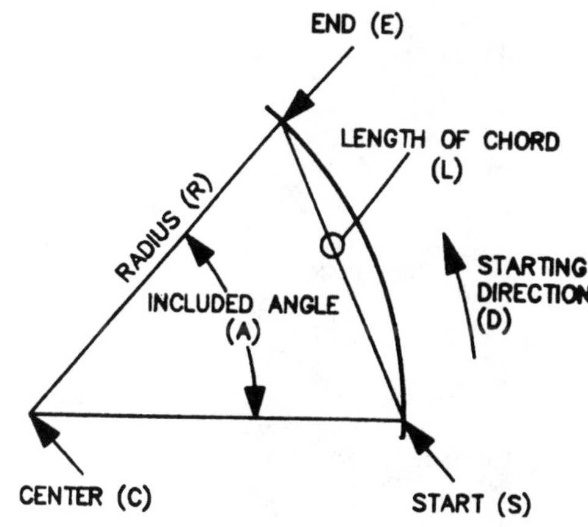

FIGURE 7–21
Elements of an Arc

St Start—the beginning point of the arc (does not always have to be the first point picked.)
C or Cen Center—the center of the arc radius.
End End—the ending point of the arc.
Len The length of the chord—a straight line connecting the ends of the arc.
Dir Starting direction—used only in the S, E, D sequence; all other sequences draw the arc in a counterclockwise direction (unless you specify clockwise when you set up the drawing using the Units setting).
Rad Radius—the radius of the arc.
Ang Angle—the included angle of the ends of the arc.

There are several methods of drawing arcs for specific situations or preferences. We will cover one other method in this chapter and others later where drawing problems will require the use of them.

Step 35. Draw an arc of a specific radius to include a specific angle (Figure 7–20).

Radius = .315, included angle = 90°.

Prompt	Response
Command:	**Arc: then St, C, Ang**
_arc Center/<Start point>:	*Pick:* **D7**
_c Center:	*Type:* **@.315<180** ↵
_a Included angle:	*Type:* **90** ↵

Curves through Points Using Pline: and Pedit:

Step 36. Draw a curve through given points (Figure 7–22).

Before you start, draw 14 points using the Point: command to approximate Figure 7–22. Make sure snap is on and ortho is off when you draw the points so that the line you draw through them can be drawn easily and accurately. Draw this figure ½" below the arcs.

FIGURE 7–22
Curve through Points

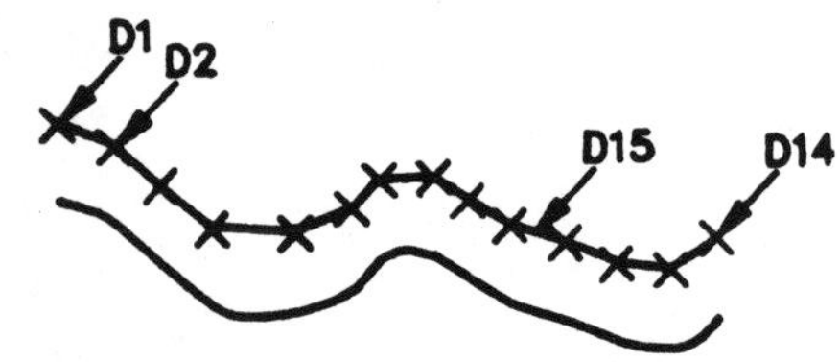

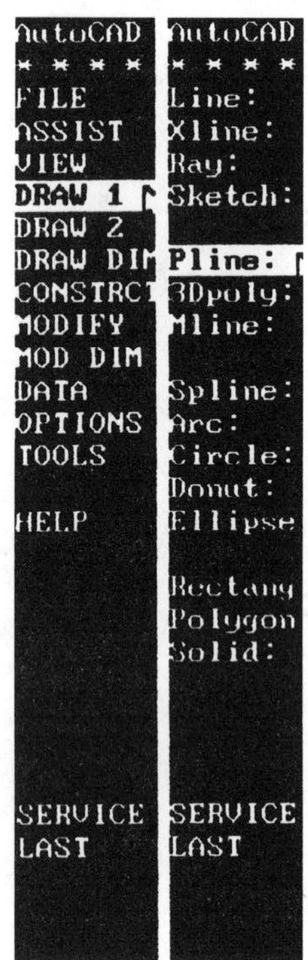

Prompt	Response
Command:	**Pline:** (or *Type:* **PL** ↵)
From point:	*Pick:* **D1**
Arc/Close/Halfwidth/Length/Undo/Width/<Endpoint ob line>:	Pick each point from D2 to D14 one by one. Then Press ↵.
Command:	**Pedit:** (from the MODIFY menu) (or Edit Polyline from the toolbar)
_pedit Select polyline:	*Pick:* **D15** (any point on the polyline)
Close/Join/Width/Edit vertex/Fit curve/Spline/Decurve/Ltype gen/Undo/	*Type:* **F** ↵
Exit<X>:	↵

The Spline feature draws the curve to fit the average distance assumed by the points. It is used in the same manner as "fit curve." Try it.

Step 37. Break a polyline (Figure 7–23):

Note: Lines may be drawn through points that are not on SNAP or Grid points by using *Node* from the *Osnap* menu when identifying the points. Snap and ortho must be off.

Prompt	Response
Command:	**Break:**
Select object:	*Pick:* **D1** (on the polyline you drew in Figure 7–22)
Enter second point (or F for first point):	*Pick:* **D2**

FIGURE 7–23
Breaking a Pline and Drawing Plines with Different Beginning and Ending Widths

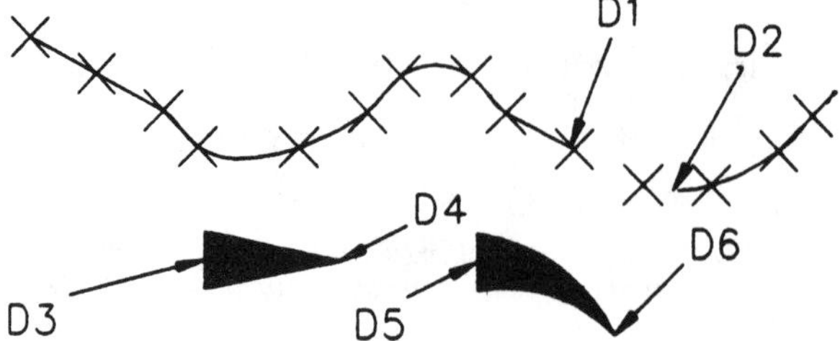

Tip: Use the same beginning and ending widths of Pline: to draw thick lines.

Step 38. Draw polylines with different beginning and ending widths.

Prompt	Response
Command:	*Type:* **PL** ↵
From point:	*Pick:* **D3** (Figure 7–23)
Arc/Close/Halfwidth/Length/Undo/ Width/<Endpoint of line>:	*Type:* **W** ↵
Starting width <0.000>:	*Type:* **.2** ↵
Ending width <0.200>:	*Type:* **0** ↵
Arc/Close/Halfwidth/Length/Undo/ Width/<Endpoint of line>:	*Pick:* **D4** (Pick 2 grids to the right.) ↵
Command:	↵
From point:	*Pick:* **D5** (Figure 7–23)
Arc/Close/Halfwidth/Length/Undo/ Width/<Endpoint of line>:	*Type:* **W** ↵
Starting width <0.000>:	*Type:* **.2** ↵
Ending width <0.200>:	*Type:* **0** ↵
Arc/Close/Halfwidth/Length/Undo/ Width/<Endpoint of line>:	*Type:* **A** ↵
Arc/Close/Halfwidth/Length/Undo/ Width/<Endpoint of line>:	*Pick:* **D6** (Select a curve to approximate the one shown.)
<Endpoint of arc>:	↵

Similar Shapes Using Pline: and Offset:

Step 39. Draw a shape inside a similar shape (Figure 7–24).

FIGURE 7–24
Parallel Shapes

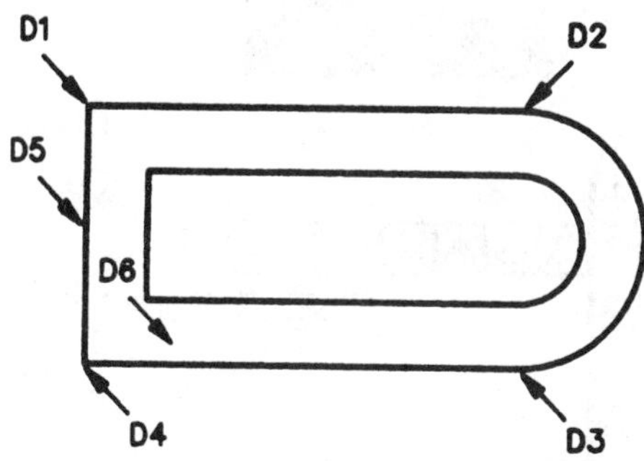

All points of the inner shape are the same distance from the outer shape; the inner shape is .25″ smaller than the outer shape. Start this figure at coordinates 7.500,8.000 with SNAP on.

Prompt	Response
Command:	*Type:* **PL** ↵
From point:	*Pick:* **D1** (or *Type:* **7.5,8** ↵)
<Endpoint of line>:	*Pick:* **D2** (or *Type:* **@2.25<0** ↵)
Arc/Close/Halfwidth/Length/Undo/ Width/<Endpoint of line>:	**Arc** (or *Type:* **A** ↵)
<Endpoint of arc>:	*Pick:* **D3** (or *Type:* **@1<270** ↵)
<Endpoint of arc>:	**Length** (or *Type:* **L** ↵)
<Endpoint of line>:	*Pick:* **D4**
<Endpoint of line>:	**Close** (or *Type:* **C** ↵)

Prompt	Response
Command:	**Offset:** (from the CONSTRCT menu)
Offset distance or Through <Through>:	*Type:* **.25** ↵
Select object to offset:	*Pick:* **D5** (anywhere on the Pline)
Side to offset?	*Pick:* **D6** (anywhere inside the shape)
Select object to offset:	↵

Arrays of Circles and Lines

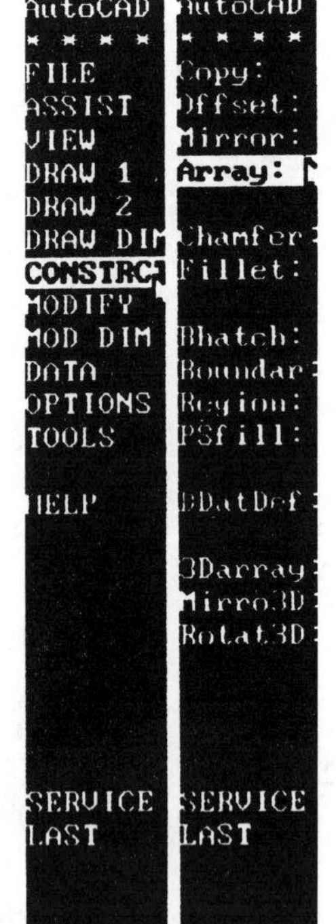

Step 40. Draw arrays of circles and lines or any other shape (Figure 7–25).

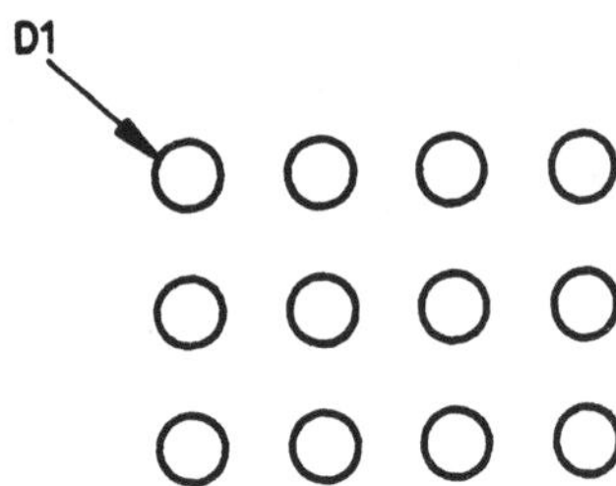

FIGURE 7–25
Rectangular Array

Draw three rows of four .25-diameter circles each; all circles are ½″ (.5) from center to center:

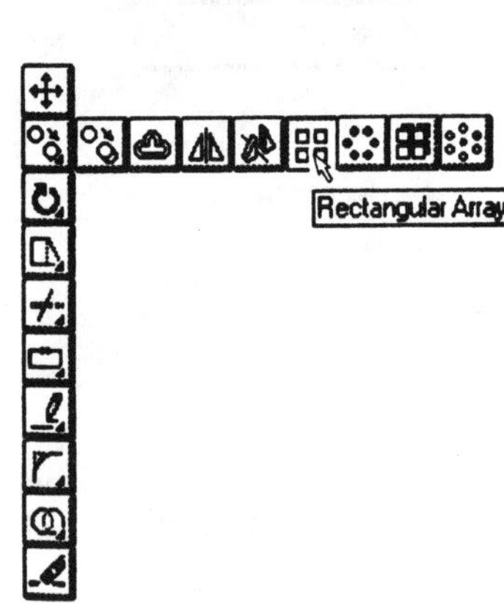

Prompt	Response
Command:	**Circle: Cen, Dia**
<Center point>:	Pick the center of the circle ⅝″ below the lower left corner of the shape of Figure 7–24.
Diameter:	*Type:* **.25** ↵
Command:	**Array:** (from the CONSTRCT menu) (or Rectangular Array from the toolbar)
Select objects:	*Pick:* **D1**
Select objects:	↵
Rectangular or Polar array (R/P)<R>:	↵ (or *Type:* **R** ↵)
Number of rows (------)<1>:	*Type:* **3** ↵
Number of columns (III)<1>:	*Type:* **4** ↵
Unit cell or distance between rows (----):	*Type:* **−.5** ↵ (Rows form downward—a response of .5 forms rows upward.)
Distance between columns (III):	*Type:* **.5** ↵ (Columns form to the right—a response of −.5 forms columns to the left.)

Step 41. Draw a row of seven ¼″ (.25) lines spaced ¼″ (.25) apart (Figure 7–26).

FIGURE 7–26
Rectangular Array

Prompt	Response
Command:	**Line:**
From point:	*Pick:* **D1** (½″ below the left bottom circle of the array of Figure 7–25)
To point:	*Pick:* **D3** (¼″ below D1)
Command:	**Array:**
Select objects:	*Pick:* **D2** ↵
Select objects:	↵
Rectangular or Polar array (R/P)<R>:	↵
Number of rows (------)<1>:	↵
Number of columns (111)<1>:	*Type:* **7** ↵
Distance between columns (111):	*Pick:* **D4** (Pick two points to specify the spacing between columns or rows.)
Second point	*Pick:* **D5** (¼″ to the right of D4—SNAP must be on)

Step 42. Draw a circular (polar) pattern of eight ¼″-(.25-) diameter circles on a 1″-diameter bolt circle (circular center line) (Figure 7–27):

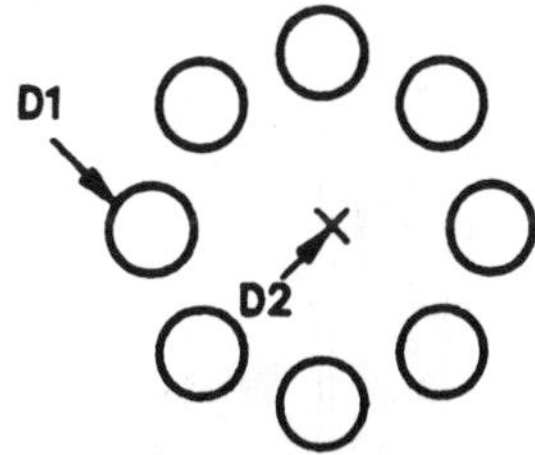

FIGURE 7–27
Polar Array

Note: You may use the selection LAST, at the bottom of several of the menus to go back to another menu without having to go back to the root menu first.

Prompt	Response
Command:	**Circle: Cen, Dia**
Center:	Pick the center for the circle (1¼″ below the left line of the array of Figure 7–26.)
Diameter <0.250>:	↵
Command:	**Array:** (Windows users: *Select:* Polar Array)
Select objects:	*Pick:* **D1**
Select objects:	↵
Rectangular or Polar array (R/P)<R>:	*Type:* **P** ↵ (or *Select:* Polar from the screen menu)
Center point of array:	*Pick:* **D2** (D2 is .5″ to the right of the picked circle from its right edge.)
Number of items:	*Type:* **8** ↵
Angle to fill (+ = ccw, − = cw) <360>:	↵ (ccw means counterclockwise, cw is clockwise, 360 is the number of degrees in a circle—you may specify fewer than 360.)
Rotate objects as they are copied? (Y)	↵ (In this case yes or no will give the same pattern; rotation of the objects keeps them perpendicular to a radius drawn from the center of a circle.)

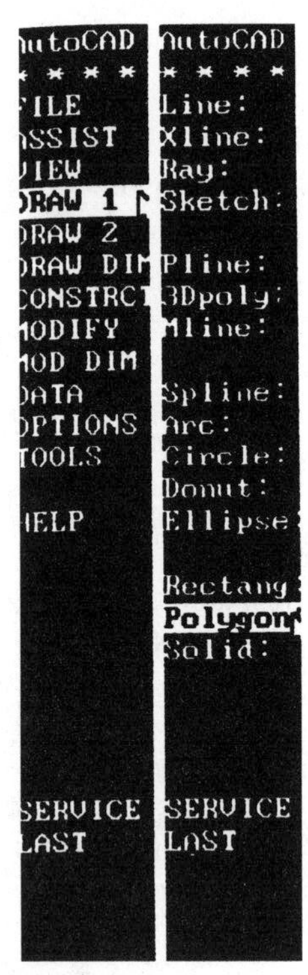

Polygons

Step 43. Draw polygons (Figure 7–28).

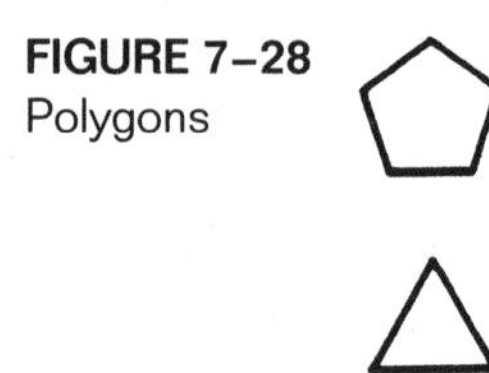
FIGURE 7–28
Polygons

Polygons are to be drawn inside an imaginary ½″-(.5-) diameter circle.

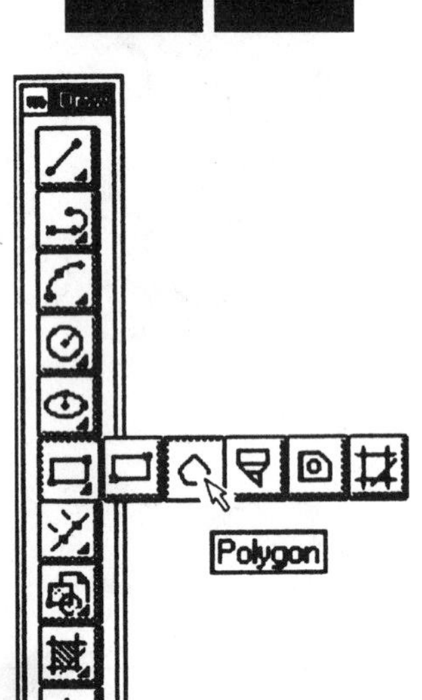

Prompt	**Response**
Command:	**Polygon:**
Number of sides<4>:	*Type:* **5** ↵
Edge/<Center of polygon>:	*Pick:* **D1** (Pick the center of the polygon 1″ to the right of the top circle of Figure 7–27.)
Inscribed in circle/circumscribed about circle (I/C)<I>:	↵
Radius of circle:	*Type:* **.25** ↵

On Your Own: Draw another ¼″-radius polygon with three sides, as shown in Figure 7–28. Locate its center .625″ below the center of the pentagon.

Solid Shapes

Step 44. Draw a solid triangle (Figure 7–29).

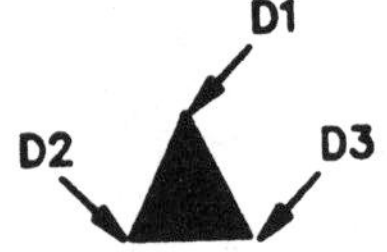

FIGURE 7–29
A Solid Triangle

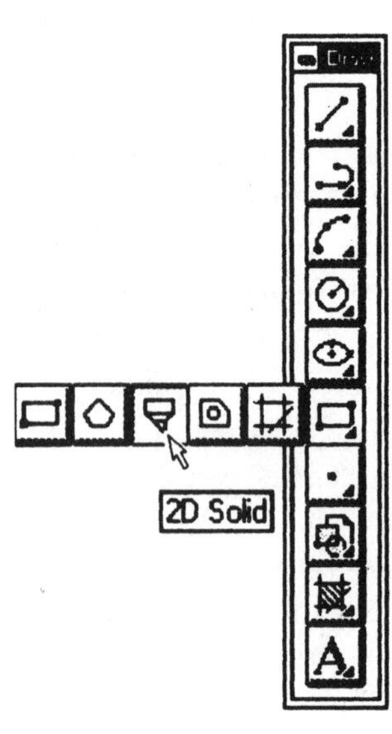

Prompt	**Response**
Command:	**Solid:** (from the DRAW 1 menu)
First point:	*Pick:* **D1** (Place this solid ½″ to the right of the pentagon, as shown in Figure 7–1.)
Second point:	*Pick:* **D2** (¼″ to the left and ½″ below D1)
Third point:	*Pick:* **D3** (½″ to the right of D2) ↵
Fourth point:	(be sure to strike ↵)

Step 45. Draw a solid ½″ square (Figure 7–30).

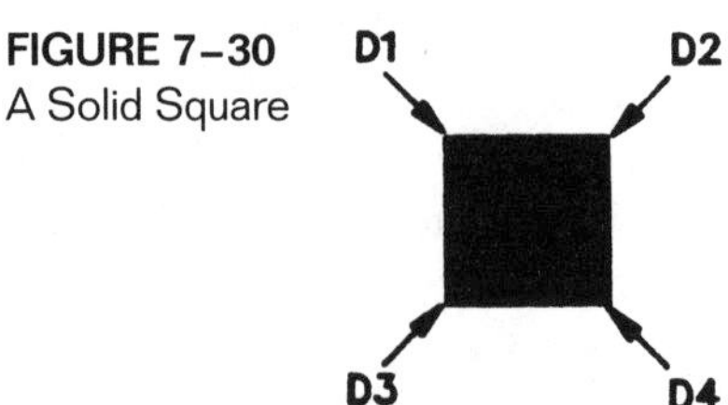

FIGURE 7–30
A Solid Square

Note: Picking must be done in the order in which it appears in Figure 7–30.

Prompt	Response
Command:	**Solid:**
First point:	*Pick:* **D1** (Place this solid ⅜″ below the triangle, as shown in Figure 7–1.)
Second point:	*Pick:* **D2**
Third point:	*Pick:* **D3**
Fourth point:	*Pick:* **D4**
Third point:	↵

Ellipses and Tangents to Them

Step 46. Draw a 1″ diameter isometric cylinder (Figure 7–31).

FIGURE 7–31
Isometric Cylinder

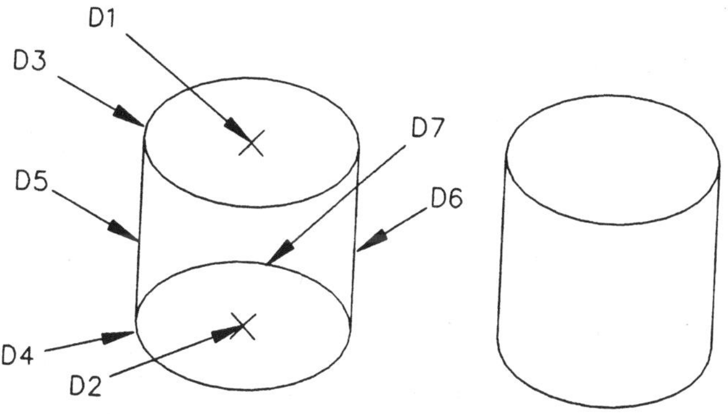

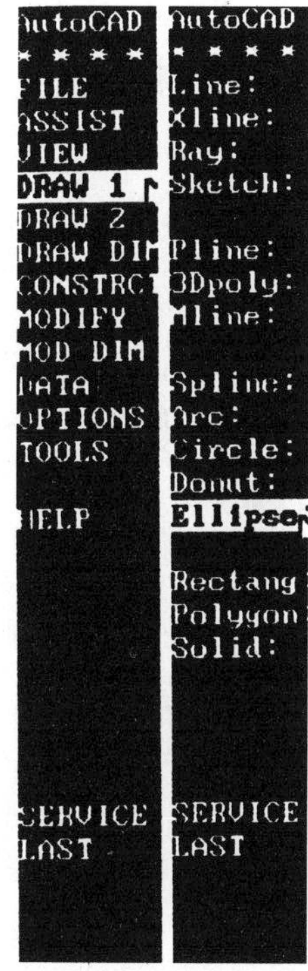

Note: Other ellipses will be covered later.

Prompt	Response
Command:	*Type:* **SNAP** ↵
Snap spacing ON/OFF/Aspect/Rotate/Style<0.125>:	**Style** (from the screen menu) (or *Type:* **S** ↵)
Standard/Isometric<s>:	**Iso** (from the screen menu) (or *Type:* **I** ↵)
Iso Vertical spacing<0.125>:	*Type:* **.125** ↵ (or just ↵ if spacing is already .125)
Command:	Press the Ctrl key and the letter E at the same time until the last bracket reads <Isoplane Top>. **Ellipse:** (from the Draw 1 menu) (Windows users: *Type:* **ELLIPSE** ↵)
Arc/Center/Isocircle/<Axis endpoint 1>:	*Type:* **I** ↵
Center of circle:	*Pick:* **D1** (approximately ¾″ below the polar array of Figure 7–27)
<Circle radius>/Diameter:	*Type:* **.5** ↵ (the radius for the ellipse)
Command:	↵
<Axis endpoint 1>/Center/Isocircle:	*Type:* **I** ↵
Center of circle:	*Pick:* **D2** (1″ below the first ellipse on the same center line)
<Circle radius>/Diameter:	*Type:* **.5** ↵
Command:	**Line:**
From point:	**QUAdrant** (from the Osnap menu)
_qua of	*Pick:* **D3** (the outermost left point on the ellipse)

Prompt	Response
To point:	**TANgent** (from the Osnap menu)
Tangent to:	*Pick:* **D4**
To point:	↵

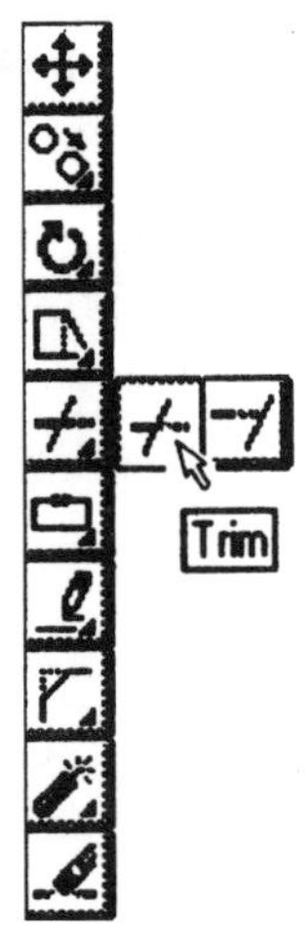

Draw another line to form the right side of the cylinder in a similar manner. Use Trim: to remove the back half of the bottom ellipse.

Prompt	Response
Command:	**Trim:** (from the MODIFY menu)
Select cutting edges:. . . Select objects:	*Pick:* **D5, D6** (Select the two vertical lines by picking them. You may have to turn SNAP (F9) off.)
Select cutting edge(s). . .	↵ (You are finished with selecting cutting edges.)
Select object to trim/Project/Edge/Undo:	*Pick:* **D7** (Select the back half of the ellipse by picking it. You may have to pick the ellipse in more than one piece.)

Return to the standard Snap: setting now by selecting Snap:, Style, and then Standard. Press ↵

Extending Lines

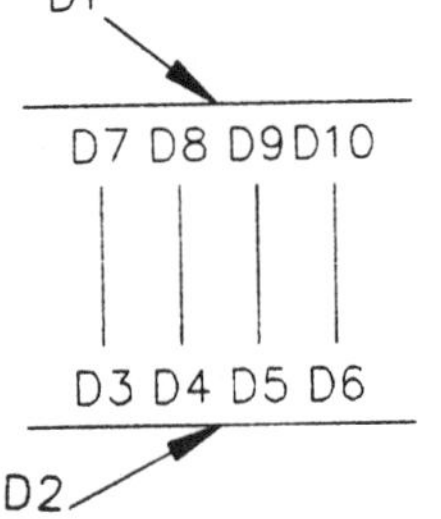

FIGURE 7–32
Extending Lines

Step 47. Extend lines (Figure 7–32).

Draw four ½″ vertical lines ¼″ apart. Draw 1¼″ horizontal lines ¼″ below and above the vertical lines. Extend the vertical lines to the horizontal lines by using the EXTEND command. *Before you begin, draw the lines shown in Figure 7–32, ¼″ below the solids. Extend the vertical lines to the horizontal line.*

Prompt	Response
Command:	**Extend:** (from the MODIFY menu) (Windows: on the same flyout as trim)
Select boundary edges	*Pick:* **D1, D2** ↵ (Figure 7–32)
Select objects to extend:	*Pick:* **D3, D4, D5, D6, D7, D8, D9, D10** (Pick the lower ends of the vertical lines; then pick the upper ends of the vertical lines.)

Trimming Lines

Step 48. Trim lines (arcs, circles, etc.).

Before you begin, draw six vertical ¾″ lines ¼″ apart and ¼″ below Figure 7–32. Draw four horizontal 1¼″ lines ¼″ apart to form Figure 7–33A. Trim lines using crossing window to select.

Note: You may select a crossing window without typing by picking any open point on the drawing and dragging the cursor to the left.

Prompt	Response
Command:	**Trim:**
Select cutting edges:. . . Select objects:	*Type:* **C** ↵ (to select crossing window)
First corner (Figure 7–33):	*Pick:* **D1** (Figure 7–33)
Second corner:	*Pick:* **D2**
Select cutting edges	↵ (You are finished with selecting cutting edges.)
Select object to trim>Project/Edge/Undo:	*Pick:* **D3 through D16** ↵ (Figure 7–33B; Pick all lines between squares, as shown in Figure 7–1.)

FIGURE 7–33
Trimming Lines

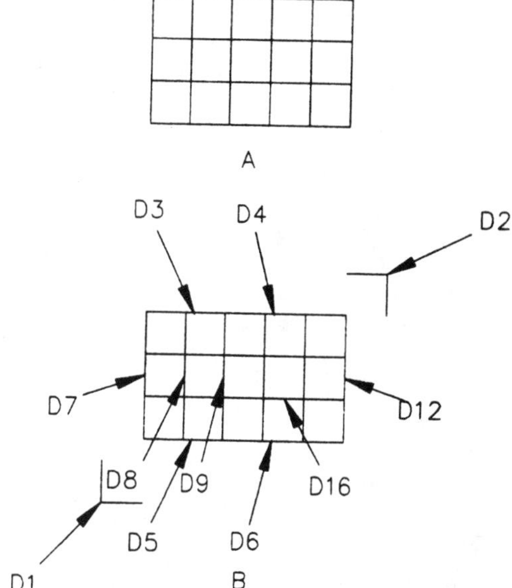

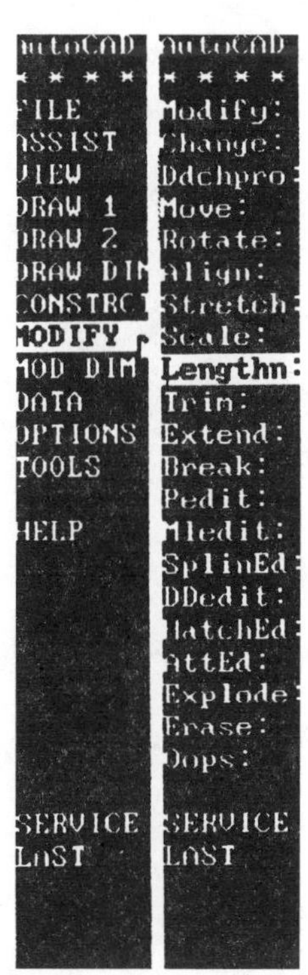

Changing Line Length

Step 49. Change the length of the line in Figure 7–3 from 2.000 to 2.500 using the Change: command.

Prompt	Response
Command:	**Change:** (or *Type:* **CHANGE** ↵)
Select objects:	Select the first line you drew in this exercise by picking it.
Select objects:	↵
Properties/<Change point>:	{Pick a point ½″ to the right of the end point of the line you selected, or *Type:* **@.5<0** ↵.}

Step 50. Change the length of the line in Figure 7–4 from 1.985 to 2.500.

Prompt	Response
Command:	**Lengthn:** (from the MODIFY menu)
DElta/Percent/Total/DYnamic/<Select object>:	**Total**
Angle/<Enter total length (1.000)>:	*Type:* **2.5** ↵
<Select object to change>/Undo:	Pick the second line you drew in this exercise.
<Select object to change>/Undo:	↵

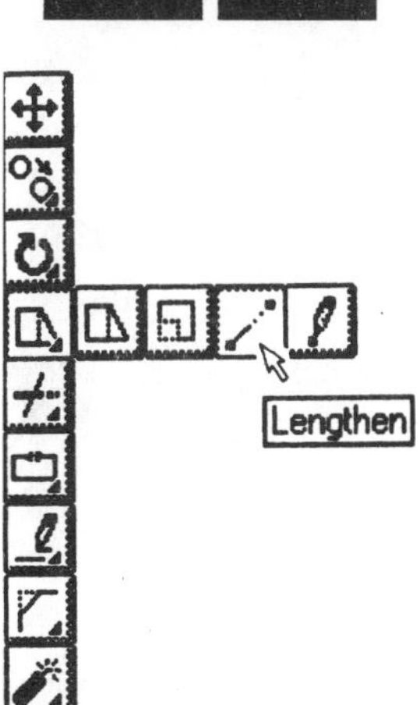

The Lengthn: command allows you either to select the entity first and then specify the new length or to specify the new length and then pick one or more entities. You also have the following four options to use in specifying the new length:

DElta This option allows you to specify the amount by which you wish to lengthen an entity. For example, a DElta setting of .25 will lengthen a 2″ line to 2.25.

Percent This option allows you to specify the percentage of the original length you wish to change to. For example, a Percent setting of 150 will lengthen a 2″ line to 3″.

Total This option allows you to specify the new total length. For example, a Total setting of 1.985 will change a 2″ line to 1.985.

DYnamic This option allows you to lengthen the entity by picking the new length with your digitizer.

Stretching Entities

Step 51. Use the Stretch: command to shorten the shape of Figure 7–22.

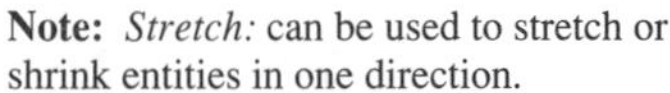

Note: *Stretch:* can be used to stretch or shrink entities in one direction.

Prompt	**Response**
Command:	**Stretch:** (from the MODIFY menu; be sure snap and ortho are on.)
First corner:	*Pick:* **D2** (Figure 7–34)

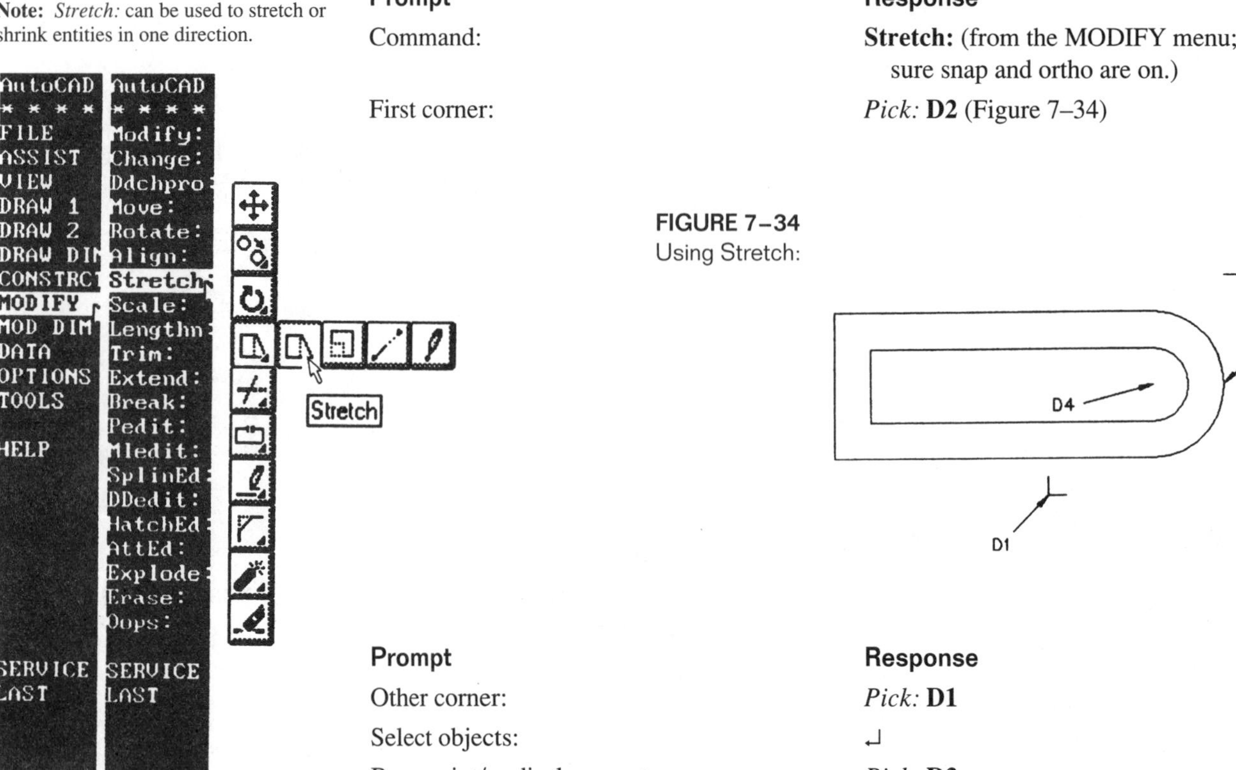

FIGURE 7–34
Using Stretch:

Prompt	**Response**
Other corner:	*Pick:* **D1**
Select objects:	↵
Base point/or displacement:	*Pick:* **D3**
Second point of displacement:	*Pick:* **D4** (½″ to the left)

Construction Lines Using Ray: and Trim:

Step 52. Draw rays.

Prompt	**Response**
Command:	**Ray**
From point:	*Type:* **6.25,8** ↵
Through point:	*Pick:* **D2, D3, D4, D5** ↵ (Figure 7–35) (¼″ apart, ½″ below D1)

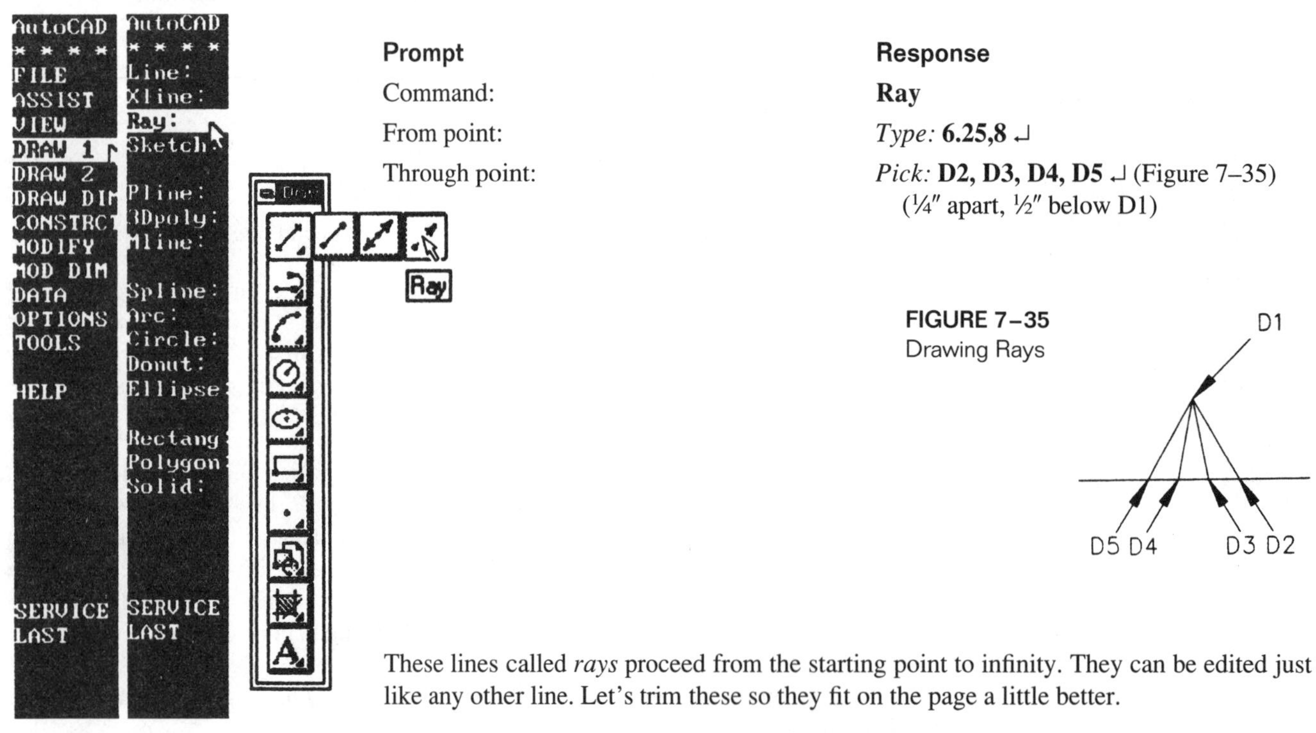

FIGURE 7–35
Drawing Rays

These lines called *rays* proceed from the starting point to infinity. They can be edited just like any other line. Let's trim these so they fit on the page a little better.

Step 53. Draw a boundary line and trim the rays.

Prompt	Response
Command:	**Line:**
From point:	*Type:* **5.5,7.5** ↵
To point:	*Type:* **7,7.5** ↵
To point:	↵
Command:	**Trim:**
Select cutting edges: . . . Select objects:	Pick the line you just drew and press ↵
<Select object to trim>Project/Edge/Undo:	Pick each ray below the cutting edge so that it appears as shown in Figure 7–35, then press ↵

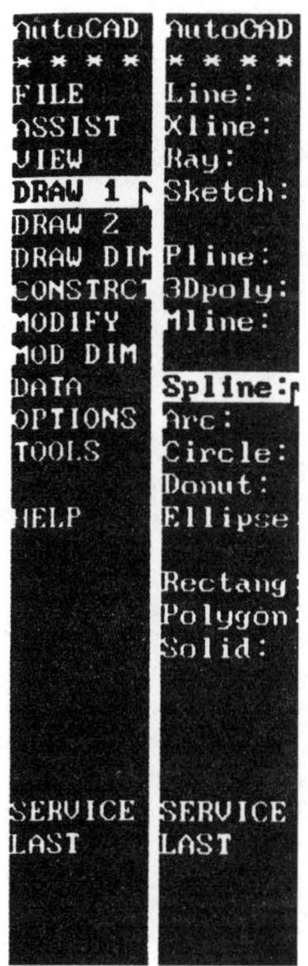

Drawing Curves Using Spline:

Step 54. Draw a smooth curve to fit a sequence of points within a specified tolerance.

Prompt	Response
Command:	**Spline:**
Object/<Enter first point>:	*Type:* **6,6.75** ↵ (or pick a point in the approximate location shown in Figure 7–1)
Enter point:	*Type:* **6.75,6.25** ↵ (or pick the second point on the spline as shown in Figure 7–1)
Close/Fit Tolerance/<Enter point>:	**Fit Tol** (or *Type:* **F** ↵)
Enter Fit tolerance<0.000>	*Type:* **.1** ↵
Close/Fit Tolerance/<Enter point>:	*Type:* **6,5.5** ↵ (or pick the third point)
Close/Fit Tolerance/<Enter point>:	*Type:* **6.5,4.75** ↵ (or pick the fourth point)
Close/Fit Tolerance/<Enter point>:	*Type:* **6.5,.75** ↵ (or pick the fifth point)
Close/Fit Tolerance/<Enter point>:	↵
Enter start tangent:	*Type:* **6,6.75** ↵ (or pick the first point on the spline)
Enter end tangent:	*Type:* **6.5,.75** ↵ (or pick the last point on the spline)

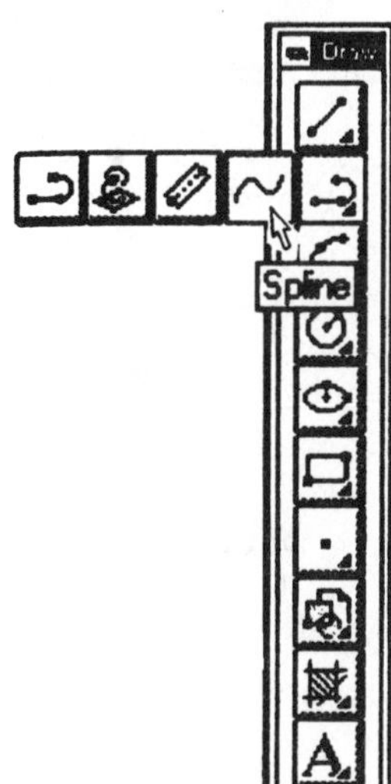

You have just drawn a spline with a fit tolerance of .1. The fit tolerance refers to how closely the spline fits the set of fit points. The default fit tolerance of 0.000 is the most accurate. The Object option allows you to convert smoothed and fit polylines to splines. Splines are more accurate and use less memory than polylines. Changing the start and end tangents will produce very different splines. Experiment with this command; you will find it to be very useful in accurately drawing smooth curves.

Drawing Multiple Lines Using Mline: and MLstyle:

Step 55. Set the multiline style.

Prompt	Response
Command:	**Mline:**
Justification/Scales/STyle/<From point>:	**MLstyle:**
The Multiline Styles dialog box appears:	Pick the Name: button. Delete the word STANDARD and *Type:* **three** (as shown in Figure 7–36)

FIGURE 7–36
Mline Styles Dialog Box

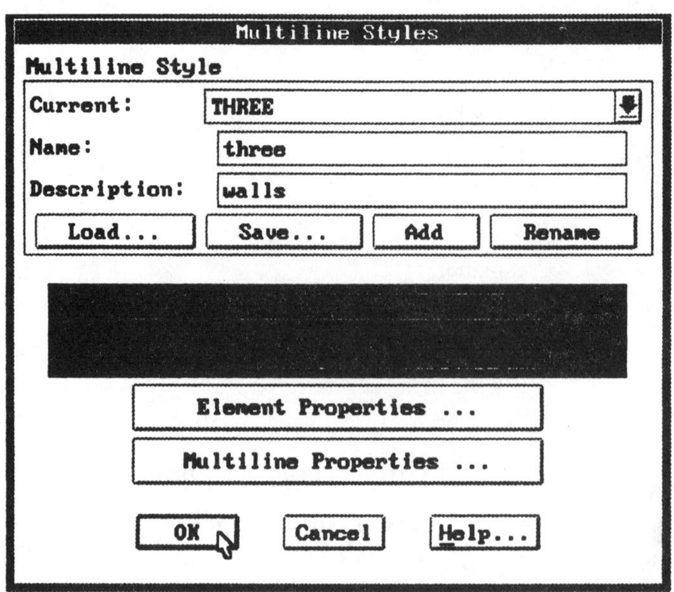

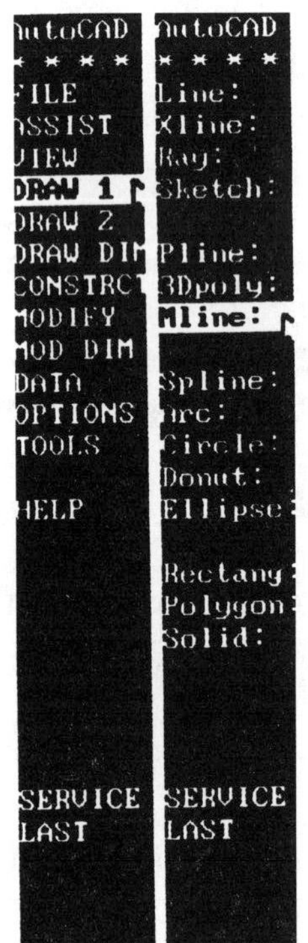

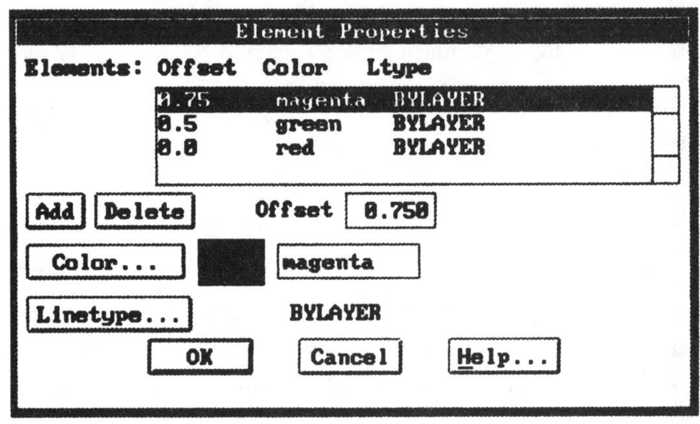

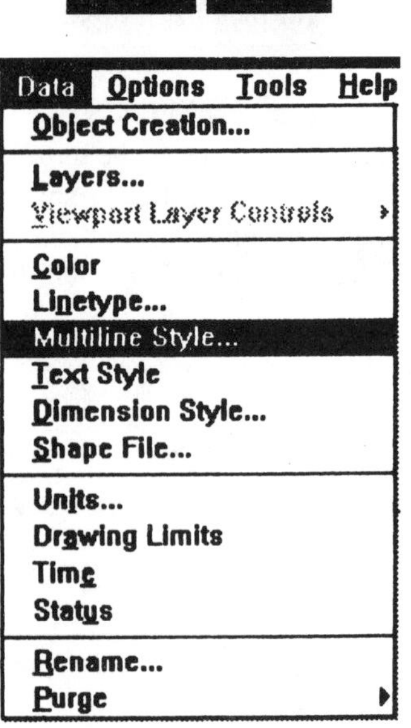

Prompt	Response
	Pick the Description: button, and *Type:* **WALLS.**
	Pick the Element Properties. . . button.)
The Element Properties dialog box appears:	Pick to the right of all numbers in the Offset button.
	Backspace to remove all numbers. *Type:* **.75**
	Pick the Add button.
	Pick to the right of all numbers in the Offset button.)
	Backspace to remove all numbers. *Type:* **.5**
	Pick the Add button
	Pick to the right of all numbers in the Offset button.
	Backspace to remove all numbers. *Type:* **0**
	Pick the Add button.

Prompt	Response
	Pick the Color button as shown in Figure 7–36.
The Select Color dialog box appears:	*Pick:* **Red** Pick the OK button. Highlight the 0.5 Offset. Pick the Color button.
The Select Color dialog box appears:	*Pick:* **Green** Pick the OK button. Highlight the 0.75 Offset. Pick the Color button.
The Select Color dialog box appears:	*Pick:* **Magenta** Pick the OK button. Highlight any other offset lines and delete them.)
The Element Properties dialog box appears:	Pick the OK button.
The Multiline Styles dialog box appears:	Pick the Save. . . button.
The Save Multiline Style dialog box appears:	Pick the OK button.
The Multiline Styles dialog box appears.	Pick the Load. . . button.
The Load Multiline Styles dialog box appears:	*Pick:* **three** *Pick:* **OK**
The Multiline Styles Dialog box appears:	*Pick:* **OK**

Notice that the 0,0 red line is the origin from which all other lines are drawn. The distance from the red line to the green line when drawn at a scale of 1.000 will be 0.500. The distance from the green line to the magenta line will be 0.250 (0.750 − 0.500) or 0.750 from the green line to the red line (the origin).

Now draw some lines at a scale of ¼ (.250).

Step 56. Draw multilines.

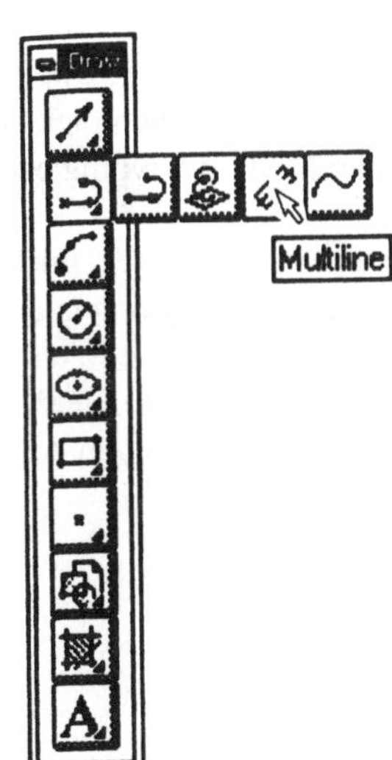

Prompt	Response
Command:	**Mline:**
Justification/Scale/STyle/<From point>:	*Type:* **S** ↵
Set Mline scale <1.000>:	*Type:* **.25** ↵
Justification/Scale/STyle/<From point>:	*Type:* **9.5,6.5** ↵
<To point>:	*Type:* **10.25,6.5** ↵
Close/Undo/<To point>:	*Type:* **10.25,5.75** ↵
Close/Undo/<To point>:	*Type:* **10.5,5.75** ↵
Close/Undo/<To point>:	*Type:* **10.5,4.5** ↵
Close/Undo/<To point>:	*Type:* **9.5,4.5** ↵
Close/Undo/<To point>:	*Type:* **C** ↵

If you make a mistake in specifying a point, type U and press ↵ to select the Undo option from the Mline: prompt.

There are two other options on the Mline: command:

Justification This option allows you to specify whether you want the lines above or below the points specified.

STyle This option allows you to select a different style from the list of styles in the Multiline Styles dialog box.

The Multiline command allows you to draw from 1 to 16 lines at the same time and allows you to specify spacing, color, and linetype for each line.

In addition, you may also turn fill on and draw solid lines of any specified width, using the following set of instructions:

Prompt	Response
Command:	**Mline:** **MLstyle:**
The Multiline Styles dialog box appears:	Pick the Multiline Properties. . . button.
The Multiline Properties dialog box appears:	Pick the on button under Fill and digitize Color. . . After you have activated fill, select a color if you wish.

Mledit:

This command displays the Multiline Edit Tools dialog box, which allows you to edit multilines in the manner displayed by the icons. For example, if you have two different multilines crossing, you can eliminate all lines in the intersection by selecting the middle icon in the first column and then picking the two crossing multilines.

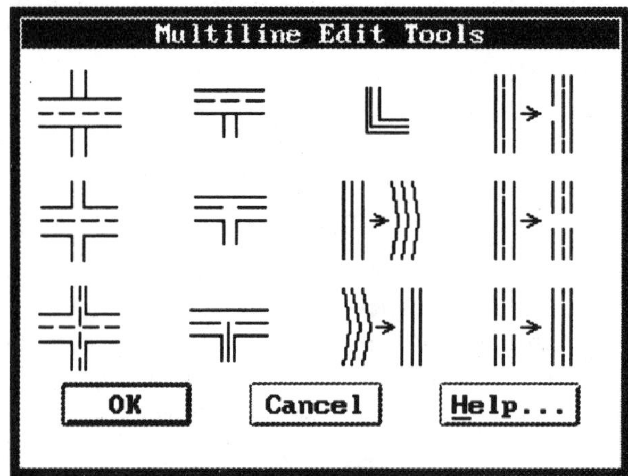

Displaying Dialog Boxes

The commands you see on the menu that are preceded by Dd such as Ddosnap:, Ddptype:, Ddchprop:, Dducs: display dialog boxes for the basic command. You may then pick areas on the boxes to perform the same functions as the basic commands without typing certain information.

For example, the Chprop: command allows you to change the color, layer, linetype, linetype scale, and thickness of any entity. If the basic command is used, prompts are issued that require you to type one or two letters to specify what it is you want to change; then you must type the name of the color, layer, etc. to which you want to change the entity. DDchprop: displays the Change Properties dialog box, which allows you to pick Color, Layer, or Linetype. You then pick the name from another dialog box.

You have completed Exercise 7–1.

Complete the Drawing

Step 57. On Your Own:

1. Print your drawing to fit on an 11″ × 8.5″ sheet.
2. Save your drawing in two places and exit from AutoCAD.

The preceding paragraphs cover many of the constructions you will encounter in this book and in industry. Other constructions are presented in later chapters, but understanding how to use these will provide a basis for your later work.

EXERCISES

7–1. Draw Figure 7–1 using the instructions contained in this chapter.

7–2. Set up an 8½″ × 11″ sheet and draw a ½″ border inside of it. Place your name ¼″ up and ¼″ over from the lower right corner in .1″-high letters. Set snap, ortho, and grid at a convenient setting. Arrange the following in order on your sheet inside the border, leaving approximately ½″ betewen drawings.

a. Draw a line 2.0″ long.
b. Draw a line 3.125″ long at a 30° angle upward to the right.
c. Draw two lines 3.5″ long, parallel to each other, .375″ apart.
d. Draw a 2″ line with a .5″ line perpendicular to it, .625″ from the left end.
e. Draw a line 3″ long and divide it into seven equal parts; an X must appear where each division occurs.
f. Draw a 3″ line and divide it into .625″ segments; an X must appear where each segment ends.
g. Draw two lines 1″ long to form a 90° angle. Make a .25 chamfer at the corner.
h. Draw two 1″ lines to form a 90° angle. Make a .250 fillet at the corner.
i. Draw a polar array of eight .25″-diameter circles on a 2″-diameter circular center line.
j. Draw three 1″-diameter semicircles using three different Arc: commands. Label each arc with the command used, for example: St,C,End.
k. Draw an arc with a radius of .45″ and include an angle of 60°.
l. Draw a 1½″ square using the Pline: command. Draw a 1¼″ and a 1″ square using the Offset: command; all squares must be concentric.
m. Draw a hexagon inscribed inside a 1″-diameter circle.
n. Draw a solid triangle inscribed inside a ½″-diameter circle. Make an array of these triangles 3 rows by 3 columns, 1″ from center to center both vertically and horizontally.
o. Draw a ¾″-diameter isometric cylinder, 1″ tall. Be sure to erase or trim the hidden portion of the bottom ellipse.

7–3. Make an AutoCAD drawing of the fan shown in Figure 7–37. Measure the picture and duplicate it on a vertical 8½″ × 11″ sheet. Place your name in the lower right corner.

FIGURE 7–37
Exercise 7–3

7–4. Make an AutoCAD drawing of the model airplane motor part shown in Figure 7–38. Make the drawing 4 times size on a vertical 8½″ × 11″ sheet. The upper dimensions are in inches. The lower dimensions are in millimeters. Approximate any dimensions not given. Place your name in the lower right corner. Do not put any dimensions on your drawing. After you have drawn the two upper lugs, use the Mirror: command (on the CONSTRCT menu) to duplicate them on the bottom of the outer diameter. Be sure ortho (F8) is on when you select mirror line for ease in selecting the second point of the mirror line.

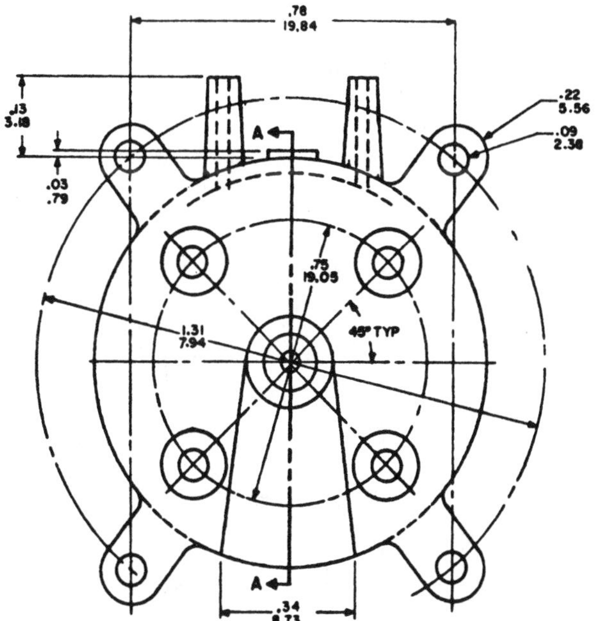

FIGURE 7–38
Exercise 7–4

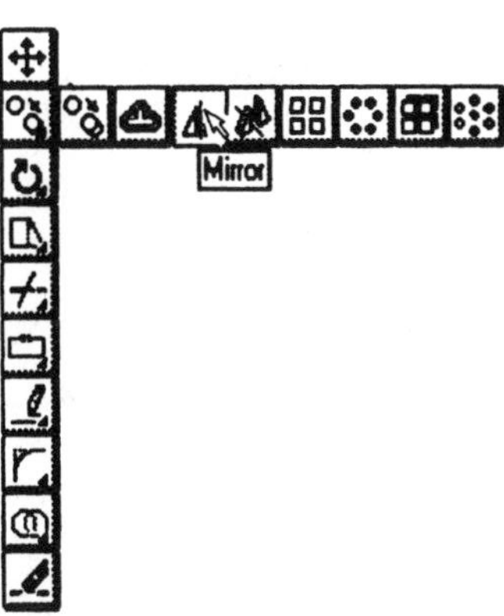

7–5. Draw Figure 7–39, following the instructions given for Exercise 7–4.

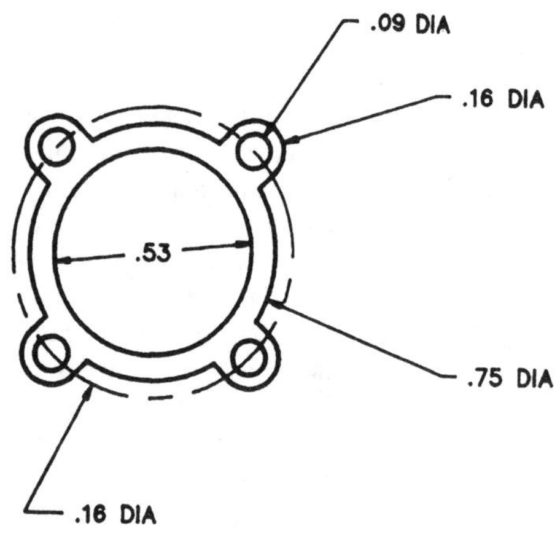

FIGURE 7–39
Exercise 7–5

7–6. Draw Figure 7–40, following the same instructions given for Exercise 7–4 except make the drawing the same dimensions as shown and place it on a horizontal 11″ × 8½″ sheet. Do not put any dimensions on your drawing.

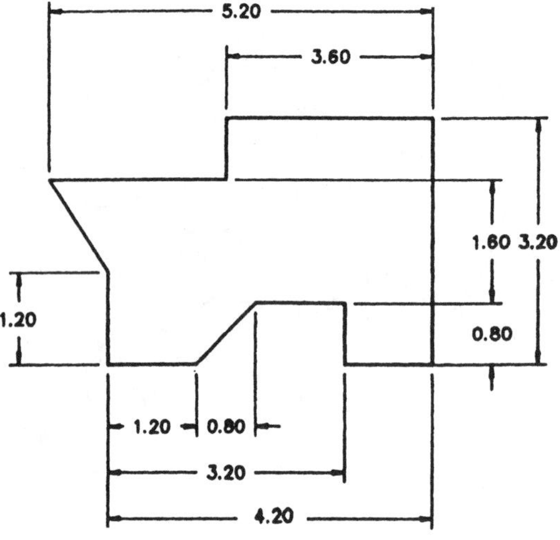

FIGURE 7–40
Exercise 7–6

7–7. Draw Figure 7–41, following the instructions given in Exercise 7–3.

FIGURE 7–41
Exercise 7–7

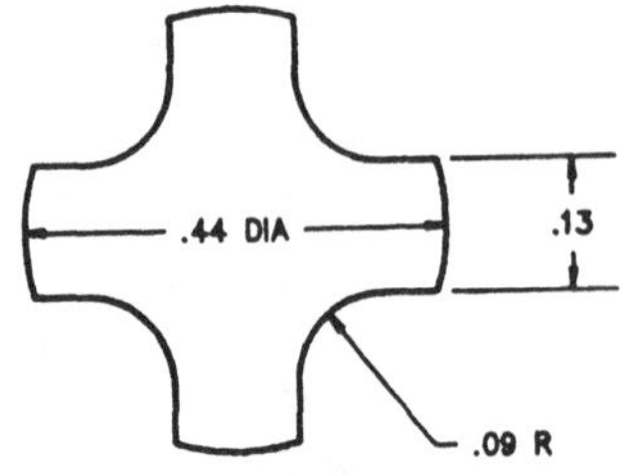

7–8. Make an AutoCAD drawing of the door shown in Figure 7–42. Measure the drawing and reproduce it twice size as accurately as possible. Place it on a horizontal 8.5″ × 11″ sheet. Place your name in the lower right corner. Use the Mirror: command (on the CONSTRCT menu) to produce a mirror image of any features. Leave ortho on when you select mirror lines for ease in locating the second point of the mirror line. You will find Mirror: to be very effective for this problem. Be sure to watch the prompts during this command and follow them carefully.

FIGURE 7–42
Exercise 7–8

7–9. Draw Figure 7–43, following the instructions given in Exercise 7–8. Place it on a horizontal 8.5″ × 11″ sheet.

FIGURE 7–43
Exercise 7–9

7–10. Draw the patterns for molding twice the size shown in Figure 7–44. Place them on a horizontal 11″ × 8½″ sheet. Place your name in the lower right corner.

7–11. Make an AutoCAD drawing of the part shown in Figure 7–45. Make the drawing the same dimensions as shown and place it on a horizontal 11″ × 8½″ sheet. Do not put any dimensions on your drawing. Place your name in the lower right corner.

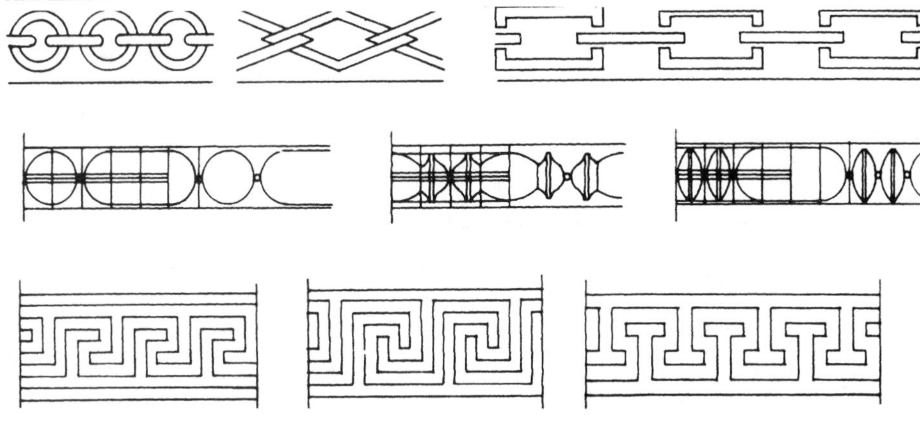

FIGURE 7–44
Exercise 7–10

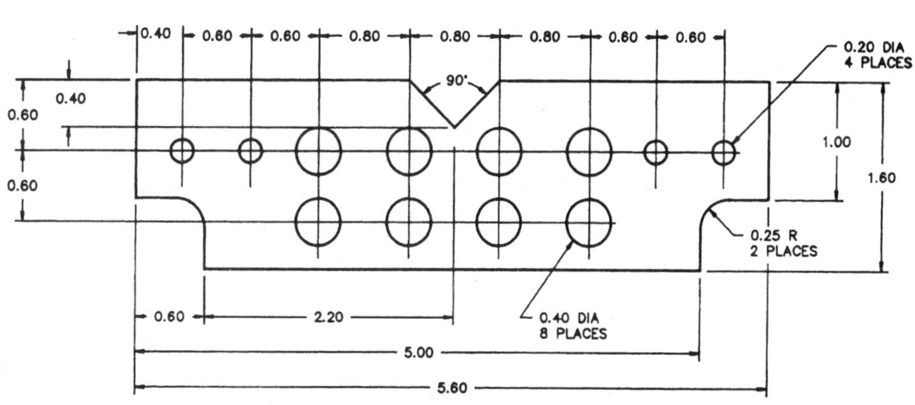

FIGURE 7–45
Exercise 7–11

REVIEW QUESTIONS

Circle the correct answer.

1. What is the maximum number of characters that may be used for a drawing name?
   a. 2 b. 4 c. 6 d. 8 e. Any number
2. If the Grid: spacing is .25″ and the Snap: must touch every line of the grid, at what should the Snap: be set?
   a. .06 b. .125 c. .1 d. .2 e. .3
3. What is the command used to trim lines between cutting edges?
   a. Edit: d. Copy:
   b. Trim: e. Extend:
   c. Erase:
4. From the Line: prompt "to point," which is the correct response to draw a horizontal line 4.501″ long to the right of the starting point?
   a. 4.501<180↵ d. @4.501<0↵
   b. 4.501↵ e. <0° 4.501↵
   c. <180°<4.501↵
5. To draw a line 5.000″ long that proceeds downward at a 45° angle to the right, which is the correct response to the prompt "to point"?
   a. @25<135 d. 5.000,135
   b. @5.00<45 e. 5.000<45°
   c. @5.00<−45
6. To draw a line parallel to another line, which of the following commands should be used?
   a. Line parallel: d. Offset parallel:
   b. Parallel: e. LP:
   c. Offset:
7. To draw a line perpendicular to another line from a point, which of the following options should be used?
   a. SQUARE
   b. RT ANGLE
   c. PERpendicular (from the Osnap menu)
   d. 90° ANGLE
   e. @90°

8. If you have just drawn a line at the wrong angle and you want to return to the starting point of the line, enter?
   a. Redo b. R c. U d. Control-C e. Erase:
9. If you need to break a line at the intersection of another line, select the line to be broken and enter?
   a. The second point—not the intersection
   b. F
   c. The first point
   d. Break:
   e. Change:
10. What is the variable setting used to make a point appear as an X?
    a. Node d. Pdmode
    b. Point Set e. Node set
    c. Pdsize
11. To divide a given line into five equal parts, which of the following commands should be used?
    a. Measure: d. Change:
    b. Divide: e. Polyline:
    c. Break:
12. To divide a given line into ½″ increments, which of the following commands should be used?
    a. Measure: d. Change:
    b. Divide: e. Polyline:
    c. Break:
13. To make a 45° angle at the corner of two intersecting lines, which of the following commands should be used?
    a. Measure: d. Change:
    b. Fillet: e. Chamfer:
    c. Break:
14. To make a ¼″ radius at the intersection of two lines, which of the following commands should be used?
    a. Measure: d. Change:
    b. Fillet: e. Chamfer:
    c. Break:
15. A response of .5 to the prompt "diameter/<radius>" will produce a circle of?
    a. .5000 radius d. .5000 circumference
    b. .5000 diameter e. .5000 chord
    c. .5 chord
16. To produce a circle with a diameter of .5000, what is the correct response to the prompt "diameter/<radius>"?
    a. D, then .5 d. Circle-diameter
    b. R, then .500 e. .5000, then ↵
    c. .50
17. The maximum number of lines that can be drawn with the Multiline: command is:
    a. 2 b. 8 c. 12 d. 16 e. Unlimited
18. A pattern of 16 holes on a circular centerline may be drawn fastest using?
    a. RECTANGULAR ARRAY
    b. MULTIPLE COPY
    c. COPY CIRCULAR
    d. REPEAT
    e. POLAR ARRAY
19. The command _____ was used to draw the arc shown.
    a. ARC Ce, S, Len
    b. ARC End, S, Cen
    c. ARC Ce, S, End
    d. ARC St, C, End
    e. ARC St, C, Ang

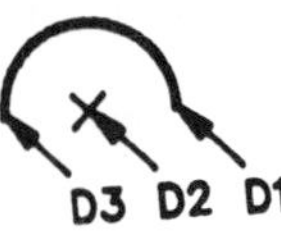

20. A polyline is used when a series of lines must all be treated as a single entity, as in Offset:
    a. True b. False
21. An array of 5 rows and 1 column with a .25 distance between rows will produce which of the following patterns?

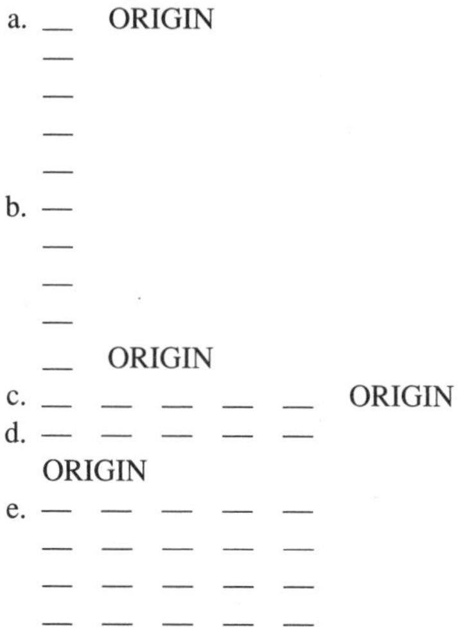

22. Which of the following commands should be used to draw a hexagon?
    a. Polygon:
    b. Hexagon:
    c. Polyline:
    d. Fillet:
    e. Chamfer:
23. Which of the following sequences will produce a solid square using the Solid: command?

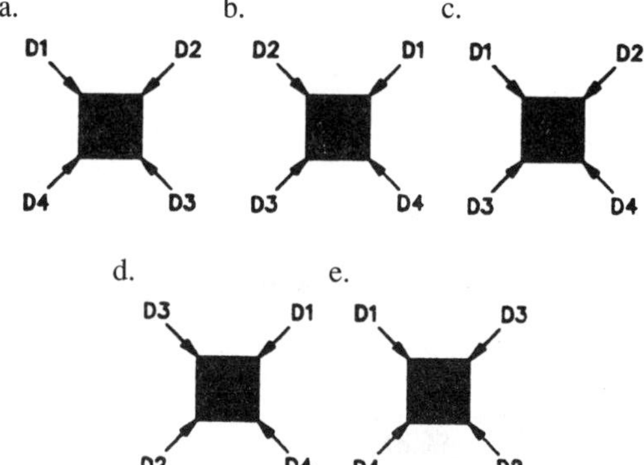

24. The isoplane top condition will produce which of the following isometric ellipses?

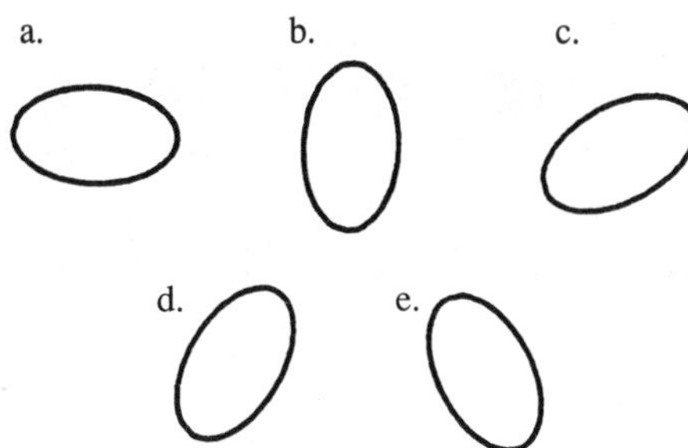

25. Which of the following commands sets an isometric grid?
    a. Grid:
    b. Edit:
    c. Utility:
    d. Snap:
    e. Units:
26. Which of the following commands is used to extend lines to a boundary line?
    a. Move:
    b. Copy:
    c. Trim:
    d. Edit:
    e. Extend:

8 Using 2-D Commands to Draw Orthographic Views Including Sectional Views

OBJECTIVES

After completing this chapter, you will be able to:

□ Make 2-D drawings to scale from 2-D and 3-D sketches using the following commands:

Arc:	Fillet:	ID:	Pan:
Bhatch:	Filter:	Limits:	Redraw:
Chamfer:	Grips	Line:	Trim:
Circle:	Hatch:	Offset:	Undo:
Dist:	Help:	Osnap:	View:
Erase:			

□ Correctly answer questions regarding the preceding commands.

□ Use Hatch: and Bhatch: along with other draw and edit commands to produce detail and assembly sectional views.

TWO-DIMENSIONAL DRAWINGS

Two-dimensional drawings are those showing only two of the three dimensions of an object in any one view. Figure 8–1 illustrates the three most commonly used 2-D views. The top view shows width and depth. The front view shows width and height. The right side view shows height and depth.

AutoCAD has excellent capabilities for drawing in two dimensions. The drawings can be extremely accurate and can be dimensioned in a manner ensuring correct results. Although a checking procedure is introduced in this chapter, dimensioning accurately is covered in a later chapter. In this chapter the mechanics of drawing in two dimensions and the procedures needed to move quickly from one view to another are covered. Orthographic projection (2-D drawing) is a major part of any good basic drafting textbook. This is a good time to review if you have questions regarding view placement or line identification. Let us begin 2-D drawing with a reasonably simple flat object (Figure 8–2).

Drawing 2-D Views

EXERCISE 8–1 DRAWING A SINGLE TWO-DIMENSIONAL VIEW

Set Up the Drawing

Step 1. On Your Own:

Note: Refer to Chapter 4 for information on how to make settings and create layers.

1. Load AutoCAD. Select New. . . and name the drawing 8-1 (your initials).
2. Make the following settings (see Chapter 4).

UNITS: Decimal; 3 digits to the right of the decimal point. Accept defaults for all other unit prompts.

LIMITS: Lower left corner: 0,0
Upper right corner: 11,8.5

GRID: .25

SNAP: 125

STYLE: STANDARD; FONT: SIMPLEX

Create the following layers:

LAYER NAME	COLOR	LINETYPE
1	RED	CONTINUOUS
2	YELLOW	CONTINUOUS

Set layer 1 current.

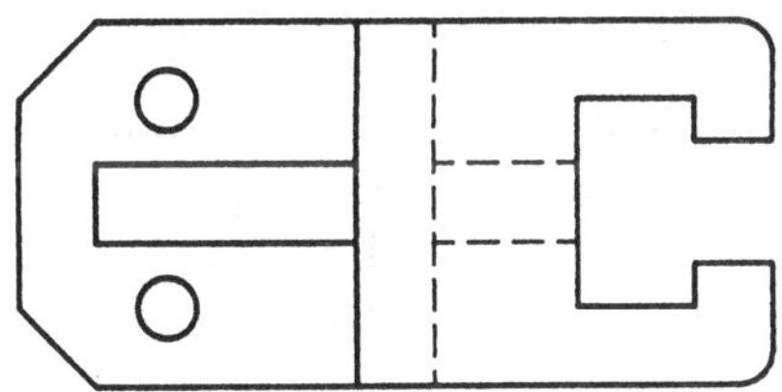

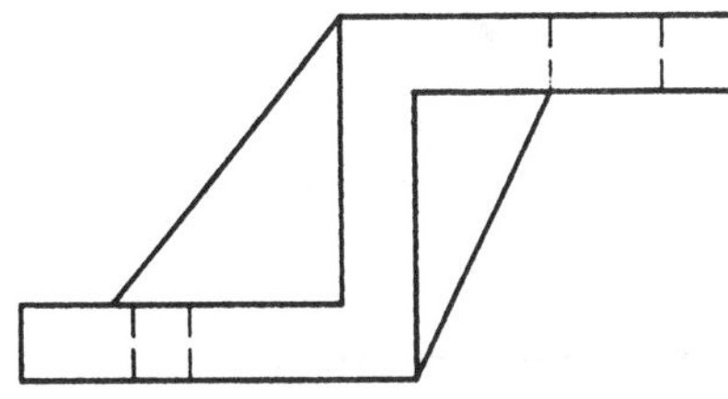

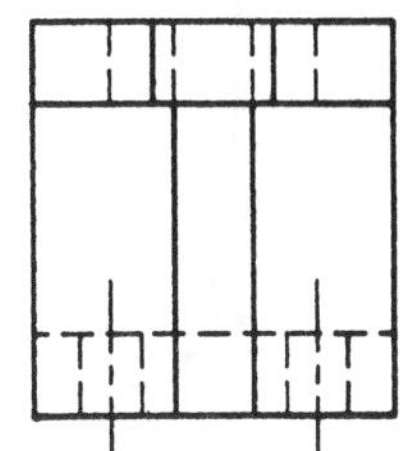

FIGURE 8–1
The Most Commonly Used Views

You are now ready to draw on layer 1. Your status line should read Layer 1 ORTHO SNAP. If ortho and snap are not on, activate them from function keys F8 and F9 or from the bottom of the Windows screen.

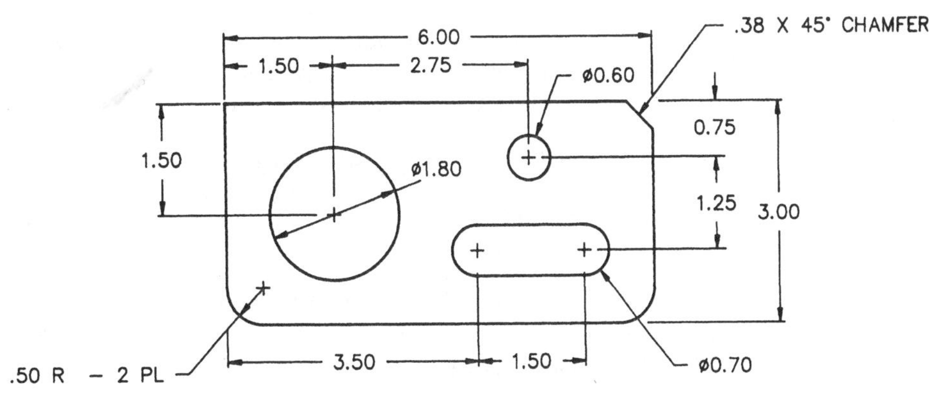

FIGURE 8–2
Two-Dimensional Drawing

Draw the Outline

Step 2. Draw the outline of Figure 8–2.

Prompt	Response
Command:	**Line:** (or *Type:* L ↵)
Line from point:	*Pick:* **D1** (Figure 8–3) (or *Type:* **2.5,5.75**↵)
To point:	*Type:* **@6<0** ↵
To point:	*Type:* **@3<270** ↵
To point:	*Type:* **@6<180** ↵
To point:	*Type:* **C** ↵ (or *Pick:* **CLOSE**—the close option will cause the last point entered to connect back to the first point entered)

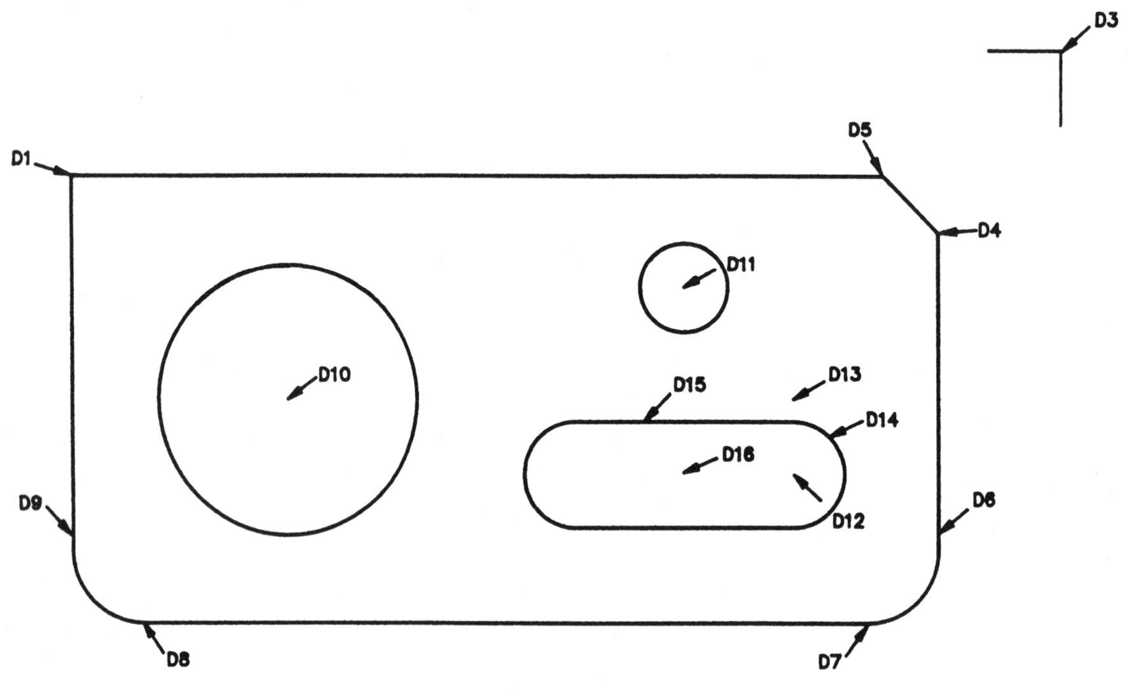

FIGURE 8–3
Draw Object

You should now have a closed red box on the screen. If you make a mistake while entering line coordinates, type U (the Undo: command) and press ↵. This returns the cursor to the last line entered. Now add the chamfer and the fillets to the outline.

Add Chamfer and Fillets

Note: Use the pull-down View menu.

Prompt	Response
Command:	**Zoom**
All/Center/Dynamics/Extents/Left/ Previous/Window/Scale(x):	*Pick:* **D2** (Figure 8–3)
Other corner:	*Pick:* **D3** (Figure 8–3)
Command:	**Chamfer:**

Polyline/Distance/Angle/Trim/Method/ <Select first line>:	*Type:* **D** ↵ (or *Select:* **Distance** from the screen menu)
Enter first chamfer distance <0.000>:	*Type:* **.38** ↵
Enter second chamfer distance <0.380>:	↵
Polyline/Distance/Angle/Trim/Method/ <Select first Line>:	*Pick:* **D4** (Figure 8–3)
Select second line:	*Pick:* **D5** (Figure 8–3)
Command:	**Fillet:**
Polyline/Radius/Trim/<Select first object>:	

Note: At this point you may have to press the space bar or ↵ to get back to the Chamfer: command.

First enter the fillet radius.

Prompt	Response
	Type: **R** ↵ (or *Select:* **Radius** from the Fillet menu)
Enter fillet radius <0.000>:	*Type:* **.5** ↵
Command:	↵ (or press the space bar to get back to the fillet: command)
Fillet Polyline/Radius/Trim/<Select first object>:	*Pick:* **D6 D7** ↵ ↵ **D8 D9**

Add Circles and the Slot

Step 3. Add the circles and the slot to the drawing.

Prompt	Response
Command:	*Type:* **LA** ↵
Layer?/Make/Set/New/ON/OFF/Color/ Ltype/Freeze/Thaw/LOck/Unlock:	*Type:* **S** ↵
New current layer <1>:	*Type:* **2** ↵
Layer?/Make/New/ON/OFF/Color/Ltype/ Freeze/Thaw/LOck/Unlock:	↵ (or press the space bar)
Command:	**Circle:** (or *Type:* C ↵)

When you select the menu, digitize CEN,RAD: to change the prompt.

Prompt	Response
3P/2P/TTR/Center point:	*Pick:* **D10** (Figure 8–3)

Pick a point 1.5″ from the top edge and 1.5″ from the left edge. Press the appropriate function keys to turn the grid on and snap on.

Prompt	Response
Diameter/<Radius>:	*Type:* **.9** ↵ (Radius is the default.)
Command:	**Circle:**
3P/2P/TTR/<Center point>:	*Pick:* **D11** (Figure 8–3)

Pick a point .75″ from the top edge and 1.75″ from the right edge. Remember the grid is set to .25″.

Prompt	Response
Diameter/<Radius>:	*Type:* **D** ↵
Diameter <1.800>:	*Type:* **.6** ↵
Command:	

Now, draw the slot.

Prompt	Response
	Arc:
Center/Start point:	*Type:* **C** ↵ (or *Select:* **Ce,S,End,** from the ARC menu)
Center:	*Pick:* **D12** (Figure 8–3)

Pick a point 1.00″ from the right edge and 1.00″ from the bottom edge.

Prompt	Response
Start point:	*Type:* **@.35<270** ↵
Angle/Length of chord/<Endpoint>:	*Pick:* **D13**

Pick on grid a point 180° opposite the start point.

Note: Use the ENDpoint option on the Osnap menu. Osnap is obtained by pressing the mouse button on the far right (or the middle button), selecting from the menu bar or picking **** on the root menu.

Prompt	Response
Command:	**Line:** (or *Type:* **L** ↵)
From point:	**Osnap-ENDpoint**

Move the cursor and notice the target box. Position the box near the top part of the arc. If you have difficulty because the snap command is on, turn snap off, digitize the point, and turn snap back on.

Prompt	Response
From point: _endp of:	*Pick:* **D14**
To point:	*Type:* **@1.5<180** ↵
To point:	↵ (or press the space bar)
Command:	**Offset:**
Offset distance or Through <Through>:	*Type:* **.7** ↵ (This sets the distance to the end of the arc.)
Select object to offset:	(Turn off snap.) *Pick:* **D15** (Figure 8–3)
Side to offset:	*Pick:* **D16** (Notice how the offset line connects exactly on the end of the arc.)
Select object to offset:	↵
Command:	**Fillet:**
Polyline/Radius/Trim/<Select first object>:	*Type:* **R** ↵
Enter fillet radius <0.500>:	*Type:* **.35** ↵
Command:	↵
<Select first object>	Pick the left end of one line of the slot.
Select second object:	Pick the left end of the other line of the slot.
Command:	*Type:* **R** ↵ (Redraw: command will remove the picked points from the screen.)

Tip: Press the GRID function key F7 twice and get the same result as Redraw: if it is faster for you.

Plot and Save the Drawing

Step 4. On Your Own:

1. Print the drawing on an A-size (11″ × 8½″) sheet. See Chapter 6 for instructions on plotting.
2. After the plot is complete save your drawing in two places, and exit from the AutoCAD program.

You have made and printed a drawing with commonly used commands. Now analyze the commands you have used and look at the following means of drawing that you must master to become an AutoCAD expert:

Absolute coordinates
Relative coordinates
Polar coordinates
ID—identify a point
Filters

Absolute Coordinates

Absolute coordinates are given with respect to the origin 0,0. Although every point has X, Y, and Z coordinates, only X and Y are used in 2-D drawings. The coordinates are

X = horizontal (the first number)
Y = vertical (the second number)
Z = depth or thickness (the third number)

The Z coordinate is given a 0 or the current elevation if it is not specified. You will use Z coordinates in later chapters on 3-D objects.

Let's look at an example of how absolute coordinates can be used in drawing to further explain this concept. The front view of Figure 8–4 was drawn using absolute coordinates. To make this drawing, use the same settings from the previous drawing, 8–1 (your initials). The initials BK will be used in the remaining examples.

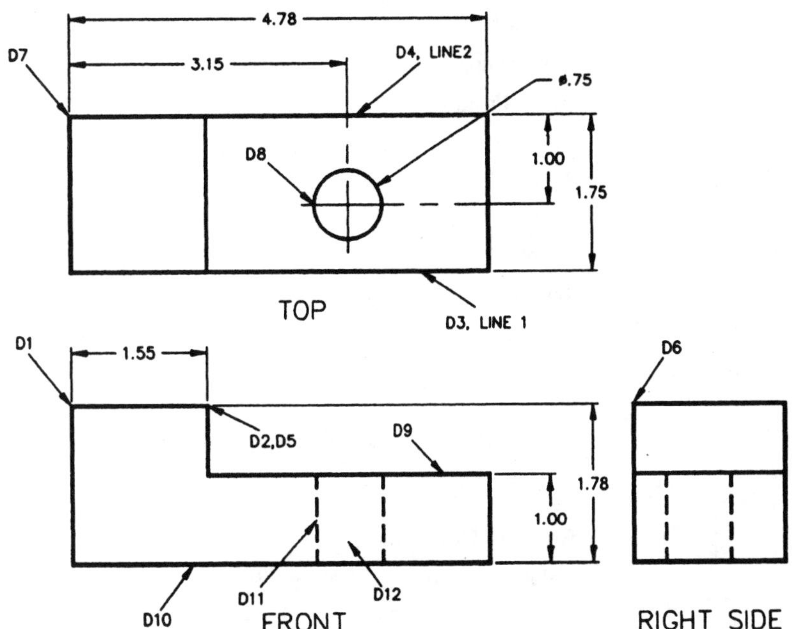

FIGURE 8–4
Drawing Using Absolute, Relative, and Polar Coordinates, ID, and Filters

EXERCISE 8–2
USING FILTERS TO DRAW VIEWS

Set Up the Drawing

Step 1. Load AutoCAD and begin a new drawing.

Prompt	Response
Command:	**NEW**
The Create New Drawing dialog box appears:	*Type:* **8–2BK = 8–1BK** ↵ (or 8–2BK = B:8–1BK if 8–1BK is on a floppy disk in the B drive in the New Drawing Name button.)

Step 2. Erase the prototype drawing.

Prompt	Response
Command:	*Type:* **E** ↵
Select objects:	*Type:* **ALL** ↵ (ALL will erase the entire drawing so that nothing remains from 8–1BK but the settings and layers.)
Select objects:	

Step 3. On Your Own:

Note: If you are using the pull-down menus, the hidden line-type will not appear as a selection until linetypes are loaded. See Chapter 4 for details.

Note: Use the pull-down Layer dialog box to set layer 2 as the current layer.

Note: Remember: Absolute coordinates show a location from 0,0.

1. Add the following layer.

LAYER NAME	COLOR	LINETYPE
3	GREEN	HIDDEN

2. Zoom: All before you begin drawing.

Draw the Front View Outline with Absolute Coordinates

Step 4. Draw the front view using absolute coordinates.

With layer 2 as the current layer, follow this procedure:

Prompt	Response
Command:	**Line:**
LINE From point:	*Type:* **1, 2** ↵ (1 unit in the X direction, 2 units in the Y direction)
To point:	*Type:* **5.78, 2** ↵
To point:	*Type:* **5.78, 3** ↵
To point:	*Type:* **2.55, 3** ↵
To point:	*Type:* **2.55, 3.78** ↵
	Type: **1, 3.78** ↵
	Type: **C** ↵

Draw the Top View Outline Using Relative Coordinates

Step 5. Draw the top view using relative coordinates.

Relative Coordinates

Relative coordinates (relative to the point entered) are taken from the previous point entered. For example, the front view just drawn could have been drawn using relative coordinates after the first point had been picked or located using absolute coordinates. The endpoint of the first line using relative coordinates would have been:

Prompt	Response
To point:	*Type:* **@4.78,0** ↵ (Move 4.78 in the X direction and 0 in the Y direction from the previous point.)

The symbol @ must precede relative coordinates.

Suppose you are going to draw the top view using relative coordinates, but you do not want to do the arithmetic necessary to use absolute coordinates to locate the lower left corner of the top view. All you know is that you want the views to be 1″ apart. AutoCAD has provided the ID command on the INQUIRY menu (INQUIRY is on the ASSIST menu) that allows you to do that.

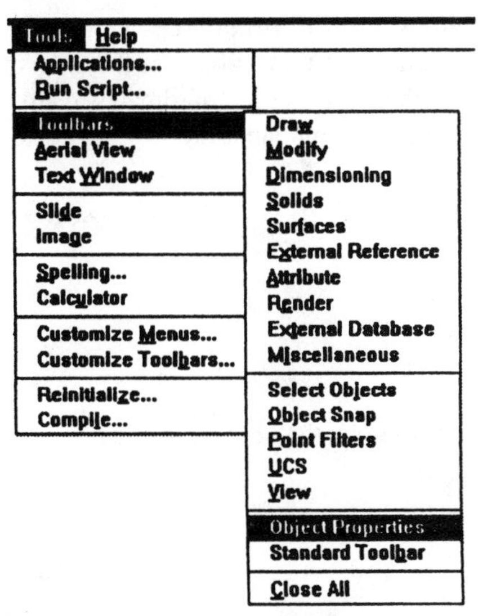

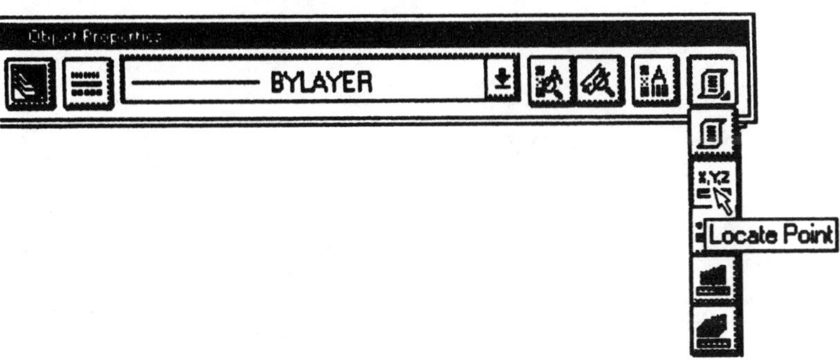

ID

Note: If you type the wrong coordinate, *Type:* U ↵ (for Undo) to return to the previous point.

ID identifies a location from which relative coordinates may be given. Therefore, every point in the top view can be drawn using relative coordinates as follows.

Prompt	Response
Command:	*Type:* **ID** ↵
Point:	*Pick:* **D1** (Pick the upper left corner of the front view. Use Osnap-INTersection.)
Command:	**Line:**
From point:	*Type:* **@0,1** ↵ (0 units in the X direction and 1 unit in the Y direction from the ID point.)
To point:	*Type:* **@4.78,0** ↵
To point:	*Type:* **@0,1.75** ↵
To point:	*Type:* **@−4.78,0** ↵
To point:	*Type:* **@0,−1.75** ↵ (or *Type:* **C** ↵)
To point:	↵

Now draw the vertical inside line of the top view using FILTERS to locate the first point.

Draw Inside Lines

Filters

Filters relate to the X, Y, and Z coordinates of a point. Filters allow you to avoid unnecessary construction lines and to save considerable time when they are used effectively. An

XZ filter, for example, says to AutoCAD, "I am pointing to the XZ location for the point now; then I will point to the Y location. Use that information to locate my point." You may filter one or two of the X, Y, and Z coordinates in any command that requires the location of a point. Some of these commands are

Line:
Circle:
Ellipse:
Copy:
Move:
Polygon:

Let's use a filter to draw the vertical inside line of the top view of Figure 8–4.
Set layer 1 current.

Prompt	Response
Command:	**Line:**
From point:	*Type:* **.X** ↵
Of:	*Pick:* **D2** (Use Osnap-INTersection and pick. You are pointing to the X coordinate of the point you want.)
Need YZ:	*Pick:* **D3** (Use Osnap-NEArest and pick any point on line 1 of the TOP view. You are pointing to the Y coordinate of the point. The Z coordinate in 2-D is 0 oı the current elevation.)
To point:	*Pick:* **D4** (Use Osnap-PERpendicular and pick any point on line 2 of the top view.)
To point:	↵

Now use a Y filter to locate the top left corner of the right-side view.

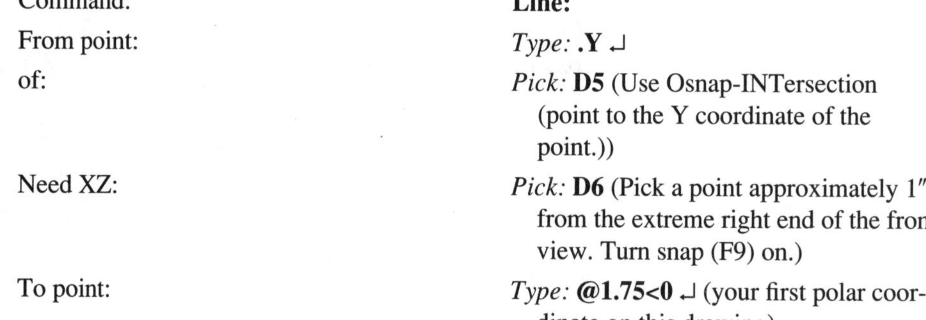

Prompt	Response
Command:	**Line:**
From point:	*Type:* **.Y** ↵
of:	*Pick:* **D5** (Use Osnap-INTersection (point to the Y coordinate of the point.))
Need XZ:	*Pick:* **D6** (Pick a point approximately 1″ from the extreme right end of the front view. Turn snap (F9) on.)
To point:	*Type:* **@1.75<0** ↵ (your first polar coordinate on this drawing)

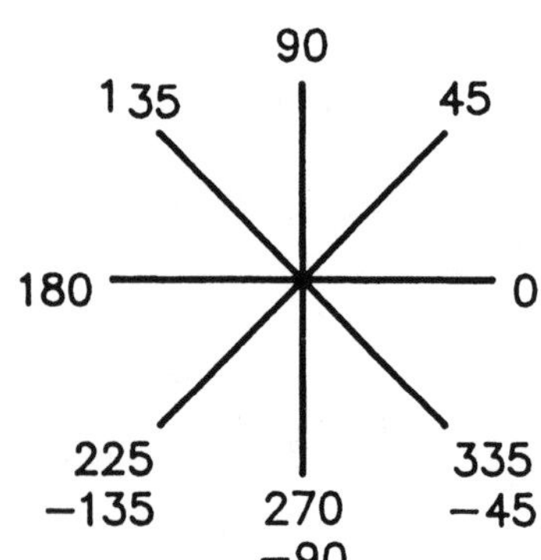

FIGURE 8–5
Polar Angles

Before you draw the rest of the polar coordinates that you will use, let's look briefly at the parts of a polar coordinate.

Polar Coordinates

A polar coordinate involves distance and direction. @ indicates that a distance will follow. @ 1.75 tells AutoCAD to move 1.75 units. < indicates that an angle will follow. <0 tells AutoCAD to move horizontally to the right. Figure 8–5 shows the values for polar angles. Now draw the remaining outside lines of the right side view.

Draw the Right Side View with Polar Coordinates

Step 6. Draw the right-side view using polar coordinates.

Prompt	Response
To point:	*Type:* **@1.78<270** ↵
To point:	*Type:* **@1.75<180** ↵
To point:	*Type:* **C** ↵

Draw the Circle

Now use relative coordinates to locate and draw the circle in the top view.

Prompt	Response
Command:	*Type:* **ID** ↵
Select point:	*Pick:* **D7** (Use Osnap-INTersection.)
Command:	**Circle-DIA**
3P/2P/TTR/<Center Point>:	*Type:* **@3.15,−1** ↵
Circle diameter:	*Type:* **.75** ↵

Draw Hidden Lines in the Front View Using Filters

Now use Filters to draw the hidden lines in the front view. Set layer 3 current and follow this procedure:

Note: If you draw a line on the wrong layer, use CHPROP (change properties) to change the line to the correct layer. You may use the Properties Dialogue Box from Modify on the Menu Bar, Ddchpro: on the Screen Menu or *Type:* CHPROP ↵ at the command prompt.

Prompt	Response
Command:	**Line:**
From point:	*Type:* **.X** ↵
of:	*Pick:* **D8** (Use Osnap-QUAdrant.)
Need YZ:	*Pick:* **D9** (Use Osnap-NEArest (any point on this line).)
To point:	*Pick:* **D10** (Use Osnap-PERpendicular.)
To point:	↵
Command:	**Offset:**
Offset distance or through <T>:	*Type:* **.75** ↵
Object to offset:	*Pick:* **D11**
Side to offset:	*Pick:* **D12**

With layer 2 current:
Turn snap on and draw the horizontal line in the right-side view.
Copy the two hidden lines in the front view to the right-side view.

Prompt	Response
Command:	**Copy:**
Select objects:	Pick the two hidden lines in the front view.
Base point or displacement:	With snap off, use Osnap-ENDpoint to select the endpoint of one of the hidden lines.
Second point of displacement:	Turn snap back on. Use the grid points to locate the correct point to pick for the copied location.

Print and Save the Drawing

Step 7. Print the drawing.
Step 8. Save the drawing in two places and exit.

Now, let's draw three 2-D views of a more complex object.

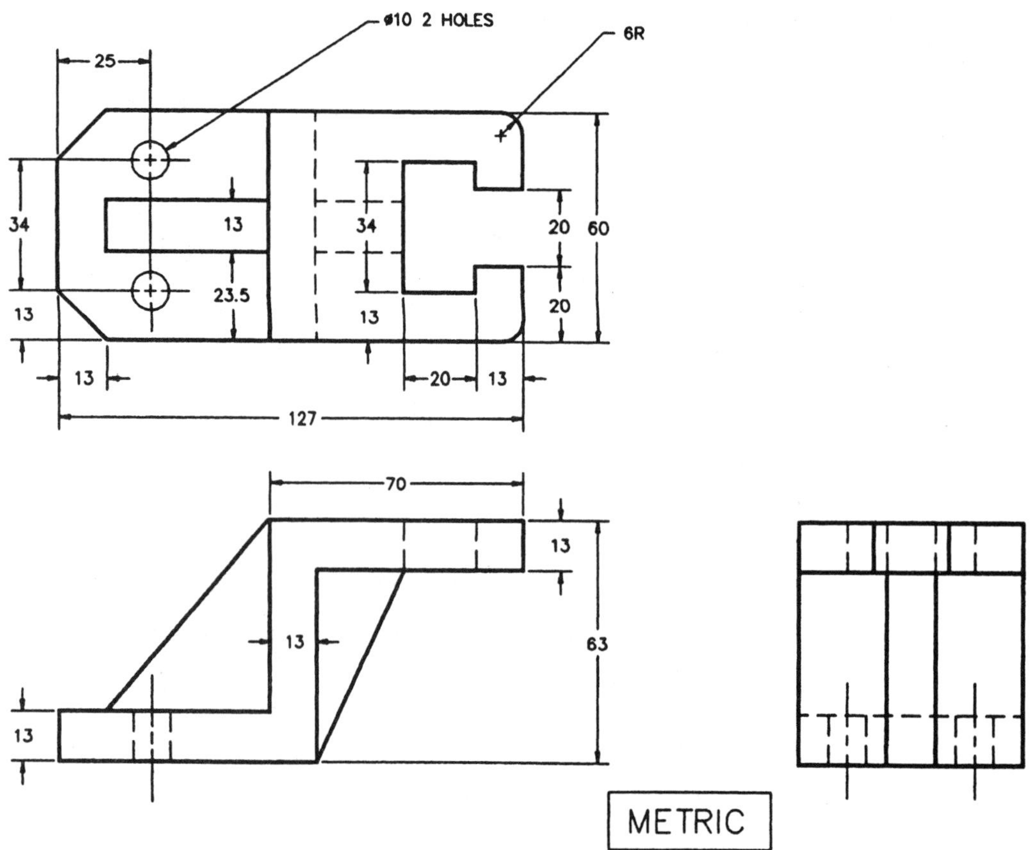

FIGURE 8–6
Three Views of an Object

EXERCISE 8–3: DRAWING THREE 2-D VIEWS OF AN OBJECT (FIGURE 8–6)

Set Up the Drawing

Step 1. Load AutoCAD, select New. . . , and name it 8–3 (your initials).
Step 2. Set units, limits, grid, snap, and layers.

Note: You may select Units: from the DATA menu and use the Units Control dialog box to set units.

Prompt	Response
Command:	*Type:* **UNITS** ↵
System of Units: 1. Scientific 2. Decimal 3. Engineering 4. Architectural 5. Fractional	
Enter choice, 1 to 5 <2>:	↵ (This defaults to decimal.)
Number of digits to the right of decimal point (0 to 8) <4>:	*Type:* **2** ↵
Systems of angle measure: 1. Decimal degrees 2. Degrees/Minutes/Seconds 3. Grads 4. Radians 5. Surveyor's units	

Enter choice, 1 to 5 <1>:	↵ (This defaults to 1.)
Number of fractional places for display of angles (0 to 8) <0>:	↵ (This defaults to 0.)
Direction for angle 0: East 3 o'clock = 0 North 12 o'clock = 90 West 9 o'clock = 180 South 6 o'clock = 70	
Enter direction for angle 0 <0>:	↵ (This defaults to current settings on screen.)
Do you want angles measured clockwise: <N>	↵ (This defaults to *no.*)
Command:	

At this point you need to return to the drawing editor (use flip screen key).

Note: You may also select a metric prototype drawing from Preferences under the Options menu on the menu bar.

Note: You may also set Layers from the Layer Control dialog box as described in Chapter 4.

Prompt	**Response**
	Type: **LIMITS** ↵
ON/OFF/<Lower left corner> <0.000,0.00>:	↵ (This will default the lower left corner to 0.00,0.00.)
Upper right corner <12.00,9.00>:	*Type:* **420, 297** ↵ (This sets up a metric drawing on an 11″ × 17″ sheet; respond with 297,210 for an A-size sheet.)
Command:	*Type:* **GRID** ↵
Grid spacing (x) or ON/OFF/Snap/Aspect <0.00>:	*Type:* **10** ↵
Command:	*Type:* **SNAP** ↵
SNAP spacing or ON/OFF/Aspect/ Rotate/Style <0.00>:	*Type:* **5** ↵
Command:	*Type:* **Z** ↵
All/Center/Dynamics/Extents/Left/ Previous/Vmax/Window/<Scale (x/xp)>:	*Type:* **A** ↵ (or *Select:* **All** from the screen menu)
Command:	*Type:* **LA** ↵
Layer?/Make/Set/New/ON/OFF/Color/ Ltype/Freeze/Thaw/LOck/Unlock:	*Type:* **N** ↵
New layer name(s):	*Type:* **1, 3** ↵
Layer?/Make/Set/New/ON/OFF/Color/ Ltype/Freeze/Thaw/LOck/Unlock:	*Type:* **C** ↵
Color:	*Type:* **R** ↵ (for red)
Layer name(s) for color 1 (red) <0>:	*Type:* **1** ↵
Layer?/Make/Set/New/ON/OFF/Color/ Ltype/Freeze/Thaw/LOck/Unlock:	*Type:* **C** ↵
Color:	*Type:* **G** ↵ (for green)
Layer name(s) for color 3 (green) <1>:	*Type:* **3** ↵

Now select a linetype for layer 3. Layer 3 is the layer to be used for hidden lines.

Prompt	**Response**
Layer?/Make/Set/New/ON/OFF/Color/ Ltype/Freeze/Thaw/LOck/Unlock:	**Ltype**
Line type (or ?) <CONTINUOUS>:	*Type:* **HIDDEN** ↵

Prompt	Response
Layer name(s) for Ltype hidden <0>:	*Type:* **3** ↵ (the name of the layer to contain the hidden line type)
Layer?/Make/Set/New/ON/OFF/Color/ Ltype/Freeze/Thaw/LOck/Unlock:	*Type:* **?**
Layer name(s) for listing <*>:	(Press the ↵ key for a complete listing of all layers created; notice LAYER 3—the linetype has now been changed to HIDDEN)
Layer?/Make/Set/New/ON/OFF/Color/ Ltype/Freeze/Thaw/LOck/Unlock:	*Type:* **S** ↵ (or *Select:* **SET** from the LAYER menu)
New current layer <0>:	*Type:* **1** ↵ (Layer 1 is the red layer.)
Layer?/Make/Set/New/ON/OFF/Color/ Ltype/Freeze/Thaw/LOck/Unlock:	↵ (or press the space bar)

You are now ready to draw on layer 1. The status line should read: Layer 1 Ortho Snap. If ortho and snap are not on, activate them from the appropriate function keys (F8 and F9).

Draw Top and Front Views

Step 3. On Your Own:

Draw object lines for top and front views. Draw the outside edges and other object lines for the top and front views of Figure 8–7 using relative and polar coordinates. Leave 50 mm between views and arrange the drawing so that the entire drawing (top, front, and right side views) is centered within the drawing limits.

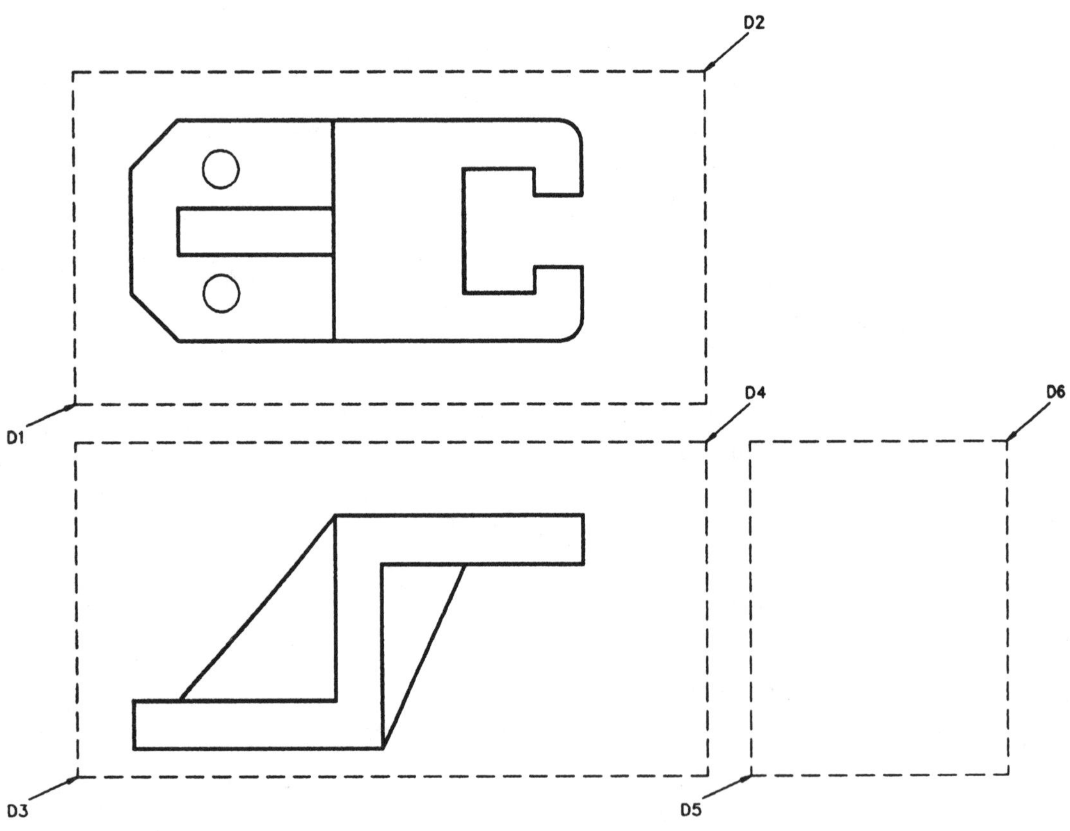

FIGURE 8–7
Creating View Areas

Create Viewing Areas

Create viewing areas for the front, top, and right side views. Window an area for the front view (name it F, or Front), an area for the top view (name it T, or Top), and an area for the right side view (name it S, or Side). As you draw these views you will find it helpful to project surfaces from one view to another. Using the View:-Restore command allows you to move from one view to another quickly without going through Zoom: Dynamic to get there. Naming the views with a single letter reduces the amount of typing needed to change views. Follow this sequence to create views (Figure 8–7):

Prompt	Response
Command:	*Type:* **VIEW** ↵
View?/Delete/Restore/Save/Window:	*Type:* **W** ↵ (or select Window from the menu)
View name to save:	*Type:* **T** ↵ (top)
First corner:	*Pick:* **D1** (Figure 8–7)
Other corner:	*Pick:* **D2**
Command:	↵
VIEW?/Delete/Restore/Save/Window:	*Type:* **W** ↵
View name to save:	*Type:* **F** ↵ (front)
First corner:	*Pick:* **D3**
Other corner:	*Pick:* **D4**
Command:	↵
VIEW?/Delete/Restore/Save/Window:	*Type:* **W** ↵
View name to save:	*Type:* **R** ↵ (right side)
First corner:	*Pick:* **D5**
Other corner:	*Pick:* **D6**

Now move from one view to another to observe the View: command in action.

Prompt	Response
Command:	↵
VIEW?/Delete/Restore/Save/Window:	*Type:* **R** ↵ (or *Select:* **Restore** from the menu)
View name to restore:	*Type:* **T** ↵ (top)

You should have the area reserved for the top view on your screen now. Complete the lines of the top view in this area using the commands you used to draw Figures 8–2 and 8–4. Take your measurements from Figure 8–6. Then use the Zoom: Dynamic to display an area that shows both the front and top views. Use the top view to line up the surfaces in the front as you complete that view. Once the views are placed, you will be able to move quickly from one view to another by using the View:-Restore command. After you have completed the top and front views, Restore the area for the right side view and use the following sequence of steps to draw that view. (After you have completed the right side view, you may need to return to the front and top views to add center lines and hidden lines to those views.)

Draw the Right Side View

Step 4. Draw object lines for the right side view.

Prompt	Response
Command: <ORTHO ON> <Coords ON>	

Zoom in closer for a better view of the drawing.

Prompt	Response
	Zoom: (from the DISPLAY menu or *Select:* **Zoom: Window** from the pull-downs.)
All/Center/Dynamics:	*Pick:* **D1** (Figure 8–8)
Other corner:	*Pick:* **D2**
Command:	*Type:* **L** ↵ (or *Select:* **Line:** from the screen DRAW 1 menu)

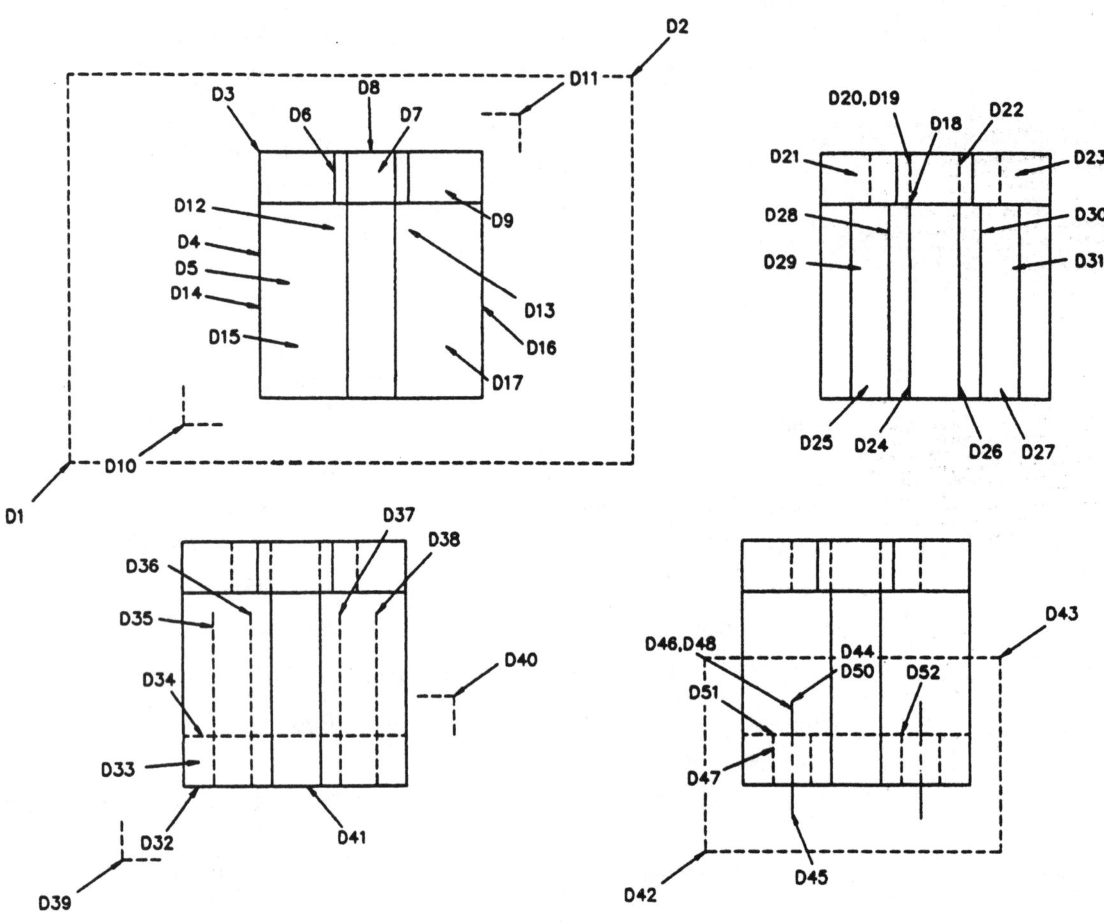

FIGURE 8–8
Drawing the Right Side View

LINE from point:	*Pick:* **D3**
To point:	*Type:* **@60<0** ↵
To point:	*Type:* **@63<270** ↵
To point:	*Type:* **@60<180** ↵
To point:	*Type:* **C** ↵ (This response closes the figure back to the beginning point.)
Command:	

Now, use the Offset: command to draw the other vertical lines in the side view.

Prompt	Response
	Offset:
OFFSET distance or Through <Through>:	*Type:* **20** ↵

Select object to offset:	*Pick:* **D4** (Notice the change in the line.)
Side to offset:	*Pick:* **D5** (Notice how the line has been copied and moved 20 mm to the right.)
Select object to offset:	(Pick the new line just created.)
	Pick: **D6**
Side to offset:	*Pick:* **D7**
Select object to offset:	↵

Now use the Offset: command to create a horizontal line.

Prompt	**Response**
Command:	↵ (Or press the space bar; this returns the prompt to the last command entered: Offset:)
Offset distance or Through <20.0000>:	*Type:* **13** ↵
Select object to offset:	*Pick:* **D8**
Side to offset:	*Pick:* **D9**
Select object to offset:	↵
Command:	

Now the two vertical lines may be trimmed to meet the horizontal line.

Prompt	**Response**
	Trim:
Select cutting edges: . . .	
Select objects:	

At this point the target cursor should appear on the screen. This cursor may be used to select objects. A window can also be used to select objects.

Prompt	**Response**
	Pick: **D10**
Other corner:	*Pick:* **D11**
Select object:	↵
Select object to trim >/Project/Edge/ Undo:	*Pick:* **D12** (The bottom part of this line is now gone in Figure 8–8.)
Select object to trim:	*Pick:* **D13**
Select object to trim:	↵

At this point, the screen may be cluttered with picked marks. Use the Redraw: command to clean up the screen.

Prompt	**Response**
Command:	**Redraw:** (or press F7 twice)
Command:	**Offset:**
Offset distance or Through <13.00>:	*Type:* **23.5** ↵
Select object to offset:	*Pick:* **D14**
Side to offset:	*Pick:* **D15**
Select object to offset:	*Pick:* **D16**
Side to offset:	*Pick:* **D17**
Select object to offset:	↵

Step 5. Use the Break: command to divide the lines describing the web lines into partially hidden and partially solid lines. (The Chprop: command can be used to put part of the line on the hidden layer.)

Note: You may also select Break—then 1 Point from the Modify menu on the menu bar.

Prompt	Response
Command:	**Break:**
Select object:	**Sel Pt**

You may need to turn snap off (F9) in order to pick the line.

Prompt	Response
Select object:	*Type:* **INT** ↵ (or *Select:* INTersec from **** (Osnap menu) on the screen menu)
_int of:	*Pick:* **D18**

Notice target box; align it so that it includes the intersection of two lines.

Prompt	Response
Command:	*Type:* **CHPROP** ↵
Select objects:	*Pick:* **D19**
1 selected, 1 found. Select objects:	↵
Properties/<change point>:	*Type:* **LA** ↵ (LAyer or select from the screen menu)
New layer <1>:	

Now you can enter layer 3, which is the hidden Layer.

Prompt	Response
	Type: **3** ↵↵

Notice that the layer has changed color but still looks like continuous linetype. This is because the line scale is too small. It can be changed by using the Ltscale: command.

Step 6. Change the linetype scale (Ltscale).

Note: The length of the line segments must increase when using metric values.

Prompt	Response
Command:	*Type:* **LTSCALE** ↵
_ltscale New scale factor <1.0000>:	

Entering a decimal value of less than 1 will result in a smaller line segment.

Note: Ltscale may also be selected from Preferences on the OPTIONS menu on the menu bar (Global Linetype Scale).

Prompt	Response
	Type: **25.4** ↵ (Try 15 if your hidden and center lines appear solid. The linetype scale is affected by the size of the drawing.)

The line is now hidden and on the proper layer. Repeat Step 5 for other hidden lines on the web. Remember to leave the snap function (F9) off until you are ready to go to the next step. Add the other hidden lines by offsetting the hidden lines just drawn.

Step 7. Add other hidden lines.

Prompt	Response
Command:	**Offset:**
Offset distance or Through <Through>:	*Type:* **10.5** ↵
Select object to offset:	*Pick:* **D20** (same as D19)
Side to offset:	*Pick:* **D21**
Select object to offset:	*Pick:* **D22**
Side to offset:	*Pick:* **D23**
Select object to offset:	↵↵

The Offset: command may be used again for creating the bottom hidden lines, a procedure similar to Step 5.

Prompt	Response
Offset distance or Through <10.5000>:	*Type:* **5.5** ↵

This is one edge of the holes in the bottom portion.

Prompt	Response
Select object to offset:	*Pick:* **D24**
Side to offset:	*Pick:* **D25**
Select object to offset:	*Pick:* **D26**
Side to offset:	*Pick:* **D27**
Select object to offset:	↵↵
Offset distance or Through <5.500>:	*Type:* **10** ↵

Change the offset distance for the other edge of the hole.

Prompt	Response
Select object to offset:	*Pick:* **D28**
Side to offset:	*Pick:* **D29**
Select object to offset:	*Pick:* **D30**
Side to offset:	*Pick:* **D31**
Select object to offset:	↵↵

Now offset the horizontal hidden line in the view. (It will not be hidden at this time.)

Prompt	Response
Offset distance or Through <10.0000>:	*Type:* **13** ↵
Select object to offset:	*Pick:* **D32**
Side to offset:	*Pick:* **D33**
Select object to offset:	↵↵
Command:	

Step 8. Trim these lines.

Prompt	Response
	Trim:
Select cutting edge(s). . . . Select objects:	*Pick:* **D34**
Select objects:	↵
Select objects to trim:	*Pick:* **D35**
Select objects to trim:	*Pick:* **D36**
Select object to trim:	*Pick:* **D37**
Select object to trim:	*Pick:* **D38**
Select object to trim:	↵

Step 9. Use the Change: command to make the solid lines hidden. Change the lines to the hidden layer.

Prompt	Response
Command:	**Change:**
Select objects:	*Pick:* **D39**
Other corner:	*Pick:* **D40**

Prompt	Response
Select objects:	*Type:* **R** ↵ (or *Select:* **REMOVE** from the screen menu)
Remove Objects:	*Pick:* **D41** (This removes the bottom line from the lines selected to be changed.)
Remove Objects:	↵
Properties/<Change point>:	*Type:* **P** ↵
Change what property (Color/Elev/LAyer/LType/ltScale/Thickness)?	*Type:* **LA** ↵
New layer <1>:	*Type:* **3** ↵↵

Add Center Lines

The drawing is complete except for the center lines. Create a new layer for the center lines called 5.

Step 10. Add the following layer and set it current.

LAYER NAME	COLOR	LINETYPE
5	BLUE	CENTER

Step 11. Create center lines and move them to their correct positions.

Prompt	Response
Command:	**Zoom:**
All/Center/Dynamic/Extents/Left/Previous/Window/<Scale(x)>:	*Pick:* **D42**
Other corner:	*Pick:* **D43**
Command:	**Line:**
LINE from point:	

Toggle the snap key on.

Prompt	Response
	Pick: **D44**

Estimate the point at which the center line should start. Be sure snap is off and ortho is on.

Prompt	Response
To point:	*Pick:* **D45**
To point:	↵

Notice that the line is probably not centered on the hole. The Dist: command will give a distance between lines and points. Use the Dist: command to determine the position of the centered line.

Prompt	Response
Command:	**Dist:** (from Inquiry on the ASSIST menu)
Dist first point:	**Osnap-MIDpoint**
Midpoint of:	*Pick:* **D46**
Second point:	**Osnap-PERpendicular**

Perpend to:	*Pick:* **D47**
5.2928	↵
Command:	**Move:**

Once Move: has been selected as the command, move the center line to its correct location. In the case described previously, the procedure would then continue as follows:

Prompt	Response
Select objects:	*Pick:* **D48**
Select objects:	↵ (or space bar)
Base point or displacement:	*Pick:* **D49** (Pick anywhere.)
Second point of displacement:	*Type:* **@.2928<180** ↵

Now use the Dist: command in the same manner as you did before to check the position of the center line. If the center line is not 5 mm from the left vertical dotted line, move it to that location.

You could have used ID and relative coordinates to draw the centerlines. This method was used to introduce the DISTance command.

Now the center line can be copied to the other hole.

Prompt	Response
Command:	*Type:* **CP** ↵ (or *Select:* **Copy:** from the MODIFY menu)
Select objects:	*Pick:* **D50**
Select objects:	↵
<Base point or displacement>/Multiple:	*Type:* **INT** (*or Select:* **INTersec** from **** (Osnap) screen menu)
Intersec of:	*Pick:* **D51**
Second point of displacement:	**INT** (from the Osnap menu), then *Pick:* **D52** ↵

Complete the Drawing, Plot and Save It

Note: See Chapter 6 for information on plotting.

You have now completed the right side view.

1. Return to the front and top views to create hidden lines and center lines in those views.
2. After you have completed all three views, print the drawing at a scale of 1 = 1 on a 17″ × 11″ sheet of paper or plot to fit on an 11″ × 8½″ sheet.

- □ Be sure to select the MM button on the Plot Configuration dialog box and B = Paper Size if you plot full size (1 = 1).
- □ Select MM and A = Paper Size if you plot to fit.

3. Save the drawing in two places and exit from AutoCAD.

GRIPS

The Grips feature allows you to edit existing entities more quickly than with any of the menu methods. Begin by drawing the entities described next.

EXERCISE 8–4 DRAWING USING GRIPS

Set Up the Drawing

Step 1. On Your Own:

1. *Select* New. . . from the File menu on the menu bar and name the drawing 8–4 (your initials).

2. Make the following settings:

GRID: .2
SNAP: .05
LIMITS: Lower left corner: 0,0
Upper right corner: 8.5,11

Draw Shapes

Step 2. Draw basic shapes.

FIGURE 8–9
Draw Line, Circle, Polyline, and Polygon

Prompt	Response
Command:	*Type:* **L** ↵
From point:	Pick a point in the approximate location shown in Figure 8–9.
To point:	*Type:* **@2<45** ↵
To point:	↵
Command:	*Type:* **C** ↵
_Circle 3P/2P/TTR/<Center point>:	(Pick a point in the approximate location shown in Figure 8–9.)
Diameter/<Radius>:	*Type:* **.5** ↵
Command:	*Type:* **PL** ↵
From point:	Pick a point to begin the polyline in the approximate location shown. (The polyline is the jagged shape.)
Arc/Close/Halfwidth/Length/Undo/ Width/<Endpoint of line>:	Pick five points to approximate the shape shown.
Command:	*Type:* **POLYGON** ↵ (from the keyboard or select from the DRAW 1 menu)
Number of sides <4>:	*Type:* **6** ↵
Edge/<Center of polygon>:	Pick a point in the approximate location shown for the hexagon.
Inscribed in circle/Circumscribed about circle (I/C) <I>:	*Type:* **C** ↵
Radius of circle:	*Type:* **.5** ↵

Use Grips

Step 3. Make sure grips are enabled.

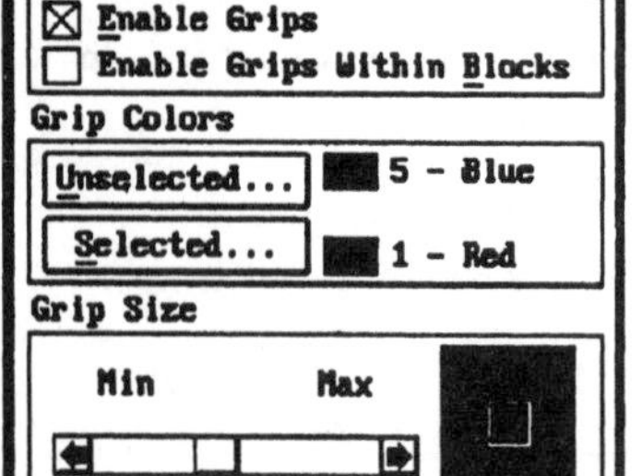

FIGURE 8–10
Enable Grips

Prompt	Response
Command:	Pick Grips from the Options menu on the menu bar (Figure 8–10). Be sure there is an X in the Enable Grips box. If there isn't, pick the box. Leave everything else as it is unless you want to change the size or color of the Grips indicators. When you are through, pick OK.

Note: The status line in the upper left of your display shows the grip mode as you toggle from one mode to another.

Step 4. Use Grips to Stretch, Copy, Move, Change Circle Radius, Rotate, Scale, and Mirror entities.

Prompt	Response
Command:	Pick the line, as shown in Figure 8–11.

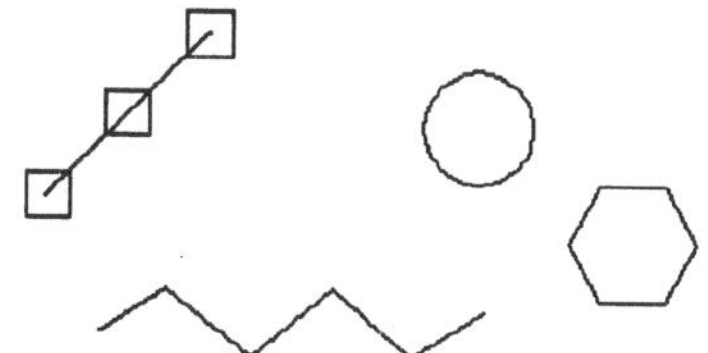

FIGURE 8–11
Pick the Line to Display Grips

Prompt	Response
Command:	Pick the grip on the top end of the line.
STRETCH	
<Stretch to point>/Base point/Copy/ Undo/eXit:	*Type:* **@1<45** ↵

You have now changed the length of the line by 1″ in the 45° direction. You could have picked the new point or used absolute or relative coordinates to designate the new endpoint of the line.

Prompt	Response
Command:	Pick the grip on the midpoint of the line.
STRETCH	
<Stretch to point>/Base point/Copy/ Undo/eXit:	Hold down the shift key while you pick two points to copy the line twice, as shown in Figure 8–12 (multiple copy).
Command:	Press Esc twice to eliminate grips from the line.
Command:	Pick a point on the circumference of the circle to enable grips. Pick any one of the five grips on the circle.
STRETCH	
<Stretch to point>/Base point/Copy/ Undo/eXit:	↵
MOVE	
<Move to point>/Base point/Copy/ Undo/eXit:	Pick a point approximately 1″ above the circle to move it to a new location.

FIGURE 8–12
Multiple Copy Using Grips

Once again, you could have used absolute, relative, or polar coordinates to specify the new point. If you want to specify a base point first, you can type B↵ from the keyboard and then press ↵ again to toggle to the Move mode.

Prompt	Response
Command:	Pick the grip on the right quadrant on the circumference of the circle.
STRETCH	
<Stretch to point>/Base point/Copy/ Undo/eXit	*Type:* **@.5,0** ↵

You have now enlarged the radius of the circle .5″ using relative coordinates (Figure 8–13).

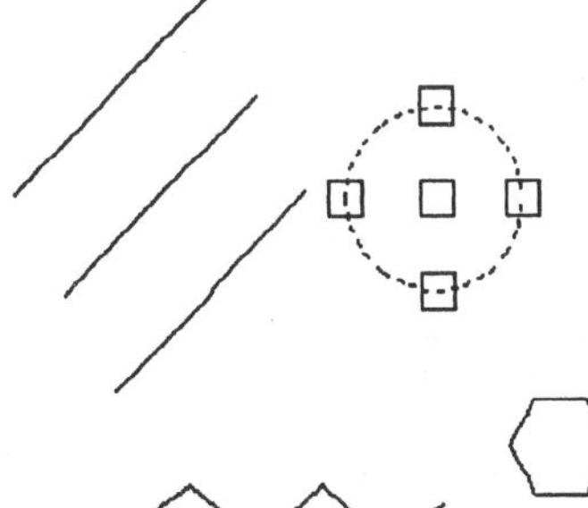

FIGURE 8–13
Enlarge the Radius Using Grips

Prompt	Response
Command:	Press Esc twice to eliminate grips from the circle.
Command:	Pick the polyline (Figure 8–14). Pick the grip on the right end of the polyline. Press ↵ twice.
ROTATE	
<Rotation angle>/Base point/Copy/ Undo/Reference/eXit:	*Type:* **90** ↵
Command:	Pick the top grip on the polyline. Press ↵ three times.

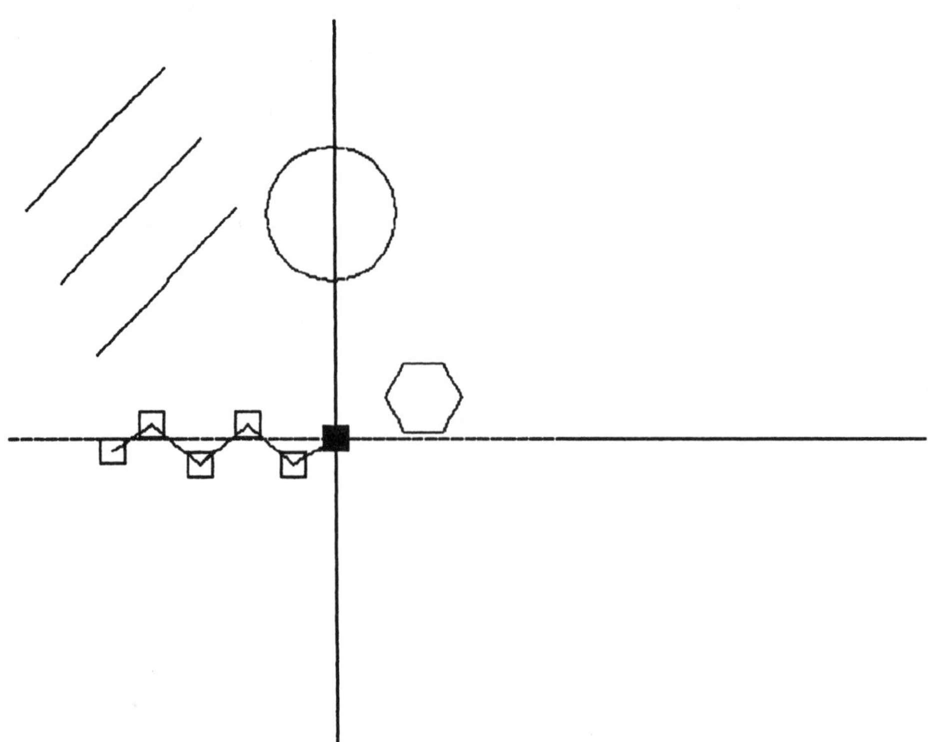

FIGURE 8–14
Rotate Using Grips

Prompt	Response
SCALE	
<Scale factor>/Base point/Copy/Undo/ Reference/eXit:	*Type:* **R** ↵
Reference length <1.000>	*Type:* **.375** ↵
SCALE	
<New length>/Base point/Copy/Undo/ Reference/eXit:	*Type:* **.5** ↵

You have changed the size of the polyline by specifying that anything that was .375 on the original polyline should be .5 on the enlarged polyline. You could have done the same thing by typing a scale factor instead of R to obtain a reference scale factor.

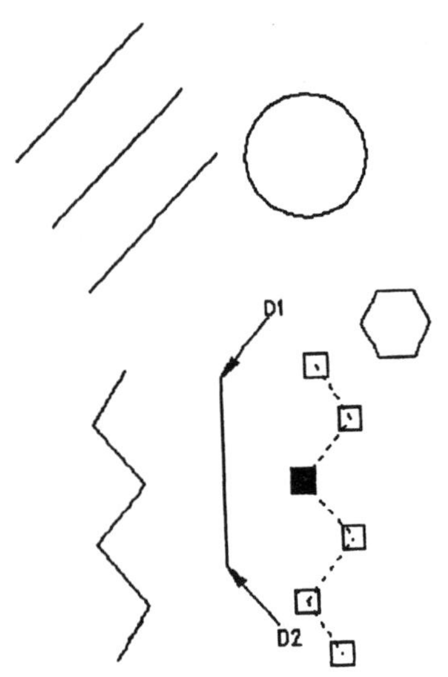

FIGURE 8–15
Mirror Using Grips

Prompt	Response
Command:	Pick the third grip from the top of the polyline (Figure 8–15). (Any grip is OK.)
	Press ↵ four times.
MIRROR	
<Second point>/Base point/Copy/ Undo/eXit:	*Type:* **B** ↵
Base point:	Hold down the shift key as you pick D1 in the approximate location shown in Figure 8–15.
MIRROR	
<Second point>/Base point/Copy/ Undo/eXit:	Release the shift key and then pick D2. ↵ (Be sure ortho is on so that your mirror line will be exactly vertical.) Press Esc twice.

You can obtain multiple mirrored images by holding down the shift key instead of releasing it before you pick D2, and you can mirror an image and delete the original image by not holding down the shift key at all.

Print and Save the Drawing

Step 5. Print 8–4 on a vertical 8.5″ × 11″ sheet.
Step 6. Save your drawing in two places and exit.

This concludes the exercise on grips. A little practice using grips in your AutoCAD work will increase your speed and make drawing a little simpler.

USE OF SECTIONAL DRAWINGS

Sectional drawings are used to show the internal construction of parts (Figure 8–16) or external features that cannot be easily understood with external views (Figure 8–17).

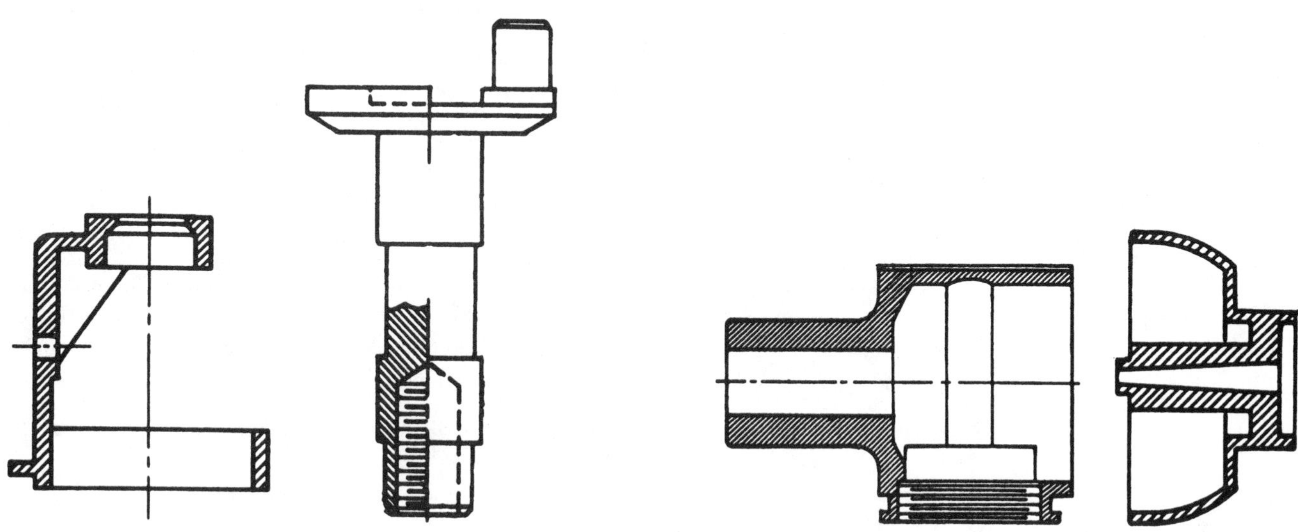

FIGURE 8–16
Internal Construction

Sectional drawings are used not only to show someone how to make a part but also to show someone how several parts function or how to assemble parts (Figure 8–18). The construction of sectional views is reviewed for your information in the following paragraphs. If you need further information regarding sectional views, consult any good technical drawing textbook.

FIGURE 8–17
External Features Shown in Section

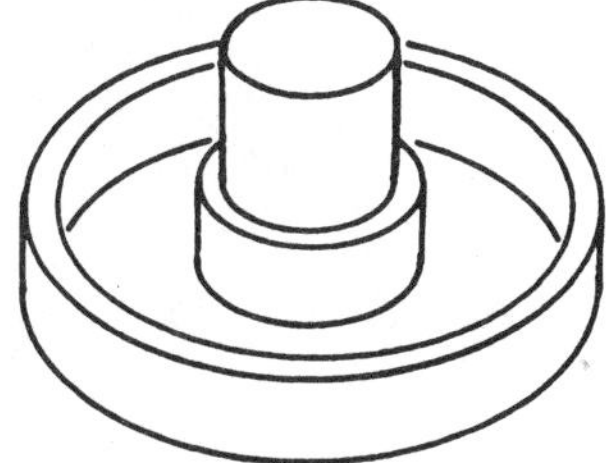

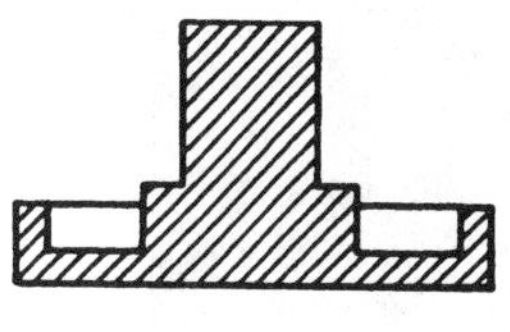

FIGURE 8–18
Assembly Drawing

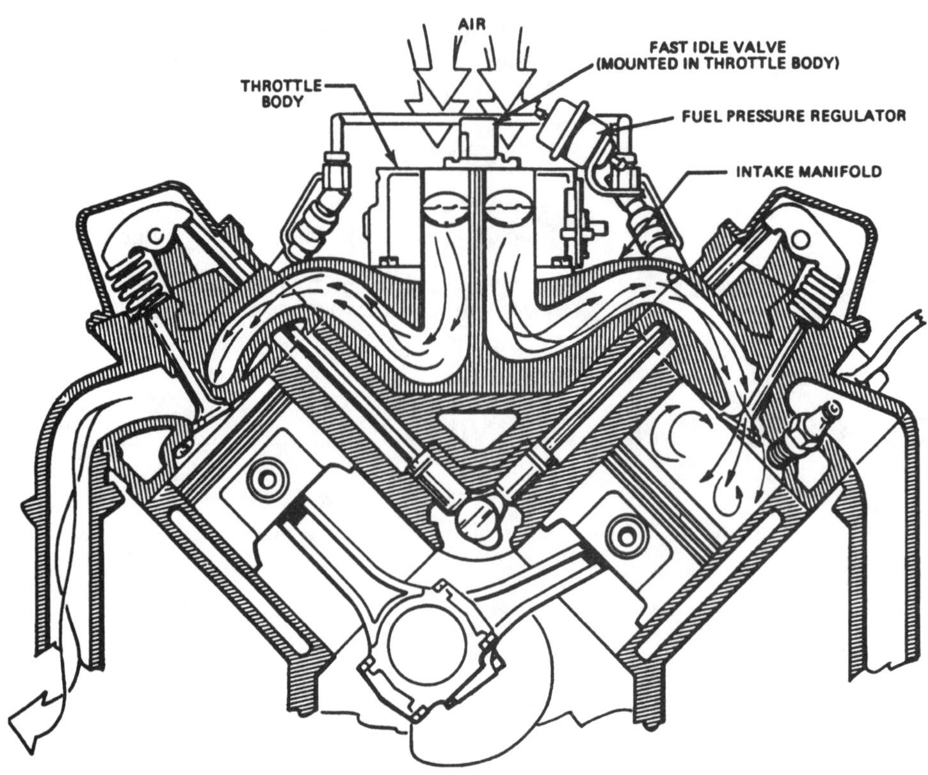

Constructing a Sectional View

Sectional views are easy to construct if you follow a simple series of steps. These steps are shown in Figure 8–19. The object shown in Figure 8–19 is a rather complex shape. Its features could be misunderstood if only external views were used. To clear up any misunderstanding, a sectional view is chosen. To draw the sectional view, use the following steps.

Step 1. Decide which view would best show the hidden feature. In your mind, cut off the part that is hiding the feature.

Step 2. Throw away the part you cut off and do not think of it again.

Step 3. Look into the part that is left.

Step 4. Draw the shape of what you see. Place the sectional view in the standard view arrangement; for example, right side, left side, top, bottom.

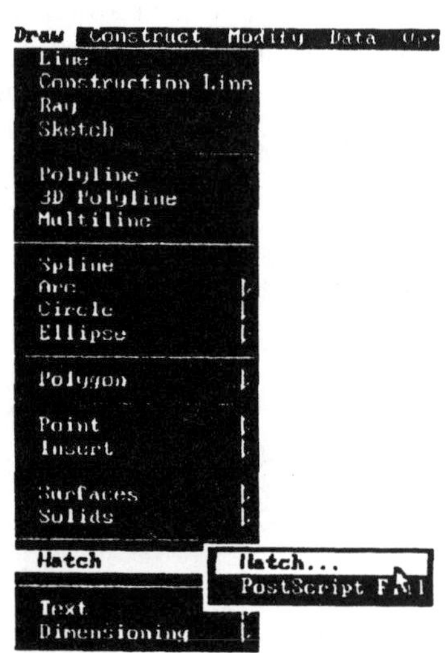

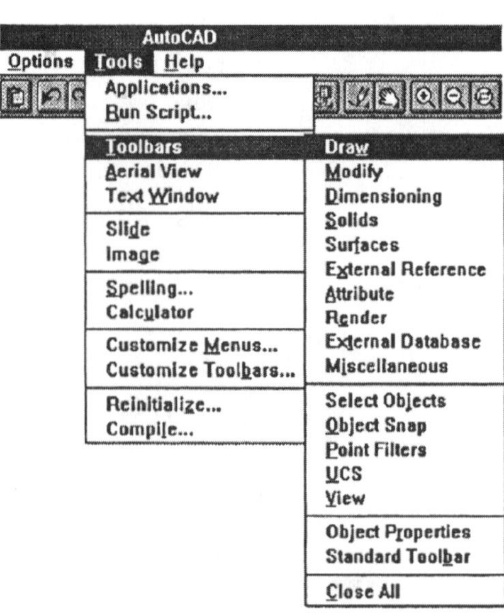

FIGURE 8–19
Constructing a Sectional Drawing

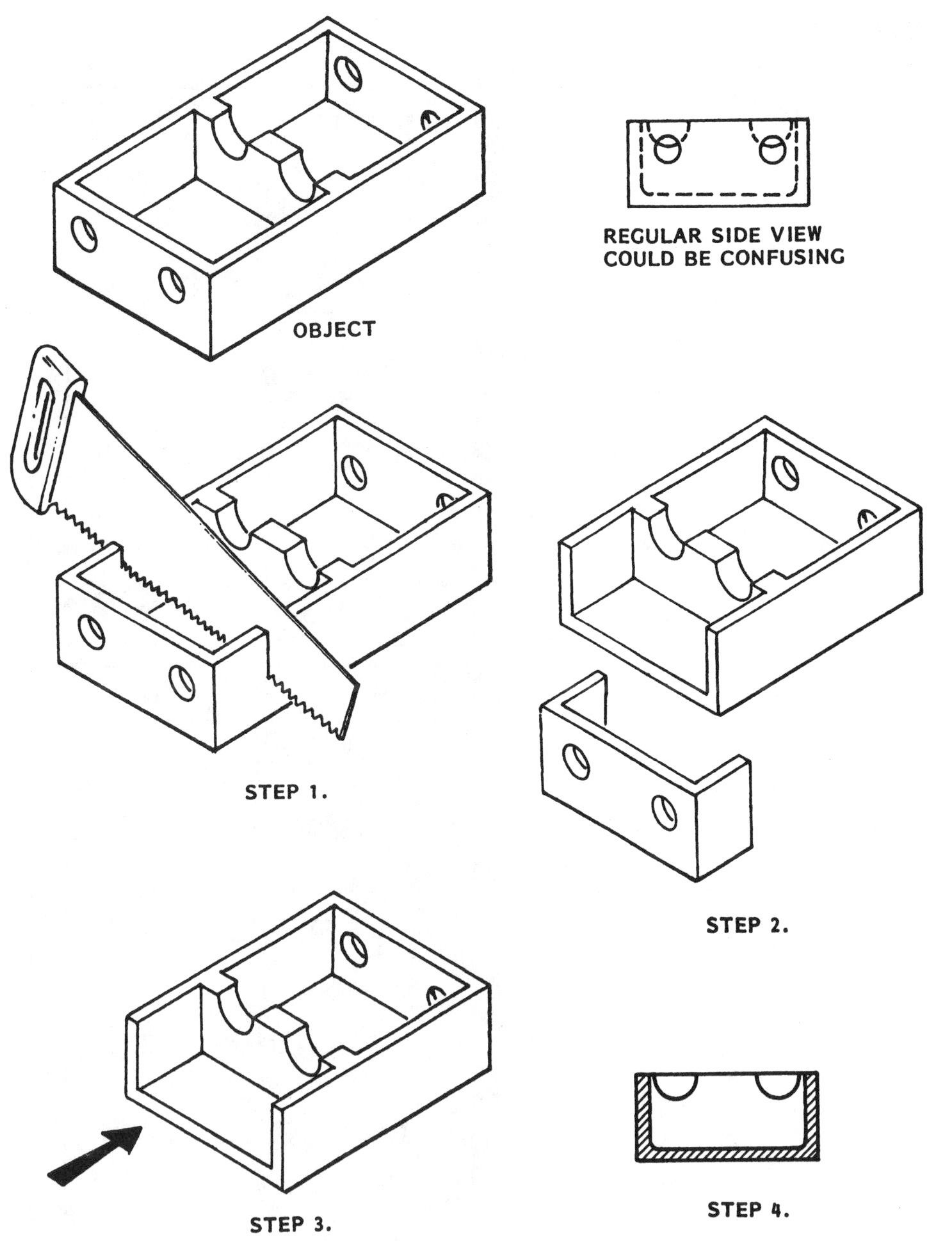

Occasionally, sections are placed away from the other views to show details. Put section or crosshatch lines on the part that was cut. You can think of putting saw marks on the part of the object that the saw actually touched. Section lines are often drawn at a 45° angle and are spaced approximately 1⁄10″ apart. They may be spaced wider apart on very large drawings.

Hatch Patterns

Section lining in AutoCAD can take many forms. You will find icons showing the standard patterns in the Boundary Hatch dialog box.

In this chapter you will use these patterns:

U: the standard equally spaced solid lines
A curved line symbolizing wood
MUDST: a standard for symbolizing concrete
EARTH: a standard for symbolizing the earth
Other patterns of your choice under hatch patterns

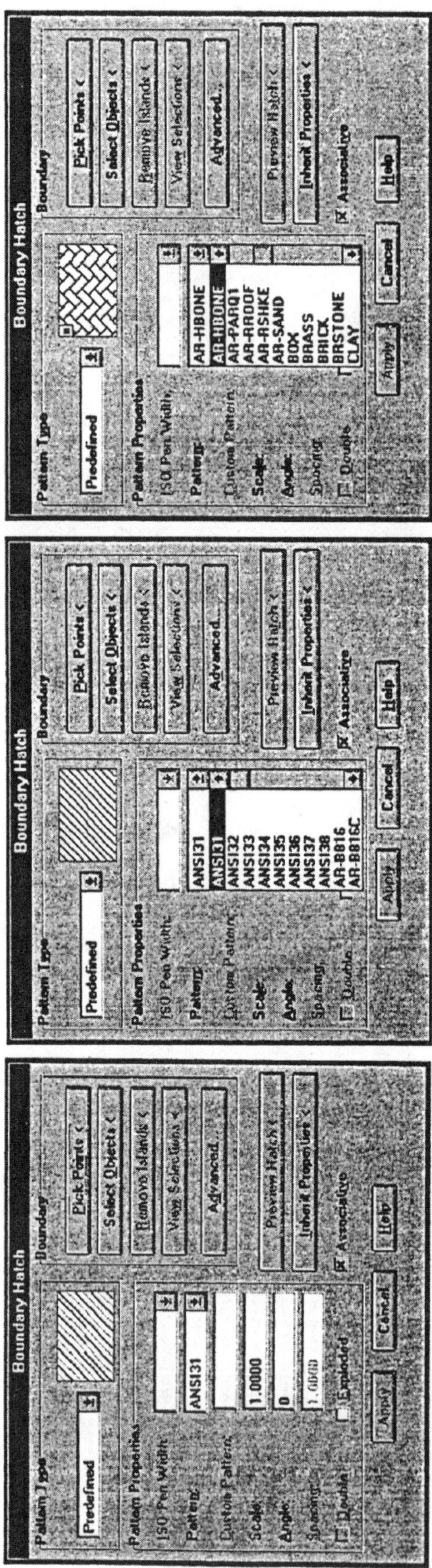
Boundary Hatch
Pattern Type
Predefined
Boundary
Pick Points <
Select Objects <
Remove Islands <
View Selections <
Advanced...
Preview Hatch <
Inherit Properties <
Associative
Pattern Properties
ISO Pen Width:
Pattern:
ANSI31
Custom Pattern:
Scale:
1.0000
Angle:
0
Spacing:
1.0000
Double
Exploded
Apply
Cancel
Help
Boundary Hatch
ANSI31
ANSI32
ANSI33
ANSI34
ANSI35
ANSI36
ANSI37
ANSI38
AR-B816
AR-B816C
Boundary Hatch
AR-HBONE
AR-PARQ1
AR-RROOF
AR-RSHKE
AR-SAND
BOX
BRASS
BRICK
BRSTONE
CLAY

Showing Hatch Patterns in the Boundary Hatch Dialog Box

The following illustration shows how to show the pattern for any of the predefined hatch patterns in AutoCAD:

Step 1. Pick Hatch from the menu. The picture on the left on page 160.

Step 2. Pick the down arrow on the Pattern: button. The picture in the center appears.

Step 3. Pick the slider bar in the Pattern: button until you find the pattern you want to view. Pick the pattern, and the new pattern appears in the Pattern Type area, as shown in the picture on the right in the same figure.

Other Buttons and Features of the Boundary Hatch Dialog Box

ISO Pen Width: If you select one of the 14 ISO (International Organization of Standardization) patterns at the bottom of the list of hatch patterns, you can select a pen width for the pattern. Each of these pattern names begins with ISO.

Custom Pattern: This button shows a custom pattern name. This option is available when Custom is selected in the Pattern Type box.

Scale: This allows you to enlarge or shrink the hatch pattern to fit the drawing. It is not available if you have selected User Defined in the Pattern Type box.

Angle: Allows you to specify an angle for the hatch pattern relative to the X axis of the current UCS. For now only the world UCS is used. Other UCSs will be used in the chapters on 3-D.

Spacing: Allows you to specify the space between lines on a user-defined hatch pattern.

Double When you pick this button so that an X appears in it, the area is hatched with a second set of lines at 90° to the first hatch pattern.

Exploded When you pick this button so that an X appears in it, the hatch pattern is applied as individual line segments instead of as a single entity. If you think you may have an overlapping hatch pattern, you should bring in the pattern exploded and then use the Trim: command to correct the overlap.

Pick Points < Allows you to pick points inside a boundary to specify the area to be hatched.

Select Objects < Allows you to select the outside edges of the boundary to specify the area to be hatched.

Remove Islands < Allows you to remove from the boundary set objects defined as islands by the Pick Points option. You cannot remove the outer boundary.

View Selections < Displays the currently defined boundary set. This option is not available when no selection or boundary has been made.

Advanced. . . Displays the Advanced Options dialog box shown below.

Preview Hatch < Allows you to preview the hatch pattern before you apply it to the drawing.

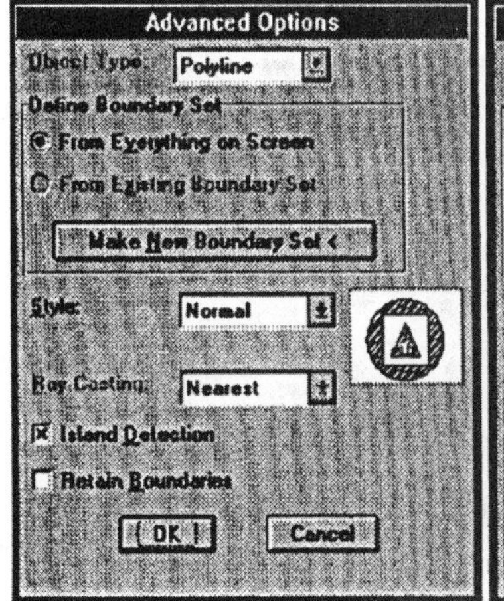

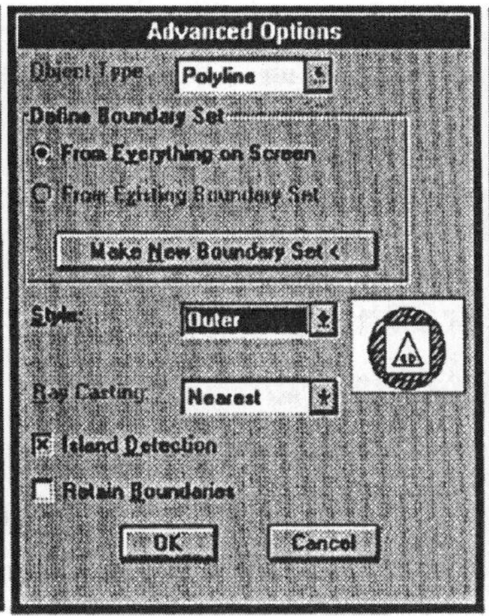

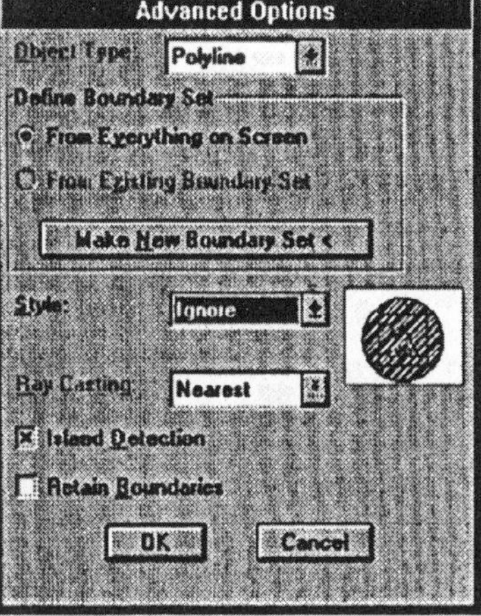

Inherit Properties < Allows you to pick an existing hatch pattern to specify the properties of that pattern. The pattern picked must be associative.

Associative When an X appears in this button, the hatch pattern stretches when the area that has been hatched is stretched.

Apply Allows you to apply the hatch pattern to the drawing.

Advanced Options

When you pick the Advanced. . . button, the Advanced Options dialog box appears:

Object Type: Controls the type of the new boundary object. When the boundary is created, AutoCAD uses a region or polyline. For now this box should read Polyline.

Define Boundary Set—From Everything on Screen When you select this option, a boundary set is created from everything that is visible on the screen.

Define Boundary Set—From Existing Boundary Set When you pick this button, the current boundary set is selected. If you have just entered the Boundary Hatch dialog box, this option is not available because there is no current boundary set.

Style:

Hatch style options:

Normal When style is set to Normal (and a selection set is composed of areas inside other areas), alternating areas are hatched as shown in the Advanced Options dialog box on the left.

Outer When style is set to Outer (and a selection set is composed of areas inside other areas), only the outer area is hatched as shown in the Advanced Options dialog box in the center.

Ignore When style is set to Ignore (and a selection set is composed of areas inside other areas), all areas are hatched as shown in the Advanced Options dialog box on the right.

Ray Casting Controls the way AutoCAD defines the hatch boundary. Ray casting is available only if Island Detection is not selected. Usually the Nearest option produces the desired result. You may also specify positive and negative X and Y directions.

Island Detection Specifies whether objects within the outermost boundary are used as boundary objects. These internal objects are known as *islands*.

Retain Boundaries Specifies whether or not the boundary objects will remain in your drawing after hatching is completed.

Begin by placing section lines on a single part. There are a few peculiarities of using the Hatch: command that must be addressed. They will be covered as they occur.

To place hatch patterns on a single part:

The given drawing (Figure 8–20) contains a front view and a side view. The side view should be shown as a sectional view. (It will be to your advantage to place hatching on a different layer from the other lines of the drawing.)

EXERCISE 8–5 HATCH A SINGLE PART

Set Up the Drawing

Step 1. On Your Own:

1. Load AutoCAD and select New. . . . Name the drawing 8-5(your initials).
2. Make the following settings:

UNITS: Decimal; 2 digits to the right of the decimal point

LIMITS: Lower left corner: 0,0
Upper right corner: 8.5,11

GRID: .25

SNAP: .125

STYLE: STANDARD; FONT: SIMLPEX; HEIGHT: 0

Create the following layers:

LAYER NAME	COLOR	LINETYPE
1	RED	CONTINUOUS
2	YELLOW	CONTINUOUS
3	GREEN	CONTINUOUS

Set layer 2 current.

Make the Drawing

3. Draw the right side view of Figure 8–20 using the dimensions shown.
4. Set layer 3 as the current layer.

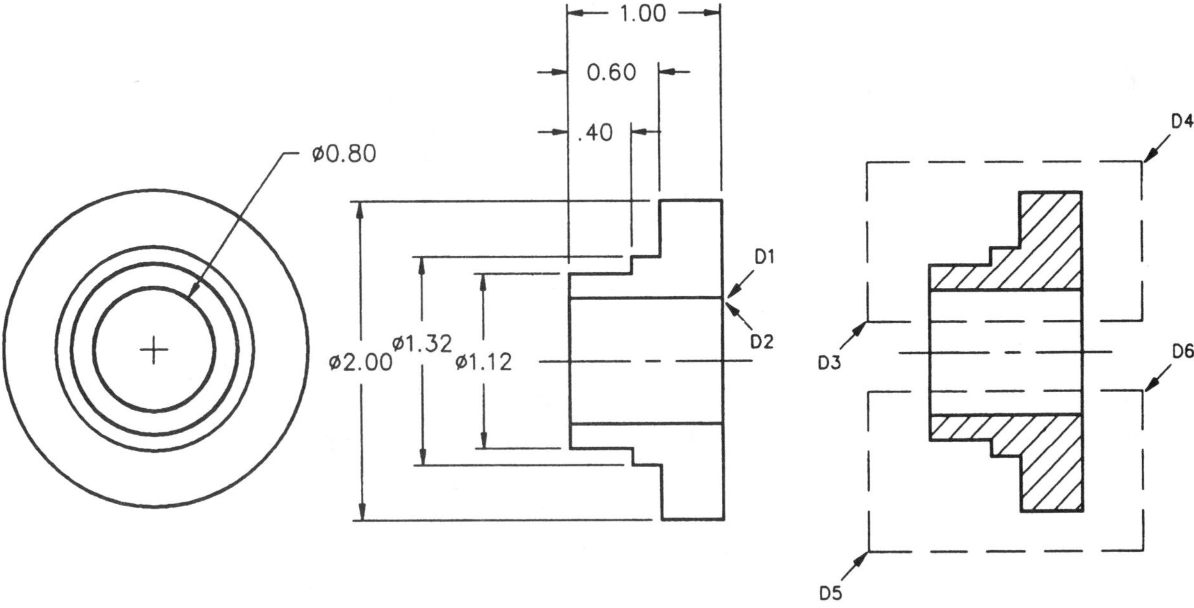

FIGURE 8–20
Placing Hatch Patterns on a Single Part

Hatch the Drawing

Step 2. Prepare the drawing for hatching.

Tip: You may prefer to draw lines on a new layer over the ones existing to form the enclosed area instead of breaking, as described in this procedure. These additional lines may be erased easily with a window after turning off all layers except the one to be erased. This is sometimes faster and allows the line that was to be broken to remain intact.

If the views to be hatched have already been drawn, it is often necessary to break some of the lines so the area to be hatched does not contain lines that extend outside the area. To do this, use the Break: command in this manner:

Prompt	Response
Command:	**Break:**
Select object:	*Pick:* **D1**

Select the vertical line and the first point of the break. You may need to select the line at a point removed from the intersection, enter F, and then pick both break points at the intersection.

Prompt	**Response**
Enter second point (or F for first point):	*Pick:* **D2** (or *Select:* @ from the BREAK menu—@ places the second point at the same place as the first point)

Be sure to perform the break on both vertical lines at the top and bottom areas to be hatched. After both areas to be hatched have been properly prepared, proceed as follows:

Step 3. Hatch the drawing.

Prompt	**Response**
Command:	**Hatch**. . .
The Boundary Hatch dialog box, Figure 8–21, appears:	Pick the Down Arrow in the Pattern Type button.
	Pick User-defined so that it appears in the Pattern Type button as shown.
	Pick the Angle: button, backspace over anything in this box, and *Type:* **315** as shown.
	Pick the Spacing: button, backspace over anything in this box, and *Type:* **.08.**

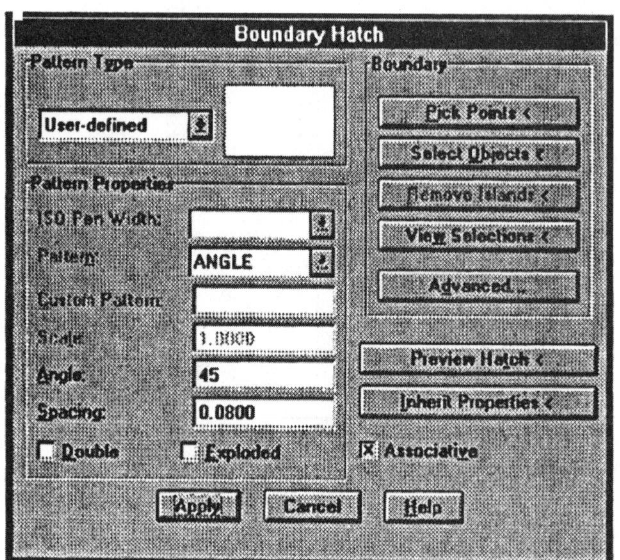

FIGURE 8–21
Boundary Hatch Dialog Box

All other buttons in the Boundary Hatch dialog box should appear as shown in Figure 8–21.

Pick: **Select Objects <**

Prompt	**Response**
Select objects:	*Pick:* **D3** (Figure 8–20)
Other corner:	*Pick:* **D4**
Select objects:	↵
The Boundary Hatch dialog box appears:	*Pick:* **Preview Hatch <**
The Boundary Hatch Continue button appears:	*Pick:* **Continue**
The Boundary Hatch dialog box appears:	*Pick:* **Apply**

The area forming the upper half of the view should be hatched now. Continue as follows:

Prompt	**Response**
Command:	↵

This will activate the Hatch: command again.

Prompt	**Response**
The Boundary Hatch dialog box appears:	*Pick:* **Select Objects <**
Select objects:	*Pick:* **D5**
Other corner:	*Pick:* **D6**
8 found. Select objects:	↵
The Boundary Hatch dialog box appears:	*Pick:* **Apply**

Print and Save the Drawing

Step 4. On Your Own:

1. Print the drawing at 1 to 1 scale in the center of an 8.5 × 11 sheet.
2. Save your drawing in two places and exit.

Both top and bottom halves of the right side view should now be hatched to complete the figure. Now, place some of the same hatch pattern on an assembly section drawing, Figure 8–22.

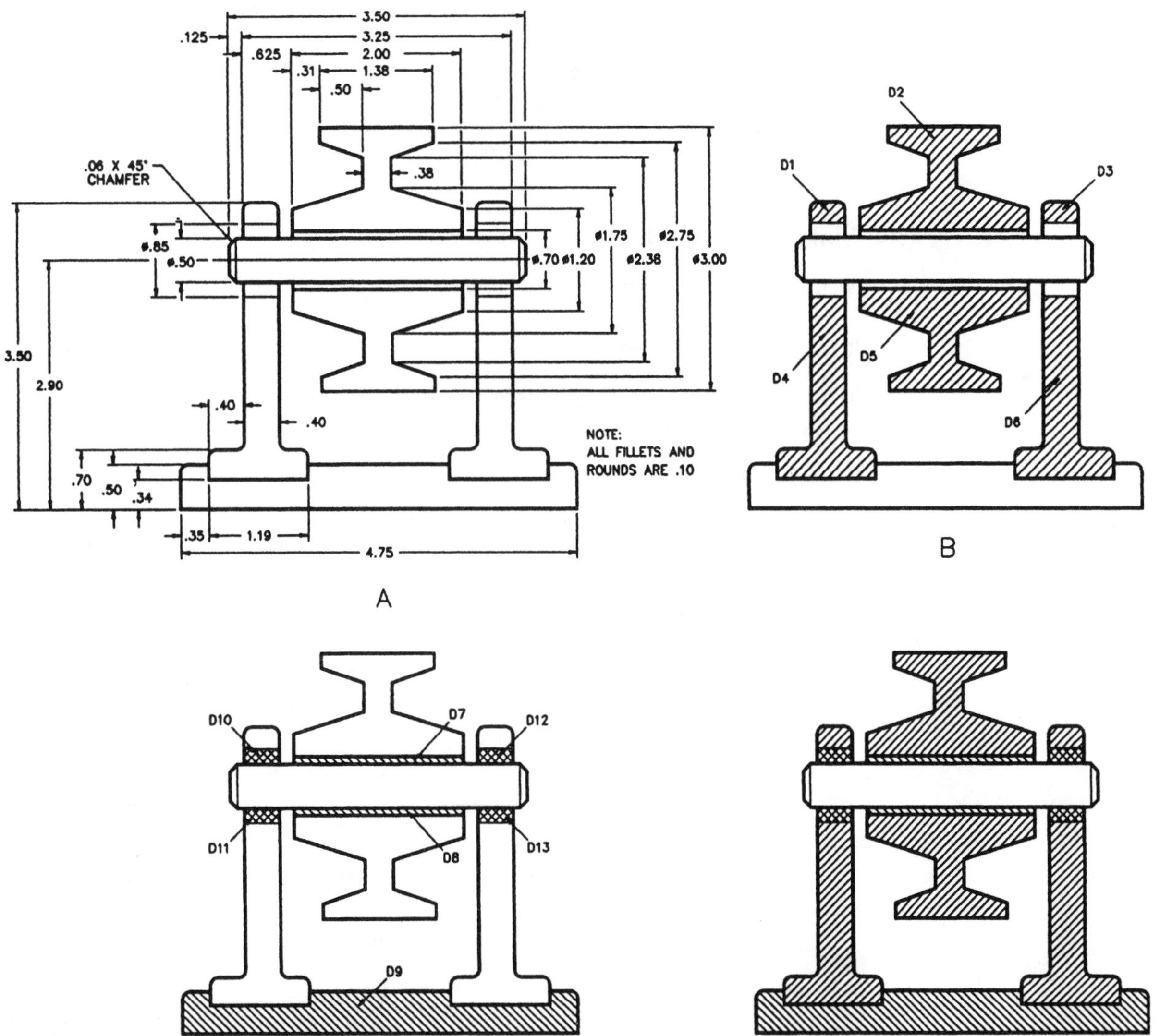

FIGURE 8–22
Placing Hatch Patterns on an Assembly Section Drawing

EXERCISE 8–6
PLACING HATCH PATTERNS ON AN ASSEMBLY SECTION DRAWING

Set Up the Drawing

Step 1. On Your Own:

1. Load AutoCAD, select New. . . , and name the drawing 8–6 (your initials).
2. Make the following settings:

UNITS: Decimal; 2 digits to the right of the decimal point
LIMITS: Lower left corner: 0,0
Upper right corner: 11,8.5
GRID: .25
SNAP: .125
STYLE: STANDARD; FONT: SIMPLEX; HEIGHT: 0
Create the following layers:

LAYER NAME	COLOR	LINETYPE
1	RED	CONTINUOUS
2	YELLOW	CONTINUOUS
3	GREEN	CONTINUOUS

Set layer 2 current.

Make the Drawing

Step 2. Draw the assembly using dimensions shown in Figure 8–22A.

Hatch the Drawing

Step 3. Place 45° hatch lines upward to the right.

Set layer 3 as the current layer.

Prompt	Response
Command:	**Hatch**. . .
The Boundary Hatch dialog box, Figure 8–21 appears:	Pick the Down Arrow in the Pattern Type button. Pick User-defined so that it appears in the Pattern Type button as shown. Pick the Angle: button, backspace over anything in this box, and *Type:* **45** as shown. Pick the Spacing: button, backspace over anything in this box, and *Type:* **.08.**

All other buttons in the Boundary Hatch dialog box should appear as shown in Figure 8–21.

Pick: **Pick Points <**

Prompt	Response
Select internal point:	*Pick:* **D1, D2, D3, D4, D5, and D6** (Figure 8–22B)

Select internal point:	↵
The Boundary Hatch dialog box appears:	*Pick:* **Preview Hatch <**
The Boundary Hatch Continue button appears:	*Pick:* **Continue**
The Boundary Hatch dialog box appears:	*Pick:* **Apply** (if the preview shows the hatching to be correct; if it is not correct, find out what is wrong and correct it.)

Step 4. Place 45° hatch lines downward to the right.

Prompt	Response
Command:	↵
The Boundary Hatch dialog box, Figure 8–23, appears:	Pick the Angle: button. Pick the left side of the 4 in 45. *Type:* − (so that the angle reads −45) ↵

The Angle: button changes to 315 (the same as −45). All other buttons in the Boundary Hatch dialog box should appear as shown in Figure 8–23.

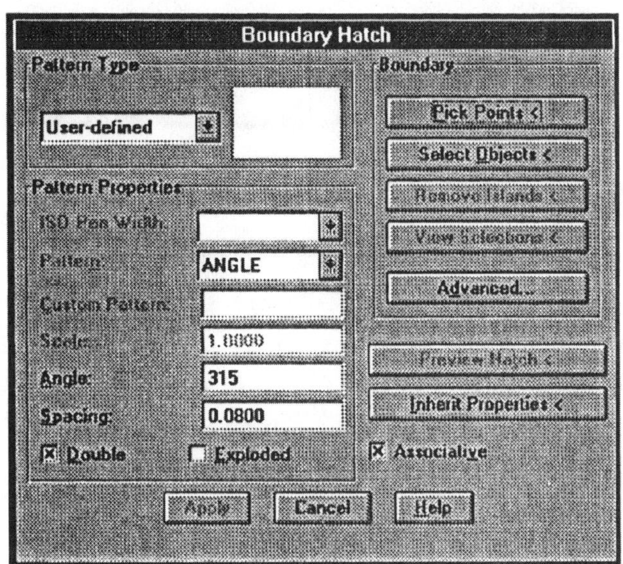

FIGURE 8–23
315 (−45) Angle Hatch

Prompt	Response
	Pick: **Pick Points <**
Select internal point:	*Pick:* **D7, D8, and D9** (Figure 8–22C)
Select internal point:	↵
The Boundary Hatch dialog box appears:	*Pick:* **Apply** (if you are reasonably sure the hatching will be correct; If not, *Pick:* **Preview Hatch <** and proceed as before.)

Step 5. Double hatch the bushings.

Prompt	Response
COMMAND:	↵
The Boundary Hatch dialog box, Figure 8–24, appears:	Pick the Double button so that an X appears in it as shown in Figure 8–24.

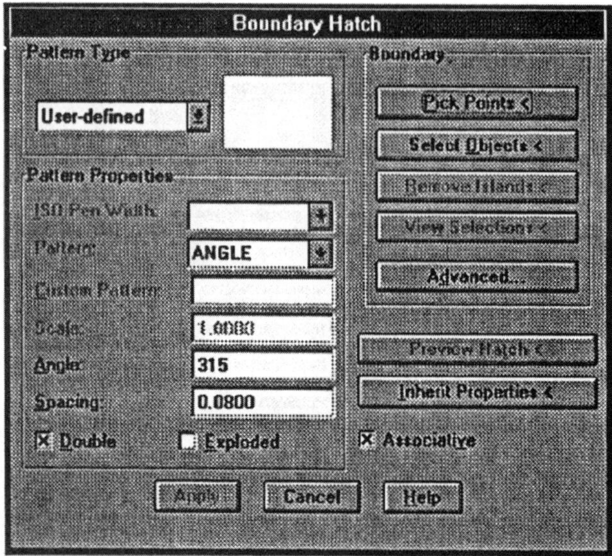

FIGURE 8–24
Double Hatch

All other buttons in the Boundary Hatch dialog box should appear as shown in Figure 8–24.

Prompt	Response
	Pick: **Pick Points <**
Select internal point:	*Pick:* **D10, D11, D12,** and **D13** (Figure 8–22C)
Select internal point:	↵
The Boundary Hatch dialog box appears:	*Pick:* **Apply** (if you are reasonably sure the hatching will be correct; If not, *Pick:* **Preview Hatch <** and proceed as before.)

The complete drawing should now appear with hatching as shown in Figure 8–22D.

Print and Save the Drawing

Step 6. On Your Own:

1. Print the drawing full scale so it is centered in an 11 × 8.5 sheet.
2. Save the drawing in two places and exit.

EXERCISES

8–1. Draw Figure 8–2 on an 11″ × 8½″ sheet of paper using the sequence of steps shown for that figure. Place your name in the lower right corner .50″ to the left and .50″ up from the bottom edge of the sheet. Center the drawing on the paper. *Do not add dimensions.* They will be added in a later chapter.

8–2. Draw Figure 8–4 on an 11″ × 8½″ sheet of paper using the sequence of the steps shown for that figure. Place your name in the lower right corner ½″ to the left and ½″ from the bottom of the sheet. Center the drawing on the paper. *Do not add dimensions.* They will be added in a later chapter.

8–3. Draw Figure 8–6 on an 11″ × 17″ sheet of paper using the sequence of steps described for that figure. Place your name in the lower right corner 12 mm to the left and 12 mm from the bottom of the sheet. Center the drawing on the paper. *Do not add dimensions.*

8–4. Draw Figure 8–15 on an 8½″ × 11″ sheet using the sequence of steps described for that figure.

8–5. Draw Figure 8–20 front and right-side views with the right side as a sectional view, using the sequence of steps described for that figure. Place your name in the lower right corner. *Do not add dimensions.*

8–6. Draw Figure 8–22D on an 11″ × 8.5″ sheet using the sequence of steps described for that figure. Place your name in the lower right corner of the sheet. *Do not add dimensions.*

8–7. Draw three orthographic views of the object shown in Figure 8–25 using the following specifications:

Full scale
17″ × 11″ sheet of paper
Name in lower right corner
Object lines—thick
All other lines and text—thin
No dimensions

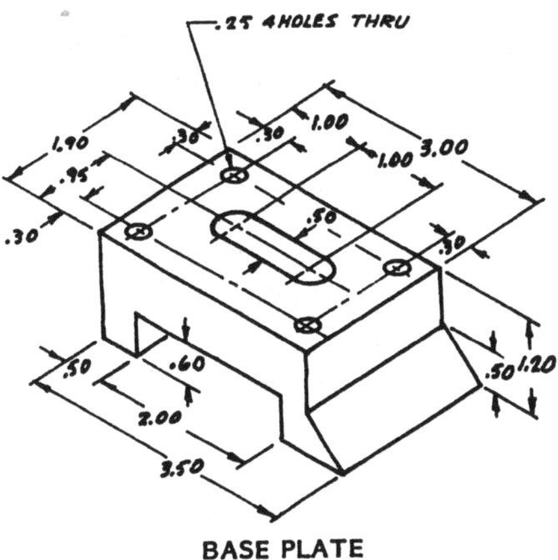

FIGURE 8–26
Exercise 8–8

8–8. Draw three orthographic views of the object shown in Figure 8–26 using the following specifications:

Full scale
17″ × 11″ sheet of paper
Name in lower right corner
Object lines—thick
All other lines and text—thin
No dimensions

For Exercises 8–9 through 8–15, make AutoCAD drawings of Figures 8–27 through 8–33. Use a scale that will allow each drawing to fit on a horizontal paper 11″ × 8.5″. Place your name in the lower right corner. *Do not place any dimensions on any of these drawings.* Special instructions for each exercise are given. Notice that metric measurements are given below the customary decimal (inch) measurements for several figures.

8–9. Draw Figure 8–27 twice size.

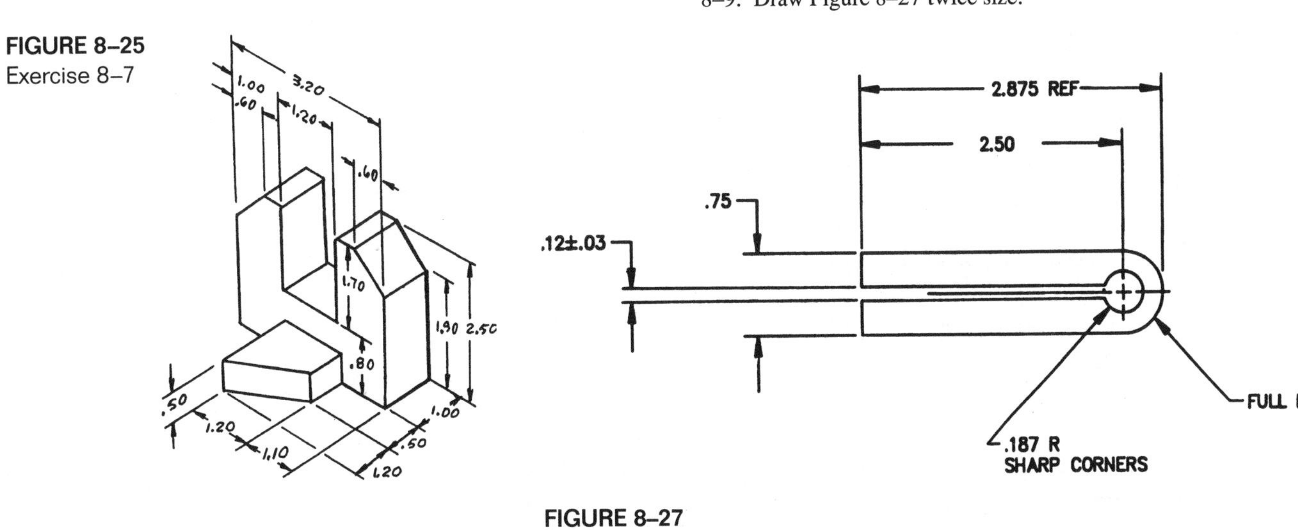

FIGURE 8–25
Exercise 8–7

FIGURE 8–27
Exercise 8–9

8–10. Draw Figure 8–28 twice size. Estimate the size of the chamfer and the screw thread symbol. The proportions should be approximately as shown.

8–11. Draw Figure 8–29 four times size. Draw the radial knurl all around the circular shape. Show 80 lines for the radial knurl.

8–12. Draw Figure 8–30 twice size.

8–13. Draw Figure 8–31 full size. Do not show the hole schedule that appears in the upper right corner.

8–14. Draw Figure 8–32 twice size. You will find Pline: and Offset: helpful on this problem.

8–15. Draw top, front and right side views of Figure 8–33. Center the drawing in a 17″ × 11″ area. Place your name in the lower right corner ½″ in and up from the bottom.

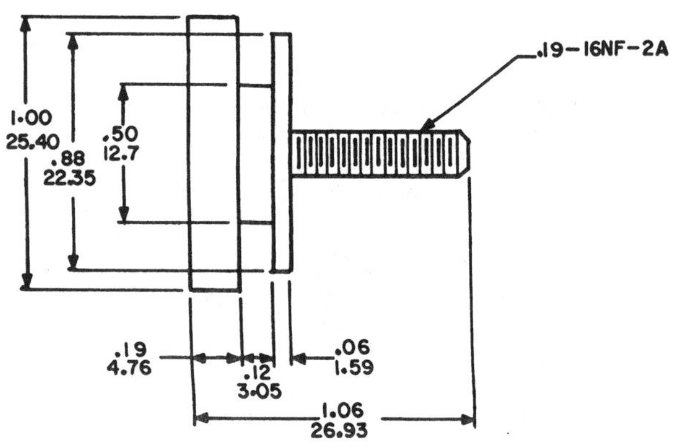

FIGURE 8–28
Exercise 8–10

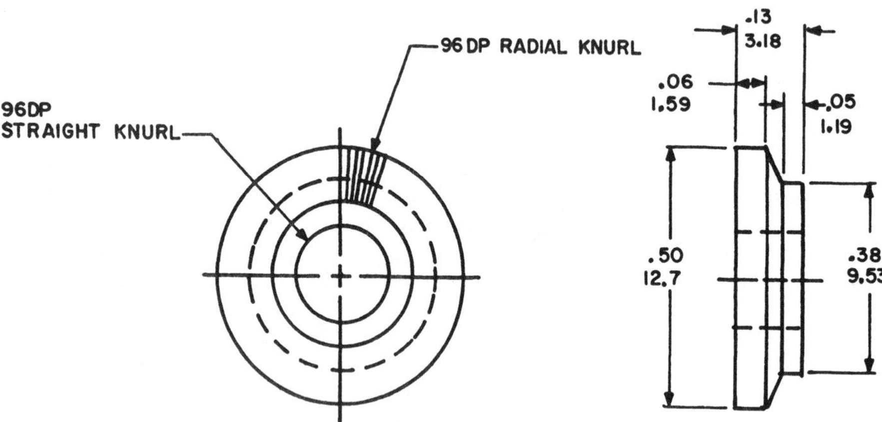

FIGURE 8–29
Exercise 8–11

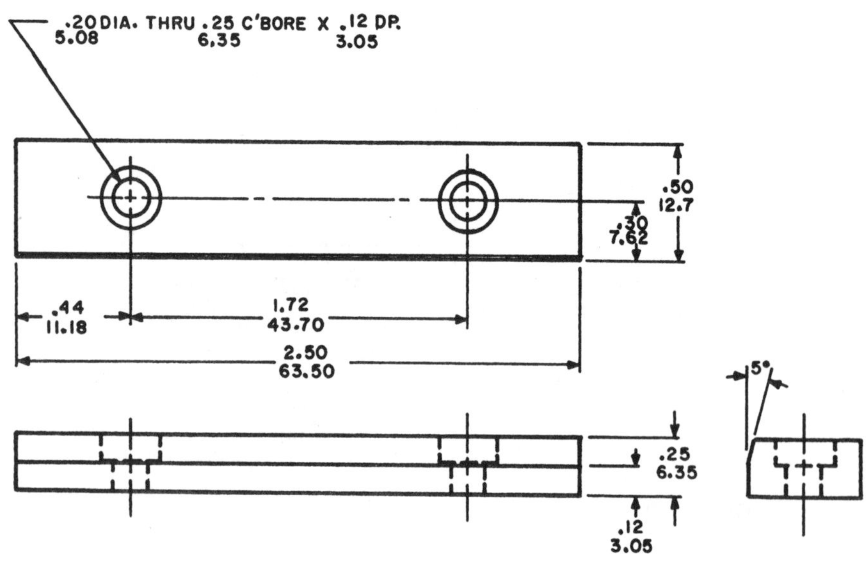

FIGURE 8–30
Exercise 8–12

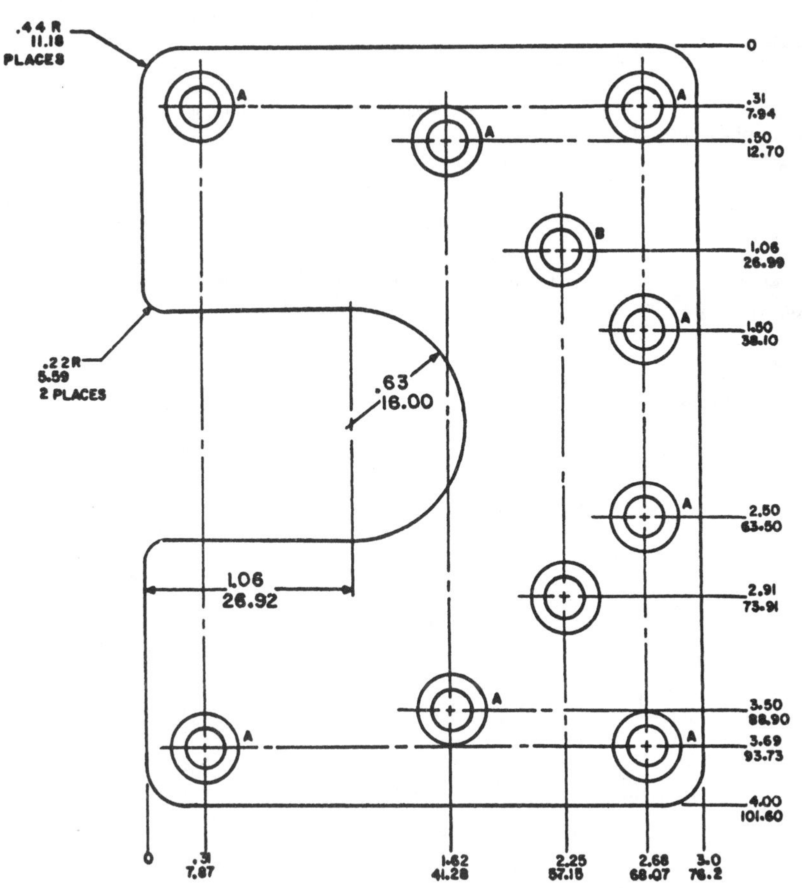

	HOLE SCHEDULE	
	SIZE	NUMBER OF HOLES
A	.19 DIA - 82°CSK TO .375	8
B	.19 DIA - C'BORE - .375 X .06 DP	2
A	4.83 DIA - 82°CSK TO 9.53	8
B	4.83 DIA - C'BORE 9.53 X 1.59 DP	2

MATERIAL: .125 STEEL PAINTED BLACK
3.18

FIGURE 8–31
Exercise 8–13

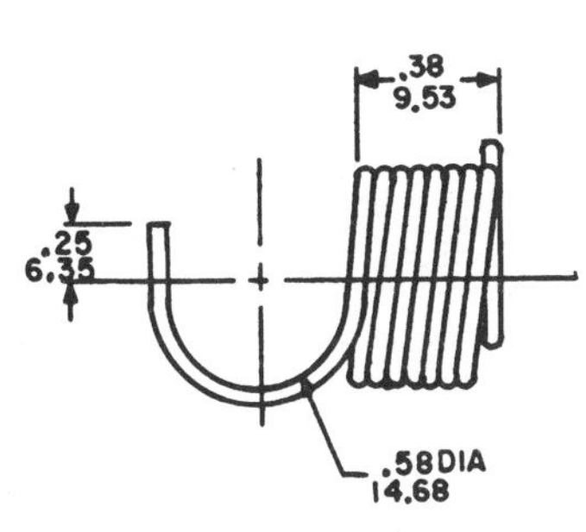

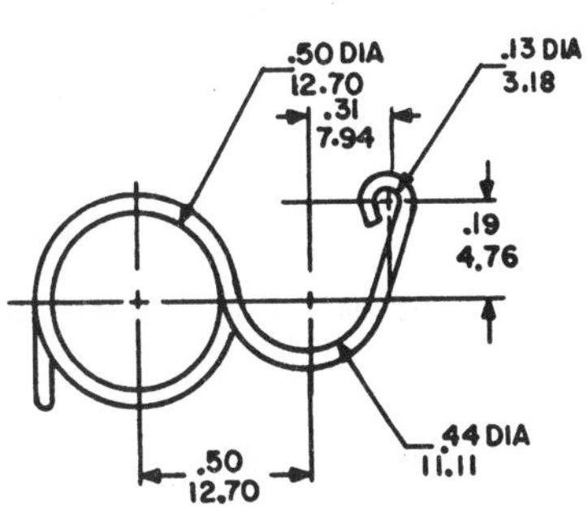

MATL: .03 SPRING WIRE
.79

FIGURE 8–32
Exercise 8–14

FIGURE 8–33
Exercise 8–15

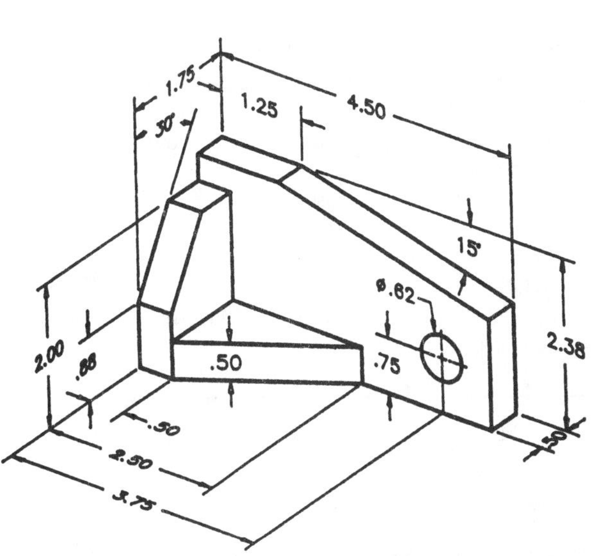

REVIEW QUESTIONS

Circle the correct answer.

1. Which command will allow you to set the number of places to the right of the decimal point?
   a. Limits: d. Units:
   b. Grid: e. Select:
   c. Snap:
2. If the grid is set at .25 and the operator wishes snap to fall on every grid and also halfway between each grid, on what value should snap be set?
   a. .10 b. .12 c. .125 d. .25 e. .50
3. What is the advantage in naming layers with either a single letter or a single number?
   a. Saves zoom time
   b. Saves typing time
   c. Saves drawing time
   d. Saves plotting time
   e. Saves all of these
4. How many standard layer colors are there? (Look on the Layer Control dialog box.)
   a. 3 b. 5 c. 7 d. 9 e. Unlimited
5. Which command is used to load linetypes?
   a. Linetype: d. Appload:
   b. Litscale: e. Compile:
   c. Load:
6. If three lines of a rectangle have been drawn, which letter may be pressed to complete the rectangle?
   a. L b. C c. D d. R e. Z
7. Which of the following will produce a vertical line 3½″ long downward from a point?
   a. 3.50 × 90
   b. @3.50<0
   c. @0<3.50
   d. @3.50<−90
   e. 90<3.50
8. When a new layer is created with the name R, it automatically assumes the color RED unless otherwise assigned.
   a. True b. False
9. Which of the following is used to identify the coordinates of a point?
   a. Status: b. Point: c. ID: d. Line: e. Dist:
10. Which of the following will display the Osnap: menu?
    a. **** d. SETTINGS
    b. OSNAP ↵ e. F9
    c. DRAW
11. A 45° angle at a corner may be obtained most easily with the use of which of the following commands?
    a. Chamfer: d. Offset:
    b. Fillet: e. Break:
    c. Draw:
12. A rounded corner may be obtained most easily with the use of which of the following commands?
    a. Chamfer: d. Offset:
    b. Fillet: e. Break:
    c. Draw:
13. Which of the following circles is produced if ".50" is entered in response to the circle prompt "Diameter/<Radius>:"?
    a. .50 diameter d. 1.00 diameter
    b. .25 radius e. .25 diameter
    c. 1.00 radius
14. The letters Ce,S,End on the Arc: menu are labels for
    a. Center,start,end
    b. Center,start,clockwise
    c. Clockwise,start,end
    d. Clockwise,start,endpoint
    e. Counterclockwise,start,end
15. The three picked points shown here will produce which of the following Ce,S,End arcs?

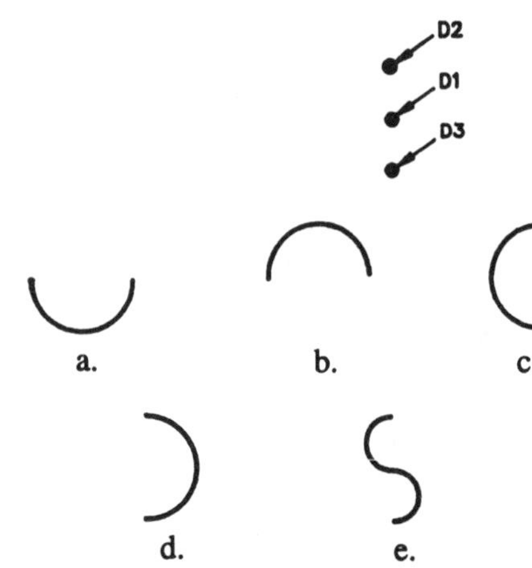

16. Which of the following commands can most easily be used to produce parallel plines?
    a. Parallel: d. Change:
    b. Draw: e. Osnap:
    c. Offset:
17. Which of the following commands can be used most quickly to remove picked points from the screen?
    a. Zoom: d. Remove:
    b. Pan: e. Redraw:
    c. Change:
18. Which of the following is the correct Paper Size setting on the Plot Configuration dialog box for an 8½″ × 11″ horizontal page size?
    a. 11 × 8½″ d. 8.5 × 11
    b. 11,8.5 e. 8-½″,11
    c. 8.5,11
19. If the drawing is to be plotted at half the size it was drawn, what is the correct setting for: Plotted Inches = Drawing Units?
    a. .05 b. 2 = 1 c. 1 = 2 d. Fit e. ½
20. Which of the following View: options allows views to be changed quickly?
    a. Dynamic d. Restore
    b. Window e. View
    c. Save

Complete.

21. Describe the differences between absolute, relative, and polar coordinates.

____

____

____

22. Name the dialogue box that is used to establish Grid: and Snap: settings.

____

23. Write a sequence of *draw responses* to the "to point" prompt that will produce a 3″ by 4½″ rectangle using polar coordinates.

____

____

24. When should the Zoom: Dynamic command be used instead of the Zoom: All command?

____

____

25. Describe the function of the ID (LOCATE POINT for Windows) command.

____

____

26. How may you discover which layers exist and their status?

____

____

27. Describe how filters are used to locate points.

____

____

28. Draw and label three points in sequence (D1,D2,D3) that will produce the Ce,S,End arc shown here.

29. For what purpose is the View: command used?

____

____

30. List the command that is used to give the distance from one point to another.

____

9 Adding Dimensions and Tolerances to Drawings

OBJECTIVES

When you have completed this chapter, you will be able to:

- □ Use the Dimensioning menu to dimension full-scale drawings of
  Mechanical parts using decimal parts of an inch.
  Mechanical parts using metric measurements.
- □ Provide positive and negative tolerances for specific dimensions.
- □ Use the geometric tolerance feature to dimension mechanical parts.
- □ Correctly answer questions regarding dimensioning variables and commands.

DIMENSIONING

Up to this point, you have made several different types of drawings. You have made block diagrams, architectural floor plans, drawings of furniture containing attributes, and 2-D drawings of mechanical parts.

For the manufacturing and construction drawings to be used to manufacture a part or to construct a building, dimensions must be added. Adding dimensions to a drawing manually is a very time-consuming process. With AutoCAD, adding dimensions is much easier. In addition, the AutoCAD dimensioning process verifies the accuracy of the drawing. The associative dimensioning feature of AutoCAD also allows a part size to be changed or corrected, automatically changing the dimension with it.

In this chapter you will dimension some of the drawings you have already made, and you will make some simple drawings to demonstrate other dimensioning features. Remember that you have made these drawings full size, so the dimensioning procedure is relatively simple. There are several settings that must be checked or set before you begin dimensioning, however:

Warning: If you set the letter style height o 0, AutoCAD will prompt you each time you see DTEXT for the height so that you may have two or more heights of the same style. This setting of 0 also has no effect on the height of the text used for dimensions (DIMTXT). *If you set the letter style height to something other than 0:*

Only one height can be drawn for that style.

The change command cannot be used to change letter height.

The letter height for dimensioning text (DIMTXT) is overridden by the style height.

Leave style height at 0.

UNITS The correct system of units must be selected and the places to the right of the decimal must be correctly set if decimals are used.

STYLE The lettering style desired must be current *and* the height for that style must be set at 0.

LAYER The correct layer for dimensions must be current.

DIMVARS The dimensioning variables that control the length, height, and spacing of the many elements of dimensions must be set correctly. These dimensioning variables are described next.

Dimensioning Variables

Although the following list is long, there are only a few variables that you will set for any drawing. Once these are set you may make a prototype drawing containing all the settings (Layers, Units, Limits, etc.) for a particular type of drawing. Notice that the variable names begin to make sense when you know what they are. For example: DIMSCALE is dimensioning scale, DIMTXT is dimensioning text, and DIMSTYLE is dimensioning style.

Tip: A prototype drawing may be created by beginning a new drawing, making all the settings, and saving it in the ACAD directory on the hard disk with no lines, etc. drawn on it. Then make each new drawing of that type = to the prototype. Your prototype drawing may be saved on a floppy disk if the hard disk cannot be used for your prototype. Then the new drawing name = A: Prototype Drawing Name.

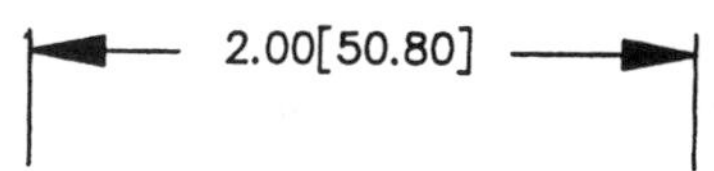

FIGURE 9–1
DIMALT

DIMALT Alternate units selected (Figure 9–1). If a drawing must show two sets of dimensions, such as inches and millimeters, this variable is turned on.

DIMALTD Alternate unit decimal places. This variable sets the number of places to the right of the decimal for the second set of dimensions. (Example: For DIMALTD=2, the dimension will read 12.70.)

DIMALTF Alternate unit scale factor. This is the number by which the primary dimension is multiplied to get the alternate dimension. (Example: For DIMALTF=25.40, if the primary dimension is 2″, the alternate dimension is 50.80.)

DIMALTTD Alternate dimension tolerance decimal places. DIMALTTD sets the number of decimal places for the tolerance values of an alternate units dimension.

You will not use this dimensioning variable in this book.

DIMALTTZ Alternate tolerance zero suppression. DIMALTTZ suppresses zeros in alternate tolerance values to the right of the value as follows:

0 Zeros are not suppressed (are shown; example: .0500)
1 Zeros are suppressed (are not shown; example: .05)

You will not use this dimensioning variable in this book.

DIMALTU Alternate units. This variable sets units for alternate dimensions as follows:

1. Scientific
2. Decimal
3. Engineering
4. Architectural

You will not use this dimensioning variable in this book.

DIMALTZ Alternate units zero suppression. DIMALTZ suppresses zeros in alternate dimension values to the right of the decimal point as follows:

0 Zeros are not suppressed (are shown; example: 2.00)
1 Zeros are suppressed (are not shown; example: 2)

You will not use this dimensioning variable in this book.

Note: There are advantages and disadvantages to setting DIMASO on.

Disadvantages:

1. If you want to erase an extension line or any other part of the dimension, you must EXPLODE the dimension first and then use the Change: command to change the color of the dimension elements to BYLAYER. (The XPLODE Lisp routine allows the dimension to remain on the layer on which it was created.) XPLODE.LSP is located under Applications in the SAMPLE directory. Applications is in the TOOLS menu on the menu bar.
2. If you reduce the drawing using the Scale: command, the dimensions change with it.

Advantages:

1. If you decide to change a dimensioning variable after part of the drawing has already been dimensioned, you can change the existing dimensions to the new dimensioning variables with the Update: command.
2. If you decide to change the text of the dimension, you can do it with the Newtext: command or the location of text with Tedit.
3. If you change the length of a dimensioned feature, the dimension changes with it. For example, if you STRETCH a 3″ line to a 4″, the dimension changes from 3″ to 4″.

DIMAPOST Suffix for alternate text. This is the marking placed after the alternate dimension. (Example: For DIMAPOST=mm, the alternate dimension reads 50.80 mm.)

DIMASO Create associative dimensions. When DIMASO is on, the complete dimension (dimension lines, arrowheads, extension lines, and text) comes in as a block.

DIMASZ Arrow size. DIMASZ sets the length of the arrowhead. (Figure 9–2).

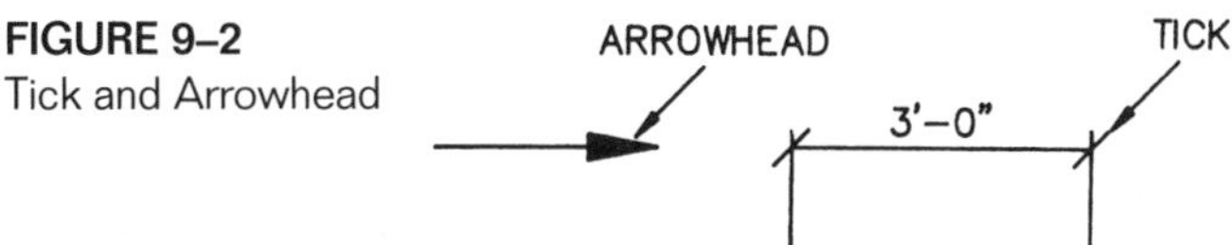

FIGURE 9–2
Tick and Arrowhead

DIMAUNIT Angular unit format. This variable sets the angle format for angular dimensions as follows:

0 Decimal degrees
1 Degrees/minutes/seconds
2 Gradians
3 Radians
4 Surveyor's units

You will not use this dimensioning variable in this book.

DIMBLK Arrow block name. If you want to use something other than the standard arrowhead or tick (Figure 9–2), change this to the desired block name and then create a block with that name. Example: DIMBLK=DOT. If you have a block with the name

DOT that is a circle, that circle will appear instead of an arrowhead. When you want to return to the arrowhead, change DIMBLK to . (a period). Consult the *AutoCAD Reference Manual* for details on how to construct a DIMBLK.

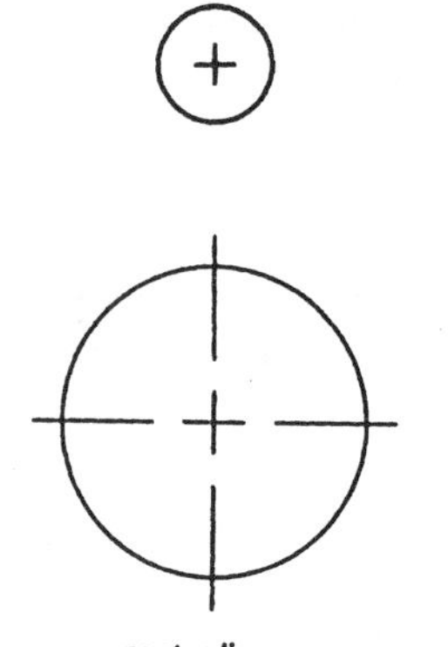

FIGURE 9–3
DIMCEN

DIMBLK 1; DIMBLK 2 First and second arrow block names. If you want to use one block (a circle) at one end of the dimension line and something else (a square) at the other end, give DIMBLK 1 and DIMBLK 2 different names and draw blocks with these names. Turn DIMSAH ON to activate these two variables.

DIMCEN Center mark size (Figure 9–3). DIMCEN sets the size of the center mark that appears at the center of circles and radii. A negative value for the center mark draws center lines that extend that amount outside the circle.

DIMCLRD Dimension line color. If you want the dimension line, extension lines, leaders, and the dimension text to be different colors, AutoCAD gives you that option with DIMCLRD, DIMCLRE, and DIMCLRT. The default of BYBLOCK (color is assigned by the layer on which it is inserted) is acceptable for most situations.

DIMCLRE Extension line and leader color.

DIMCLRT Dimension color.

DIMDEC Decimal places. This variable sets the number of decimal places for the tolerance value of the dimension.

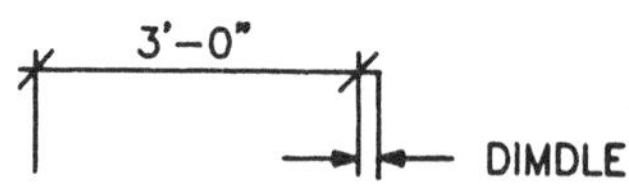

FIGURE 9–4
DIMDLE

DIMDLE Dimension line extension (Figure 9–4). DIMDLE allows you to extend the dimension line past the extension line. This is useful for some architectural styles.

DIMDLI Dimension line increment for continuation (Figure 9–5). DIMDLI allows you to set the space between dimension lines when *BASELINE* or *CONTINUE* dimensioning is used.

FIGURE 9–5
DIMDLI

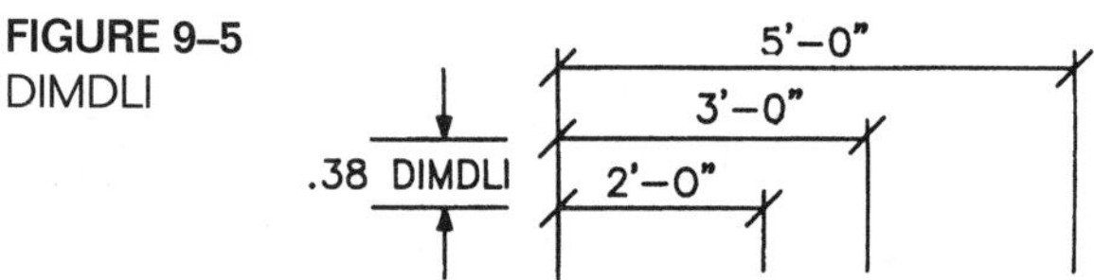

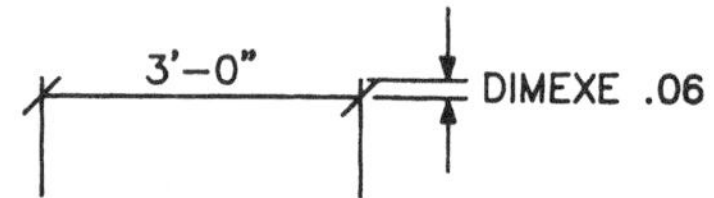

FIGURE 9–6
DIMEXE

DIMEXE Extension above dimension line (Figure 9–6). DIMEXE allows you to set the length of the extension line past the arrowhead.

DIMEXO Extension line origin offset (Figure 9–7). DIMEXO allows you to set the space between the object and the extension line.

FIGURE 9–7
DIMEXO

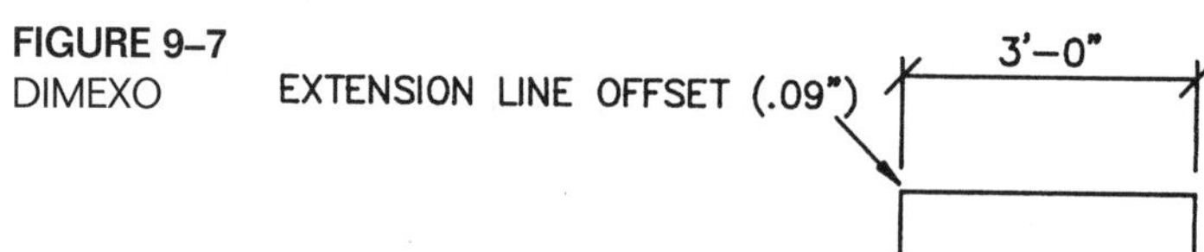

DIMFIT Fit text. This variable controls the placement of text and arrowheads inside or outside extension lines based on the available space between extension lines as follows:

0 Places text and arrowheads between the extension lines if space is available. Otherwise, AutoCAD places both text and arrowheads outside extension lines.

1 If space is available, places text and arrowheads between the extension lines. When enough space is available for text, AutoCAD places text between the extension lines and arrowheads outside them. When not enough space is available for text, AutoCAD places both text and arrowheads outside extension lines.

2 If space is available, places text and arrowheads between the extension lines. When space is available for the text only, AutoCAD places the text between the extension lines and the arrowheads outside. When space is available for the arrowheads only, AutoCAD places them between the extension lines and the text outside. When no space is available for either text or arrowheads, AutoCAD places them both outside the extension lines.

3 Creates leader lines when there is not enough space for text between extension lines. The dimensioning variable DIMJUST controls whether the text is drawn to the right or to the left of the leader.

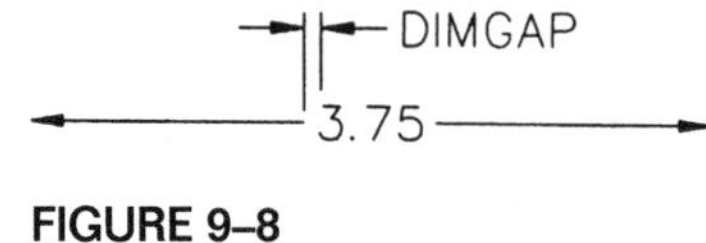

FIGURE 9–8
DIMGAP

DIMGAP Gap from dimension line to text (Figure 9–8). DIMGAP sets this space.

DIMJUST Justification of text on dimension line. DIMJUST controls the horizontal position of the text in the dimension as follows:

0 Positions the text above the dimension line and centers it between the extension lines.
1 Positions the text above the dimension line and next to the first extension line.
2 Positions the text above the dimension line and next to the second extension line.
3 Positions the text above the dimension line and rotates it so that it is centered above the first extension line.
4 Positions the text above the dimension line and rotates it so that it is centered above the second extension line.

DIMLFAC Linear unit scale factor (Figure 9–9). DIMLFAC is the factor by which the measured distance is multiplied to obtain the dimension shown on the drawing. This is used to dimension drawings that have been drawn to a scale other than full size. If a drawing has been drawn one-fourth size, the DIMLFAC is set to 4 to obtain the full-size dimension.

FIGURE 9–9
DIMLFAC

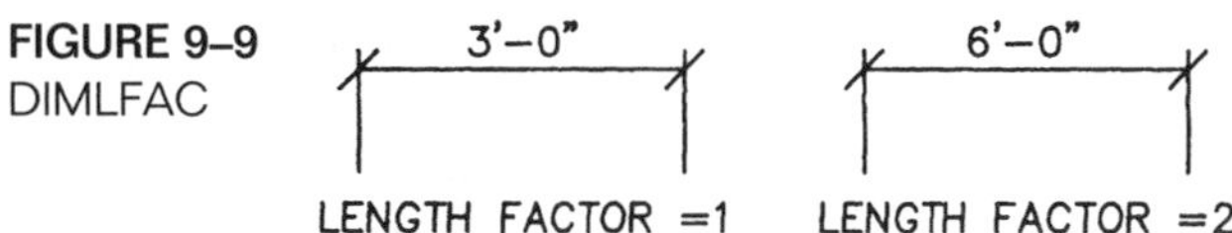

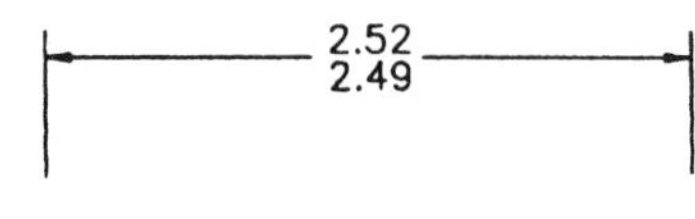

FIGURE 9–10
DIMLIM

FIGURE 9–11
DIMSAH

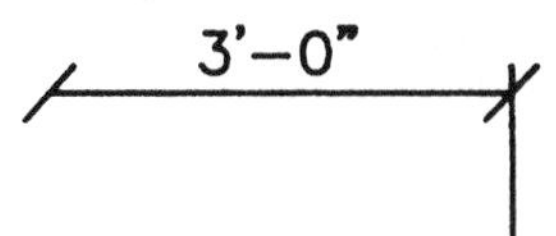

FIGURE 9–12
DIMSE1

Note: Use DIMSE1 and DIMSE2 to avoid overlapping two extension lines. Although overlapping is not noticeable in many cases, it increases the size of the drawing file, which is usually undesirable.

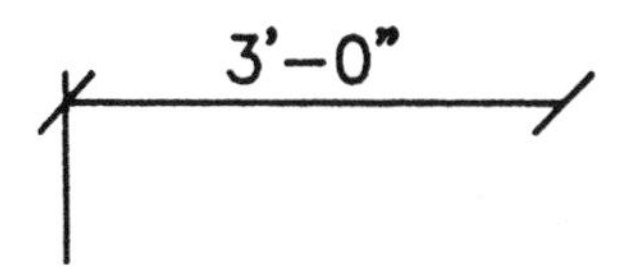

FIGURE 9–13
DIMSE2

DIMLIM Generate dimension limits (Figure 9–10). This setting is turned on if a limit dimension is necessary. A limit dimension shows the upper and lower limits of tolerance for a dimension. For example, if the dimension is 2.50 with a tolerance of +.02 (set with DIMTP) and −.01 (set with DIMTM), the limits are 2.52 and 2.49, as shown.

DIMPOST Default suffix for dimension text. This variable allows units such as feet, inches, or millimeters to be added after the dimension. (Example: When DIMPOST=″, the dimension is displayed as 12.00″. When DIMPOST=mm, the dimension reads 12.00 mm.)

DIMRND Rounding value. This variable is used for rounding dimensions. (Example: When DIMRND=.005, all dimensions are rounded to the nearest .005 unit. When DIMRND=1.0, the dimension is rounded to the nearest full unit, so 2.40 becomes 2.)

DIMSAH Separate arrow blocks (Figure 9–11). When this variable is on, DIMBLK1 and DIMBLK2 define the shape that is used on each end of the dimension line. It is used for shapes other than the arrowhead or tick at each end of the dimension line.

DIMSCALE Overall scale factor. This variable allows you to set all the other variables at the size you want them to be plotted and then set DIMSCALE to the same value as the plotting ratio. For example, a drawing of a house drawn full scale (40′ × 30′) is plotted at a scale of ¼″ = 1′ to fit comfortably on a 17′ × 11′ sheet. DIMSCALE must be set to 48 (the same ratio as ¼″ = 1′, or 4 × 12) for dimensions to show in their correct proportions. You may also set DIMSCALE = 0 so that AutoCAD may set a DIMSCALE for you. This DIMSCALE is the ratio between model space and paper space limits. You must first set paper space limits and create a paper space viewport before DIMSCALE = 0 will work. (Tilemode must also be 0.)

DIMSE1 Suppress the first extension line (Figure 9–12). When DIMSE1 is on, the first extension line of any dimension is not drawn.

DIMSE2 Suppress the second extension line (Figure 9–13). When DIMSE2 is on, the second extension line of any dimension is not drawn.

DIMSHO Update dimensions while dragging. When DIMASO is on and DIMSHO is on, the dimensions are changed continuously as a part is stretched. This variable could be used to stretch a part to a predetermined value.

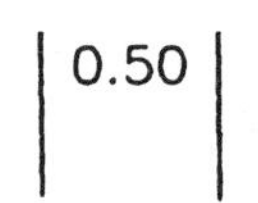

FIGURE 9–14
DIMSOXD

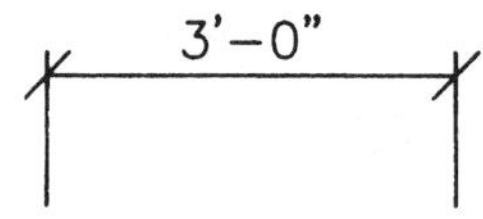

FIGURE 9–15
DIMTAD

DIMSOXD Suppress outside extension dimension (Figure 9–14). Dimension lines outside the extension lines are not drawn when DIMSOXD is on.

DIMSTYLE Current dimension style. This variable allows you to have several sets of different dimensioning variables saved under style names that can be recalled quickly with the restore option.

DIMTAD Place text above dimension line (Figure 9–15). This variable turned on (used in conjunction with DIMTIH and DIMTOH turned off) places all dimensions above the dimension line.

DIMTDEC Tolerance decimal places. Sets the number of decimal places in the tolerance value for a dimension.

DIMTFAC Tolerance text scaling factor (Figure 9–16). Multiplying DIMTEXT, the dimension text height, times DIMTFAC equals the height of the tolerance text. In the case of Figure 9–16, DIMTFAC=.5.

FIGURE 9–16
DIMTFAC

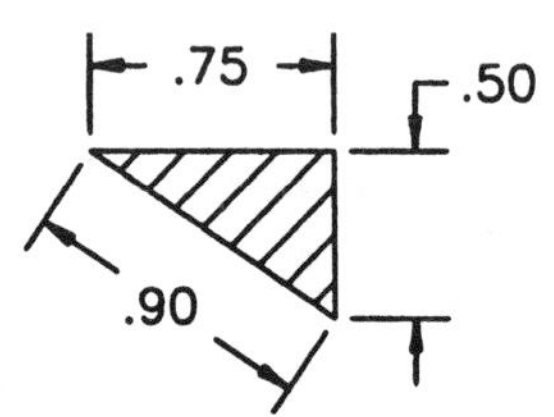

FIGURE 9–17
DIDMTIH

DIMTIH Text inside dimensions is horizontal (Figure 9–17). All dimensions inside extension lines are drawn horizontally when DIMTIH is on.

DIMTIX Place text inside extension. This variable forces the text inside the extension lines whether it fits or not.

DIMTM Minus tolerance (Example: 1.500 − .005).

DIMTOFL Force line inside extension line (Figure 9–18). A line is drawn inside the extension lines.

FIGURE 9–18
DIMTOFL

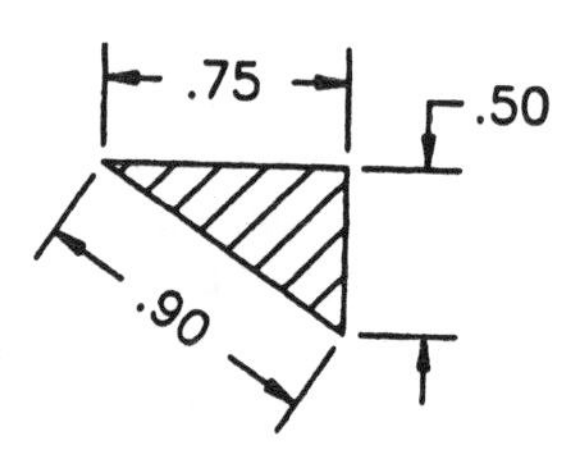

FIGURE 9–19
DIMTOH

DIMTOH Text outside extensions is horizontal (Figure 9–19). Text outside the extension lines is horizontal; inside it is aligned with the dimension line unless DIMTH is also on.

DIMTOL Generate dimension tolerances (Figure 9–20). When DIMTOL is on and DIMTP and DIMTM are the same (Example: .02), the dimension is displayed as 3.37 ± .02. If they are different (Example: DIMTP=.02, DIMTM=.01), the dimension is displayed as $3.37^{+.02}_{-.01}$.

FIGURE 9–20
DIMTOL

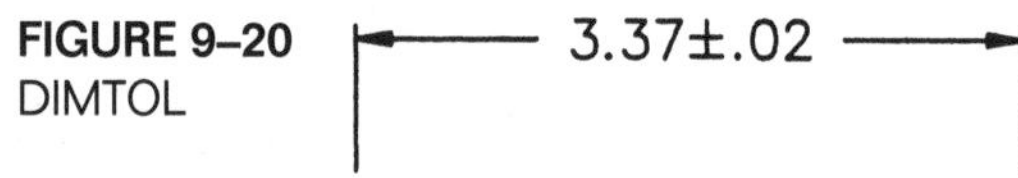

DIMTOLJ Tolerance vertical justification. Controls the vertical placement of tolerance values relative to the dimension text as follows:

0 Top
1 Middle
2 Bottom

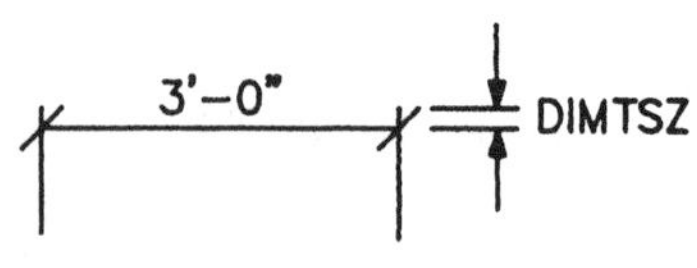

FIGURE 9–21
DIMTSZ

DIMTP Plus tolerance (Example: 1.500 + .005).

DIMTSZ Tick size (Figure 9–21).

DIMTVP Text vertical position. This is the factor by which the DIMTXT height is multiplied to obtain the location of text above or below the dimension line.

DIMTXSTY Text style. Specifies the text style of the dimension. The style chosen must be defined in the current drawing. See Chapter 6 for setting styles with the STYLE command.

DIMTXT Text height. This variable sets the height of the text if the current text height under the STYLE setting is 0. DIMTXT is multiplied by DIMSCALE.

DIMTZIN Tolerance zero suppression. Suppresses zeros in tolerance values to the right of the value as follows:

0 Zeros are not suppressed (are shown; example: .0500)
1 Zeros are suppressed (not shown; example: .05)

DIMUNIT Unit format. Sets units for primary dimensions as follows:

1. Scientific
2. Decimal
3. Engineering
4. Architectual

DIMUPT User-positioned text. When this variable is on, it allows you to pick the point where you wish the dimension line and the text to appear. If you want the text to appear nearer one end of the dimension line, select a single point that will place the dimension line where you want it, and the text will be placed on the same point. The setting is:

0 Off
1 On

DIMZIN Zero suppression. This factor allows several different variations of feet and inches display, as follows:

DIMZIN Value	Meaning	Examples			
0	Suppress zero feet and inches	¼″,	3″,	2′,	1′-0½″
1	Include zero feet and inches	0′-0¼″,	0′-3″,	2′-0″,	1′-0½″
2	Include zero feet; suppress zero inches	0′-0¼″,	0′-3″,	2′,	1′-0½″
3	Suppress zero feet; include zero inches	¼″,	3″,	2′-0″,	1′-0½″

Now that you have been introduced to dimensioning variables, let's dimension some drawings to see how this works. Begin with a mechanical part (Figure 9–22). Use the drawing you did in Exercise 1, Chapter 8.

FIGURE 9–22
Drawing to Be Dimensioned

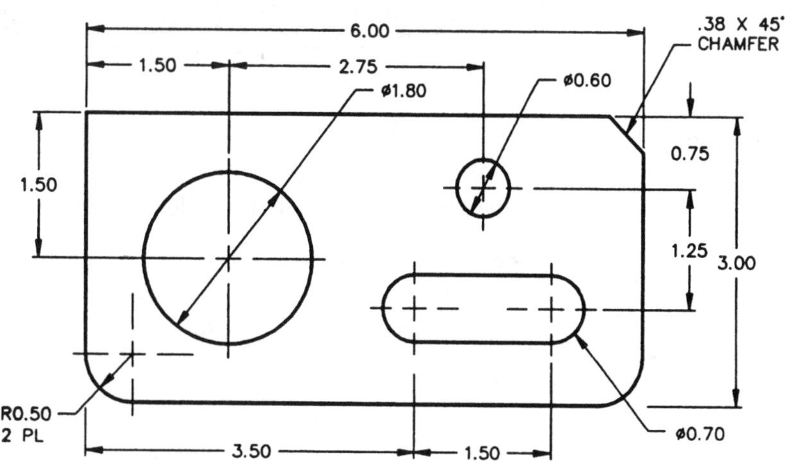

EXERCISE 9–1
DIMENSIONING A MECHANICAL PART

Set Up the Drawing

Step 1. On Your Own:

1. Load AutoCAD and Select: New. . . . Name the drawing 9-1 (your initials)=8-1 (your initials) (B: 8-1 (your initials) if the drawing is on a floppy disk in the B: drive).
2. Make or check the following settings.

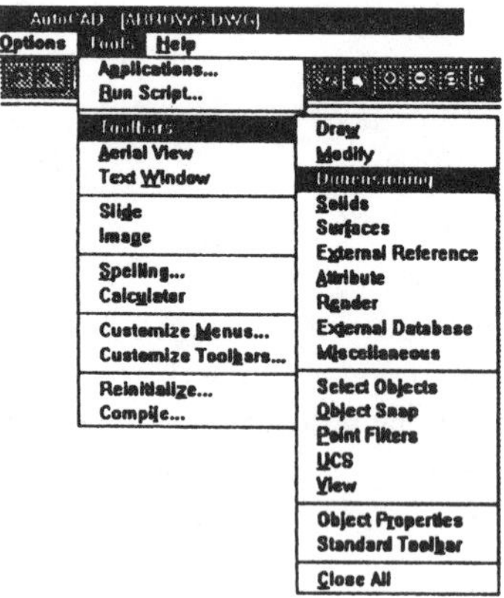

UNITS: Decimal units; 2 digits to the right of the decimal point
LIMITS: Lower left corner: 0,0
Upper right corner: 11,8.5
GRID: .25
SNAP: .0625
STYLE: STANDARD; FONT: SIMPLEX; HEIGHT: 0
Check the following layers:

LAYER NAME	COLOR	LINETYPE
1	RED	CONTINUOUS
2	YELLOW	CONTINUOUS
3	GREEN	CONTINUOUS

Set layer 3 current.

Check and Change Dimensioning Variables

Step 2. Check the current status of dimensioning variables and make necessary changes.

Prompt	Response
Command:	*Type:* **DIM** ↵
DIM:	*Type:* **STATUS** ↵

A listing of all dimensioning variables appears. Compare the listing in your computer with the list shown in Figure 9–23. Make any necessary changes so that your list matches Figure 9–23.

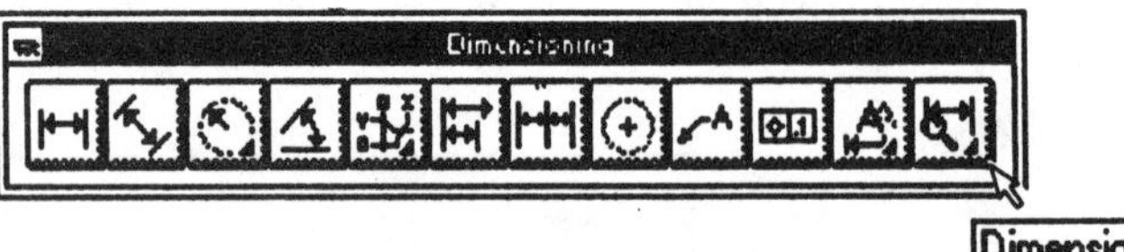

Note: Set DIMSTYLE after you have set all other dimensioning variables. Select DIMSTYLE; then Save: under DIMSTYLE by typing SE1-2 ↵ (or any other name you choose) to save all your settings under this style name. You may have another DIMSTYLE (Example: SE1) that has DIMSE1 on, DIMTIX off, and DIMTOFL on that will allow you to suppress the first extension line and dimension the larger circle in a different manner. You may quickly move from one set of dimensioning variables to another set by recalling DIMSTYLEs using DIMSTYLE: Restore.

To change a dimensioning variable from the keyboard:

Prompt	Response
Command:	*Type:* **DIMASZ** ↵
New Value for DIMASZ <0.18>:	*Type:* **.125** ↵
DIM:	(Because units are set to two places to the right of the decimal, .125 will be shown on the list as .13. The actual measurement, however, will be .125.)

FIGURE 9–23
Dimensioning Variables for Figure 9–22

DIMALT	Off	Alternate units selected
DIMALTD	2	Alternate unit decimal places
DIMALTF	25.40	Alternate unit scale factor
DIMALTTD	2	Alternate tolerance decimal places
DIMALTTZ	0	Alternate tolerance zero suppression
DIMALTU	2	Alternate units
DIMALTZ	0	Alternate unit zero suppression
DIMAPOST		Prefix and suffix for alternate text
DIMASO	On	Create associative dimensions
DIMASZ	0.13	Arrow size
DIMAUNIT	0	Angular unit format
DIMBLK		Arrow block name
DIMBLK1		First arrow block name
DIMBLK2		Second arrow block name
DIMCEN	-0.13	Center mark size
DIMCLRD	BYBLOCK	Dimension line and leader color
DIMCLRE	BYBLOCK	Extension line color
DIMCLRT	BYBLOCK	Dimension text color
DIMDEC	2	Decimal places
DIMDLE	0.00	Dimension line extension
DIMDLI	0.38	Dimension line spacing
DIMEXE	0.06	Extension above dimension line
DIMEXO	0.06	Extension line origin offset
DIMFIT	3	Fit text
DIMGAP	0.09	Gap from dimension line to text
DIMJUST	0	Justification of text on dimension line
DIMLFAC	1.00	Linear unit scale factor
DIMLIM	Off	Generate dimension limits
DIMPOST		Prefix and suffix for dimension text
DIMRND	0.00	Rounding value
DIMSAH	Off	Separate arrow blocks
DIMSCALE	1.00	Overall scale factor
DIMSD1	Off	Suppress the first dimension line
DIMSD2	Off	Suppress the second dimension line
DIMSE1	Off	Suppress the first extension line
DIMSE2	Off	Suppress the second extension line
DIMSHO	On	Update dimensions while dragging
DIMSOXD	Off	Suppress outside dimension lines
DIMSTYLE	STANDARD	Current dimension style (read-only)
DIMTAD	0	Place text above the dimension line
DIMTDEC	4	Tolerance decimal places
DIMTFAC	1.00	Tolerance text height scaling factor
DIMTIH	On	Text inside extensions is horizontal
DIMTIX	Off	Place text inside extensions
DIMTM	0.00	Minus tolerance
DIMTOFL	Off	Force line inside extension lines
DIMTOH	On	Text outside horizontal
DIMTOL	Off	Tolerance dimensioning
DIMTOLJ	1	Tolerance vertical justification
DIMTP	0.00	Plus tolerance
DIMTSZ	0.00	Tick size
DIMTVP	0.00	Text vertical position
DIMTXSTY	STANDARD	Text style
DIMTXT	0.13	Text height
DIMTZIN	0	Tolerance zero suppression
DIMUNIT	2	Unit format
DIMUPT	Off	User positioned text
DIMZIN	0	Zero suppression

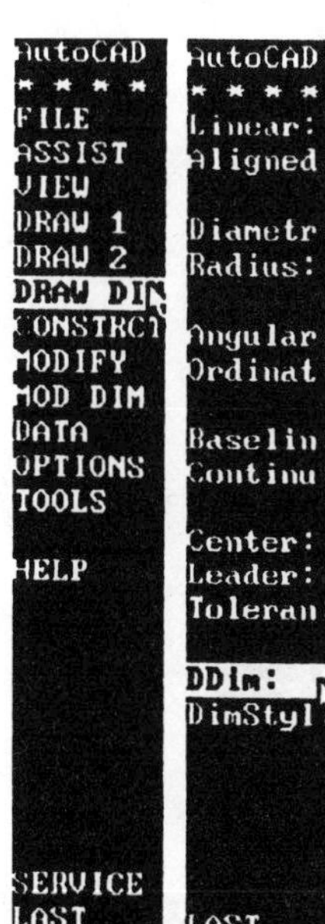

To change a dimensioning variable from the Dimension Styles dialog box:

Prompt	Response
Command:	**DDim:** (from the screen menu) **SET DIMVARS**

The Dimension Styles dialog box shown in Figure 9–24 appears.

This box will allow you to pick the variable group you want to change, select the variable, and type the new setting. Notice that the variables are grouped under different headings:

□ Geometry (Figure 9–25). (Pick the Geometry button.)
□ Format (Figure 9–26). (Pick the Format button.)
□ Annotation (Figure 9–27). (Pick the Annotation button.)

After you have set the dimensioning variables, go on to Step 3.

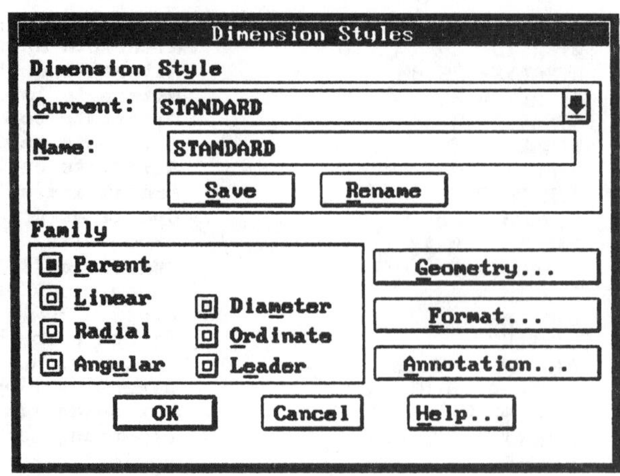

FIGURE 9–24
Dimension Styles Dialog Box

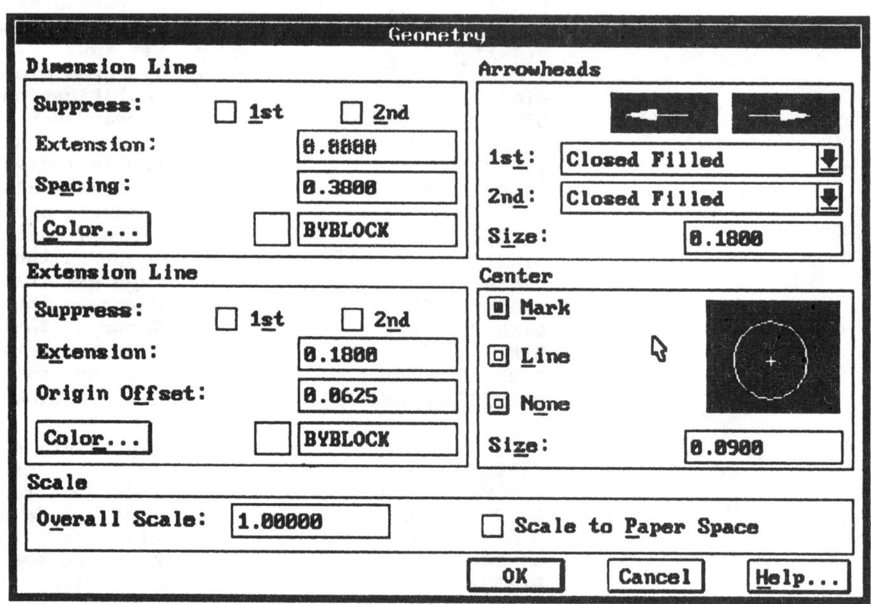

FIGURE 9–25
Geometry Variables Dialog Box

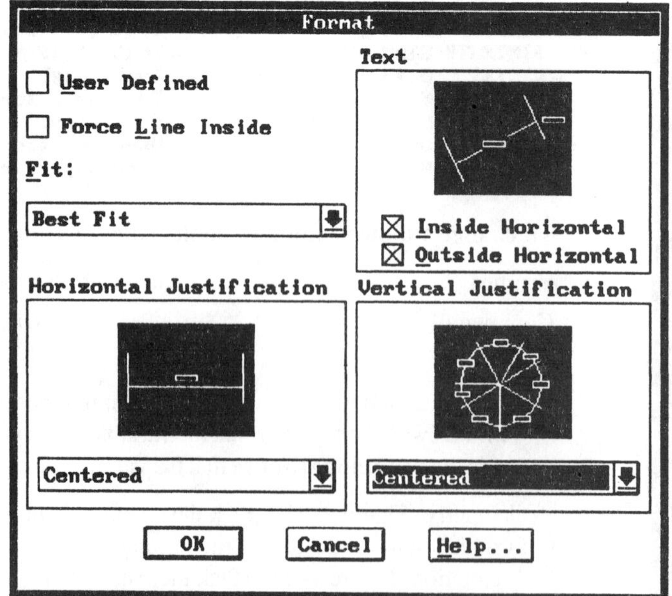

FIGURE 9–26
Format Variables Dialog Box

FIGURE 9–27
Annotation Variables Dialog Box

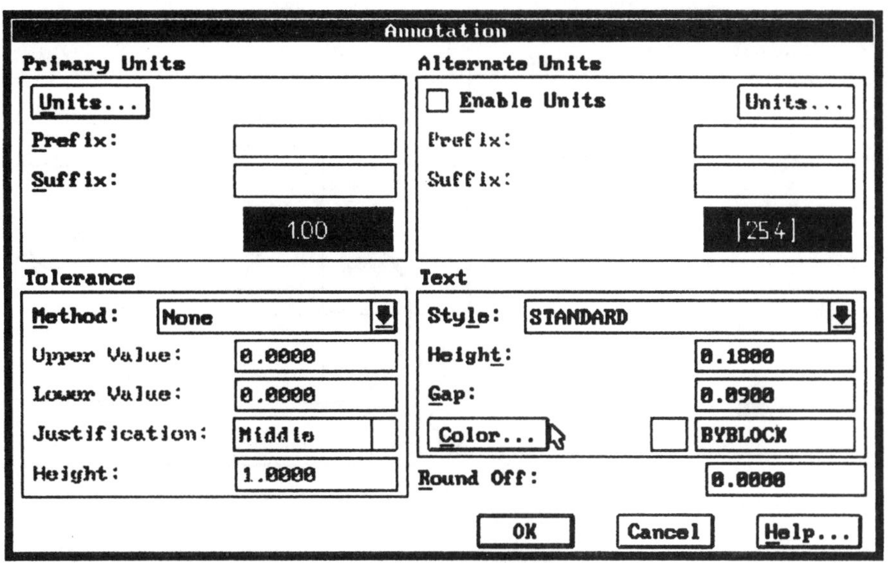

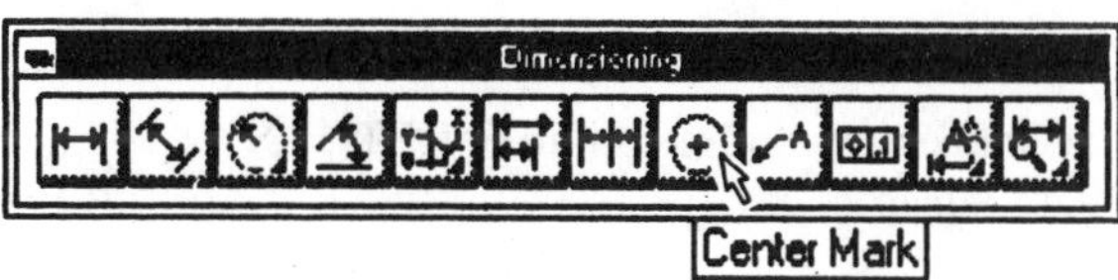

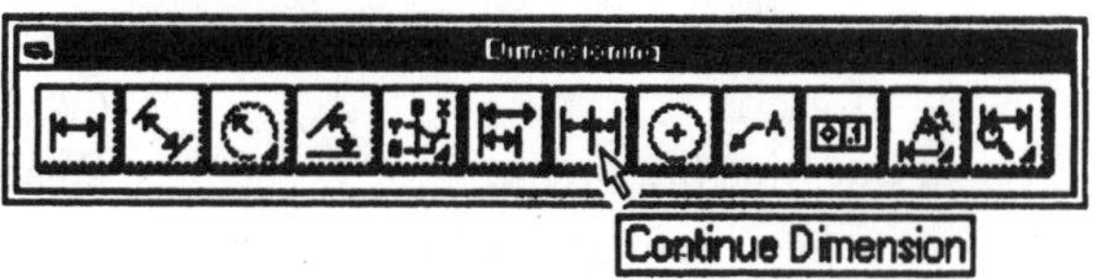

Dimension the Drawing

Step 3. Place center marks at the centers of all circles (Figure 9–28).

Windows Users: Activate the Dimensioning toolbar.

Prompt	Response
Command:	**DRAW DIM Center:**
_dim center Select arc or circle:	*Pick:* **D1**↵ **D2**↵ **D3**↵ **D4**↵

Step 4. Make the horizontal dimensions (Figure 9–28).

Prompt	Response
Command:	**DRAW DIM Linear:**
First extension line origin or RETURN to select:	Pick: **D5** (Snap should be *on* if the drawing was done with snap on.)
Second extension line origin:	*Pick:* **D6** (Pick the end of the center mark—use Osnap-ENDpoint.)
Dimension line location (Text/Angle/Horizontal/Vertical/Rotated):	*Pick:* **D7** (½″ from the object)
Dim:	**Continu:** (from the DIM menu; *Pick:* **LAST** to return to the DIM menu.)

FIGURE 9–28
Dimension Shapes

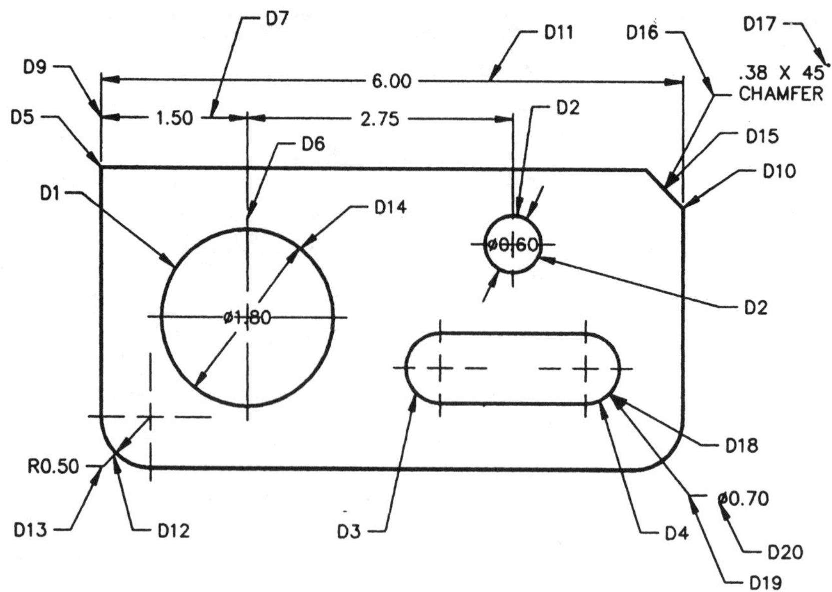

Prompt	**Response**
Second extension line origin or RETURN to select:	*Pick:* the end of the center mark of the 0.60 diameter circle.
Second extension line origin or RETURN to select:	↵
Select continued dimension:	↵
Command:	*Pick:* **LAST:**
Command:	**Linear:**
First extension line origin or RETURN to select:	*Pick:* **D9**
Second extension line origin:	*Pick:* **D10**
Dimension line location (Text/Angle/Horizontal/Vertical/Rotated):	*Pick:* **D11** (⅜″ from the first dimension line)

Draw the remainder of the horizontal dimensions shown at the bottom of Figure 9–22 in a similar manner.

Step 5. Make all vertical dimensions (Figure 9–22).

Use a procedure similar to the one you used to make horizontal dimensions.

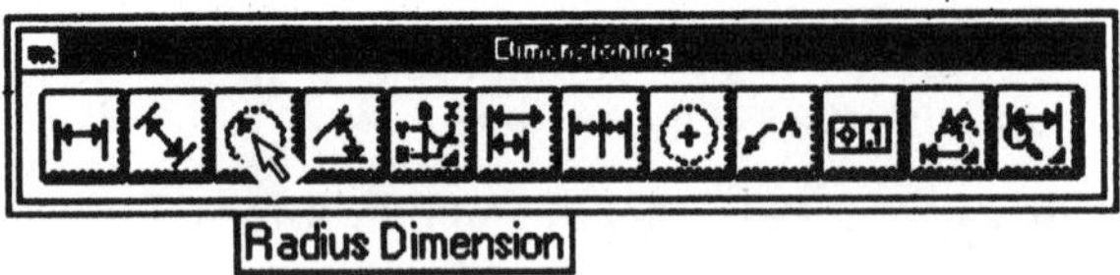

Step 6. Dimension radii, diameters, and chamfer (Figure 9–28).

To dimension these features follow this procedure:

Dimension radii:

Prompt	**Response**
Command:	**DRAW DIM Radius:**
Select arc or circle:	*Pick:* **D12**
Dimension line location (Text/Angle):	*Pick:* **D13**

Use DTEXT to add the characters 2 PL (meaning *two places*) beneath the dimension.

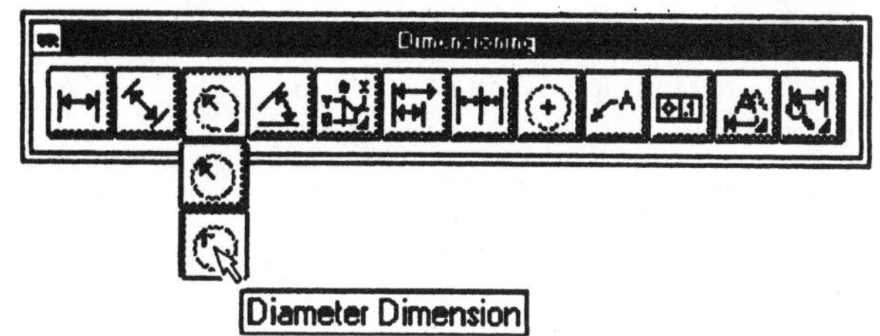

Dimension diameters of circles:

Prompt	Response
Command:	*Pick:* **DRAW DIM Diametr:**
Select arc or circle:	*Pick:* **D14** (Notice that the point you pick aligns the dimension line with the center of the circle.)
Dimension line location (Text/Angle):	*Pick:* **D14** (again)

Repeat the Diametr: command for the .60 diameter.

Dimension chamfer:

Prompt	Response
Command:	**Leader:**
From point:	*Pick:* **D15** (*Select:* **Osnap-MIDpoint.**)
To point:	*Pick:* **D16**
To point:	↵
(Format/Annotation/Undo) <Annotation>:	↵
Annotation (or RETURN for options):	↵
Tolerance/Copy/Block/None/<Mtext>:	↵
Mtext:	*Type:* **.38 × 45**↵
Mtext:	*Type:* **CHAMFER**↵
Mtext:	↵
Command:	**Dtext:**
Justify/Style/<Start point>:	*Pick:* **D17**
Height <0.13>:	↵
Rotation angle <0>:	↵
Text:	*Type:* **% %D** ↵
Text:	↵

Dimension slot diameter:

Prompt	Response
Command:	**Leader:**
From point:	*Pick:* **D18**
To point:	*Pick:* **D19**

Prompt	Response
To point (Format/Annotation/Undo) <Annotation>:	↵
Annotation (or RETURN for options):	↵
Tolerance/Copy/Block/None/<Mtext>:	↵
Mtext:	↵
Command:	**Dtext:**
Justify/Style/<Start point>:	*Pick:* **D20**
Height <0.13>:	↵
Rotation angle <0>:	↵
Text:	*Type:* **% %C0.70** ↵
Text:	↵

Step 7. Modify diameters and center mark. (Figure 9–29).

Now let's fix the diameters so they are less congested and make the center mark on the .50 radius .125 long. (It was a negative .125 so that a center line was drawn.)

FIGURE 9–29
Using DimTedit: to Relocate Dimension Text

WINDOWS USERS:
Type: DIMTEDIT ↵

Prompt	Response
Command:	**MOD DIM**
Command:	**DimTedt:**
Select dimension:	Pick any point on the 1.80 diameter dimension.
Enter text location (Left/Right/Home/Angle):	*Pick:* **D1**
Command:	*Type:* **DIMCEN** ↵
New value for DIMCEN <−0.13>:	*Type:* **.125** ↵
Command:	*Type:* **DIM** ↵
Dim:	*Type:* **UP** ↵ (to UPDATE selected dimensions to the current dimensioning variables)
Select objects:	*Pick:* Any point on the 0.50 radius.

Step 8. On Your Own:

Use DIMTEDIT to fix the 0.60 diameter so that its text is as shown in Figure 9–22.

Prompt	Response
Dim:	*Type:* **E** ↵ (or press Ctrl-C or Esc to exit from the dimensioning menu)

Hint: Dimensioning diameters, radii, and special features before making horizontal and vertical linear dimensions is often helpful. Planning the complete dimensioning procedure for a drawing before dimensioning often saves time.

Print and Save the Drawing

Step 9. On Your Own:

1. Print the drawing full scale on an 11″ × 8.5″ sheet.
2. Save the drawing in two places and exit.

Prompt	Response
Command:	**SaveAs:** (Save the drawing in two places and then exit from AutoCad.)

Geometric Dimensioning and Tolerancing

Now that you have dimensioned a mechanical part and a floor plan, let's look at a specific type of dimensioning of mechanical parts. This type, called *Geometric Dimensioning and Tolerancing,* allows parts to be manufactured with required accuracy and economy so that mating parts fit with the least cost. We introduce this topic to acquaint you with what this type of dimensioning looks like, what the standard symbols mean, and how you can use AutoCAD to easily construct the required frames containing those symbols. There are several good books on geometric dimensioning and tolerancing to which you can refer for further information.

What Geometric Dimensioning and Tolerancing Looks Like

Let's say, for example, that one surface on a part needs to be perpendicular to another surface within two parallel lines (called a tolerance zone) that are .005″ apart. One of these surfaces must be identified as a theoretically exact flat plane so that a note on the other surface can refer to it. Figure 9–30 shows one surface identified as surface A (called a *datum*). The other surface is described as being perpendicular (the *symbol*) within a tolerance zone of .005 to datum A. Other examples of this type of dimensioning are shown in Figure 9–31.

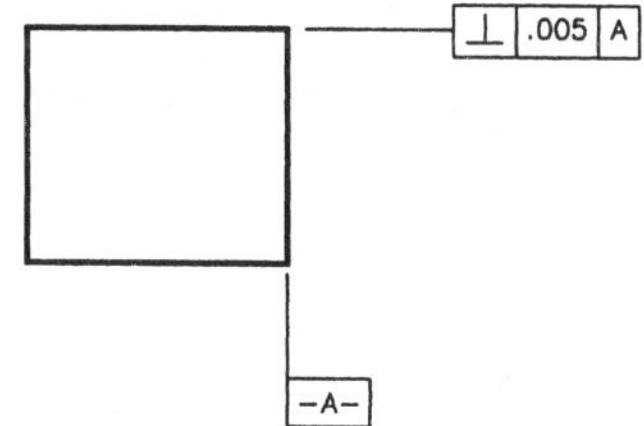

FIGURE 9–30
The Top Plane Is Perpendicular to the Right Side Within .005

What the Standard Symbols Mean

Figure 9–32 lists the standard symbols, describes the general terms applied to those symbols, and identifies the types of tolerances:

Location A location tolerance, for example, is often applied to the centers of holes.

Orientation An orientation tolerance, such as parallelism or perpendicularity, is often applied to two planes.

Form A form tolerance, such as roundness or straightness, is often applied to a shaft so that it will fit into a cylindrical opening.

Profile Profile describes the tolerance zone within which the shape of a surface must lie.

Runout Runout describes the movement of the dial of a precise measuring instrument as a shaft to be inspected is rotated in it.

All dimensions have tolerances whether they are stated directly on the drawing or contained in a general note. A dimension of .500 with a standard tolerance of ±.010 could measure (when inspected) .510 or .490 or any measurement between those two numbers and pass the inspection. When these tolerances are applied to cylinders such as shafts and holes, the following terms are often necessary:

Maximum Material Condition This is the condition in which the most material is present within the tolerance limits, such as the largest shaft and the smallest hole.

Least Material Condition This is the opposite of maximum material condition, the smallest shaft and the largest hole.

Regardless of Feature Size This term means that no matter how large or small the feature is within its tolerance limits, the tolerance shown for the particular geometry holds.

Projected Tolerance Zone The standard positional tolerance means that the center line of a hole, for example, must lie within a cylindrical tolerance zone that extends through the thickness of the part. In some situations where there are mating parts, the cylindrical tolerance zone is extended to accommodate the mating part, so that screws, studs, or other fasteners will fit when the parts are assembled.

FIGURE 9–31
Examples of Geometric Dimensioning and Tolerancing

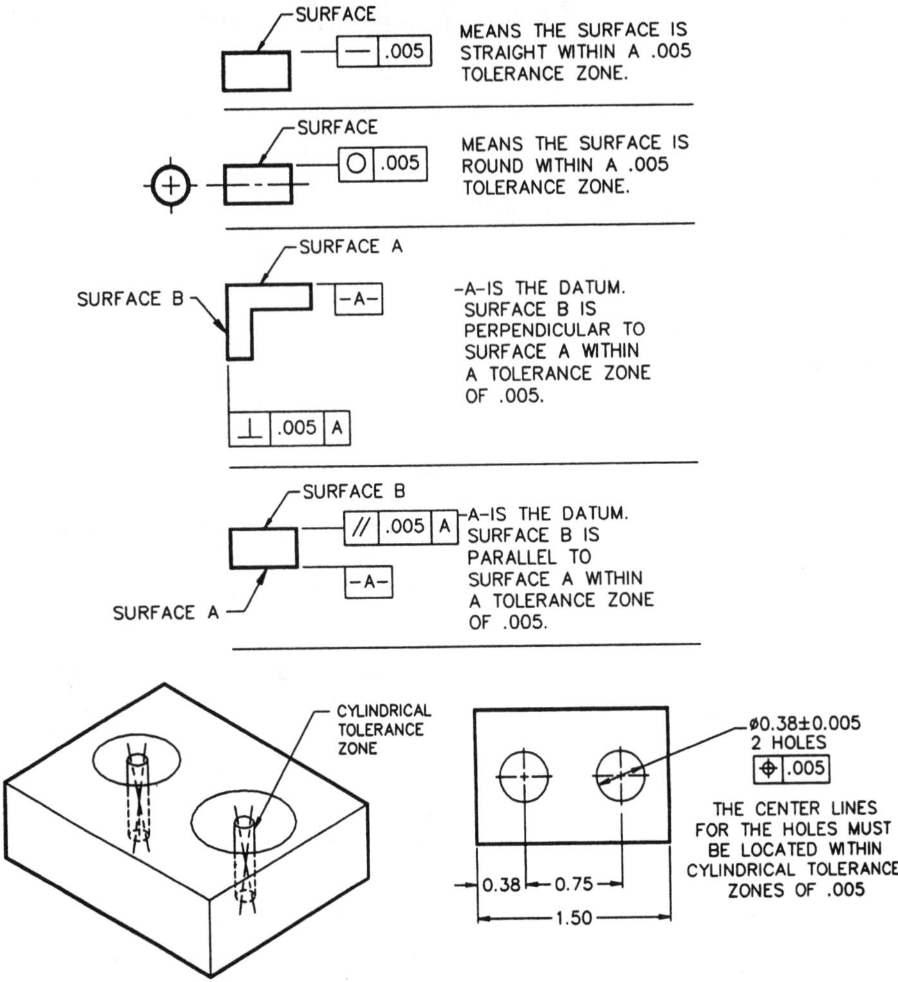

FIGURE 9–32
Standard Geometric Tolerance Symbols

Symbol	Characteristic	Type
⌖	Position	Location
◎	Concentricity or coaxiality	Location
⌯	Symmetry	Location
//	Parallelism	Orientation
⊥	Perpendicularity	Orientation
∠	Angularity	Orientation
⌭	Cylindricity	Form
⏥	Flatness	Form
○	Circularity or roundness	Form
—	Straightness	Form
⌓	Profile of a surface	Profile
⌒	Profile of a line	Profile
↗	Circular runout	Runout
⌰	Total runout	Runout

Ⓜ MAXIMUM MATERIAL CONDITION

Ⓛ LEAST MATERIAL CONDITION

Ⓢ REGARDLESS OF FEATURE SIZE

FIGURE 9–33
Material Condition Symbols

Figure 9–33 shows the Material Condition Symbols, and Figure 9–34 describes the Projected Tolerance Zone.

FIGURE 9–34
Projected Tolerance Zone

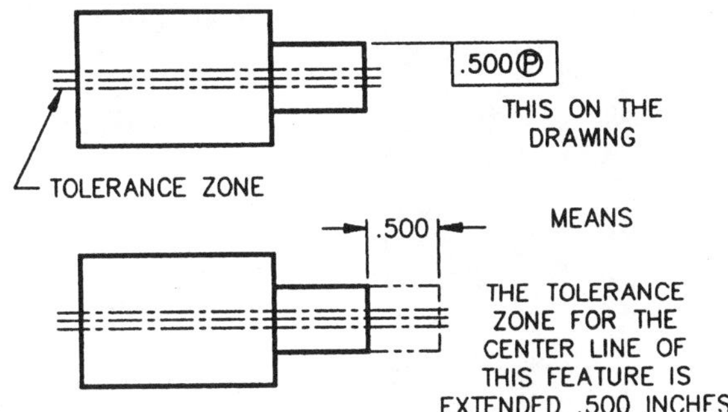

EXERCISE 9–2: USING THE TOLERANCE OPTION OF AUTOCAD DIMENSIONING TO CREATE THE CONTROL FRAMES USED IN GEOMETRIC DIMENSIONING AND TOLERANCING

Step 1. On Your Own:

1. *Before you start,* draw and dimension the shape shown in Figure 9–35. Use grid, snap, units, limits, and layer settings from Exercise 9–1.

FIGURE 9–35
Dimensions for Exercise 9–2

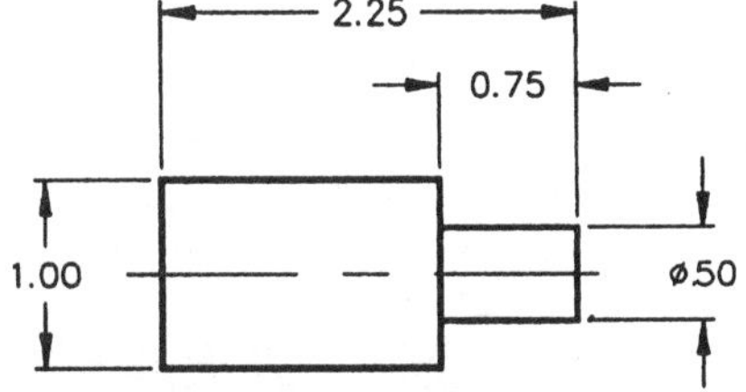

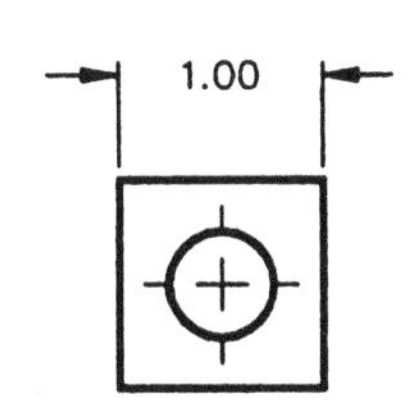

2. Make Exercise 9–1 the prototype drawing and erase all before you start drawing. Name this drawing 9–2 (your initials). (In the New Drawing Name. . . button, type 9–2 (your initials) = 9–1 (your initials).)

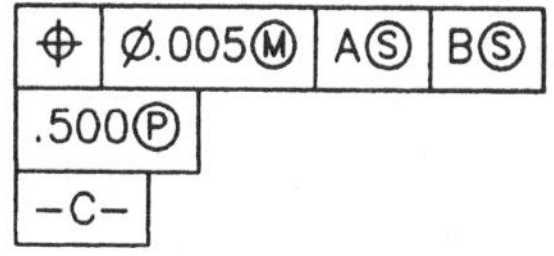

FIGURE 9–36
Feature Control Frame

Step 2. Complete the feature control frame shown in Figure 9–36.

Let's start with one feature control frame, Figure 9–36, that uses all the values in the Geometric Tolerance dialog box, Figure 9–37.

FIGURE 9–37
Geometric Tolerance Dialog Box

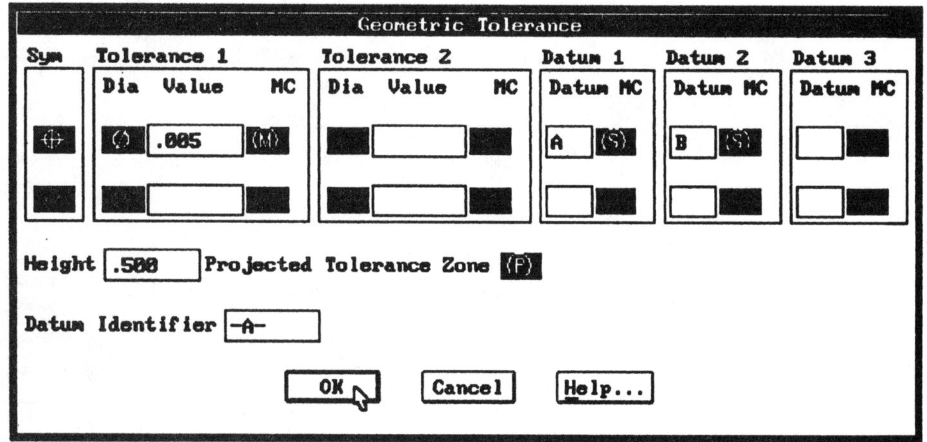

Prompt	Response
Command:	*Pick:* **DRAW DIM Toleran:**

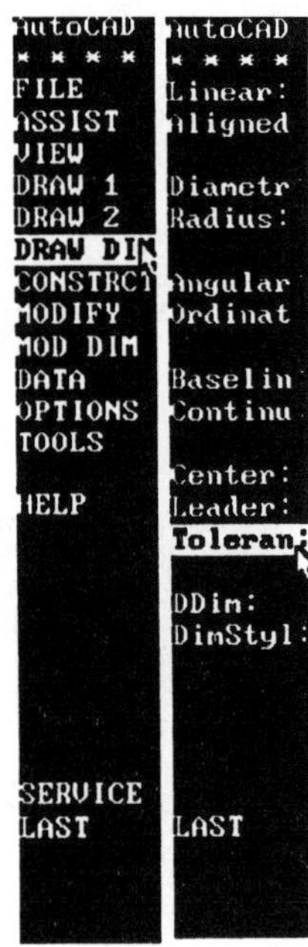

The Symbol dialog box, Figure 9–38, appears:	*Pick:* the Position symbol as shown. *Pick:* the OK button.

FIGURE 9–38
Symbol Dialog Box With the Position Symbol Selected

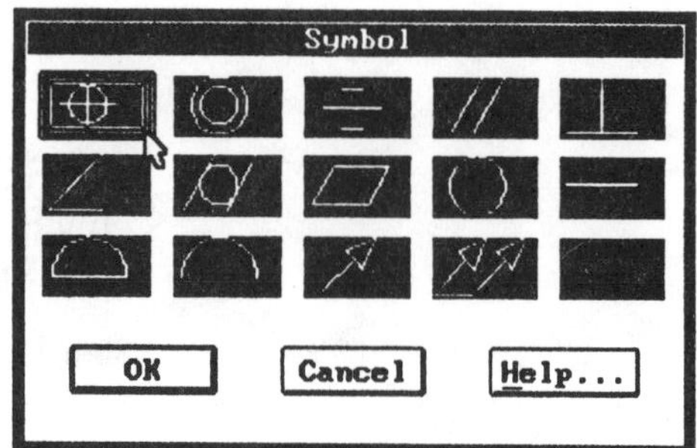

The Geometric Tolerance dialog box, Figure 9–39, appears:	Pick the Dia button in the Tolerance 1 area so that the diameter symbol appears as shown. Pick the Value button. *Type:* **.005** Pick the MC button.

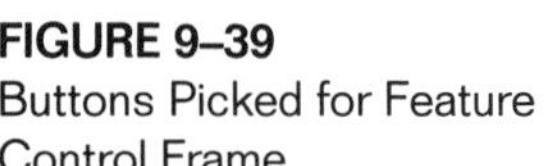
FIGURE 9–39
Buttons Picked for Feature Control Frame

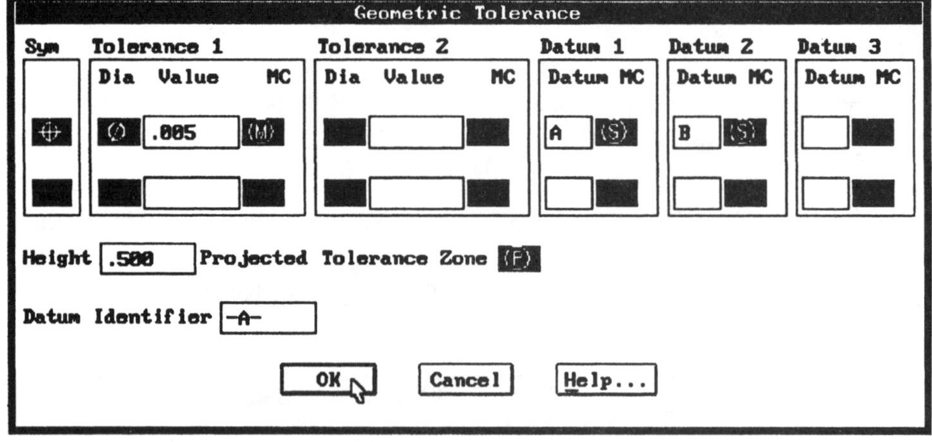

The Material Condition dialog box, Figure 9–40 appears:	Pick the Maximum Material Condition symbol as shown. Pick the OK Button.

FIGURE 9–40
Material Condition Dialog Box with Maximum Material Condition Symbol Picked

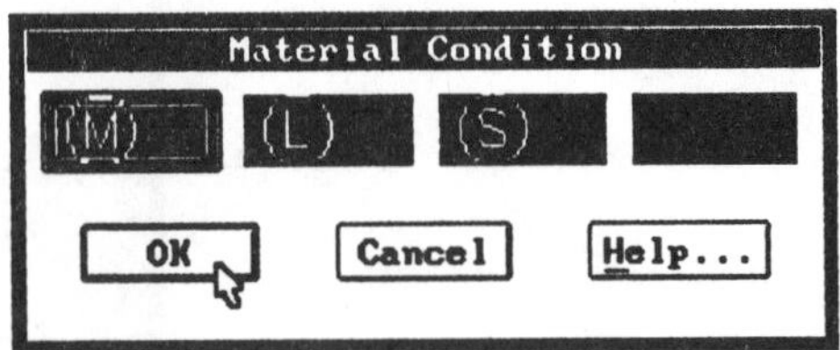

The Geometric Tolerance dialog box, Figure 9–39, appears:

Pick the Datum button in the Datum 1 area.

Type: **A**

Pick the MC button in the Datum 1 area.

The Material Condition dialog box, Figure 9–41, appears:

Pick the Regardless of Feature Size symbol as shown.

Pick the OK button.

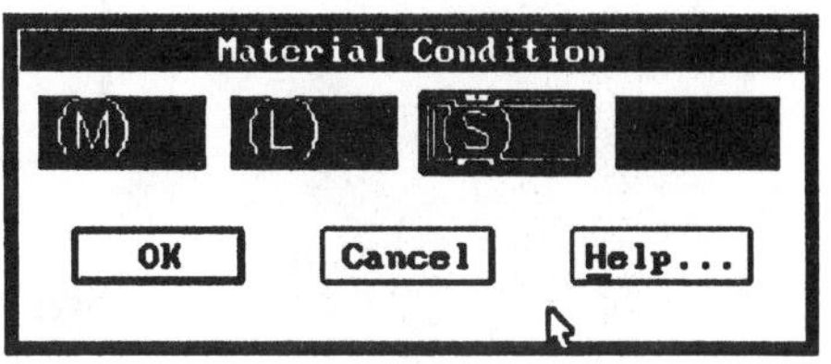

FIGURE 9–41
Material Condition Dialog Box with Regardless of Feature Symbol Picked

The Geometric Tolerance dialog box, Figure 9–39, appears:

Pick: the Datum button in the Datum 2 area.

Type: **B**

Pick the MC button in the Datum 1 area.

The Material Condition dialog box, Figure 9–41, appears:

Pick the Regardless of Feature Size symbol as shown.

Pick the OK button.

The Geometric Tolerance dialog box, Figure 9–39, appears:

Pick the Height button below the Tolerance 1 area.

Type: **.500**

Pick the Projected Tolerance Zone button so that the Projected Tolerance Zone symbol appears.

Pick the Datum Identifier button.

Type: **-A-**

Pick the OK button.

Enter tolerance location:

Pick: **D1** (Figure 9–42)

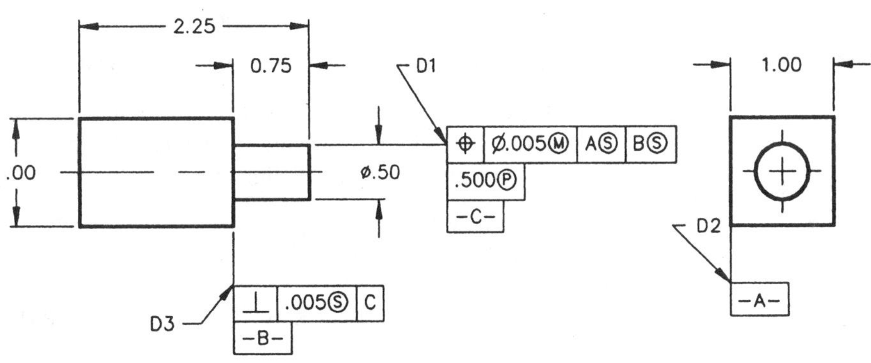

FIGURE 9–42
Applying Feature Control Frames

On Your Own:

Step 3. Add the -A- datum identifier by completing the Geometric Tolerance dialog box as shown in Figure 9–43 and D2, Figure 9–42.

FIGURE 9–43
Adding Datum -A-

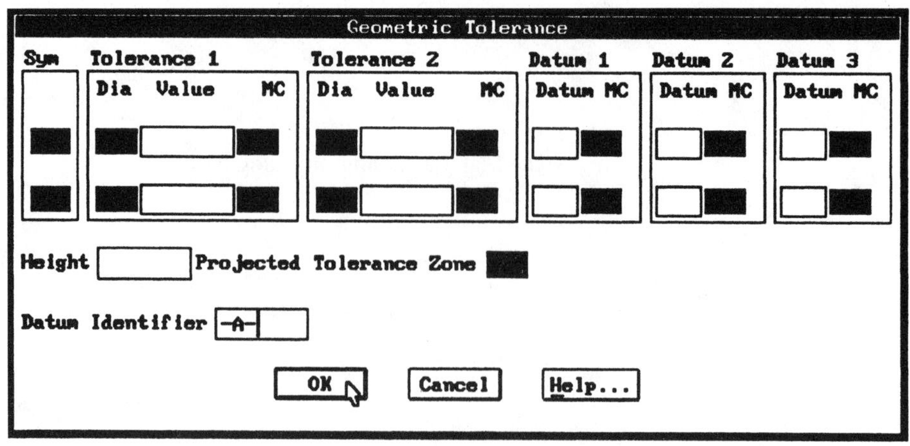

Step 4. Add the perpendicularity tolerance by completing the Geometric Tolerance dialog box as shown in Figure 9–44 and D3, Figure 9–42.

FIGURE 9–44
Adding Perpendicularity Tolerance

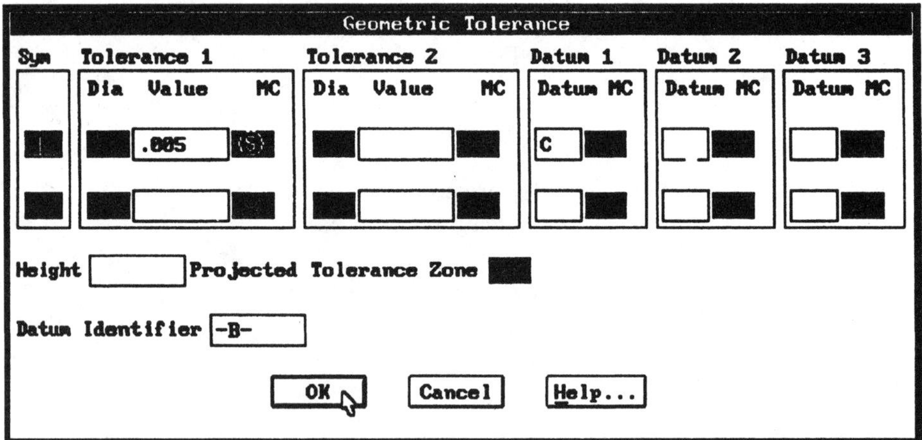

Step 5. Add or extend any necessary lines so that the drawing appears as shown in Figure 9–42 (do not add D1, D2, and D3 and their leaders.)

Exercise 9–2 is now complete.

Step 6. Plot the drawing and save it in two places.

Additional Dimensioning Features

To dimension a drawing in millimeters using one-place decimals:

Dimensioning a metric drawing is similar to dimensioning a drawing drawn in inches, with a few differences, which are shown next. Set dimensioning variables in the same manner as you chose for dimensioning in inches (Figure 9–23), except:

DIMDEC = 1
DIMUNITS = 2
DIMSCALE = 25.4
LTSCALE = 25.4 (from DISPLAY on the OPTIONS menu)

Note: LTSCALE for metric drawings may have to be more or less than 25.4, depending on the size of the drawing.

Set units as follows:

Prompt	Response
Systems of units:	
1. Scientific	
2. Decimal	

3. Engineering
4. Architectural
5. Fractional

Enter choice, 1 to 5 <2>:	*Type:* **2** (or ↵ if 2 is the default)
Number of digits to right of decimal point (0 to 8) <4>:	*Type:* **1** ↵

Press ↵ in response to the other prompts.

Feature 1. This will eliminate some prompts. You will discover where it can be used most effectively, for example: overall dimensions of parts (Figure 9–45).

FIGURE 9–45
Selected Line for Dimension

Prompt	Response
Command:	**DRAW DIM** **Linear:**
First extension line or RETURN to select:	↵ (Figure 9–45)
Select line, arc, or circle:	*Pick:* (the line, arc, or circle to be dimensioned) **D1**
Dimension line location:	*Pick:* **D2**

Feature 2. Notice that the sequence of extension lines selection determines where the small dimension is placed. See examples in Figure 9–46.

FIGURE 9–46
Dimension Placement

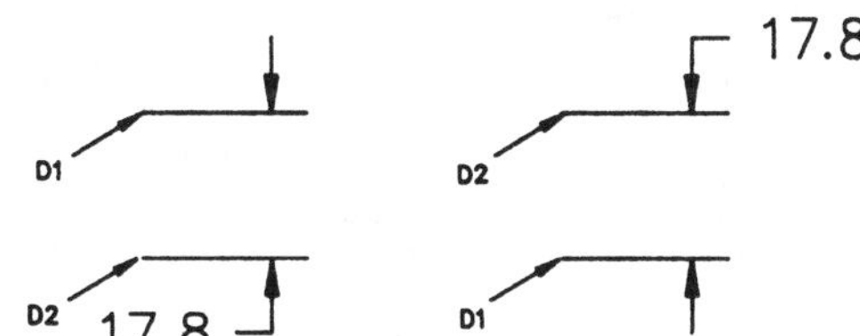

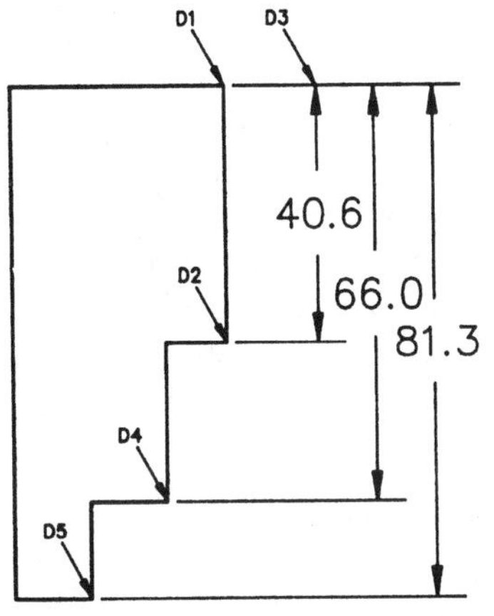

FIGURE 9–47
Baseline Dimensioning

Feature 3. For baseline dimensioning (Figure 9–47):

Baseline Dimension

Prompt	Response
Command:	**Linear:** (from the DRAW DIM menu)
First extension line origin or RETURN to select:	*Pick:* **D1**
Second extension line origin:	*Pick:* **D2**
Dimension line location:	*Pick:* **D3**
Command:	**baselin:** (*Pick:* **LAST** to return to the DRAW DIM menu.)
Second extension line origin or RETURN to select:	*Pick:* **D4**
Dim:	↵
Second extension line origin or RETURN to select:	*Pick:* **D5**

Feature 4. Associative dimensioning: Use the STRETCH command to shrink or enlarge any drawing already dimensioned.

Observe that the dimension text changes with the size of the drawing (DIMASO must be on). When DIMAZO is on, the dimension, dimension lines, arrowheads, and extension lines are inserted as a block.

Feature 5. Adding tolerances to specific dimensions: To add tolerances to a specific dimension (Figure 9–48) make settings as shown in Figure 9–48 and then dimension.

FIGURE 9–48
Tolerances

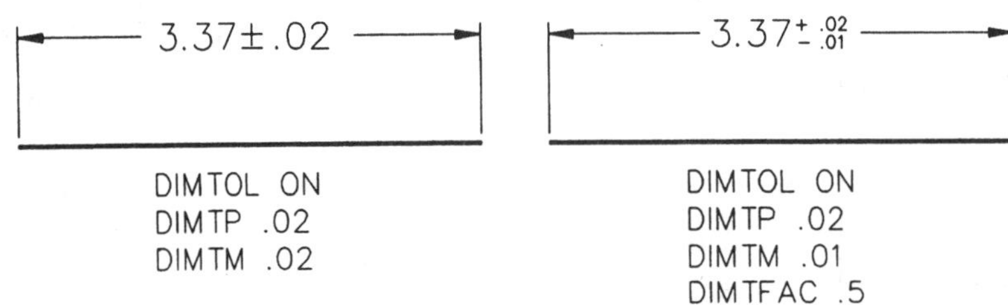

Feature 6. The command DimTedit: is used to control the placement and orientation of the text within an associative dimension.

Note: An associative dimension is one that has been drawn with the variable DIMASO on. All the elements of an associative dimension are a single entity (a block).

Note: UCS (user-coordinate system) will be explained in depth later chapters on 3-D.

Prompt	Response
Command:	**DimTedt:** (from the MOD DIM menu) or *Type:* **DIMTEDIT** ↵
Select dimension:	Pick a single associative dimension.
Enter text location (Left/Right/Home/Angle):	Pick the new location or: (left = left justified) *Type:* **L** ↵ (right = right justified) *Type:* **R** ↵ (home = the original text location) *Type:* **H** ↵ (angle = type the angle or pick two points) *Type:* **A** ↵.

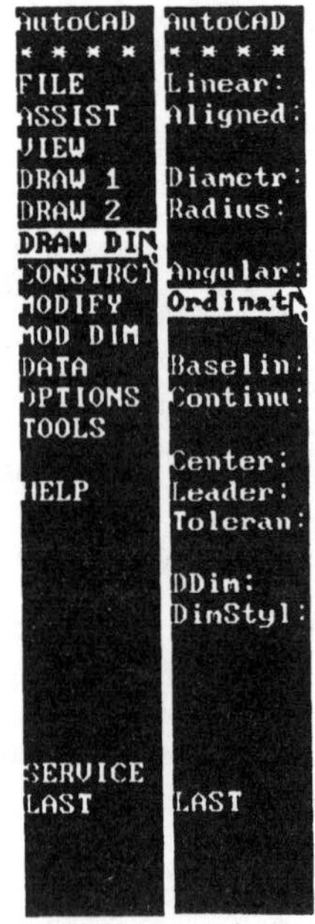

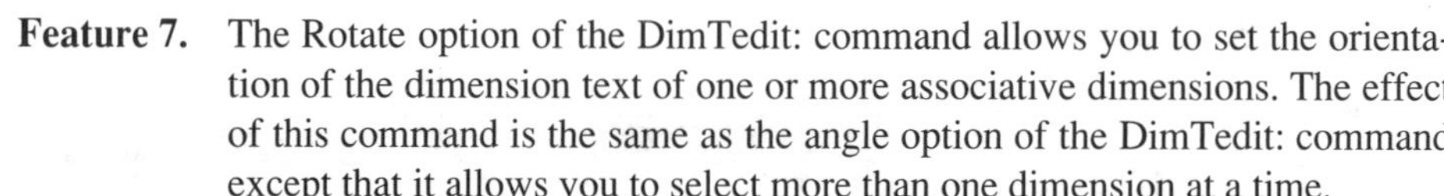

Feature 7. The Rotate option of the DimTedit: command allows you to set the orientation of the dimension text of one or more associative dimensions. The effect of this command is the same as the angle option of the DimTedit: command except that it allows you to select more than one dimension at a time.

Feature 8. The Ordinate dimensioning command is used to create dimensions from a 0,0 datum similar to Figure 9–49. The current UCS is used to define where 0,0 is located. To place 0,0 at the upper left corner of this drawing, do the following:

FIGURE 9–49
Ordinate Dimensioning

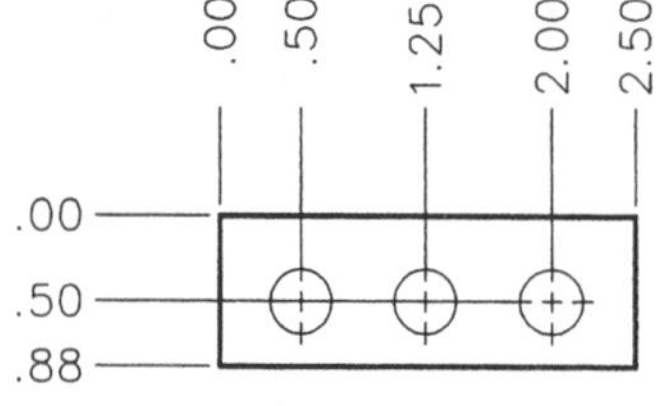

Prompt	Response
Command:	*Type:* **UCS** ↵
Origin/ZAxis/3point/OBject/View/X/Y/Z/ Prev/Restore/Save/Del/?/<World>:	*Type:* **O** ↵ {for origin}

Note: To move the UCS icon, select or type UCSICON ↵ then type or ↵ to move the icon to the new origin.

Remember: Return the origin to its original location before plotting. (Select UCS and then World, which is the default.)

Origin point <0,0,0>: Pick the upper left corner of the part. This is now the origin 0,0 of the current UCS. (The UCS icon, the arrow in the lower left corner of the display, will not move to the new origin unless directed to do so.) Now ORDINATE dimensioning can be used by picking two points for each end of the ordinate dimension line.

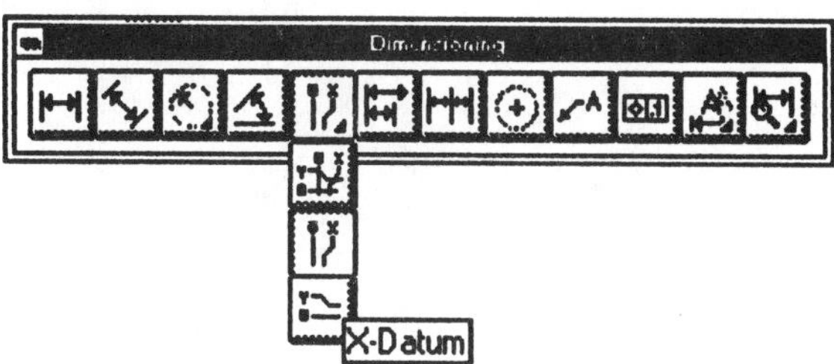

EXERCISES

Tip: The scale factor for X and Y for ¼″ = 1′ is .0208 (¼″ divided by 12″). When you insert the drawing into the format, type .0208 ↵ when prompted for the X scale factor. You may want to insert the format around the drawing instead of inserting the drawing into the format, in which case the scale factor is 48 (12″ divided by ¼″). If you insert the format around the drawing, the plotting ratio will be 1 = 48.

Hint: If you have created dimensions with DIMASO ON and reduce the drawing using the SCALE command, the dimensions will change with the size of the drawing. INSERTing a drawing, however, treats the entire drawing as a block, and the dimensions remain in their original form unless the block is EXPLODED. Do not EXPLODE the block. Make any changes on the original drawing. (It is a better practice to Insert: the format around the drawing at a scale of 2 and then Plot: at 1 = 2.)

9–1. Dimension the mechanical part shown as Figure 9–22. Use the basic drawing from Chapter 8. Use the procedures described in this chapter. Insert the drawing into an A-size format. Plot the drawing or save it on a floppy disk for later use according to your instructor's plan.

9–2. Complete Exercise 9–2 as described in the section on geometric dimensioning and tolerancing. Plot the drawing or save it on a floppy disk for later use according to your instructor's plan.

9–3. Draw and dimension the part shown in Figure 9–50 using metric dimensions. Make the drawing full scale. Set the dimensioning variables using the procedures described for Figure 9–23. Set DIMSCALE = 25.4. Insert an A-size format around this drawing at a scale factor of 25.4 (Assignment 9-3). Plot or save according to your instructor's directions.

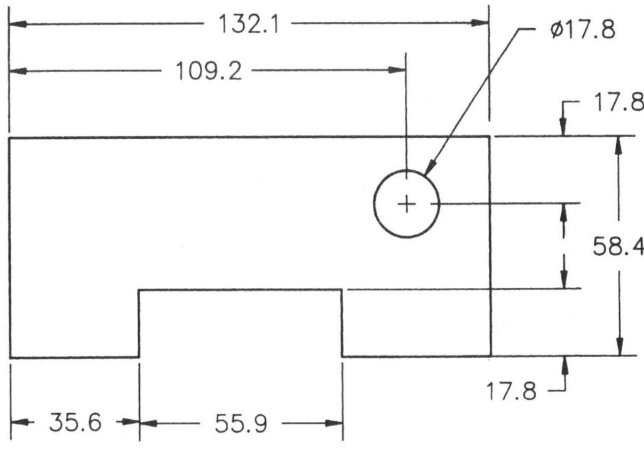

FIGURE 9–50
Exercise 9–3

9–4. Draw and dimension the part shown in Figure 9–51 using 1-place decimal dimensions in millimeters. Use settings from Exercise 3. Use the baseline dimensioning system. Estimate horizontal dimensions. Set DIMSCALE = 25.4. Insert an A-size format around this drawing at a scale of 25.4 (Assignment 9-4). Plot or save as your instructor directs.

FIGURE 9–51
Exercise 9–4

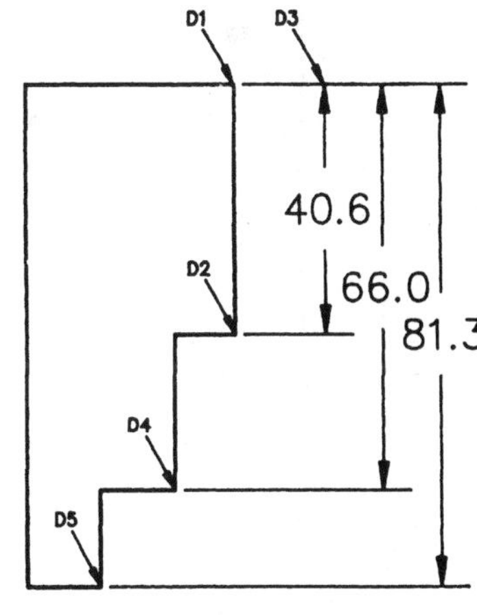

9–5. Dimension the drawings done for Chapter 8, Exercises 8–3 and 8–7. Use settings from Exercise 9–1. Change drawing limits to 17,11. Plot these drawings on an 11″ × 17″ horizontal sheet. Insert each one into a B-size format before plotting (Assignment 9–5).

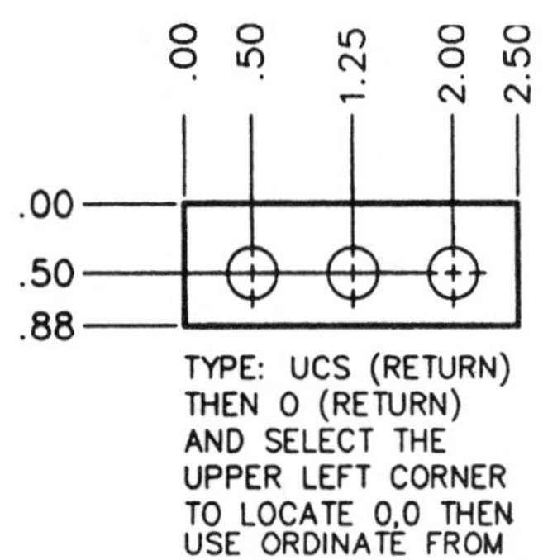

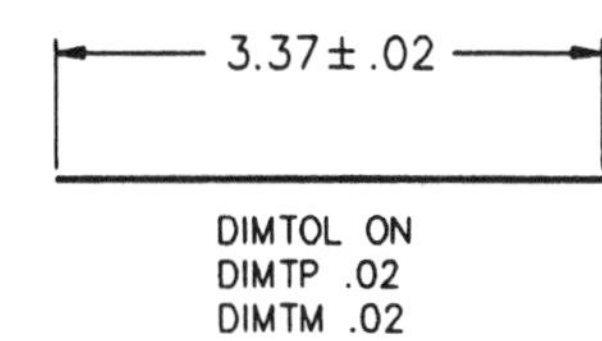

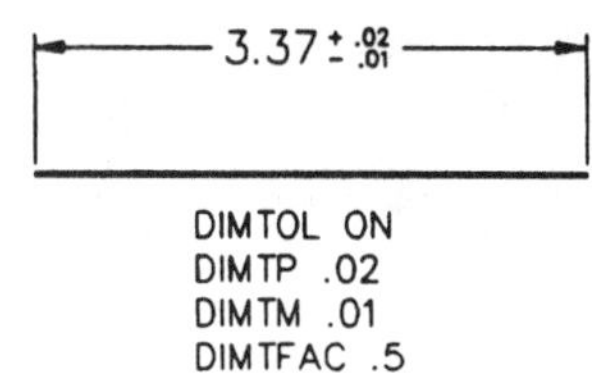

FIGURE 9–52
Exercise 9–6

9–6. Draw full size, set indicated variables, and dimension the figure shown in Figure 9–52. Use settings from Exercise 9–1.

DIMDEC = 2
ARROW SIZE = .2
DIMUNITS = 2
EXTENSION LINE OFFSET = .06
TEXT HEIGHT = .25
EXTENSION LINE EXTENSION = .06
Use 2-place decimals for all dimensions.

Insert into an A-size format (Assignment 9–6).

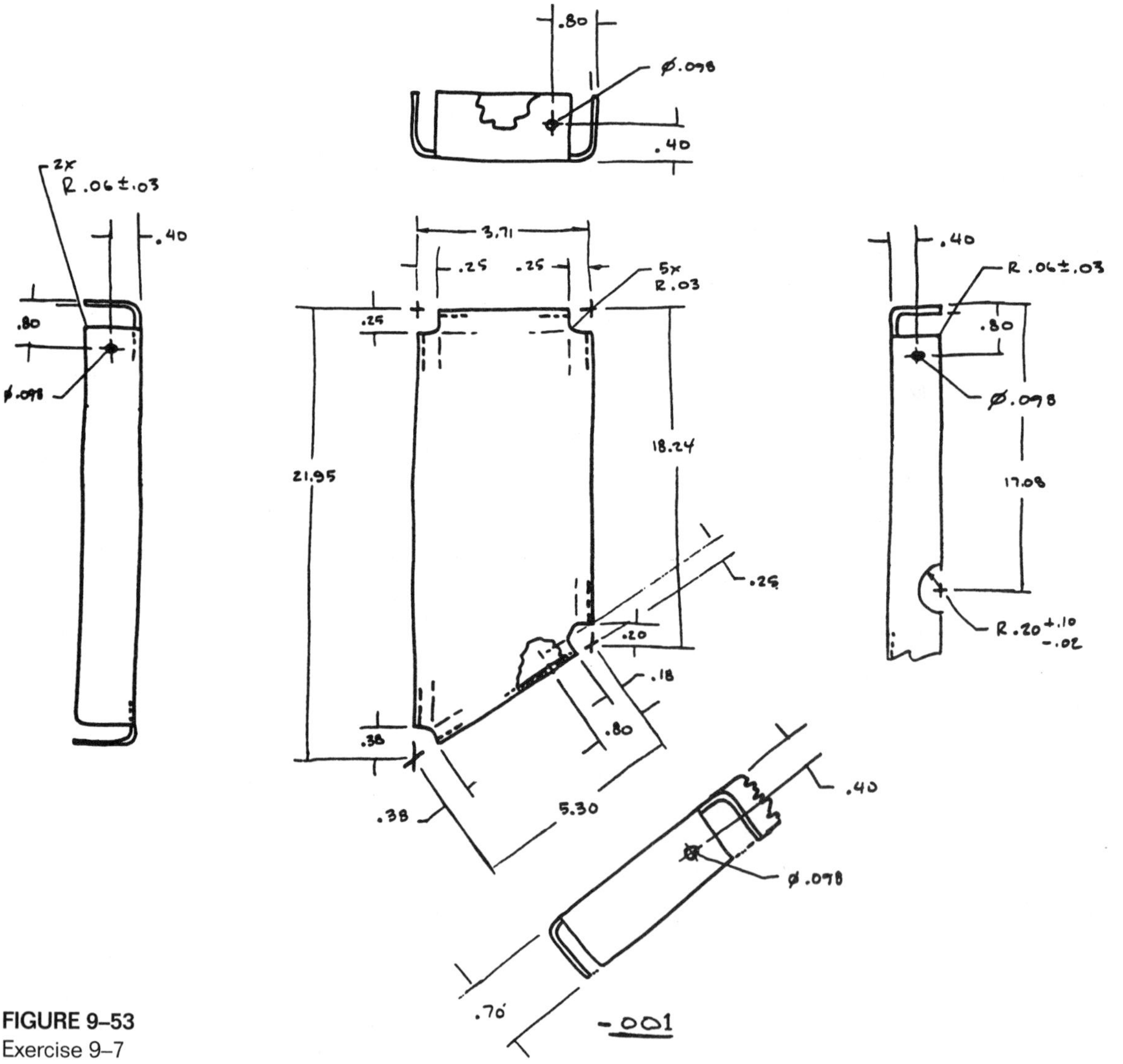

FIGURE 9–53
Exercise 9–7

9–7. Draw full size and dimension the part shown in Figure 9–53. Put it on a 22″ × 34″ sheet size using the following:

DIMDEC = 2
DIMUNIT = 2
DIMTXT = .18
DIMEXE = .16
DIMEXO = .16
DIMASZ = .18
DIMSCALE = 1.00
Use 3-place decimals for hole sizes.
Use 2-place decimals for all other dimensions.

Insert this drawing into a C-size format at a scale of .5 or insert the format around the drawing at a scale of 2 (Assignment 9–7).

9–8. Draw the part shown in Figure 9–54. Make the drawing twice size and place it on an 8.5″ × 11″ horizontal sheet. Name the drawing 9–8A, then copy it under the name 9–8B. Use these DIMVARS to dimension each drawing (Inch dimensions are above metric dimensions.):

DIMDEC = 2
DIMUNIT = 2
DIMTXT = .10
DIMEXE = .08
DIMEXO = .08
DIMASZ = .12
DIMLFAC = .5
DIMSCALE = 2.00

a. Use 2-place decimal inch dimensions for Drawing 9–8A.
b. Use 2-place decimal millimeter dimensions for Drawing 9–8B.

Use DIMSCALE = 25.4 and DIMLFAC = 12.7 for part b.

Insert each drawing into an A-size format, using a scale of 25.4 for drawing 9–8B (Assignments 9–8A and 9–8B).

9–9. Draw the part shown in Figure 9–55. Make the drawing full size and place it on an 8.5″ × 11″ horizontal sheet. Name the drawing 9–9A, then copy it under the name 9–9B. Use these DIMVARS to dimension each drawing:

DIMDEC = 2
DIMUNIT = 2
DIMTXT = .10
DIMEXE = .08
DIMEXO = .08
DIMASZ = .12
DIMSCALE = 1.00

a. Use 2-place decimal inch dimensions for Drawing 9–9A. (Inch dimensions are above metric dimensions.)

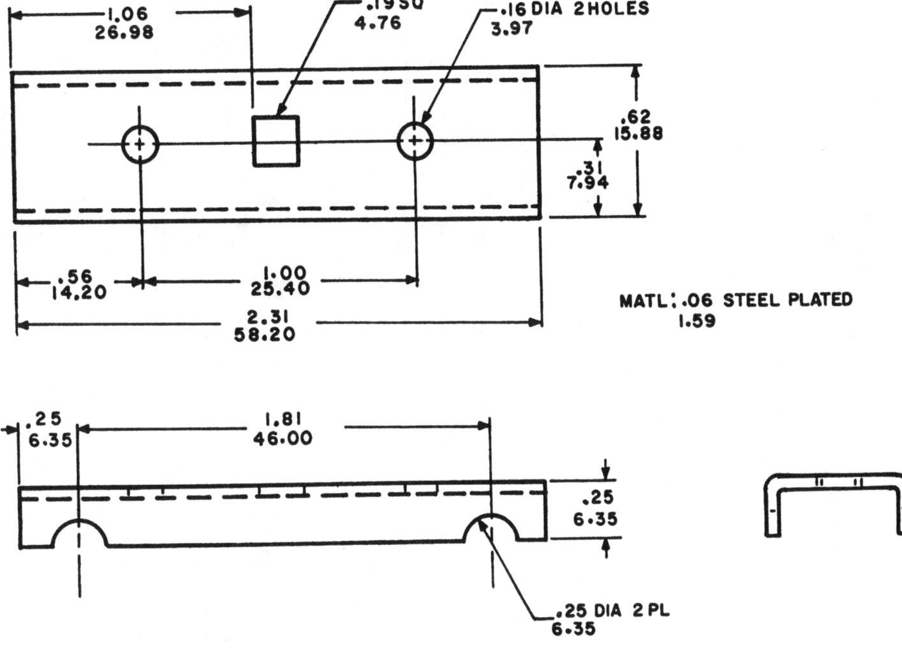

FIGURE 9–54
Exercise 9–8A and 9–8B

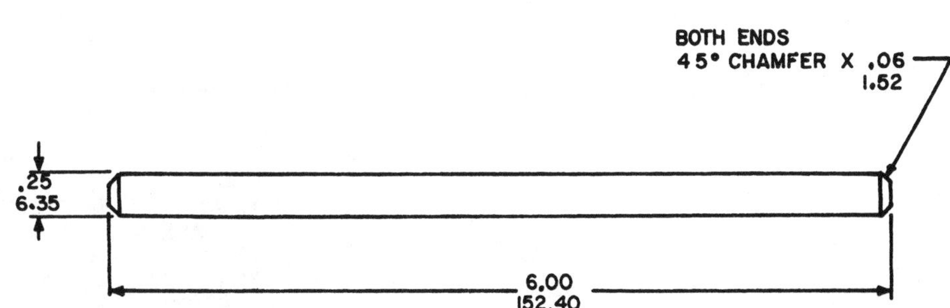

FIGURE 9–55
Exercise 9–9A and 9–9B

b. Use 2-place decimal millimeter dimensions for Drawing 9–9B. Use DIMLFAC = 25.4 for part b.

Insert each drawing into an A-size format (Assignments 9–9A and 9–9B).

9–10. Draw and dimension the part shown in Figure 9–56. Use the Tolerance: option of Dimensioning to add a feature control frame as stated in Figure 9–56. Insert an A-size format around the drawing (Assignment 9–10).

9–11. Draw and dimension the part shown in Figure 9–57. Use the Tolerance: option of Dimensioning to add feature control frames as stated in Figure 9–57. Insert an A-size format around the drawing (Assignment 9–11).

9–12. Draw and dimension the part shown in Figure 9–58. Use the Tolerance: option of Dimensioning to add feature control frames as stated in Figure 9–58. Insert an A-size format around the drawing (Assignment 9–12).

9–13. Draw and dimension the top view only of the part shown in Figure 9–59. Use 3-place decimals on all dimensions. Use the Tolerance: option of Dimensioning to add feature control frames as stated below:

Make the horizontal center lines of the holes datums -A- and -B-.

Make the bottom edge datum -C-.

Locate holes with a positional tolerance of .005 at maximum material condition with reference to datums -A- and -B-. Holes should have a projected tolerance zone height of .375. Show the projected tolerance zone symbol.

Make the left side of the part perpendicular to the bottom edge within a tolerance zone of .005 regardless of feature size.

Insert an A-size format around the drawing (Assignment 9–13).

FIGURE 9–56
Exercise 9–10

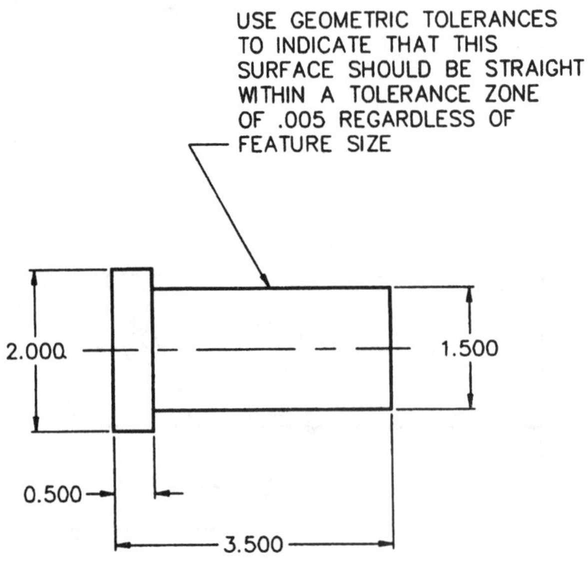

USE GEOMETRIC TOLERANCES
TO INDICATE THAT THIS
SURFACE SHOULD BE STRAIGHT
WITHIN A TOLERANCE ZONE
OF .005 REGARDLESS OF
FEATURE SIZE
2.000
1.500
0.500
3.500

FIGURE 9–57
Exercise 9–11

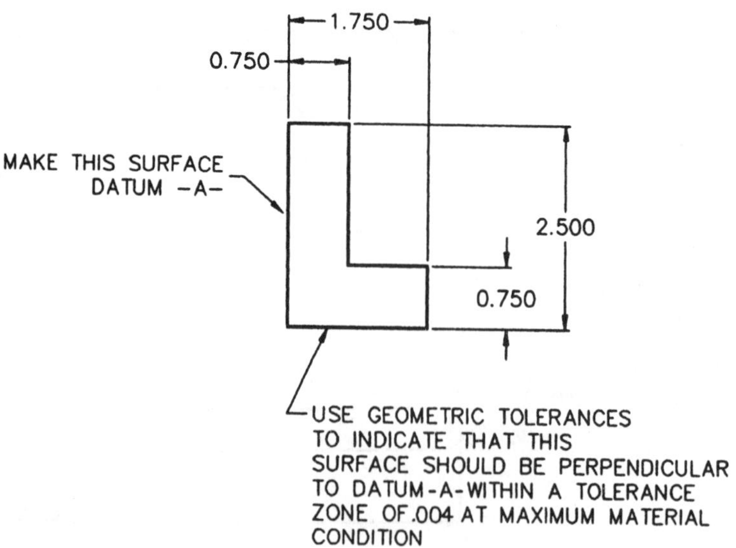

FIGURE 9–58
Exercise 9–12

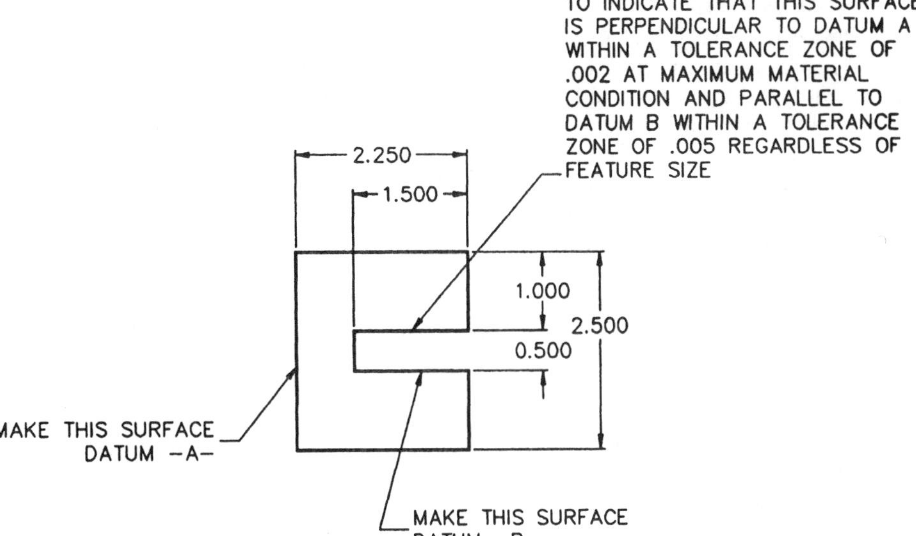

FIGURE 9–59
Exercise 9–13

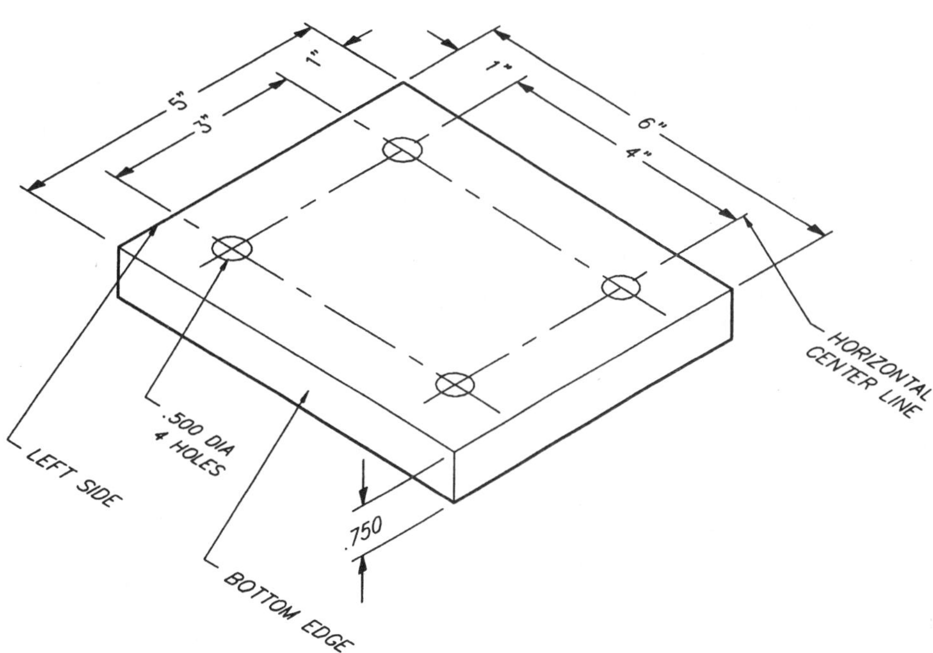

REVIEW QUESTIONS

Circle the correct answer.

1. Which of the following sets the text style of the dimension?
   a. DIMTXT
   b. DIMTXSTY
   c. DIMUNIT
   d. DIMDEC
   e. DIMUPT
2. DIMASZ determines:
   a. The height of the alternate text
   b. The height of the arrowhead
   c. The length of the arrowhead
   d. The direction of the azimuths
   e. The length of the bearing
3. DIMEXO sets:
   a. The distance from the X and Y coordinates
   b. The execute file for dimensions
   c. The distance from the object to the beginning of the extension line
   d. The distance from the end of the extension line to the dimension line
   e. The distance from the beginning of the extension line to the end of the extension line
4. DIMDLI sets:
   a. The dimension length in inches
   b. The length of the arrowhead

c. The distance from the beginning of the dimension line to the extension line
d. The length of dimension lines
e. The spacing between dimension lines

5. With DIMSCALE set at 48 and DIMTXT at ⅛″, text for dimensions will measure:
a. 1/16″ b. ⅛″ c. ¼″ d. 3″ e. 6″

6. Which of the following places the text above the dimension line?
a. DIMSE1 d. DIMLIM
b. DIMSE2 e. DIMTOL
c. DIMTAD

7. Which of the following produces a dimension with no extension line at the beginning of the dimension?
a. DIMSE1 d. DIMLIM
b. DIMSE2 e. DIMTOL
c. DIMTAD

8. Which of the following must be set to ON for tolerances to be added to dimensioning text?
a. DIMSE1 d. DIMLIM
b. DIMSE2 e. DIMTOL
c. DIMTAD

9. Which of the following must be set ON for metric dimensions to be displayed with inch dimensions?
a. DIMLIM d. DIMALTF
b. DIMTOL e. DIMALTD
c. DIMALT

10. Which of the following sets the number of decimal places in the alternate dimension?
a. DIMDEC d. DIMALTF
b. DIMTOL e. DIMALTD
c. DIMALT

11. Which of the following sets the number of decimal places to the right of the decimal point for the standard dimension?
a. DIMDEC d. DIMALTF
b. DIMTOL e. DIMALTD
c. DIMALT

12. To pick the exact location of the upper right corner of a part, which of the following Osnap modifiers should be used?
a. PERPENDICULAR d. MIDPOINT
b. INTERSECTION e. LINE
c. CENTER

13. When DIMSCALE = 0, AutoCAD computes a DIMSCALE that is the ratio:
a. Between model space and paper space limits
b. Between DIMLFAC and DIMALTF
c. Between the plotting scale and the drawing size
d. Between DIMTXT and STYLE height
e. Between drawing size and plotting units

14. Which of the following dimension commands produces feature control frames for geometric tolerances?
a. Toleran: d. Baselin:
b. Linear: e. Continu:
c. Ordinat:

15. If DIMSCALE is set at 1.0000, what must the setting be for an arrowhead to be ⅛″ long?
a. DIMASZ = .125 d. DIMTSZ = 1.00
b. DIMASZ = 1.00 e. DIMASZ = 0
c. DIMTSZ = .125

16. Which of the following variables must be activated if some symbol other than the tick or the arrowhead is to be used for the ends of a dimension line?
a. DIMSHO d. BIMALT
b. DIMPOST e. DIMALT 2
c. DIMBLK

17. If all dimensions are to originate from the same edge, which of the following modifiers should be used?
a. Continue: d. Originate:
b. Datum: e. Baseline:
c. Origin:

18. If you wish to begin all extension lines 1/16″ from the object lines, which of the following is the correct setting?
a. DIMZIN = 0 d. DIMLIM = .0625
b. DIMEXE = 1 e. DIMLIM = 1
c. DIMEXO = .0625

19. To place center marks at the center of all arcs and circles, which of the following DIM options should be activated?
a. Center: d. Diametr:
b. Intersection: e. Radius:
c. Point:

20. Which of the following is the correct response if a 1.395-diameter dimension is needed? The prompt is XXXXX<Radius>?
a. 1.395 b. .625 c. D d. R e. C
Complete.

21. Write the command that establishes the origin from which ORDINATE dimensions are drawn.

____

22. Write the dimensioning variable that sets the overall scale of the arrowheads and text size used on a drawing.

____

23. Write the dimensioning variable that sets the height of the text used for dimensions.

____

24. Write two commands that can be used to correct an associative dimension.

____

25. Describe the function of DimTedit:.

____

26. Write the correct DIMSCALE setting for a drawing done in millimeters.

____

27. Describe the function of associative dimensioning.

____

____

____

28. Draw the correct symbol for maximum material condition and describe what it means with reference to a hole and a shaft.

____

____

____

29. Define the term "Projected Tolerance Zone."

____

____

30. Define the term "datum."

____

PART III THE AUTOCAD PROGRAM: SOLID MODELING

10 An Introduction to Solid Modeling

OBJECTIVES

When you have completed this chapter, you will be able to:

- □ Use the Elevation and Thickness settings to draw basic 3-D models.
- □ Use the Vports: command to create multiple viewports so that you can display several views of the same 3-D model.
- □ Use Vpoint: to change the viewing angle of a 3-D model.
- □ Describe the standard viewing angles for engineering drawings.
- □ Change the location of the user coordinates systems (UCS) while working in 3-D.
- □ Describe the uses of model space and paper space.
- □ Use MVSetup to insert a standard ANSI title block.
- □ Use Dview: to make a perspective view of a 3-D model.

INTRODUCTION

While making the drawings in previous chapters you have been working in 2-D AutoCAD, making 2-D drawings of objects. This chapter introduces you to drawing in three dimensions; now you will be creating a solid model. Although all the AutoCAD DRAW, CONSTRCT, AND MODIFY commands work in 3-D, your concept of what you are drawing must now change. You are creating a model, not drawing pictures.

EXERCISE 10–1, PART 1 USING THE ELEV: (ELEVATION) AND THICKNESS SETTING TO DRAW A 3-D MODEL

When you have completed Exercise 10–1, parts 1 through 3, your drawing will look similar to Figure 10–1. Parts of the 3-D model drawn in Exercise 10–1, Part 1, have different heights. These heights are called *thickness.* Until now you have worked in only the X and Y directions. The Z dimension will now be added, to give thickness (vertical shape) to your models. Elev: (Elevation), will allow you to specify different elevations, starting from 0 elevation, for different parts of the model. The Thickness setting is part of the Elev: command; it will allow you to assign different heights to parts of the model.

Drawing part of the model (the outside wall, lower rectangular shape, and second rectangular shape) will demonstrate drawing 3-D shapes using AutoCAD commands that are

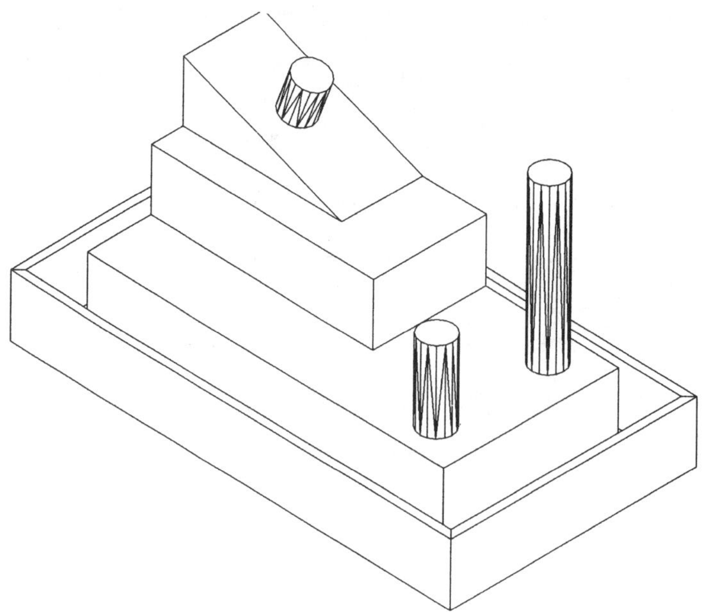

FIGURE 10–1
Using Elevation and Thickness to Draw a 3-D Model

also used to draw in 2-D. Drawing the top wedge and the cyclinders of the model will demonstrate using basic SOLIDS commands.

To prepare to draw Exercise 10–1, turn on the computer and start AutoCAD.

Set Up the Drawing

Step 1. On Your Own:

1. Pick New. . . from the menu bar File Menu. Name the drawing: 10-1 (your initials).
2. Make the following settings:

UNITS: Decimal; 3 digits to the right of the decimal point
LIMITS: Lower left corner: 0,0
Upper right corner: 8.5,11
GRID: .2
SNAP: .05
STYLE: STANDARD; FONT: SIMPLEX; HEIGHT: 0
Create the following layers:

LAYER NAME	COLOR	LINETYPE
Y	YELLOW	CONTINUOUS
R	RED	CONTINUOUS
G	GREEN	CONTINUOUS

Set layer Y current.

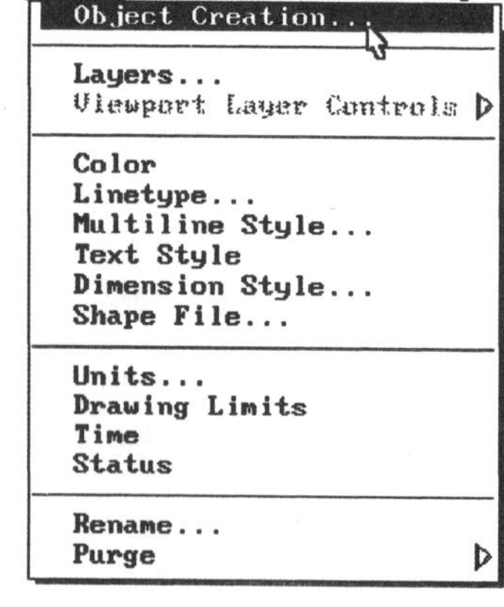

Elevation and Thickness

Step 2. Set the elevation and thickness for drawing the outside wall of the model.

Prompt	Response
Command:	*Type:* **ELEV** ↵
ELEV New current elevation <0.000>:	↵ (to accept 0 elevation)
New current thickness <0.000>:	*Type:* **.75** ↵

Object Creation Modes

Color...	BYLAYER
Layer...	0
Linetype...	BYLAYER
Text Style...	STANDARD
Linetype Scale:	1.0000
Elevation:	0.0000
Thickness:	0.0000

OK   Cancel   Help...

Now everything you draw will be at elevation 0′-0″ with a thickness of .75. Don't be concerned when you don't see any thickness for the shapes when you draw them in the following part of this exercise. You are looking directly down on the plan view of the model (0,0,1 coordinates). You will see the thickness of the model shapes when you change your viewpoint of the model later in the exercise.

Draw Part of the 3-D Model Using AutoCAD Commands That Are Also Used in 2-D

Step 3. Draw the outside wall of the model (Figure 10–2).

Prompt	Response
Command:	**Pline:** (or *Type:* **PL** ↵)
From point:	*Type:* **1.5,8** ↵
Current line-width is <0.000>:	
Arc/Close/Halfwidth/Length/Undo/Width/ <Endpoint of line>:	*Type:* **W** ↵
Starting width <0.000>:	*Type:* **.1** ↵
Ending width <0.100>:	↵
Arc/Close/Halfwidth/Length/Undo/Width/ <Endpoint of line>:	*Type:* **@5.5<0** ↵
Arc/Close/Halfwidth/Length/Undo/Width/ <Endpoint of line>:	*Type:* **@3<−90** ↵
Arc/Close/Halfwidth/Length/Undo/Width/ <Endpoint of line>:	*Type:* **@5.5<180** ↵
Arc/Close/Halfwidth/Length/Undo/Width/ <Endpoint of line>:	*Type:* **C** ↵

Step 4. Set the elevation and thickness for drawing the larger, inside rectangular shape.

Prompt	Response
Command:	*Type:* **ELEV** ↵
ELEV New current elevation <0.000>:	↵
New current thickness <0.750>:	*Type:* **1** ↵

Step 5. Draw the larger, inside rectangular shape (Figure 10–2).

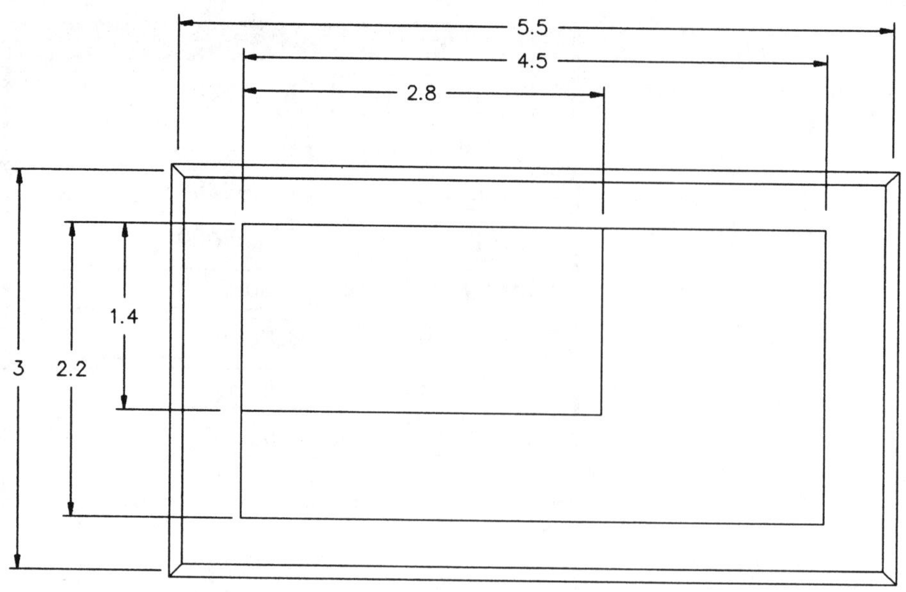

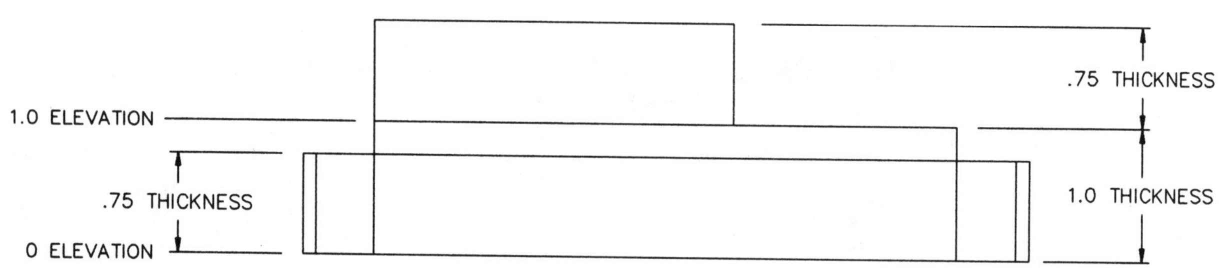

FIGURE 10–2
Drawing Part of the 3-D Model Using Commands That Are Also Used to Draw in 2-D

Prompt	**Response**
Command:	**Solid:**
First point:	*Type:* **2,7.6** ↵
Second point:	*Type:* **6.5,7.6** ↵
Third point:	*Type:* **2,5.4** ↵
Fourth point:	*Type:* **6.5,5.4** ↵
Third point:	↵

Step 6. Set layer R current for drawing the smaller rectangular shape.

Prompt	**Response**
Command:	*Type:* **LA** ↵
LAYER ?/Make/Set/New/ON/OFF/Color/ Ltype/Freeze/Thaw/LOck/Unlock:	*Type:* **S** ↵
New current layer <Y>:	*Type:* **R** ↵
?/Make/Set/New/ON/OFF/Color/ Ltype/Freeze/Thaw/LOck/Unlock:	↵

Step 7. Set elevation and thickness for drawing the smaller rectangular shape.

Set the elevation so that the bottom of the second rectangle is sitting on the top (thickness) of the first. The first, larger rectangle has an elevation of 0 and a thickness of 1.

Prompt	Response
Command:	*Type:* **ELEV** ↵
ELEV New current elevation <0.000>:	*Type:* **1** ↵
New current thickness <1.000>:	*Type:* **.75** ↵

Now everything you draw will be at elevation 1 with a thickness of .75.

Step 8. Draw the smaller rectangular shape sitting on top of the first rectangle (Figure 10–2).

Command:	**Solid:**
First point:	*Type:* **2,7.6** ↵
Second point:	*Type:* **4.8,7.6** ↵
Third point:	*Type:* **2,6.2** ↵
Fourth point:	*Type:* **4.8,6.2** ↵
Third point:	↵

Draw Part of the 3-D Model Using SOLIDS Commands Cylinder and Wedge

A primitive solid is a single solid 3-D shape that has had nothing added to or subtracted from it. Six solid primitives (box, sphere, wedge, cone, cylinder, torus) are the basic shapes often used in solid modeling. They are drawn by using six commands: Box:, Sphere:, Wedge:, Cone:, Cylinder:, and Torus:.

Next, we will add two cylinders and the wedge shape to the 3-D model. Elevation will be set to determine the drawing plane, but thickness will be set to 0 for drawing the wedge and cylinders. The Cylinder: and Wedge: commands both prompt for height, and the height of each will be entered at that time.

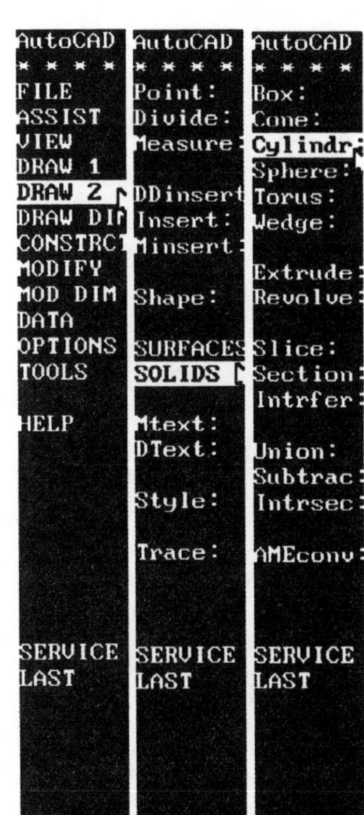

Step 9. Set elevation and thickness for drawing two cylinders.

Prompt	Response
Command:	*Type:* **ELEV** ↵
New current elevation <1.000>:	↵ (to accept the elevation of 1)
New current thickness <.750>:	*Type:* **0** ↵

Now everything you draw will be at an elevation of 1.

Step 10. Draw two cylinders sitting on top of the first, larger rectangle (Figure 10–3).

Prompt	Response
Command:	**Cylindr:**
Elliptical/<Center point><0,0,0>:	*Type:* **6,7.2** ↵
Diameter/<Radius>:	*Type:* **.2** ↵
Center of other end/<Height>:	*Type:* **2** ↵

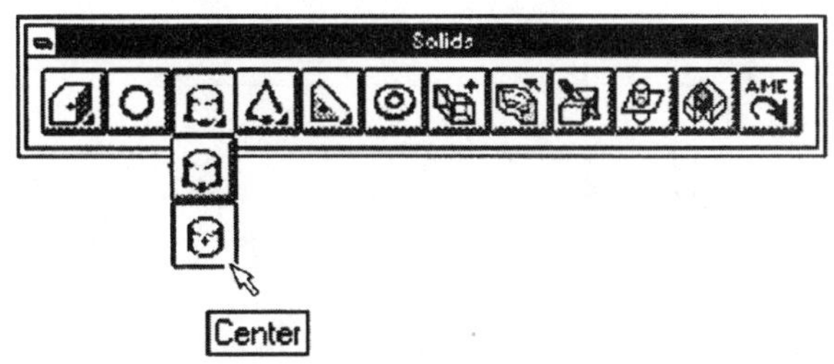

Prompt	Response
Command:	↵
Elliptical/<Center point><0,0,0>:	*Type:* **6,5.8** ↵
Diameter/<Radius>:	*Type:* **.2** ↵
Center of other end/<Height>:	*Type:* **1** ↵

Step 11. On Your Own:

Set layer G current for drawing the wedge shape.

Step 12. Set elevation and thickness for drawing the wedge shape.

Command:	*Type:* **ELEV** ↵
New current elevation <1.000>:	*Type:* **1.75** ↵
New current thickness <0.000>:	↵

Step 13. Draw the wedge shape (Figure 10–3).

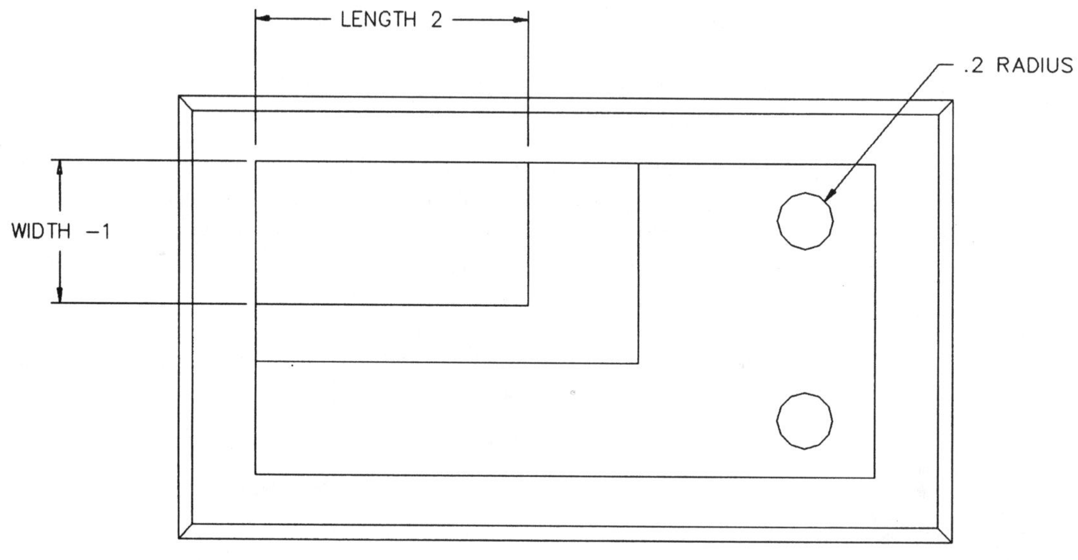

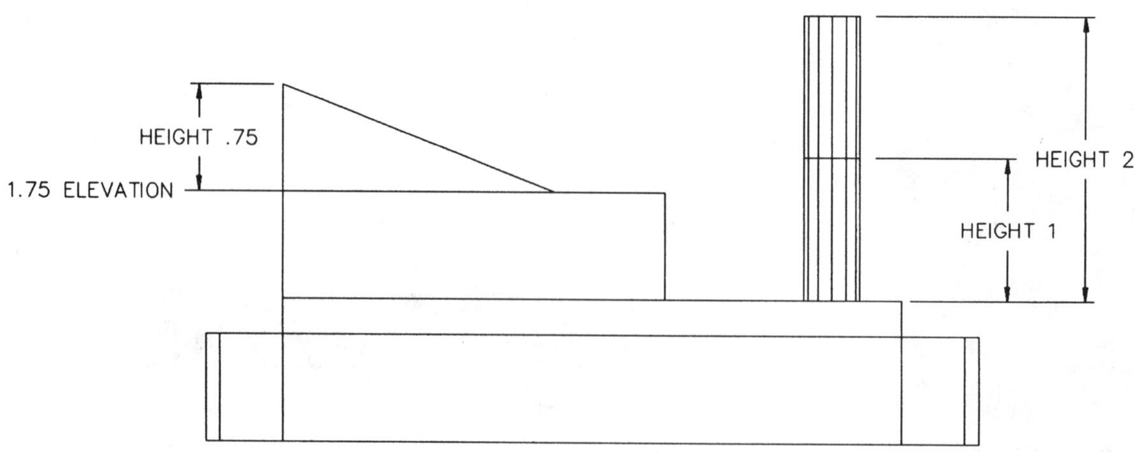

FIGURE 10–3
Drawing Part of the 3-D Model Using SOLIDS Commands

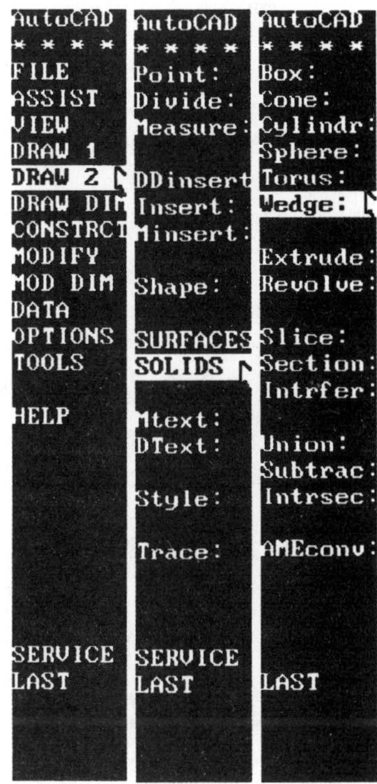

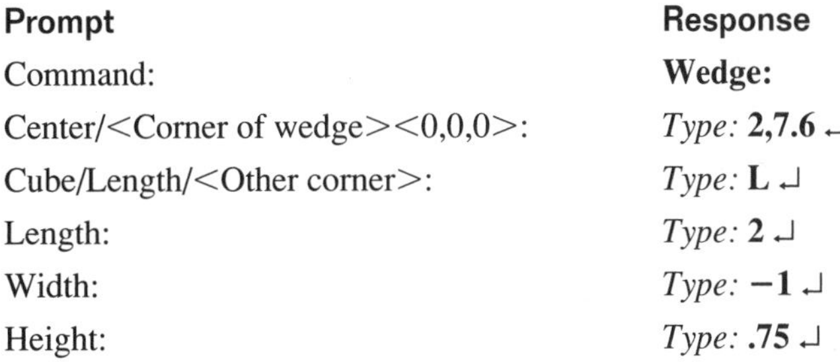

Prompt	Response
Command:	**Wedge:**
Center/<Corner of wedge><0,0,0>:	*Type:* **2,7.6** ↵
Cube/Length/<Other corner>:	*Type:* **L** ↵
Length:	*Type:* **2** ↵
Width:	*Type:* **−1** ↵
Height:	*Type:* **.75** ↵

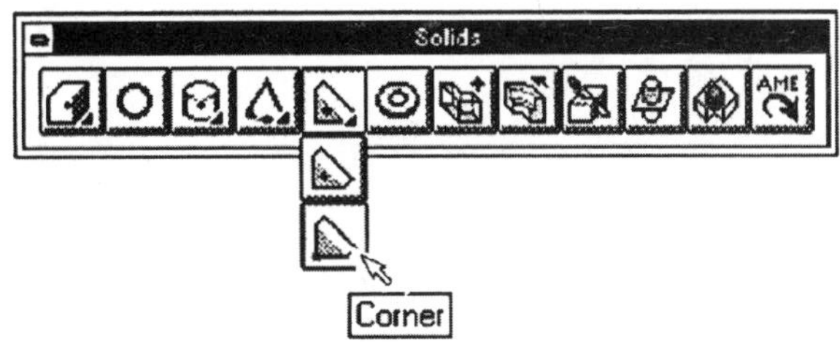

The third cylinder that sits on top of the wedge will be drawn in Part 3 of the exercise.

Step 14. On Your Own:

Set elevation and thickness to 0.

EXERCISE 10–1, PART 2
CREATING MULTIPLE-SCREEN VIEWPORTS; VIEWING THE 3-D MODEL

Vports:

Step 1. On Your Own:

Use Zoom: All so you start at full magnification.

Step 2. Divide the screen into four viewports (Figure 10–4).

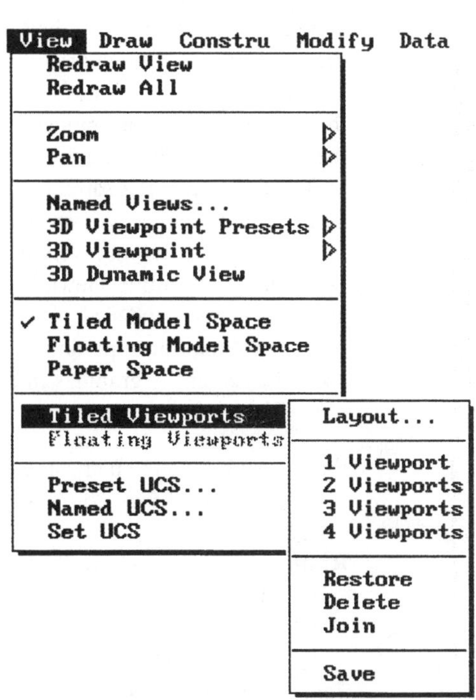

FIGURE 10–4
Dividing the Screen into Four Viewports

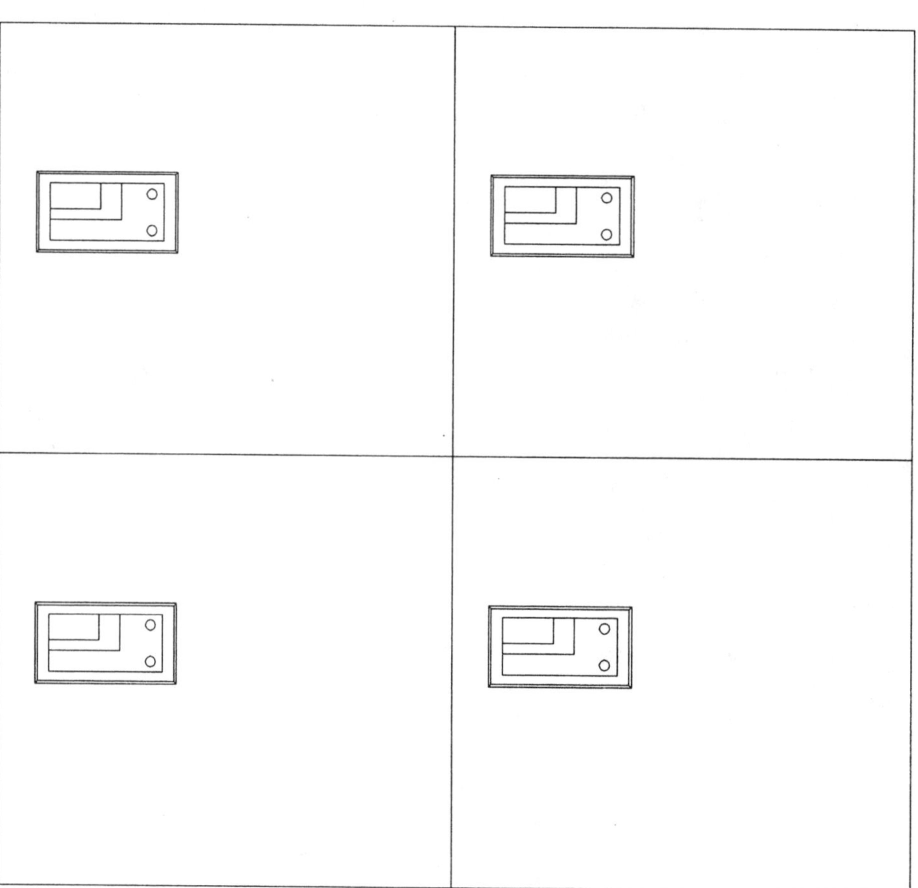

Prompt	Response
Command:	**Vports:** (or *Type:* **VPORTS** ↵)
Save/Restore/Delete/Join/SIngle/?/2/3/4:	*Type:* **4** ↵

The screen is now divided into four viewports. The active viewport is outlined with a solid line, and you can see the lines of the cursor when the cursor is moved into the active viewport. Inactive viewports display an arrow when the cursor is moved into those areas. To make a different viewport active, position the arrow in the desired viewport and press the pick button on your mouse. You may also use Ctrl-V (press the Control and V keys at the same time) to select a different viewport from the current one.

The drawing is the same in each viewport. If you edit the model in any one viewport, you are doing it in all viewports. You may, however, freeze different layers in each viewport. Freezing different layers in each viewport is discussed later in this chapter. You may zoom in or out in one viewport without affecting other viewport magnifications. To decrease or increase the size of the graphics in an individual viewport by a specific value, activate the Zoom: prompt, and enter a number followed by X (entering .8X will reduce the size). To center the graphics in each viewport, use Pan and Zoom: Dynamic. The options of the Vports: command are:

Save Allows you to name a set of viewports and save the name for future use. Restore recalls the saved viewports. Any number of sets of viewports may be named, saved, and recalled.

Restore Restores a saved set of viewports. AutoCAD prompts you for the name of the saved viewport.

Delete Deletes a named viewport set. AutoCAD prompts you for the name of the saved viewport set to be deleted.

Join Joins two viewports into a larger one. The resulting view is the dominant viewport.

Single Returns the display to a single viewport. The resulting view reverts to the current active viewport before single was selected.

? Lists the identification numbers and the screen positions of the current arrangement of viewports and all previously saved viewports by name if you accept the default <*> when AutoCAD prompts you for the viewport configuration to list.

2,3,4 Divides the current viewport into two, three, or four viewports with the same view, snap, grid, and layer settings. Selections 2 and 3 also allow you to select a vertical or horizontal arrangement. Selection 3 allows for two smaller viewports to the left or right of one larger one. A total of 64 viewports may be created on any one drawing.

Step 3. On Your Own (Figure 10–5).

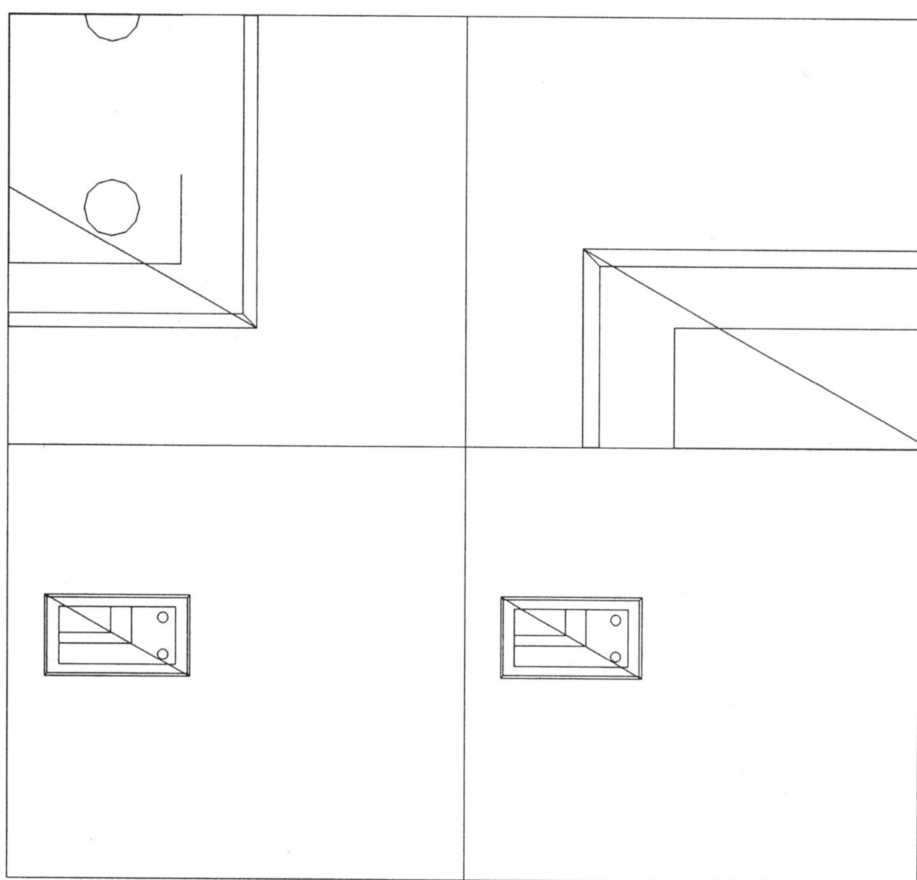

FIGURE 10–5
Experimenting with Changing Views and Drawing in the Viewports

Experiment with the viewports to get an idea of how viewports can be useful in drawing as well as in presentation:

1. Pick the upper left viewport to make it active, and zoom a window around the lower right corner of the model in the upper left viewport.
2. Pick the upper right viewport to make it active, and zoom a window around the upper left corner of the model in the upper right viewport.
3. Draw a line from the lower right corner of the model to the upper left corner: Pick the upper left viewport to make it active, and start the Line: command in the upper left viewport. Then, pick the upper right viewport to make it active, and end the line in the upper right viewport.
4. Erase any lines you have drawn that are not part of the model.

When you begin a command in any viewport, you must first pick the viewport to make it active. Ending the line in the upper right viewport requires two picks—one to make the viewport active and one to complete the Line: command. Experiment with this a little, then

return all displays to their original Zoom: All magnification. Use RedrAll: in the Display menu to refresh the display in all viewports at the same time.

RedrwAll: and RegnAll:

The Redraw: and Regen: commands redraw or regenerate the drawing in the current viewport only. RedrwAll: redraws, and RegnAll: regenerates, the drawing in all viewports at the same time.

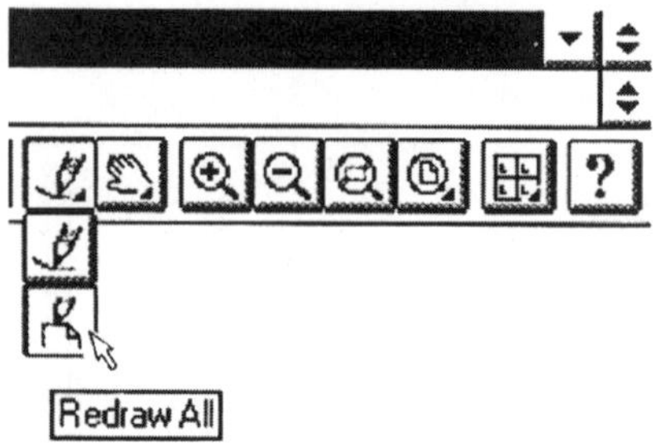

Vpoint:

Vpoint: (Viewpoint) is the first command used in this chapter for viewing your 3-D model from other than the plan view. When Vpoint: is picked from the side menu, the prompt is "Rotate/<View point><default>:". The options rotate, axes, plan, View Pt. Dialogue. . . , and Hide:, are on the Vpoint: side menu. The options for selecting a viewing point (the location of the eye that is looking at your model) when using the Vpoint: command are described next.

<Viewpoint>

Using this option, you may type the X, Y, and Z coordinates of the viewpoint from the keyboard and press enter.

Step 4. On Your Own:

Select the upper right viewport as the current viewport.

Step 5. Select the Viewpoint for the upper right viewport by typing the X, Y, and Z coordinates of the viewpoint from the keyboard (Figure 10–6).

Prompt	Response
Command:	**Vpoint:** (Windows users: *Type:* **VPOINT** ↵)
Rotate/<View point> <0.000,0.000,0.000>:	*Type:* **1,−1,1** ↵

A viewpoint of 1, −1, 1 means the viewing eye has been moved one unit to the right, one unit in front, and one unit above the object.

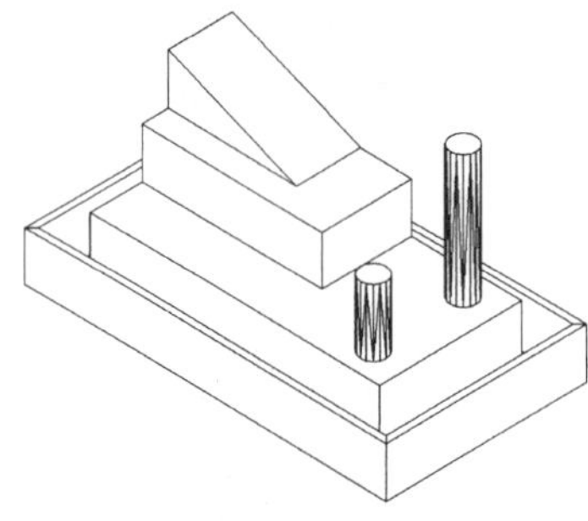

FIGURE 10–6
Selecting a Viewpoint by Typing the X, Y, and Z Coordinates of the Viewpoint

Note: The 3D Viewpoint-Vector command is also located in a pull-down menu under View in the menu bar.

Hide:

Now that you have a 3-D viewpoint of the model, you will be able to see that model more clearly, and make sure it is drawn correctly, by using the Hide: command. The Hide: command hides surfaces that are behind other surfaces.

Step 6. Use the Hide: command to remove lines that are covered by surfaces in front of them (Figure 10–6).

Prompt	Response
Command:	**Hide:** (or *Type:* **HIDE** ↵)

Vpoint:

<Viewpoint>

Step 7. On Your Own (Figures 10–7 and 10–8):

Figure 10–7 shows the results of typing other viewpoint coordinates. Set the viewpoints for each viewport as described in items 1–3 of the following list. Use the menu bar View commands to center the model in each viewport, as shown in Figure 10–7.

1. The upper left viewport already shows the plan view (0,0,1).
2. Set the viewpoint for the lower left viewport to −1,−1,1. This shows that the viewing eye has been moved one unit to the left, one unit in front, and one unit above the object. If necessary, use the menu bar View commands Pan and Zoom: Dynamic to center the model in the viewport. Perform a Hide: on the model. Set the viewpoint for the lower right viewport to 1,−1,−1. This shows that the viewing eye has been moved one unit to the right, one unit in front, and one unit below the object. If necessary, use the menu bar View commands Pan and Zoom: Dynamic to center the model in the viewport. Perform a Hide: on the model.
3. Experiment with typing different viewpoints if you like. Always return to the plan view before typing in a new viewpoint. This assures you a selected viewpoint that is relative to the plan view.
4. Return to the arrangement shown in Figure 10–8. Select "plan" from the Vpoint: options, or type 0,0,1 for the X, Y, and Z coordinates to return to the plan view.

plan

The "plan" option returns the viewpoint to the plan view of the model. This is the same as viewpoint 0,0,1. It automatically performs a Zoom: All, and the view of the model fills the viewport.

axes

The AutoCAD compass and axis tripod appear when the enter key is pressed at the Vpoint: prompt, or when "axes" is picked from the Vpoint options. A viewpoint can be selected by picking a point on the AutoCAD compass.

FIGURE 10–7
Different Viewpoint Coordinates

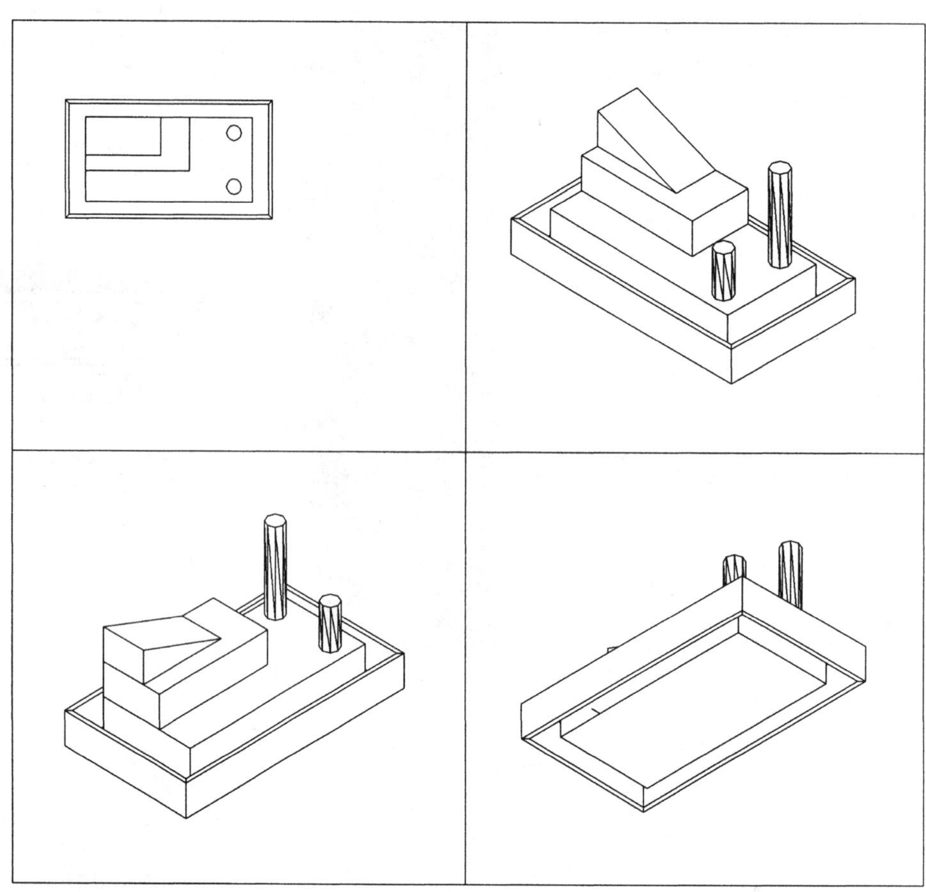

FIGURE 10–8
Returning to These Viewpoint Coordinates

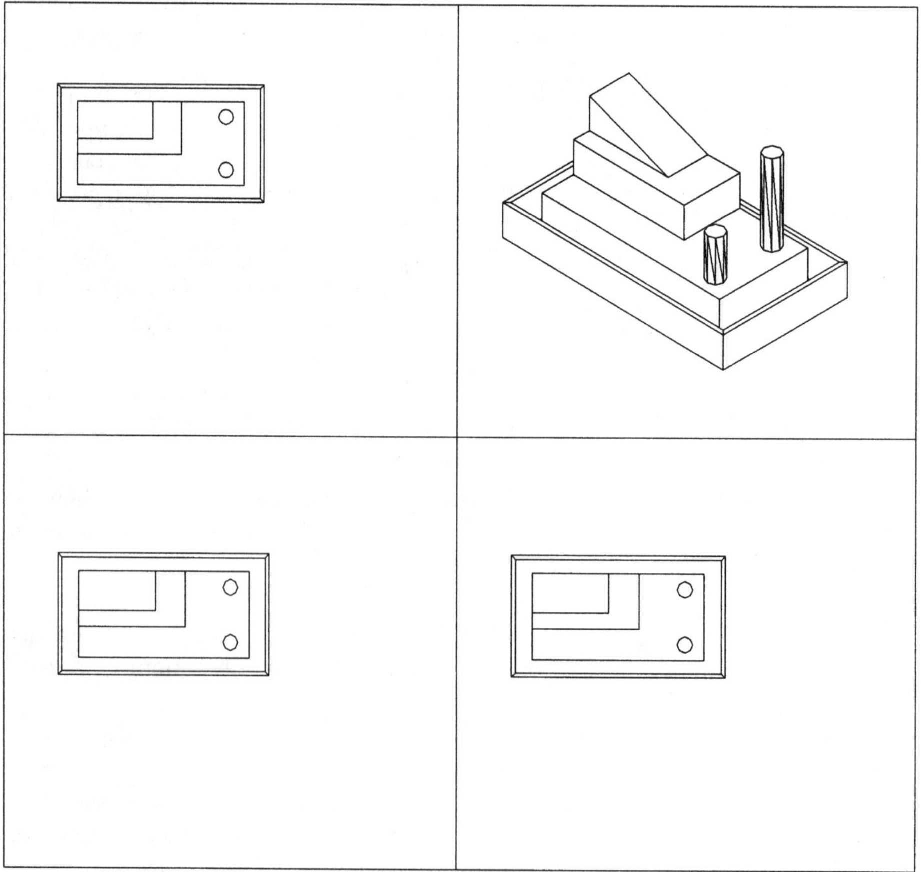

Step 8. On Your Own:

Pick the lower right viewport to make it active.

Step 9. Use the Vpoint: command to view the AutoCAD compass (Figure 10–9).

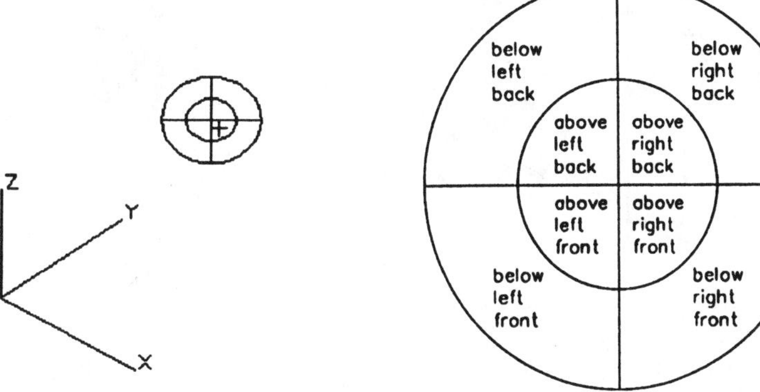

FIGURE 10–9
The AutoCAD Compass and Axis Tripod

Prompt	**Response**
Command:	*Type:* **VPOINT ↵**
Rotate/<View point> <0.000,0.000,0.000>:	↵

The AutoCAD compass (Figure 10–9) and axis tripod appear. As you move the cursor inside the compass, the tripod with its X, Y, and Z axes moves to give you an idea of what the resulting display will be. When the tripod appears to have the desired orientation, pick that spot inside the compass to produce the desired viewpoint.

Study Figure 10–9 a few moments to obtain an understanding of what each area on the compass signifies. Any point selected within the smaller, inner circle is a viewpoint above the object. Any point selected between the larger outer circle and the inner circle is a viewpoint below the object. Any point above the horizontal line is behind the object. Any point below the horizontal line is in front of the object. Any point to the right of the vertical line is looking at the viewer's right side of the object; left of the vertical line is the viewer's left side. Figure 10–10 shows examples of eight different picks on the compass.

Step 10. Select the viewpoint for the lower right viewport by picking a point on the AutoCAD compass (Figure 10–11).

Prompt	**Response**
The AutoCAD compass is visible:	**Pick a point on the AutoCAD compass to create a view similar to the view shown in Figure 10–11.**

Step 11. On Your Own:

1. Experiment with selecting viewpoints using the AutoCAD compass.
2. Return the display to plan views in all but the upper right viewport as shown in Figure 10–8.

Viewpoint Presets

When DDview: is picked from the VIEW side menu, the Viewpoint Presets dialog box appears (Figure 10–12). This dialog box allows you to specify the viewing angle of a 3-D object relative to the World UCS or another current UCS that you are using. It allows you to set the angle along the X axis and the angle from the XY plane by either picking a standard angle as shown on the chart or picking the existing numbers in the appropriate boxes, backspacing over them, and typing the desired numbers.

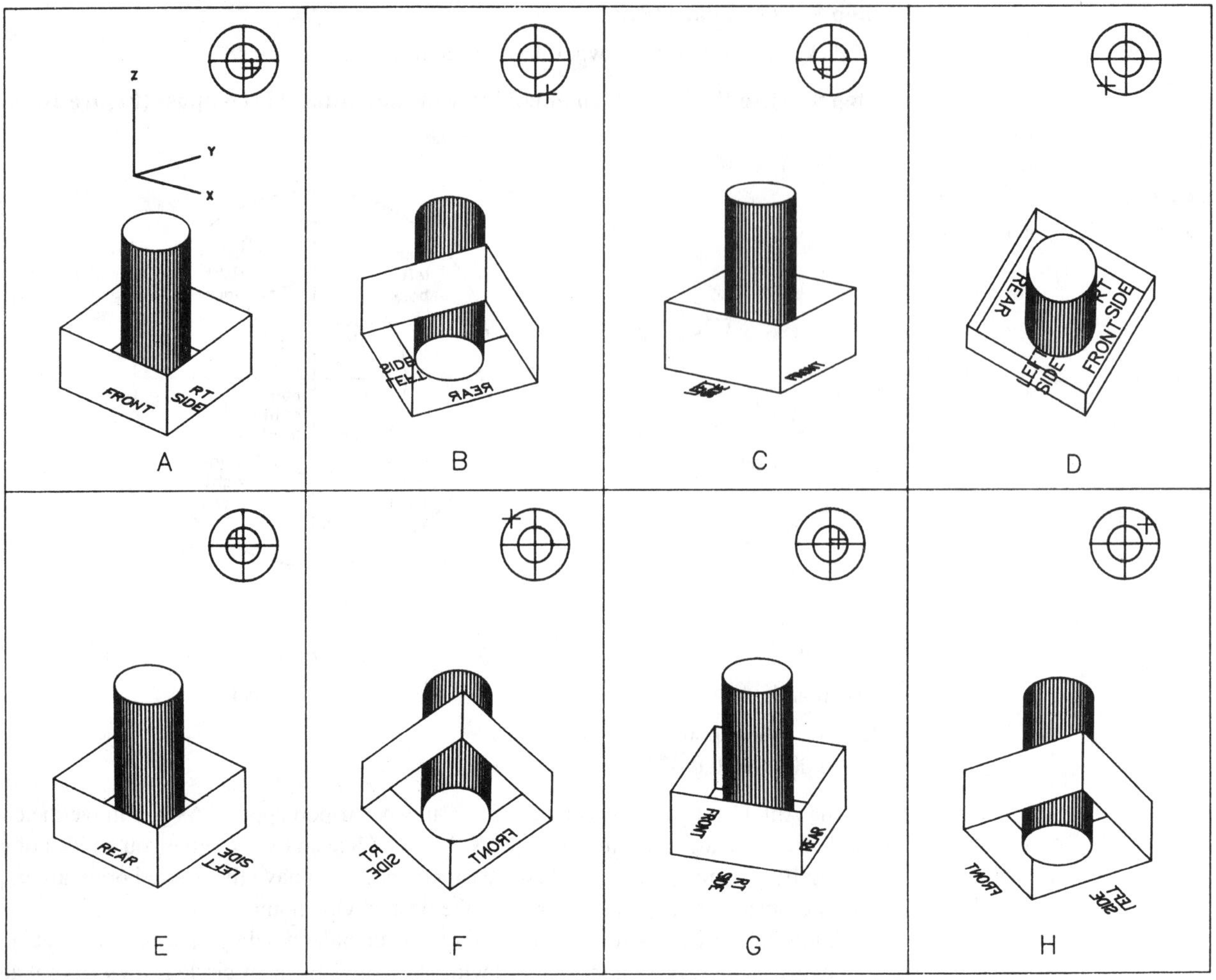

FIGURE 10–10
Eight Different Picks on the AutoCAD Compass

FIGURE 10–11
Selecting a Viewpoint by Picking a Point on the AutoCAD Compass

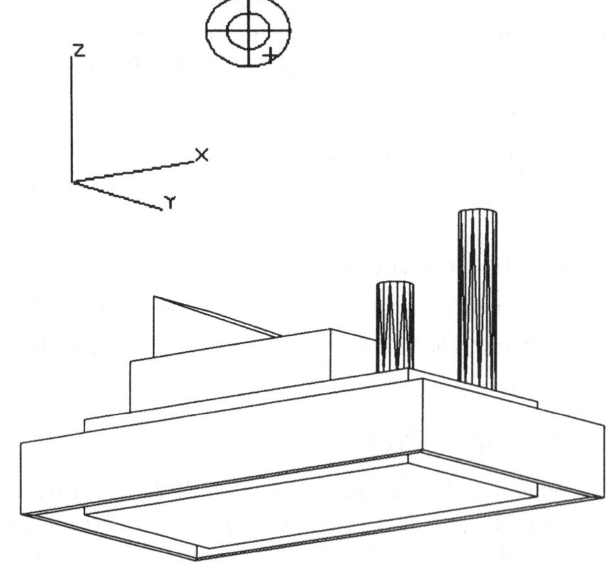

The circle on the left allows you to position the view with respect to the X axis. This places the viewpoint to the left or right, in front or behind the model. For example: the angle 225 places the viewpoint to the left in front of the model; the angle 45 places the viewpoint to the right behind the model; the angle 0 places the viewpoint directly to the right of the model.

The semicircle on the right allows you to position the view with respect to the angle from the XY plane. This places the viewpoint above, below, or directly in line with the model.

The Viewpoint Presets dialog box is also available by using the pull-down menu under View in the Menu Bar, as shown in Figure 10–12.

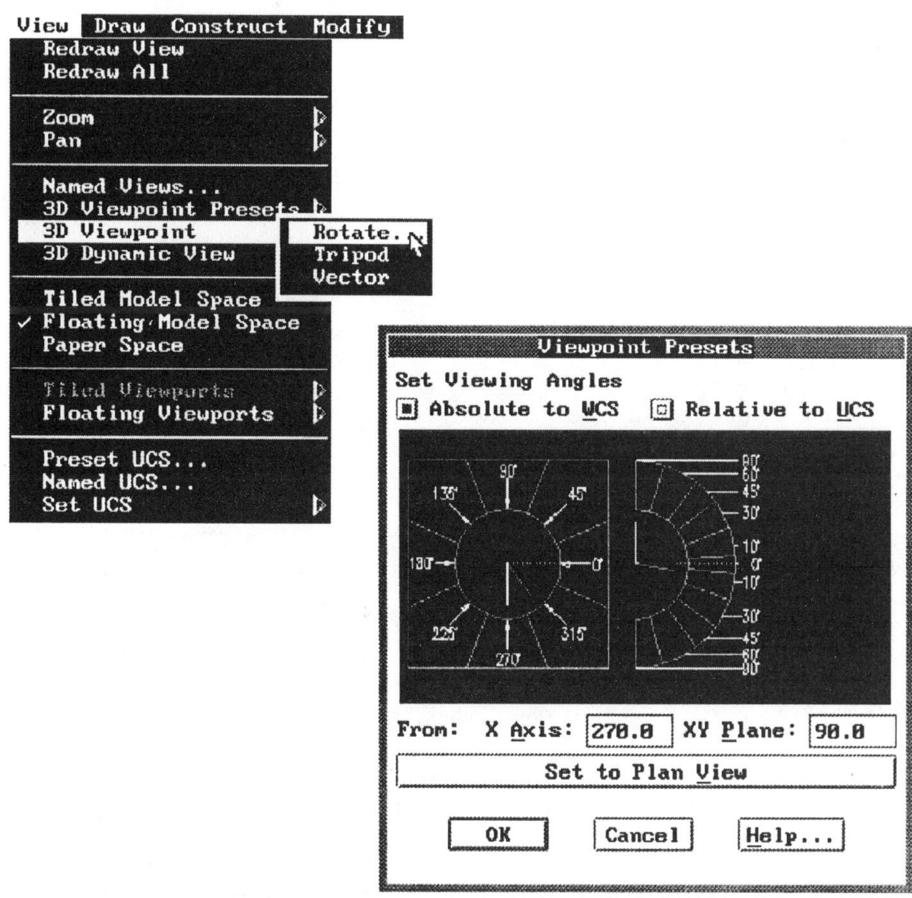

FIGURE 10–12
Viewpoint Presets Dialog Box

Standard Viewing Angles for Engineering Drawings

The standard viewing angles for engineering drawings are used in Figure 10–13 as examples:

- □ The default setting of 270 on the X axis and 90 from the XY plane gives you a top view of the model.
- □ A selection of 270 on the X axis and 0 from the XY plane gives you a front view of the model.
- □ A selection of 0 on the X axis and 0 from the XY plane gives you a right side view of the model.
- □ A selection of 90 on the X axis and 0 from the XY plane gives you the rear view of the model.
- □ A selection of 180 on the X axis and 0 from the XY plane gives you the left side of the model.
- □ A selection of 90 on the X axis and −90 from the XY plane gives you the bottom view of the model.

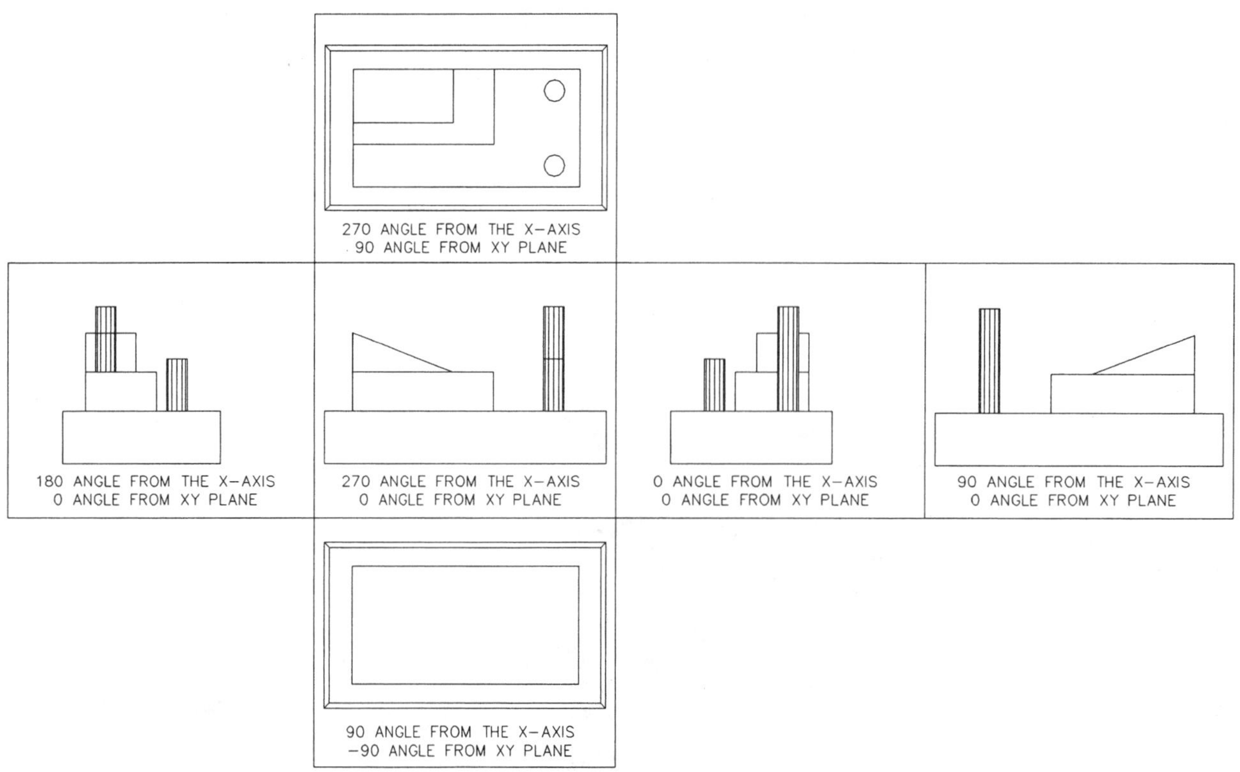

FIGURE 10–13
Standard Viewing Angle for Engineering Drawings

Rotate. . .

The Rotate. . . option is the same as the Viewpoint Presets dialog box. It allows you to specify the viewpoint by entering two angles; one determines the angle in the XY plane from the X axis, the other angle determines the Z angle from the XY plane. Some of the other angles for 3-D viewpoints are shown in Figure 10–14.

EXERCISE 10–1, PART 3
CONTROLLING THE LOCATION AND ORIENTATION OF THE UCS WHILE WORKING IN 3-D

Thus far you have been using Elevation (Elev:) to locate the base and construction plane of the parts of the 3-D model. This exercise will show you how to locate the construction plane by moving the user coordinate system (UCS) to the desired elevation and orientation.

Understanding and controlling the UCS is extremely important in creating 3-D models. The UCS is the *location and orientation* of the X, Y, and Z axes. If you are going to draw parts of a 3-D model on a slanted surface, you can create a slanted UCS. If you are going to draw a 3-D entity such as the handles on a front panel, you can locate your UCS so that it is flush with the front plane of the panel. Thickness is then taken from that construction plane, and the handles can be easily created in the correct location.

UCS:

The UCS: command prompt is "Origin/ZAxis/3point/OBject/View/X/Y/Z/Prev/Restore/Save/Del/?/<World>:" The UCS: command options Origin, Entity, Previous, Restore, Save, Delete, World, and ? were described in Chapter 4. The options described in this chapter are Origin, ZAxis, 3point, OBject, VIew, X/Y/Z, and Follow:

Step 1. On Your Own (Figure 10–15):

FIGURE 10–14
Viewing Angles for 3-D Models

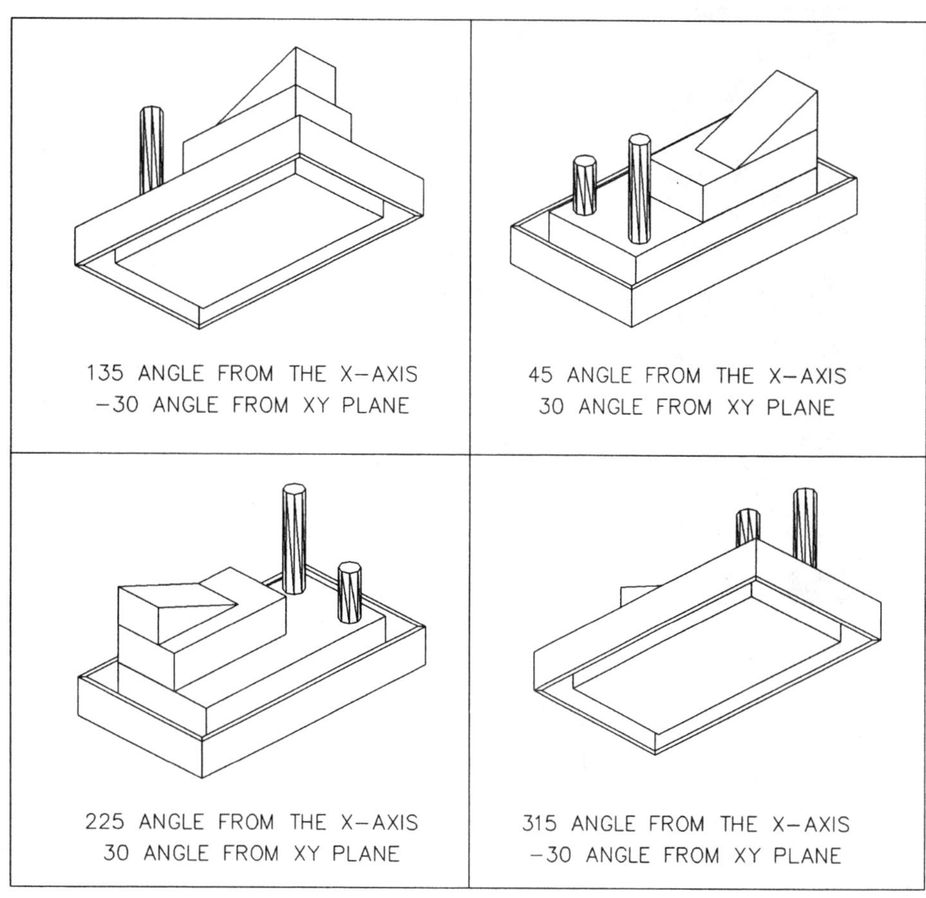

FIGURE 10–15
A Display with Four Viewports

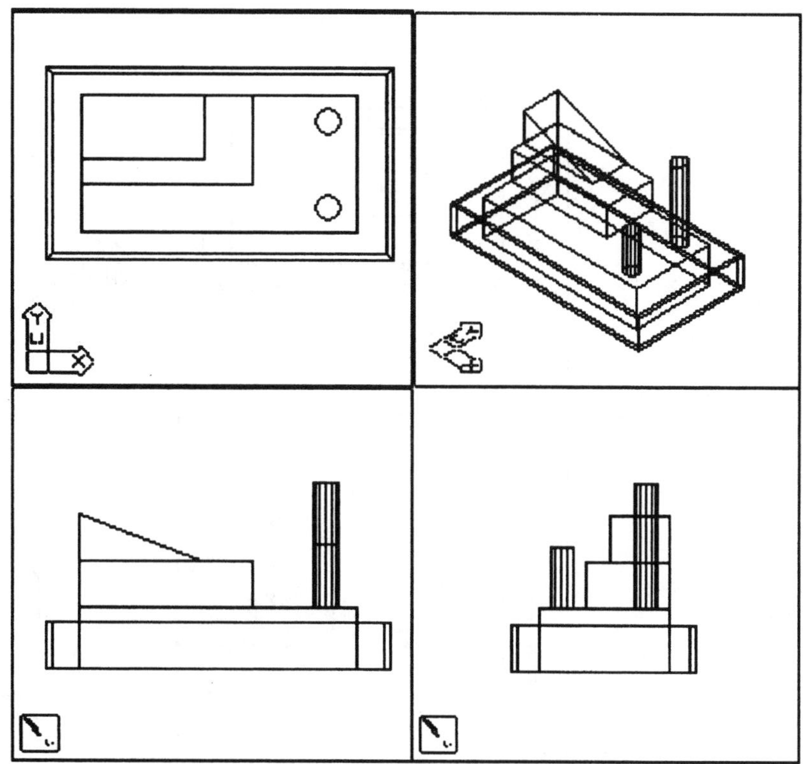

Note: The Set UCS command is also located under View in the menu bar.

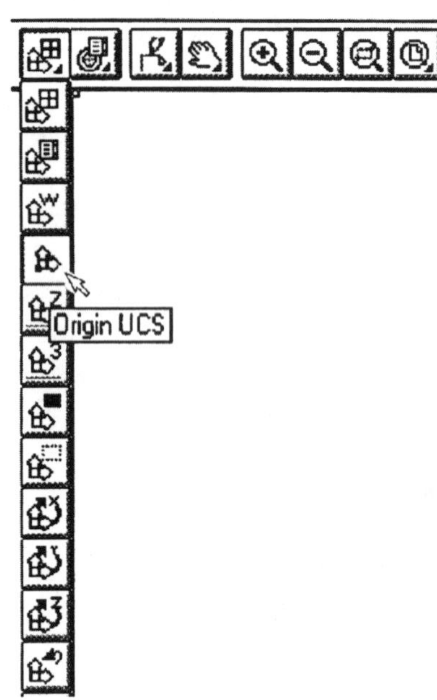

1. Set your display to four viewports, with viewpoints set as shown in Figure 10–15. Refer to the paragraph labeled standard viewing Angles for Engineering Drawings.
2. Set the Ucsicon: command to origin (type UCSICON ↵, then OR ↵) so you can see the UCS icon move as you change the origin of 0,0,0 in the next part of this exercise.
3. Set the upper right viewport as active, and work in that viewport.

The UCS icon is shown with a W (indicating the world UCS) in the top two views. The broken pencil in the other views indicates that the view is not parallel to the current UCS and anything you draw in these views may not be as it appears.

Origin

This option allows you to define a new UCS by shifting the origin of the current UCS, leaving the direction of its X, Y, and Z axes unchanged.

Step 2. Use UCS: Origin to define a new UCS (Figure 10–16).

Prompt	Response
Command:	**UCS:**
Origin/ZAxis/3point/OBject/View/ X/Y/Z/Prev/Restore/Save/Del/?/ <World>:	*Type:* **O** ↵
Origin point <0,0,0>:	**Osnap-INTersection (Pick the lower left corner of the wall as shown in Figure 10–16.)**

The origin of the world UCS is shifted, to the corner of the wall, but the direction of its X, Y, and Z axes remained unchanged.

World

Step 3. Use UCS: World to return to the world UCS location.

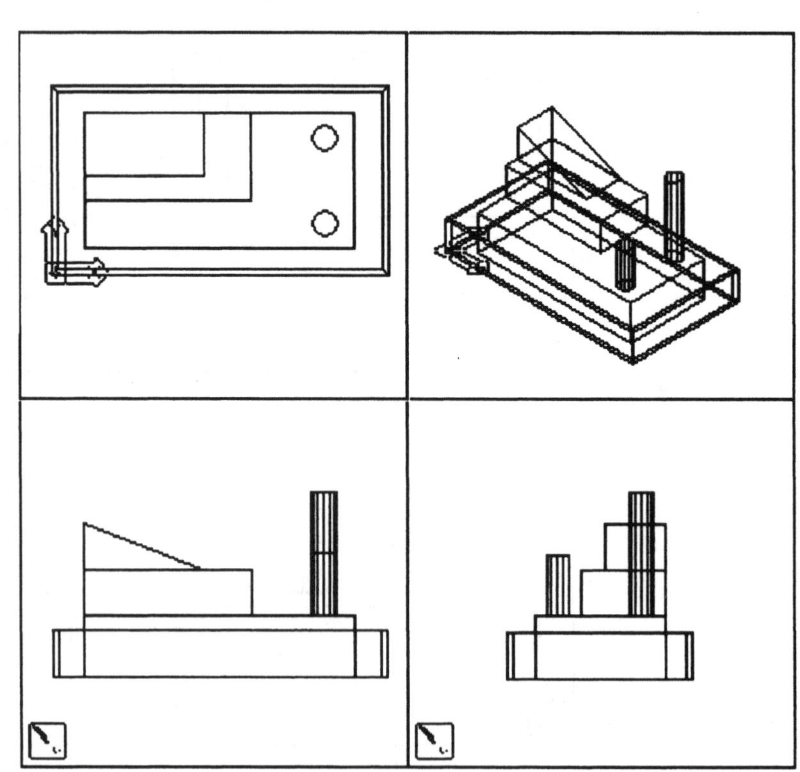

FIGURE 10–16
Using UCS: Origin to Define a New UCS

Prompt	Response
Command:	**UCS:** (or *Type:* **UCS** ↵)
Origin/ZAxis/3point/OBject/View/ X/Y/Z/Prev/Restore/Save/Del/?/ <World>:	↵

The world UCS returns.

ZAxis

This option allows you to change the direction of the Z axis. Based on the new Z axis, AutoCAD determines the direction of the X and Y axes.

Step 4. On Your Own:

1. Turn off the G and Y layers.
2. Make the upper right viewport active, and work in that viewport.

Step 5. Use UCS: ZAxis to define a new UCS (Figure 10–17).

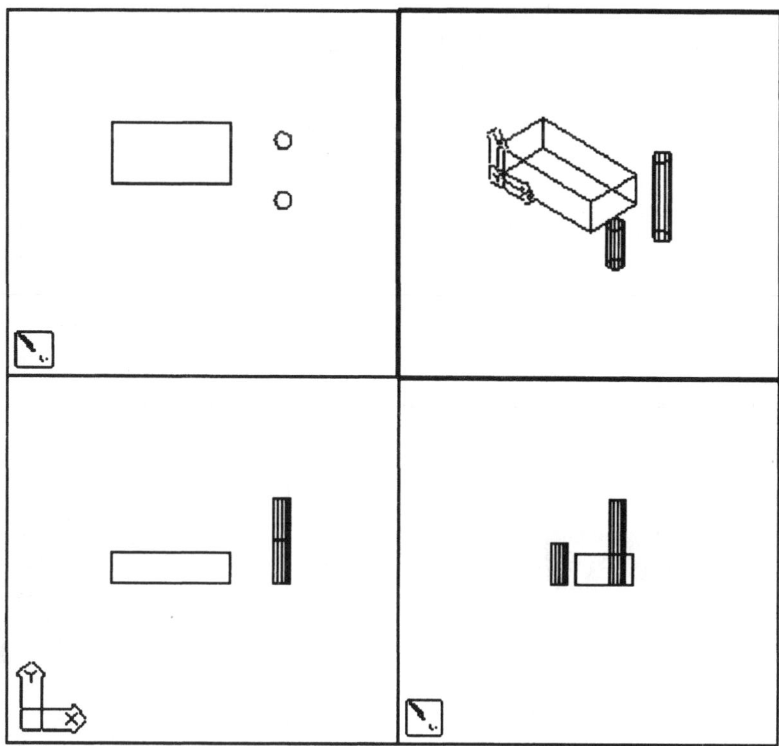

FIGURE 10–17
Using UCS: ZAxis to Define a New UCS

Prompt	Response
Command:	**UCS:** (or *Type:* **UCS** ↵)
Origin/ZAxis/3point/OBject/View/ X/Y/Z/Prev/Restore/Save/Del/?/ <World>:	*Type:* **ZA** ↵
Origin point <0,0,0>:	**Osnap-INTersection (Pick the lower left corner of the small red rectangle.)**
Point on positive portion of Z axis <default>:	**With ortho and snap on, use the cross hairs of the pointer to reorient the Z axis so it comes "out" from the lower left corner of the rectangle and pick a point.**

The UCS appears as in Figure 10–17.

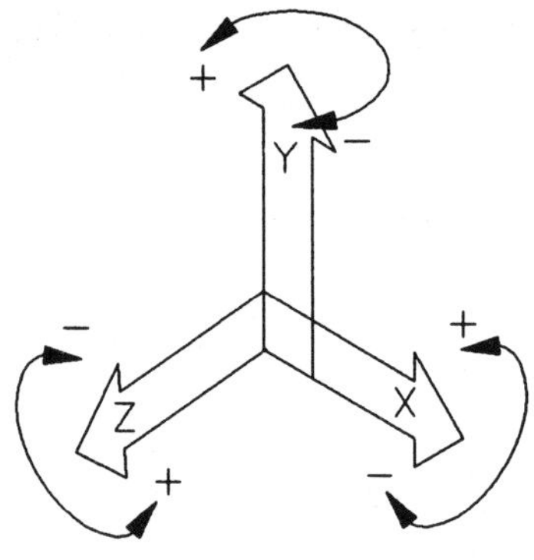

FIGURE 10–18
Rotating the UCS about the X, Y, and Z Axes

The origin of the current UCS is moved to the corner of the rectangle, and when the direction of the Z axis is changed, the X and Y axes follow.

X/Y/Z

These options allow you to rotate the user coordinate system about any of the three axes. Figure 10–18 shows how the UCS is rotated about the X, Y, and Z axes. A positive rotation angle rotates the UCS counterclockwise; a negative rotation angle rotates the UCS clockwise. Keep the UCS just created and use the X/Y/Z option in the following exercises to rotate the UCS about the three axes:

Step 6. Use UCS: X to define a new UCS by rotating the UCS about the X axis (Figure 10–19).

Prompt	Response
Command:	**UCS:**
Origin/ZAxis/3point/OBject/View/X/Y/Z/Prev/Restore/Save/Del ? <World>:	*Type:* **X** ↵
Rotation angle about X axis <0>:	*Type:* **−90** ↵
The UCS rotates 90° clockwise around the X axis to appear as in Figure 10–19.	
Command:	*Type:* **U** ↵ (To return to the UCS created using the ZAxis option, Figure 10–17.)

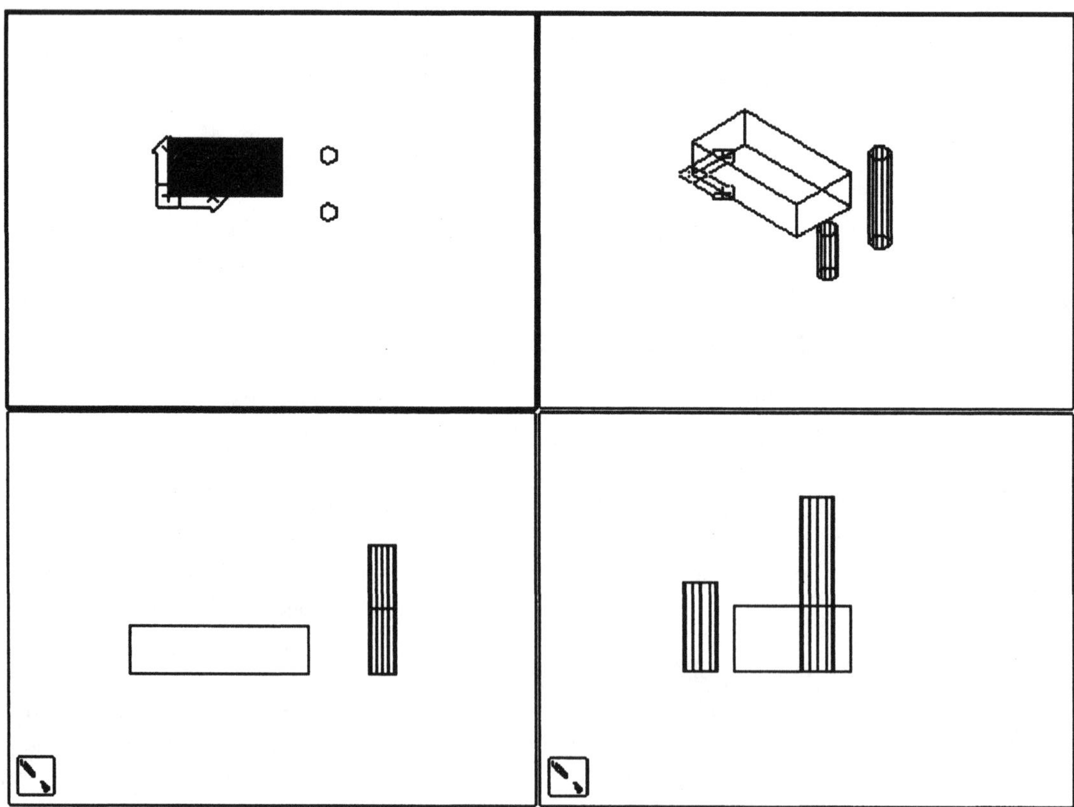

FIGURE 10–19
Using UCS: X to Define a New UCS

Step 7. Use UCS: Y to define a new UCS by rotating the UCS about the Y axis (Figure 10–20).

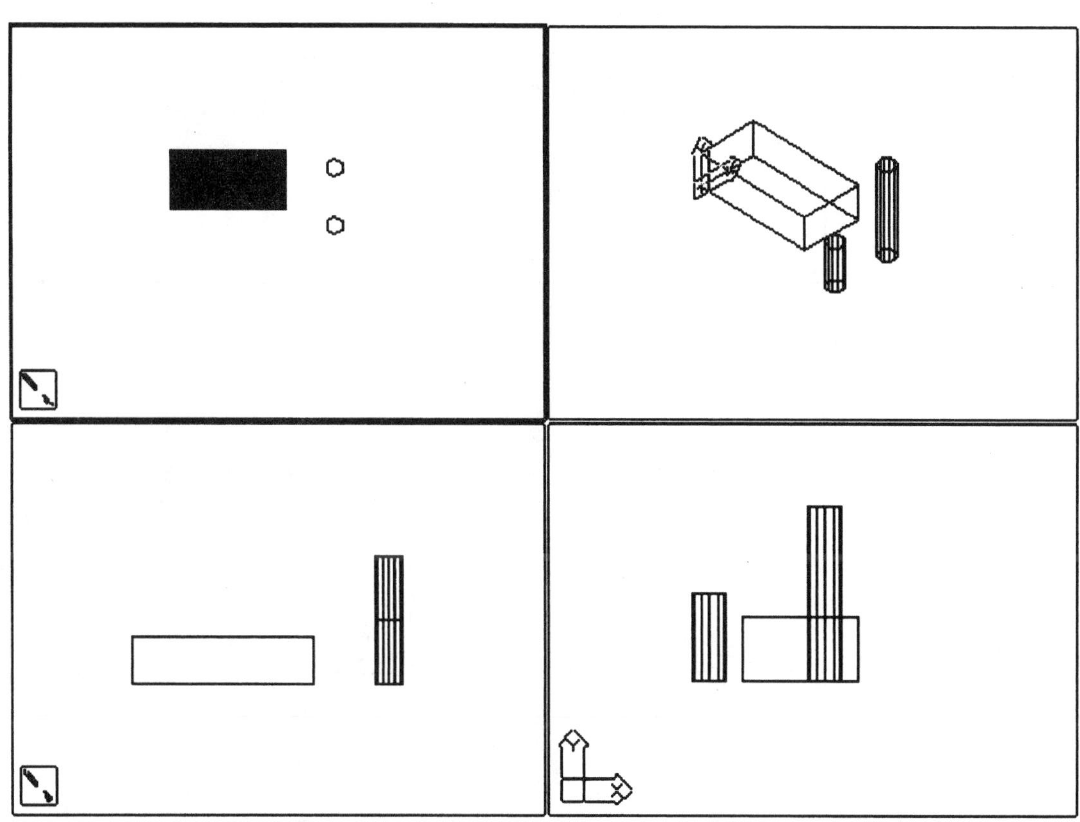

FIGURE 10–20
Using UCS: Y to Define a New UCS

Prompt	Response
Command:	**UCS:**
Origin/ZAxis/3point/OBject/View/ X/Y/Z/Prev/Restore/Save/Del ? <World>:	*Type:* **Y** ↵
Rotation angle about Y axis <0>:	*Type:* **90** ↵
The UCS rotates 90° counterclockwise around the Y axis to appear as in Figure 10–20.	

Step 8. Use UCS: Z to define a new UCS by rotating the UCS about the Z axis (Figure 10–21).

Prompt	Response
Command:	**UCS:**
Origin/ZAxis/3point/OBject/View/ X/Y/Z/Prev/Restore/Save/Del ? <World>:	*Type:* **Z** ↵
Rotation angle about Z axis <0>:	*Type:* **90** ↵
The UCS rotates 90° counterclockwise around the Z axis to appear as in Figure 10–21.	

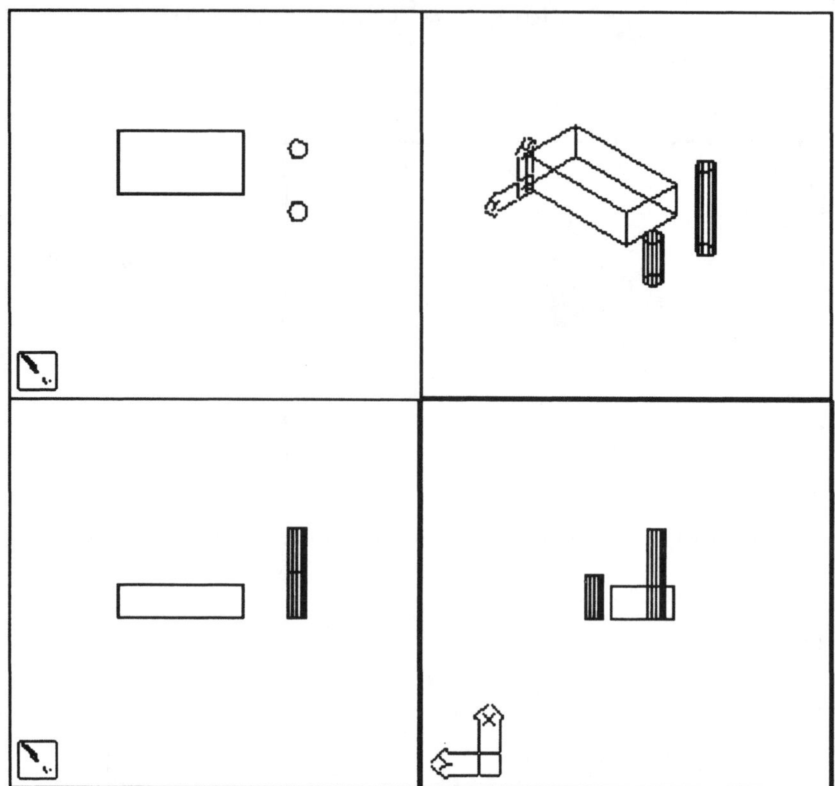

FIGURE 10–21
Using UCS: Z to Define a New UCS

OBject

The OBject option allows you to define a UCS by pointing to any entity except a 3-D polyline or polygon mesh. The Z axis of the UCS created with OBject has the same extrusion direction as the entity that is selected.

Step 9. On Your Own:

1. Use UCS: World to return to the world UCS.
2. Turn layer G on.
3. Make the upper right viewport active.

Step 10. Use UCS: OBject to define a new UCS (Figure 10–22).

Prompt	Response
Command:	**UCS:**
Origin/ZAxis/3point/OBject/View/ X/Y/Z/Prev/Restore/Save/Del ? <World>:	*Type:* **OB** ↵
Select object to align UCS:	**Pick any point on the wedge.**

The wedge was drawn using the Wedge: command. The UCS's position shown in Figure 10–23 may vary from the position of your UCS, because the first point of the solid (when drawn) determines the new UCS origin. The new X axis lies along the line between the first two points of the solid.

See the AutoCAD Reference Manual for a description of how each entity—arc, circle, dimension, line, point, 2D Polyline, solid, text, insert, attribute, and attribute definition—determines the position of the UCS origin when the entity option is used.

3point

This option allows you to change the origin of the UCS by specifying a new direction for the X and Y axes; the Z axis follows. In the next part of this exercise, a new UCS will be

FIGURE 10-22
Using UCS: Entity to Define a New UCS

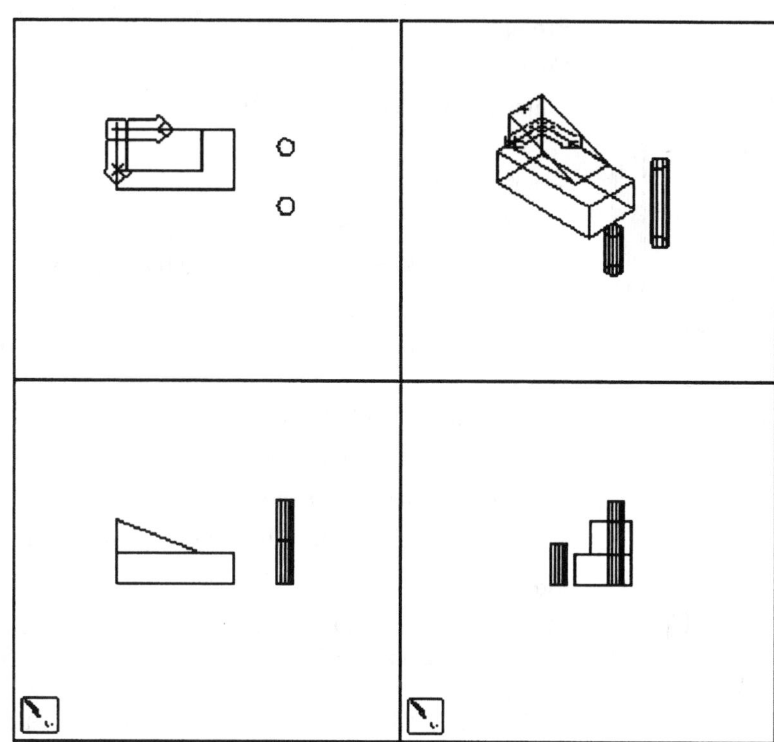

created using the 3point option. This UCS will be used to draw a cylinder whose base is on the slanted surface of the wedge and parallel to it.

Step 11. On Your Own:

1. Use UCS: World to return to the world UCS.
2. Make the upper right viewport active.
3. Turn ortho and snap off.

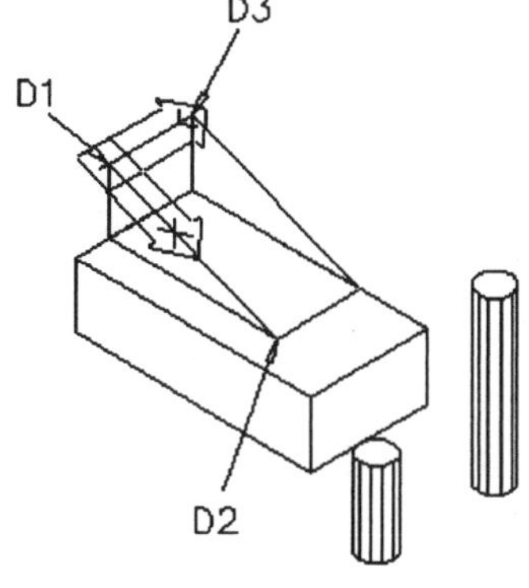

FIGURE 10-23
Using UCS: 3point to Define a New UCS

Step 12. Use UCS: 3point to define a new UCS (Figure 10-23).

Prompt	Response
Command:	**UCS:**
Origin/ZAxis/3point/OBject/View/X/Y/Z/Prev/Restore/Save/Del/?/<World>:	*Type:* **3** ↵
Origin point <0,0,0>:	**Osnap-ENDpoint; D1**
Point on positive portion of the X axis <>:	**Osnap-ENDpoint; D2**
Point on positive Y portion of the UCS XY plane <>:	**Osnap-ENDpoint; D3**
The newly created UCS appears as shown in Figure 10–23.	

Step 13. On Your Own:

1. Set elevation and thickness to 0.
2. Make the upper right viewport active.

Step 14. Use Cylinder: to draw a cylinder using the new UCS (Figure 10-24).

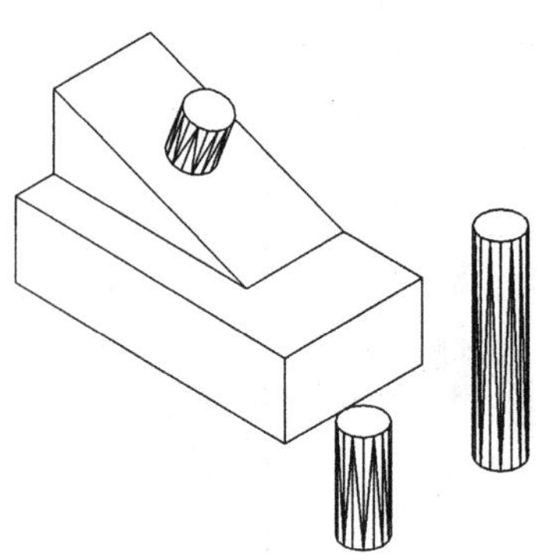

FIGURE 10–24
Using Cylinder: to Draw a Cylinder

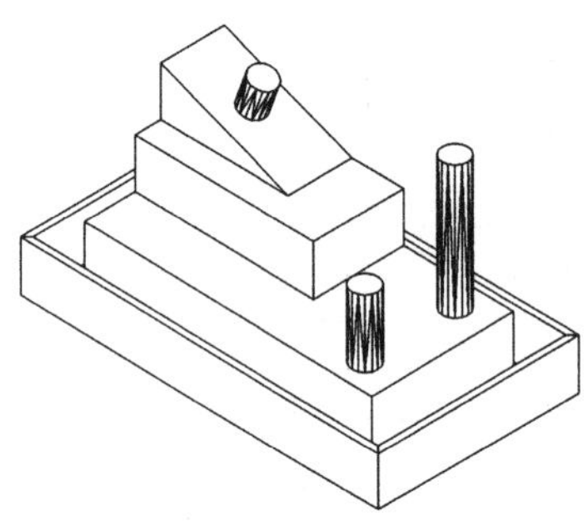

FIGURE 10–25
The Complete 3-D Model

Prompt	Response
Command:	**Cylinder:**
Elliptical/<Center point><0,0,0>:	*Type:* **1,.5** ↵ (to locate the center point with respect to the new origin)
Diameter/<Radius>:	*Type:* **.2** ↵
Center of other end/<Height>:	*Type:* **.5** ↵

Step 15. On Your Own. Complete the 3-D model (Figure 10–25):

1. Turn layer Y on.
2. With the upper right viewport current, use the Vports: command to return to a single viewport.
3. Return to the world UCS.
4. Center the model in the viewport.
5. Perform a Hide: on the model.

Next, UCS: View is used to add your name to your drawing.

View

This option creates a new coordinate system whose XY plane is parallel to the display screen. This is the UCS that must be used when a 2-D format (border) is to be placed around the 3-D drawing. A good way to combine the 3-D drawing and the 2-D format is to arrange the 3-D drawing as you wish it to appear, set the UCS to View, and insert a previously drawn format around it. Also use the View option when you want to add text to your drawing; you can enter text parallel to the screen while in a 3-D viewpoint.

Step 16. Use UCS: View to define a new UCS parallel to the display screen (Figure 10–26) and type your name in the lower right corner.

FIGURE 10–26
Using UCS: View to Define a UCS Parallel to the Screen

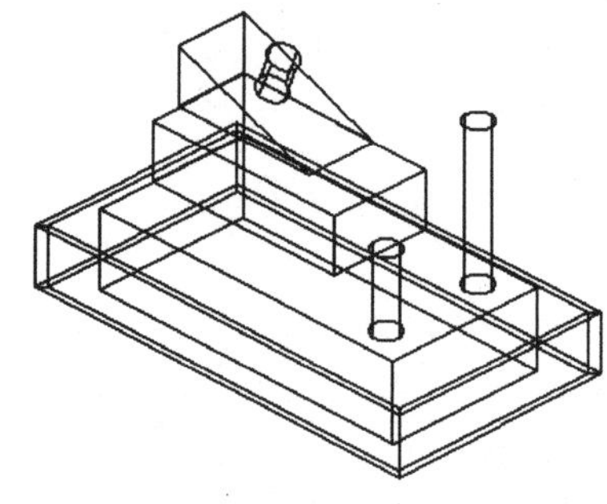

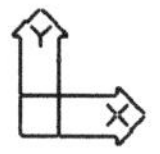

Prompt	Response
Command:	**UCS:**
Origin/ZAxis/3point/OBject/View/ X/Y/Z/Prev/Restore/Save/Del/?/ <World>:	*Type:* **V** ↵
The UCS appears parallel to the screen as shown in Figure 10–26.	

Step 17. On Your Own:

Type your name in the lower right corner of the drawing.

User Coordinate System Orientation Icon Menu

The UCS Orientation icon menu is located in a pull-down menu under View in the menu bar (Figure 10–27). It allows you to create a new UCS that is absolute to the world UCS or relative to a current UCS (other than world).

FIGURE 10–27
User Coordinate System Orientation Icon Menu

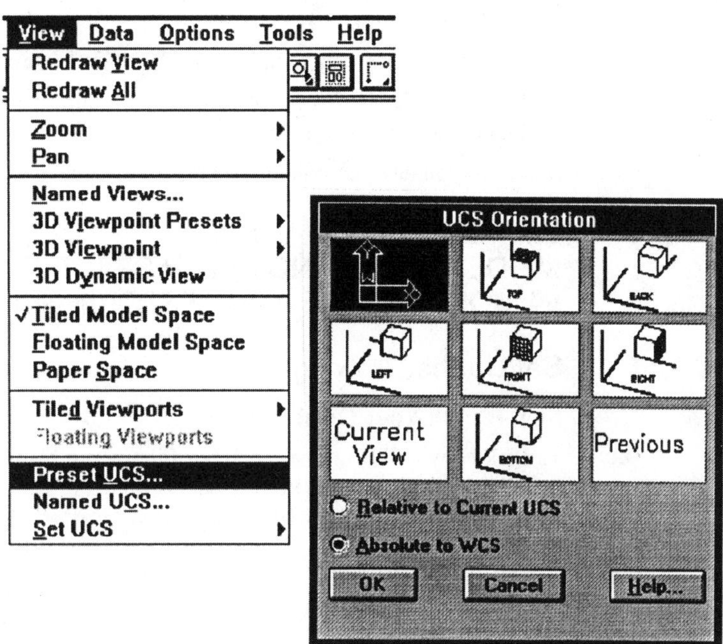

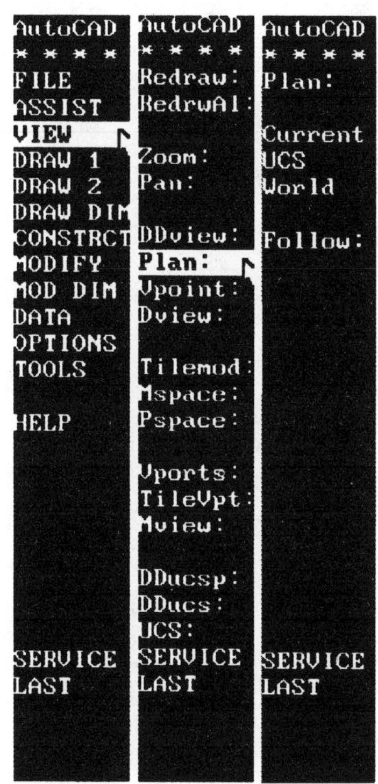

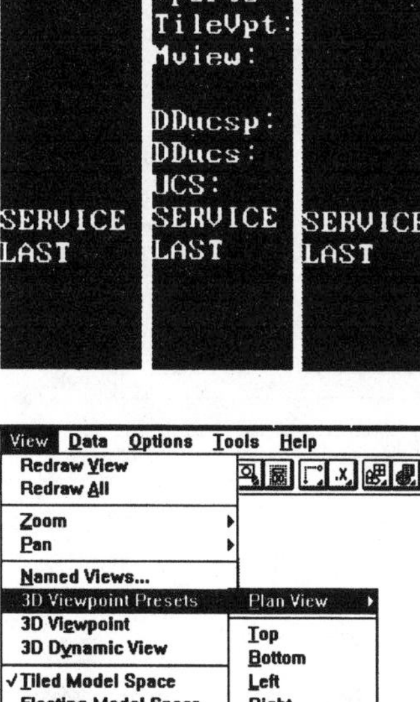

Step 18. On Your Own:

1. Activate the UCS Orientation Icon menu.
2. Pick the Absolute to WCS button, to make that current.
3. Pick the RIGHT icon, then pick the OK button.

The UCS is reoriented to show the right side of your model. You can now execute the Plan: command to get a plan view of the right side of your model. This can be done for the top, bottom, front, back, right, and left views of your model. The UCS Orientation icon menu also allows you to set the world UCS, return to the Previous UCS, and set a UCS that is parallel to the display screen (Current View).

Plan:

When Plan: under the VIEW menu is selected, the prompt is "<Current UCS>/Ucs/World:".

<Current UCS>

When the Current UCS option is entered, the display is returned to the plan view (VPOINT: 0,0,1) with respect to the current UCS.

Ucs

This option prompts "?/Name of UCS:" and returns the display to the plan view for the named UCS.

World

This option returns the display to the plan view for the world UCS.

Follow:

The Follow option allows you to set the UCSFOLLOW system variable so that when a new UCS is created, the display automatically goes to the PLAN view of the new UCS.

When you select Follow: from either the Plan: options or UCSfoll: from the OPTIONS menu, the prompt is ">>New value for UCSFOLLOW <0>:". When UCSFOLLOW is set to 1, any UCS change will automatically cause the screen to return to the plan view of the new UCS. When UCSFOLLOW is set to 0, a UCS change does not affect the display.

Step 19. On Your Own:

1. Return your drawing to appear as shown in Figure 10–26.
2. Plot Exercise 10–1 to scale. Check Hide Lines so an x appears in that check box on the Plot Configuration dialog box.
3. When you have completed Exercise 10–1, save your work in at least two places.

EXERCISE 10–2, PART 1
MODEL SPACE AND PAPER SPACE; SAVING A VIEWPORT SET IN MODEL SPACE AND RESTORING IT INTO PAPER SPACE

Set Up the Drawing

Step 1. On Your Own:

1. Pick New. . . from the menu bar File menu. Name the drawing 10–2 (your initials) = 10–1 (your initials) (Remember to procede 10–1 (your initials) with A: or B: if the drawing is on a floppy disk.)

When you have completed Exercise 10–2, parts 1–3, your drawing will look similar to Figure 10–28.

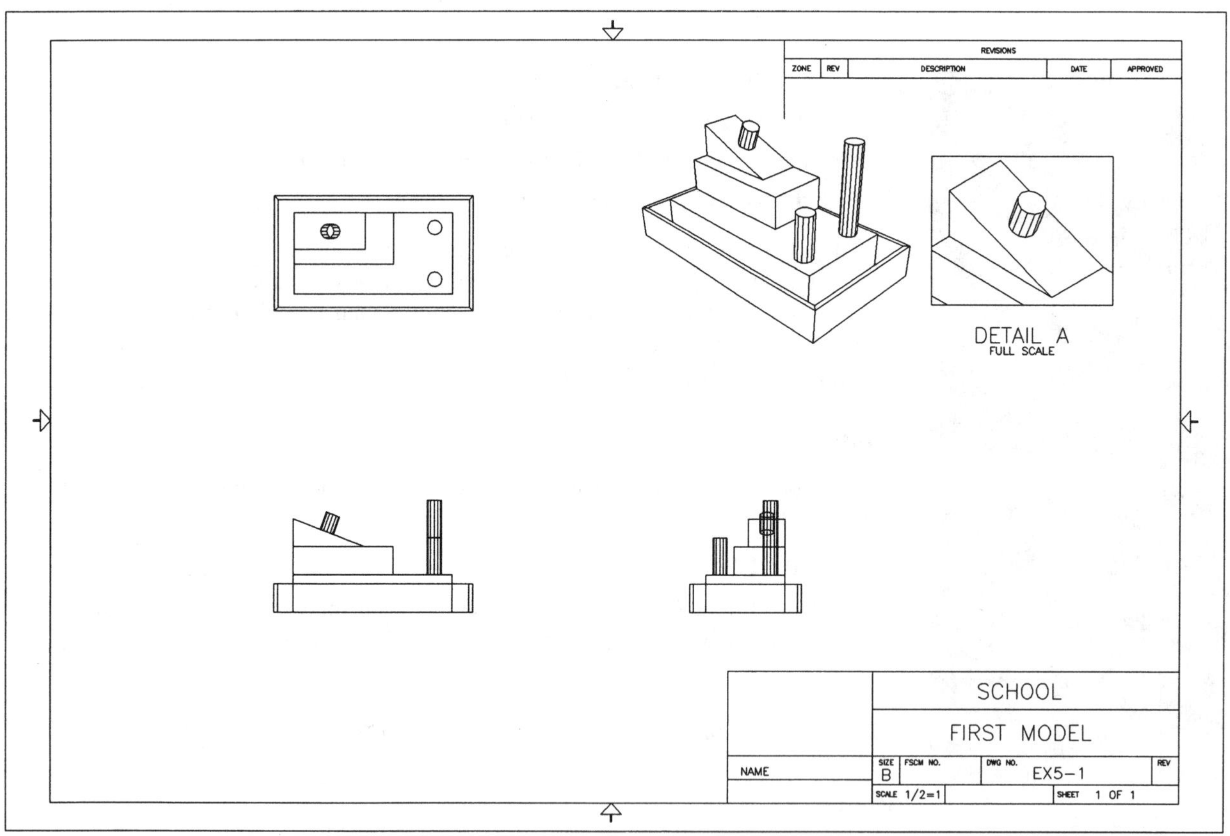

FIGURE 10–28
Exercise 10–2

Model Space

Model space is the environment in which you have been working to this point. Model space is where your 2-D or 3-D model (drawing) is created and modified. When you start a new drawing, you are in model space.

While in model space the Vports: command can be used to divide the display screen into multiple viewports, as you have already done. Model space and the Vports: command is limited in that although several viewports may be visible on the display screen, only one viewport can be active on the display screen at a time, and only one viewport can be plotted.

Step 2. On Your Own (Figure 10–29): Make the following settings.

1. Turn on all layers.
2. Set the UCS to world.
3. Return to the four-viewport configuration shown in Figure 10–29.
4. Turn the grid off in all four viewports. When the viewport set is restored into paper space, you will not have a double grid, showing both the model space and paper space grid.

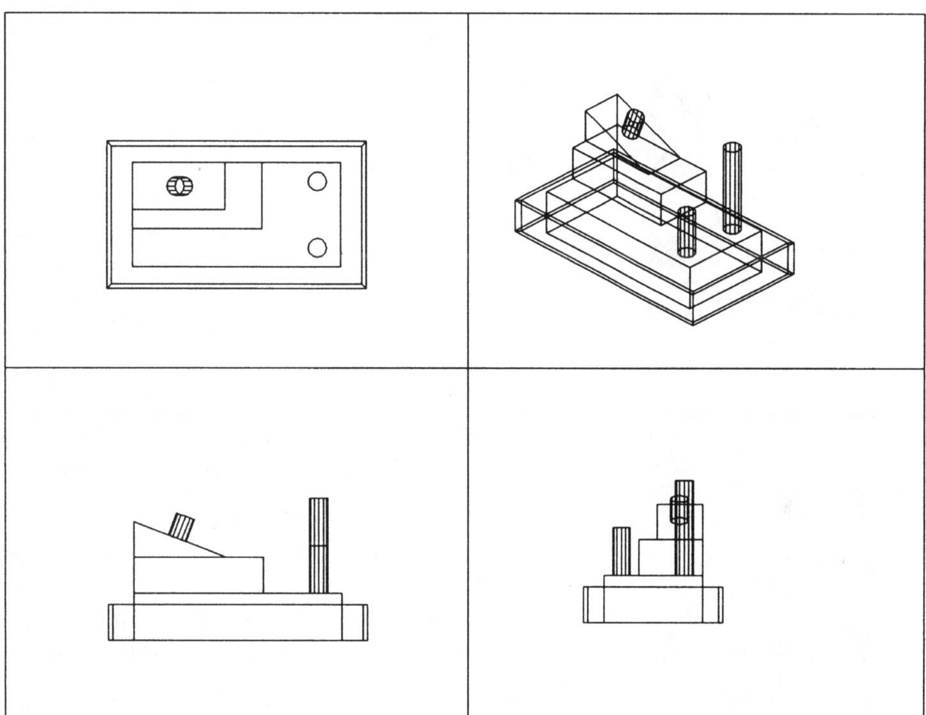

FIGURE 10–29
Four Viewports Configuration

Step 3. Save the current four-viewport configuration in model space.

Prompt	Response
Command:	*Type:* **VPORTS ↵ (or** *Select:* **Tiled Viewports, then Save)**
Save/Restore/Delete/Join/SIngle/?/2/3/4:	*Type:* **S ↵**
?/Name for new viewport configuration:	*Type:* **VP1 ↵**

Paper Space

Paper space is similar to using a piece of illustration board to paste up a presentation. The Mview: command operates only in paper space and, like VPorts: (which operates only in model space), is used to create and control viewport display; the display screen may be divided into multiple viewports. Each viewport can be treated as a single sheet of paper (on the illustration board) and may be copied, stretched, erased, moved, or scaled. The drawing within the viewport cannot be edited while in paper space (you must return to model space to edit the drawing); however, something may be drawn over the viewport—such as the dimensions or labels to a drawing. A viewport may even overlap one or more of the other viewports. The viewports may also be placed into a single drawing format sheet, and all the viewports may be plotted at the same time.

Types of Viewports

There are two types of viewports: tiled and nontiled.

Tiled Viewport Characteristics

Tiled viewports are those that exist in model space. They have the following characteristics:

- □ They fill the graphics screen and lie side-by-side like ceramic tile.
- □ They are fixed and cannot overlap.
- □ They can be deleted only by changing the viewport configuration.
- □ Only one tiled viewport can be active at a time.
- □ Only the active viewport can be plotted.
- □ Anything drawn in a tiled viewport cannot be edited in a nontiled viewport.

Nontiled Viewport Characteristics

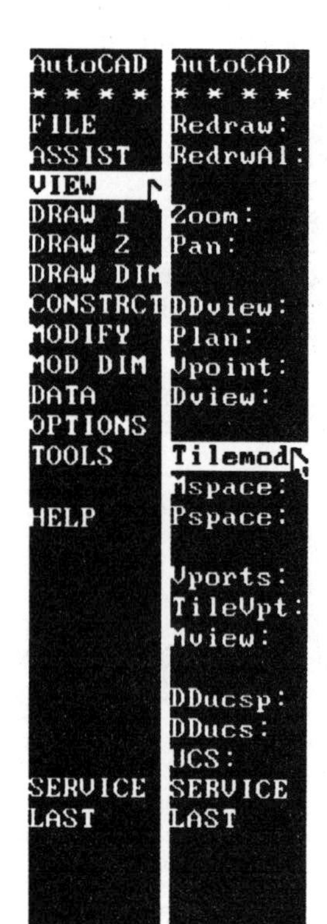

Nontiled viewports are those that exist in paper space. They have the following characteristics:

- □ They may or may not fill the graphics screen.
- □ They can overlap.
- □ They can be moved, copied, scaled, stretched, or erased.
- □ They can have different layers frozen in any viewport.
- □ All nontiled viewports can be plotted at the same time.
- □ Anything drawn in paper space (a nontiled viewport) cannot be edited in model space.

Tilemode

Settings for Tilemod: are 1 (on) or 0 (off). The Tilemod: setting determines whether the viewports displayed are tiled (on) or nontiled (off).

- □ The default setting for Tilemod: is 1 (on).
- □ You can work in model space with Tilemod: set to either 1 (on) or 0 (off).
- □ When Tilemod: is 0 (off), the Vports: command is disabled, and the Mview: command must be used to create and display viewports.
- □ Tilemod: must be 0 (off) for you to work in paper space.

The View menu on the menu bar contains five commands that combine the concepts of tilemode, Mview, Vports, model space, and paper space. They are:

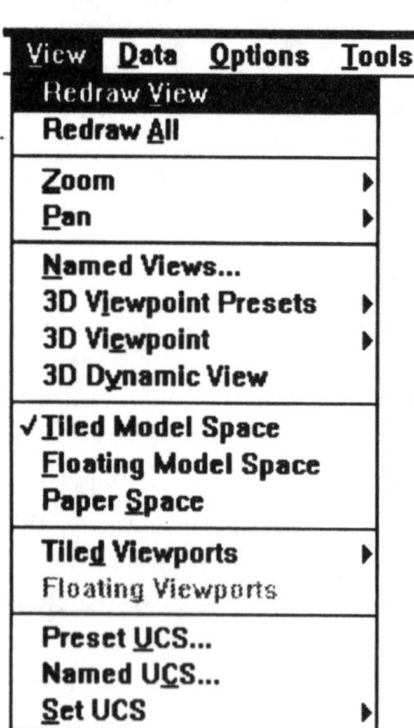

Tiled Model Space
Tilemode is on; you are in model space. You cannot go to paper space unless tilemode is off.

Floating Model Space
Tilemode is off; you are in model space and can flip to paper space by typing PS ↵.

Paper Space
Tilemode is off; you are in paper space and can flip to model space by typing MS ↵.

Tiled Viewports
Tilemode must be on for this command to be accessible. This is the Vports: command that allows you to divide the screen into several areas with a different view in each viewport.

Floating Viewports
Tilemode must be off for this command to be accessible. This is the Mview: command.

Step 4. Set Tilemod: to 0 (off) to switch to paper space.

Prompt	Response
Command:	**Tilemod: (Windows users:** *Type:* **TILEMODE ↵)**
New value for TILEMODE <1>:	*Type:* **0 ↵**
Regenerating drawing.	

You now have a blank screen similar to a blank sheet of illustration board.

Paper Space Limits

In this exercise a B-size title block is inserted around the viewport set, so the limits of the paper space need to be set for that size.

Step 5. Set paper space limits.

Prompt	Response
Command:	**Limits:**
ON/OFF/<LOwer left corner><default>:	*Type:* **0,0** ↵
Upper right corner <default>:	*Type:* **17,11** ↵

Note: The Floating Viewports and Floating Model Space (Mview) commands are also located under View in the menu bar.

Mview:

The Mview: command operates only in paper space and is used to create and control viewport display. The viewport named VP1 that was saved in model space using the Vports: command can now be inserted into paper space using the Mview: command.

Step 6. Use the Mview: command to restore the saved viewport named VP1 into paper space.

Prompt	Response
Command:	**Mview: (Windows users:** *Type:* **MVIEW** ↵)
ON/OFF/Hideplot/Fit/2/3/4/Restore/ <First point>:	*Type:* **R** ↵
?/Name of window configuration to insert <*ACTIVE>:	*Type:* **VP1** ↵
Fit/<First Point>:	*Type:* **.5,.5** ↵ (to locate the lower left corner of the drawing)
Second point:	*Type:* **10,7.5** ↵ (to locate the upper right corner of the drawing)

This viewport set restored in paper space at a size of 9.5 × 7 will fit easily into the B-size title block.

The other Mview: command options are:

OFF

Think of each viewport as a single sheet of paper (on the illustration board). The viewport may be copied, stretched, erased, moved, or scaled. The drawing within the viewport cannot be edited while in paper space. The OFF option turns off the views (drawings) inside the viewport and saves regeneration time while you are editing the viewports. The views can be turned back on when the viewports are situated so you are pleased with the format.

ON

Turns the model space view (drawing inside the viewport) on.

Hideplot

Used to remove hidden lines in a selected viewport when the drawing is plotted.

Fit

Creates a single viewport to fill the current paper space limits. Other viewports can be erased before or after the Fit option is used.

2,3,4

Creates two, three, or four viewports in a specified area or to fit the current paper space limits.

Restore

Restores saved model space viewports (saved with the Vports: command) into paper space.

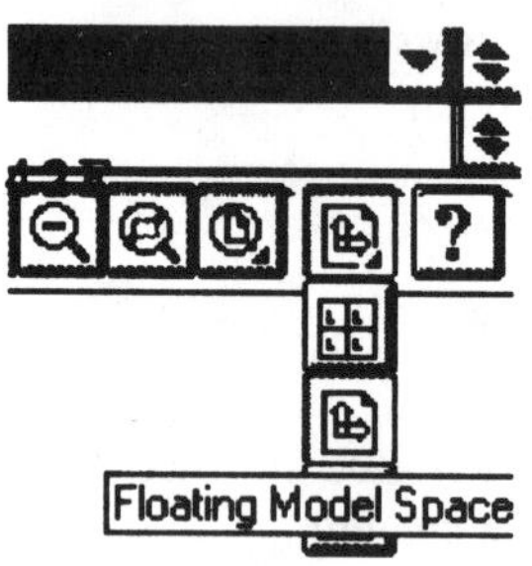

Note: The Floating Model space command is also located under View in the menu bar.

<First point>
Creates a new viewport defined by picking two corners or by typing the X and Y coordinates of lower left and upper right corners.

Mspace:

This command switches you from paper space to model space. You may work in model space with Tilemod: either on or off.

Tilemod: must be set to 0 (off) to use the Mspace: command. Because you are presently in paper space, you know that Tilemode: is 0 because paper space cannot be active unless Tilemode: is 0. To return to model space simply select Mspace:.

Step 7. Return to model space with Tilemod: set to 0.

Prompt:	Response:
Command:	**Mspace:** (or *Type:* **MS** ↵)

On Your Own:

Pick the upper left viewport to make it active.

While working in model space with Tilemod: set to 0 you can use the XP option of the Zoom: command to scale the current model space view relative to paper space.

Step 8. Set the zoom magnification for the upper left viewport.

Prompt	Response
Command:	*Type:* **Z** ↵
All/Center/Dynamic/Extents/Left/ Previous/Vmax/Window/<Scale (X/XP)>:	*Type:* **.5XP** ↵
The view is now magnified to .5 times the paper space units.	

The .5XP entered gives you a scale of ½ the paper space units (in this case ½″ = 1″). A scale of 1/96XP entered gives you a scale of ⅛′ = 1′ (8 × 12 = 96) on your viewport.

Be aware that the XP zoom magnification is significant only when tilemode is set to 0 and you are in model space.

Step 9. On Your Own: Set the zoom magnification for the other three viewports.

Zoom to a magnification of .5XP in the other three viewports.

Pspace:

The Pspace: command switches you from model space to paper space. Tilemod: must be 0 (off) for Pspace: to work. Tilemod: is still set to 0. You have been working in model space with Tilemod: set to 0.

Step 10. Use the Pspace: command to return to paper space.

Prompt	Response
Command:	**Pspace:** (or *Type:* **PS** ↵)

EXERCISE 10–2, PART 2
INSERTING A TITLE BLOCK IN PAPER SPACE AND ANNOTATING PAPER SPACE VIEWPORTS

MV Setup

In this part of Exercise 10–2, the MV Setup AutoLISP routine is used to insert a standard (American National Standards Institute) title block

Note: The Paper Space command is also located under View in the menu bar.

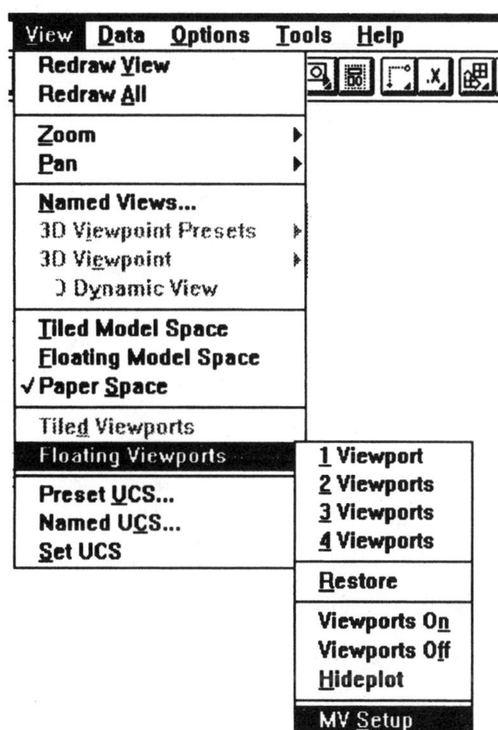

Step 1. Use MV Setup to insert a standard ANSI title block (Figure 10–30).

Prompt	Response
Command:	**MV Setup**
Align/Create/Scale viewports/Options/ Title block/Undo:	*Type:* **T** ↵
Delete objects/Origin/Undo/<Insert title block>:	↵
Available title block options:	
0: None	
1: ISO A4 Size (mm)	
2: ISO A3 Size (mm)	
3: ISO A2 Size (mm)	
4: ISO A1 Size (mm)	
5: ISO A0 Size (mm)	
6: ANSI-V Size	
7: ANSI-A Size	
8: ANSI-B Size	
9: ANSI-C Size	
10: ANSI-D Size	
11: ANSI-E Size	
12: Arch/Engineering (24″ × 36″)	
13: Generic D-size Sheet (24″ × 36″)	
Add/Delete/Redisplay<Number of entry to load>:	*Type:* **8** ↵
Create a drawing named ansi-b.dwg? <Y>	↵
Align/Create/Scale viewports/Options/ Title block/Undo:	↵

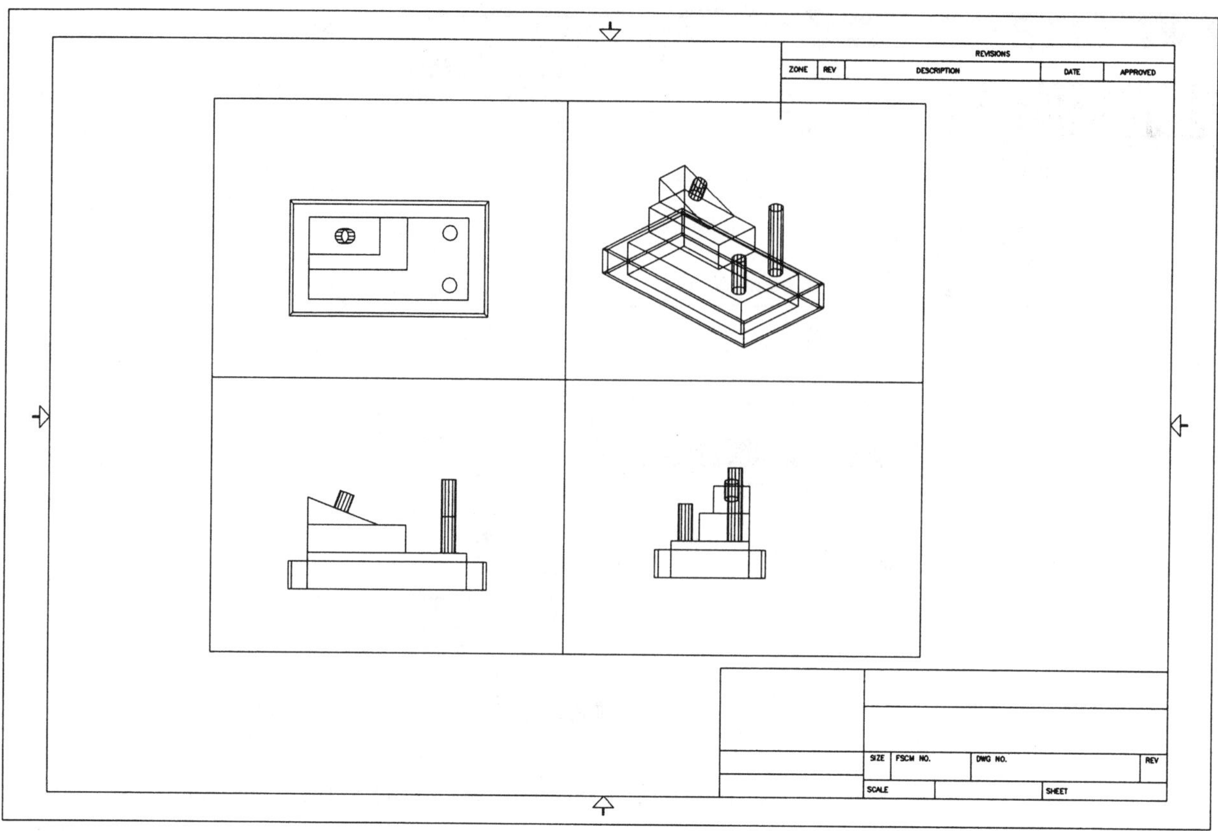

FIGURE 10–30
Using MV Setup to Insert a Standard ANSI Format

You now have a standard B-size ANSI title block with the four viewports in it. Before using the Move: command to move the viewports so that they are centered in the title block, use the Mview: command option OFF to turn off the model space views (drawings inside the viewports), as shown in Figure 10–31. When the prompt "Select objects" appears, pick the edge of the viewport. Turning the viewports off decreases regeneration time and allows you to work faster on complex drawings.

Step 2. On Your Own (Figure 10–31): Arrange viewports inside the title block.

1. Use the Move: command to move all viewports to the approximate locations shown in Figure 10–31.
2. Use the Mview: command option ON to turn on the model space views.

Because the viewports have been moved, it is likely that your model space views are not lined up vertically and horizontally. MV Setup can also be used to align the views (drawings) within each viewport. The Align option automatically returns you to model space.

Step 3. Use the MV Setup Routine to align the model space views (Figure 10–32).

Prompt	**Response**
Command:	**MV Setup**
Align/Create/Scale viewports/ Options/Title block/Undo:	*Type:* **A** ↵
Angled/Horizontal/Vertical alignment/ Rotate view/Undo:	*Type:* **H** ↵ (AutoCAD changes to model space.)

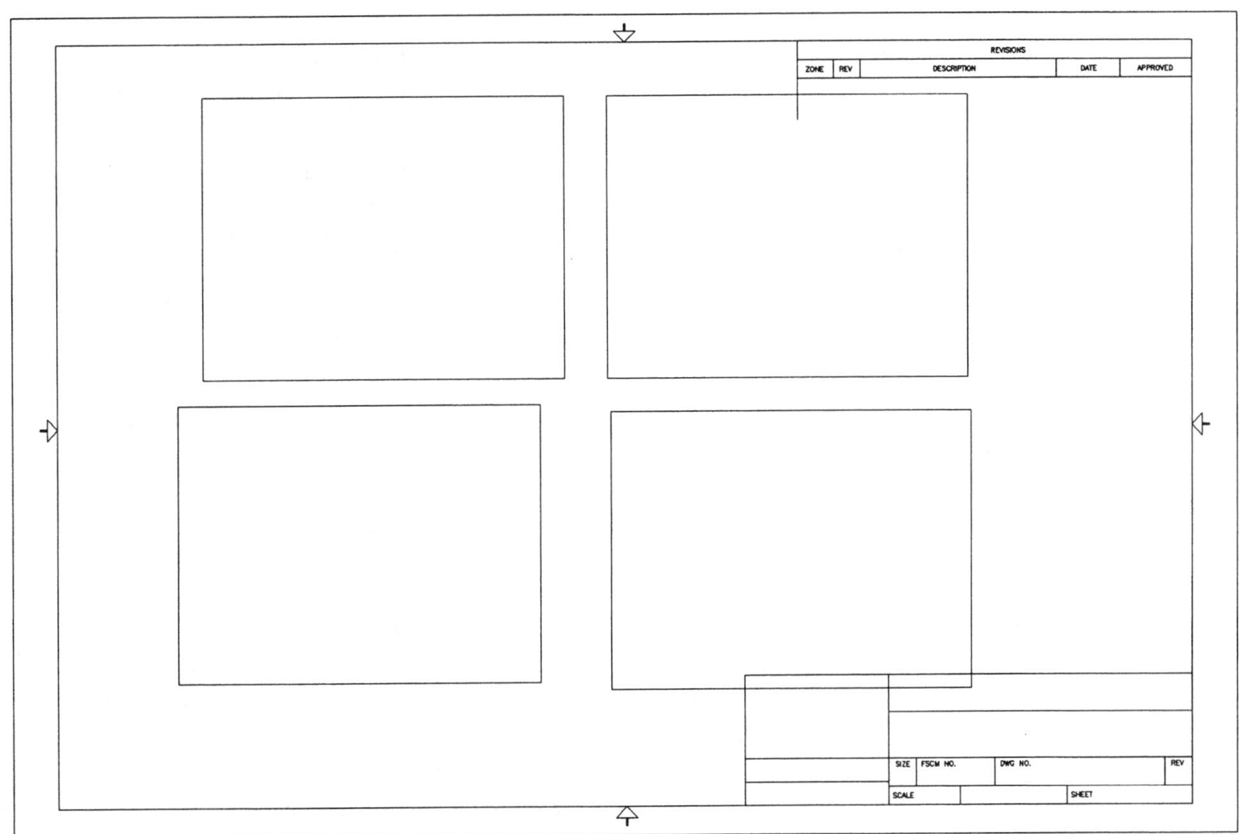

FIGURE 10–31
Model Space Turned Off (Drawing Inside the Viewports)

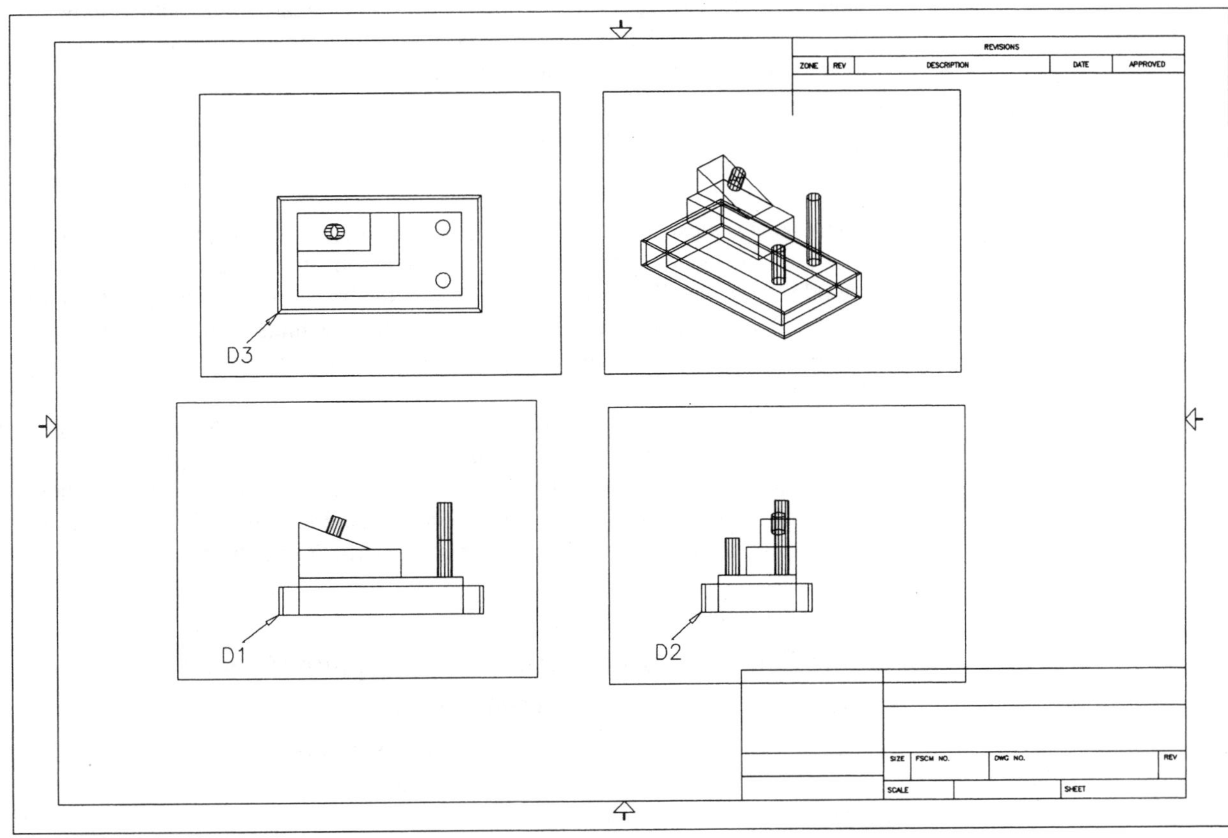

FIGURE 10–32
Using MV Setup to Align the Model Space Views

Prompt	Response
Basepoint:	Osnap-**ENDpoint**
of	**D1**
Other point:	**Pick the lower left viewport to make it active.**
	Osnap-**ENDpoint**
of	**D2**
Angled/Horizontal/Vertical alignment/ Rotate view/Undo:	*Type:* **V** ↵
Basepoint:	Osnap-**ENDpoint**
of	**Pick the upper left viewport to make it active.**
	D3
Other point:	**Pick the lower left viewport to make it active.**
	Osnap-**ENDpoint**
of	**D1** ↵↵

When Tilemode: is set to 1 (on), MV Setup acts just like SETUP on earlier versions of AutoCAD; units, scale, and paper size can be set using prompts for each setting.

When Tilemode: is 0 (off), MV Setup has the following options:

Align viewports
This option lets you pan the view so that it aligns with a basepoint in another viewport. You may align viewports horizontally and vertically and at a specified distance and angle from a basepoint in another viewport, and you may rotate the view in a viewport about a basepoint. This option also has an undo feature.

Create viewports
This option allows you to delete existing viewports. It also allows you to create one or more standard size viewports. If more than one is created, this option allows you to specify the distance between viewports. It also allows you to create an array of viewports. This option also has an undo feature.

Scale viewports
This option allows you to set the scale of the drawing displayed in the viewports, similar to the Zoom: XP feature.

Options
When Options is picked, the "Set Layer/Limits/Units/Xref:" prompt appears. This prompt applies to the insertion of the title block. This option allows you to set a layer current for the title block, specify whether or not to reset the limits of the drawing extents after the title block is inserted, specify whether to translate the units to inches or millimeters, or specify if the title block is to be inserted into the drawing, or if an Xref is used.

Title block
This option allows you to delete objects from paper space and to select the origin point for this sheet. It then prompts you to select one of 13 standard formats. The first 5 are standard ISO (International Standards Organization) metric formats. The next 6 are standard ANSI formats used in many manufacturing industries. The 12th is a standard architectural format, and the last format is a generic D-size sheet.

Undo
This is an undo option for the major routine.

Adding Details and Annotating Paper Space Viewports

Step 4. Add another viewport (Figure 10–33).

Prompt	Response
Command:	**Mview:**
ON/OFF/Hideplot/Fit/2/3/4/Restore/ <First point>:	*Type:* **13,7** ↵ (Or pick a point.)

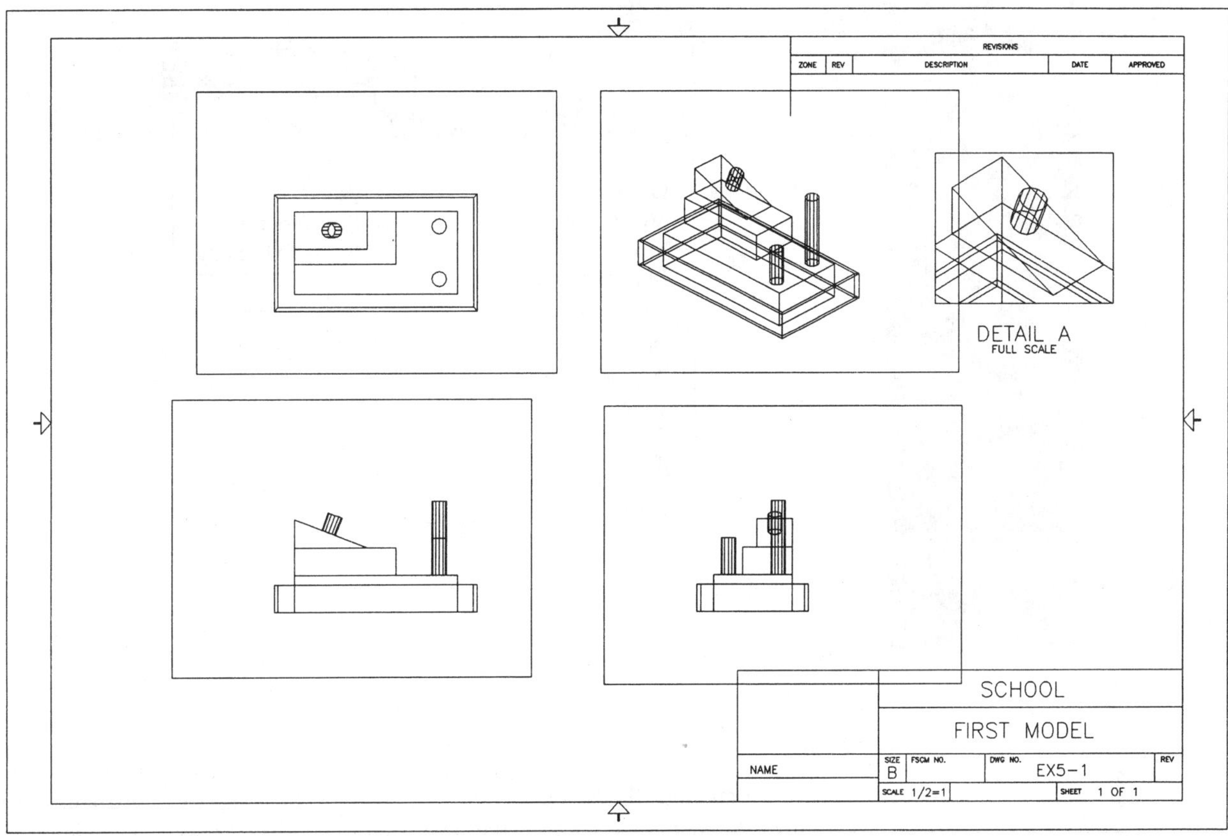

FIGURE 10-33
Adding Details and Annotating Paper Space Viewports

Other corner: *Type:* **15.5,9** ↵ (Or pick a point.)

You are now in paper space and have a viewport containing a view of the active model space viewport.

Step 5. On Your Own: Modify the new viewport (Figure 10-33).

1. Before returning to model space, zoom a window around the detail. This is to provide you a clear display view of the viewport when you are working in model space.
2. Return to model space.
3. Use the Vpoint: command to select a viewpoint of 1,−1,1 in the new viewport, if it is not already that.
4. Zoom a window around the wedge as shown.
5. Use Zoom: XP to scale the view to 1XP, which is full scale.

Step 6. On Your Own: Label the drawing.

1. Return to paper space.
2. Label the drawing using DText: with text height as follows:

   .2 for DETAIL A
   .1 for FULL SCALE
   .2 for SCHOOL, and FIRST MODEL
   .15 for EX5-1
   .1 for 1 OF 1
   .1 for NAME
   .15 for SIZE B

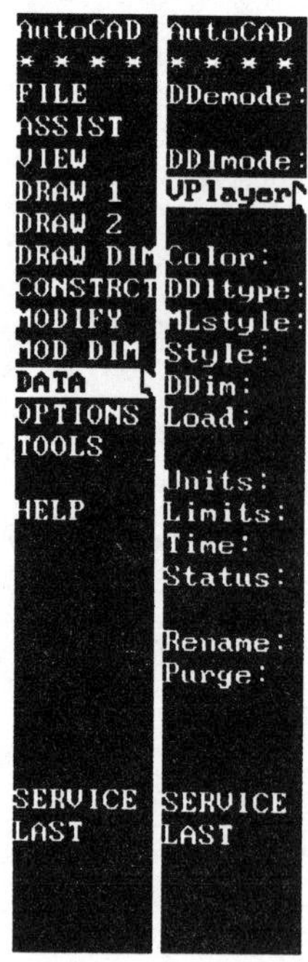

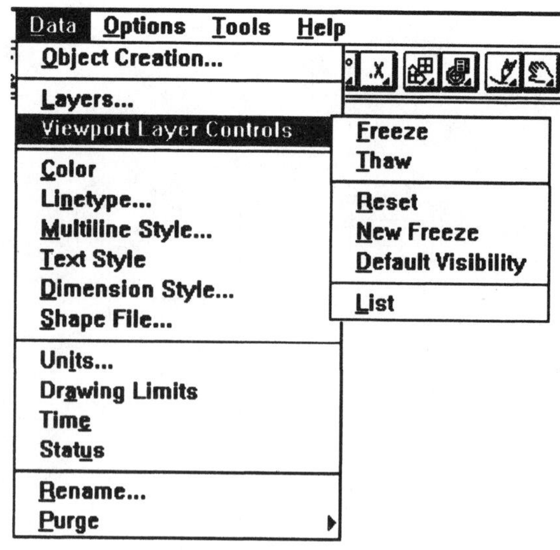

VPlayer:

The VPlayer: command allows you to freeze different layers in any viewport. This is especially useful with an annotation layer that you want to be visible only in one viewport. It works in either model space or paper space. To use the VPlayer: command, you must set Tilemod: to 0 (off).

In model space, you can use the Layer Control dialog box to freeze layers in individual viewports by picking the layer, then picking the Cur VP: Frz button. Tilemode must be set to 0 (off). When you pick the New VP: Frz button, that layer is frozen for all new viewports created. Both the Cur VP: Frz and the New VP: New buttons should be picked to freeze layers for newly created viewports.

In paper space, you can use the Layer Control dialog box to freeze layers only globally (in all viewports at the same time). The globally frozen layer must be thawed and set on globally before the VPlayer: command options can affect its visibility. In paper space, you may freeze layers in individual viewports by using the VPlayer: command options.

The VPlayer: command options are:

?
Lists layers frozen in selected paper space viewports.

Freeze
Prompts you to list the names of layers you want to freeze, then prompts you for the viewports in which you want to freeze the layers. The viewport options are:

- **All** All viewports, in model space or paper space.
- **Select** Switches to paper space (when you are in model space) and allows you to pick viewports for layer freeze.
- **Current** Selects the current viewport in model space for layer freeze.

Thaw
Prompts you to name the layers you want to thaw, then prompts you for the viewports in which you want to thaw the layers.

Reset
After you use the Freeze or Thaw option to change a layer's visibility, you can use the Reset option to restore the default visibility setting for a layer in a selected viewport.

Newfrz
Creates new layers that are frozen in all viewports. If you then want to thaw a layer in a single viewport, use the Thaw option.

Vpvisdfl

If a layer is frozen in some viewports and thawed in others, you can use the Vpvisdfl option to set the default visibility per viewport for any layer. This default setting then determines the layer's visibility in any new viewport created with the Mview: command.

EXERCISE 10–2, PART 3
MAKE A PERSPECTIVE VIEW OF THE 3-D MODEL

Dview:

The Dview: command perspective mode (perspective mode is turned on by selecting the Distance option of Dview:) gives a realistic view of the 3-D model. The previous views that were obtained using Vpoint: are parallel projections (the lines do not converge in the distance). Dview: gives a perspective view of the model.

Note: 3D Dynamic View (Dview): is also located under View on the menu bar.

Step 1. On Your Own: Prepare the drawing for making a perspective view.

1. While in paper space enlarge the upper right viewport by zooming a window around it so you are able to see it clearly on the display screen.
2. Change to model space.
3. Pick the upper right viewport to make it active.

Step 2. Use Dview: to obtain a perspective view of the model (Figure 10–34).

Prompt	Response
Command:	**Dview: (Windows users:** *Type:* **DVIEW ↵)**
Select objects:	(Window the entire model.)
Select objects:	↵
CAmera/TArget/Distance/POints/PAn/ Zoom/TWist/CLip/Hide/Off/Undo/ <eXit>	Type: **D** ↵
New camera/target distance <default>: (A slider bar at the top of the screen also appears.)	*Type:* **20** ↵ (the desired distance, or select by using the slider bar)

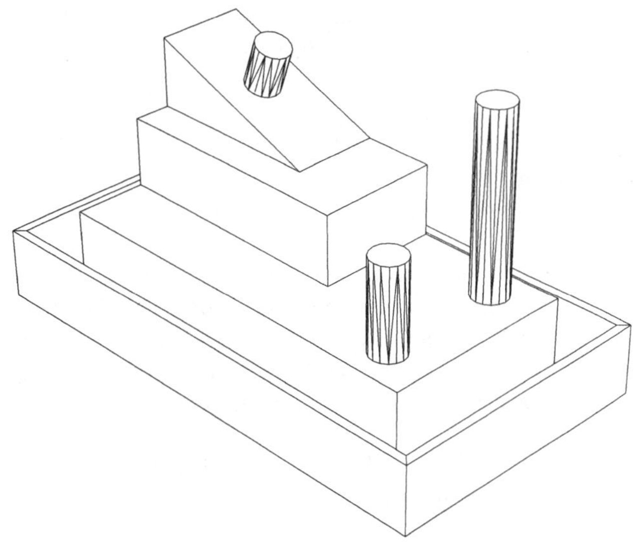

FIGURE 10–34
Using Dview: to Obtain a Perspective View of the Model

Step 3. Pan the view to center the model.

Prompt	Response
CAmera/TArget/Distance/POints/PAn/ Zoom/TWist/CLip/Hide/Off/Undo/ <eXit>	*Type:* **PA** ↵
Displacement base point:	Pan the view to center the model in the space.
CAmera/TArget/Distance/POints/PAn/ Zoom/TWist/CLip/Hide/Off/Undo/ <eXit>	*Type:* **X** ↵

When X is entered, AutoCAD exits from the Dview: command but still remains in perspective mode.

Because the object was already in a 3-D viewpoint, it was not necessary to use the CAmera or TArget options of the Dview: command to obtain the desired viewpoint.

Distance

The Distance option moves the camera (your viewing eye) in or out along the line of sight and places the object into a perspective view. AutoCAD prompts you for the new camera-to-object distance and displays the current distance as the default.

The slider bar is labeled from 0× to 16×, with 1× representing the current distance. Moving the slider bar cursor to the right increases the distance between the camera and your object. Moving the cursor to the left moves the camera closer to the object. For example, moving the slider bar cursor to 2× sets the new distance to two times the previous distance. The readout at the top of the screen (in the Coordinates area) gives you contiuous information telling you how far from the object the camera is located.

On large objects the default for Distance is often so small (your eye is too close to the object) that very little of the object appears. Typing a large distance or selecting 16× on the slider bar several times will give you the desired view.

POints

Allows you to change the target (the point toward which you are looking) and the camera location by either picking those points (using Osnap) or entering them with the use of X, Y, and Z coordinates.

CAmera

Rotates your viewpoint around the existing view. You may use either slider bars or type the desired angle to rotate the camera up and down (angle relative to the XY plane of the current UCS) or from side to side to obtain your desired view.

TArget

Rotates the point you are looking toward about the camera. The effect is like turning your head to see different views of the drawing from the same point. TArget is used to see different parts of the same room using the same perspective vanishing points, whereas CAmera is used to change your perspective viewpoint. Slider bars or typing is also used to select the TArget angle.

PAn

Acts like the Pan: command but allows you to remain in the perspective mode.

Zoom

This option has two modes. If perspective is on, this option changes the camera lens length. Changing the lens length changes the field of view and allows more or less of the view to be visible. The default lens length is 50. Decreasing this number makes more of the view visible. Increasing the number zooms in so that less of the view is visible.

If perspective is off, Zoom performs like the Zoom: Center command.

TWist

Allows you to tilt the object around the line of sight using either a digitizer to pick the desired angle or the keyboard to type the desired angle.

CLip

Allows you to create views by positioning invisible walls perpendicular to the line of sight so that any portion of the object that is in front of the front clipping plane is obscured, and any portion behind the back clipping plane is invisible.

Prepare the Drawing for Plotting

Step 4. On Your Own (Figure 10–35): Prepare the drawing for plotting.

Return to paper space and perform a Zoom: All.

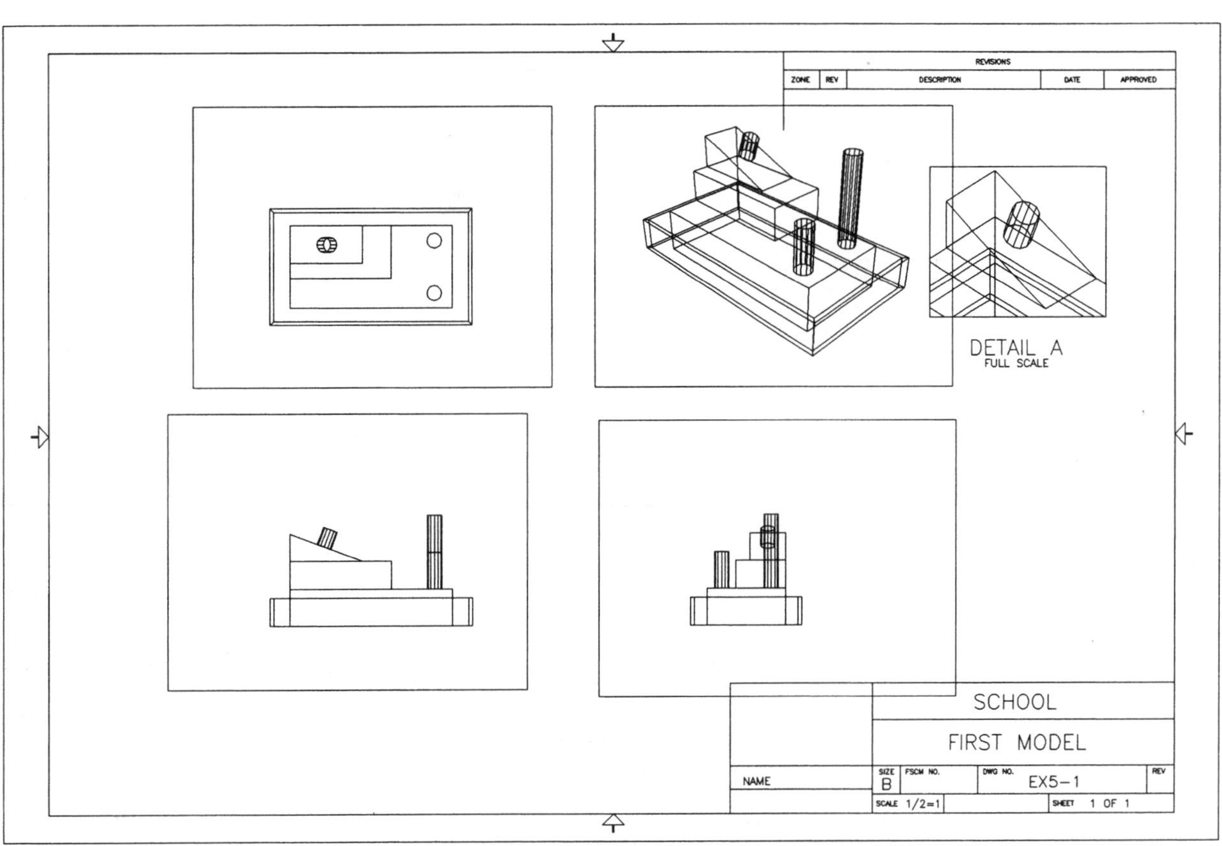

FIGURE 10–35
Preparing the Drawing for Plotting

Step 5. Use the Hideplot option of Mview: to remove hidden lines in a selected viewport when the drawing is plotted.

Prompt	**Response**
Command:	**Mview:**
ON/OFF/Hideplot/Fit/2/3/4/Restore/ <First Point>:	*Type:* **H** ↵
ON/OFF:	*Type:* **ON** ↵
Select objects:	**(Pick the boundary of the upper right viewport and the DETAIL A viewport.)**

You may now plot all viewports at the same time with the upper right viewport and the DETAIL A viewport displaying views with hidden lines removed as shown in Figure 10–36. Do not plot quite yet.

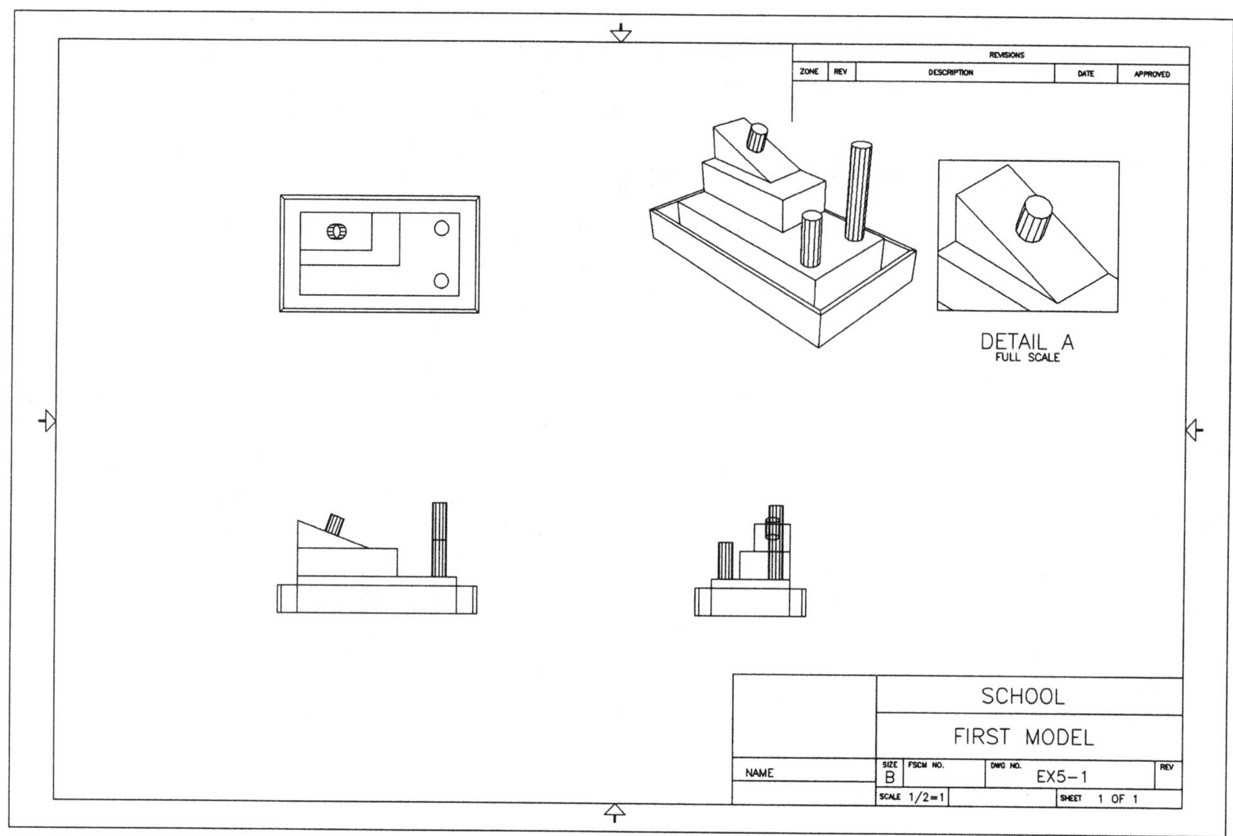

FIGURE 10-36
Exercise 10-2

Step 6. On Your Own: Remove lines around all major viewports, plot, and save the drawing.

1. Create a layer named BORDER.
2. Freeze the layer named BORDER.
3. Use the Chprop: command to change all viewport borders except the DETAIL A viewport to the layer BORDER, which is frozen. When you are prompted "Select objects:", pick the outside edge of each viewport. This eliminates the boxes surrounding each viewport.
4. Plot Exercise 10-2 to scale.
5. When you have completed Exercise 10-2, save your work in at least two places.

EXERCISES

10-1. Complete Exercise 10-1 using the steps described in this chapter.

10-2. Complete Exercise 10-2 using the steps described in this chapter.

REVIEW QUESTIONS

1. Which of the following is a characteristic of paper space?
   a. Viewports are tiled
   b. Tilemode is set to 1
   c. Viewports can overlap
   d. Models are created
   e. The Vports: command will work

2. How many model space viewports can be created on any one drawing?
   a. 2
   b. 4
   c. 16
   d. 64
   e. Unlimited

3. To save a viewport configuration which of the following letters must be typed?
   a. S d. J
   b. R e. N
   c. D
4. Which of the following Vports: options allows for both vertical and horizontal arrangements?
   a. SIngle d. 4
   b. J e. S
   c. 3
5. A command can be started in one viewport and completed in a different viewport.
   a. True b. False
6. Which of the following is a characteristic of a nontiled viewport?
   a. Fills the graphics screen and touches all other viewports
   b. Is fixed and cannot overlap
   c. Can be erased or moved.
   d. Only one viewport may be plotted at one time
   e. Only one viewport may be active at one time
7. Model space may be active with Tilemod: set at either 0 or 1.
   a. True b. False
8. Which of the following Mview: options creates several viewports at the same time?
   a. ON d. 2,3,4
   b. OFF e. <First point>
   c. Fit
9. Which of the following will produce a model space view within a viewport that is at a scale of ¼″ = 1′ in relation to paper space?
   a. Zoom: 1/4XP d. Zoom: 1/4=12XP
   b. Zoom: 1/48XP e. Zoom: 1/4-12 XP
   c. Zoom: 1/4″ = 1′ XP
10. Which of the following can be used to accurately align viewports in model space?
   a. Mview: d. MV Setup
   b. Vports: e. Align:
   c. Move:
11. List the command and its option that will insert a set of saved model space viewports into paper space.

   ____
12. List the command used to switch from model space to paper space when Tilemod: is off.

   ____
13. List five characteristics of nontiled viewports that are different from those of tiled viewports.

   ____

   ____

   ____

   ____

   ____
14. Write the command that splits the active viewport into two, three, or four areas.

   ____
15. Write the command that allows you to restore a viewport configuration saved in model space to a display in paper space.

   ____
16. Describe the uses of model space and paper space in creating and plotting 3-D models.

   Model space: ______________________________

   Paper space: ______________________________

   ____
17. Describe the difference between parallel and perspective projection.

   Parallel: ______________________________

   Perspective: ______________________________
18. Describe how to set the UCS for a 3-D view so that your name can be typed parallel to the screen display.

   ____
19. Describe how to obtain a perspective view of an object from a distance of 40″ in front of it.

   ____

   ____
20. Describe the difference between elevation and thickness.

   ____

   ____

11 Using SOLIDS Commands to Draw Solid Geometric Shapes

OBJECTIVES

When you have completed this chapter, you will be able to:

- □ Draw the following primitive solids: box, sphere, wedge, cone, cylinder, torus.
- □ Make settings to display solids smoothly.
- □ Draw extruded solids.
- □ Draw revolved solids.
- □ Rotate solids about the X, Y, or Z axis.
- □ Form chamfers and fillets on solid edges.
- □ Join two or more solids.
- □ Subtract one or more solids from another solid.
- □ Prepare a solid model for rendering (using the Hide: command).
- □ Form a solid model from the common volume of two intersecting solids.

INTRODUCTION

A solid may be a single object called a *primitive,* or it may be a combination of objects called a *composite.*

SOLIDS Commands Used to Create Basic Shapes

A *primitive solid* is a single solid shape that has had nothing added to or subtracted from it. Six solid primitives (box, sphere, wedge, cone, cylinder, torus) are the basic shapes often used in solid modeling. They are drawn by using six commands:

Box:
Cone:
Cylinder:
Sphere:
Torus:
Wedge:

AutoCAD also allows you to form solids by extruding (adding height) and revolving (rotating about an axis) 2-D drawing entities such as polylines, circles, ellipses, rectangles, polygons, and donuts. The commands that extrude and revolve drawing entities to form solids are:

Extrude:
Revolve:

SOLIDS Commands Used to Create Composite Solids

Composite solids are formed by joining primitive solids, other solids, or a combination of the two. These combinations may also be added to or subtracted from other solids to form the composite model needed. The following commands used to create composite solids are described in this chapter:

Union:

Allows you to join several solids to form a single solid.

Intersect:

Allows you to create composite solids from the intersection of two or more solids. Intersect: creates a new solid by calculating the common volume of two or more existing solids.

Subtract:

Allows you to subtract solids from other solids.

Interfere:

Does the same thing as Intersect:, except it retains the original objects.

SOLIDS Commands Used to Edit Solids

Slice:

Used to create a new solid by cutting the existing solid into two pieces and removing or retaining either or both pieces.

Section:

Used to create the cross-sectional area of a solid. That area may then be hatched using the Hatch: or Bhatch: commands with any pattern you choose. Be sure the section is parallel with the current UCS when you hatch the area.

Other Commands That Can Be Used to Edit Solids

Rotate3d:

Used to rotate solids about the X, Y, or Z axes.

Mirror3D:

Used to create mirror images of solids about a plane specified by three points.

Trim:

Used to trim lines, polylines, and similar entities in 3-D space, but this command will not trim a solid shape.

Extend:

Used to extend lines, polylines, and similar entities in 3-D space, but this command will not extend a solid shape.

Fillet:

Used to create fillets and rounds. Specify the radius for the fillet and then pick the edge or edges to be filleted.

Chamfer:

Used to create chamfers. Specify the distances for the chamfer and then pick the edge or edges to be chamfered.

Align:

Used to move a solid so that a selected plane on the first solid is aligned with a selected plane on a second solid.

Explode:

Used to explode a solid into regions. (*Example:* An exploded solid box becomes six regions: four sides, a top, and a bottom.)

All the following commands may be used to edit or view solids in the same manner as you have used them previously:

Chprop:	Pan:
Dview:	Scale:
Erase:	UCS:
Move:	Vpoint:
Mview:	Zoom:

Settings That Control How the Solid Is Displayed

FACETRES

Used to make shaded solids and those with hidden lines removed appear smoother. Values range from 0.01 to 10.0. The default value is 0.5. Higher values take longer to regenerate but look better. If you change this value, you can update the solid to the new value by using the Shade: or Hide: command again.

ISOLINES

Sets the number of lines per surface on solids. Values range from 0 to 2047. The default value is 4. The value 10 is a good middle ground. If you change this value, you can update the solid to the new value by regenerating the drawing.

Changing AME Models from Previous Versions of AutoCAD to R13

Ameconvert:

Used to convert AME solid models to AutoCAD solid objects. The solids selected must be AME Release 2 or 2.1 regions or solids. AutoCAD ignores all other objects.

Exercise 11–1, parts 1 through 6, provides step-by-step instructions for using the solids commands just described.

When you have completed Exercise 11–1, parts 1 through 6, your drawing will look similar to Figure 11–1.

EXERCISE 11–1, PART 1
SETTING FACETRES AND ISOLINES; USING BOX:, SPHERE:, WEDGE:, CONE:, CYLINDER:, AND TORUS: TO DRAW PRIMITIVE SOLIDS

Set Up the Drawing

Step 1. On Your Own:

1. Pick New. . . from the menu bar File menu. Name the drawing: 11–1 (your initials).
2. Make the following settings:

UNITS: Decimal; 3 digits to the right of the decimal point
LIMITS: Lower left corner: 0,0
Upper right corner: 11, 8.5
GRID: .4
SNAP: .05
STYLE: STANDARD; FONT: SIMPLEX; HEIGHT: 0
Create the following layers:

LAYER NAME	COLOR	LINETYPE
Y	YELLOW	CONTINUOUS
R	RED	CONTINUOUS
G	GREEN	CONTINUOUS

Set layer Y current.

Note: Use *Zoom: Window* to enlarge the graphics display in a viewport. Use *Zoom: X* (*Example:* Type **.5X** to enlarge the graphics display or **2X** to enlarge the graphics display.) Pan: or Zoom: Dynamic will center the graphics in a viewport.

3. Use the Vports: command to make two vertical viewports. Zoom: All in both viewports. Either viewport may be active as you draw.
4. Use the Vpoint: command to set a 1,−1,1 viewpoint for the right viewport.

FACETRES and ISOLINES

Note: Either viewport may be active. Use the Zoom: commands in either viewport to easily see your drawing.

FACETRES and ISOLINES are the variables for displaying solids. The larger the number, the more realistic the display of the solid, and the longer it takes to process (regenerate, plot, Hide:, save, etc.) the drawing.

FIGURE 11–1
Using Basic SOLIDS Commands to Draw Geometric Solids

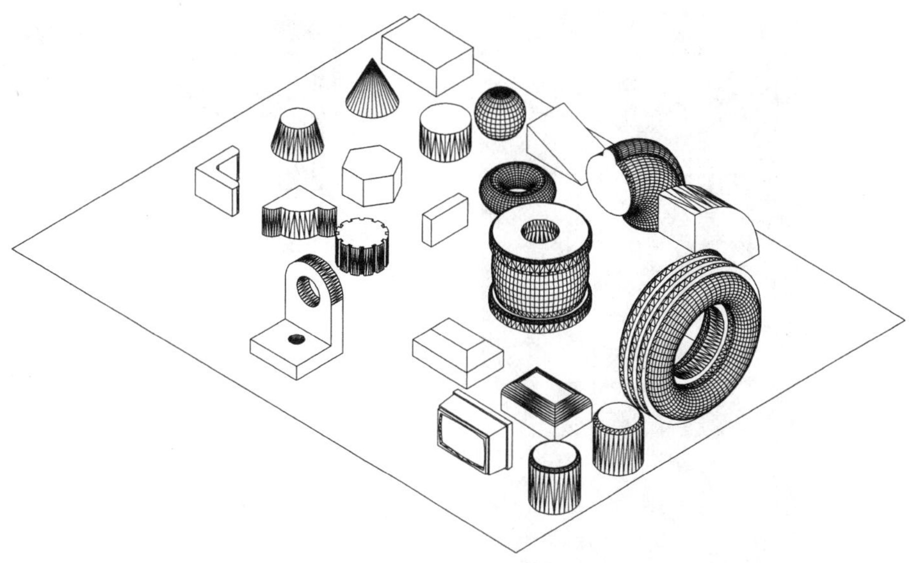

Step 2. Set the FACETRES and ISOLINES variables.

Prompt	Response
Command:	*Type:* **FACETRES** ↵
New value for FACETRES <0.500>:	*Type:* **2** ↵
Command:	*Type:* **ISOLINES** ↵
New value for ISOLINES <4>:	*Type:* **10** ↵

Box:

Step 3. Draw a solid box, 1.2 × .8 × .5 height (Figure 11–2).

Note: The Box command is also located in the Solids pull-down menu under Draw in the menu bar.

Prompt	Response
Command:	**Box:**
Center/<Corner of box> <0, 0, 0>:	Type: **.6,7.4** ↵
Cube/Length/<Other corner>:	*Type:* **1.8,8.2** ↵
Height:	*Type:* **.5** ↵

FIGURE 11–2
Drawing a Solid Box

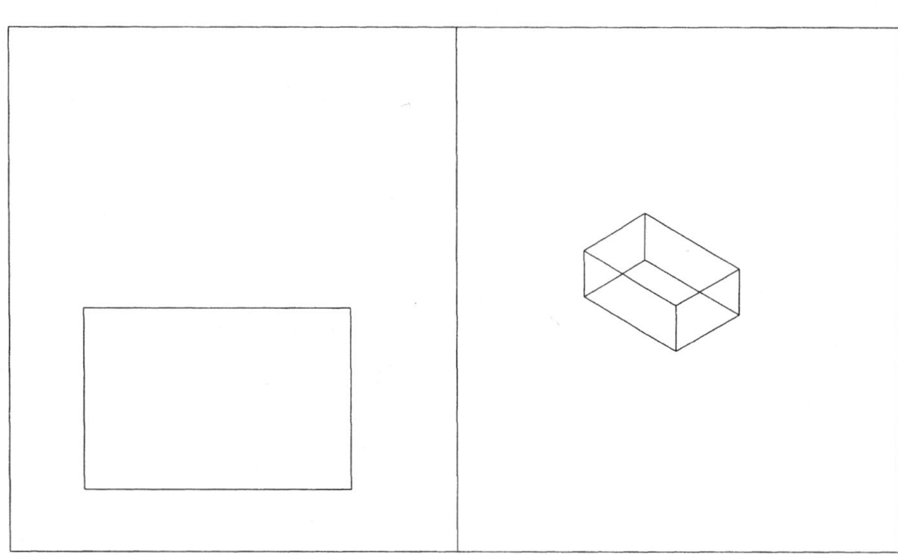

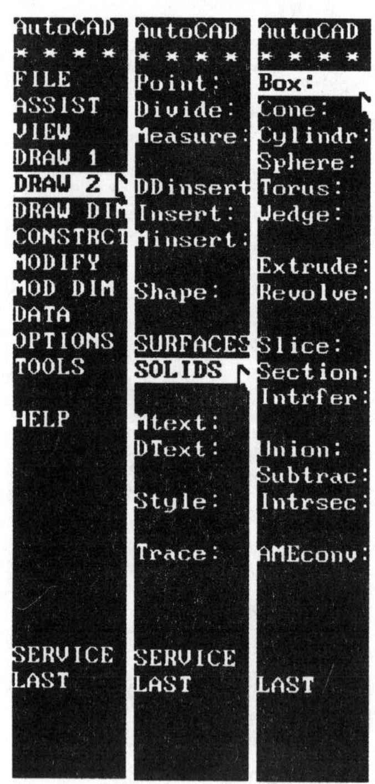

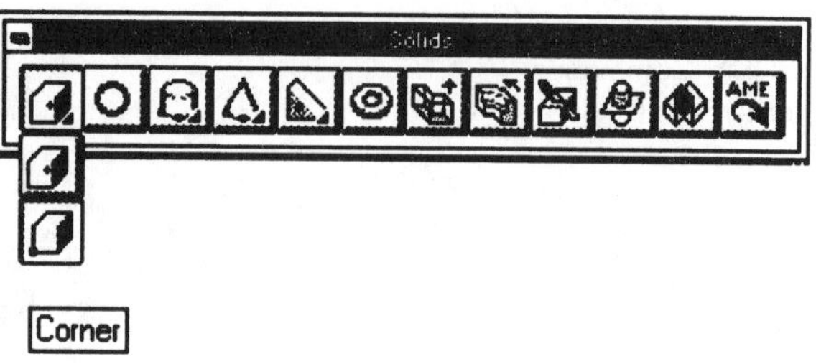

Center
Allows you to draw a box by first locating its center.
Cube
Allows you to draw a cube by specifying the length of one side.
Length
Allows you to draw a box by specifying its length (X), width (Y), and height (Z).

Sphere:

Step 4. Draw a solid sphere, .4 radius (Figure 11–3).

Prompt	Response
Command:	**Sphere:**
Center of sphere> <0, 0, 0>:	*Type:* **2.8,7.8** ↵
Diameter/<Radius> of sphere:	*Type:* **.4** ↵

FIGURE 11–3
Drawing a Solid Sphere

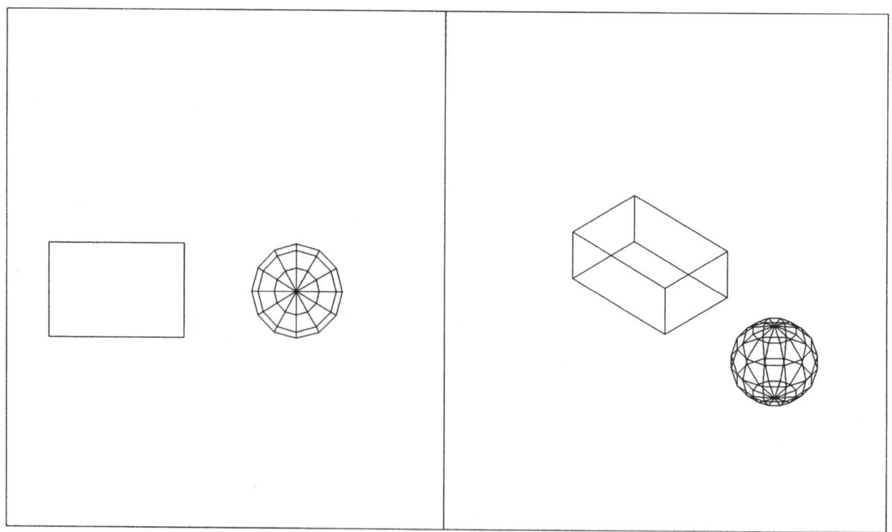

Wedge:

Step 5. Draw a solid wedge, .8 × 1.2 × .5 height (Figure 11–4).

Prompt	Response
Command:	**Wedge:**
Center/<Corner of wedge> <0, 0, 0>:	*Type:* **3.8,7.4** ↵
Cube/Length/<other corner>:	*Type:* **5,8.2** ↵
Height:	*Type:* **.5** ↵

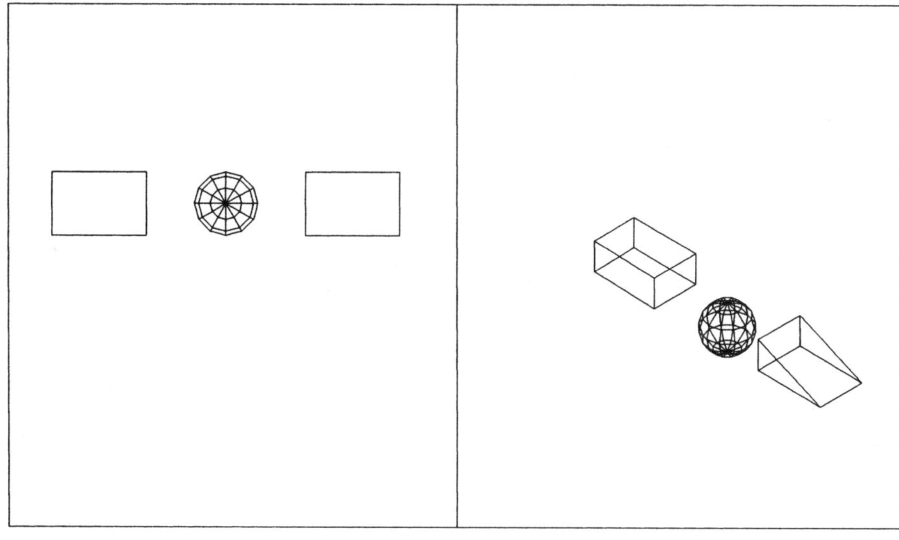

FIGURE 11–4
Drawing a Solid Wedge

Cone:

Step 6. Draw a solid cone, .4 radius, .8 height (Figure 11–5).

Prompt	Response
Command:	**Cone:**
Elliptical/<center point> <0, 0, 0>:	*Type:* **1.2, 6.6** ↵
Diameter/<Radius>:	*Type:* **.4** ↵
Apex/<Height>:	*Type:* **.8** ↵

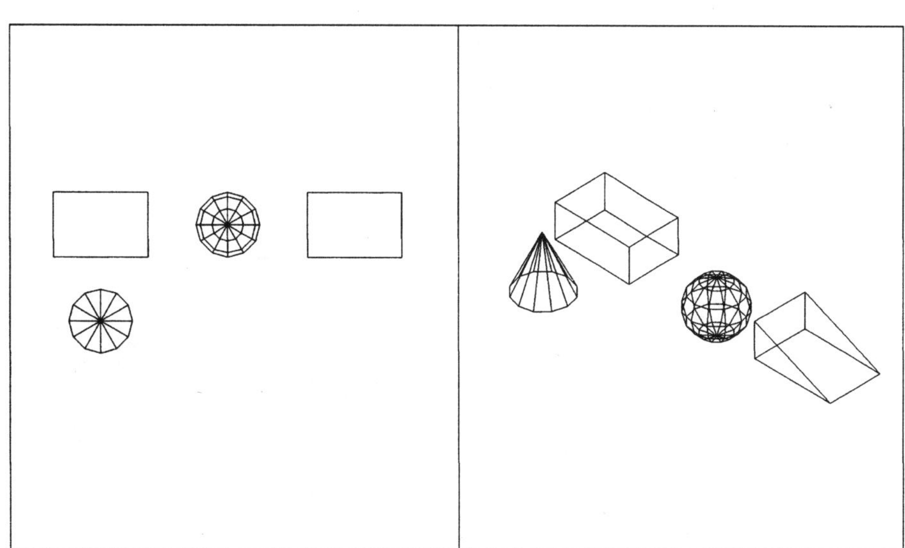

FIGURE 11–5
Drawing a Solid Cone

Cylinder:

Step 7. Draw a solid cylinder, .4 radius, .5 height (Figure 11–6).

Prompt	Response
Command:	**Cylinder:**
Elliptical/<Center point> <0, 0, 0>:	*Type:* **2.8,6.6** ↵
Diameter/<Radius>:	*Type:* **.4** ↵
Center of other end/<Height>:	*Type:* **.5** ↵

FIGURE 11–6
Drawing a Solid Cylinder

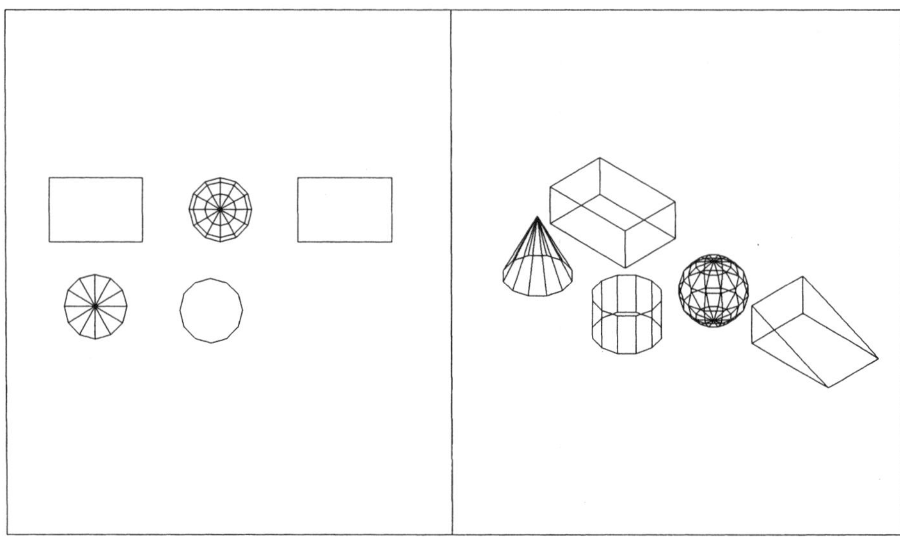

Torus:

Step 8. Draw a solid torus (a 3-D donut), .4 torus radius, .2 tube radius (Figure 11–7).

Prompt	Response
Command:	**Torus:**
Center of torus> <0, 0, 0>:	*Type:* **4.4,6.6** ↵
Diameter/<Radius> of torus:	*Type:* **.4** ↵
Diameter/<Radius> of tube:	*Type:* **.2** ↵

FIGURE 11–7
Drawing a Solid Torus

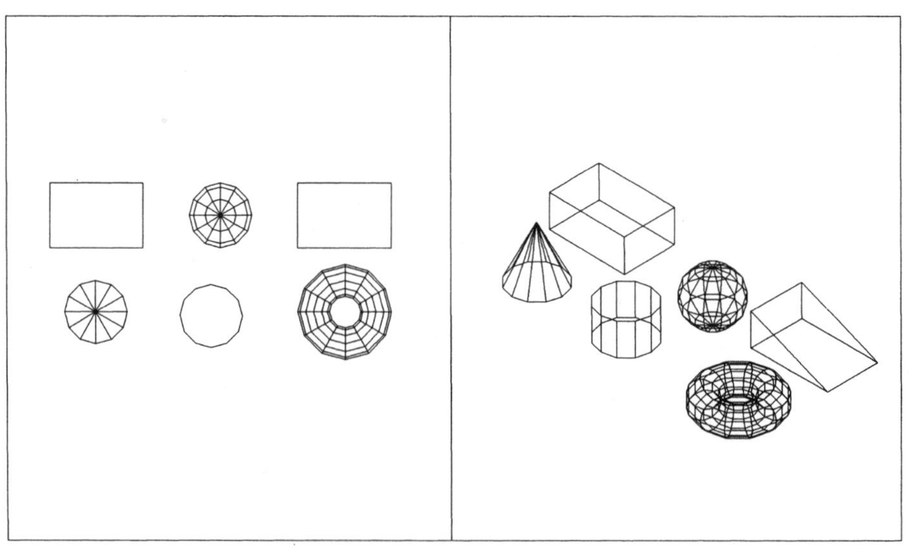

FIGURE 11–8
Radius of Torus, Radius of Tube

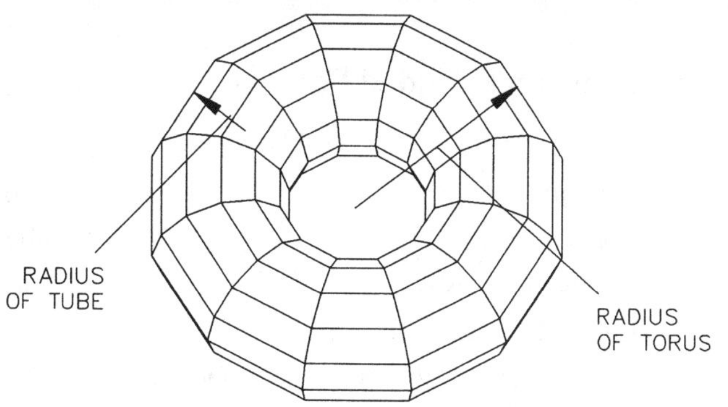

Note: The Extrude command is also located in the Solids pull-down menu under Draw in the menu bar.

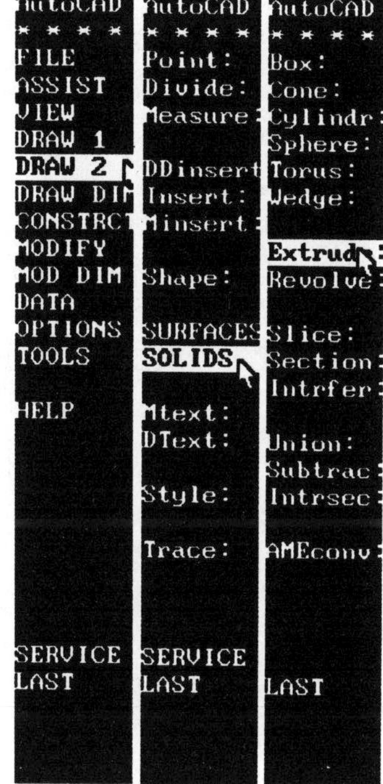

The radius of the torus is the distance from the center of the 3-D donut to the center of the tube that forms the donut. The radius of the tube is the radius of the tube forming the donut, Figure 11–8.

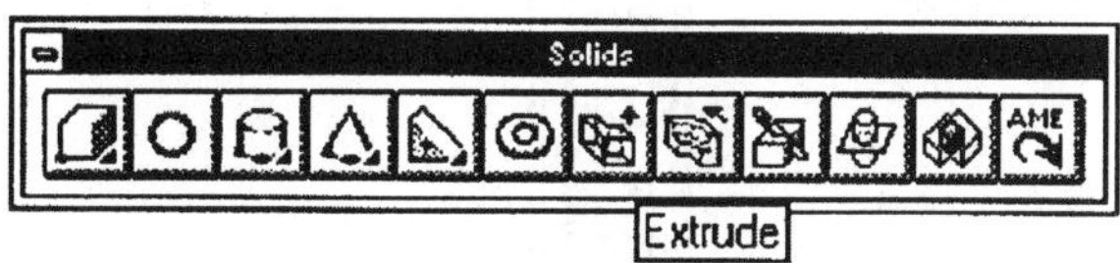

EXERCISE 11–1, PART 2
USING EXTRUDE: TO DRAW EXTRUDED SOLIDS

Draw an Extruded Circle

Step 1. Draw a circle (Figure 11–9).

Prompt	Response
Command:	*Type:* **C** ↵ (the keyboard macro for circle)
CIRCLE 3P/2P/TTR/<Center point>:	*Type:* **1.2,5** ↵
Diameter/<Radius>:	*Type:* **.4** ↵

Step 2. Extrude the circle, .5 height, 15° extrusion taper angle (Figure 11–9).

Prompt	Response
Command:	**Extrude:**
Select objects:	**Pick the circle.**
Select objects:	↵
Path/<Height of extrusion>:	*Type:* **.5** ↵
Extrusion taper angle <0>:	**15** ↵

FIGURE 11–9
Drawing an Extruded Circle

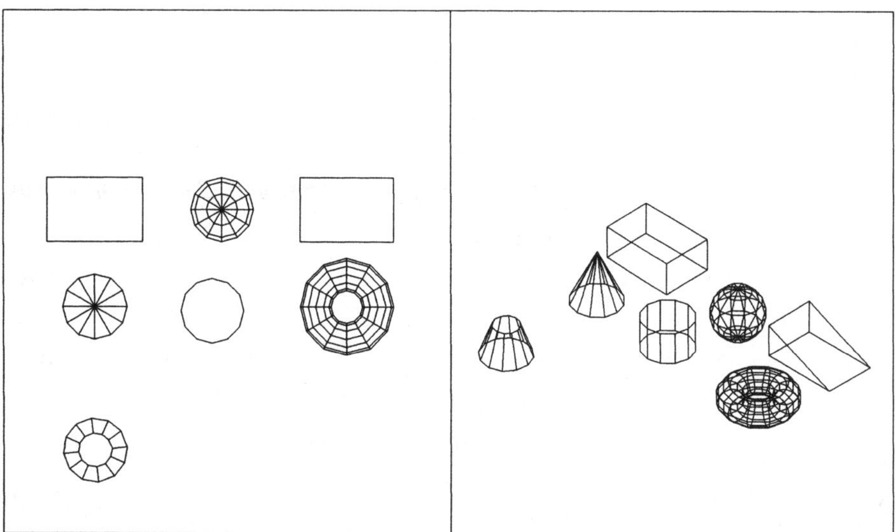

Draw an Extruded Polygon

Step 3. Draw a polygon (Figure 11–10).

Note: The Polygon command is also located in a pull-down menu under Draw in the menu bar.

Prompt	Response
Command:	**Polygon:**
Number of sides <4>:	*Type:* **6** ↵
Edge/<Center of polygon>:	*Type:* **2.8,5** ↵
Inscribed in circle/Circumscribed about circle (I/C)<I>:	*Type:* **C** ↵
Radius of circle:	*Type:* **.4** ↵

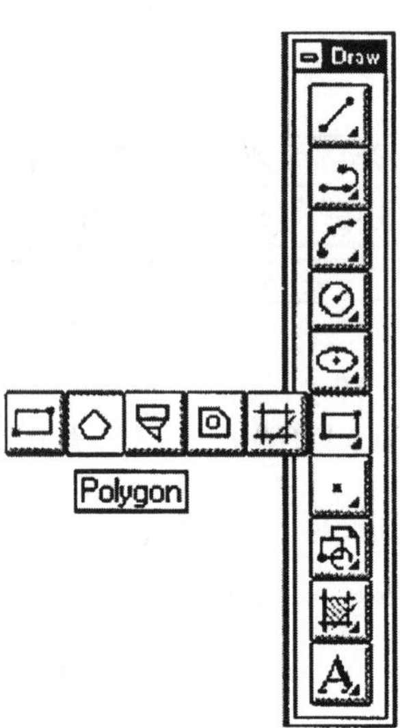

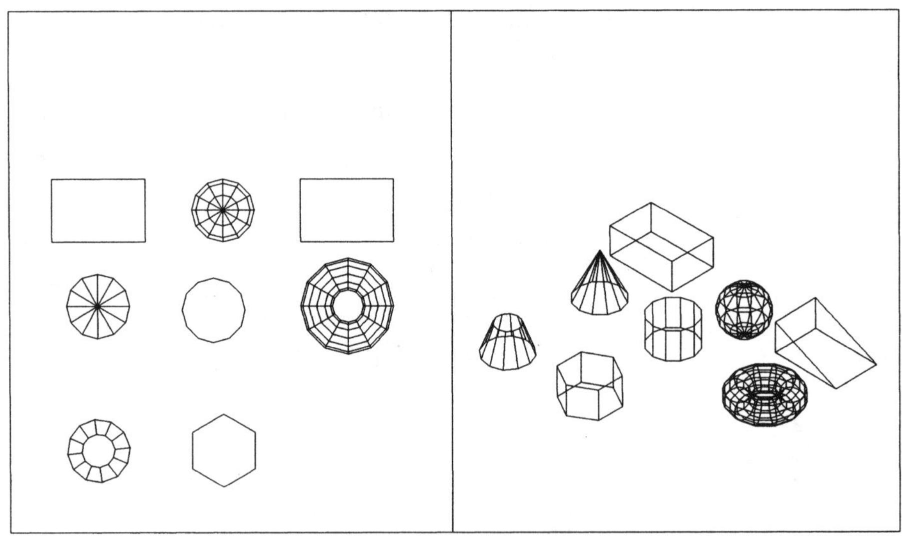

FIGURE 11–10
Drawing an Extruded Polygon

Step 4. Extrude the polygon, .5 height, 0° extrusion taper angle (Figure 11–10).

Prompt	Response
Command:	**Extrude:**
Select objects:	Pick the hexagon.
Select objects:	↵
Path/<Height of Extrusion>:	*Type:* **.5** ↵
Extrusion taper angle <0>:	↵

Draw an Extruded Rectangle

Step 5. Draw a rectangle (Figure 11–11).

Prompt	Response
Command:	*Type:* **RECTANG** ↵
First corner:	*Type:* **4.3,4.6** ↵
Other corner:	*Type:* **4.5,5.4** ↵

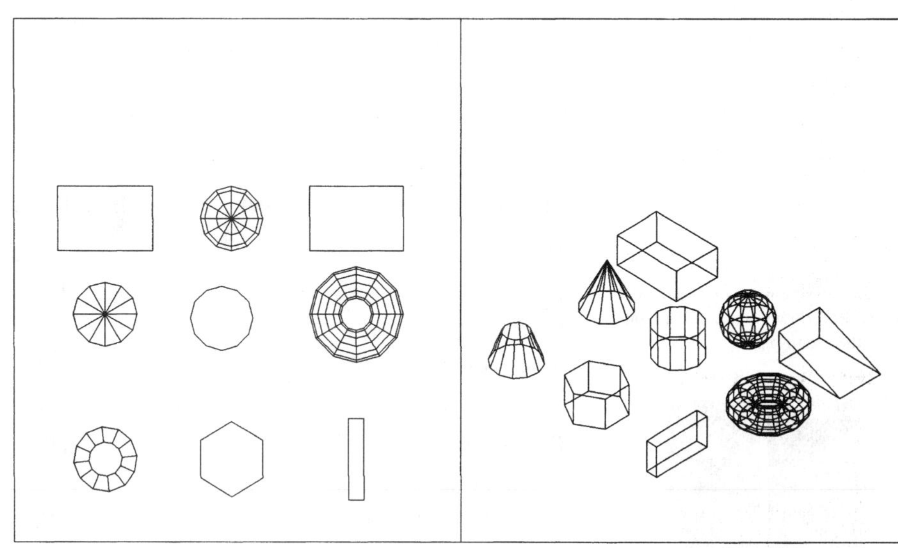

FIGURE 11–11
Drawing an Extruded Rectangle

Step 6. Extrude the rectangle, .5 height, 0° extrusion taper angle (Figure 11–11).

Prompt	Response
Command:	**Extrude:**
Select objects:	**Pick: the rectangle.**
Select objects:	↵
Path/<Height of extrusion>:	*Type:* **.5** ↵
Extrusion taper angle <0>:	↵

Draw an Extruded Structural Angle

Step 7. Draw the outline of the cross section of a structural angle (Figure 11–12).

Prompt	Response
Command:	*Type:* **L** ↵
LINE From point:	*Type:* **1,3** ↵
To point:	*Type:* **@.8,0** ↵
To point:	*Type:* **@0,.2** ↵
To point:	*Type:* **@.6<180** ↵
To point:	*Type:* **@.6<90** ↵
To point:	*Type:* **@.2<180** ↵
To point:	*Type:* **C** ↵

FIGURE 11–12
Drawing an Extruded Structural Angle

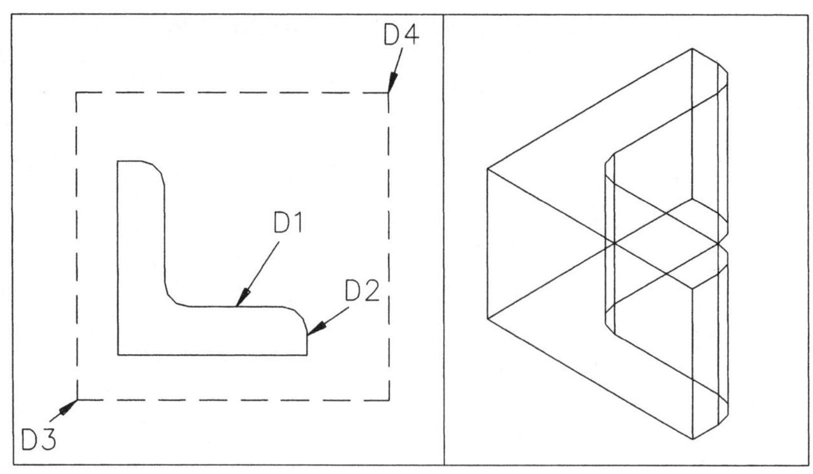

Step 8. Add a .1-radius fillet to the outline (Figure 11–12).

Note: The Fillet command is also located in a pull-down menu under Construct in the menu bar.

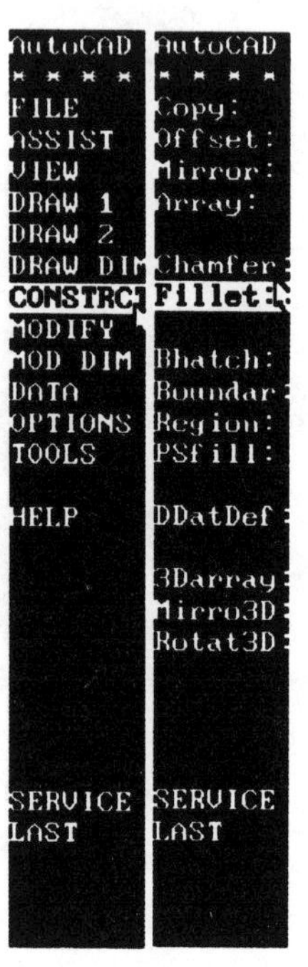

Prompt	Response
Command:	**Fillet:**
Polyline/Radius/Trim/ <Select first object>:	*Type:* **R** ↵
Enter fillet radius <0.000>:	*Type:* **.1** ↵
Command:	↵
Polyline/Radius/Trim/ <Select first object>:	**D1**
Select second object:	**D2**
Command:	↵

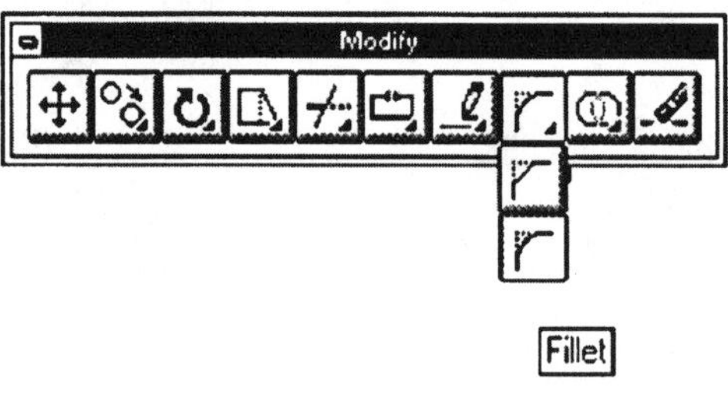

Fillet

Step 9. On Your Own (Figure 11–12):

Draw .1-radius fillets at the other two intersections shown.

Step 10. Use Pedit: to combine all the lines and fillets into a single entity (Figure 11–12):

Prompt	Response
Command:	*Type:* **PEDIT** ↵
Select objects:	**(Pick one of the lines forming the structural angle.)**
Select objects: 1 found	
Select objects:	↵
Entity selected is not a polyline Do you want to turn it into one?<Y>	↵

Close/Join/Width/Edit vertex/Fit/Spline/ Decurve/Ltype gen/Undo/eXit <X>:	*Type:* **J** ↵ (to select the Join option)
Select objects:	**D3**
Other corner:	**D4**
Select objects:	↵
8 segments added to polyline	
Open/Join/Width/Edit vertex/Fit/Spline/ Decurve/Ltype gen/Undo/eXit <X>:	↵ (to exit from the Pedit: command)

Step 11. Extrude the cross section of the structural angle, .5 height, 0° extrusion taper angle (Figure 11–12).

Prompt	Response
Command:	**Extrude:**
Select objects:	**(Pick the polyline.)**
Select objects:	↵
Path/<Height of extrusion>:	*Type:* **.5** ↵
Extrusion taper angle <0>:	↵

Draw Two Extruded Shapes

Step 12. On Your Own (Figures 11–13 and 11–14):

1. Draw the two shapes shown as Figures 11–13 and 11–14 in the approximate locations shown in Figure 11–1. Draw one section of the knurled knob, Figure 11–14, and then create a polar array using the Array: command.
2. Use the Pedit: command to join all entities of each figure into a single polyline.
3. Extrude each figure to a height of .5.

FIGURE 11–13
Drawing an Extruded Shape

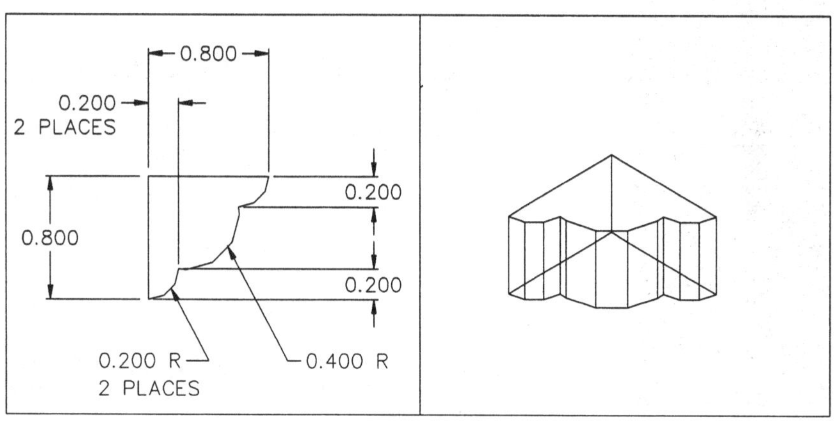

FIGURE 11–14
Drawing an Extruded Shape

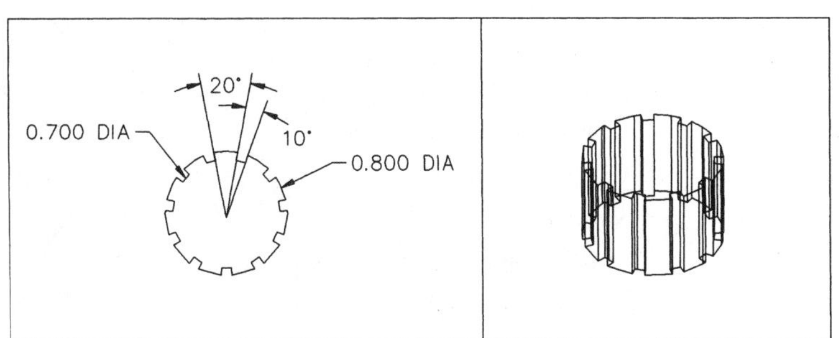

EXERCISE 11–1, PART 3
USING REVOLVE: TO DRAW REVOLVED SOLIDS; USING ROTAT3D: TO ROTATE SOLIDS ABOUT THE X,Y, AND Z AXES

Draw Revolved Shape 1

Step 1. Draw two circles (Figure 11–15A).

Prompt	Response
Command:	*Type:* **C** ↵
3P/2P/TTR/<Center point>:	*Type:* **6.3,7.7** ↵
Diameter/<Radius>:	*Type:* **.5** ↵
Command:	↵
3P/2P/TTR/<Center point>:	*Type:* **6.3,8.2** ↵
Diameter/<Radius>:	*Type:* **.15** ↵

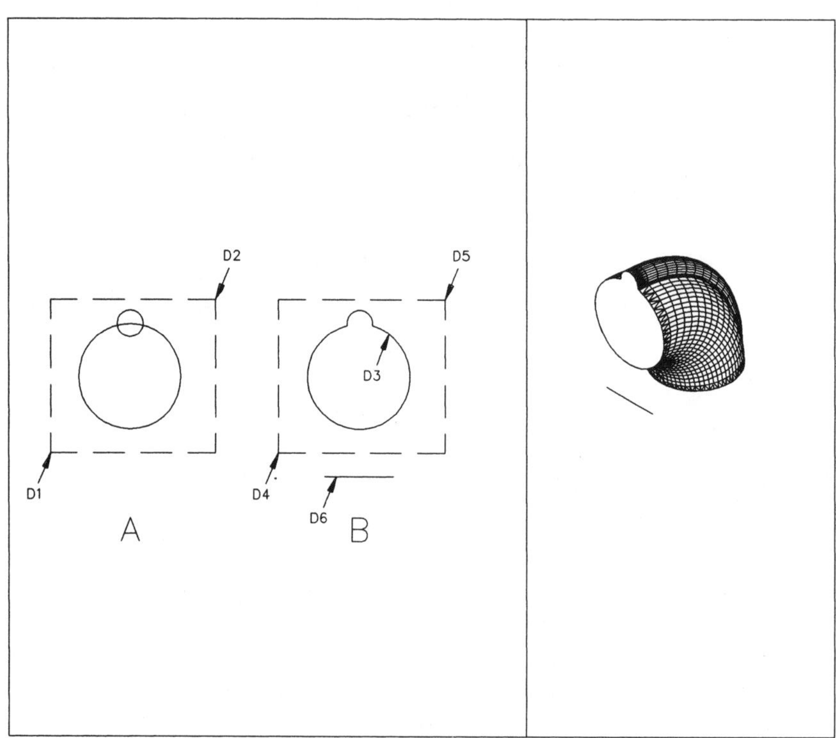

FIGURE 11–15
Drawing Revolved Shape 1

Step 2. Use the Trim: command to trim parts of both circles (Figures 11–15A and 11–15B).

Prompt	Response
Command:	**Trim:**
Select cutting edges: (Projmode = UCS, Edgemode = No extend)	
Select objects:	**D1** (first corner of a window)
Other corner:	**D2** (second corner of a window)
Select objects:	↵
<Select object to trim>/Project/Edge/Undo:	**Trim the circles as shown in Figure 11–15B.**

Step 3. Join all segments of the circles into one polyline (Figure 11–15B).

Prompt	Response
Command:	**Pedit:**
Select objects:	**D3** ↵
Object selected is not a polyline Do you want to turn it into one? <Y>	↵
Close/Join/Width/Edit vertex/Fit/Spline/ Decurve/Ltype gen/Undo/eXit <X>:	*Type:* **J** ↵
Select objects:	**D4**
Other corner:	**D5**
Select objects:	↵
1 segments added to polyline	
Open/Join/Width/Edit vertex/Fit/Spline/ Decurve/Ltype gen/Undo/eXit <X>:	↵ (to exit from the Pedit: command)

Step 4. Draw the axis of revolution (Figure 11–15B).

Prompt	Response
Command:	**Line:**
LINE From point:	*Type:* **6,6.7** ↵
To point:	*Type:* **@.6<0** ↵
To point:	↵

Step 5. Use Revolve: to form a revolved solid created by revolving a single polyline 90° counterclockwise about an axis (Figure 11–15B).

Note: The Revolve command is also located in the Solids pull-down menu under Draw in the menu bar.

Prompt	Response
Command:	**Revolve:**
Select objects:	**D3**
Select objects:	↵
Axis of revolution—Object/X/Y/<Start point of axis>:	*Type:* **O** ↵
Select an object:	**D6** (Be sure to pick the left end of the line for counterclockwise rotation.)
Angle of revolution <full circle>:	*Type:* **90** ↵

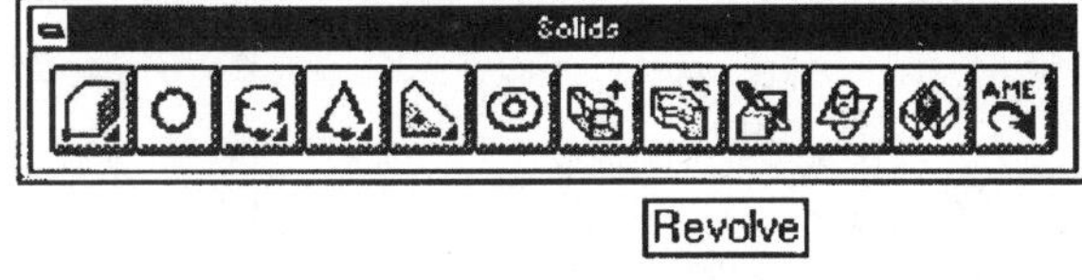

Draw Revolved Shape 2

Step 6. Draw a rectangle (Figure 11–16).

Prompt	Response
Command:	*Type:* **RECTANG** ↵
First corner:	*Type:* **7.4,7.4** ↵
Other corner:	*Type:* **8.2,8.1** ↵

FIGURE 11–16
Drawing Revolved Shape 2

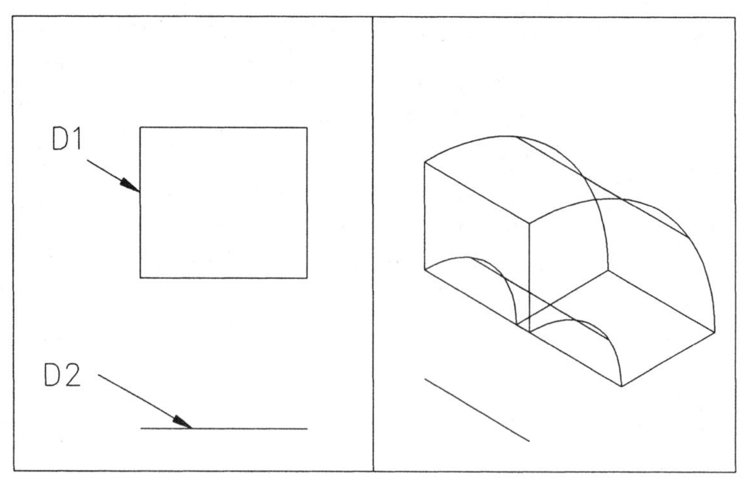

Step 7. Draw the axis of revolution (Figure 11–16).

Prompt	Response
Command:	*Type:* **L** ↵
LINE From point:	*Type:* **7.4,6.7** ↵
To point:	*Type:* **@.8< 0** ↵
To point:	↵

Step 8. Use the Revolve: command to form a revolved solid created by revolving the rectangle 90° counterclockwise about an axis (Figure 11–16).

Prompt	Response
Command:	**Revolve:**
Select objects:	**D1** ↵
Axis of revolution—Object/X/Y/<Start point of axis>:	*Type:* **O** ↵
Pick entity to revolve around:	**D2** (Pick left end of the line.)
Angle of revolution <full circle>:	*Type:* **90** ↵

FIGURE 11–17
Drawing Revolved Shape 3

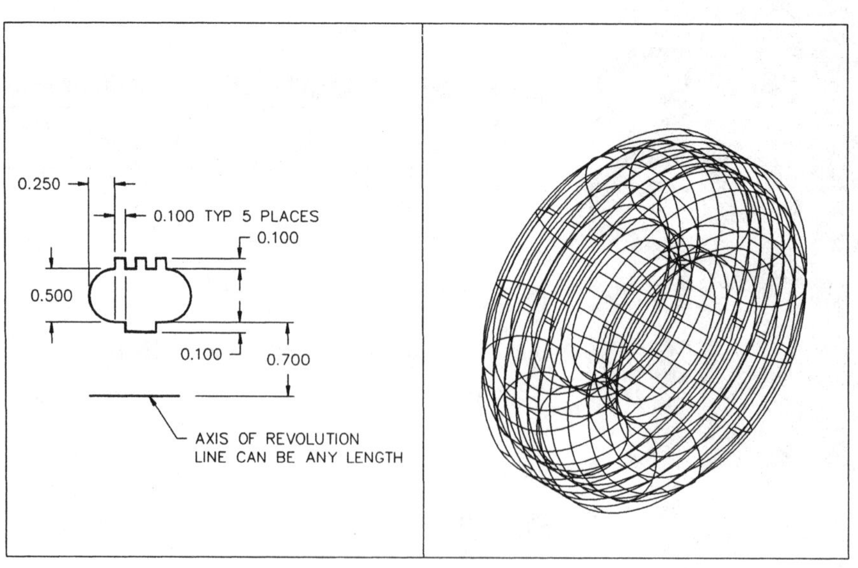

Draw Revolved Shapes 3 and 4

Step 9. On Your Own (Figures 11–17 and 11–18):

1. Draw the cross-sectional shapes of the two objects shown in Figures 11–17 and 11–18 using the Line: and Arc: commands in the approximate locations shown in Figure 11–1.
2. Use the Pedit: command to join all entities of each shape into a single closed polyline.
3. Locate the axis of rotation for each shape in the position shown.
4. Use Revolve: to revolve each shape full circle about the axis.

FIGURE 11–18
Drawing Revolved Shape 4

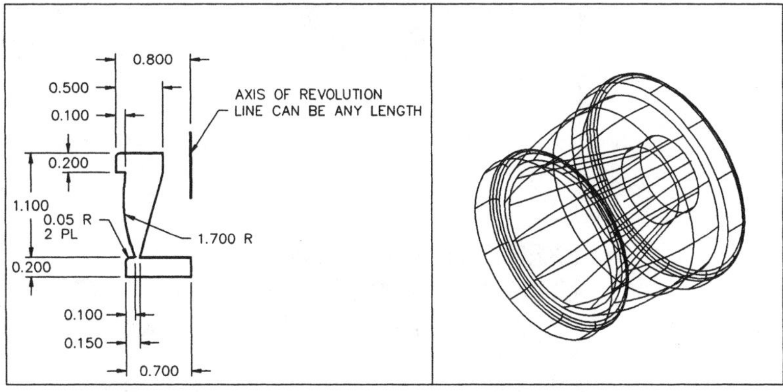

Rotat3D:

Step 10. Use Rotat3D: to rotate shape 4 90° about the X axis so that it assumes the position shown in Figure 11–19.

Note: The 3D Rotate command is also located in a pull-down menu under Construct in the menu bar.

Prompt	**Response**
Command:	**Rotat3D:**
Select objects:	**(Pick shape 4.)**
Select objects:	↵
Axis by Entity/Last/View/XAxis/YAxis/ ZAxis/<2points>:	*Type:* **X** ↵
Point on X axis <0, 0, 0>:	*Type:* **END** ↵
endpoint of	**D1**
<Rotation angle>/Reference:	*Type:* **90** ↵

AutoCAD AutoCAD
* * * * * * * *
FILE Copy:
ASSIST Offset:
VIEW Mirror:
DRAW 1 Array:
DRAW 2
DRAW DIM Chamfer:
CONSTRCT Fillet:
MODIFY
MOD DIM Bhatch:
DATA Boundar:
OPTIONS Region:
TOOLS PSfill:
HELP DDatDef:
3Darray:
Mirro3D:
Rotat3D:
SERVICE SERVICE
LAST LAST

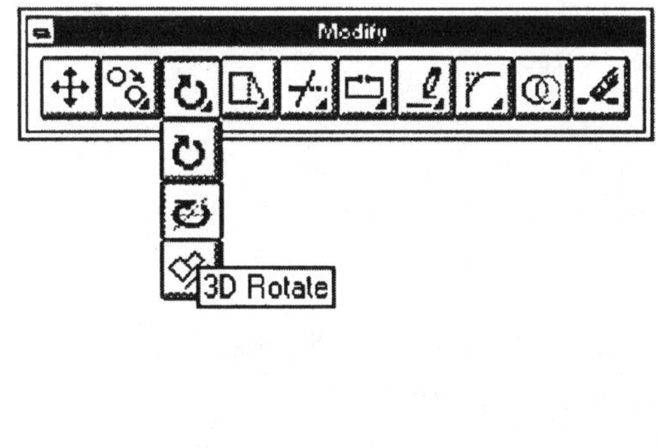

FIGURE 11–19
Using Rotat3D: to Rotate Shape 4 90° About the X Axis

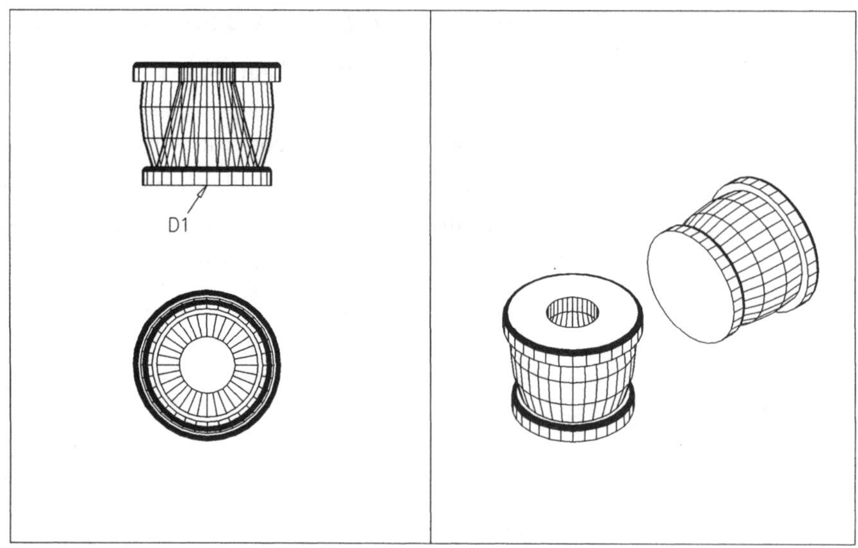

EXERCISE 11–1, PART 4
USING CHAMFER: AND FILLET: TO DRAW CHAMFERS AND FILLETS ON SOLID EDGES

Chamfer and Fillet the Top Four Edges of Two Separate Boxes

Step 1. On Your Own (Figure 11–1):

Use Box: to draw two boxes measuring 1.2 × .8 × .5 height each, in the approximate locations shown in Figure 11–1.

Note: The Chamfer command is also located in a pull-down menu under Construct in the menu bar.

Note: All edges to be chamfered must be picked in the same selection set, otherwise the resulting corners form an overlap.

Step 2. Chamfer the top four edges of the first box (Figure 11–20).

Prompt	Response
Command:	**Chamfer:**
(TRIM mode) Current chamfer Dist1 = 0.000, Dist2 = 0.000 Polyline/Distance/Angle/Trim/Method/ <Select first line>:	*Type:* **D** ↵
Enter first chamfer distance <0.000>:	*Type:* **.2** ↵
Enter second chamfer distance <0.200>:	↵
Command:	↵
(TRIM mode) Current chamfer Dist1 = 0.200, Dist2 = 0.200 Polyline/Distance/Angle/Trim/Method/ <Select first line>:	**D1 (Figure 11-20)**
Select base surface:	
Next/<OK>:	

If the top surface of the box turns dotted, showing it as the selected surface, continue. If one of the side surfaces is selected, type **N** ↵ until the top surface is selected.

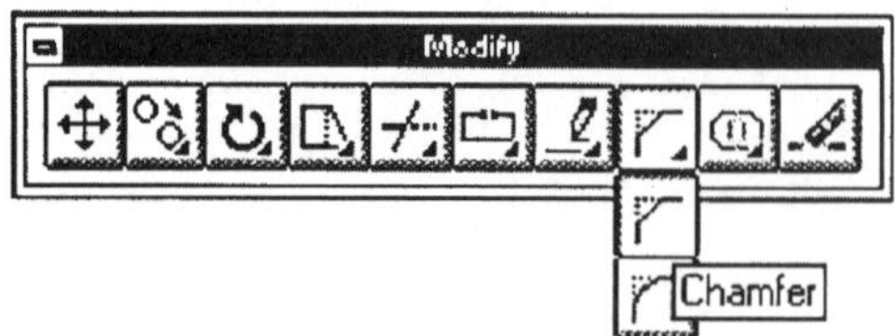

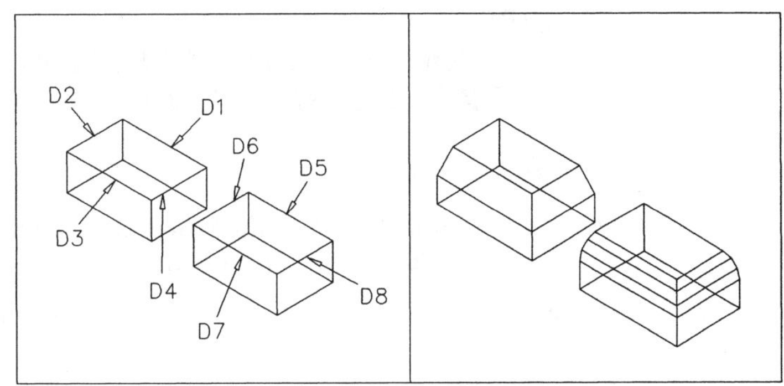

FIGURE 11–20
Chamfering and Filleting the Top Four Edges of Two Separate Boxes

Prompt	**Response**
Select base surface:	
Next/<OK>:	↵
Enter base surface distance <0.200>:	↵
Enter other surface distance <0.200>:	↵
Loop/<Select edge>:	**D1,D2,D3,D4**
Loop/<Select edge>:	↵

Step 3. Fillet the top four edges of the second box (Figure 11–20).

Prompt	**Response**
Command:	**Fillet:**
(TRIM mode) Current fillet radius = 0.050 Polyline/Radius/Trim/ <Select first object>:	**D5 (Figure 11–20)**
Enter radius <0.050>:	*Type:* **.2** ↵
Chain/Radius/<Select edge>:	**D5,D6,D7,D8**
Chain/Radius/<Select edge>:	↵

Chamfer and Fillet on the Top Edge of Two Separate Cylinders

Step 4. On Your Own (Figure 11–21):

1. Draw two cylinders using Cylinder: with a radius of .4 and a height of .8 in the approximate location shown in Figure 11–1.
2. Chamfer the top edge of the first cylinder (Figure 11–21) using chamfer distances of .06.
3. Fillet the top edge of the second cylinder (Figure 11–21) using a fillet radius of .06.

   The edges of the cylinders should appear as shown in Figure 11–21.

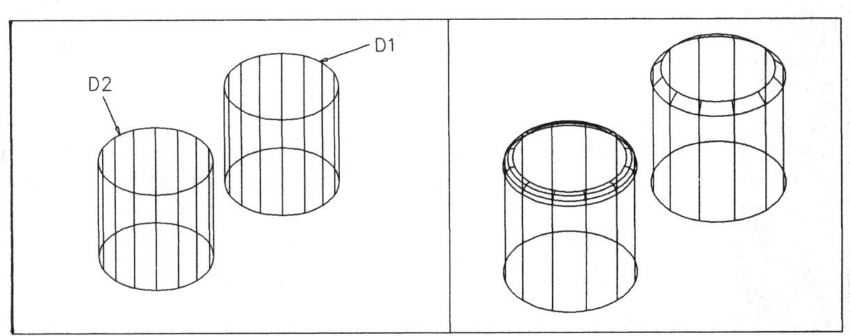

FIGURE 11–21
Chamfering and Filleting the Top Edge of Two Separate Cylinders

EXERCISE 11–1, PART 5
USING UNION: TO JOIN TWO SOLIDS; USING SUBTRAC: TO SUBTRACT SOLIDS FROM OTHER SOLIDS

Draw Solid Shape 1

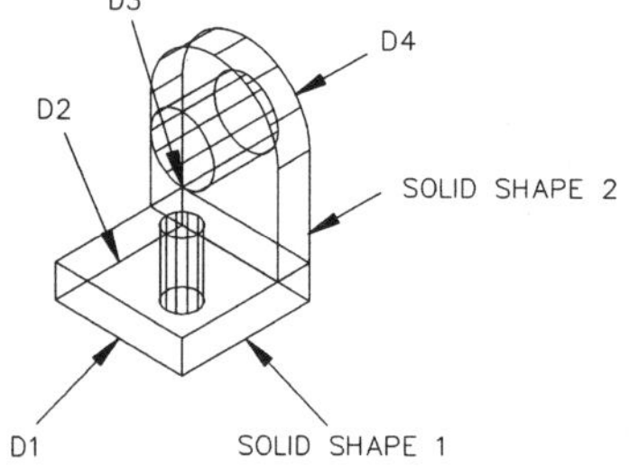

FIGURE 11–22
Drawing Solid Shapes 1 and 2

Step 1. Draw solid shape 1 (the base of the shape) and a cylinder that will be the hole in the base (Figure 11–22).

Prompt	Response
Command:	**Box:**
Center/<Corner of box> <0, 0, 0>:	*Type:* **4.5,.7** ↵
Cube/Length/<Other corner>:	*Type:* **@1,1** ↵
Height:	*Type:* **.25** ↵
Command:	**Cylinder:**
Elliptical/<center point><0, 0, 0>:	*Type:* **.X** ↵
of	*Type:* **MID** ↵
of	**D1**
(need YZ):	*Type:* **MID** ↵
of	**D2**
Diameter/<Radius>:	*Type:* **.125** ↵
Center of other end/<Height>:	*Type:* **.5** ↵ (Make the height of the hole tall enough so you can be sure it goes through the model.)

Draw Solid Shape 2

Step 2. On Your Own:

Set the UCSICON: command to ORigin so you will be able to see the UCS icon move when the origin is relocated.

Note: The Set UCS command is also located in a pull-down menu under View in the menu bar.

```
AutoCAD    AutoCAD
* * * *    * * * *
FILE       Redraw:
ASSIST     RedrwAl:
VIEW
DRAW 1     Zoom:
DRAW 2     Pan:
DRAW DIM
CONSTRCT   DDview:
MODIFY     Plan:
MOD DIM    Vpoint:
DATA       Dview:
OPTIONS
TOOLS      Tilemod:
           Mspace:
HELP       Pspace:

           Vports:
           TileVpt:
           Mview:

           DDucsp:
           DDucs:
           UCS:
SERVICE    SERVICE
LAST       LAST
```

Step 3. Rotate the UCS 90° about the X axis, and move the origin of the UCS to the upper left rear corner of the box (Figure 11–22).

Prompt	Response
Command:	**UCS**
Origin/ZAxis/3point/OBject/View/ X/Y/Z/Prev/Restore/Save/Del/?/ <World>:	*Type:* **X** ↵
Rotation angle about X axis <0>:	*Type:* **90** ↵
Command:	↵ (to repeat the last command)
Origin/ZAxis/3point/OBject/View/ X/Y/Z/Prev/Restore/Save/Del/?/ <World>:	*Type:* **O** ↵
Origin point <0, 0, 0>:	*Type:* **END** ↵
of	**D3**

Step 4. Draw solid shape 2 (the vertical solid) and a cylinder that will be the hole in the vertical solid (Figure 11–22).

Prompt	Response
Command:	**Pline:**
From point:	*Type:* **0,0** ↵

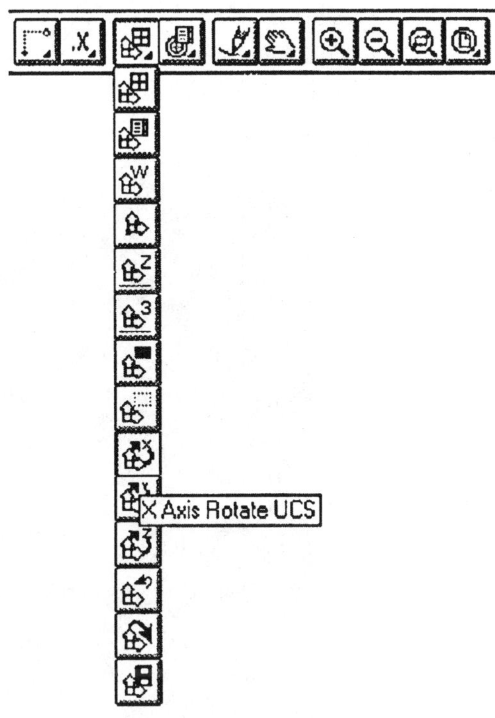

Arc/Close/Halfwidth/Length/Undo/ Width/<Endpoint of line>:	*Type:* **@1<0** ↵
Arc/Close/Halfwidth/Length/Undo/ Width/<Endpoint of line>:	*Type:* **@.75<90** ↵
Arc/Close/Halfwidth/Length/Undo/ Width/<Endpoint of line>:	*Type:* **A** ↵
<Endpoint of arc>:	*Type:* **@1<180** ↵
<Endpoint of arc>:	*Type:* **CL** ↵
Command:	**Extrude:**
Select objects:	**Pick the polyline just drawn.**
Select objects:	↵
Height of extrusion:	*Type:* **.25** ↵
Extrusion taper angle <0>:	↵
Command:	**Cylinder:**
Baseplane/Elliptical/<Center point> <0, 0, 0>:	*Type:* **CEN** ↵
of	**D4**
Diameter/<Radius>:	*Type:* **.25** ↵
Center of other end/<Height>:	*Type:* **.5** ↵

Make sure the base of the cylinder is located on the back surface of the upright piece. If the cylinder is located on the front surface of the upright piece, move the cylinder .25 in the negative Z direction.

Union:

Step 5. Join the base and the vertical shape to form one model.

Note: The Union command is also located in a pull-down menu under Construct in the menu bar.

Prompt	**Response**
Command:	**Union:**

Prompt	Response
Select objects:	**Pick the base (shape 1) and the vertical solid (shape 2).**
Select objects:	↵

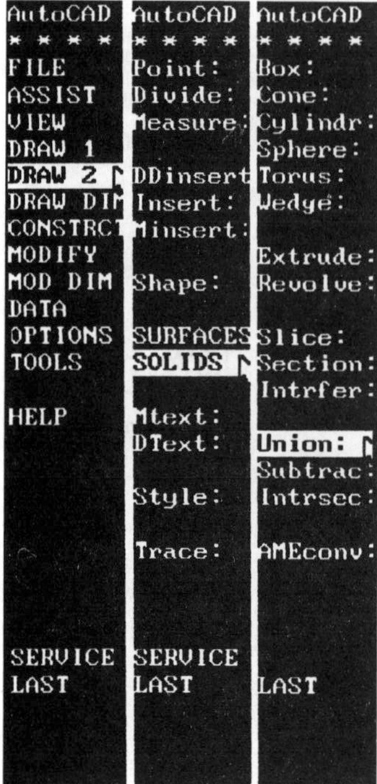

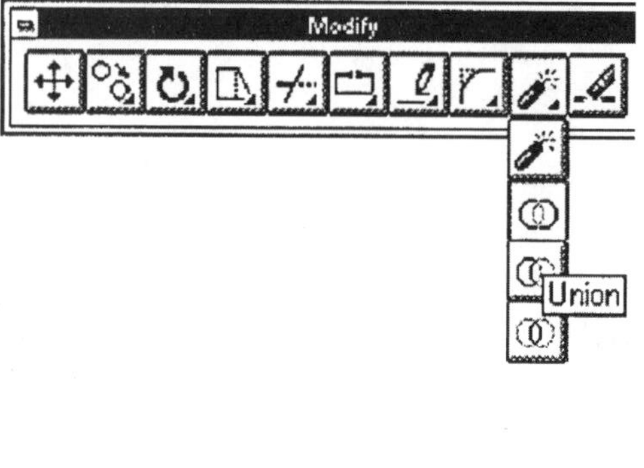

Subtract:

Step 6. Subtract the holes from the model.

Note: The Subtract command is also located in a pull-down menu under Construct in the menu bar.

Prompt	Response
Command:	**Subtract:**

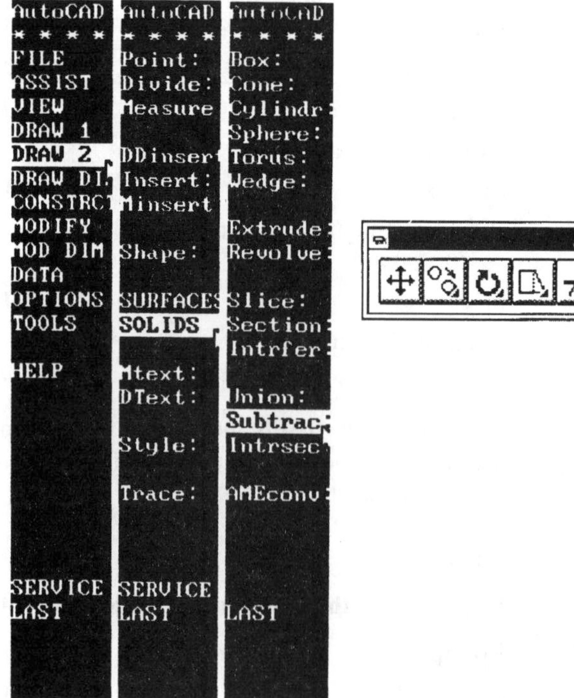

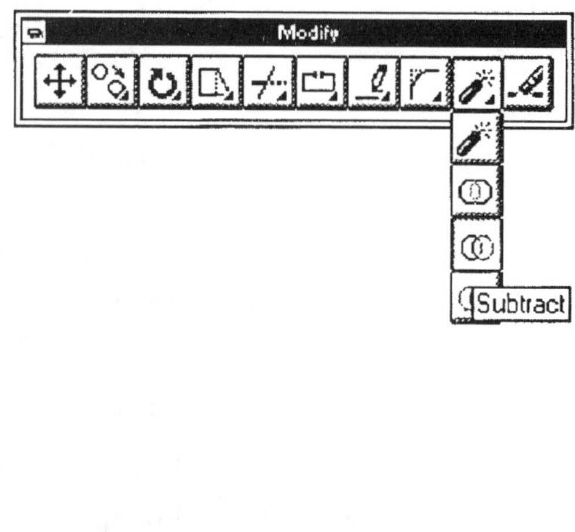

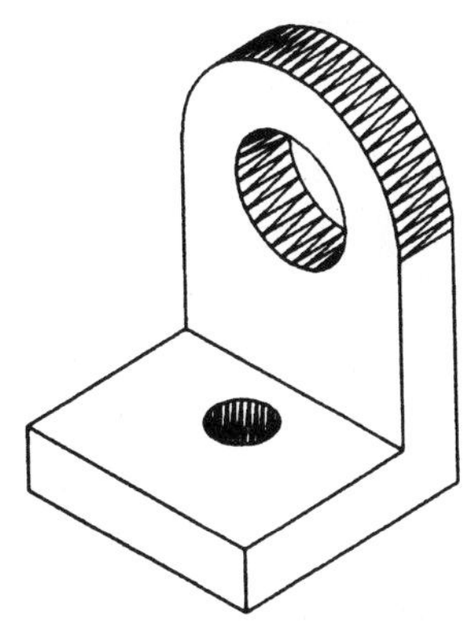

FIGURE 11–23
The Completed Solid Model

Select solids and regions to subtract from . . .	
Select objects:	**(Pick any point on the model.)**
Select objects:	↵
Select solids and regions to subtract . . .	
Select objects:	**(Pick the two cylinders.)**
Select objects:	↵

Hide:

Step 7. Perform a Hide: to be sure the model is correct (Figure 11–23).

Prompt	Response
Command:	**Hide:**

The model should appear as shown in Figure 11–23.

Step 8. On Your Own:

Return the UCS to the world origin.

EXERCISE 11–1, PART 6
USING INTERSECTION: TO FORM A SOLID MODEL FROM THE COMMON VOLUME OF TWO INTERSECTING SOLIDS

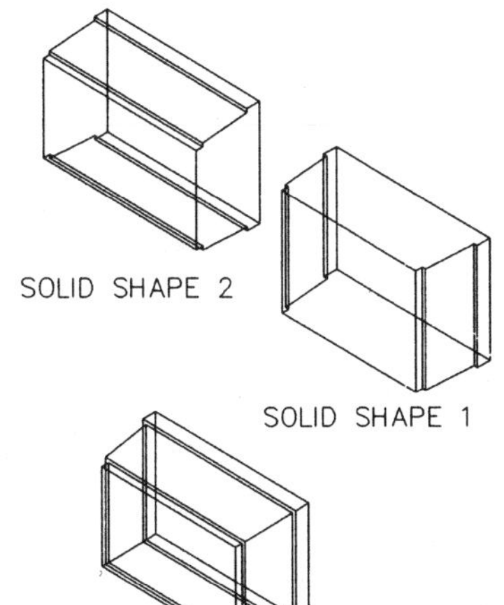

FIGURE 11–24
Using Intersection: to Form a Solid Model from the Common Volume of Two Intersecting Solids

Drawing the solid model in Exercise 11–1, Part 6, demonstrates some powerful tools that can be used to form complex models. In this exercise two separate solid shapes are drawn and moved so that they intersect. Intersection: is used to combine the shapes to form one solid model from the common volume of the two intersecting solids. Figure 11–24 shows the two separate solid shapes and the solid model that is formed from the common volume of the two solid shapes.

Copy and Rotate Two Boxes

Step 1. On Your Own (Figure 11–25):

With snap on, copy the box twice from the upper left corner of your drawing to the open space in front of the chamfered and filleted objects as shown in Figure 11–25. Use the plan view when you copy the box so you know where the new boxes are located. These boxes will be used to help draw the two separate solids.

Step 2. Use Rotat3D: to rotate the boxes 90° about the X axis (Figure 11–26).

Prompt	Response
Command:	**Rotat3D:**
Select objects:	**(Pick the two boxes.)**
Axis by Entity/Last/View/XAxis/YAxis/ ZAxis/<2points>:	*Type:* **X** ↵
Point on X axis <0, 0, 0>:	*Type:* **END** ↵
of	**D1**
<Rotation angle>/Reference:	*Type:* **90** ↵

Solid Shape 1

Shape 1 is drawn using the box on the right, as the following describes.

Step 3. Use UCS: to relocate the UCS to the top of the box on the right (Figure 11–27). (Be sure the world UCS is active before you relocate the UCS.)

Prompt	Response
Command:	**UCS:**

FIGURE 11–25
Copying the Box Twice from the Upper Left Corner of the Drawing

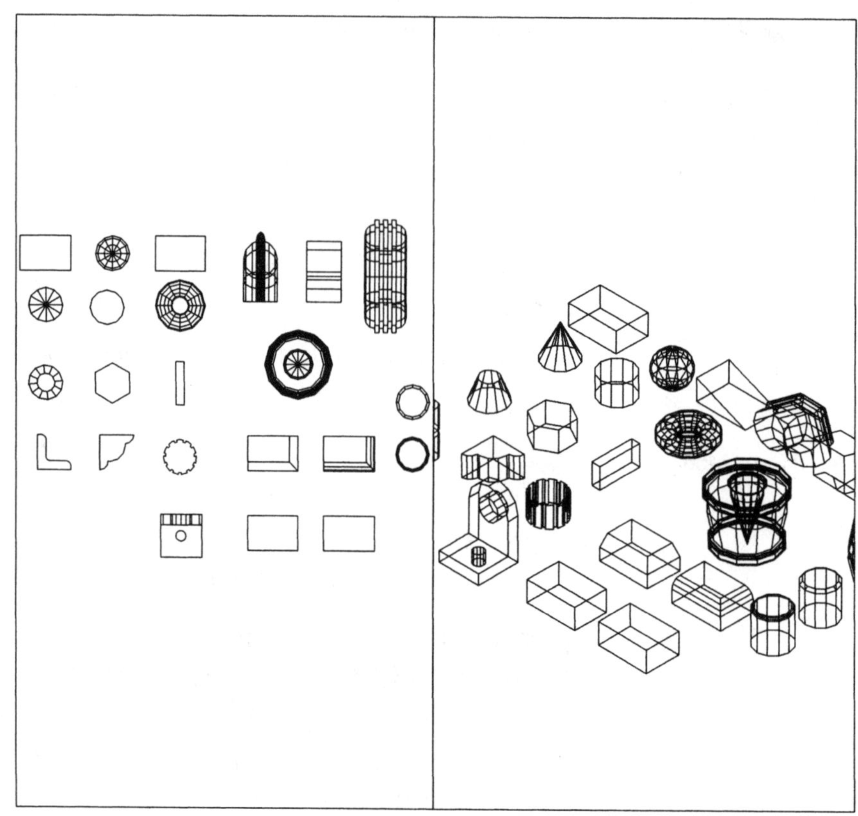

FIGURE 11–26
Using Rotat3D: to Rotate the Boxes 90° about the X Axis

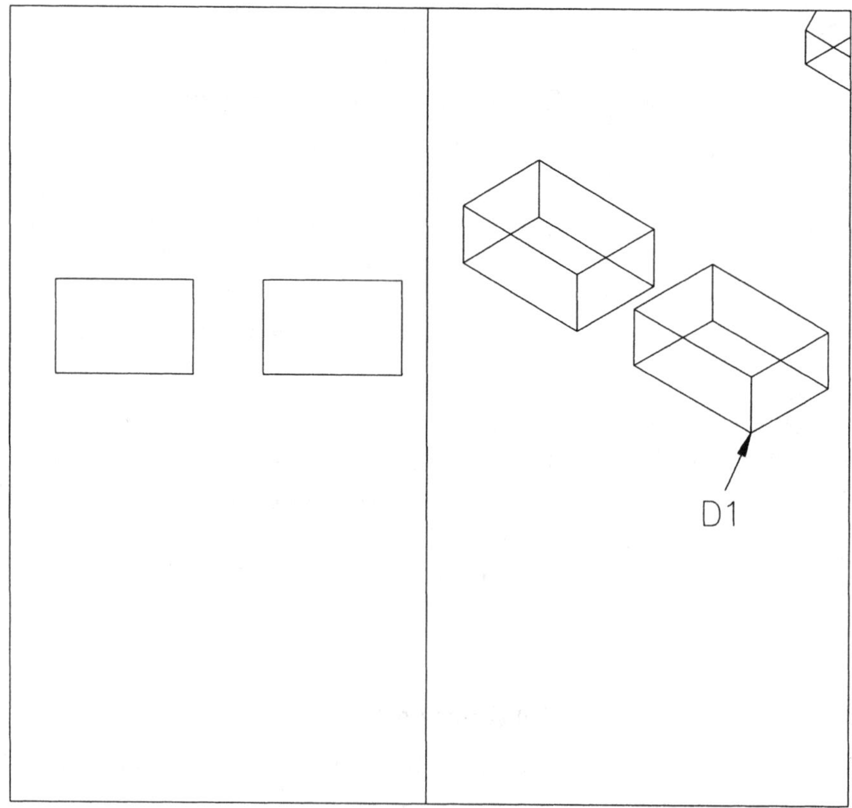

FIGURE 11–27
Using UCS: to Relocate the UCS to the Top of the Box on the Right

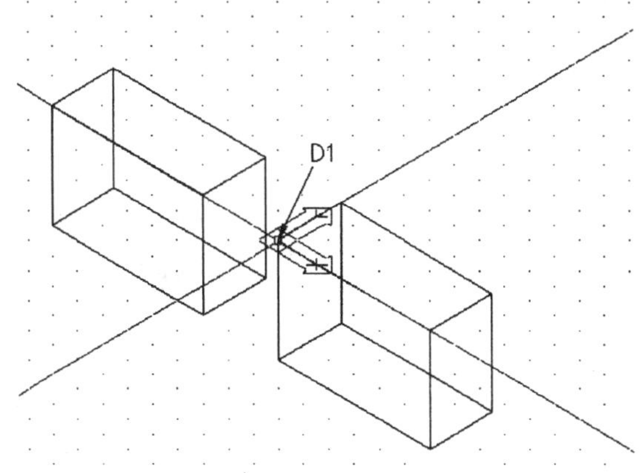

Note: The Plan View command is also located in the 3D Viewpoint Presets pull-down menu under View in the menu bar.

Prompt	Response
Origin/ZAxis/3point/OBject/View/X/Y/Z/ Prev/Restore/Save/Del/?/<World>	*Type:* **O** ↵
Origin point <0, 0, 0>:	*Type:* **END** ↵
of	**D1**

Step 4. Use Plan: to change the view in the right viewport to the plan view of the new UCS.

Prompt	Response
Command:	**Plan:** (Windows users: *Type:* **PLAN** ↵)
<Current UCS>/Ucs/World:	↵

Step 5. On Your Own (Figure 11–28):

1. Set snap to .025
2. Set layer R current.
3. With snap on, use the Pline: command to draw the right side *only* of the outline shown in Figure 11–28 on the top surface of the box on the right. Use Pedit: to make it a single polyline if necessary.
4. Complete the outline as follows:

Step 6. Mirror the polyline you just drew (Figure 11–28).

Prompt	Response
Command:	**Mirror:**
Select objects:	**(Pick the polyline you just drew.)**
Select objects:	↵
First point of mirror line:	**Osnap-MIDpoint D1**

FIGURE 11–28
Drawing the Outline Shown on the Top Surface of the Box on the Right

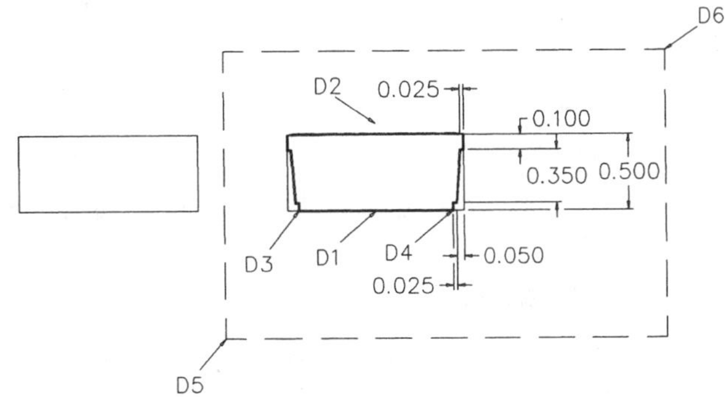

Prompt	Response
Second point:	**(With ortho on, pick a point above the first point.) D2**
Delete old objects? <N>	↵

Step 7. Use Pline: to draw the bottom line of the outline (Figure 11–28).

Prompt	Response
Command:	*Type:* **PL** ↵
From point:	**Osnap-ENDpoint D3**
Arc/Close/Halfwidth/Length/Undo/ Width/<Endpoint of line>:	**Osnap-ENDpoint D4**
Arc/Close/Halfwidth/Length/Undo/ Width/<Endpoint of line>:	↵

Step 8. On Your Own:

Use Pline: to draw the top line of the outline.

Step 9. Use Pedit: to combine all the polylines forming the outline, into a single polyline (Figure 11–28).

Prompt	Response
Command:	**Pedit:**
Select polyline:	**(Pick one of the polylines you just drew.)** ↵
Close/Join/Width/Edit vertex/Fit/Spline/ Decurve/Ltype gen/Undo/eXit <X>:	*Type:* **J** ↵
First corner:	**D5**
Other corner:	**D6**
Select objects:	↵
Open/Join/Width/Edit vertex/Fit/Spline/ Decurve/Ltype gen/Undo/eXit <X>:	↵ (to exit from the Pedit: command)

Step 10. On Your Own:

1. Erase the solid box; it was used for construction only.
2. Return to the world UCS.
3. Use the Vpoint: command to set the viewpoint for the right viewport to 1,−1,1.

Step 11. Use Extrude: to complete shape 1 by extruding the polyline, −.8 height, 0° extrusion taper angle (Figure 11–29).

Prompt	Response
Command:	**Extrude:**
Select objects:	**D1**
Select objects:	↵
Height of extrusion:	*Type:* **−.8** ↵
Extrusion taper angle <0>:	↵

The display of solid shape 1 should appear as shown in Figure 11–30.

Solid Shape 2

The second solid is drawn using the other box to help with construction, as the following describes.

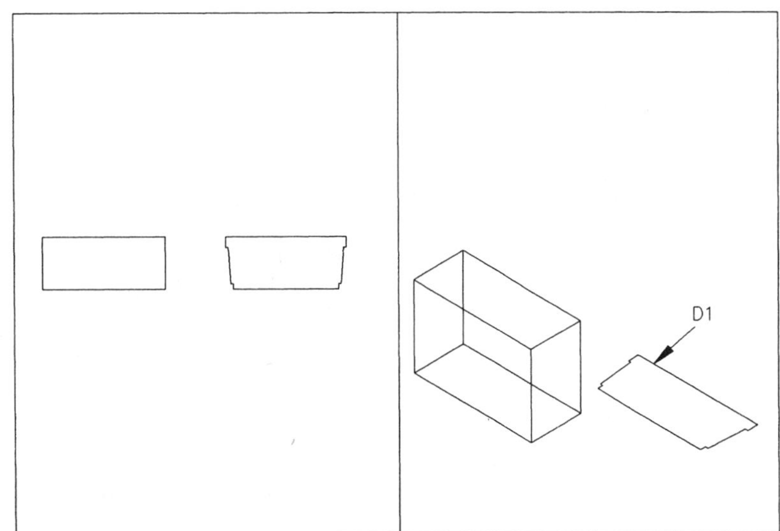

FIGURE 11–29
Using Extrude: to Extrude the Polyline

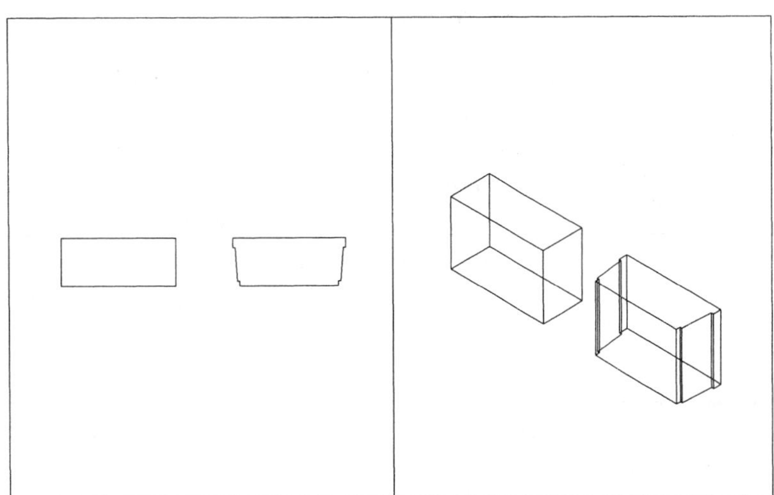

FIGURE 11–30
Solid Shape 1

Step 12. On Your Own:

1. Set layer G current.
2. Freeze layer R, to more easily see what you are doing on the left box.

Step 13. Use UCS to relocate the UCS to the right side of the box (Figure 11–31).

Prompt	Response
Command:	*Type:* **UCS** ↵
Origin/ZAxis/3point/OBject/View/ X/Y/Z/Prev/Restore/Save/Del/?/ <World>:	*Type:* **3** ↵
Origin point <0, 0, 0>:	*Type:* **END** ↵
of	**D1**
Point on positive portion of the X axis < >:	*Type:* **END** ↵
of	**D2**
Point on positive Y portion of the UCS XY plane: < >:	*Type:* **END** ↵
of	**D3**

FIGURE 11–31
Using UCS: to Relocate the UCS to the Right Side of the Box

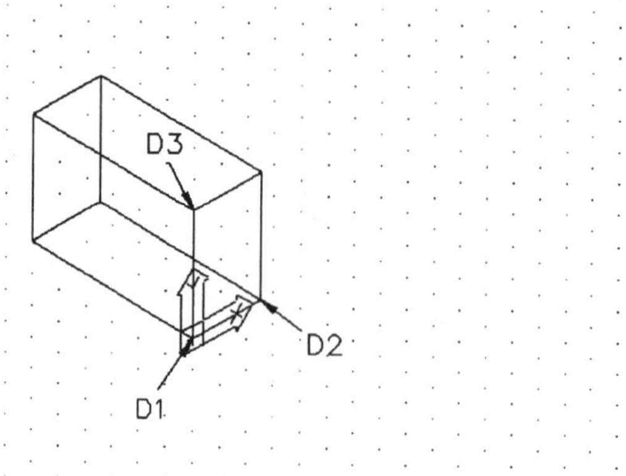

Step 14. Use Plan: to change the view to the plan view of the new UCS.

Prompt	**Response**
Command:	**Plan:**
<Current UCS>/Ucs/World:	↵

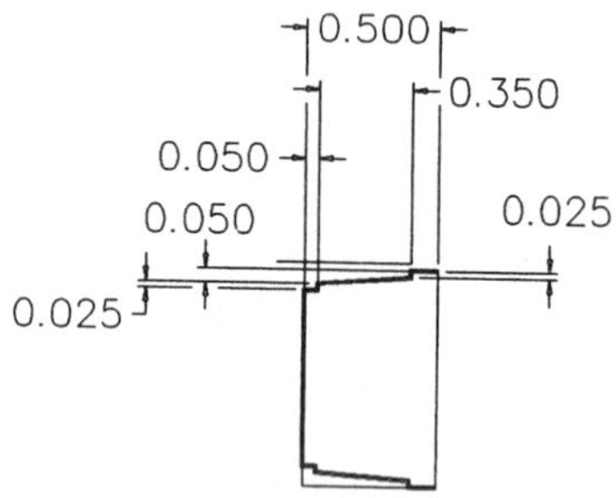

FIGURE 11–32
Drawing the Outline Shown on the Side Surface of the Box

Step 15. On Your Own (Figures 11–32 and 11–33):

1. If another solid model in the exercise interferes with the plan view of solid shape 2, move the interfering solid model temporarily.
2. With snap on, use the Pline: command to draw the top side *only* of the outline shown in Figure 11–32 on the side surface of the box.
3. Mirror the top part of the outline using the midpoint of the vertical edge of the box as the first point on the mirror line. Pick any other point to the right of the first point with ortho on.
4. Complete drawing the outline (the front and rear lines) using Pline: and Osnap-Endpoint.
5. Use the Pedit: command to join all the polylines drawn, into a single polyline.
6. Erase the box.
7. Use the Extrude: command to extrude the polyline −1.2 (in the negative Z direction).
8. Return to the world UCS.
9. Use the Vpoint: command to set the viewpoint for the right viewport to 1,−1,1.

FIGURE 11–33
Solid Shapes 1 and 2

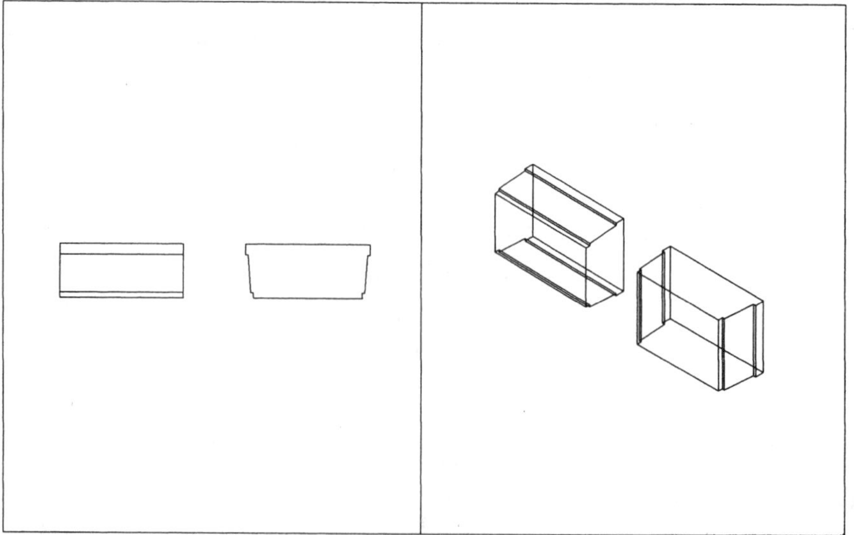

10. Thaw layer R.
11. The display should appear as shown in Figure 11–33.

Move One Solid to Intersect With the Other Solid

Step 16. Use the Move: command to move the solid on the left to intersect with the other solid (Figure 11–34).

FIGURE 11–34
Moving One Solid to Intersect with the Other Solid

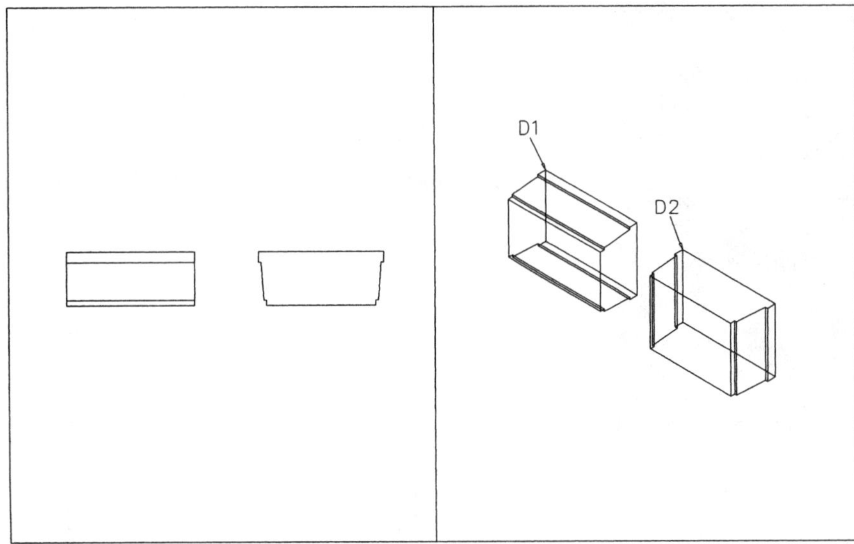

Prompt	**Response**
Command:	**Move:**
Select objects:	**(Pick the shape on the left.)**
Select objects:	↵
Base point or displacement:	*Type:* **END** ↵
of	**D1**
Second point of displacement:	*Type:* **END** ↵
of	**D2**

Step 17. On Your Own (Figure 11–35):

Zoom in on the two intersecting solids so your display appears similar to Figure 11–35.

FIGURE 11–35
Zooming In on the Two Intersecting Solids

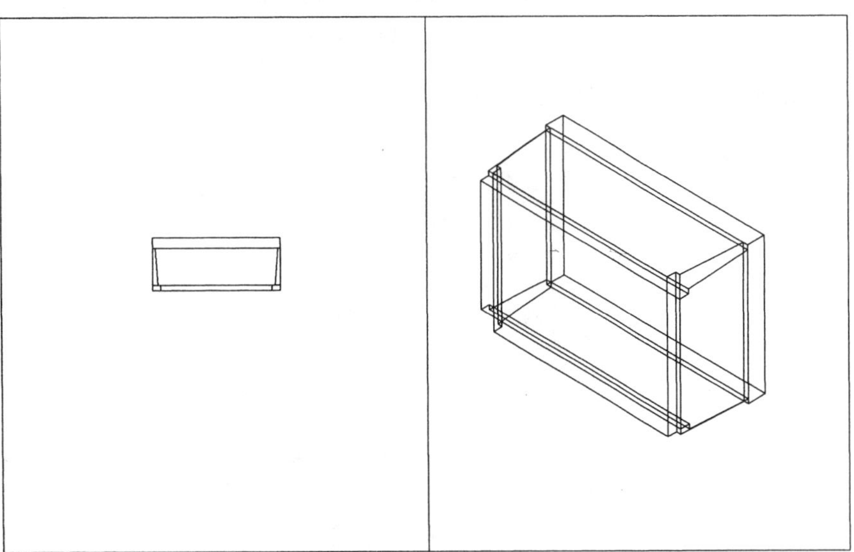

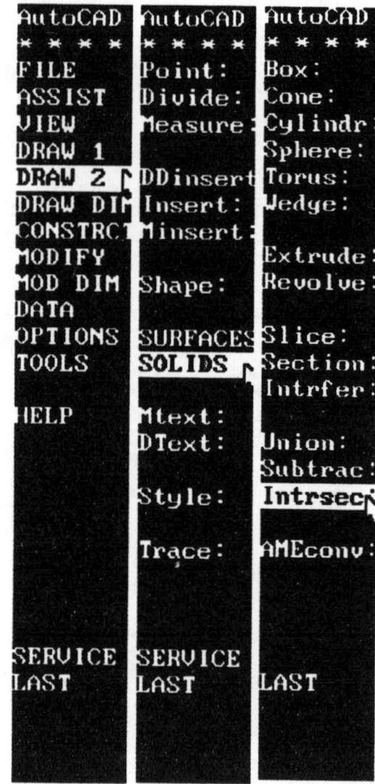

Note: The Intersection command is also located in a pull-down menu under Construct in the menu bar.

Intersection:

Step 18. Use Intrsec: to form a solid model from the common volume of the two intersecting solids (Figure 11–36).

Prompt	Response
Command:	**Intrsec:**
Select objects:	**(Pick both shapes.)**
2 solids intersected	

The display should appear as shown in Figure 11–36.

Complete Drawing the Combined Solid

Step 19. On Your Own (Figures 11–37, 11–38, and 11–39):

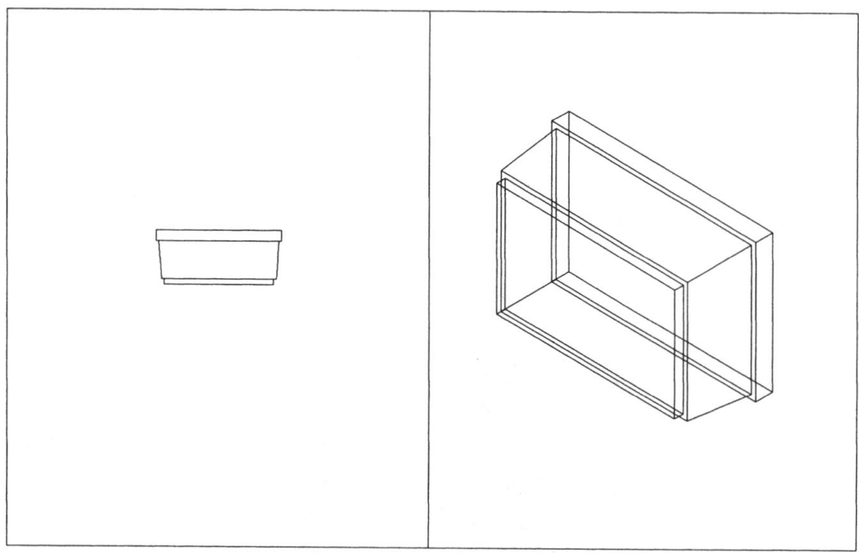

FIGURE 11–36
Using Intersection: to Form a Solid Model from the Common Volume of the Two Intersecting Solids

1. Select a UCS that is common with the front surface of the solid, Figure 11–37, so that you can easily draw the outline shown in Figure 11–38.
2. Use Arc: St,E,Rad, to draw the curved outline for the front face. Use the dimensions shown in Figure 11–38.

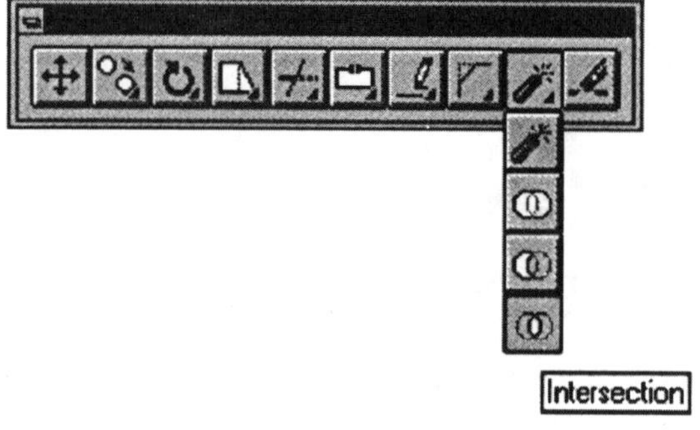

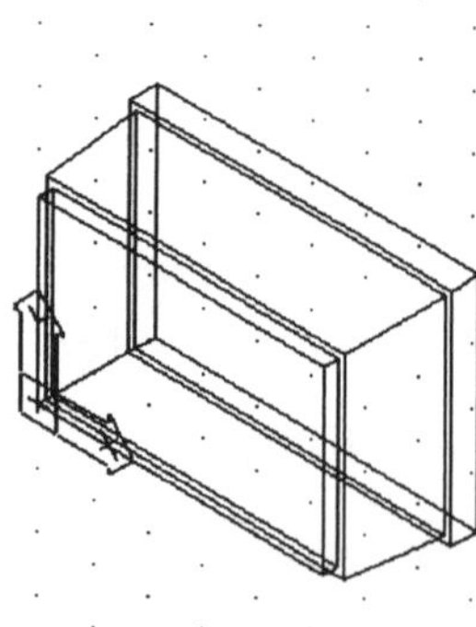

FIGURE 11–37
Selecting a UCS That Is Common with the Front Surface of the Solid

FIGURE 11–38
Drawing the Curved Outline on the Front Face

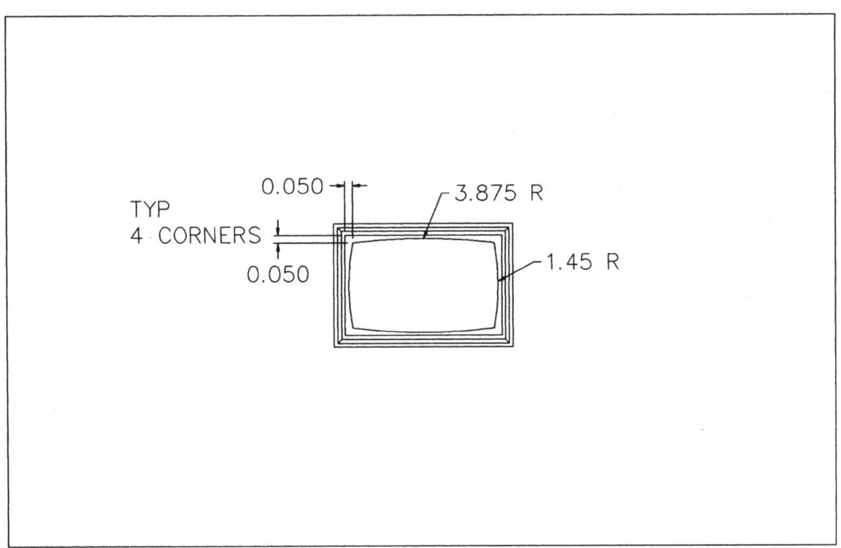

3. Join all four arcs to form a single polyline using Pedit:.
4. Use Extrude: to extrude the single polyline −.05 (in the negative Z direction).
5. Use Subtrac: to subtract the extruded polyline from the combined solid, Figure 11–39.

Step 20. Preform a Hide: to be sure the solid model is correct.

Prompt	**Response**
Command:	**Hide:**

The display should appear as shown in Figure 11–40.

Complete Exercise 11–1

Step 21. On Your Own:

1. Use the Vports: command to return to a single viewport of the 3-D viewport.
2. Set the UCS: to View, and add your name to the lower right corner of the drawing.
3. Plot the 3-D viewport on a standard size sheet of paper. Be sure to pick the Hide Lines box in the Plot Configuration dialog box so the final plot appears as shown in Figure 11–1.
4. Save the drawing in two places.

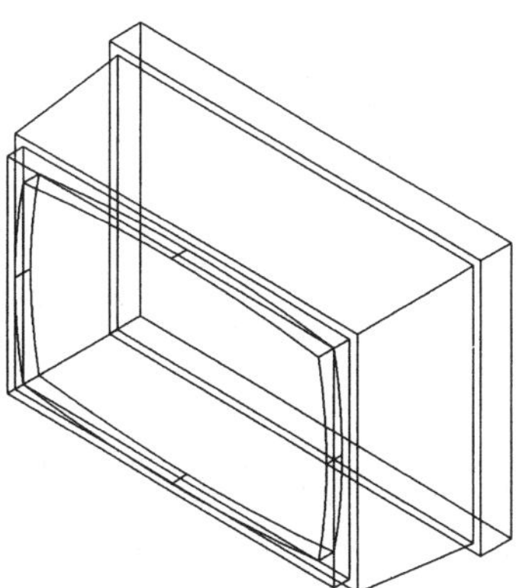

FIGURE 11–39
Using Subtrac: to Subtract the Extruded Polyline from the Combined Solid

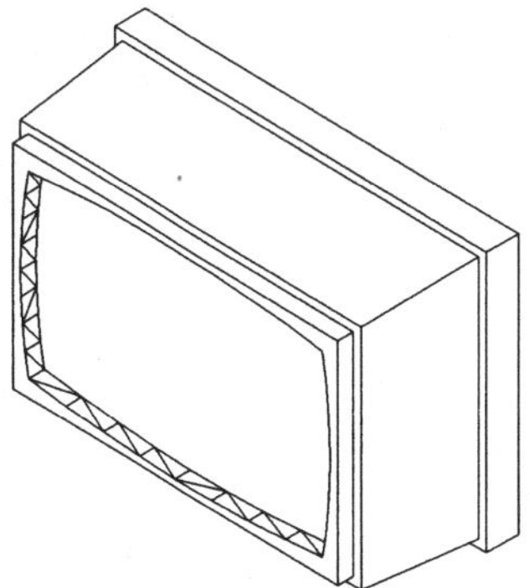

FIGURE 11–40
Performing a Hide: on the Solid Model

EXERCISES

11–1. Complete Exercise 11–1, parts 1 through 6, using the steps described in this chapter.

11–2. Draw Solid Model I.

1. Draw a solid model of the object shown in Figure 11–41. Use the dimensions shown in that figure. Do not include any dimensions on your drawing.
2. Study Figure 11–42 for ideas on how to construct the solid model. Draw cylinders for any holes, and subtract them from the solid using Subtrac:. Combine all individual pieces such as the triangular pieces, the base, and the back using Union:.
3. Create four viewports with viewpoints similar to those shown in Figure 11–41.
4. Plot the final drawing in paper space. Use Mview: Hideplot on any viewport that requires it. Your final drawing should be similar to Figure 11–41, without the dimensions.

11–3. Draw Solid Model II

1. Draw a solid model of the object shown in Figure 11–43. Use the dimensions shown in that figure. Do not include any dimensions on your drawing.
2. Create four viewports with viewpoints similar to those shown in Figure 11–41.
3. Plot the final drawing in paper space. Use Mview: Hideplot on any viewport that requires it. Your final drawing should be similar to Figure 11–43, without dimensions and hidden lines.

11–4. Draw a Solid Model of a Bracket

1. Draw a solid model of the bracket shown in Figure 11–44. Use the dimensions shown in that figure. Do not include any dimensions on your drawing.
2. Create four viewports with viewpoints similar to those shown in Figure 11–44.
3. Plot the final drawing in paper space. Use Mview: Hideplot on any viewport that requires it. Your final drawing should be similar to Figure 11–44, without dimensions.

11–5. Draw a Solid Model of a Spoked Hub

1. Draw a solid model of the spoked hub shown in Figure 11–45. Use the dimensions shown in that figure. Do not include any dimensions on your drawing.
2. Your final drawing should look similar to Figure 11–45, without dimensions.

11–6. Draw a Solid Model of a Gear

1. Draw a solid model of the gear shown in Figure 11–46. Use the dimensions shown in Figure 11–47. Do not include any dimensions on your drawing.

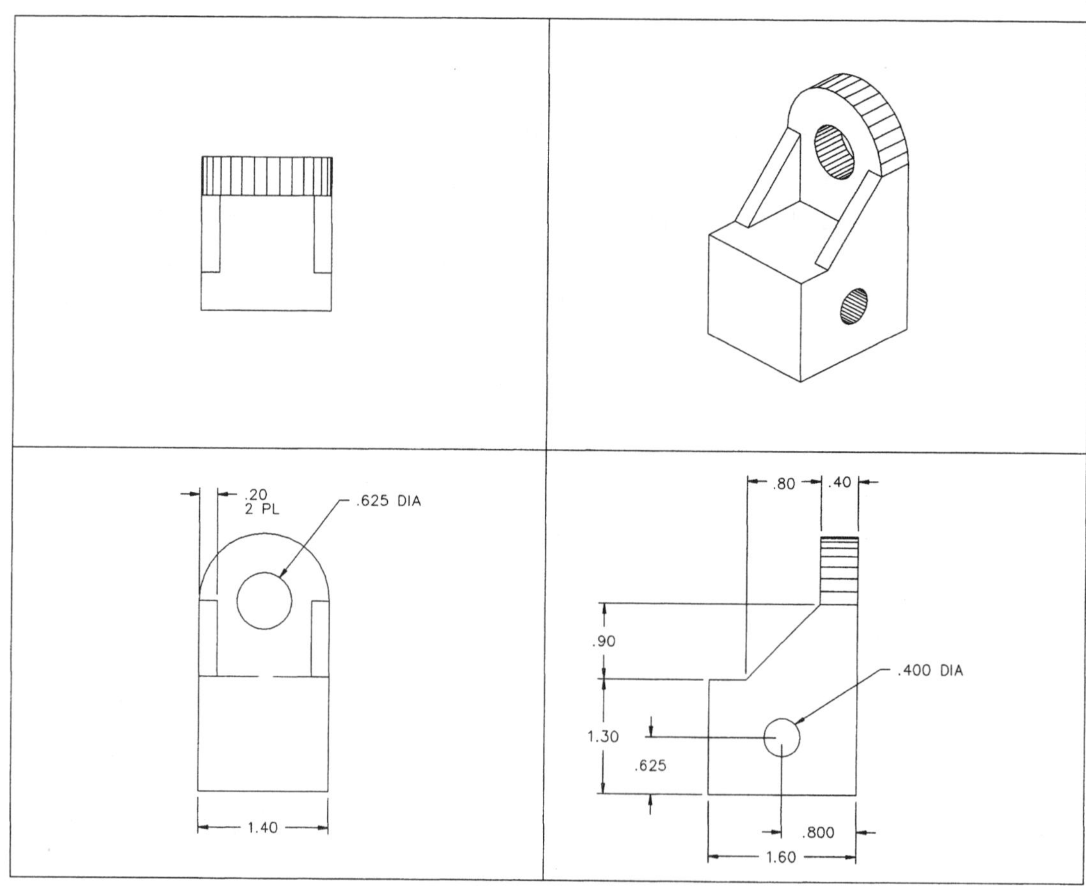

FIGURE 11–41
Exercise 11–2: Drawing Solid Model I

FIGURE 11–42
Exercise 11–2: Solid Model I
Before Using the Hide: Command

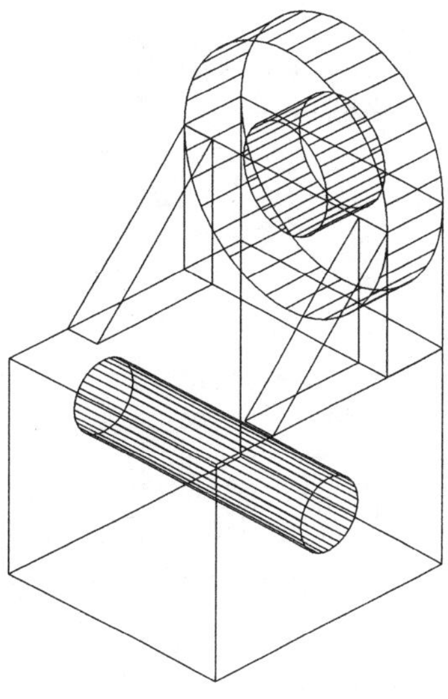

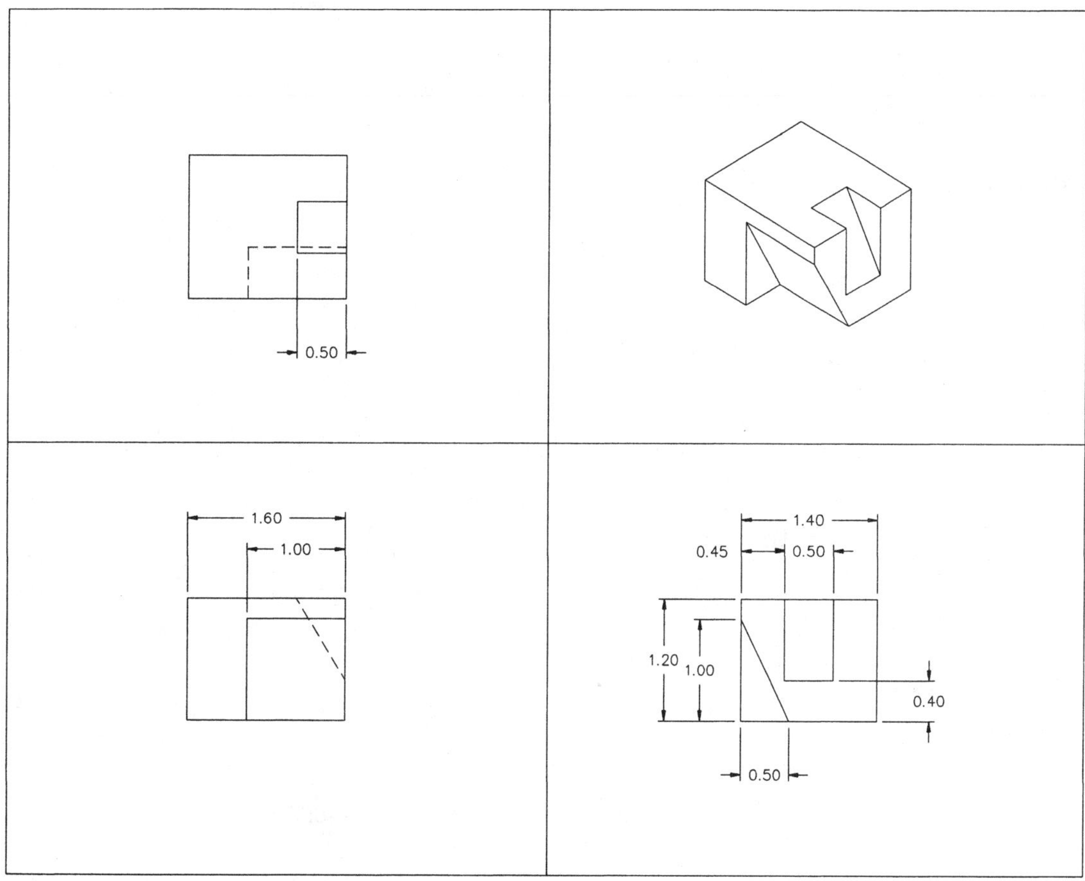

FIGURE 11–43
Exercise 11–3

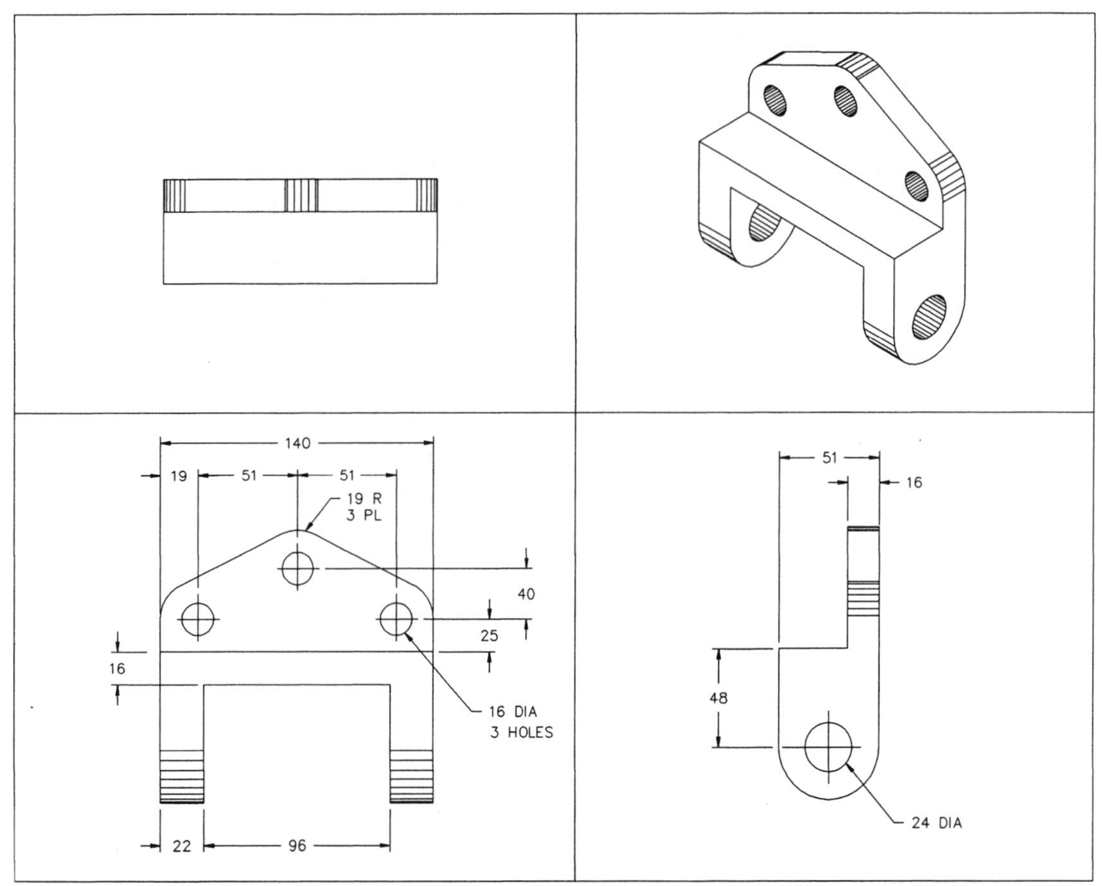

FIGURE 11–44
Exercise 11–4

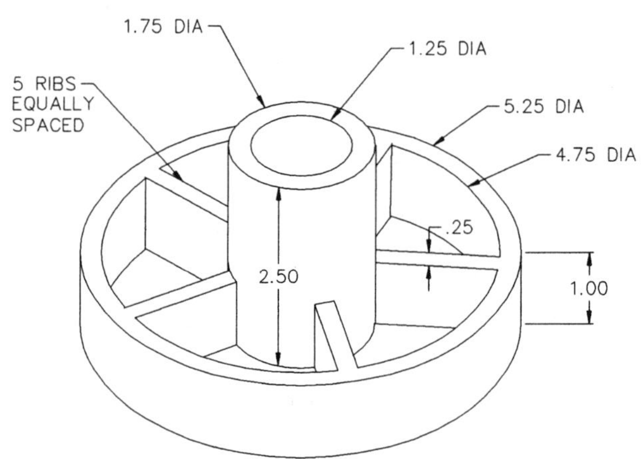

FIGURE 11–45
Exercise 11–5

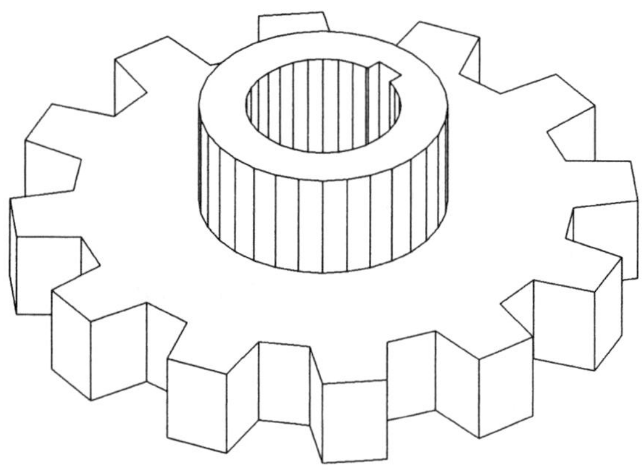

FIGURE 11–46
Exercise 11–6: Drawing a Solid Model of a Gear

FIGURE 11-47
Exercise 11-6: Gear Dimensions

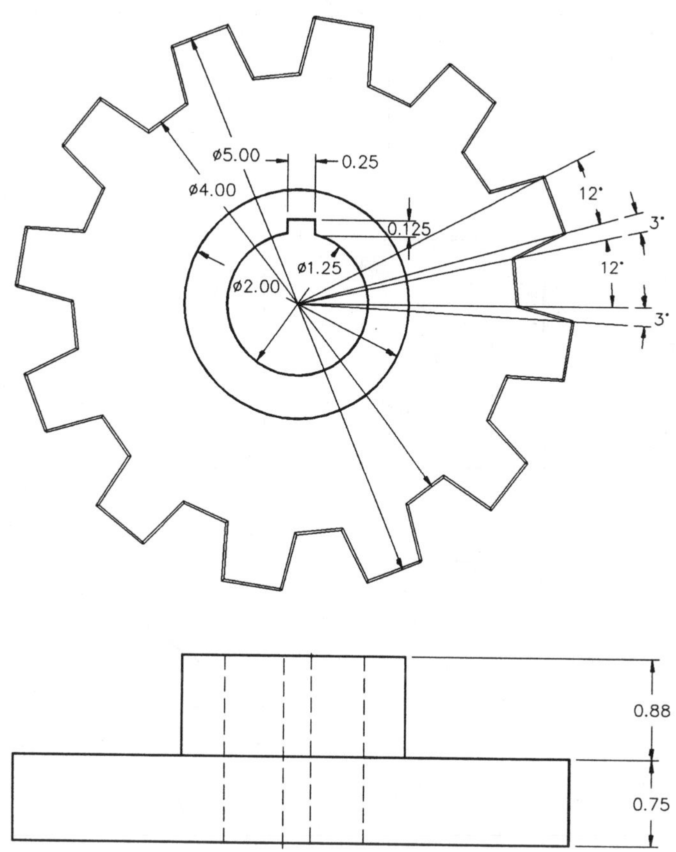

2. Use Union: to combine the shoulder and the gear body.
3. Your final drawing should look similar to Figure 11-46.

11-7. Draw Solid Models of Eight Objects

1. Draw solid models of the eight objects shown in Figure 11-48. Use the dimensions shown in the top and front views of A through E.
2. Arrange the objects so that they are well spaced on the page and take up most of a 9″ × 7″ area on an 11″ × 8.5″ sheet.
3. Your final drawing should show eight solid objects in a viewpoint similar to the one in Exercise 11-1.

11-8. Draw a Solid Model of a Wrench

1. Draw a solid model of the wrench shown in Figure 11-49. Use the dimensions shown in Figure 11-50. Do not include any dimensions on your drawing.
2. Use Union: to combine all the shapes into a single model.
3. Your final drawing should look similar to Figure 11-49.

11-9. Draw a Solid Model of a Lamp Table and Lamp

1. Draw a solid model of the lamp table and lamp shown in Figure 11-51. Scale the top and front views using a scale of 1″=1′ to obtain the correct measurements for the model.
2. Use Revolve: for the table pedestal and the lamp. Use Pline: and Extrude: for one table leg and duplicate it with Polar Array:. The table top can be an extruded j circle or a solid cylinder.

11-10. Draw a Solid Model of a Wheel Assembly

1. Draw a solid model of the wheel assembly shown in Figure 11-52. Use the dimensions shown in that figure. Do not include any dimensions on your drawing.
2. Use the Revolve: command to draw these models.
3. The completed drawing should look similar to Figure 11-52.

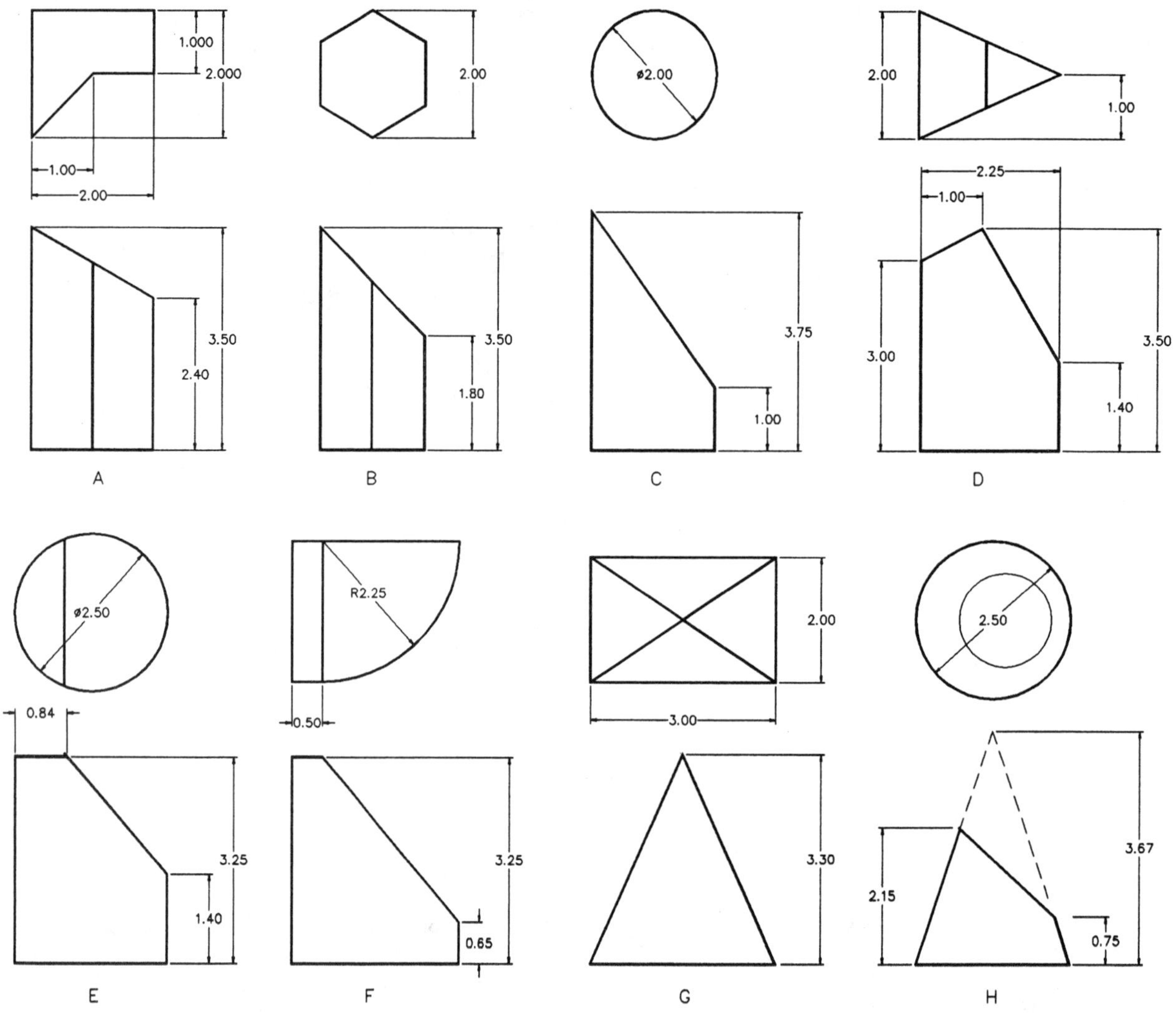

FIGURE 11–48
Exercise 11–7

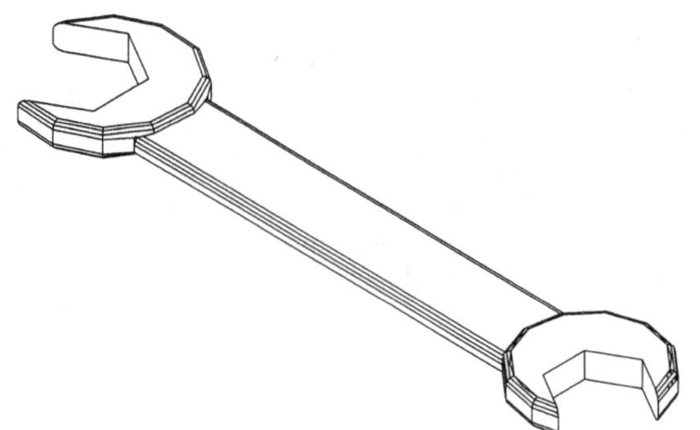

FIGURE 11–49
Exercise 11–8: Drawing a Solid Model of a Wrench

FIGURE 11–50
Exercise 11–8: Wrench Dimensions

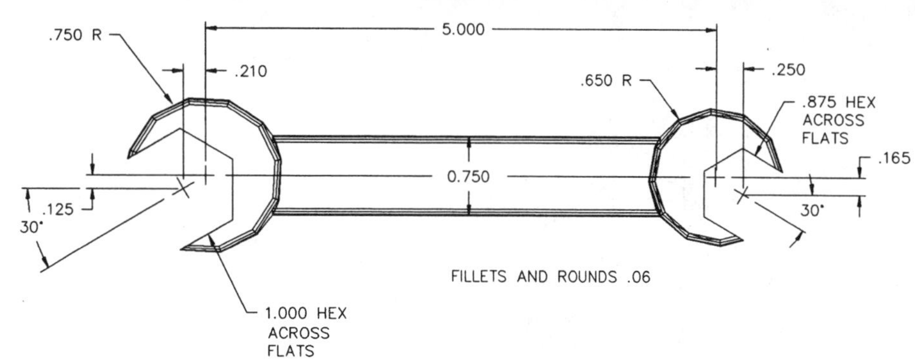

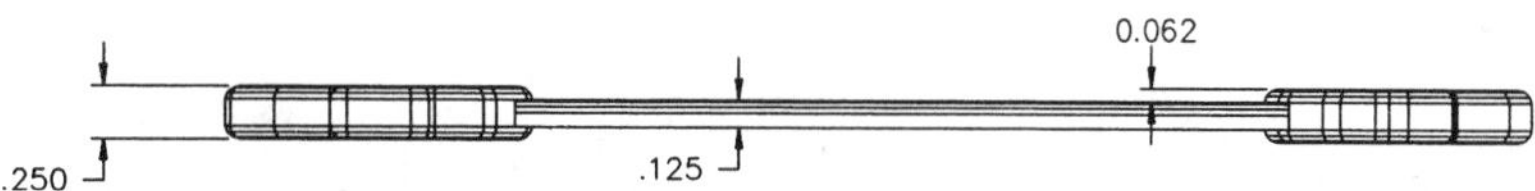

FIGURE 11–51
Exercise 11–9

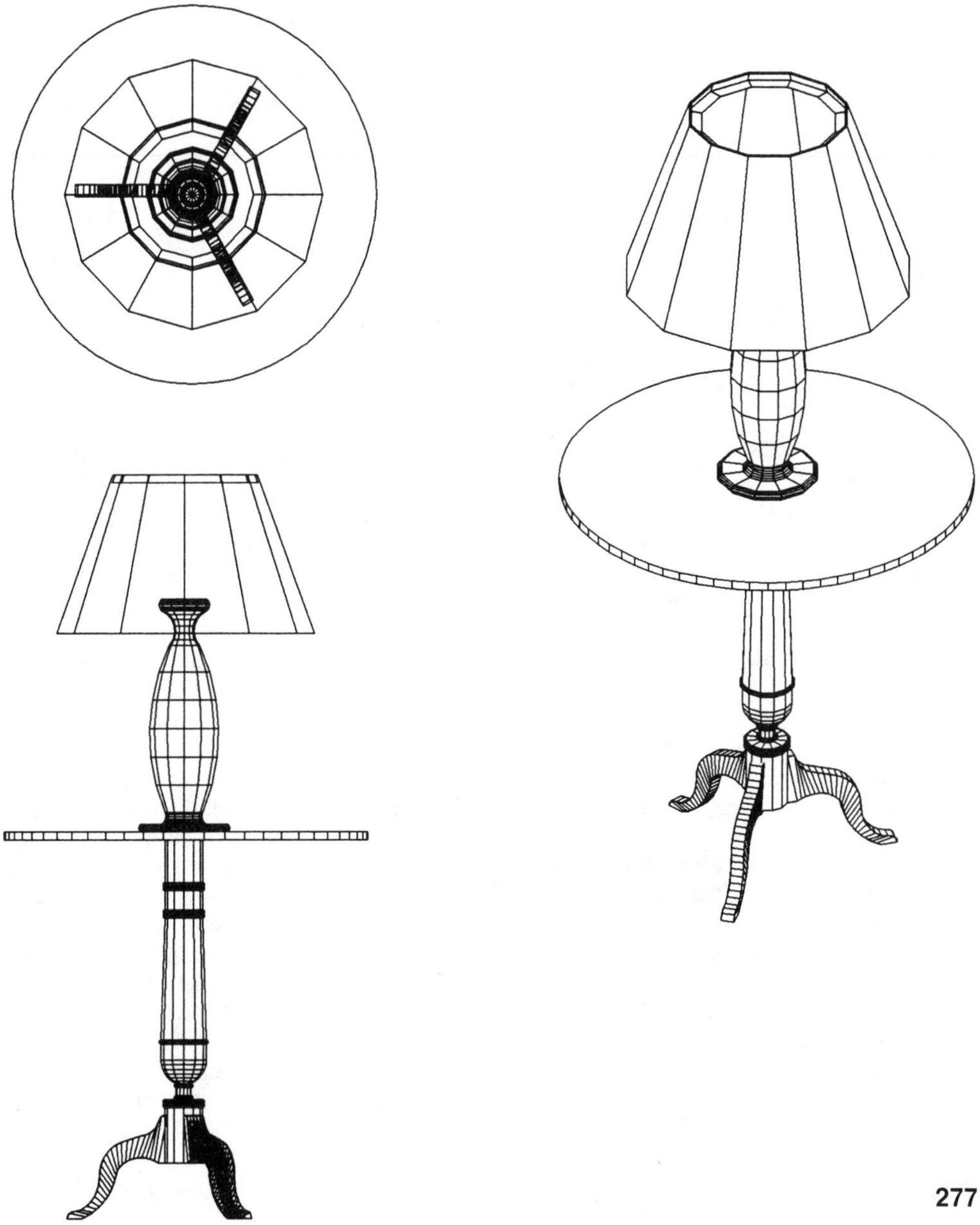

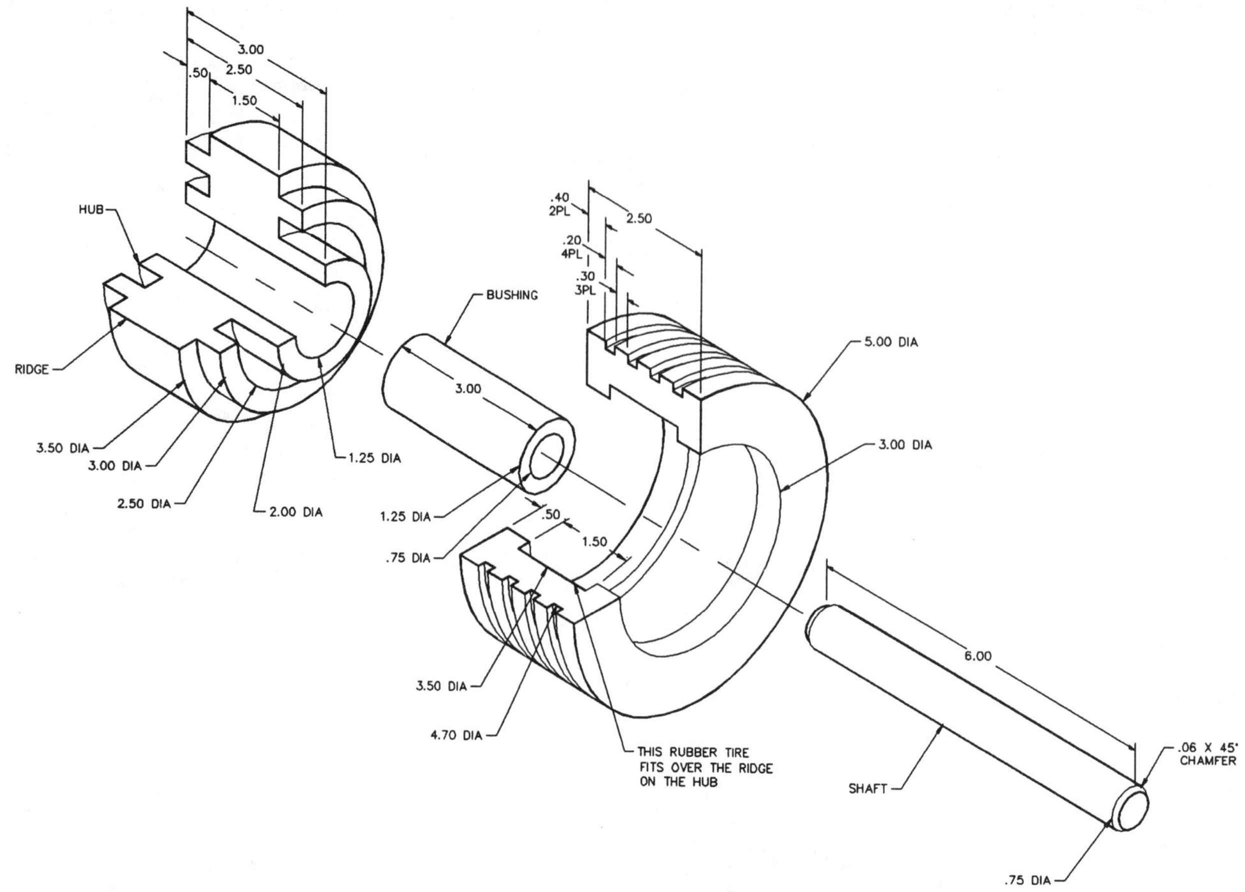

FIGURE 11–52
Exercise 11–10

REVIEW QUESTIONS

1. Which of the following is *not* a SOLIDS command used to draw solid primitives?
   a. Box:
   b. Cylinder:
   c. Rectan:
   d. Wedge:
   e. Sphere:
2. Which of the following is used to make rounded corners on a solid box?
   a. Chamfer:
   b. Extrude:
   c. Intersection:
   d. Round:
   e. Fillet:
3. Which is the last dimension called for when the Box: command is activated?
   a. Height
   b. Width
   c. Length
   d. First corner of box
   e. Other corner
4. What is the first dimension called for when the Sphere: command is activated?
   a. Segments in Y direction
   b. Segments in X direction
   c. Radius
   d. Center of sphere
   e. Diameter
5. Which of the following cannot be extruded?
   a. Polylines
   b. Circles
   c. Regions
   d. Polygons
   e. Solids
6. Which of the following commands is used to join several polylines into a single entity?
   a. Pedit:
   b. Offset:
   c. Union:
   d. Intersection:
   e. Extrude:
7. Which of the following is used to make a solid by revolving a polyline about an axis?
   a. Revolve:
   b. Extrude:
   c. Intersection:
   d. Round:
   e. Fillet:
8. Which of the following adjusts the smoothness of objects rendered with the Hide: command?
   a. SURFTAB1
   b. MESH
   c. SEGS
   d. WIRE
   e. FACETRES

9. Which of the following allows you to rotate an object around X, Y, or Z axes?
   a. Rotate:
   b. Rotat3D:
   c. Extrude:
   d. Solrot:
   e. Offset:
10. Which of the following sets the number of lines on rounded surfaces of solids?
    a. FACETRES
    b. ISOLINES
    c. Union:
    d. Fillet:
    e. Interfere:
11. List the six SOLIDS commands used to make solid primitives.

    ________ ________ ________

    ________ ________ ________

12. List the SOLIDS command used to extrude a polyline into a solid.

    ____

13. List the SOLIDS command used to create a solid by revolving a polyline about an axis.

    ____

14. List the SOLIDS command that allows you to join several solids into a single object.

    ____

15. List the SOLIDS command used to subtract solids from other solids.

    ____

16. List the command and its option that is used to move the UCS icon so that it is displayed at the origin of the current coordinate system.

    Command: ________ Option: ________

17. List the SOLIDS setting used to adjust the smoothness of solid models rendered with the Hide: command.

    ____

18. List the command and its option that allows you to join several lines into a single polyline.

    Command: ________ Option: ________

19. List the command and the rotation angle that may be used to rotate an object 90° clockwise about the Z axis.

    Command: ________ Rotation angle: ________

20. List the SOLIDS command used to create an object from the common volume of two intersecting solids.

    ____

12 Drawing Complex Solid Models Using Basic SOLIDS Commands

OBJECTIVES:

When you have completed this chapter, you will be able to:

□ Create complex models using the basic SOLIDS commands described in Chapter 11.

INTRODUCTION

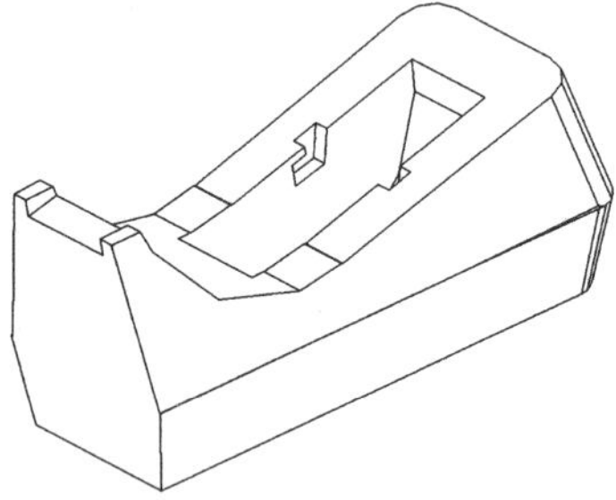

FIGURE 12–1
Solid Model of a Tape Dispenser

This chapter is a tutorial exercise designed to give you experience in drawing complex models. No new commands are introduced, but you will become more familiar with the SOLIDS commands you have already used as well as with the Ucs:, Vports:, Mview:, Pspace:, and Mspace: commands. The object chosen for this exercise is one many of you will have on your desk, the common tape dispenser, Figure 12–1. This model will later be analyzed to give you an opportunity to compare the weight AutoCAD assigns to the model with the model's measured weight. A quick look at this object reveals many angles, curves, fillets, and cutouts. Let's begin at the bottom and move up.

Creating a Solid Model Using Basic Solids Commands:

EXERCISE 12–1

Set Up the Drawing

Step 1. On Your Own:

1. Pick New. . . from the menu bar File menu. Name the drawing: 12-1 (your initials).
2. Make the following settings:

UNITS: Decimal; 3 digits to the right of the decimal point
LIMITS: Lower left corner: 0,0
Upper right corner: 11,8.5
GRID: .2
SNAP: .05
FACETRES—2; ISOLINES—10
STYLE: STANDARD; FONT: SIMPLEX; HEIGHT: 0
Create the following layers:

LAYER NAME	COLOR	LINETYPE
Y	YELLOW	CONTINUOUS
R	RED	CONTINUOUS
G	GREEN	CONTINUOUS

Set layer Y current.

3. Use the Vports: command to make two vertical viewports. Zoom: All in both viewports. Pick the right viewport to make it active.
4. Use the Vpoint: command to set a 1,−1,1 viewpoint for the right viewport so you can see what the object looks like as you draw it.

Draw the Lower Part of the Tape Dispenser

The dimensions from Figure 12–2 will be used to construct the lower part of this model.

Step 2. On Your Own:

Draw a continuous polyline.

Use the dimensions from Figure 12–2 to draw a continuous polyline in the left viewport. You may find it easier to draw the object using the Line: and Fillet: commands and then use Pedit: to join the segments into a single entity. The double line shown in Figure 12-2 shows the shape after extrusion.

FIGURE 12–2
Dimensions for Lower Part

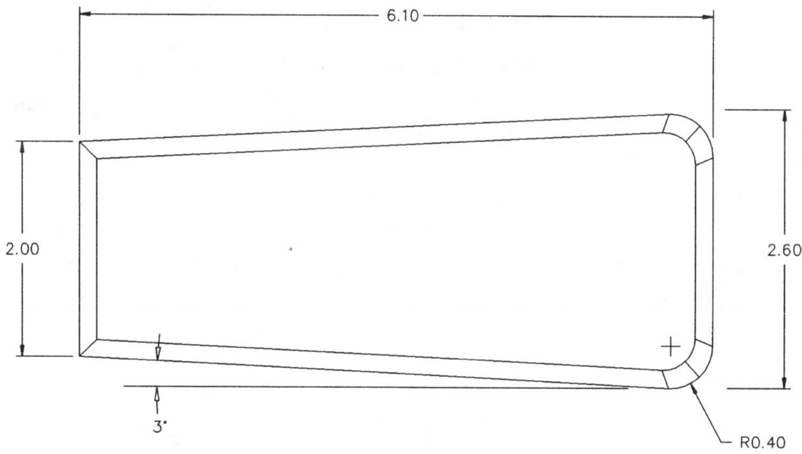

Step 3. Extrude the pline .95 in the negative Z direction and move it to 0 elevation.

Prompt	**Response**
Command:	**Extrude:**
Select objects:	**Pick the polyline.**
Select objects:	↵
Height of extrusion:	*Type:* **−.95** ↵
Extrusion taper angle <0>:	*Type:* **10** ↵

Now move the model .95 in the positive Z direction so you can keep its base at 0 elevation.

Prompt	Response
Command:	**Move:**
Select objects:	**Pick the model.**
Select objects:	↵
Base point or displacement:	**Pick any point.**
Second point of displacement:	*Type:* **@0,0,.95** ↵

Draw the Upper Part of the Tape Dispenser

Step 4. Rotate the UCS 90° about the X axis, select a plan view of that coordinate system, and draw the upper part of the dispenser, Figure 12–3.

Prompt	Response
Command:	**UCS:**
Origin/ZAxis/3point/OBject?View/ X/Y/Z/Prev/Restore/Save/Del/?/ <World>:	*Type:* **X** ↵
Rotation angle about X axis <0>:	*Type:* **90** ↵
Command:	**Plan:**
<Current UCS>Ucs/World:	↵

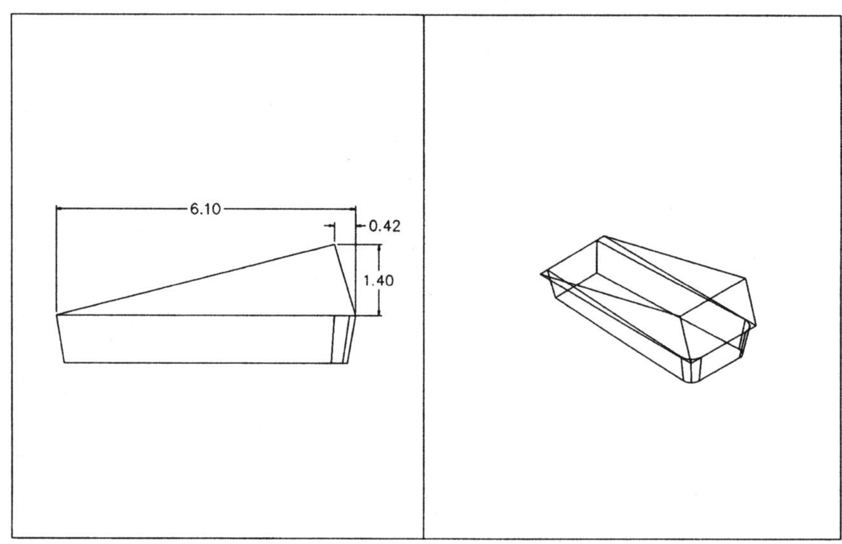

FIGURE 12–3
Dimensions for Upper Part

Step 5. On Your Own:

Use the dimensions from Figure 12–3 to draw a continuous pline for the upper part of the dispenser and extrude it 2.6″ in the positive Z direction. Just be sure that you have a continuous polyline before you try to use Extrude: to extrude the shape. Your drawing should look similar to Figure 12–4.

Step 6. Move the extruded shape to its correct position.

After you have extruded the shape, move it to its correct position as follows:

Prompt	Response
Command:	**Move:**
Select objects:	**Pick the upper part of the dispenser.**
Select objects:	↵
Base point or displacement:	*Type:* **MID** ↵

FIGURE 12–4
Extruding and Moving the Upper Part

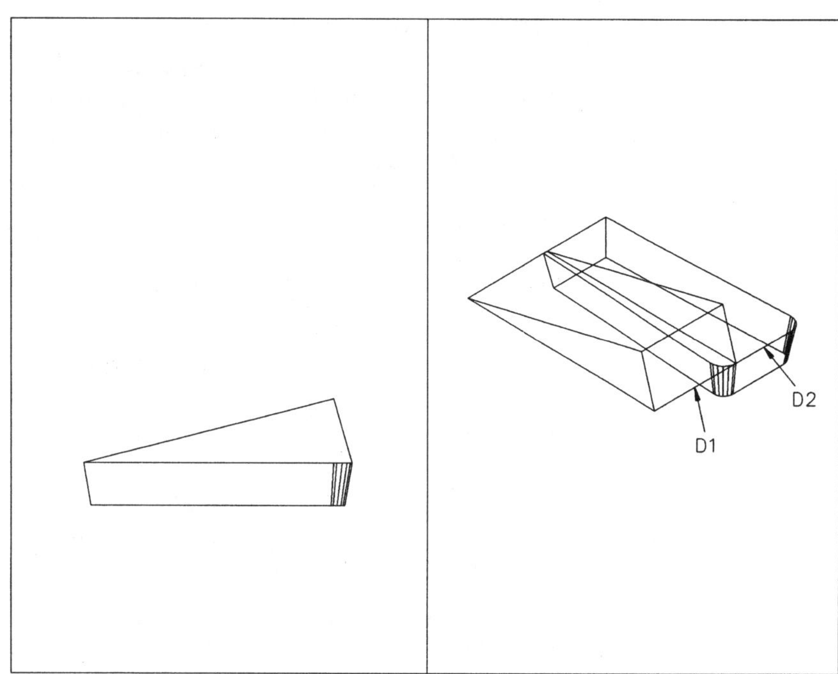

of	**D1**
Second point of displacement:	*Type:* **MID** ↵
of	**D2**

Step 7. Move the UCS origin to the intersection of the front edge of the upper part of the dispenser.

Prompt	Response
Command:	**UCS:**
Origin/ZAxis/3point/OBject?View/ X/Y/Z/Prev/Restore/Save/Del/?/ <World>:	*Type:* **O** ↵
Origin point <0,0,0>:	*Type:* **END** ↵
of	**D1** (Figure 12–5)

The UCS icon will not move to that origin unless you instruct it to do so. To be sure you have the origin in the correct location use the Ucsicon: command as follows:

Prompt	Response
Command:	**Ucsicon:**
ON?OFF?All/Noorigin/ORigin <ON>:	*Type:* **OR** ↵

FIGURE 12–5
Moving the UCS Origin

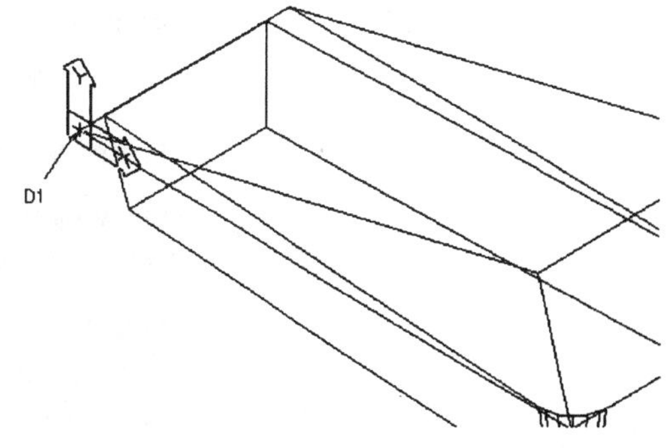

Step 8. On Your Own:

Draw the shape forming the front edge of the dispenser.

In a similar manner to the way you made the upper part of the dispenser, draw a continuous polyline from the dimensions shown in Figure 12–6. Extrude the object 2.6″ in the negative Z direction.

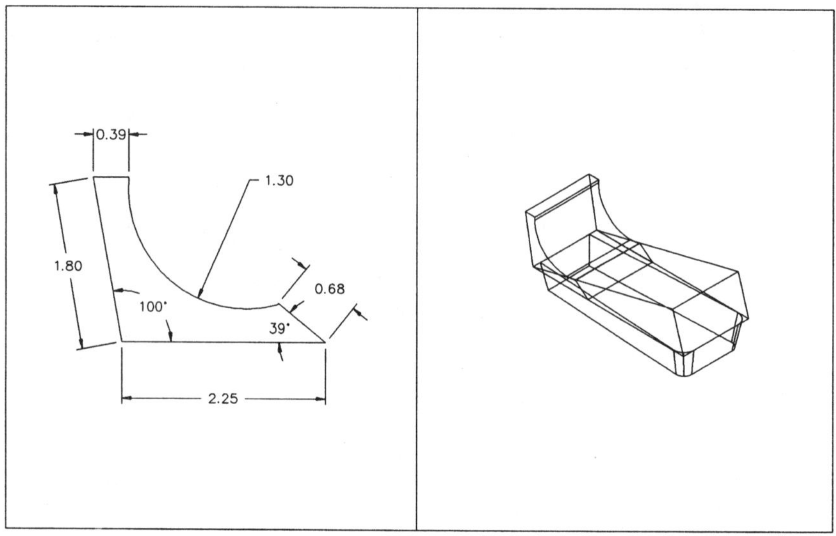

FIGURE 12–6
Dimensions for the Front Edge

If you have done everything as described thus far, your model should now appear as shown in Figure 12–7.

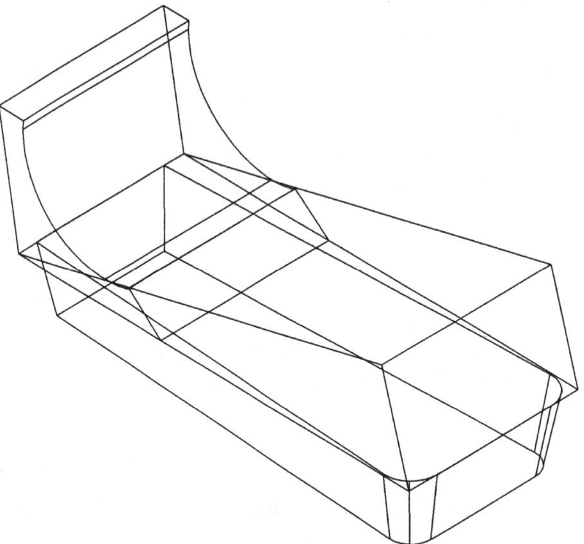

FIGURE 12–7
Extruding the Front Edge

Step 9. On Your Own:

Use Union: to combine the three pieces of the dispenser into a single shape.

Remove Excess Material from the Model

Draw inclined wedges, rotate them to their correct positions, and subtract them from the sides of the dispenser to form the slanted sides.

Step 10. On Your Own:

Rotate the UCS 90° about the Y axis and locate the origin of the UCS at the intersection of the back edge of the upper part of the dispenser as shown in Figure 12–8.

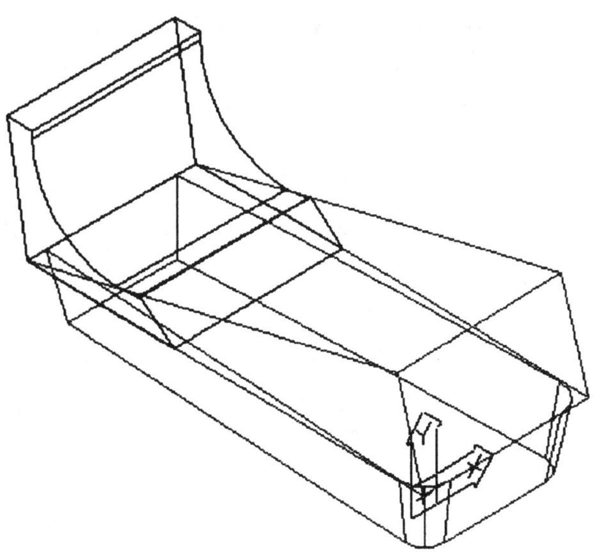

FIGURE 12–8
Rotating the UCS 90° About the Y Axis and Move the Origin

Step 11. Make four viewports.

At this point it will be helpful to have four viewports as shown in Figure 12–9. Do that now and position the model in each viewport as follows:

Prompt	Response
Command:	**Vports:**
Save/Restore/Delete/Join/SIngle/?/2/3/4:	Type: **SI** ↵ (to return to a single viewport)
Command:	↵
Save/Restore/Delete/Join/SIngle/?/2/3/4:	*Type:* **4** ↵

Step 12. Set the viewports so that they show the views displayed in Figure 12–9.

1. Pick the upper left viewport to make it active.
2. Use the settings of the Viewpoint Presets dialog, Figure 12–10, to obtain a top view of the object.

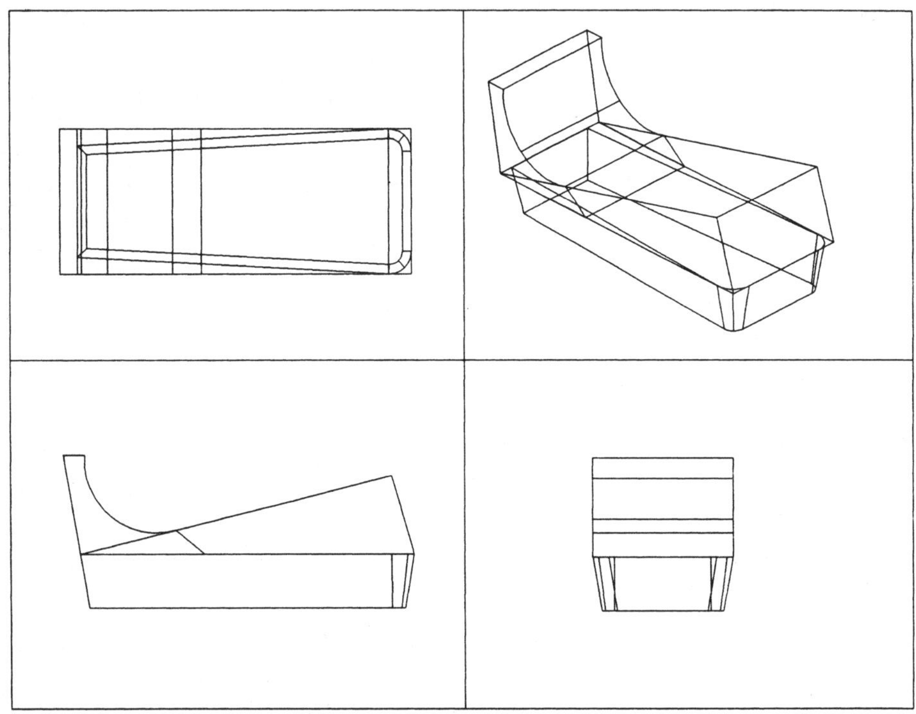

FIGURE 12–9
Creating Three Viewports

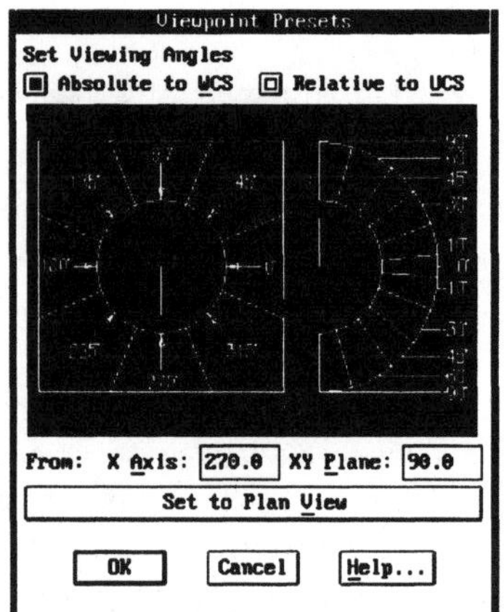

FIGURE 12–10
The Settings for the Top View in the Upper Left Viewport

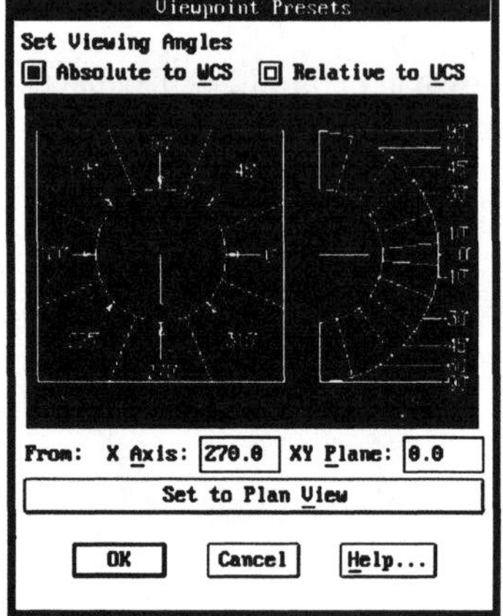

FIGURE 12–11
The Settings for the Front View in the Lower Left Viewport

3. Pick the lower left viewport to make it active.
4. Use settings of the Viewpoint Presets dialog box, Figure 12–11, to obtain a front view of the object.
5. Pick the lower right viewport to make it active.
6. Obtain the right side view of the object as follows:

Prompt	Response
Command:	*Type:* **PLAN** ↵
<Current UCS>Ucs/World:	↵

7. Leave the upper right viewport as a 3-D view.

Now set all viewports to the same scale with respect to paper space so you can plot all four viewports at the same scale when you finish the model.

Step 13. Begin by saving this viewport configuration and restoring it in paper space.

Prompt	Response
Command:	**Vports:**
Save/Restore/Delete/Join/SIngle/?/2/3/4:	*Type:* **S** ↵
?/Name for new viewport configuration:	*Type:* **1** ↵
Command:	*Type:* **TILEMODE** ↵
New value for TILEMODE <1>:	*Type:* **0** ↵
Command:	**Mview:** (You are now going to restore your model space viewport configuration in paper space in an 11″ × 8.5″ area with a .5″ border all around.)
ON/OFF/Hideplot/Fit/2/3/4/Restore/ <First Point>:	*Type:* **R** ↵
?/Name of window configuration to insert <>:	*Type:* **1** ↵
Fit/<First Point>:	*Type:* **.5,.5** ↵
Second point:	*Type:* **10.5,8** ↵

Step 14. On Your Own:

Zoom: All to make sure you have the complete picture.

Step 15. Return to model space and use the XP option of the Zoom: command to obtain equally scaled views of the object.

Prompt	Response
Command:	*Type:* **MS** ↵
	Pick the upper left viewport to make it active.
Command:	*Type:* **Z** ↵
All/Center/Dynamic/Extents/Left/ Previous/Vmax/Window/<Scale (X/XP)>:	*Type:* **.6XP** ↵
	Pick the lower left viewport to make it active.
Command:	↵ (to repeat the previous command)
All/Center/Dynamic/Extents/Left/ Previous/Vmax/Window/<Scale (X/XP)>:	*Type:* **.6XP** ↵

Step 16. On Your Own:

1. Use the Zoom: XP option to obtain the same zoom scale factor in the other two viewports.
2. Use the Pan: command to align objects within viewports so they appear approximately as shown in Figure 12–9. These views can be aligned very accurately using the MVsetup AutoLISP routine as described in Chapter 16. For now, the approximate alignment is OK.
3. With the lower right viewport active, draw the wedge shape as a continuous polyline using the Pline: command. You will find it easy to use absolute and relative coordinates to draw the wedge with your origin at the location shown in Figure 12–8. Use the figure as shown in Figure 12–12. Mirror the left wedge to form the right wedge. Use the midpoints of any of the edges forming the depth of the object that are on the same plane as the mirror line.
4. Use Extrude: to extrude both wedges 7″ in the negative Z direction to make sure they extend beyond the end of the object.
5. Use Rotat3D: to rotate the left wedge −3° about the Y axis, and the right wedge 3° about the Y axis.
6. Use Subtrac: to subtract the wedges from the existing object so that your object appears as shown in Figure 12–13.

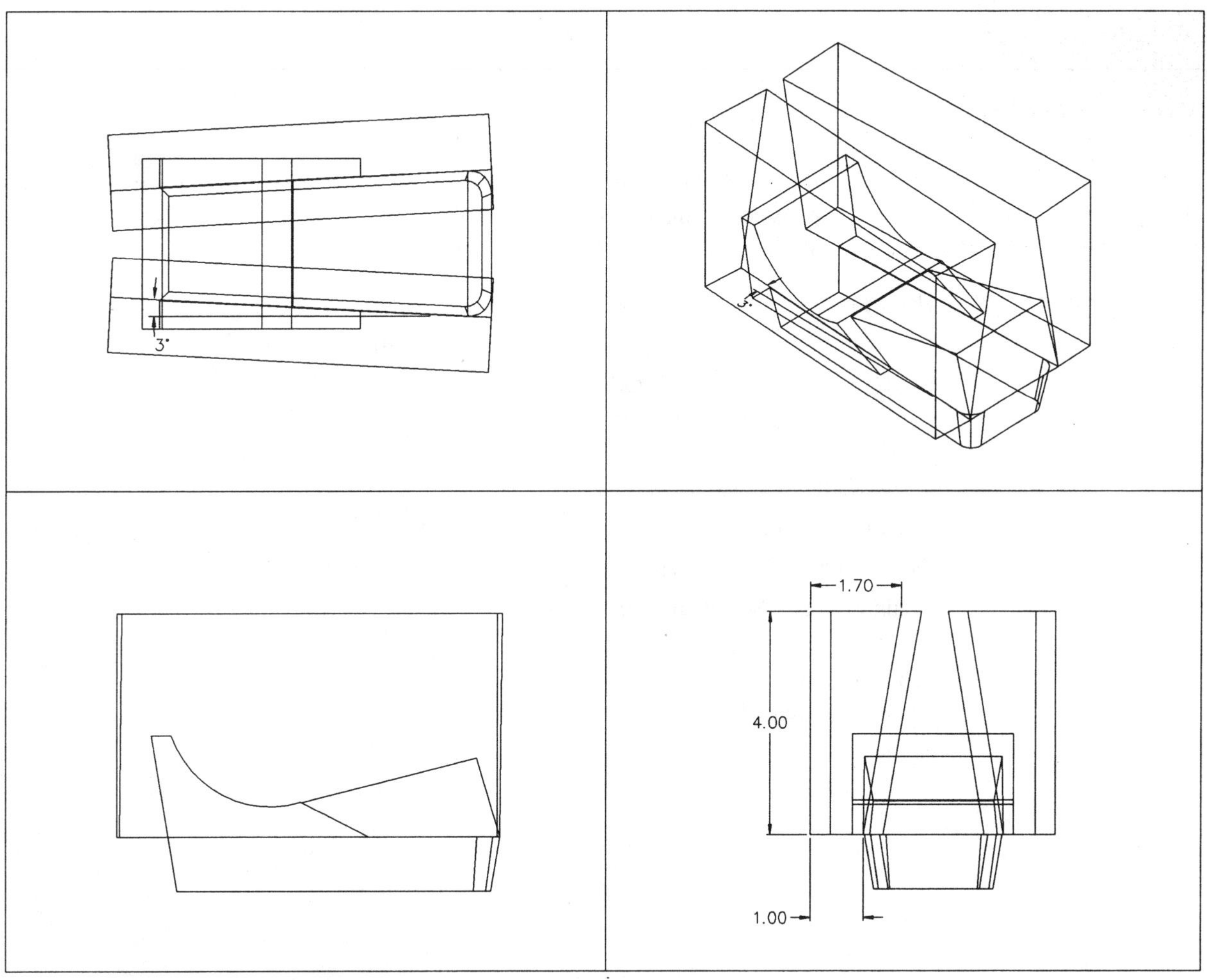

FIGURE 12–12
Dimensions for the Wedge Shapes

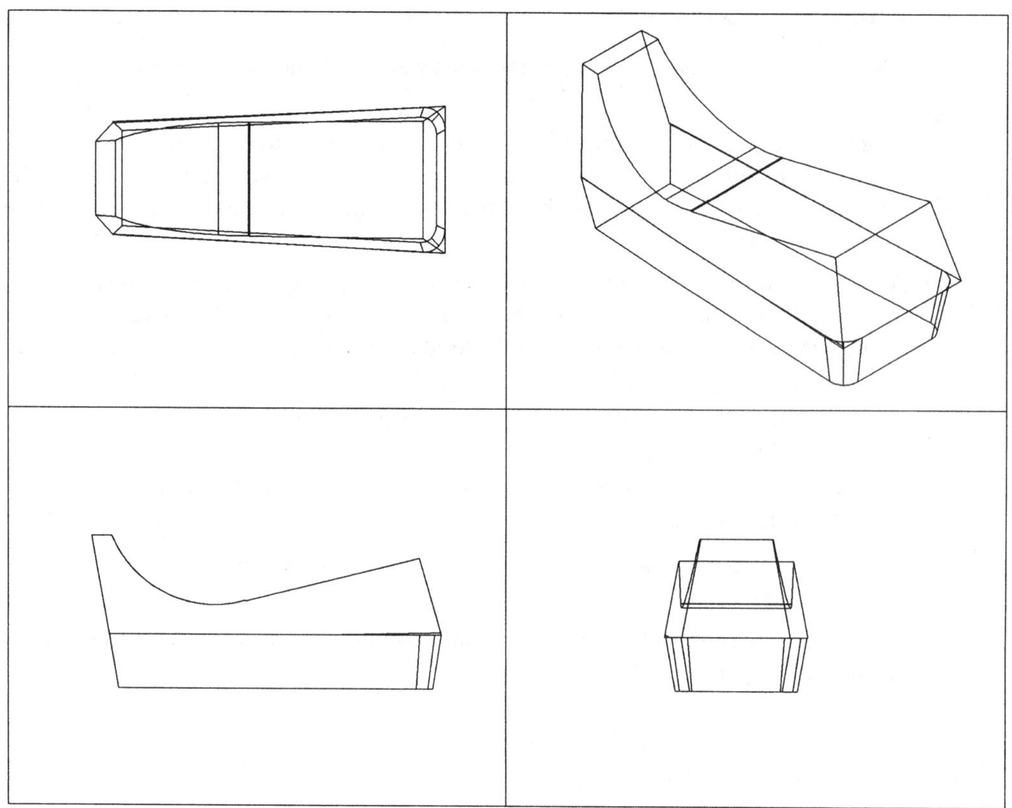

FIGURE 12–13
Subtracting the Wedge Shapes

Step 17. Use the Fillet: command to round the corners of the upper part of the dispenser. (If you have trouble with Fillet: working, create an extruded fillet shape and subtract it to form rounded edges.)

Prompt	Response
Command:	**Fillet:**
(TRIM mode) Current fillet radius = 0.400 Polyline/Radius/Trim/ <Select first object>:	**D1 (Figure 12–14)**
Chain/Radius/<Select edge>:	
Enter radius <0.400>:	↵
Chain/Radius/<Select edge>:	**D2**
Chain/Radius/<Select edge>:	↵

FIGURE 12–14
Filleting the Upper Part

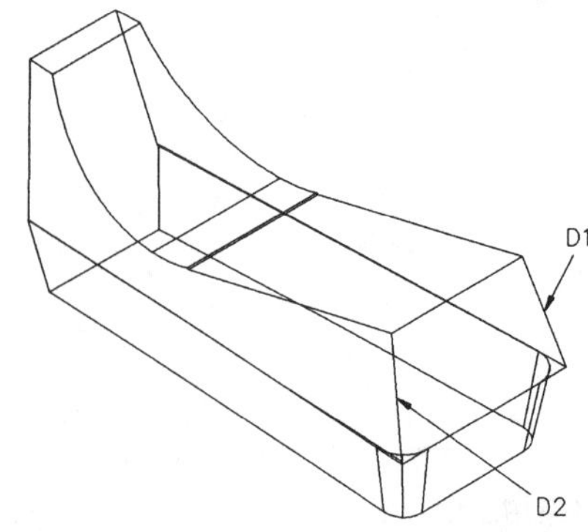

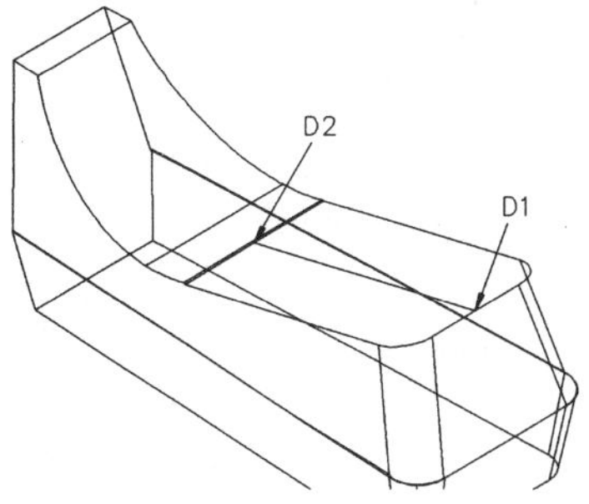

FIGURE 12–15
Drawing a Construction Line

Draw the Tape Cavity

Step 18. Draw a construction line from the midpoints of two lines on the slanted surface.

Prompt	Response
Command:	**Line:**
From point:	*Type:* **MID** ↵
of	**D1** (Figure 12–15)
To point:	*Type:* **MID** ↵
of	**D2**
To point:	↵

Step 19. Rotate the UCS −90° about the Y axis so you can determine at what angle in the XY plane you must draw a line to locate the center of the tape cavity.

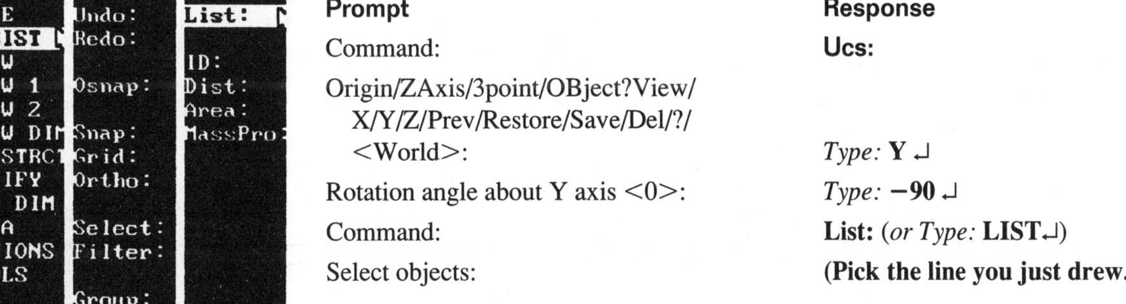

Prompt	Response
Command:	**Ucs:**
Origin/ZAxis/3point/OBject?View/ X/Y/Z/Prev/Restore/Save/Del/?/ <World>:	*Type:* **Y** ↵
Rotation angle about Y axis <0>:	*Type:* **−90** ↵
Command:	**List:** (*or Type:* **LIST**↵)
Select objects:	**(Pick the line you just drew.)**

You have just listed the construction line to determine its angle in the XY plane. The angle should be 194° or close to that.

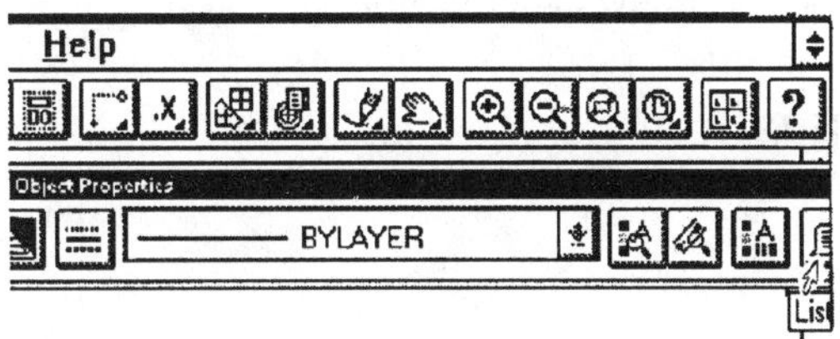

Step 20. Erase the construction line and draw a line to locate the center of the tape cavity.

Prompt	Response
Command:	**Erase:**
Select objects:	**Pick the construction line you just listed.**
Select objects:	↵
Command:	**Line:**
From point:	*Type:* **MID** ↵
of	**D1 (Pick the front edge,** Figure 12–16.)
To point:	*Type:* **@2.4<194** ↵
To point:	↵

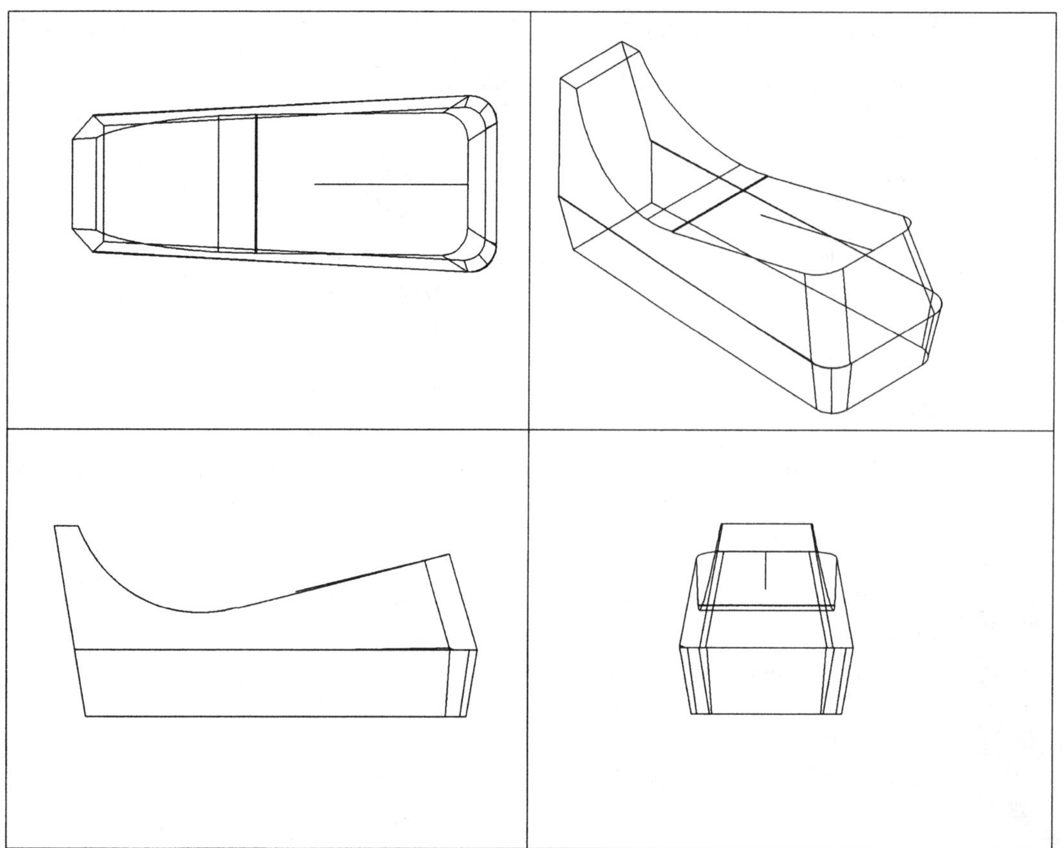

FIGURE 12–16
Drawing a Line to Locate the Center of the Cavity

You have located the center of the tape cavity, Figure 12–17, which is located 2.4″ from the back edge of the inclined surface.

FIGURE 12–17
Drawing the Cavity Cylinder

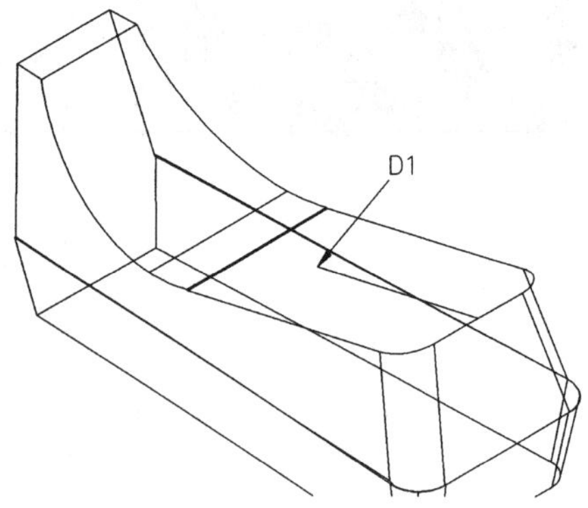

Step 21. Draw the cavity.

Prompt	**Response**
Command:	**Cylinder:**
Elliptical/<Center point><0,0,0>:	*Type:* **END** ↵
of	**D1** (Figure 12–17)
Diameter/<Radius>:	*Type:* **1.625** ↵
Center of other end/<Height>:	*Type:* **1** ↵

Step 22. Move the cavity, Figure 12–18, so that it is in the center of the dispenser. Because it is 1″ deep, move it ½″ in the negative Z direction.

Prompt	Response
Command:	**Move:**
Select objects:	**(Pick the cylinder.)**
Select objects:	↵
Base point or displacement:	**(Pick any point.)**
Second point of displacement:	*Type:* **@0,0,−.5** ↵

Step 23. On Your Own:

1. Use Subtrac: to subtract the cylinder from the model, Figure 12–19.
2. Erase the construction line locating the center of the cavity.

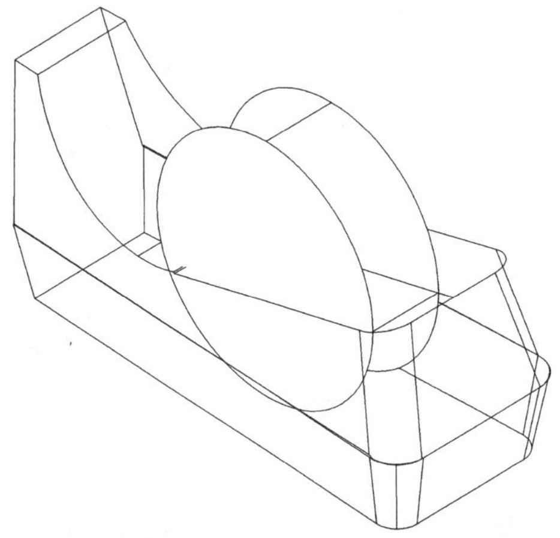

FIGURE 12–18
Moving the Cavity Cylinder

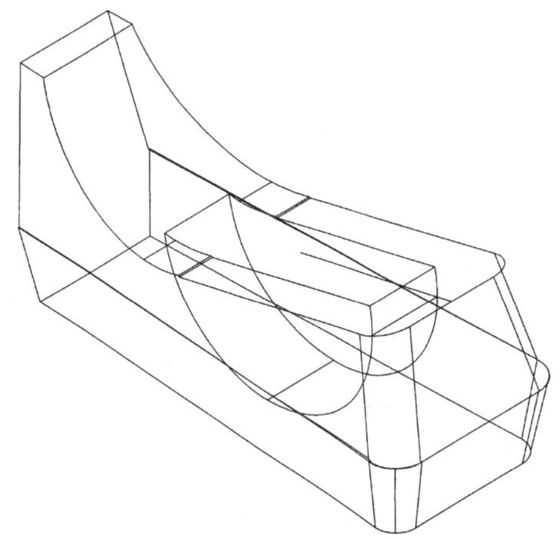

FIGURE 12–19
Subtracting the Cavity Cylinder

Draw the Holes That Are Used to Hold the Tape Roll Spinner

Step 24. Select a UCS that has its origin at the center of one side of the cavity and is aligned with the top edge of the cavity, Figure 12–20.

Prompt	Response
Command:	**Ucs:**
Origin/ZAxis/3point/OBject?View/ X/Y/Z/Prev/Restore/Save/Del/?/ <World>:	*Type:* **3** ↵

FIGURE 12–20
Locating the UCS

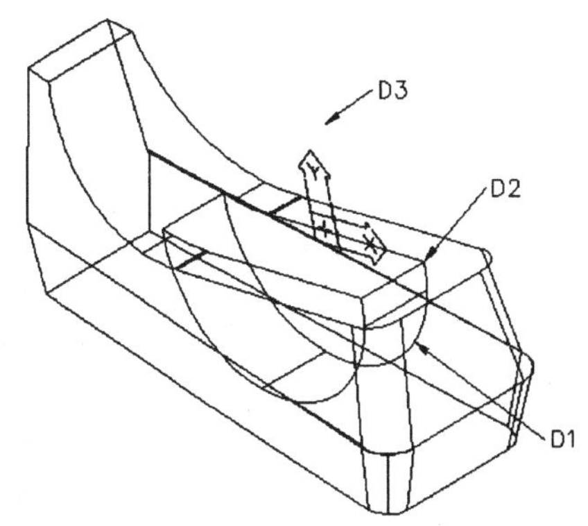

Prompt	Response
Origin point <0,0,0>:	*Type:* **CEN** ↵
of	*Pick:* **D1** (Figure 12–20)
Point on positive portion of the X axis <1.000,0.000,0.000>:	*Type:* **END** ↵
of	*Pick:* **D2**
Point on positive Y portion of the UCS XY Plane <0.000,1.000,0.000>:	(Make sure ortho (F8) is on, and *Pick:* **D3.**)

Step 25. On Your Own:

1. Use the dimensions from Figure 12–21 to draw a continuous polyline in the location shown.

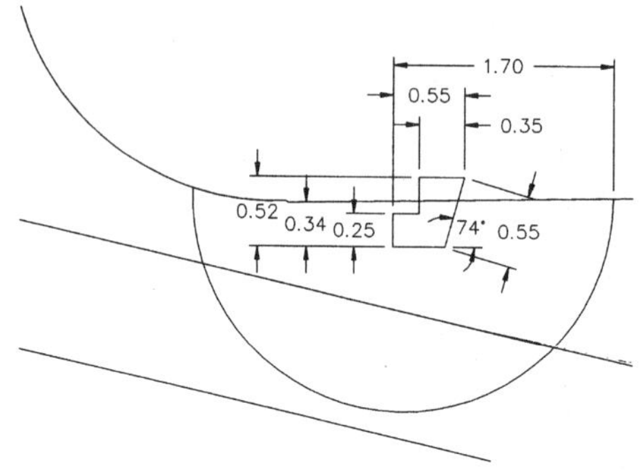

FIGURE 12–21
Dimensions for Spinnen Mounting Holes

2. Use Extrude: to extrude the shape −.15.
3. Copy the shape to the other side of the cavity 1.15 in the positive Z direction (@0,0,1.15) so that the two shapes are directly across from each other.
4. Use Subtrac: to subtract both shapes from the model, Figure 12–22.

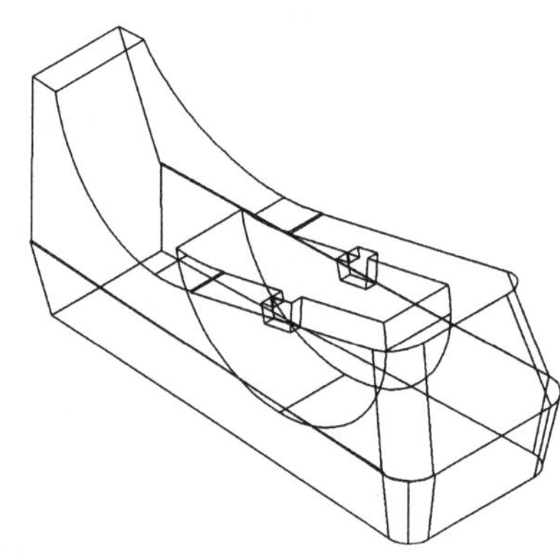

FIGURE 12–22
Subtracting the Extruded Shapes

Form the Tape Tear Edge

Step 26. Select a UCS that is parallel with the front edge of the dispenser and has its origin at the end of the curve.

Prompt	Response
Command:	**Ucs:**
Origin/ZAxis/3point/OBject?View/ X/Y/Z/Prev/Restore/Save/Del/?/ <World>:	*Type:* **3** ↵
Origin point <0,0,0>:	*Type:* **END** ↵

of	*Pick:* **D1** (Figure 12–23)
Point on positive portion of the X axis <1.000,0.000,0.000>:	*Type:* **END** ↵
of	*Pick:* **D2**
Point on positive Y portion of the UCS XY Plane <0.000,1.000,0.000>:	*Type:* **END** ↵
of	*Pick:* **D3**
Command:	↵
Origin/ZAxis/3point/OBject?View/ X/Y/Z/Prev/Restore/Save/Del/?/ <World>:	*Type:* **OR** ↵
Origin point <0,0,0>:	*Type:* **END** ↵
of	*Pick:* **D4**

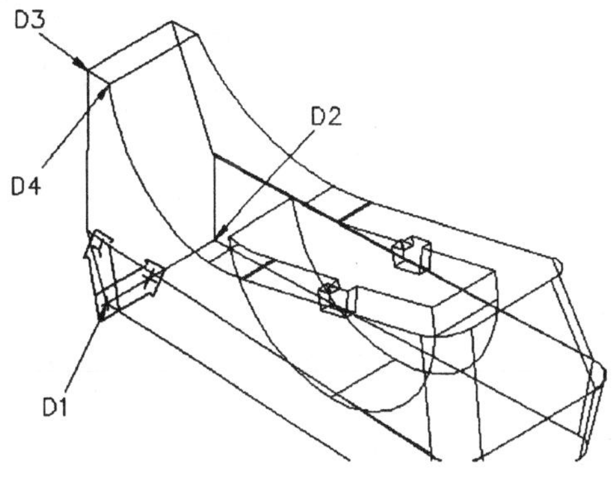

FIGURE 12–23
Defining a New UCS

The UCS icon should be in the location shown in Figure 12–24.

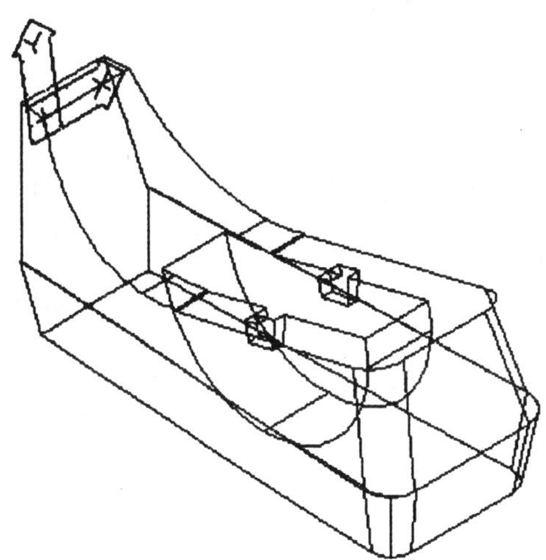

FIGURE 12–24
Moving the UCS Origin

Step 27. Use Box: to draw a box that is centered in the upper end of the front edge.

Prompt	Response
Command:	**Box:**
Center/<Corner of box><0,0,0>:	*Type:* **.175,−.1,−.5** ↵
Cube/Length/<Other corner>:	*Type:* **L** ↵

Prompt	Response
Length:	*Type:* **1** ↵
Width:	*Type:* **1** ↵
Height:	*Type:* **.75** ↵

The box should be centered in the model as shown in Figure 12–25. Notice which is the length, width, and height of the box. In similar situations you may need to draw the box in space with the correct UCS and move it to its correct location using Osnap-MIDpoint and then moving it again in either the X, Y, or Z direction.

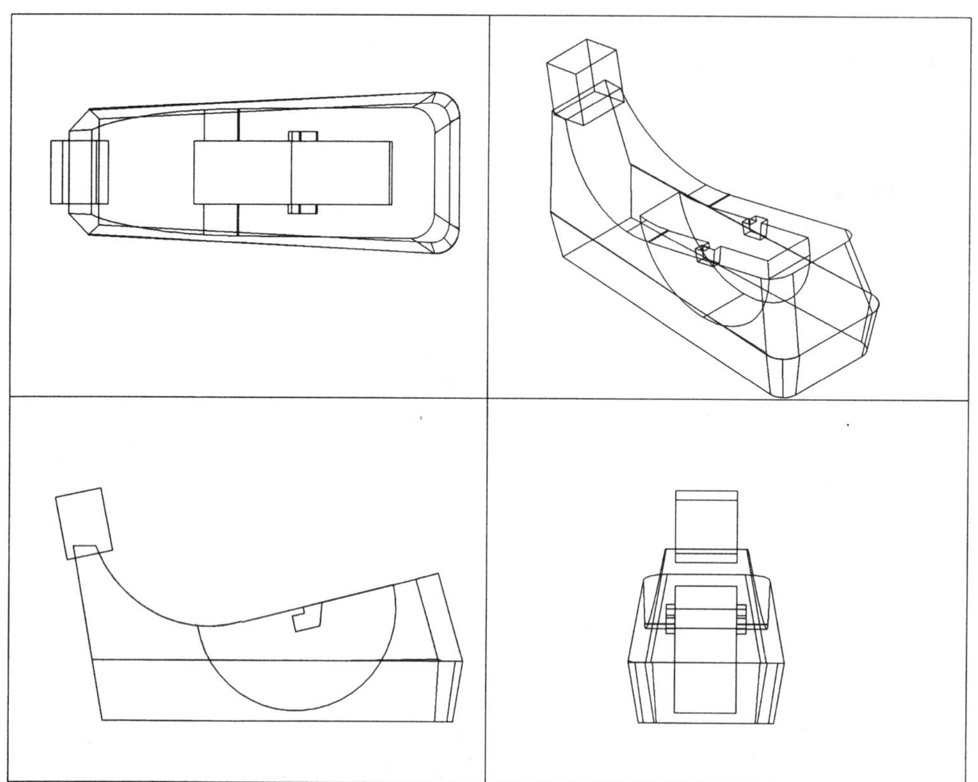

FIGURE 12–25
Drawing a Box to Form a Depression in the Front Edge

Step 28. On Your Own:

1. Use Subtrac: to subtract the box from the model, Figure 12–26.
2. Pick the upper right viewport and select a viewpoint that shows the front of the dispenser, Figure 12–27.
3. Use the Hide: command to be sure the model is correct as shown in Figure 12–27.
4. Take the model into paper space (*Type:* **PS** ↵).
5. Type your name and assignment number in the lower right corner using the simplex font, .12 high, right-justified.
6. Use Mview-Hideplot to remove hidden lines in the upper right viewport.
7. Plot all four viewports on an 11″ × 8.5″ sheet.
8. Save your drawing in two places and exit.

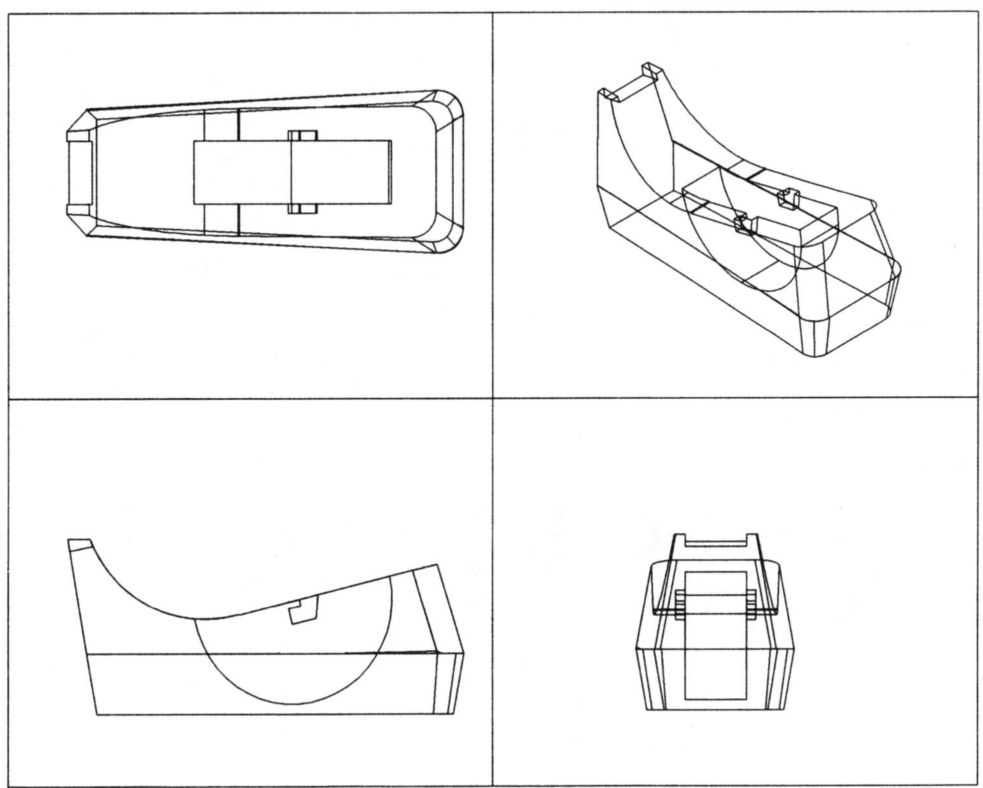

FIGURE 12–26
Subtracting the Box

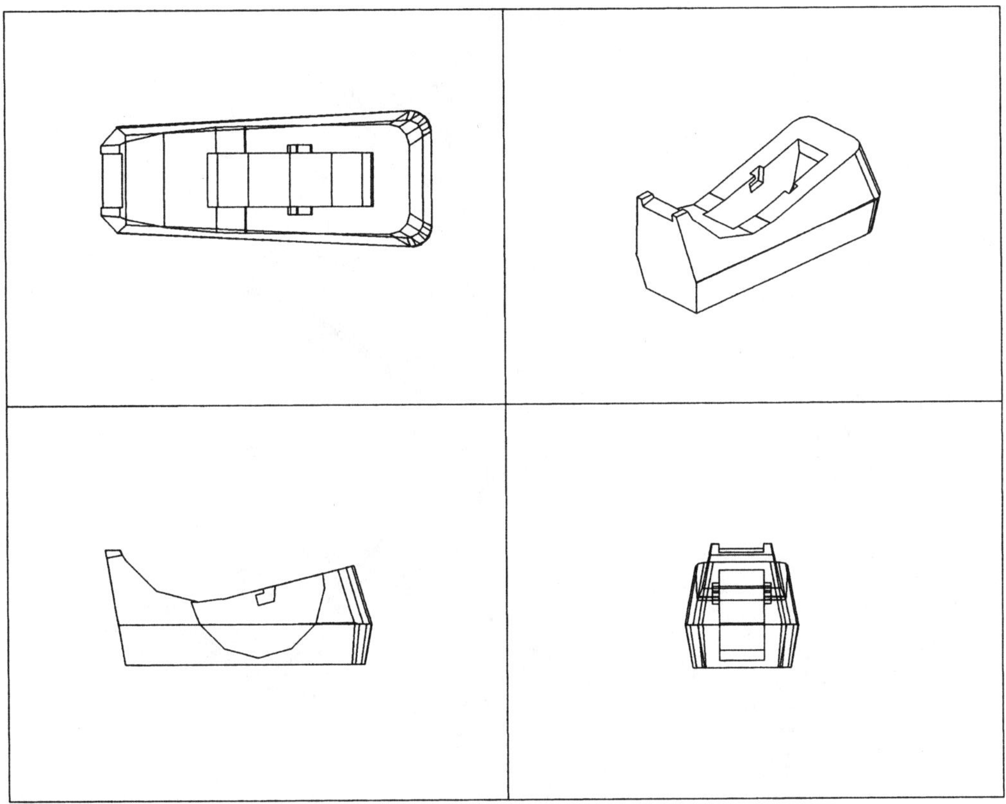

FIGURE 12–27
The Finished Solid Model

EXERCISES

12–1. 1. Follow the instructions in this chapter to draw Figure 12–1. Your final drawing should look like Figure 12–27.

2. Plot the drawing full size on an 11″ × 8.5″ sheet.

12–2. 1. Make a solid model of the screwdriver shown in Figure 12–28.

2. Measure the flat views of the object shown in that figure and make your model twice that size. Your final drawing should look like Figure 12–29.

3. You will have to draw two shapes for the handle: one from the side view and one from the end view. Use Revolve: to obtain the shape for the side view and Extrude: to obtain the extruded shape of the end view. Use Intersection: to form the shape that is the common volume of the two shapes. (You may also draw a cylinder and do a polar array to create six cylinders, then subtract them from the extruded shape of the handle.)

4. The Phillips head of the screwdriver will require 90° revolved solids that have been polar arrayed and subtracted from the screwdriver shaft. See the end and side views for the shape and location of these shapes.

5. Plot the drawing full size on an 11″ × 8.5″ sheet.

12–3. 1. Make a solid model of the telephone shown in Figure 12–30.

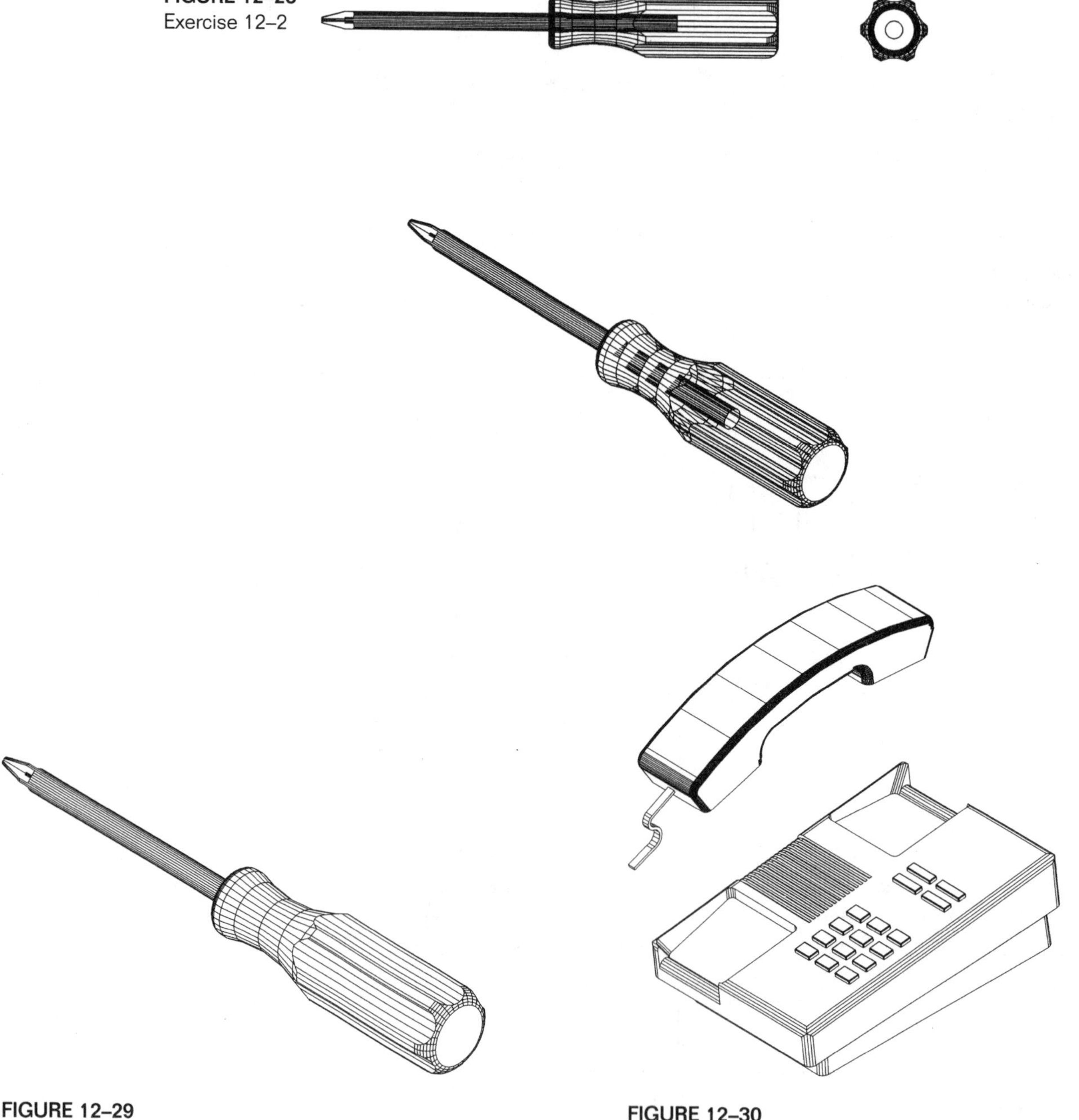

FIGURE 12–28
Exercise 12–2

FIGURE 12–29
Exercise 12–2

FIGURE 12–30
Exercise 12–3

2. Measure the object shown in that figure and make your model twice that size. Your final drawing should look like Figure 12–31.
3. Plot the drawing full size on an 11″ × 8.5″ sheet.

12–4. 1. Make a solid model of the lounge chair shown in Figure 12–31.
2. Use the grid and the callouts to draw the object full size. Each grid mark is 2″. The slats are 40″ long. Your final drawing should look like the 3-D view of Figure 12–31.
3. Plot the drawing to fit on an 11″ × 8.5″ sheet.

12–5. 1. Make a solid model of the mounting flange shown in Figure 12–32.
2. Use the dimensions shown to draw the object full size.
3. Choose a viewpoint similar to Figure 12–30 before you plot your drawing.
4. Plot the drawing full size on an 11″ × 8.5″ sheet.

12–6. 1. Make a solid model from the sketch of the Gain Control Module shown in Figure 12–33.
2. Individual parts that mount on the front and rear panels of this module are shown in Figures 12–34 through 12–39.
3. Use the dimensions shown to draw the module full size. The X's on the individual views show the insertion point where the part mounts on the front or rear panel of the module.
4. Draw only the outside of the module. Approximate any dimensions that are not shown. Place parts on front and rear panels in the approximate locations shown on the sketch, Figure 12–33.
5. Use the ROMAN DUPLEX (ROMAND) font to place labels (GAIN CONTROL, POWER ON, F1, J2, etc.) on front and rear panels. You may have to move labels off of the front panels a little (.01) to allow them to show on the final plot.
6. Choose a viewpoint similar to Figure 12–30 before plotting the drawing.
7. Plot the drawing to fit on an 11″ × 8.5″ sheet.

12–7. 1. Make a solid model of the house shown in Figure 12–40.
2. Measure the object shown in that figure and make your model twice that size. Your final drawing should look like the top illustration in Figure 12–40 with all hidden lines removed.
3. Plot the drawing to fit on an 11″ × 8.5″ sheet.

FIGURE 12–31
Exercise 12–4

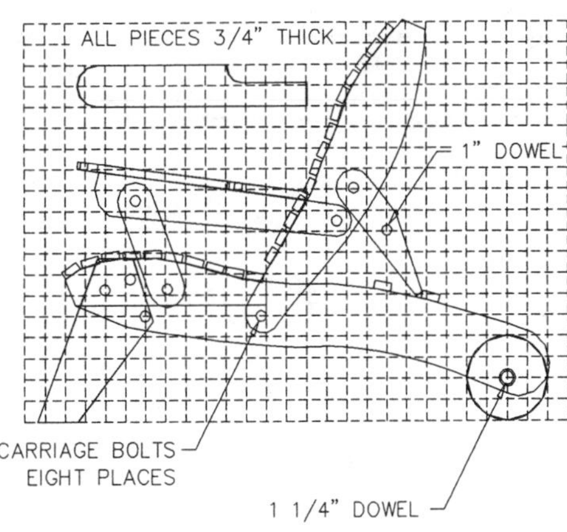

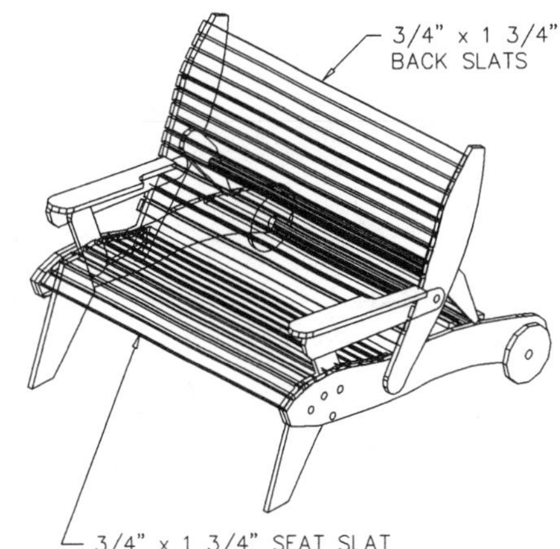

FIGURE 12–32
Exercise 12–5

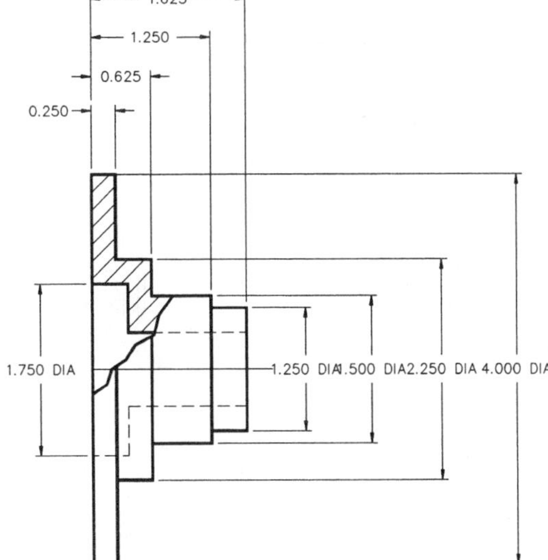

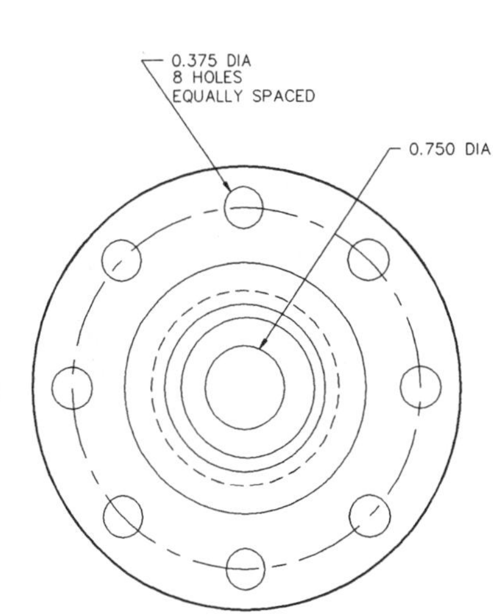

FIGURE 12–33
Exercise 12–6: Gain Control Module

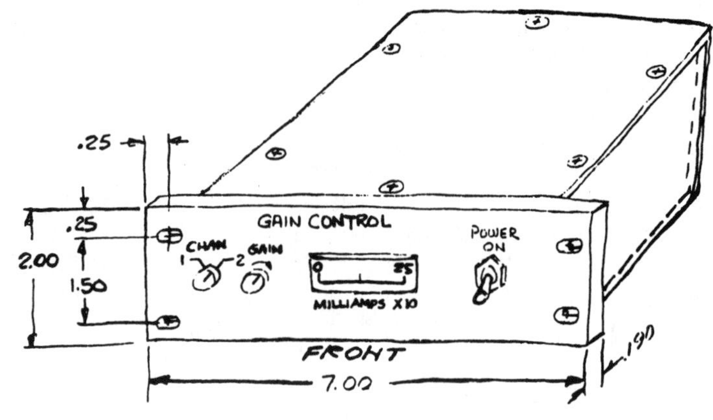

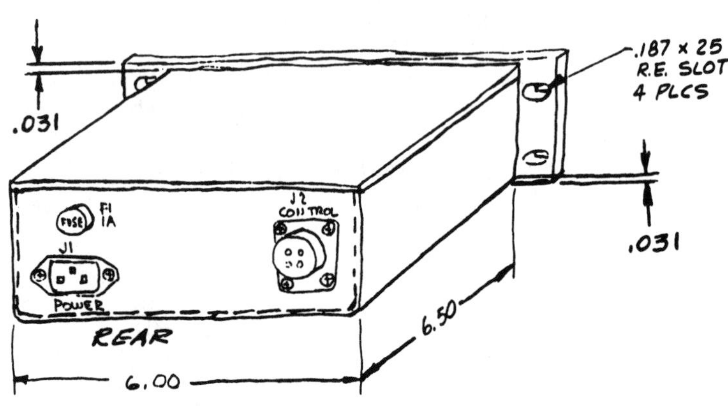

FIGURE 12–34
Exercise 12–6: Part J1

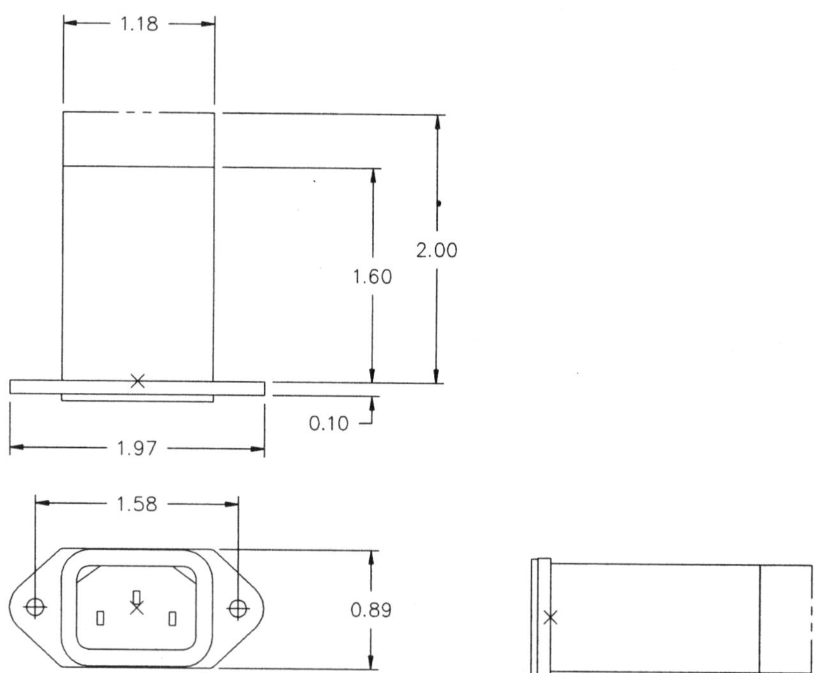

FIGURE 12–35
Exercise 12–6: Part J2

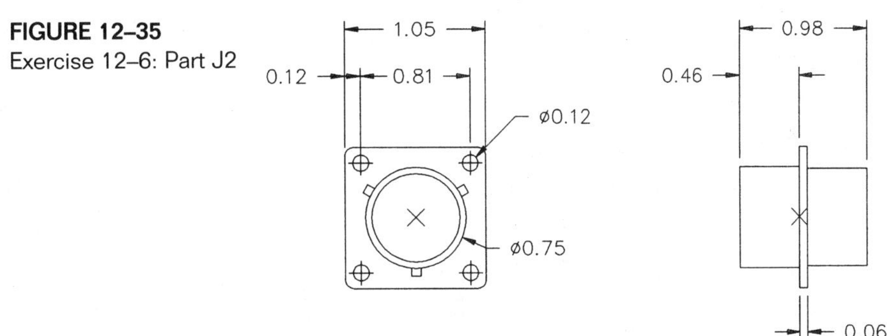

FIGURE 12–36
Exercise 12–6: Part M1

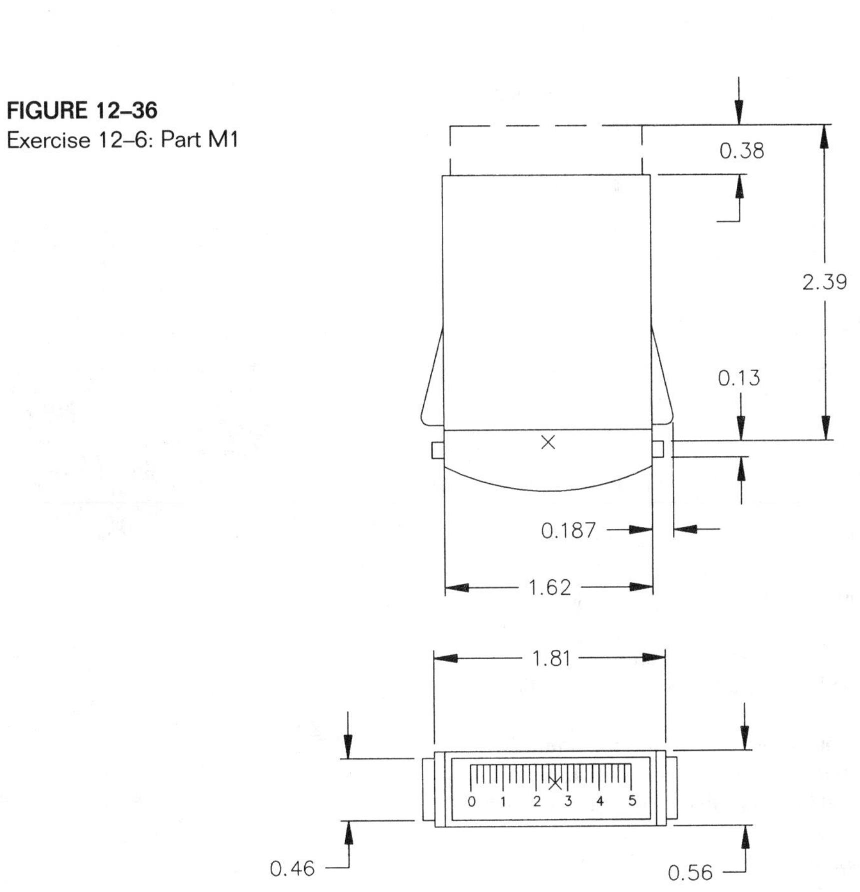

FIGURE 12–37
Exercise 12–6: Part S1

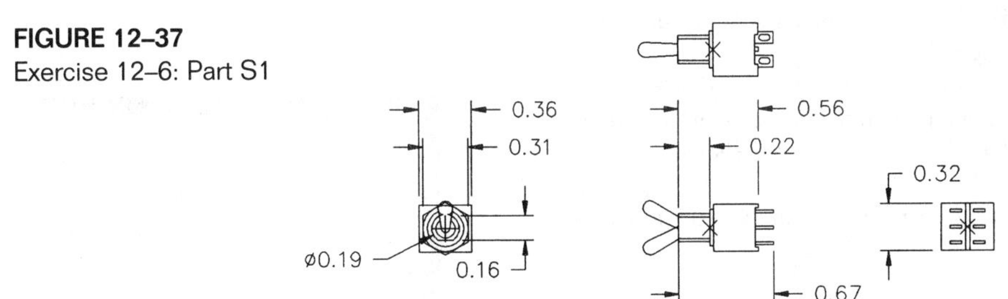

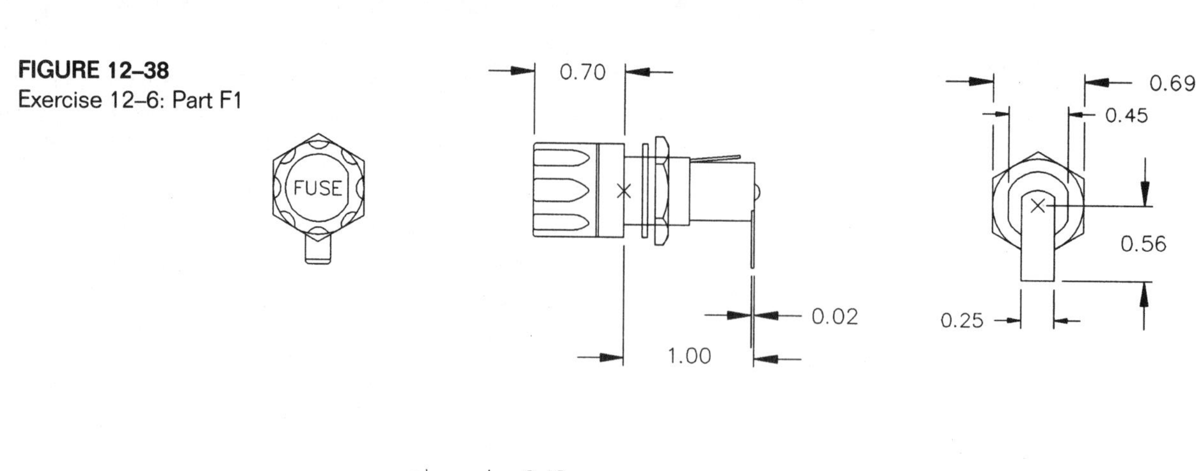

FIGURE 12–38
Exercise 12–6: Part F1

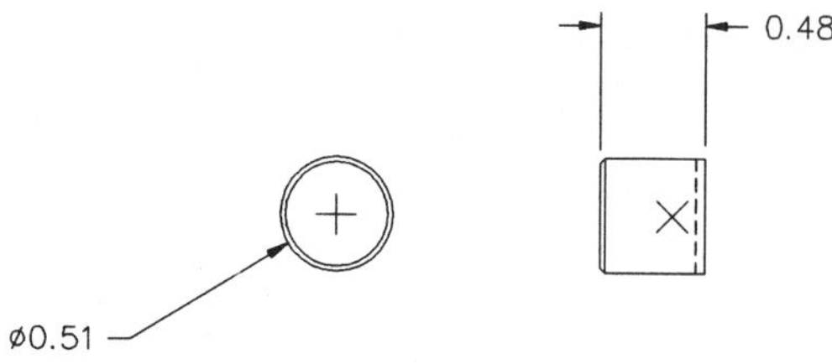

FIGURE 12–39
Exercise 12–6: Knob

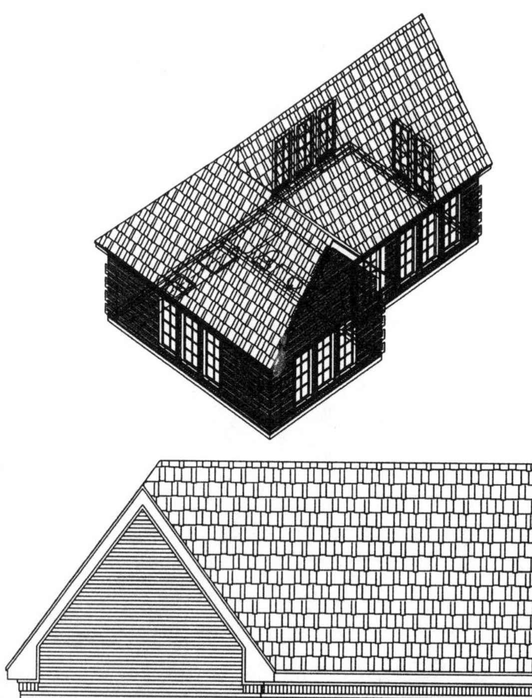

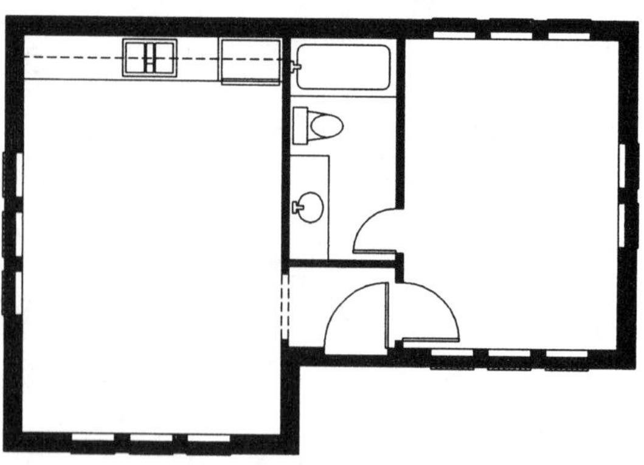

FIGURE 12–40
Exercise 12–7

12–8. 1. Make a solid model of the C-clamp shown in Figure 12–41.
2. Use the dimensions shown to draw the object full size. Use three viewports as shown in Figure 12–41. Your final drawing should look like that figure without dimensions.
3. Plot the drawing to fit on an 11″ × 8.5″ sheet.

12–9. 1. Make a solid model of the micrometer shown in Figure 12–42.
2. Use the dimensions shown to draw the object full size.
3. Use three viewports as shown in Figure 12–42. Your final drawing should look like that figure without dimensions.
4. Plot the drawing to fit on an 11″ × 8.5″ sheet.

12–10. 1. Make a solid model of the test gauge shown in Figure 12–43.
2. Measure the object shown in that figure and make your model that size. Your final drawing should look like the 3-D view in Figure 12–43.
3. Use the SANSSERIF BOLD font (SASBO ___) for letters and numbers on the gauge. Your final drawing should look like the 3-D view shown in Figure 12–43.

The following instructions should make this exercise a little easier:

Move the numbers and markings on the gauge slightly above the gauge face (.04) as shown in the sectional view. Otherwise they will be hidden when you use the Hide: command.

Construct the gauge body sectional view with a closed polyline that shows a metal thickness of .02. Then use Revolve: to construct the gauge body.

Draw the pointer so that it is located .04 above the gauge numbers and markings.

Draw the gauge face with a circle that has a radius that is .05 smaller than the inside radius of the gauge body. This will allow the lip on the gauge to show after you have used the Hide: command.

Because solids such as arrowheads, donuts, and areas drawn with the Solid: command will not fill in a 3-D view, you may have to redraw the pointer in paper space with the Line: or Pline: command and an ellipse and use a hatch pattern to obtain a solid pointer as shown in the figure.

Plot the drawing full scale on an 11″ × 8.5″ sheet.

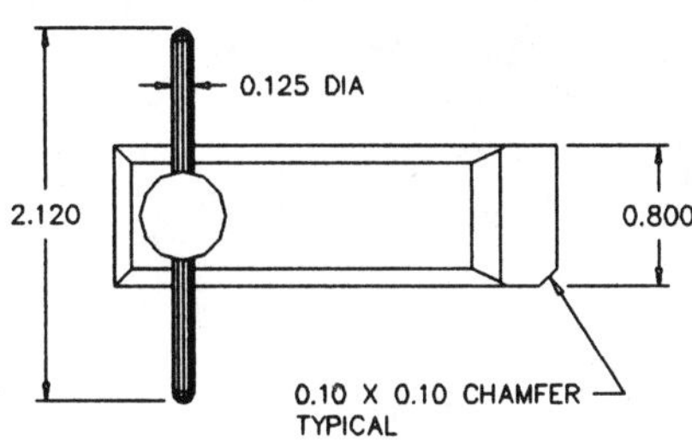

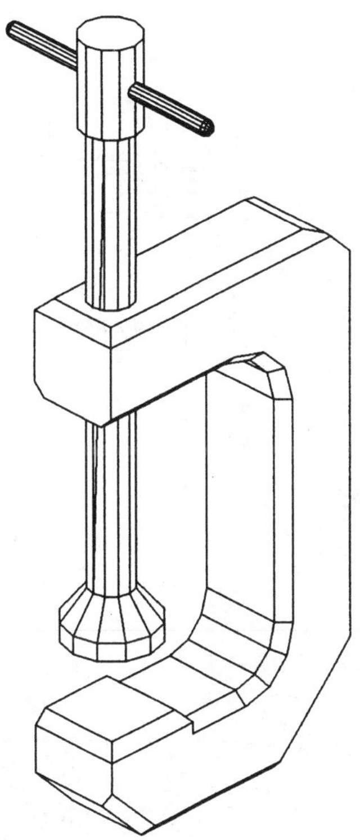

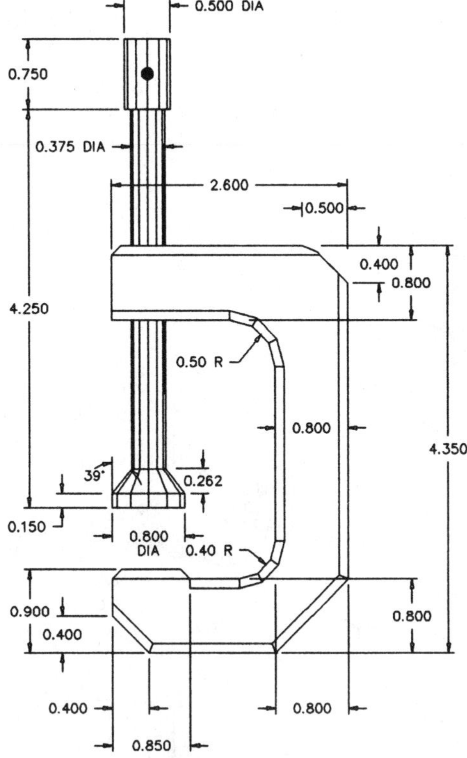

FIGURE 12–41
Exercise 12–8

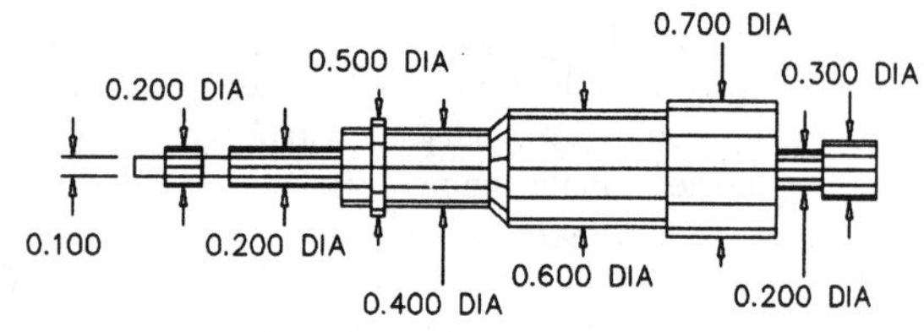

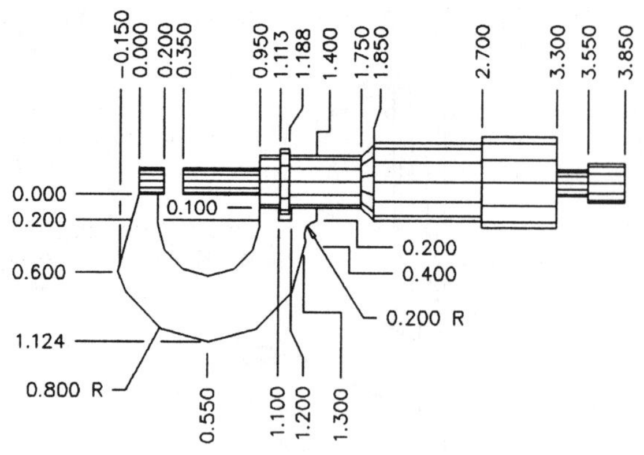

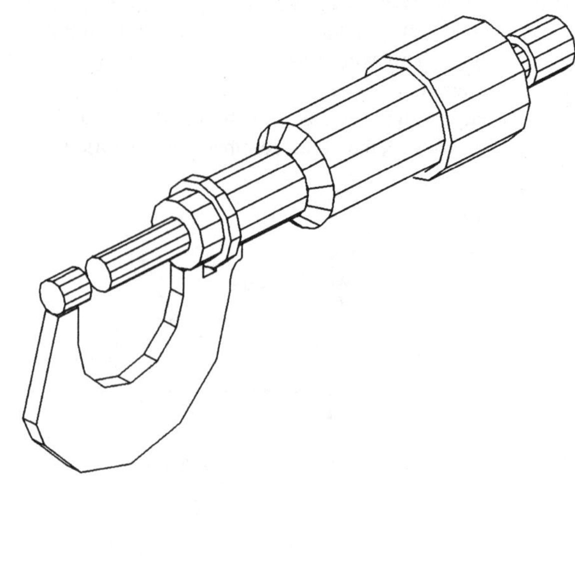

FIGURE 12–42
Exercise 12–9

FIGURE 12–43
Exercise 12–10

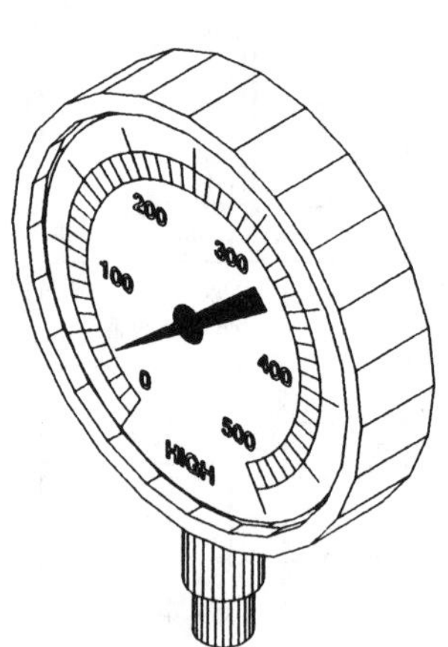

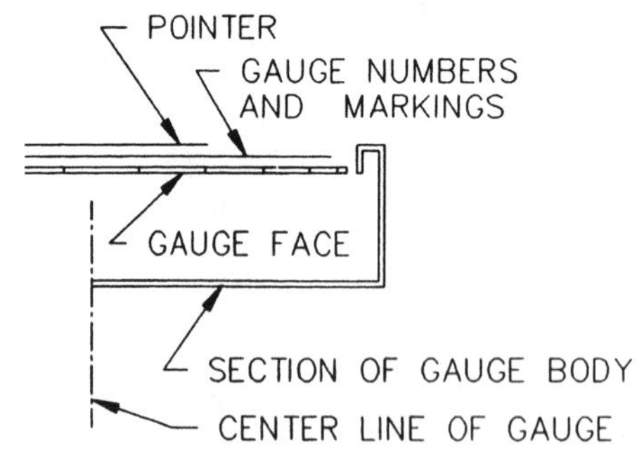

REVIEW QUESTIONS

1. Which option of the Ucsicon: command allows you to move the UCS icon to the selected UCS origin?
   a. ON
   b. OFF
   c. ORigin
   d. Restore
   e. Noorigin
2. Which command allows you to join several touching lines into a single entity?
   a. Chprop:
   b. Pedit:
   c. Offset:
   d. Union:
   e. Mesh:
3. Which option of the UCS: command always returns you to a single viewport?
   a. Restore
   b. Join
   c. One
   d. Delete
   e. SIngle
4. From which menu on the menu bar can the Viewpoints Presets dialog box be selected?
   a. View
   b. Assist
   c. Construct
   d. Options
   e. Tools
5. Which letters when typed from the Command: prompt return the display to model space from paper space?
   a. MODEL
   b. MS
   c. PS
   d. PASP
   e. MDSP
6. List the command and its option that allows you to create 2 viewports.

   Command: ______________ Option: ______________
7. Write the numbers that you type in response to the Vpoint: prompt that gives you a view similar to an isometric view.

   ______________________ ______________________
8. List the options that Extrude: prompts you for after the object to be extruded has been selected.

   ____
9. Describe how to return to the world UCS after you have used a UCS that has been rotated 90° about the X axis.

   ____
10. List the command that allows you to obtain a view directly above the current UCS.

    ____

13 Editing Solid Models

OBJECTIVES

When you have completed this chapter, you will be able to:

- □ Change the color, layer, location, and size of a solid.
- □ Move solids so that a face is aligned with another solid's face.
- □ Move solids from one axis to another.
- □ Explode solids to form separate regions.
- □ Describe how to change, copy, move, mirror, rotate, and scale solids using basic AutoCAD CONSTRUCT and MODIFY commands.

INTRODUCTION

Those of you who have used the Advanced Modeling Extension (AME) in earlier versions will find several useful commands missing in Release 13. The commands that allowed you to change the size and position of primitives within a composite solid and to separate a composite solid into primitives are no longer available. Once you adjust to the fact that they are no longer there, you will quickly find other ways to do what is necessary. Solids are much simpler in Release 13 than in AME, and AutoDesk Designer (covered in Chapters 14 through 17) allows you to do all the things you could do in AME and much more.

Being able to modify a composite solid is as important as being able to create it. Although there are times when it is faster to delete the entire model and start over, being able to efficiently modify the solid is essential. The exercises in this chapter give you practice in using the following standard AutoCAD commands for modifying solids:

Copy:	Change:
Chamfer:	Chprop:
Fillet:	Align:
3Darray:	Scale:
Mirror3D:	Explode:
Rotate3D:	Union:
Modify:	Subtract:

You will need to draw a composite solid as described next so that these commands can be demonstrated.

EXERCISE 13–1, PART 1 DRAWING A COMPOSITE SOLID

Set Up the Drawing

Step 1. On Your Own:

1. Pick New. . . from the menu bar File menu. Name the drawing: 13-1 (your initials).
2. Make the following settings:

UNITS: Decimal; 3 digits to the right of the decimal point

LIMITS: Lower left corner: 0,0
Upper right corner: 11,8.5

GRID: .5

SNAP: .05

STYLE: STANDARD; FONT: SIMPLEX; HEIGHT: 0

Create the following layers:

LAYER NAME	COLOR	LINETYPE
Y	YELLOW	CONTINUOUS
R	RED	CONTINUOUS
G	GREEN	CONTINUOUS

Set layer Y current.

3. Use the Vports: command to make two vertical viewports. Zoom: All in both viewports.
4. Use the Vpoint: command to set a 1,−1,1 viewpoint for the right viewport.

Construct the Base Containing Two Chamfered Edges and Four Round Holes

Step 2. Draw the base, Figure 13–1.

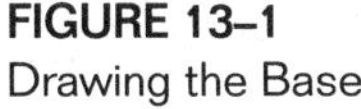

FIGURE 13–1
Drawing the Base

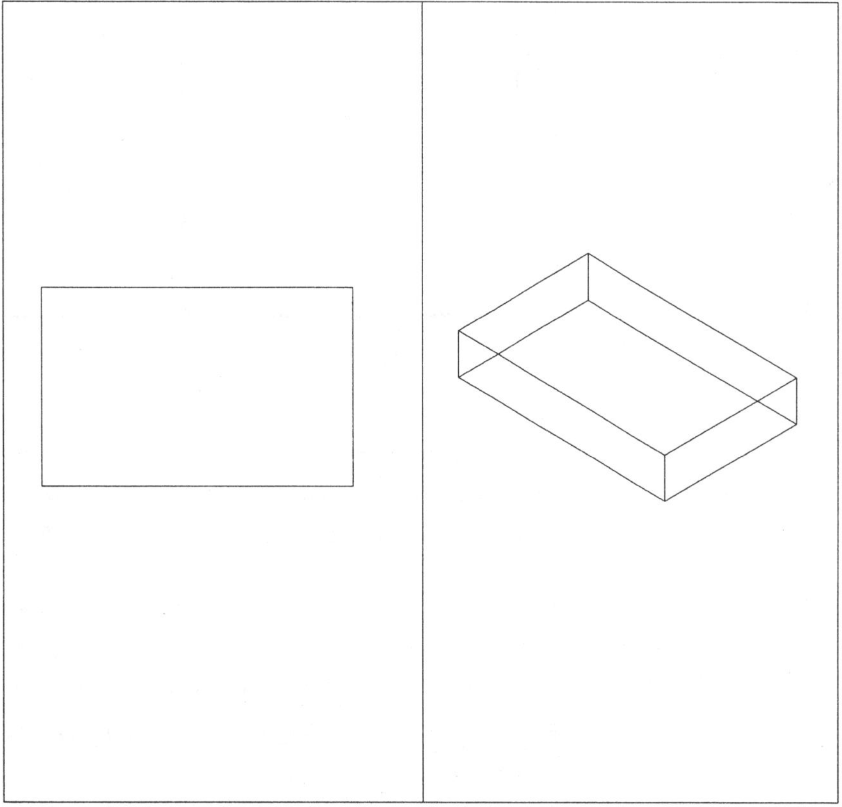

Prompt	Response
Command:	**Box:**
Center/<Corner of box> <0,0,0>:	*Type:* **2,3** ↵

Prompt	Response
Cube/Length/<Other corner>:	*Type:* **@4,2.5** ↵
Height:	*Type:* **.75** ↵
The box is shown as Figure 13–1.	

Zoom a window to get closer to the base if necessary.

Step 3. Chamfer two edges.

Prompt	Response
Command:	**Chamfer:**
Polyline/Distance/Angle/Trim/Method/ <Select first line>: Select base surface:	**Pick the right end of the box and** *Type:* **N** ↵ **until the right end surface of the box is highlighted (Figure 13–2).**

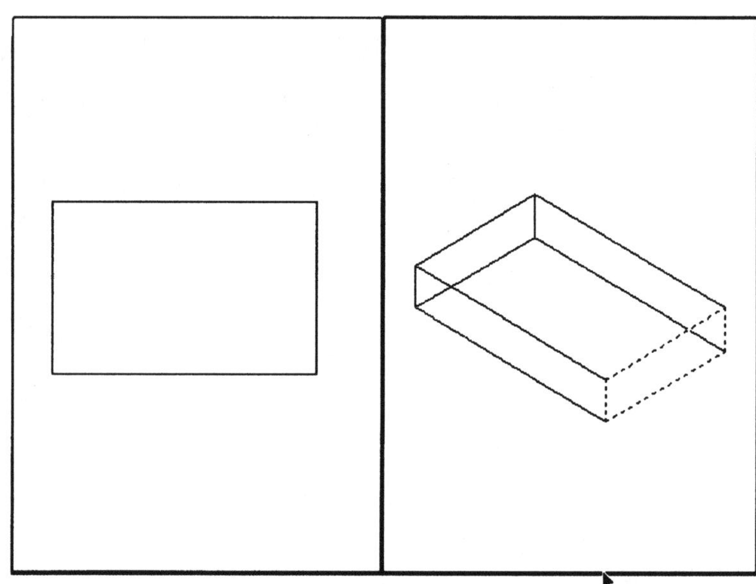

FIGURE 13–2
Highlighted Surface to Be Chamfered

Prompt	Response
Next/<OK>:	↵
Enter base surface distance:	*Type:* **.5** ↵
Enter other surface distance <0.500>:	↵
Loop/<Select edge>:	**Pick the right vertical edge of the base surface.**
Loop/<Select edge>:	**Pick the left vertical edge of the base surface.**

The two edges should be chamfered as shown in Figure 13–3.

Step 4. Make two holes in this solid and place them on the R layer.

Set layer R current.

Prompt	Response
Command:	**UCS:**
Origin/ZAxis/3point/OBject/View/ X/Y/Z/Prev/Restore/Save/Del? <World>	*Type:* **O** ↵

FIGURE 13–3
Chamfered Edges

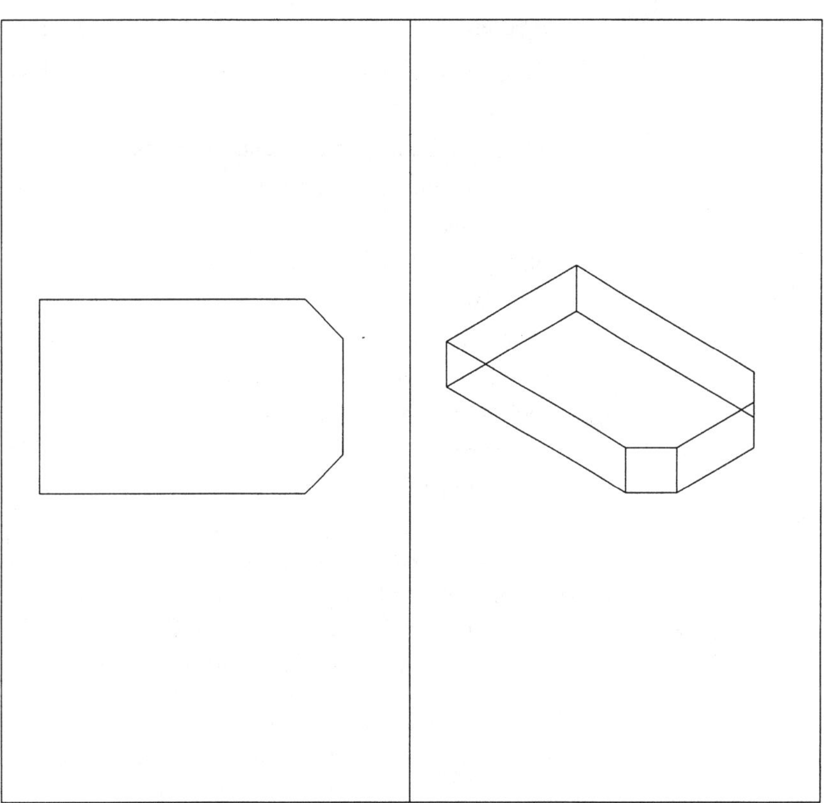

Origin point <0,0,0>:	**Osnap-ENDpoint**
of	**Pick the corner shown in Figure 13–4.**
Command:	**Cylinder:**
Elliptical/<center point><0,0,0>:	*Type:* **3,.5** ↵
Diameter/<Radius>:	*Type:* **.25** ↵
Center of other end/<Height>:	*Type:* **−1** ↵
Command:	*Type:* **CP** ↵

FIGURE 13–4
Moving the UCS Origin

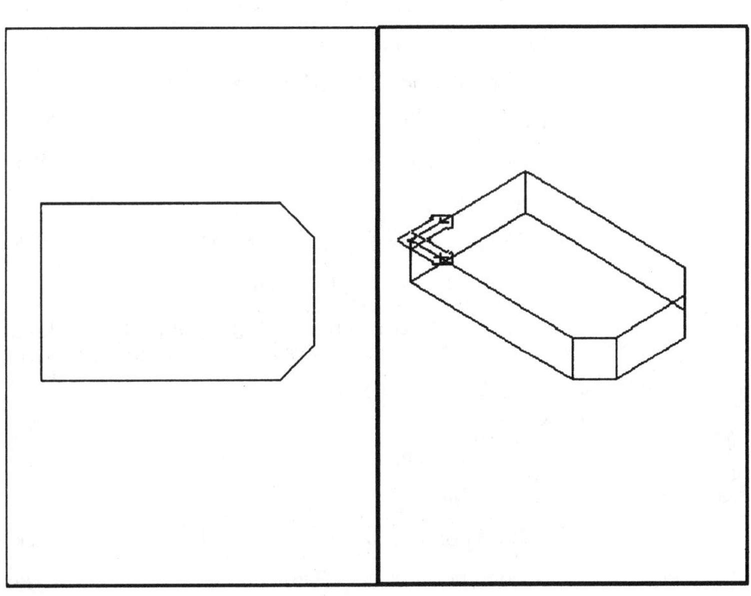

Prompt	Response
Select objects:	Pick the cylinder.
Select objects:	↵
<Base point or displacement>/Multiple:	Pick any point.
Second point of displacement:	*Type:* **@0,1.5** ↵
Command:	**Subtrac:**
Select solids and regions to subtract from . . . Select objects:	**Pick the box.**
Select objects:	↵
Select objects to subtract . . . Select objects:	**Pick the two holes.**
Select objects:	↵

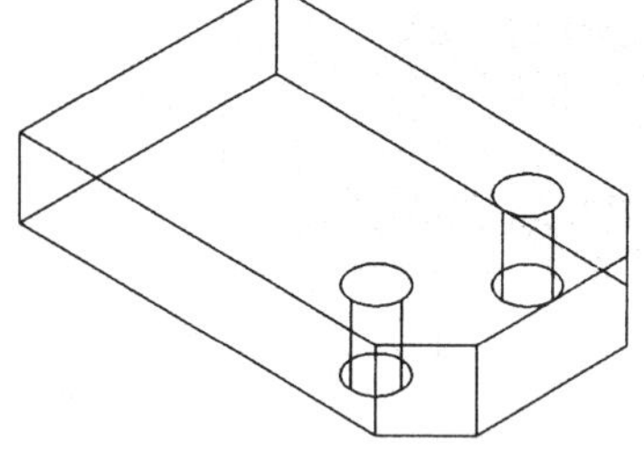

FIGURE 13–5
The Composite Solid

The two holes and the chamfered box are now one composite solid, Figure 13–5. Notice that the two cylinders that were on the R layer became part of the box when they were subtracted and are now on the Y layer. Any edit command such as Move: can be used to move the whole solid, but if you need to delete or change the size or position of the two holes you must now fill in the existing holes, make new cylinders, and subtract them.

You will learn to edit solids in this chapter by filling in the existing holes, making new cylinders, and subtracting them to move the holes 1.5″ toward the left side of the base.

EXERCISE 13–1, PART 2
MOVE THE TWO HOLES 1.5″ TOWARD THE LEFT END OF THE BASE, MAKE TWO SQUARE HOLES IN THE RIGHT END OF THE BASE, CHANGE THE SIZES OF THE TWO ROUND HOLES, AND CHANGE THE SIZES OF THE TWO CHAMFERS

Edit the Holes in the Base

Step 1. Fill in the existing holes.

Move the Two Holes

Prompt	Response
Command:	**Cylinder:**
Elliptical/<center point><0,0,0>:	*Type:* **3,.5** ↵
Diameter/<Radius>:	*Type:* **.25** ↵
Center of other end/<Height>:	*Type:* **−.75** ↵
Command:	*Type:* **CP** ↵
Select objects:	**Pick the cylinder.**
Select objects:	↵
<Base point or displacement>/Multiple:	Pick any point.
Second point of displacement:	*Type:* **@0,1.5** ↵

Step 2. Copy the two cylinders to their new location (Figure 13–6).

Prompt	Response
Command:	*Type:* **CP** ↵
Select objects:	**Pick the two cylinders.**
Select objects:	↵
<Base point or displacement>/Multiple:	Pick any point.
Second point of displacement:	*Type:* **@1.5<180** ↵

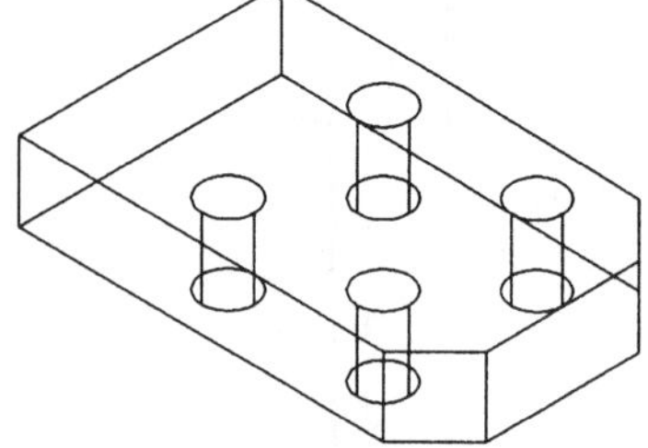

FIGURE 13–6
Copying the Two Cylinders

Step 3. Unify the front two holes with the base.

Prompt	Response
Command:	**Union:**
Select objects:	**Pick the base and the front two cylinders.**

Both cylinders have now been moved 1.5″ toward the left side of the box. The holes could have been filled in with one box or any other shape of the correct height.

Replace the Front Two Round Holes with Square Holes in a Slightly Different Location (Figure 13–7)

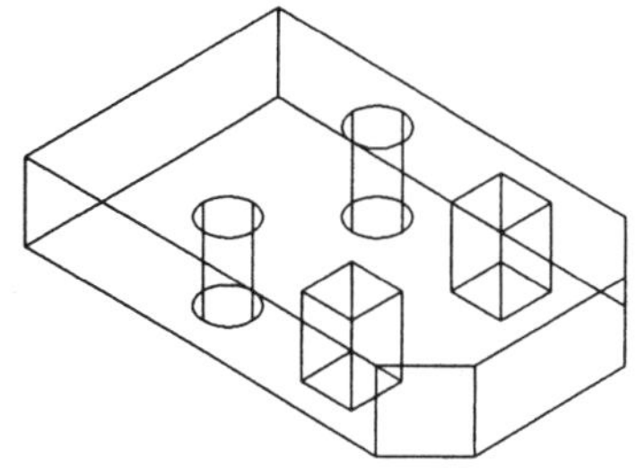

FIGURE 13–7
Square Holes Added

Step 4. Draw a square.

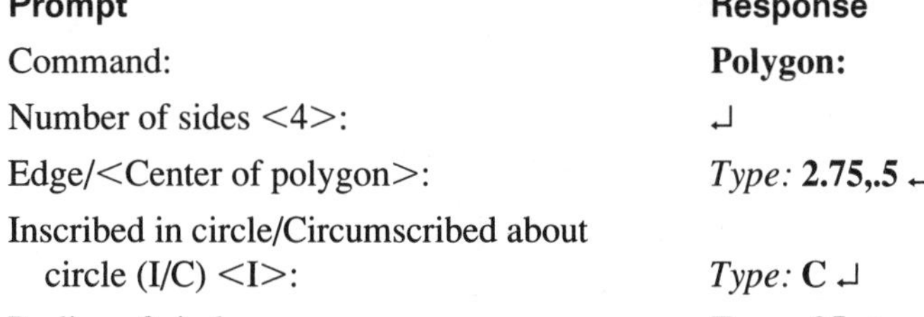

Prompt	Response
Command:	**Polygon:**
Number of sides <4>:	↵
Edge/<Center of polygon>:	*Type:* **2.75,.5** ↵
Inscribed in circle/Circumscribed about circle (I/C) <I>:	*Type:* **C** ↵
Radius of circle:	*Type:* **.25** ↵

Step 5. Extrude the square.

Prompt	Response
Command:	**Extrude:**
Select objects:	**Pick the square.**
Select objects:	↵
Height of extrusion:	*Type:* **−.75** ↵
Extrusion taper angle <0>:	↵

Step 6. Copy the extruded square.

Prompt	Response
Command:	*Type:* **CP** ↵
Select objects:	**Pick the extruded square.**
Select objects:	↵
<Base point or displacement>/Multiple:	Pick any point.
Second point of displacement:	*Type:* **@1.5<90** ↵

Step 7. Subtract the extruded squares from the base.

Prompt	Response
Command:	**Subtrac:**
Select solids and regions to subtract from . . . Select objects:	**Pick the base.**
Select objects:	↵
Select objects to subtract . . . Select objects:	**Pick the two extruded squares.**
Select objects:	↵

Change the Sizes of the Round Holes by Making One Larger (.30 Radius) and One Smaller (.20 Radius)

Making the hole larger is easy: just make a larger cylinder in the same location and subtract it.

Step 8. Draw the larger cylinder.

Prompt	Response
Command:	**Cylinder:**
Elliptical/<center point><0,0,0>:	*Type:* **1.5,.5** ↵
Diameter/<Radius>:	*Type:* **.3** ↵
Center of other end/<Height>:	*Type:* **−.75** ↵

Before you subtract this cylinder, copy it to the center of the other hole and use it to fill in the other hole. Then make another cylinder of .20 radius in the same location as the second hole, unify the base with the fill-in hole and subtract both holes, Figure 13–8.

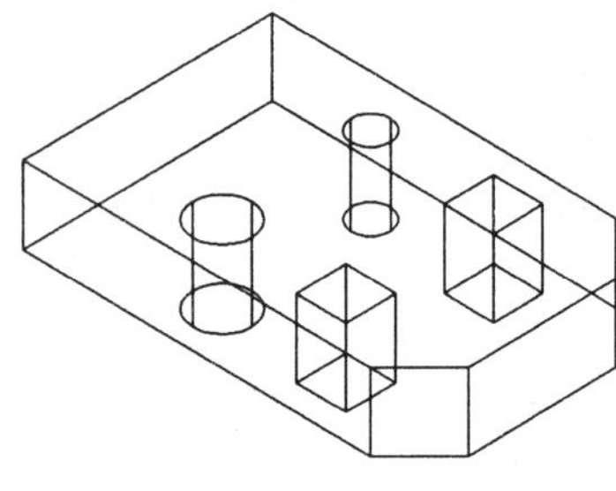

FIGURE 13–8
The Base with Two Modified Holes, One Larger and One Smaller

Step 9. Copy the cylinder to the center of the other hole.

Prompt	Response
Command:	*Type:* **CP** ↵
Select objects:	**Pick the new cylinder.**
Select objects:	↵
<Base point or displacement>/Multiple:	**Pick any point.**
Second point of displacement:	*Type:* **@1.5<90** ↵

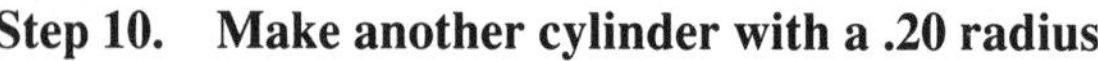

Step 10. Make another cylinder with a .20 radius.

Prompt	Response
Command:	**Cylinder:**
Elliptical/<center point><0,0,0>:	*Type:* **1.5,2** ↵
Diameter/<Radius>:	*Type:* **.2** ↵
Center of other end/<Height>:	*Type:* **−.75** ↵

Step 11. Unify the base and the copied cylinder.

Prompt	Response
Command:	**Union:**
Select objects:	**Pick the base and the copied .3 radius cylinder.**

Step 12. Subtract the two new cylinders.

Prompt	Response
Command:	**Subtrac:**
Select solids and regions to subtract from . . . Select objects:	**Pick the base.**
Select objects:	↵
Select objects to subtract . . . Select objects:	**Pick the .2 radius cylinder and the .3 radius cylinder.**
Select objects:	↵

The base should appear as shown in Figure 13–8.

Edit the Chamfers

Make One of the Chamfered Edges Larger (.75 for Both Distances) and One Smaller (.375 for Both Distances)

This presents a different problem from the one involving the holes. Both chamfers must be filled in before the new chamfers can be created. In this example an extruded polyline will be used to fill in the chamfers.

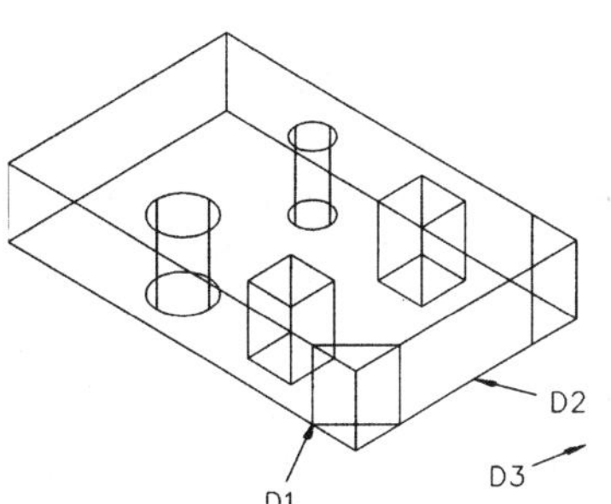

FIGURE 13–9
Filling In the Chamfers

Step 13. Draw the polyline.

Prompt	Response
Command:	**Pline:**
From point:	*Type:* **END** ↵
of	**D1** (Figure 13–9)
Arc/Close/Halfwidth/Length/Undo/ Width/<Endpoint of line>:	*Type:* **@.5<0** ↵
Arc/Close/Halfwidth/Length/Undo/ Width/<Endpoint of line>:	*Type:* **@.5<90** ↵
Arc/Close/Halfwidth/Length/Undo/ Width/<Endpoint of line>:	*Type:* **C** ↵

Step 14. Extrude the polyline.

Prompt	Response
Command:	**Extrude:**
Select objects:	**Pick the polyline.**
Select objects:	↵
Height of extrusion:	*Type:* **.75** ↵
Extrusion taper angle <0>:	↵

Step 15. Mirror the extruded polyline.

Prompt	Response
Command:	**Mirror:**
Select objects:	**Pick the extruded polyline.**
First point of mirror line:	*Type:* **MID** ↵
of	**D2** (Figure 13–9)
Second point:	**D3** (Be sure ortho is on when you pick D3.)

Step 16. Unify the extruded polylines with the base.

Prompt	Response
Command:	**Union:**
Select objects:	**Pick the two extruded plines and the base.**

Step 17. Construct the .75 chamfer.

Prompt	Response
Command:	**Chamfer:**
Polyline/Distance/Angle/Trim/Method/ <Select first line>:	
Select base surface:	**Pick the right end of the base and** *Type:* **N** ↵ **until the right end surface of the box is highlighted.**
Next/<OK>:	↵
Enter base surface distance:	*Type:* **.75** ↵
Enter other surface distance <0.500>:	*Type:* **.75** ↵
Loop/<Select edge>:	**Pick the left vertical edge of the base surface.**
Loop/<Select edge>:	↵

Step 18. Construct the .375 chamfer.

Prompt	Response
Command:	↵
Polyline/Distance/Angle/Trim/Method/ <Select first line>:	
Select base surface:	**Pick the right end of the base and** *Type:* **N ↵ until the right end surface of the box is highlighted.**
Next/<OK>:	↵
Enter base surface distance:	*Type:* **.375 ↵**
Enter other surface distance <0.500>:	*Type:* **.375 ↵**
Loop/<Select edge>:	**Pick the right vertical edge of the base surface.**
Loop/<Select edge>:	↵

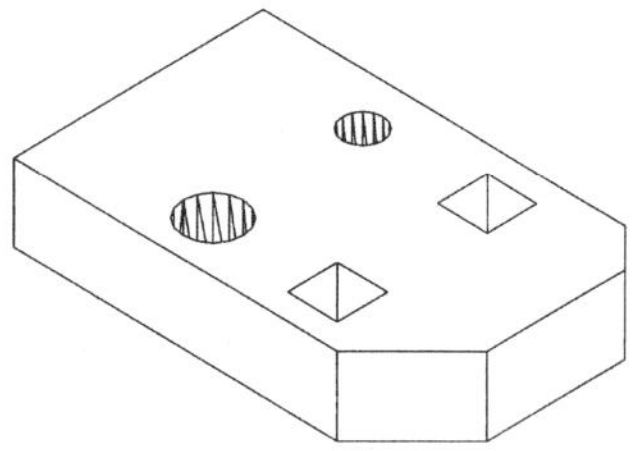

FIGURE 13–10
The Complete Modified Base

Step 19. Remove hidden lines.

Prompt	Response
Command:	**Hide:**

The model should appear as shown in Figure 13–10.

Create the Back of the Model

EXERCISE 13–1, PART 3
DRAWING THE BACK OF THE MODEL AND MOVING IT TO ITS CORRECT POSITION

Step 1. Set Layer R current.

Step 2. Draw the back of the model in the plan view, Figure 13–11.

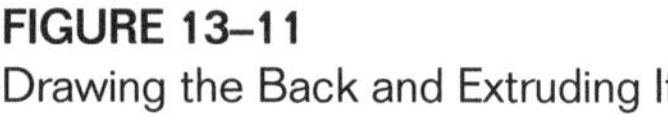

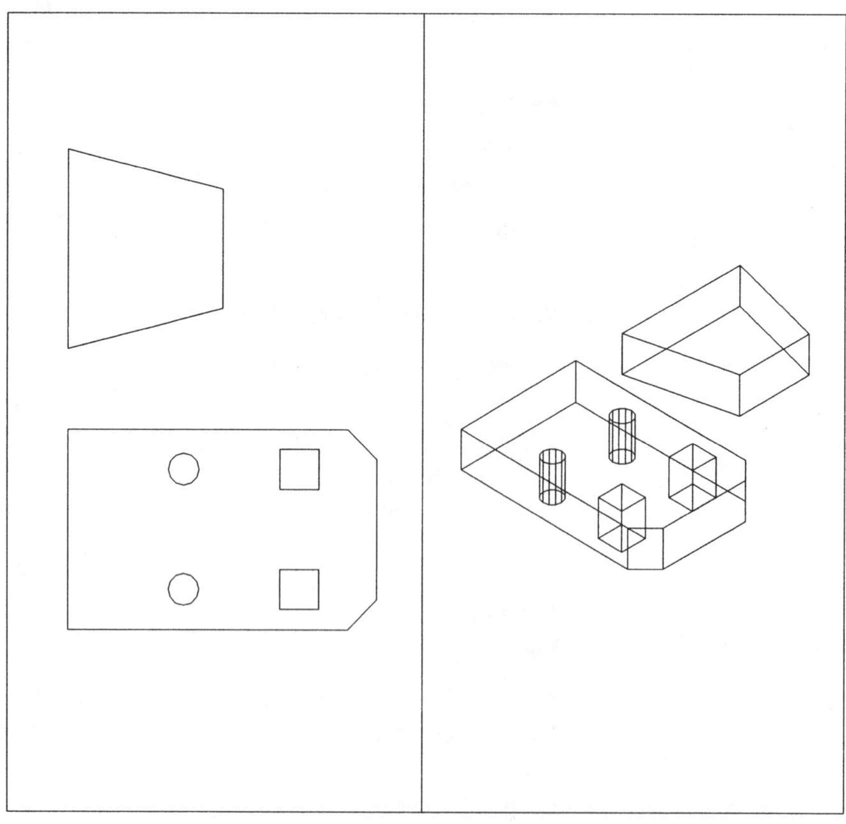

FIGURE 13–11
Drawing the Back and Extruding It

Prompt	Response
Command:	**Pline:**
From point:	*Type:* **0,3.5** ↵ **(Or pick any point in the approximate location shown.)**
Arc/Close/Halfwidth/Length/Undo/ Width/<Endpoint of line>:	*Type:* **@2,.5** ↵
Arc/Close/Halfwidth/Length/Undo/ Width/<Endpoint of line>:	*Type:* **@0,1.5** ↵
Arc/Close/Halfwidth/Length/Undo/ Width/<Endpoint of line>:	*Type:* **@−2,.5** ↵
Arc/Close/Halfwidth/Length/Undo/ Width/<Endpoint of line>:	*Type:* **C** ↵

Step 3. Extrude the polyline.

Prompt	Response
Command:	**Extrude:**
Select objects:	Pick the polyline.
Select objects:	↵
Height of extrusion:	*Type:* **.75** ↵
Extrusion taper angle <0>:	↵

Step 4. Move the back to its upright position on the base.

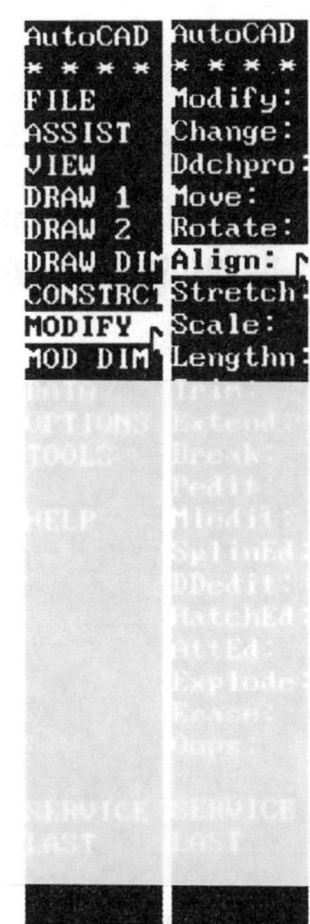

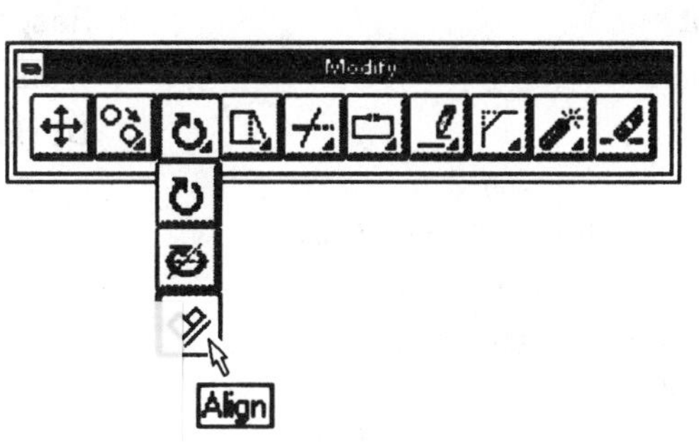

Prompt	Response
Command:	**Align:**
Select objects:	Pick the back.
Select objects:	↵
1st source point:	*Type:* **END** ↵
of	**D1** (Figure 13–12)
1st destination point:	*Type:* **END** ↵
of	**D2**
2nd source point:	*Type:* **END** ↵
of	**D3**
2nd destination point:	*Type:* **END** ↵
of	**D4**
3rd source point:	*Type:* **END** ↵
of	**D5**
3rd destination point:	*Type:* **NEA** ↵
of	**D6**

The model should appear as shown in Figure 13–13.

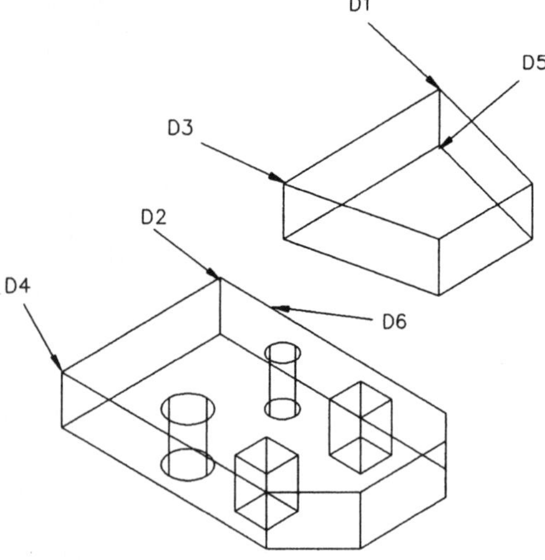

FIGURE 13–12
Moving the Back to Its Correct Position Using the Align: Command

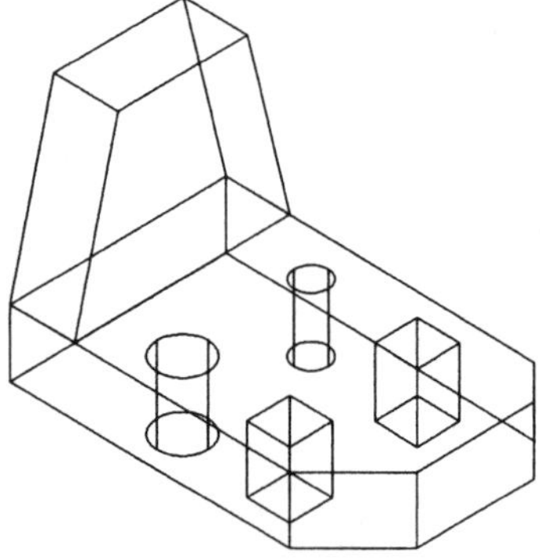

FIGURE 13–13
The Back in Its Correct Position

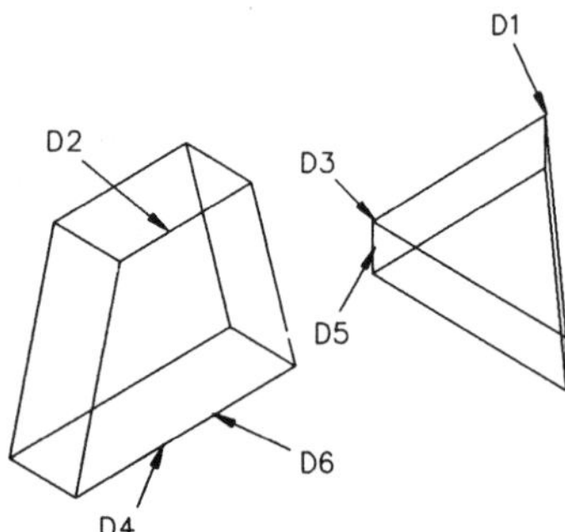

FIGURE 13–14
Using Align to Move the Web Support

Create the Web Support

EXERCISE 13–1, PART 4
DRAWING THE WEB SUPPORT AND MOVING IT TO ITS CORRECT POSITION

Step 1. Draw the web support.

Prompt	Response
Command:	**Pline:**
From point:	**D1 (Figure 13–14). (Pick any point in the approximate location shown.)**
Arc/Close/Halfwidth/Length/Undo/ Width/<Endpoint of line>:	*Type:* **@2<−90 ↵**
Arc/Close/Halfwidth/Length/Undo/ Width/<Endpoint of line>:	*Type:* **@2.25<0 ↵**
Arc/Close/Halfwidth/Length/Undo/ Width/<Endpoint of line>:	*Type:* **C ↵**

Step 2. Extrude the polyline.

Prompt	Response
Command:	**Extrude:**
Select objects:	**Pick the polyline.**
Select objects:	↵
Height of extrusion:	*Type:* **.5 ↵**
Extrusion taper angle <0>:	↵

Step 3. On Your Own:

Zoom in close to the model and turn off the Y layer to pick points for the Align: command.

Step 4. Move the web support to its correct position.

Prompt	Response
Command:	**Align:**
Select objects:	**Pick the web.**
Select objects:	↵
1st source point:	*Type:* **END ↵**

of	**D1** (Figure 13–14)
1st destination point:	*Type:* **NEA** ↵
of	**D2**
2nd source point:	*Type:* **MID** ↵
of	**D5**
2nd destination point:	*Type:* **MID** ↵
of	**D6**
3rd source point:	*Type:* **END** ↵
of	**D3**
3rd destination point:	*Type:* **END** ↵
of	**D4**

Step 5. On Your Own:

1. Turn on the Y layer.
2. Use the Union: command to unify the model into a single object. When you select objects, pick the base first so the entire model will be on the Y layer. The object you pick first determines the layer on which the unified model is placed.
3. Use the Hide: command to make sure the model is as it should be.

The model should appear as shown in Figure 13–15.
The details of the options of the Align: command follow:

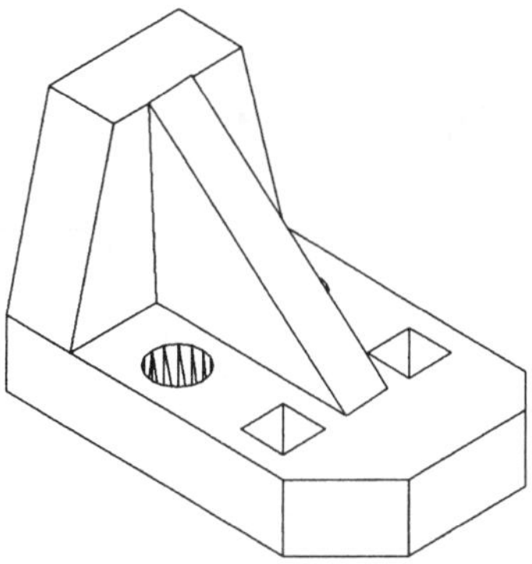

FIGURE 13–15
The Model with the Web Support in Place

Align:

The Align: command allows you to move a solid or set of solids using up to three source and destination points.

One set of points: If you use only one source and one destination point, the object is simply moved from one point to another. To use one set of destination points, press ↵ when AutoCAD asks for the second source point.

Two sets of points: If you use two sets of source and destination points, the object is moved and rotated about one axis. To use two sets of destination points, press ↵ when AutoCAD asks for the third source point.

Three sets of points: If you use three sets of source and destination points, the object is moved and rotated about two axes.

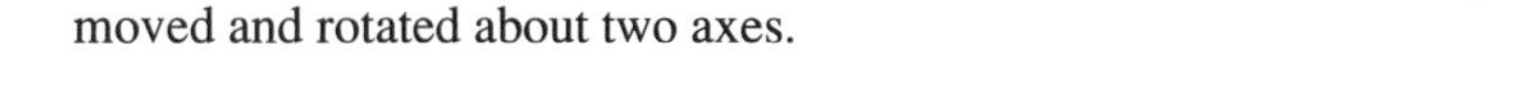

Create the Cylindrical Mount to Complete the Model

EXERCISE 13–1, PART 5
DRAWING THE CYLINDRICAL MOUNT

Step 1. Draw two construction lines to locate a cylinder to be placed on the bottom of the model.

This cylinder must be located at the MIDpoint of a construction line drawn from the center of one of the square holes to the center of one of the round holes located diagonally opposite the square hole.

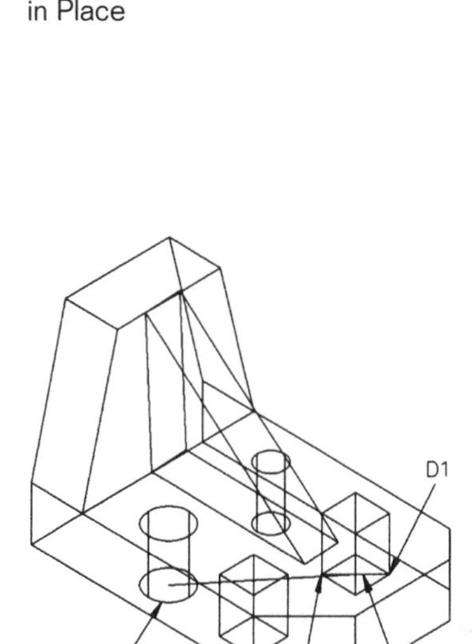

FIGURE 13–16
Drawing Construction Lines

Prompt	Response
Command:	**Line:**
LINE From point:	*Type:* **END** ↵
of	**D1** (Figure 13–16)
To point:	*Type:* **END** ↵
of	**D2**
To point:	↵

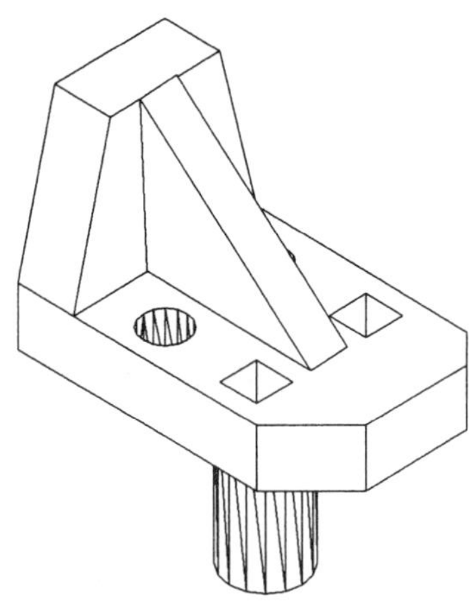

FIGURE 13–17
The Final Model

Prompt	Response
Command:	↵
LINE From point:	**Osnap-MIDpoint**
of	**D3** (Figure 13–16)
To point:	**Osnap-CENter**
of	**D4**

Step 2. On Your Own:

1. Draw a cylinder with its center point as the midpoint of the construction line you just drew from the center of the cylinder to the center of the square. Make it with a .5 radius, with a height of −2.00.
2. Use Union: to combine all shapes into a single model.
3. Erase all construction lines.
4. Use Hide: to render the model.

The final model should look like Figure 13–17.

Create a New Model

EXERCISE 13–1, PART 6 MAKING A COPY OF THE MODEL, USING THE EXPLODE: COMMAND TO MAKE SEPARATE REGIONS, AND USING SOME OF THOSE REGIONS TO CREATE A NEW MODEL AND A SAMPLE HATCHED REGION

Form the New Model without Corrections

Step 1. On Your Own:

1. Copy the model to the approximate location shown in Figure 13–18.
2. Set layer G current.

FIGURE 13–18
Copying the Completed Model

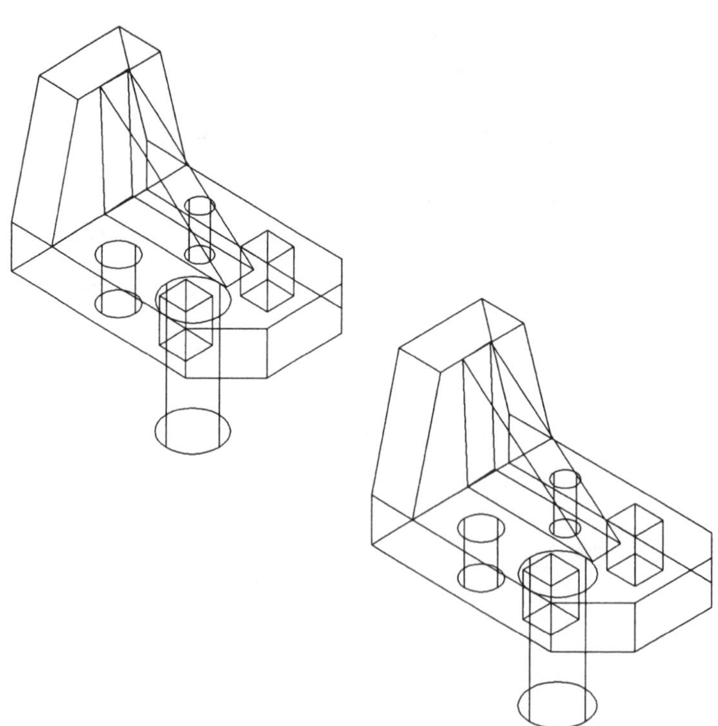

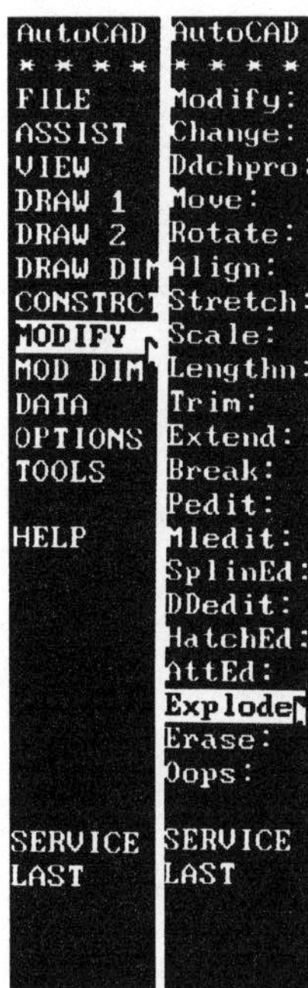

Step 2. Explode the copied model.

Prompt	**Response**
Command:	**Explode:**
Select objects:	**Pick the copied model.**

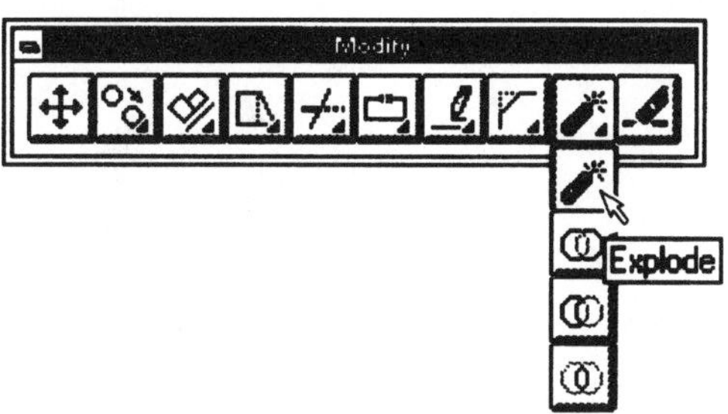

Notice that the exploded regions are placed on the layer that is current when the Explode: command is used.

Every surface on the copied model is now a region, and the copied model no longer exists.

Step 3. On Your Own:

1. Erase all the regions except those shown in Figure 13–19.

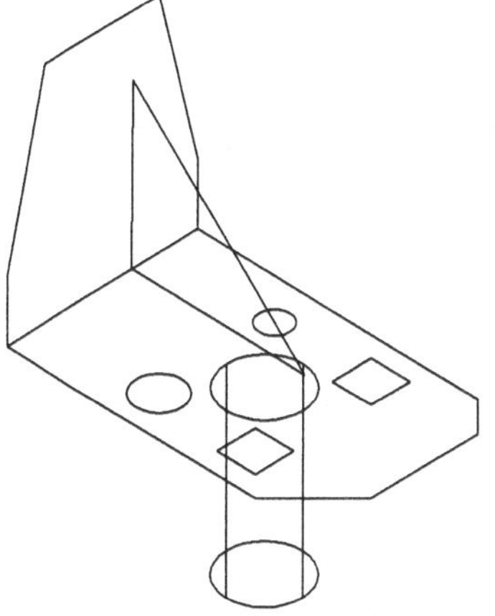

FIGURE 13–19
Saving These Regions and the Bottotm Cylinder

2. Copy the base region 4″ in the Y direction as shown in Figure 13–20.

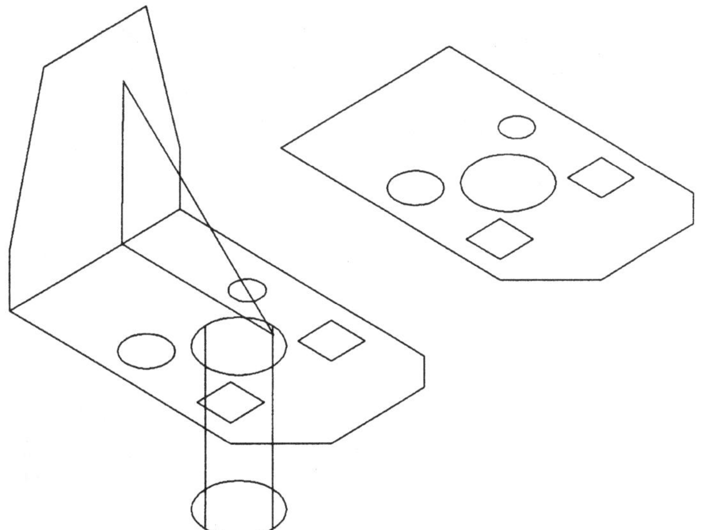

FIGURE 13–20
Copying the Base Region

3. Hatch the copied region using the ANSI31 pattern, Scale 1.000, Angle 0, as shown in Figure 13–21.

FIGURE 13–21
Hatching the Copied Region

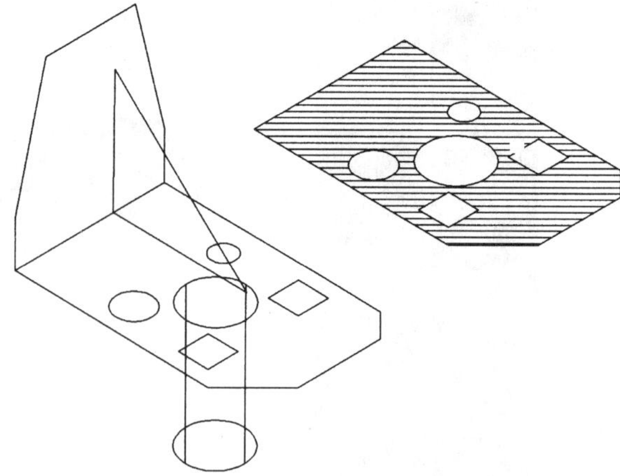

4. Select the front viewpoint for the left viewport as shown in Figure 13–22.

FIGURE 13–22
Selecting the Front Viewpoint for the Left Viewport

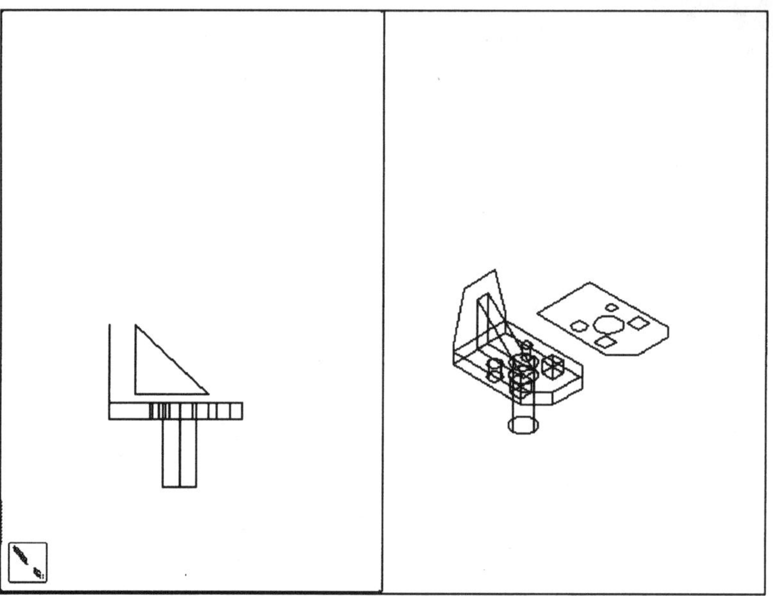

5. Extrude the region forming the web positive .5 and the base region negative .5 as shown in Figure 13–23. Positive .5 for the base region may work, but negative .5 formed the extrusion upward in my case.

FIGURE 13–23
Extruding the Web and the Base Regions Positive .5″

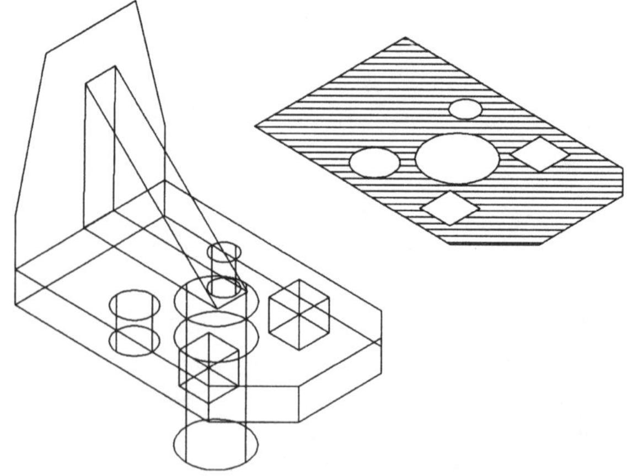

Because the base is now .5 instead of .75, the web is not in the correct location, and the angles on the back are .25 too high.

Correct the Back Region and Extrude It Positive .5

This can be done most easily by changing the back to another layer, turning off all other layers, and locating the UCS on the back plane.

Step 4. Change the back to the R layer.

Prompt	Response
Command:	**Chprop:**
Select objects:	**Pick the back region.**
Change what property (Color/LAyer/ LType/ltScale/Thickness)?	*Type:* **LA** ↵
New layer <G>:	*Type:* **R** ↵

Step 5. Turn off layers G and Y.

Prompt	Response
Command:	↵
LAYER ?/Make/Set/New?ON/OFF/ Color/Ltype/Freeze/Thaw/LOck/ Unlock:	*Type:* **OFF** ↵
Layer name(s) to turn Off:	*Type:* **G,Y**
Really want layer G (the CURRENT layer) off? <N>	Type: **Y** ↵

Step 6. Create a new UCS.

Prompt	Response
Command:	**UCS:**
Origin/ZAxis/3point/OBject/View/X/Y/Z/ Prev/Restore/Save/Del?<World>	*Type:* **3** ↵
Origin point <0,0,0>:	**Osnap-ENDpoint**
of	**D1** (Figure 13–24)
Point on positive portion of the X axis <1.000,0.000,0.000>:	**Osnap-ENDpoint**
of	**D2**
Point on positive Y portion of the UCS XY plane <0.000,1.000,0.000>:	**Osnap-ENDpoint**
of	**D3**

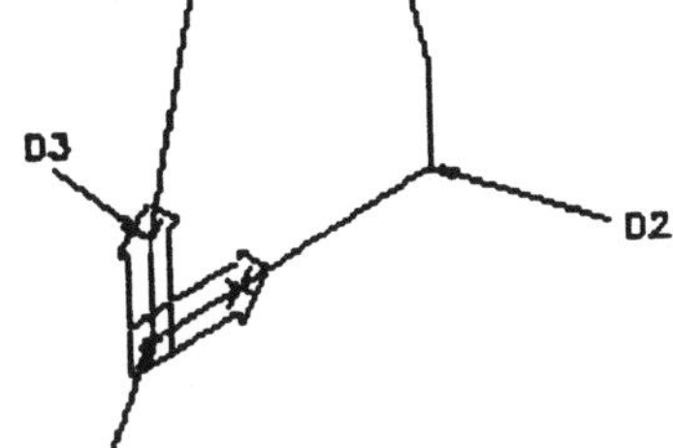

FIGURE 13–24
Locating the UCS

Step 7. Select the plan view of the new UCS.

Prompt	Response
Command:	**Plan:**
<Current UCS>/Ucs/World:	↵
Command:	**Explode:**
Select objects:	**Pick the region forming the back, Figure 13–25.**
Select objects:	↵

Step 8. Stretch the exploded region.

Prompt	Response
Command:	**Stretch:**

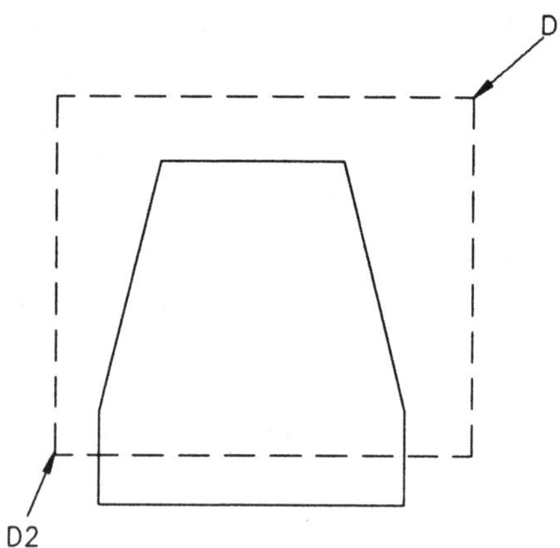

FIGURE 13–25
Stretching the Exploded Region

Prompt	Response
Select objects to stretch by crossing-window or -polygon . . . Select objects:	**D1** (Figure 13–25)
Other corner:	**D2**
Base point or displacement:	**Pick any point.**
Second point of displacement:	*Type:* **@.25<270** ↵

Step 9. Join all lines forming the back into a single polyline.

Prompt	Response
Command:	**Pedit:**
Select polyline:	**Pick any line forming the back.**
Object selected is not a polyline Do you want to turn it into one?<Y>	↵
Close/Join/Width/Edit vertex/Fit/Spline/ Decurve/Ltype gen/Undo/eXit <X>:	*Type:* **J** ↵
Select objects:	**Use a crossing window to select all lines forming the back.**
Select objects:	↵
Close/Join/Width/Edit vertex/Fit/Spline/ Decurve/Ltype gen/Undo/eXit <X>:	↵

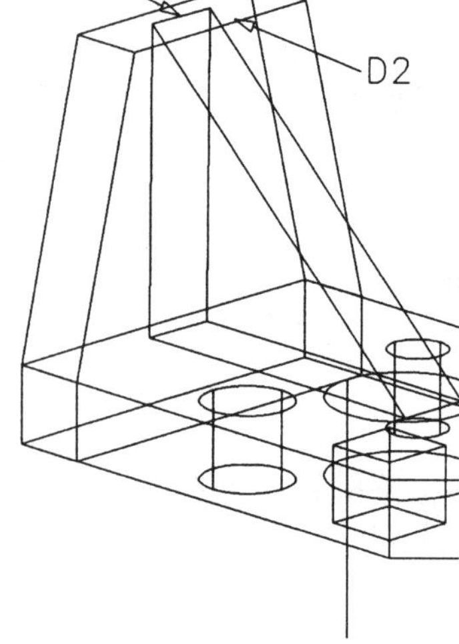

FIGURE 13–26
Moving the Web to Its Correct Location

Step 10. Extrude the polyline.

Prompt	Response
Command:	**Extrude:**
Select objects:	Pick the polyline just created.
Path/<Height of Extrusion>:	**Type: .5** ↵
Extrusion taper angle <0>:	↵

Step 11. On Your Own:
Turn on layer G.

Step 12. Move the web to the correct location.

Prompt	Response
Command:	*Type:* **M** ↵
Select objects:	**Pick the web, Figure 13–26.**
Select objects:	↵

Base point or displacement:	*Type:* **MID** ↵
of	**D1** (Figure 13–26)
Second point of displacement:	*Type:* **MID** ↵
of	**D2**

Step 13. On Your Own:

Combine all parts of the second model into a single object using Union:
Exercise 13–1 is now complete and should appear as shown in Figure 13–27.

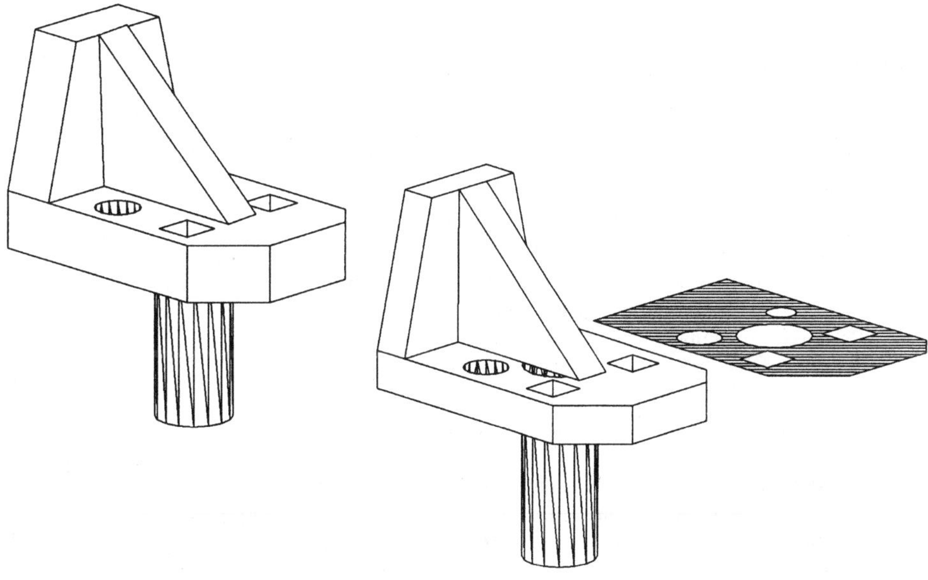

FIGURE 13–27
The Completed Model

Step 14. On Your Own:

1. Set UCS to view, and place your name in the lower right corner.
2. Print Exercise 13–1 using the viewpoint shown in Figure 13–27 at a scale of .5 = 1. Center the plot on an 8.5″ × 11″ sheet. Be sure that the HIDE button on the Plot dialog box has an X in it.
3. Save the drawing in two places and exit.

Now let's talk about other standard AutoCAD commands that may be used to edit solids.

Standard AutoCAD Commands That May Be Used to Edit Solids.

The following standard AutoCAD commands may be used to edit solids:

Array:	Erase:	Rotate:
3Darray:	Mirror:	Rotat3D:
Change:	Mirror3D:	Scale:
Chprop:	Modify:	Select:
Copy:	Move:	Undo:

All these commands may be used in ways similar to those used in 2-D or in AutoCAD standard 3-D drawing. The only difference is that you have to take into account the fact that you are editing a solid shape in three dimensions. For example, you cannot use the Change: command to change the endpoint of a solid as you can the endpoint of a line.

Commands That Cannot Be Used to Edit Solids:

The commands that cannot be used to edit solids are:

Break:
Divide:

Extend:
Measure:
Offset:
Pedit: (can be used after the solid is reduced to a polyline)
Stretch: (can be used to move a solid)
Trim:

These commands stop you with an error message telling you that the command cannot be used on this entity.

The following exercises will give you practice in editing solids.

EXERCISES

13–1. Complete Exercise 13–1 using the steps described in this chapter.

13–2. Edit the solid model drawn in Exercise 11–2.

1. Call up the solid model you drew in Exercise 11-2 and name it 13-2 (your initials). Select New. . . ; type 13-2 (your initials)=A:11-2 (your initials) in the New Drawing Name button if the drawing 11-2 (your initials) is on a floppy disk in the A: drive.
2. Change the radius of the hole in the back upright to .500.
   Move the .25 radius hole in the base .50 in the positive Y direction.
   Make a copy of the .25 radius hole and move the copy 1.00 in the negative Y direction.
   Subtract the copied hole and the original .25 radius hole from the model.
   Delete the two webs.
3. Set UCS to View and place your name in the lower right corner. Plot the drawing full size on a vertical 8.5″ × 11″ sheet. Your final drawing should look like the right side of Figure 13–28 with hidden lines removed.

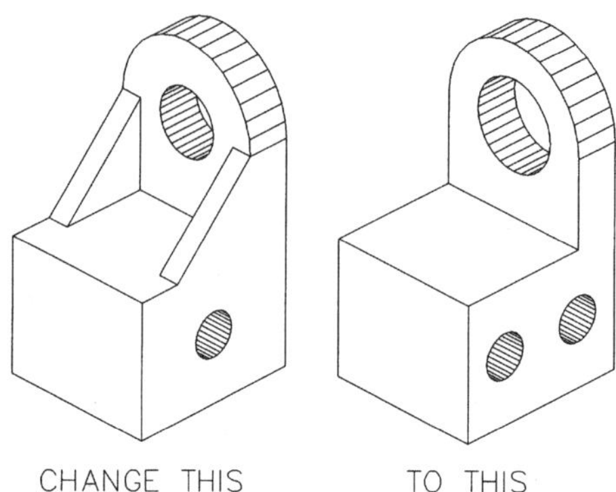

FIGURE 13–28
Exercise 13–2

13–3. Edit the solid model drawn in Exercise 11–3.

1. Call up the solid model, Figure 13–29A, you drew in Exercise 11-3 and name it 13-3 (your initials). Select New. . . ; type 13-3 (your initials)=A:11-3 (your initials) in the New Drawing Name button if the drawing 11-3 (your initials) is on a floppy disk in the A: drive.

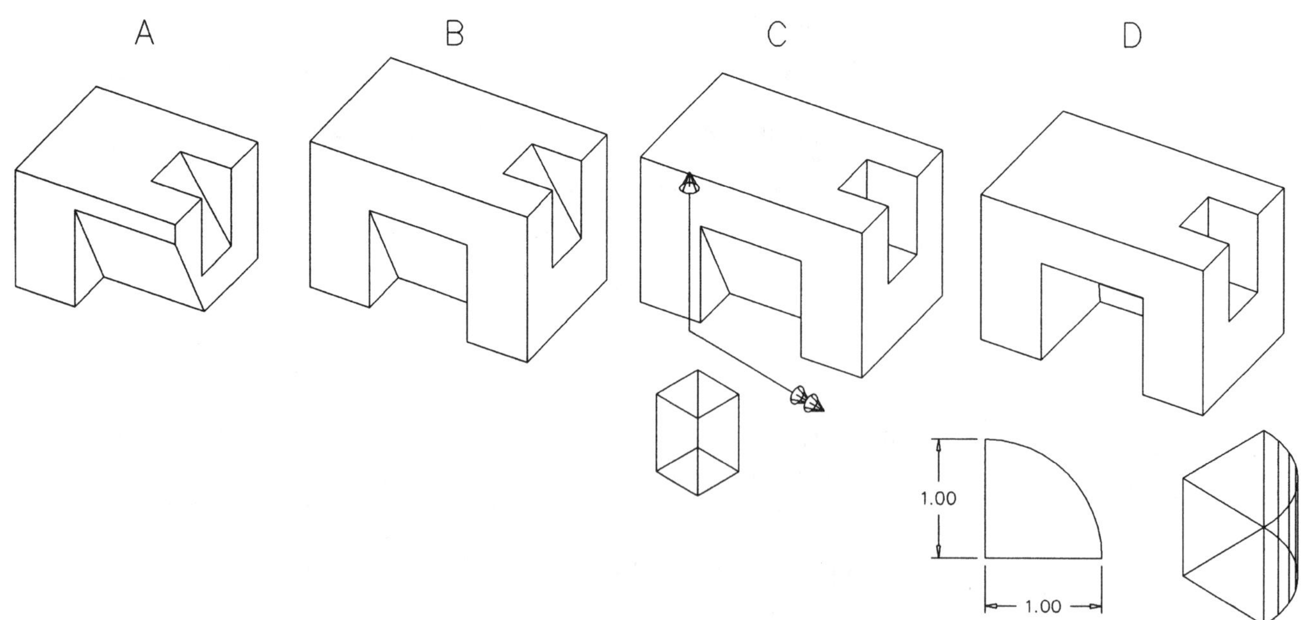

FIGURE 13–29
Exercise 13–3

2. Change the overall size of the model. With the world UCS active, change the length along the X axis to 2.2 and the length along the Z axis to 1.5. Leave the length along the Y axis as it is (1.4). This is a case where you are better off to start over with a new box.
3. Use Box: to draw a box measuring .5 in length, .5 in width, and .8 in height. Move the box to its correct location and use Subtrac: to replace the wedge shape on the upper surface of the model with the box, Figure 13–29C.
4. Draw the 1″ quarter-round shape, use Pedit: to join the straight lines and the arc into a single polyline if you draw the segments separately, and use Extrude: to extrude the shape 1″. Use Align: to move the shape to its correct location, then subtract it as shown in Figure 13–29D. The wedge-shaped hole on the front surface has been replaced with the quarter-round shape.
5. Set UCS to View and place your name in the lower right corner. Plot the drawing full size on an 11″ × 8.5″ sheet. Your final drawing should look like Figure 13–29D with hidden lines removed.

13–4. Edit the solid model drawn in Exercise 11–4.

1. Call up the solid model, Figure 13–30, you drew in Exercise 11–4 and name it 13-4 (your initials). Select New. . . ; type 13-4 (your initials)=A: 11-4 (your initials) in the New Drawing Name button if the drawing 11-4 (your initials) is on a floppy disk in the A: drive.
2. Set the UCS to the right side from the UCS Orientation icon menu. Use Cylinder: to draw a 12-mm-radius cylinder from the center of one hole to the center of the other hole as shown in the figure, using Osnap-CENter to locate the ends of the cylinder. Begin with the hole center farthest to the left.
3. Change the radius of the two outer holes in the back of the model to 10 mm. Delete the center hole.
4. Add a lip (box) on the front of the model that measures 19 × 16 × 140 mm as shown.
5. Draw a construction line from the center of one hole in the back of the model to the other hole in the back. Use Pline: to draw a polyline from the midpoint of the construction line to the midpoints of the edges of the base as shown. (You may have to use Osnap-PERpendicular to pick one or more of the edges.) Close the polyline and use Extrude: to extrude it 16 mm. Use Move: to move the extruded triangle 8 mm in the negative Z direction. Erase the construction line.
6. Use Union: to unify all pieces of the model.
7. Set UCS to View and place your name in the lower right corner. Plot the drawing, removing hidden lines, to fit on an 8.5″ × 11″ sheet. Your final drawing should look like the right side of Figure 13–30.

13–5. Edit the solid model drawn in Exercise 11–5.

1. Call up the solid model, Figure 13–31, you drew in Exercise 11–5 and name it 13-5 (your initials). Select New. . . ; type 13-5 (your initials)=A:11-5 (your initials) in the New Drawing Name button if the drawing 11-5 (your initials) is on a floppy disk in the A: drive.

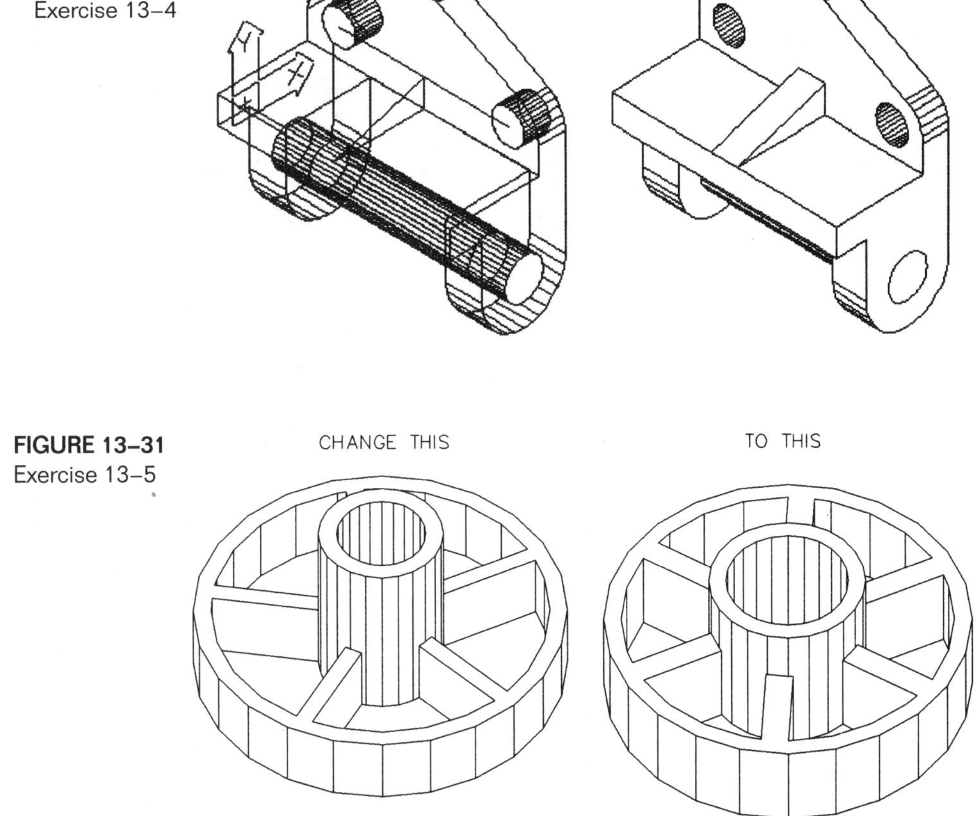

FIGURE 13–30
Exercise 13–4

FIGURE 13–31
Exercise 13–5

2. Change the size of one of the spokes to 1.5 length along the X axis, .375 length along the Y axis, and 1.25 length along the Z axis. Make a box the same size as each one of the remaining spokes and array it so it is in the same location as the original spokes. Subtract the boxes to delete the original spokes.
3. Change the size of the cylinders forming the outer ring so that their length along the Z axis is 1.25 (their height).
4. Change the radius of the inner cylinder to .875, and the radius of the outer cylinder forming the inner ring to 1.125. Change the height of both of these cylinders to 2.00. (Delete the original cylinders by drawing a cylinder large enough so you can use Subtrac: to delete them.)
5. Use the Array: command to form a polar array of six spokes as shown in Figure 13–31. Use Union: to unify the entire model.
6. Set UCS to View and place your name in the lower right corner. Plot the drawing full size on a vertical 8.5″ × 11″ sheet. Your final drawing should look like the right side of Figure 13–31 with hidden lines removed.

13–6. Edit the solid model drawn in Exercise 11–6.

1. Call up the solid model, Figure 13–32, you drew in Exercise 11–6 and name it 13-6 (your initials). Select New. . . ; type 13-6 (your initials)=A:11-6 (your initials) in the New Drawing Name button if the drawing 11-6 (your initials) is on a floppy disk in the A: drive.
2. Make a copy of the solid model and use Explode: to change the copied model to regions. Erase all regions that you do not need.
3. Move the region of the base of the gear and the hole with the keyway out of the area containing the solid model as shown in Figure 13–32. Explode the region again, and use Pedit: to rejoin the gear teeth. Use the Scale: command to reduce the polyline to .75 the size of the original. Use Extrude: to extrude this shape positive .75.
4. Use Scale: to reduce the size of the hole and keyway in the gear hub to .75 the size of the original. Use Pedit: if necessary to make a polyline out of the hole and keyway. Extrude the new hole and keyway positive 1.625.
5. Use Union: to combine the gear and the hub into a single object.
6. Subtract the hole and keyway from the model.
7. Set UCS to View and place your name in the lower right corner. Plot the drawing full size on a vertical 8.5″ × 11″ sheet. Your final drawing should look like the right side of Figure 13–32 with hidden lines removed.

13–7. Use Align: to move simple shapes to other faces and axes.

1. Call up the solid model you drew in Exercise 11–6 and name it 13-7 (your initials). Select New. . . ; type 13-7 (your initials)=A:11-6 (your initials) in the New Drawing Name button if the drawing 11-6 (your initials) is on a floppy disk in the A: drive. Making your new drawing equal to a previous drawing allows you to start the new drawing with all settings already made.
2. Use the Erase: command to erase the existing drawing.
3. Set UCS to World, and draw the following figures at 0 elevation and at any convenient location:

A. Box:	Length, 2.00
	Width, 1.50
	Height, 1.00
B. Cylinder:	Radius, 1.00
	Height, 1.00
C. Cylinder:	Radius, .25
	Height, .50
D. Box:	Length, .50
	Width, .25
	Height, .25
E. Cylinder:	Radius, .75
	Height, 2.00

4. Rotate the world UCS 90° about the X axis, and draw the following figures at any convenient location:

F. Cylinder:	Radius, .75
	Height, .50
G. Cone:	Radius, .75
	Height, .75

Your drawing should look similar to Figure 13–33.

5. Use Align: to move figures in the following manner:

Move Figure F to the top face of Figure B.
Move Figure C to the front face of Figure A.
Move Figure G to the top surface of Figure E.
Move Figure D to the right side face of Figure A.

FIGURE 13–32
Exercise 13–6

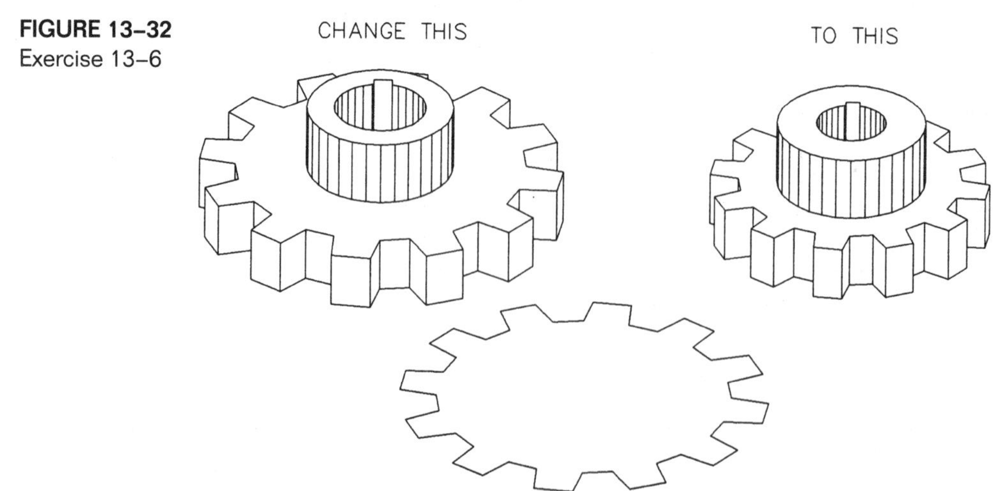

FIGURE 13–33
Exercise 13–7

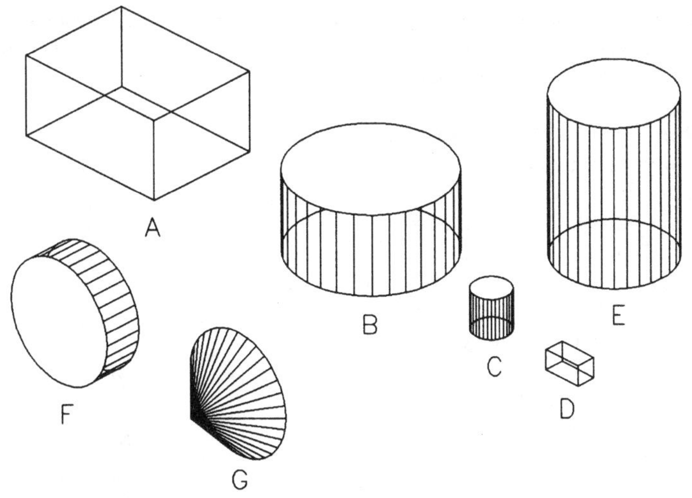

6. Use Union: to unify Figures A, C, and D and Figures B and F. Use Subtrac: to subtract Figure G from Figure E.
7. Set the UCS to View and place your name in the lower right corner. Plot the drawing full size on a vertical 8.5″ × 11″ sheet. Your final drawing should look like Figure 13–34 with hidden lines removed.

13–8. Edit the solid model drawn in Exercise 11–8.

1. Call up the solid model, Figure 13–35, you drew in Exercise 11–8 and name it 13-8 (your initials). Select New. . . ; type 13-8 (your initials)=A:11-8 (your initials) in the New Drawing Name button if the drawing 11-8 (your initials) is on a floppy disk in the A: drive.
2. Explode the wrench, and change the size of the following features of the wrench:

   Delete all the small .0625 fillets.
   Change the main body of the wrench as follows:
      Length along the X axis: change to 4.5
      Length along the Y axis: change to .5
      Length along the Z axis: change to .1
   Change the size of the 1.00 hex end of the wrench by using the Scale: command and reducing the resulting polyline to .75 of its original size. Extrude the new polyline positive .188. Replace the left end of the wrench with the new shape.
   Change the size of the .875 hex end of the wrench by using the Scale: command and reducing the resulting polyline to a .50 hex. Use the Reference option of the Scale: command and type .875 to the "Reference length" prompt. Type .5 to the "New length" prompt. Extrude the new polyline positive .188. Replace the right end of the wrench with the new (.50) hex end.

3. Move the wrench ends to their correct location on the ends of the wrench body. They should intersect the body .20 and should be centered vertically on the thickness of the body. You may have to use Move: several times to get the correct location for these objects.

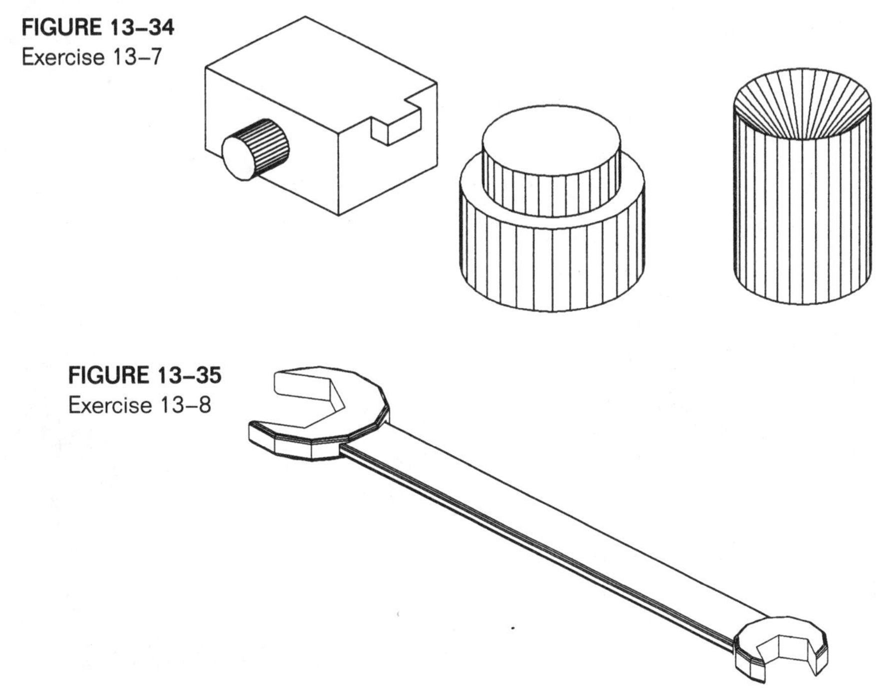

FIGURE 13–34
Exercise 13–7

FIGURE 13–35
Exercise 13–8

4. Use Fillet: to make a .03 radius on all edges that previously had a .0625 radius.
5. Set the UCS to View and place your name in the lower right corner. Plot the drawing full size on a vertical 8.5″ × 11″ sheet. Your final drawing should look like Figure 13–35 with hidden lines removed.

13–9. Edit the solid model drawn in Exercise 11–9.

1. Call up the solid model you drew in Exercise 11–9 and name it 13-9 (your initials). Select New. . . ; type 13-9 (your initials)=A:11-9 (your initials) in the New Drawing Name button if the drawing 11-9 (your initials) is on a floppy disk in the A: drive.
2. Select a viewpoint similar to the one shown in Figure 13–36. Set UCS to World if it is not already there. Rotate the UCS 90° about the X axis.
3. Draw the following in any convenient location in front of the table and lamp, Figure 13–36:

Box:	Length, 6
	Width, 4
	Height, 3
Box:	Length, 4
	Width, 3
	Height, 2
Cylinder:	Radius, 2.50
	Length, 6.00

Draw a second cylinder inside the first, using the center of the front end as the base point.

Cylinder:	Radius, 2.25
	Length, −5.875

Use the Move: command to move the smaller cylinder .125 in the positive Z direction.
Subtract the smaller cylinder from the larger one using Subtrac:

4. Use Align: to move the two boxes and the glass (cylinder) to the top of the table:
You may need to select a plan view of the current UCS to see where the box is in relation to the table top by using the Plan: command.
5. Set UCS to View and place your name in the lower right corner. Plot the drawing full size on a vertical 8.5″ × 11″ sheet. Your final drawing should look like Figure 13–37 with hidden lines removed.

FIGURE 13–36
Exercise 13–9

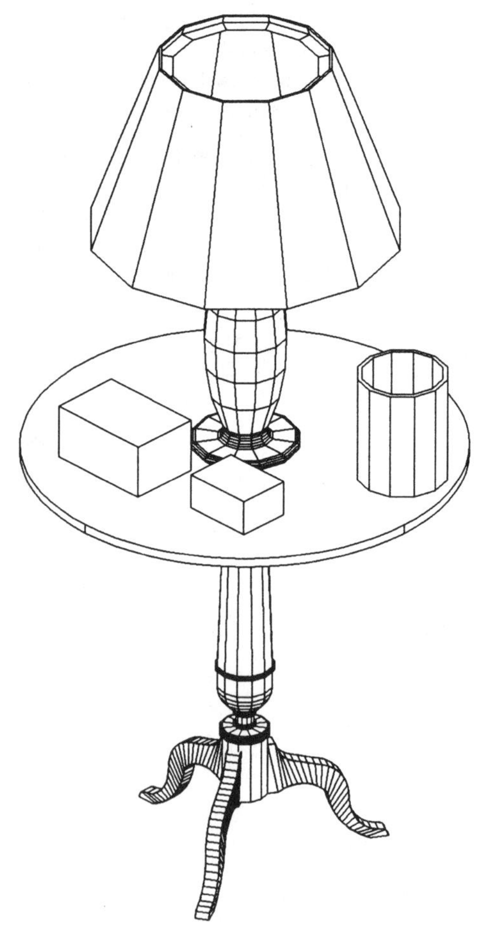

FIGURE 13–37
Exercise 13–9

13–10. Edit the solid model drawn in Exercise 11–10.

1. Call up the solid model you drew in Exercise 11–10 and name it 13-10 (your initials). Select New. . . ; type 13-10 (your initials)=A:11-10 (your initials) in the New Drawing Name button if the drawing 11-10 (your initials) is on a floppy disk in the A: drive.
2. This drawing, Figure 13–38, was done with the Revolve: command. Explode the model and change each of the polylines used to construct the model to the dimensions shown in Figure 13–39.
3. Use Revolve: to construct the new model shown in Figure 13–40.
4. Set UCS to View and place your name in the lower right corner. Plot the drawing ½ size on a horizontal 11″ × 8.5″ sheet. Your final drawing should look like Figure 13–40 with hidden lines removed.

FIGURE 13–38
Exercise 13–10

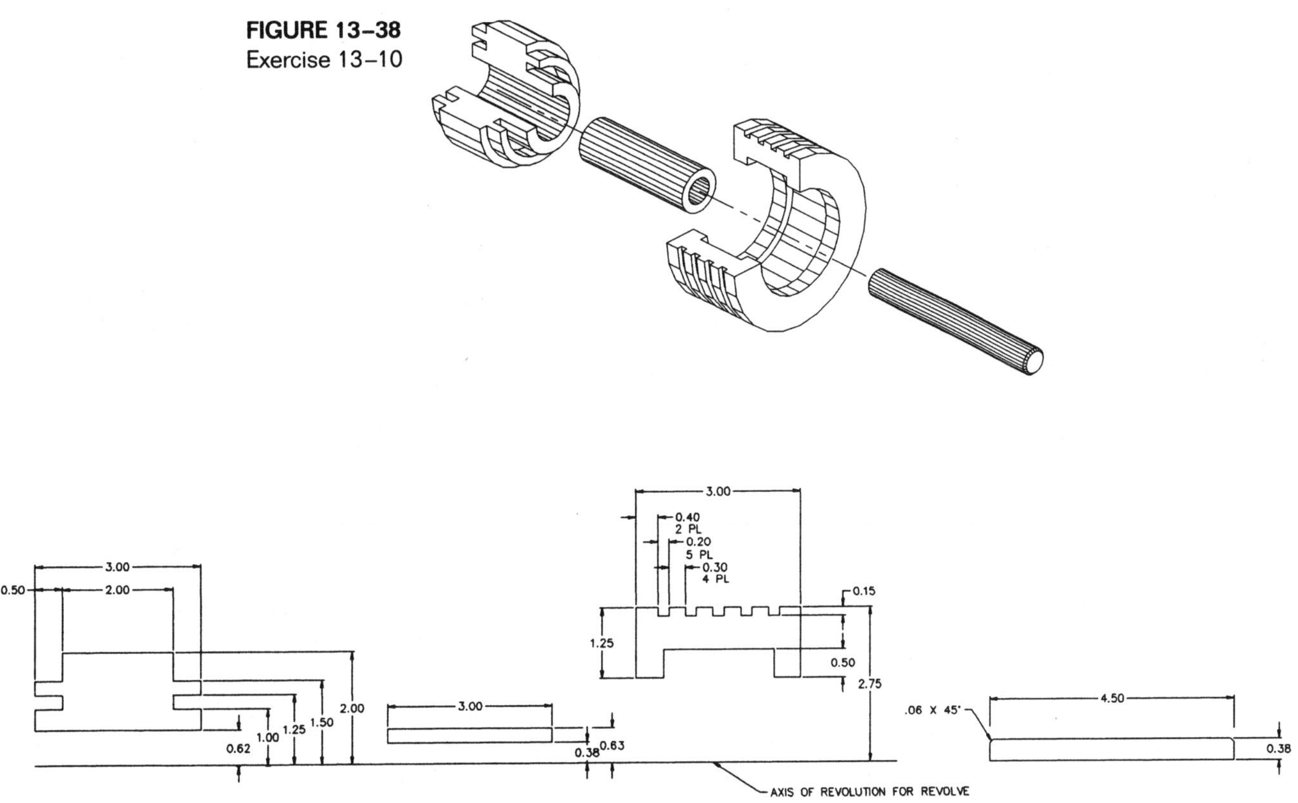

FIGURE 13–39
New DImensions for Exercise 13–10

FIGURE 13–40
Exercise 13–10

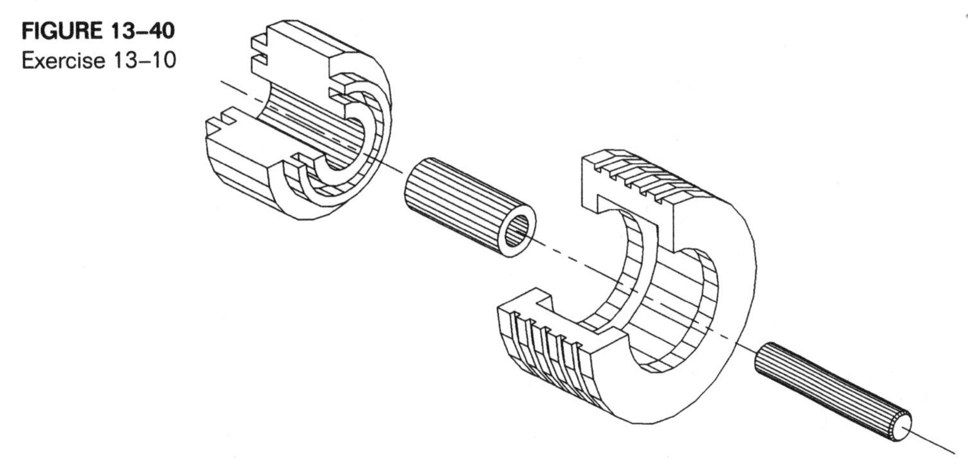

REVIEW QUESTIONS

1. Which of the following cannot be used to edit a solid model?
   a. Explode: d. Mirror:
   b. Align: e. Divide:
   c. Move:
2. Which of the following allows you to change the color of a composite solid?
   a. Chprop: d. Boundary:
   b. Layer: e. Bhatch:
   c. Color:
3. Which of the following sets the number of lines shown in a model with hidden lines removed?
   a. ISOLINES: d. Surftab2:
   b. Surftab1: e. Hide:
   c. FACETRES:
4. Which of the following allows you to move a solid to a surface on another solid and rotate it at the same time?
   a. Explode: d. Mirror:
   b. Align: e. Divide:
   c. Move:
5. Which of the following allows you to separate a composite solid into individual regions?
   a. Separate: d. Explode:
   b. Chprop: e. Change:
   c. Modify:
6. If the base surface highlighted is not the correct one when you are using the Chamfer: command, which letter must be typed and entered to move to the correct surface?
   a. N d. L
   b. S e. P
   c. ↵
7. A larger chamfer is easily obtained on a solid by just chamfering the existing chamfer.
   a. True b. False
8. Using only one set of source and destination points with the Align: command:
   a. Moves the object and rotates it about one axis
   b. Move the object and rotates it about two axes
   c. Moves the object and does not rotate it
   d. Moves the object and changes the UCS
   e. Moves the object and the viewpoint
9. Exploding a composite solid model:
   a. Separates a composite model into separate solid objects
   b. Separates a composite model into line segments
   c. Separates a composite model into regions
   d. Separates a composite model into polylines
   e. Separates a composite model into the last unified model
10. Regions formed when a solid model has been exploded may be extruded.
    a. True b. False
11. Write the name of the command that gives you a plan view of the current UCS.

    ____
12. Why did you have to explode the region forming the back of the model in Exercise 13–1 before extruding it?

    ____
13. Write the name of the command that allows you to combine several solid objects into a single composite solid.

    ____
14. List six commands that cannot be used to edit solids.

    ____________ ____________ ____________

    ____________ ____________ ____________
15. Describe how a solid object is moved when you use one, two, and three sets of source and destination points with the Align: command.

    One: ______________________________

    Two: ______________________________

    Three: ______________________________
16. What does AutoCAD ask you for first when you select a solid after activating the Fillet: command?

    ____
17. What does AutoCAD ask you for first when you select a solid after activating the Chamfer: command?

    ____
18. List two different types of entities that may be extruded.

    ____________________ ____________________
19. Describe how to make an existing hole in a solid larger.

    ____
20. Describe how to make an existing hole in a solid smaller.

    ____

    ____

PART IV THE AUTOCAD DESIGNER PROGRAM

14 An Introduction to the AutoCAD Designer Program

OBJECTIVES

When you have completed this chapter, you will be able to:

- Define the term *parametric, feature-based solid modeler*.
- Describe the basic tools used in Designer solid part modeling.
- Describe how Designer creates 2-D drawings from a solid model.
- Correctly answer questions about Designer commands contained on the Designer pull-down menu.

INTRODUCTION

AutoCAD Designer is an additional software package that runs inside AutoCAD. Although many of the standard AutoCAD commands are used with Designer, this program has its own menu and many commands and features that are unique to it.

First, you create a basic solid model called a *base* from a 2-D sketch that may or may not be accurately drawn. Second, you define size dimensions and geometric shape relationships (some automatically, some using Designer commands). Third, you use a command such as Extrude, Revolve, or Sweep to make the 2-D drawing into a solid similar to the way you created solids in earlier chapters. Fourth, you add other shapes to the model and create holes where they are needed.

When the model is complete, 2-D manufacturing drawings are created automatically. When changes are made to any dimension on either the part or the 2-D manufacturing drawing, both the part and the drawing are changed automatically with a command called Update.

Parametric Defined

Designer is a *parametric solid modeler*. Parametrics used in Designer may be thought of as the size variables of a model (shown as dimensions) and the shape or geometric variables of the model (shown as and called *constraints*). All dimensions are added to the sketch by the use of a Designer command. Some constraints are applied automatically as you create the sketch; other constraints have to be added to fully define geometric relationships between features of the model. Some examples of constraints are:

Concentric
Showing that an arc such as a corner radius and a hole have the same center.

Colinear
Showing that two shapes have edges that are in exactly the same plane.
Horizontal
Showing that a shape has a line that is horizontal.
Tangent
Showing that a shape has a line that is tangent to an arc.

Other constraint options will be discussed later.

Feature Based

Designer is a *feature-based modeler,* which means that any feature of the model such as a hole is changed appropriately when any other dimension on the model is changed. An example of this feature is shown in Figure 14–1. When the part shown in Figure 14–1A is shortened, the through hole in the model changes with the length of the model, Figure 14–1B.

FIGURE 14–1
Example of a Feature-Based Model

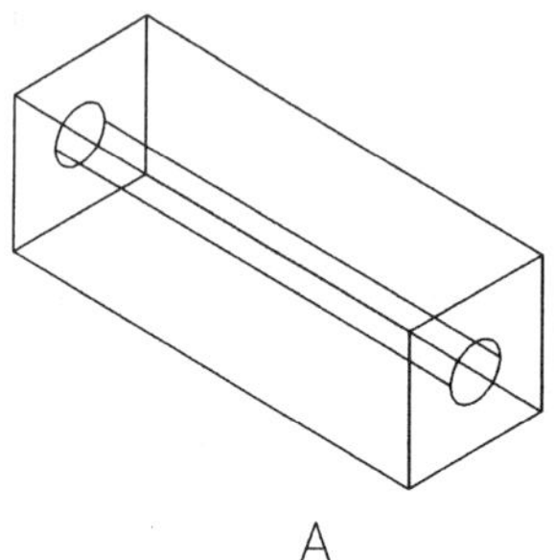
A

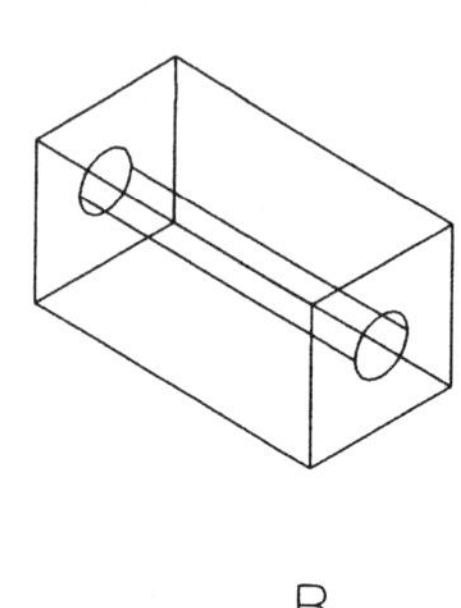
B

Basic Tools Used in Solid Part Modeling

The Designer tools you will use to create the basic solid model are:

Sketch plane	Hole
Work planes	Work points
Extrude	Work axes
Revolve	Dimensions
Sweep	Constraints

Other commands, such as Chamfer: and Fillet:, will be described when they are used. The basic tools are as follows: (Commands as typed from the keyboard are shown in parentheses.)

Sketch Plane (ADSKPLN)

A sketch plane in Designer is similar to the UCS used in AutoCAD. It has only two dimensions (X and Y), however, and is activated by the ADSKPLN command. There is only one sketch plane, which is moved from surface to surface so that new features may be created.

You have to have a sketch plane before you can sketch any feature other than the base feature. The sketch plane for the base feature is automatically placed on the XY plane of the current UCS. The sketch plane is a coordinate system that may be moved when needed to create the next solid feature, but the sketch plane itself is not a part of the model.

Work Planes (ADWORKPLN)

Work planes are 2-D planes used to locate sketch planes or to help in constructing features on the model. They are similar to construction lines used in manual drafting. You can define any number of work planes on a model, and display, move, erase, or otherwise edit them. You do not have to create a work plane to locate a sketch plane if the part has an existing surface that is in the same plane as the sketch you want to draw.

Work planes can be parametric, meaning that they become part of the model (any feature created on a parametric work plane moves with the work plane when the dimensions of the part are changed), or nonparametric (the work plane is fixed in relation to the part).

AutoCAD Designer places work axes, work planes, and work points on the ADP_WORK layer. Do not change this layer in any way, or you will permanently destroy or corrupt the modeling information in your drawing.

Parametric Work Plane Options

You can use 12 different options to create parametric work planes. These options, called *constraints,* are selected from two dialog boxes, Figure 14–2, which appear one at a time when the ADWORKPLN command is executed. The order in which you select the constraints does not affect where the work plane is located. For example, if On Edge/Axis is selected first, and Planar Parallel is selected second, the work plane created is in the same location as if Planar Parallel had been selected first. The second dialog box that appears is dependent on which constraint is picked from the first dialog box.

FIGURE 14–2
Work Plane Dialog Boxes

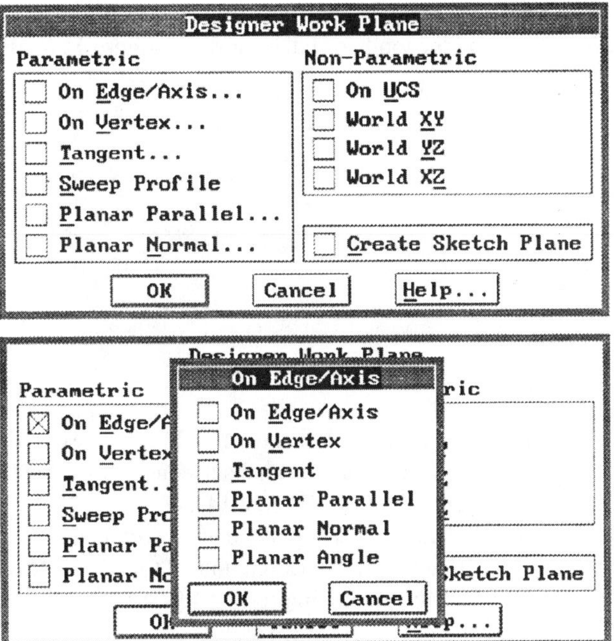

The 12 options are as follows:

On Edge/Axis and On Edge/Axis, Figure 14–3

(On Edge/Axis means that the work plane is constructed on an edge or on an axis that you select.)

Let's say you need to make a sketch and extrude it to cut a slot in the top of Figure 14–3A that is perpendicular to the center lines of the two holes.

Step 1. Construct axes through the two holes, Figure 14–3B.

Step 2. Construct a work plane using the On Edge/Axis and On Edge/Axis options of ADWORKPLN as shown in Figure 14–3C. Just pick the two axes to place the work plane through the two axes.

Step 3. Create a sketch plane on the work plane using ADSKPLN.

Step 4. Sketch the cross-sectional shape of the cut, Figure 14–3D, and place any necessary dimensions on it.

Step 5. Extrude the shape from its midplane to form the cut.

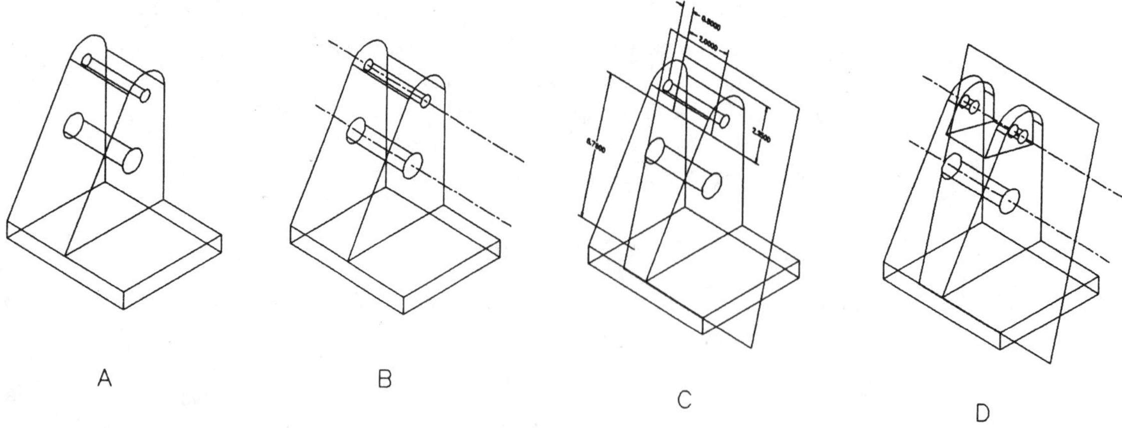

FIGURE 14–3
On Edge/Axis and On Edge/Axis

On Edge/Axis and On Vertex, Figure 14–4

In this example a slanted hole that is perpendicular to a work plane that goes through the vertex and the top back edge shown in Figure 14–4B must be cut through the model.

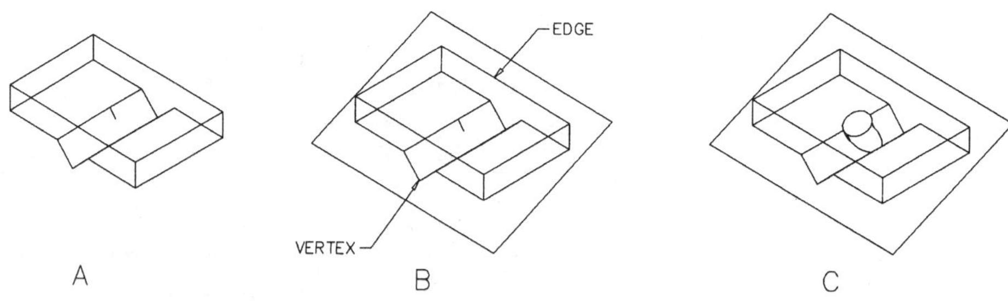

FIGURE 14–4
On Edge/Axis and On Vertex

Step 1. Create a work plane through the vertex of the triangular shape on the bottom of the model and its top back edge using the ADWORKPLN options On Vertex and On Edge/Axis, Figure 14–4B.

Step 2. Create a sketch plane on the work plane using ADSKPLN.

Step 3. Use the ADHOLE command to make a through hole that is perpendicular to the sketch plane, Figure 14–4C.

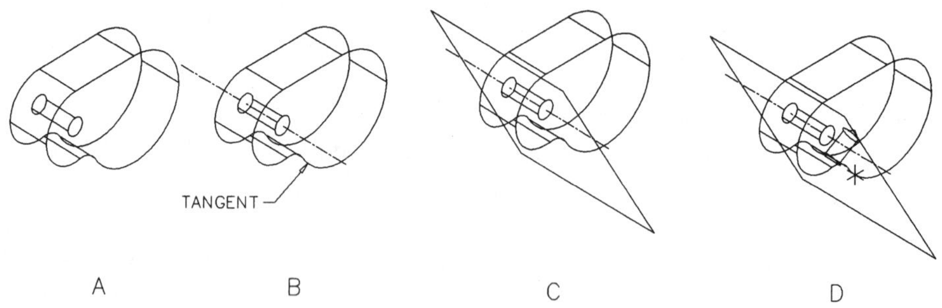

FIGURE 14–5
On Edge/Axis and Tangent

On Edge/Axis and Tangent, Figure 14–5

In this example a hole must be created that is perpendicular to a work plane that lies on the center line (an axis) of the existing hole and is tangent to the circular part of the body.

Step 1. Construct an axis through the existing hole, Figure 14–5B.

Step 2. Create a work plane using the Tangent and On Edge/Axis options of the ADWORKPLN command, Figure 14–5C.

Step 3. Create a sketch plane on the work plane using ADSKPLN.
Step 4. Use the ADHOLE command to make a blind hole that is perpendicular to the sketch plane, Figure 14–5D.

On Edge/Axis and Planar Parallel, Figure 14–6

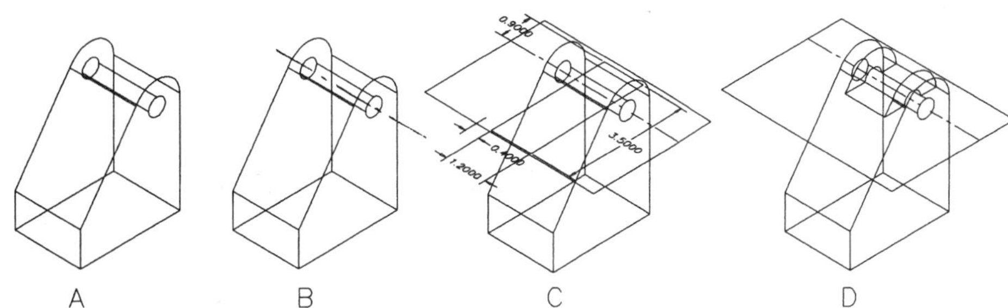

FIGURE 14–6
On Edge/Axis and Planar Parallel

In this case a cut through the model is needed that is parallel to the bottom of the model and aligned with the center line of the existing hole.

Step 1. Construct an axis through the existing hole, Figure 14–6B.
Step 2. Create a work plane using the On Edge/Axis and Planar Parallel options of the ADWORKPLN command, Figure 14–6C.
Step 3. Create a sketch plane on the work plane using ADSKPLN.
Step 4. Sketch a rectangle on the sketch plane, add necessary dimensions, make a profile of it, and extrude it to make the cut, Figure 14–6D.

On Edge/Axis and Planar Normal (Normal in Drawing Terms Means Perpendicular), Figure 14–7

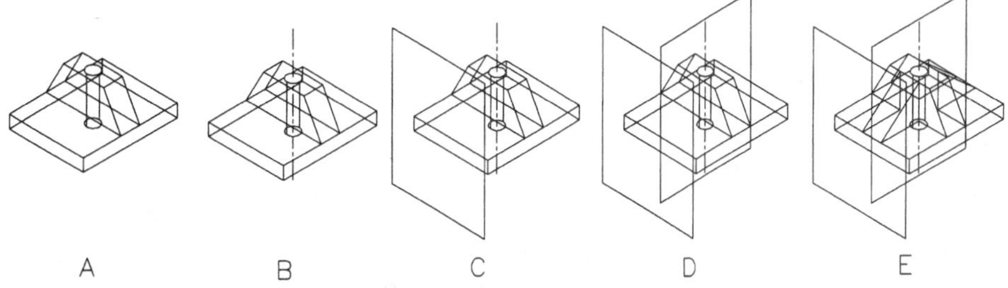

FIGURE 14–7
On Edge/Axis and On Planar Normal

In this case a cut through the model is needed that is parallel to the bottom of the model and aligned with the center line of the existing hole.

Step 1. Construct an axis through the existing hole, Figure 14–7B.
Step 2. Create a work plane using the On Edge/Axis and Planar Parallel options of the ADWORKPLN command, Figure 14–7C.
Step 3. Create another work plane, Figure 14–7D, using the On Edge/Axis and Planar Normal options of the ADWORKPLN command through the axis in the existing hole and perpendicular to the work plane constructed in step 2.
Step 4. Create a sketch plane on the work plane using ADSKPLN.
Step 5. Sketch a triangle on the sketch plane, add necessary dimensions, make a profile of it, and extrude it from its center to make the wedges, Figure 14–7E.

On Edge/Axis and Planar Angle, Figure 14–8

In this case another extrusion is needed on this part. The new extrusion should be centered about the center line of the part and at a 30° angle to the existing extrusion.

Step 1. Construct an axis through the cylindrical portion of the part, Figure 14–8B.
Step 2. Create a work plane using the On Edge/Axis and Planar Angle options of the ADWORKPLN command, Figure 14–8C.

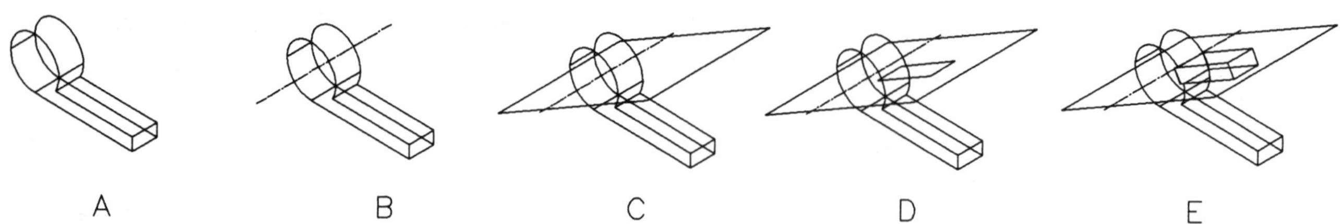

FIGURE 14–8
On Edge/Axis and On Planar Angle

Step 3. Create a sketch plane on the work plane using ADSKPLN.
Step 4. Sketch a rectangle on the sketch plane, add necessary dimensions, make a profile of it, and extrude it from its center to make the new extrusion, Figure 14–8E.

On Vertex and Planar Parallel, Figure 14–9

In this case a counterbored hole must be drilled in the model that is parallel to the bottom of the model and on the vertex of the triangular shape.

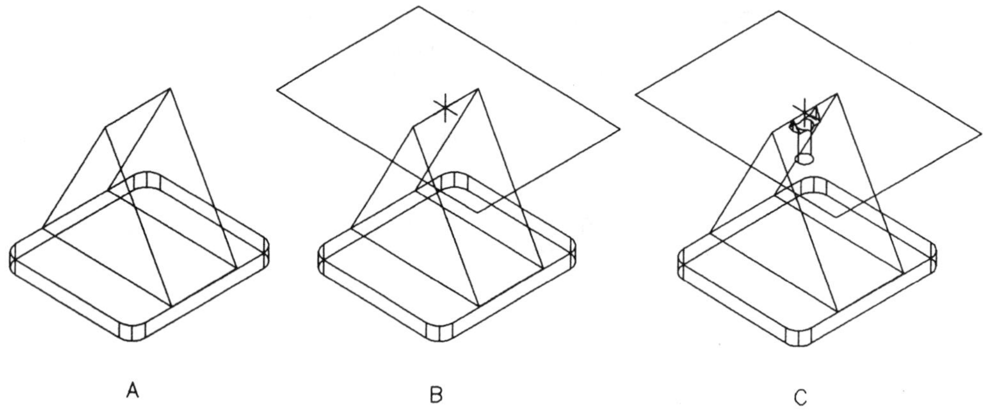

FIGURE 14–9
On Vertex and Planar Parallel

Step 1. Create a work plane using the On Vertex and Planar Parallel options of the ADWORKPLN command, Figure 14–9B.
Step 2. Create a sketch plane on the work plane using ADSKPLN.
Step 3. Locate a work point on the sketch plane that is on the midpoint of the line forming the vertex of the triangular shape, Figure 14–9B.
Step 4. Use ADHOLE to drill a counterbored hole that starts on the vertex and is perpendicular to the bottom of the model. The ADHOLE command is described later in this chapter.

On 3 Vertices, Figure 14–10

FIGURE 14–10
On 3 Vertices

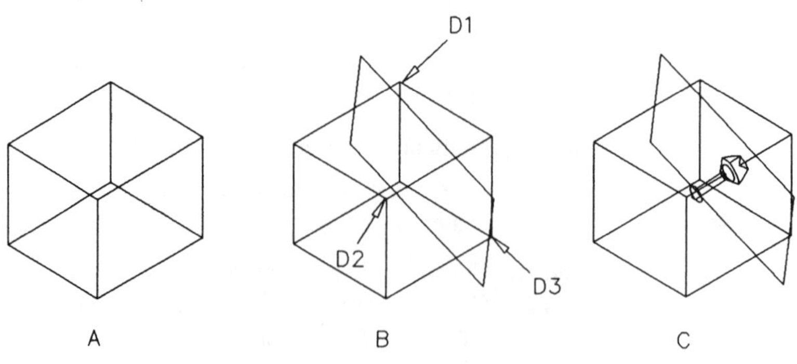

In this case a counterbored hole must be drilled in the model that is perpendicular to a work plane constructed through three vertices of the rectangular solid.

Step 1. Create a work plane using the On 3 Vertices option of the ADWORKPLN command, Figure 14–10B.
Step 2. Create a sketch plane on the work plane using ADSKPLN.
Step 3. Use ADHOLE to drill a counterbored hole that is perpendicular to the work plane.

Tangent and Planar Parallel, Figure 14–11

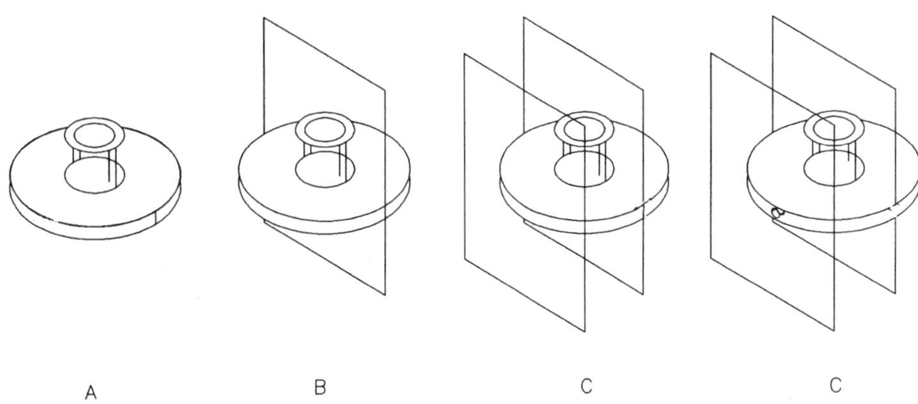

FIGURE 14–11
Tangent and Planar Parallel

In this case a hole must be drilled in the model that is parallel to an existing work plane and tangent to the circular base.

Step 1. Create a work plane through the center of the part using the ADWORKPLN command, Figure 14–9B.
Step 2. Create a second work plane using the Tangent and Planar Parallel options of the ADWORKPLN command, Figure 14–11C.
Step 3. Create a sketch plane on the new work plane using ADSKPLN.
Step 4. Use ADHOLE to drill a hole that starts on the tangent point and is perpendicular to the new work plane.

Tangent and Planar Normal, Figure 14–12

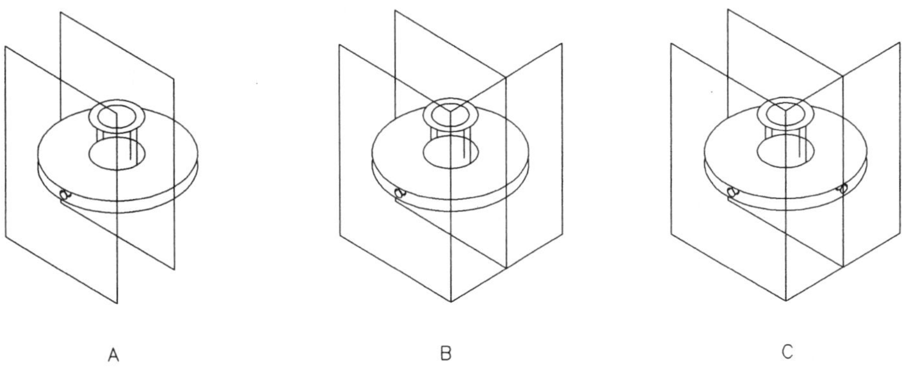

FIGURE 14–12
Tangent and Planar Normal

Now, another hole must be drilled in the model that is perpendicular (normal) to the existing work plane and tangent to the circular base.

Step 1. Create a third work plane using the Tangent and Planar Parallel options of the ADWORKPLN command, Figure 14–12C.
Step 2. Create a sketch plane on the new work plane using ADSKPLN.
Step 3. Use ADHOLE to drill a hole that starts on the tangent point and is perpendicular to the new work plane.

Sweep, Figure 14–13

In this case a model must be constructed that resembles square tubing bent in two places.

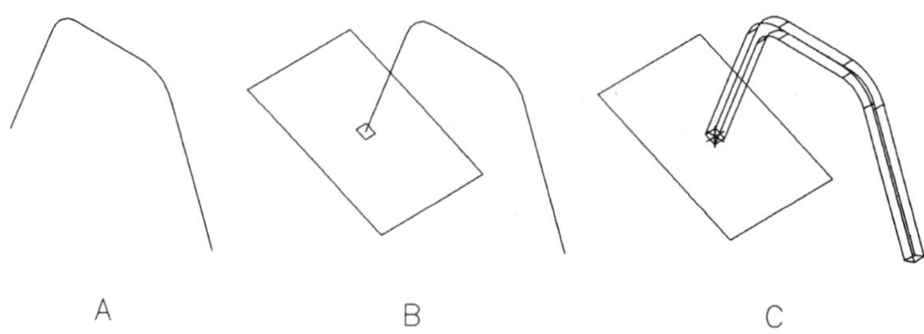

FIGURE 14–13
SWEEP

The ADSWEEP command is similar to Extrude: in solid modeling except that the sweep path can be constructed using curves and different angles. The Sweep Profile option of the ADWORKPLN command allows you to create a work plane through the starting point of the sweep path perpendicular to it.

Step 1. Create a sweep path using the ADPATH command, Figure 14–13A.
Step 2. Create a work plane at the start point of the sweep path using the Sweep Profile option of the ADWORKPLN command, Figure 14–13B.
Step 3. Create a sketch plane on the work plane using ADSKPLN.
Step 4. Draw a square centered on the start point of the sweep path, make a profile of it, and add any necessary dimensions, Figure 14–13B.
Step 5. Use the ADSWEEP command to extrude the square along the sweep path, Figure 14–13C. The ADSWEEP command is described later in this chapter.

Planar Parallel and Offset, Figure 14–14

Now, a flange must be added to the end of the swept square tubing. One way to do that is to construct a work plane that is parallel to the existing work plane and offset from it by the distance that is the flange thickness.

FIGURE 14–14
Planar Parallel and Offset

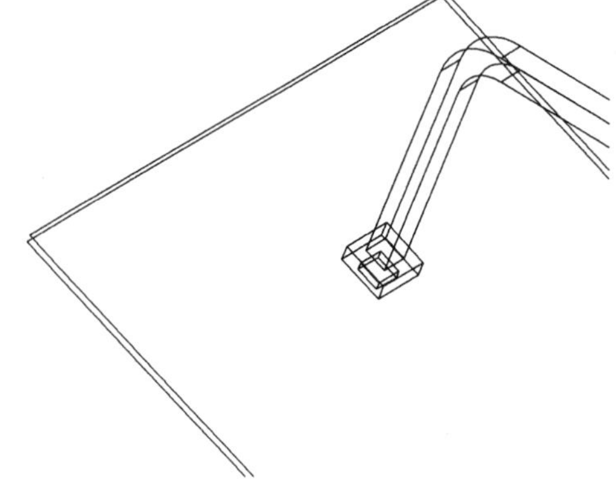

Step 1. Create a work plane using the Planar Parallel and Offset options of the ADWORKPLN command, Figure 14–14. The new work plane is parallel to the existing work plane and offset by .25″ in this case.
Step 2. Create a sketch plane on the work plane using ADSKPLN.
Step 3. Draw another larger square that is centered about the start path of the swept square and offset from it .25″.
Step 4. Use ADEXTRUDE to extrude the larger square .25″.

Nonparametric Work Plane Options

Nonparametric work planes are not attached to any feature of the part. If you change the size of a part, the nonparametric work plane does not move; it is fixed in its location with respect to the part. If the part is moved or rotated, the nonparametric work plane moves with the part.

Nonparametric work planes are defined in one of four ways, as shown in Figure 14–15.

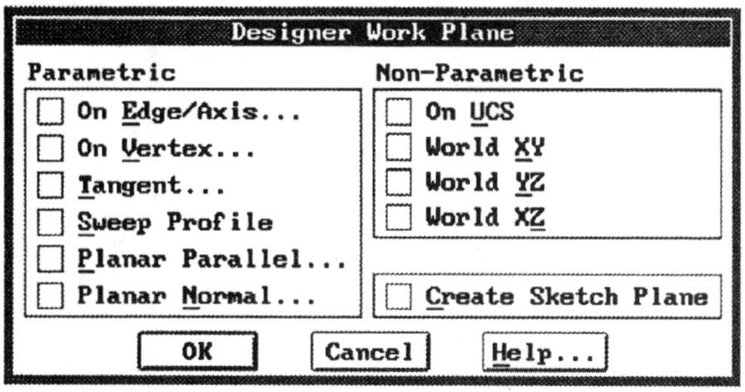

FIGURE 14–15
Nonparametric Work Plane Options

Designer Work Plane
Parametric
On Edge/Axis...
On Vertex...
Tangent...
Sweep Profile
Planar Parallel...
Planar Normal...
Non-Parametric
On UCS
World XY
World YZ
World XZ
Create Sketch Plane
OK
Cancel
Help...

On UCS
The work plane is placed on the XY plane of the current UCS.
World XY
The work plane is placed on the XY plane of the world UCS.
World YZ
The work plane is placed on the YZ plane of the world UCS.
World XZ
The work plane is placed on the XZ plane of the world UCS.

The nonparametric work plane is often useful and can be combined with parametric work planes to construct model features.

Now we return to a description of the other basic tools.

Extrude (ADEXTRUDE)

ADEXTRUDE is similar to the Extrude: command in AutoCAD solid modeling. The Designer Extrusion dialog box, Figure 14–16, appears when ADEXTRUDE is activated. There are four options in the Termination area, four options in the Operation area, and two in the Size area. When different options are selected in the Termination and Operation areas, the pictures in the upper left of the dialog box change to show what effect those options have on the extrusion of the part. You will have the opportunity to use all these options in the next two chapters.

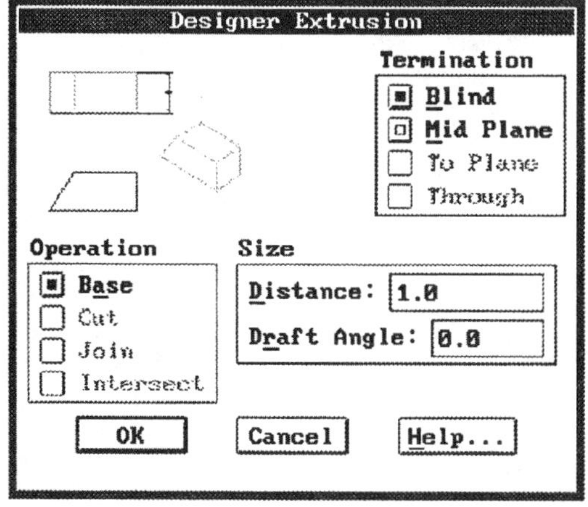

FIGURE 14–16
Designer Extrusion Dialog Box

Revolve (ADREVOLVE)

ADREVOLVE is similar to the Revolve: command in AutoCAD solid modeling. The Designer Revolution dialog box, Figure 14–17, appears when ADREVOLVE is activated. There are four options in the Termination area, four options in the Operation area, and one in the Size area. All these options will be used in later exercises.

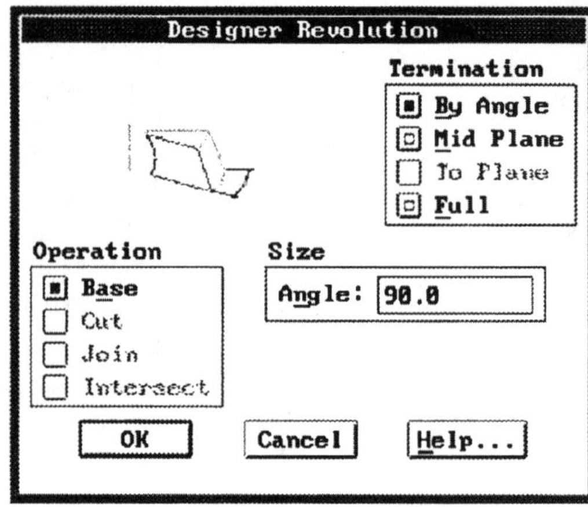

FIGURE 14–17
Designer Revolution Dialog Box

Sweep (ADSWEEP)

The ADSWEEP command is similar to Extrude: in solid modeling except that the sweep path can be constructed using curves and different angles. A profile may be swept along the path to create shapes such as the one shown in Figures 14–13 and 14–14.

Hole (ADHOLE)

The ADHOLE command creates drilled, countersunk, and counterbored holes in the location on the sketch plane that you specify. The Designer Hole dialog box, Figure 14–18, appears when ADHOLE is activated. There are three options for each of the Operation, Drill

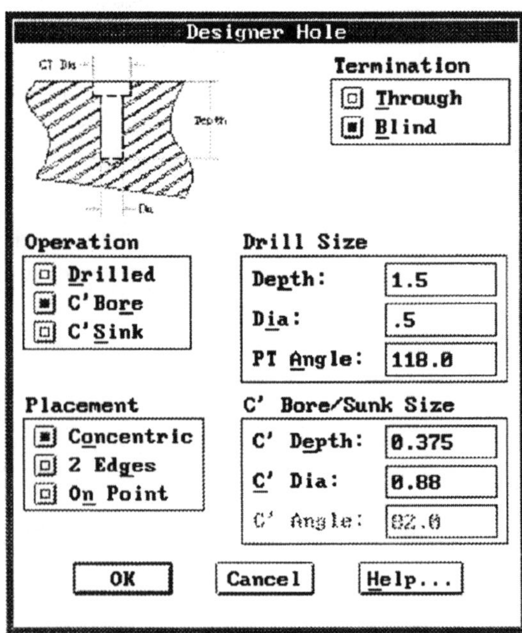

FIGURE 14–18
Designer Hole Dialog Box

Size, Placement, and C′ Bore/Sunk Size areas and two options for the Termination area. The picture in the upper left of this dialog box changes when different options are selected. For example, if you select Drilled in the Operation area, the picture changes from a counterbored hole to a drilled one.

Work Points (ADWORKPT)

The ADWORKPT command creates work points for locating holes. AutoCAD Designer places work axes, work planes, and work points on the ADP_WORK layer. Do not change this layer in any way or you will permanently destroy or corrupt the modeling information in your drawing.

Work Axes (ADWORKAXIS)

The ADWORKAXIS command creates a work axis through the center line of a selected cylinder, cone, or torus. Examples of the features through which a work axis may be created are:

Holes
Revolved arcs and lines
Extruded circles and arcs
Fillets on straight edges

Work axes are useful for constructing work planes, dimensioning, and applying geometric constraints when features are added to the model.

Dimensions

There are two types of dimensions in AutoCAD Designer: parametric and reference.

Parametric Dimensions (ADPARDIM)

Parametric dimensions added with the ADPARDIM command control the size of the model. When a parametric dimension is changed, the model changes to that size, and the drawing created from that model changes also. The ADPARDIM command allows you to add linear, horizontal, parallel, aligned, vertical, radial, diametral, and angular dimensions.

Reference Dimensions (ADREFDIM)

Reference dimensions are added with the ADREFDIM command. Reference dimensions supplement parametric dimensions on the drawings of the model but do not control the size of the model.

Constraints (ADADDCON)

Designer adds constraints and numbers them automatically as you create the profile of a sketch. When features are added to an existing model, you must add constraints between the new feature and the existing parts of the model using the ADADDCON command. For example, if an edge of a new feature should be the same as the edge on an existing model, the colinear option of the ADADDCON command should be selected. Use the ADDELCON command to delete an unnecessary constraint.

Creating 2-D Drawings From the Solid Model

AutoCAD Designer has two modes: *Part mode,* where the model is created, and *Drawing mode,* where 2-D drawings of the model are created. You are already familiar with the concepts of model space and paper space, so the model space icon and the paper space icon let you know immediately that Part mode is model space, and Drawing mode is paper space.

After the model is created, the ADMODE command is used to switch from Part mode to Drawing mode. The ADVIEW command is then used to create any views you think are necessary to fully describe and dimension the part. When the ADVIEWcommand is activated, the Designer Drawing View dialog box, Figure 14–19, appears. A brief description of each of the view types follows:

FIGURE 14–19
Designer Drawing View Dialog Box

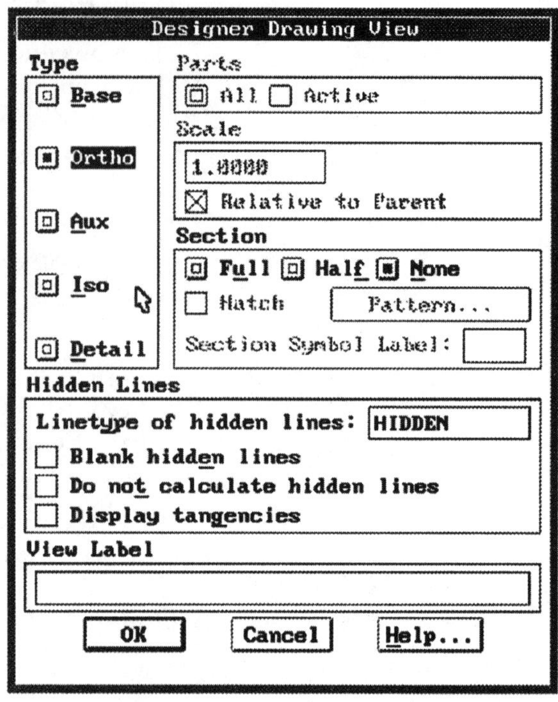

Base Views (Figure 14–20)

A base view is one that allows you to establish the orientation of the part with respect to the drawing views. For example, if you want the front of the part to be the front view of the drawing, you have the option of selecting the plane you want to be the front view and specifying the direction in which you want the X and Y coordinates to be placed.

FIGURE 14–20
Base View

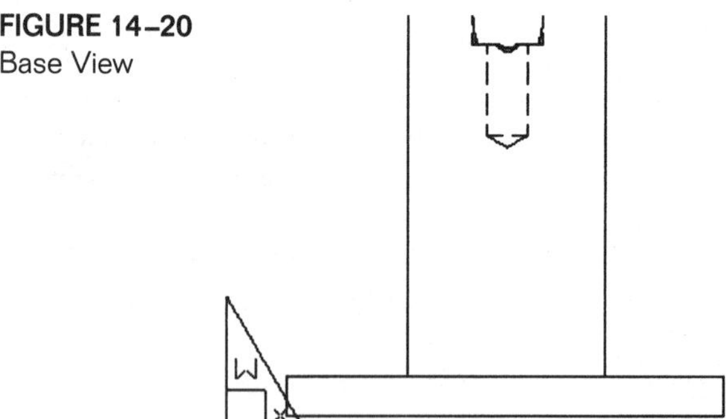

Parent Views (Figure 14–21)

Parent views are views from which you may create another view. The base view is a parent view. The parent view determines the orientation, alignment, hidden linetype, and scale of the other views. When you move or change the scale of a parent view, all dependent views change to the newly specified position or scale.

FIGURE 14-21
A Parent View

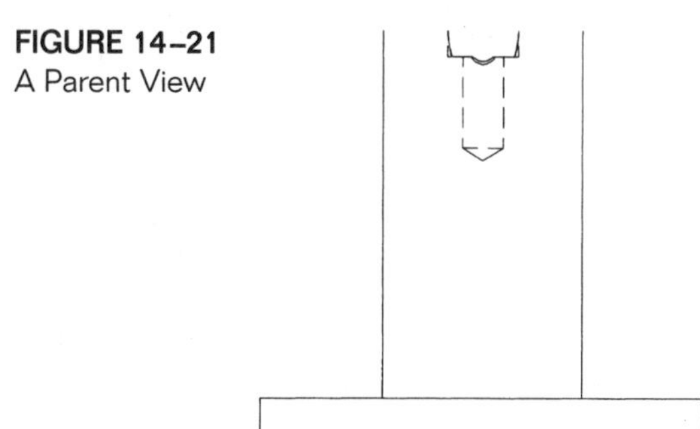

Orthographic Views (Figure 14-22)

Orthographic views are the standard 2-D plan views that are constructed from the parent view. When you place an othographic view above, below, or to either side of a parent view, AutoCAD automatically shows the view correctly aligned and with hidden lines in their correct location.

FIGURE 14-22
Orthographic Views

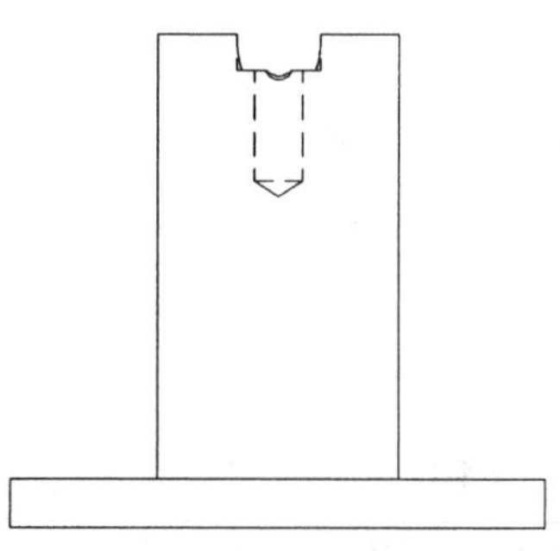

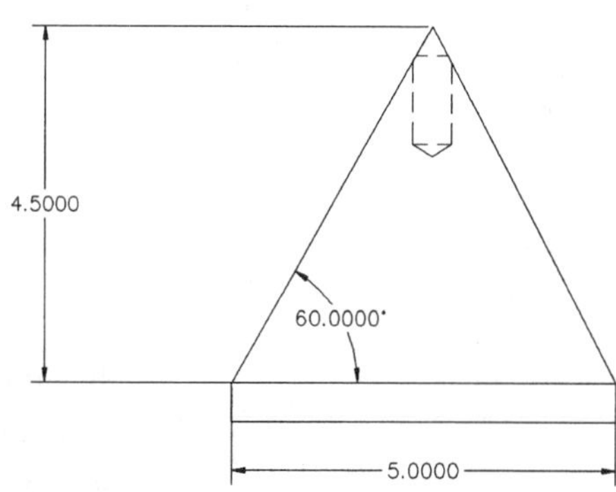

Auxiliary Views (Figure 14-23)

Auxiliary views show any face on a part of its true shape and size. They are commonly used on slanted surfaces. You can make an auxiliary view by picking the surface where it appears as an edge in the parent view, then picking on either side of the edge. Designer creates the view perpendicular to the selected edge.

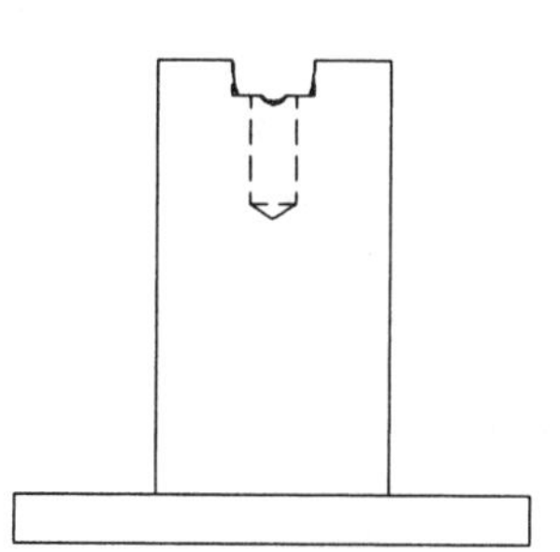

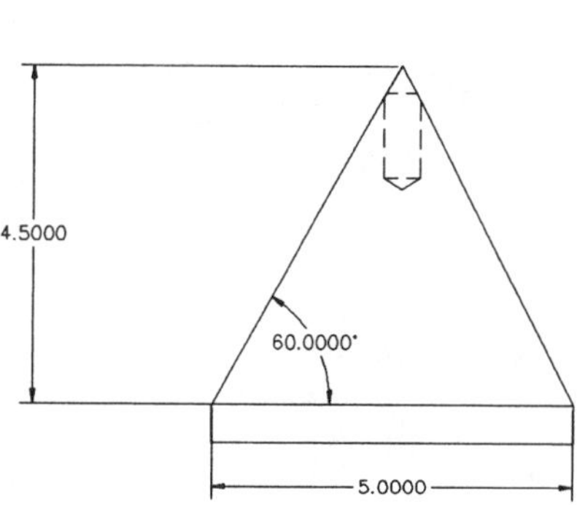

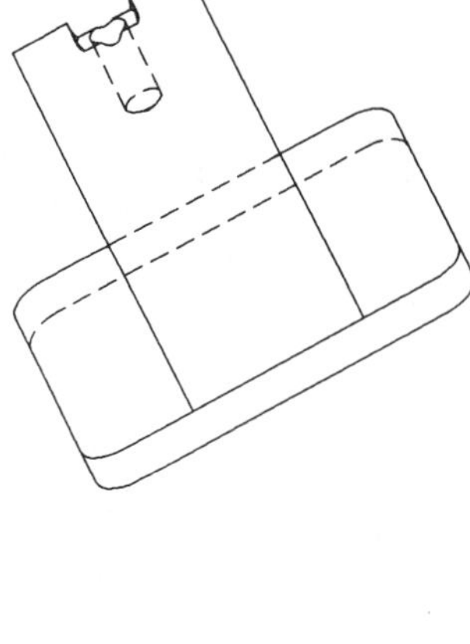

FIGURE 14-23
Auxiliary Views

Detail Views (Figure 14-24)

Detail views show an area of the part that requires more explanation or larger detail than the standard views. Designer allows you to enlarge the detail view to the part's true size or a multiple of that size. The detail view is in the same orientation as the parent view.

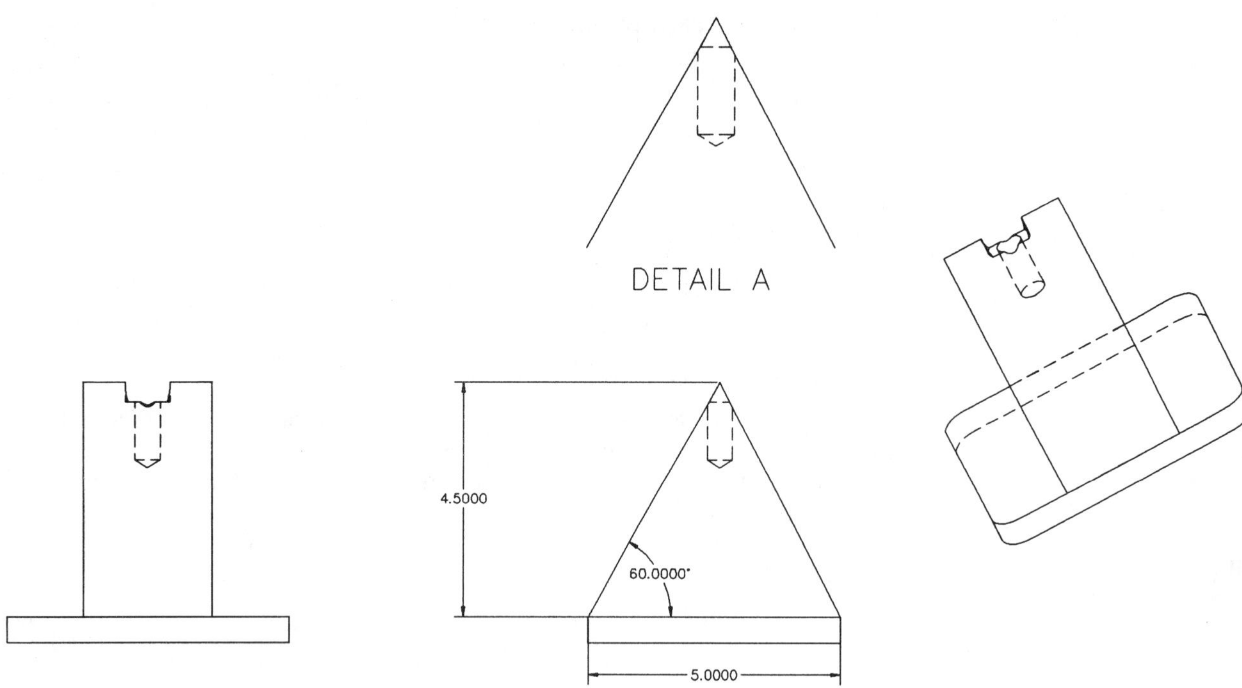

FIGURE 14–24
Detail View

Isometric Views (Figure 14–25)

Designer makes an isometric view for you if you choose and allows you to specify its scale and orientation. An isometric view is a 2-D view that gives the appearance of three dimensions by placing receding planes on 30° angles.

FIGURE 14–25
Isometric View

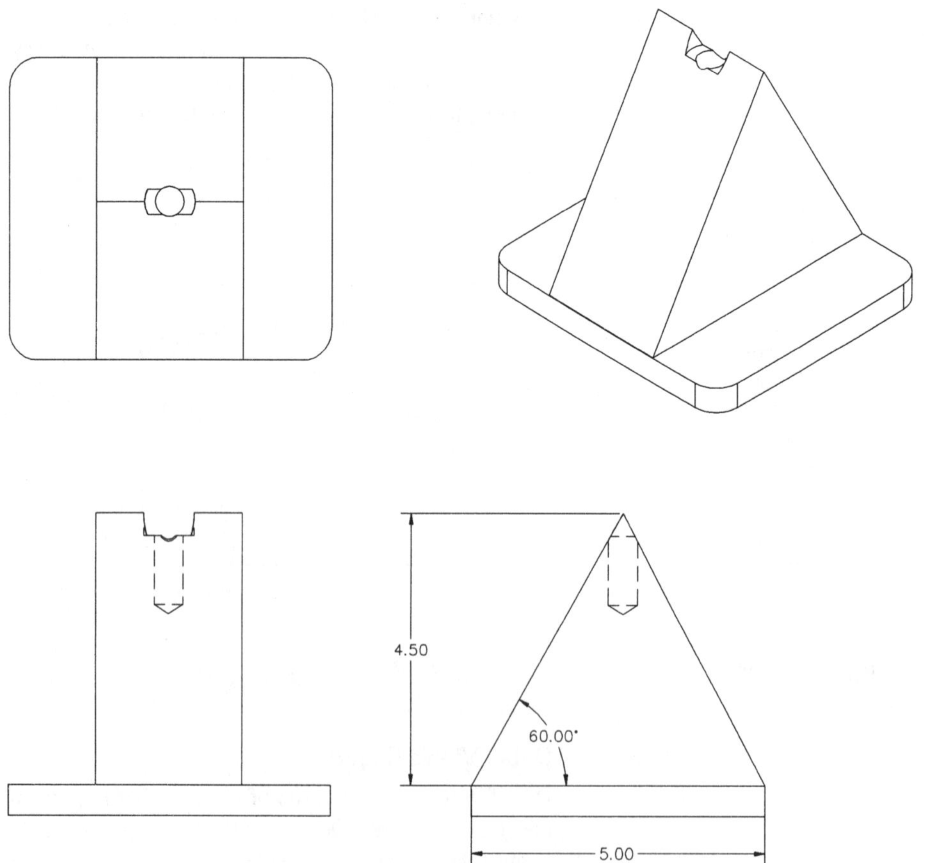

Cross-Sectional Views (Figure 14–26)

Cross-sectional views may be created from base, orthographic, and auxiliary views. They are made by selecting a work plane or point on the part through which you want to cut the cross section. The cutting plane will be parallel to the resulting cross-sectional view.

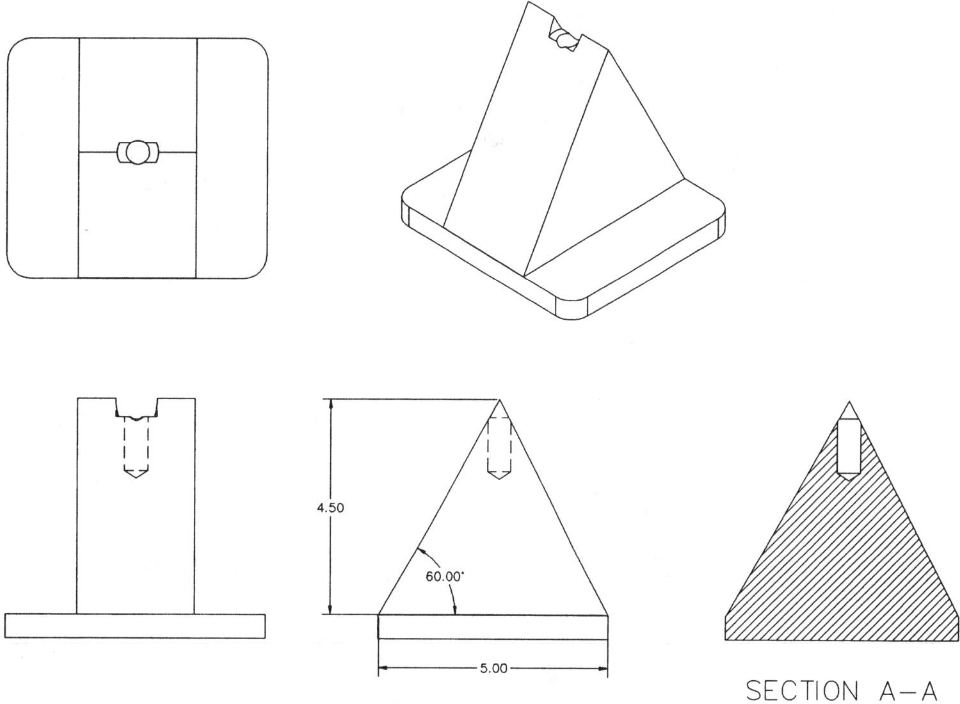

FIGURE 14–26
Cross-Sectional View

Displaying Mass Properties

You can obtain the mass property information for a single part or several parts with the ADMASSPROP command. When you activate the ADMASSPROP command for a single part, the information shown in Figure 14–27 appears. These data are reported in world co-

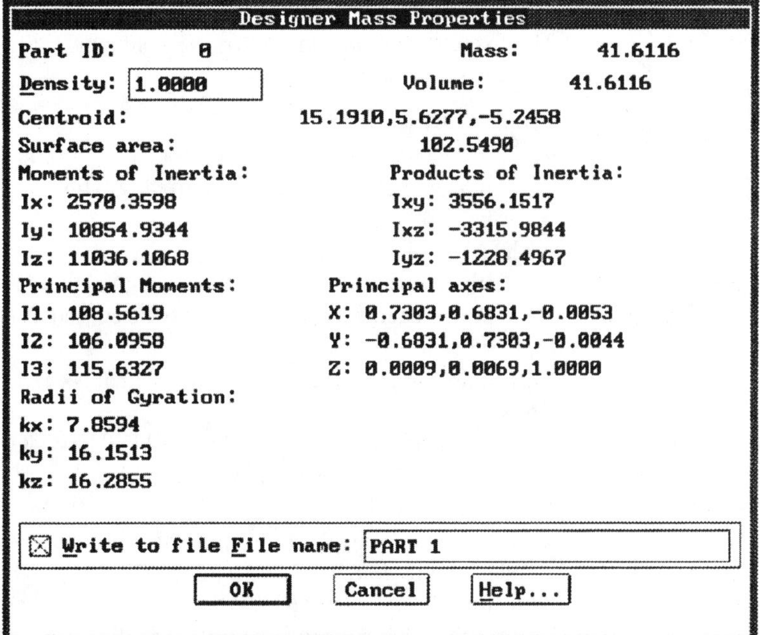

FIGURE 14–27
Designer Mass Properties Dialog Box

ordinate system coordinates. You can write the information to a file and print it out as shown in the File name: button.

If you select more than one part with the ADMASSPROP command, the information shown in Figure 14–28 appears. You can change the density value in both dialog boxes in Figures 14–27 and 14–28, and all affected values are updated automatically.

Now let's look at where the Designer commands are located.

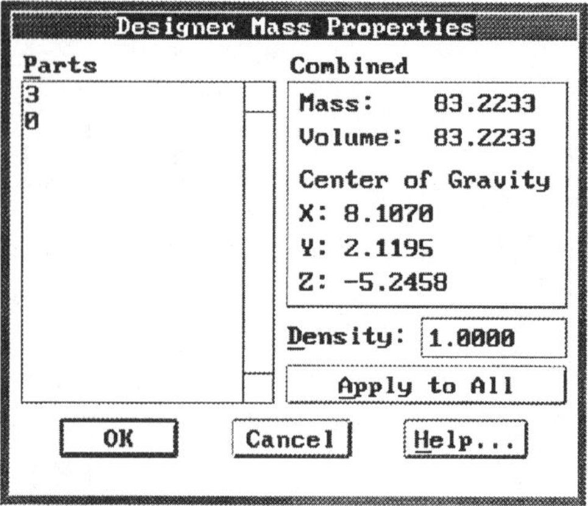

FIGURE 14–28
Designer Mass Properties Dialog Box for Multiple Parts

THE DESIGNER MENUS FOR DOS AND WINDOWS

The pull-down menu for Designer is the same in DOS as it is in Windows. You will find a toolbar in Windows and a screen menu in DOS for Designer. Use the menu you find most comfortable and efficient. For this book the common pull-down menu seems the logical choice, therefore, all references to picked commands will be from the pull-down menu.

Designer Pull-Down Menu, Figure 14–29

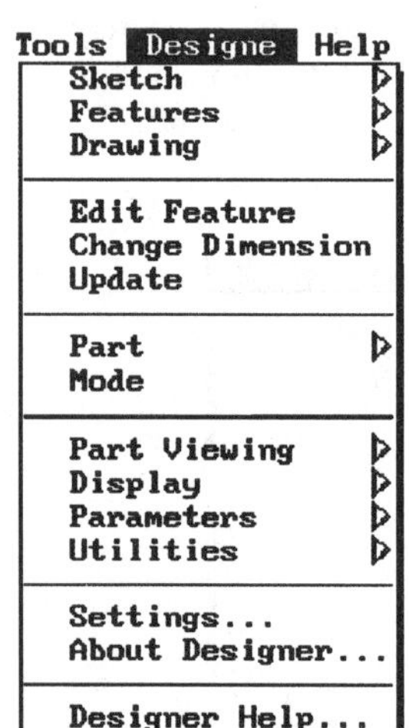

FIGURE 14–29
Designer Pull-Down Menu

Notice that several of the items on the menu have arrows at the right edge of the line. This indicates that there is a submenu attached to that item. All other items lead you directly into a command or activate a dialog box. Each item on the menu is described as follows:

Sketch, Figure 14–30

The Sketch menu has the following commands: (The command as typed from the keyboard is shown in parentheses.)

Profile (ADPROFILE)

The Profile command allows you to make a profile (similar to a region) of a 2-D object such as a circle, rectangle, or closed polyline that may then be extruded, revolved, or swept.

Path (ADPATH)

The Path command is used to create a path along which a shape may be swept (similar to being extruded except the path may be curved or at varied angles instead of straight)

Sketch Plane (ADSKPLN)

This command creates a sketch plane, which is needed for drawing any new feature.

Constraints

This submenu allows you to Show (ADSHOWCON), Add (ADADDCON), or Delete (ADDELCON) constraints to a sketch.

Fix Point (ADFIXPT)

This command allows you to move the assigned anchor point of any sketch to another point on the sketch.

Add Dimension (ADPARDIM)

This command lets you add a parametric dimension to the active sketch.

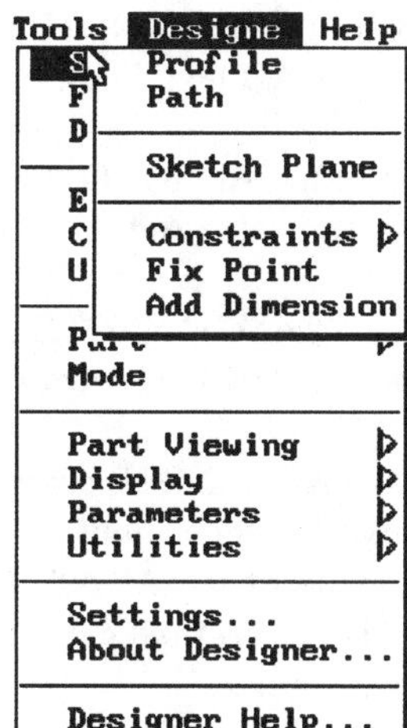

FIGURE 14–30
Sketch Submenu

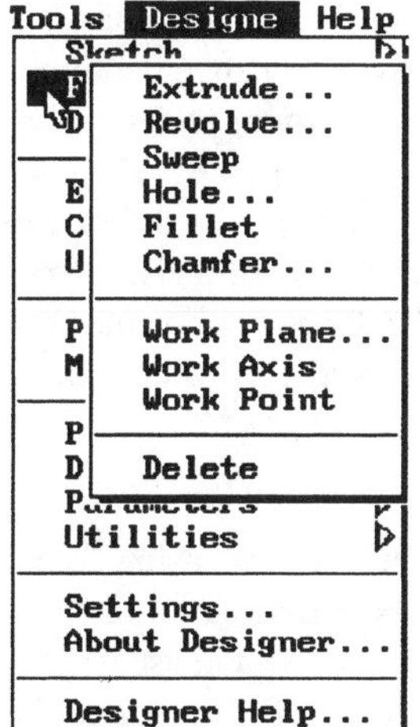

FIGURE 14–31
Features Submenu

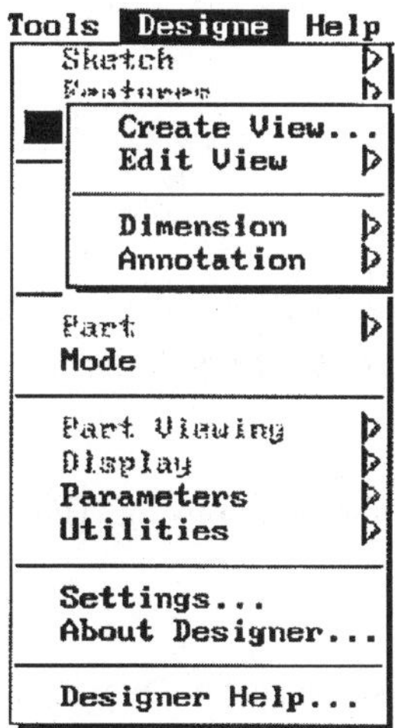

FIGURE 14–32
Drawing Submenu

Features, Figure 14–31

The Features submenu has the following commands:

Extrude. . . (ADEXTRUDE)
This command allows you to extrude a shape any specified distance and add or subtract the extruded feature from the part.

Revolve. . . (ADREVOLVE)
This command allows you to revolve a shape about an axis to create a feature that may be added to or subtracted from the active part.

Sweep. . . (ADSWEEP)
Lets you extrude a profile along a path to create a shape.

Hole. . . (ADHOLE)
Creates drilled, countersunk, or counterbored holes in the active part.

Fillet. . . (ADFILLET)
Creates fillets on selected edges of Designer solid models. It is not to be confused with the AutoCAD command Fillet:.

Chamfer. . . (ADCHAMFER)
Creates fillets on selected edges of Designer solid models. It is not to be confused with the AutoCAD command Chamfer:.

Work Plane. . . (ADWORKPLN)
This command activates the Designer Work Plane dialog boxes described earlier to create a work plane.

Work Axis (ADWORKAXIS)
This command creates a work axis through the center of any cylindrical feature.

Work Point (ADWORKPT)
This command creates a work point that is used for locating holes.

Delete (ADDELFEAT)
This command allows you to select features to delete from the part.

Drawing, Figure 14–32

You must be in drawing mode to use any of the commands on this submenu. This submenu contains the following commands:

Create View. . . (ADVIEW)
This command activates the Designer Drawing View dialog box and allows you to create a drawing view of the part in paper space.

Edit View
This submenu takes you to the following commands:

Attribute (ADEDITVIEW) allows you to change the scale, associated text, and hidden line display of the selected drawing view.

Delete (ADDELVIEW) allows you to delete a view.

Move (ADMOVEVIEW) allows you to move a view.

Dimension
This submenu takes you to the following commands:

Ref Dim (ADREFDIM) allows you to add a reference dimension to the drawing (this dimension has no control over the part).

Delete Ref Dim (ADDELREF) allows you to delete a reference dimension.

Move (ADMOVEDIM) allows you to move a dimension while maintaining its associativity to the part.

Freeze (ADFRZDIM) hides the selected dimension on a drawing.

Thaw (ADTHAWDIM) displays selected dimensions frozen with the ADFRZDIM command.

Attributes (ADDIMATT) allows you to change the appearance, precision, and tolerance of drawing view dimensions.

Annotation
This submenu takes you to the following options of the ADANNOTE command and two other commands associated with annotations: (*Annotations* are items such as ballooned callouts, center lines, and surface finish symbols.)

Create (ADANNOTE) takes you to the Create option of the ADANNOTE command and allows you to make an annotation from AutoCAD text, lines, circles and blocks.

Delete (ADANNOTE) takes you to the Delete option of the ADANNOTE command and allows you to delete annotations and their associated AutoCAD text, lines, circles, etc.

Move (ADANNOTE) takes you to the Move option of the ADANNOTE command and allows you to move an annotation around the drawing view or part edge.

Add (ADANNOTE) takes you to the Add option of the ADANNOTE command and allows you to add selected AutoCAD objects to existing annotations.

Remove (ADANNOTE) takes you to the Remove option of the ADANNOTE command and allows you to remove selected AutoCAD objects from the annotation without deleting the annotation.

Move Leader (ADMOVELDR) allows you to move an annotation leader by changing the start point of the leader arrowhead to a new point.

Hole Note (ADHOLENOTE) creates a standard note with diameter, depth, and angle information for a selected hole in the drawing.

Edit Feature (ADEDITFEAT)

This item on the Designer menu leads you directly into the Edit Feature command, which works only in part mode. This command allows you to display and change the dimension values of the active part's features. You can use dimensions or equations to define the relationships between dimensions. Each dimension has a tag such as d0, d1, or d2. The tag value may be used in an equation to establish another dimension, for example d1=d0 + d2 + .25. Edit Feature allows you to change the parametric dimensions of the part. It also allows you to select the sketch of a feature on the active part and change the dimensions on the sketch of that feature. The Update command must be used before the changed dimension changes the size of the active part.

Change Dimension (ADMODDIM)

This item on the Designer menu leads you directly into the Change Dimension command, which allows you to change parametric dimensions on either the active part or on the drawing. As with Edit Feature, the Change Dimension command allows you to use dimensions or equations to establish relationships between dimensions on the part or drawing. The Update command must be used before the changed dimension changes the size of the active part.

Update (ADUPDATE)

This item on the Designer menu leads you directly into the Update command. Update regenerates the active part and any drawing views you have created to reflect changes you have made to any dimensions.

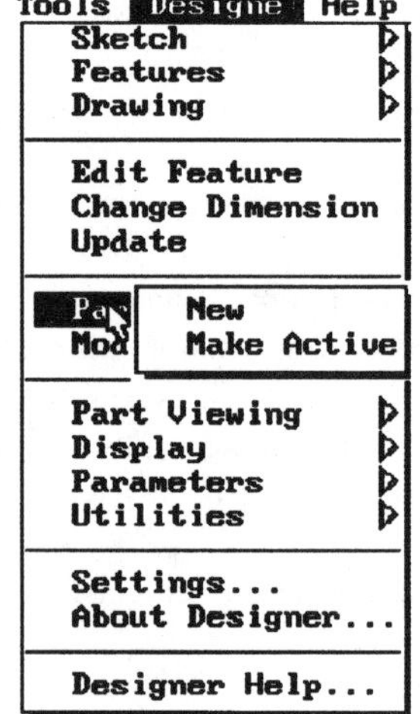

FIGURE 14–33
Part Submenu

Part, Figure 14–33

This submenu has the following two commands:

New (ADNEWPART)
ADNEWPART allows you to start a new part in the current drawing file and make it active. It does not create any geometry. New geometry is created as with the first part created in the drawing file.

Make Active (ADACTPART)
ADACTPART allows you to switch between parts in a multiple-part drawing. This command works only in part mode.

Mode (ADMODE)

This command lets you switch from Part mode (similar to model space) to Drawing mode (similar to paper space) and vice versa. If you want to add or delete a feature from the part you must be in Part mode. To annotate the drawing or tidy it up you must be in Drawing mode.

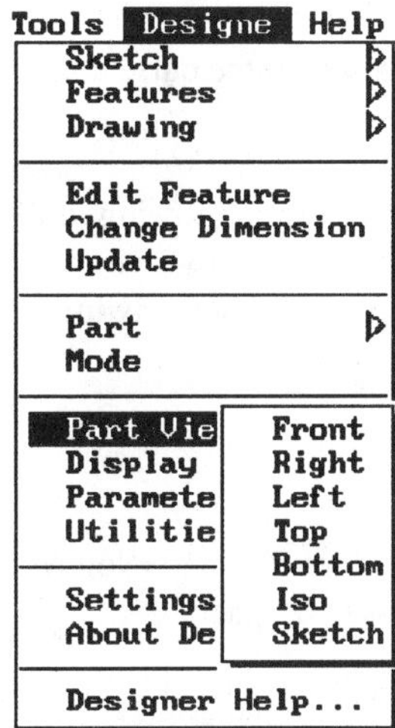

FIGURE 14–34
Part Viewing

Part Viewing (ADPARTVIEW), Figure 14–34

This command allows you to change your view of the model in Part mode. The choices shown on the menu relate to the world UCS, with the Front option showing the plan view of the world UCS. This may be a little disconcerting if you are used to using the plan view of the world UCS as the top view, but it is easy to adjust to if you choose to use the Designer Part Viewing command to view the model (you can use the AutoCAD Viewpoint: command for viewing models if you choose). The first six options on the Part Viewing command are obvious. Sketch, the seventh option, allows you to align the view with the active sketch plane.

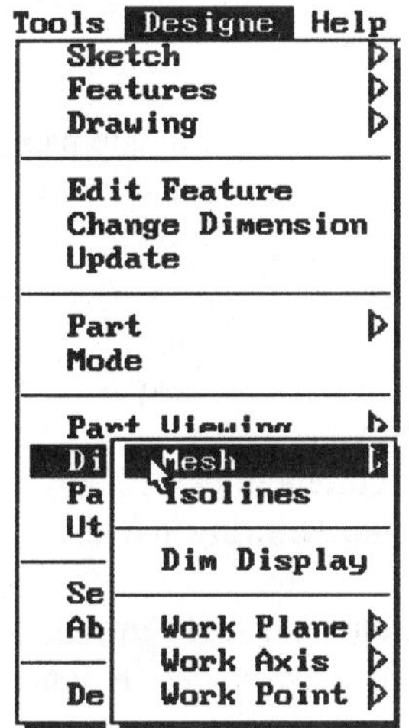

FIGURE 14–35
Display Submenu

Display, Figure 14–35

This submenu has the following commands:

Mesh (ADMESH)

This command can be ON or OFF. ON displays the model surfaces as meshes, which allows the model to appear solid when Hide:, Shade, or Render commands are used. When the ON option is selected, Designer prompts you to enter a tolerance for the mesh (stated as the allowable deviation between facets and model). The default of 0.1 is OK for some models, not for others (this depends on the size of the model). Smaller models with curved surfaces often will require a setting of 0.001. OFF displays the model as a wire frame with no meshed surfaces.

Isolines (ADISOLINES)

This command sets the number of lines to be displayed on wireframes (not meshes). Mesh command should be OFF when the part is selected to update the isoline value.

Dim Display (ADDIMDSP)

This command changes the display mode for dimensions. The modes are:

Parameters shows only the dimension parameter name.

Equations shows the equation for dimensions that have been constructed in this manner.

Numeric shows the numeric value of the dimension.

Work Plane (ADPLNDSP)

This command displays or hides work planes on the active part. ON displays them; OFF hides them.

Work Axis (ADAXISDSP)

This command displays or hides work axes on the active part. ON displays them; OFF hides them.

Work Point (ADPTDSP)

This command displays or hides work points on the active part. ON displays them; OFF hides them.

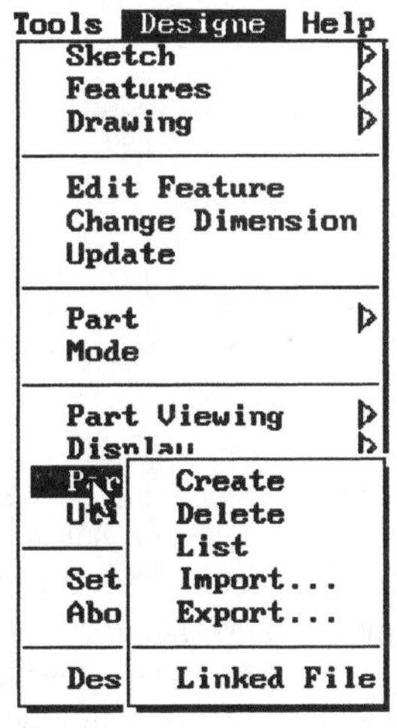

FIGURE 14–36
Parameters Submenu

Parameter, Figure 14–36

This submenu contains the following options to the Parameters (ADPARAM) command and also contains the Linked File (ADPARAFILE) command:

Create (ADPARAM)

This option lets you define global parameters and assign numeric values or equations to them. For example, the global parameter to which you assign the name Length could have the value of 10 if you make an equation that says Length = 8. You could then set up a parameter of Width and write an equation that says Width = .5 Length, so that a model based on these parameters would measure 8 × 4.

Delete (ADPARAM)

This option allows you to delete selected parameters from the current drawing.

List (ADPARAM)

This option lists all parameters defined in the current drawing.

Import. . . (ADPARAM)

This option brings a global parameter file into the current drawing. These global parameter files are created with the Export. . . option and have the extension .prm.

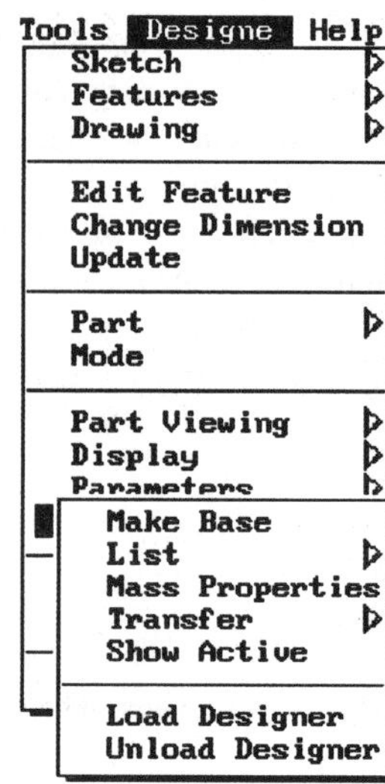

FIGURE 14–37
Utilities Submenu

Export. . . (ADPARAM)
This option allows you to export a set of global parameters defined in the current drawing to a file with the extension .prm.

Linked File (ADPARFILE)
Although you can import any number of parameter files into the current drawing, only the last file imported becomes the linked parameter file. This command allows you to select the file containing the parameters you want and link them to the current drawing.

Utilities, Figure 14–37

This submenu contains the following commands:

Make Base (ADMAKEBASE)
This command converts the active part into a static part (like a library of parts you can use on any designer part) and compresses the part to take up less disk space.

List (ADLIST)
This menu contains the following options of the List (ADLIST) command:

Feature (ADLIST) allows you to list information about features on specified parts. You must be in Part mode to use this option.

Part (ADLIST) lists the part identification and feature information for the part you specify. You must be in Part mode to use this option.

Drawing View (ADLIST) lists information about selected views on the current drawing. You must be in Drawing mode to use this option.

Mass Properties (ADMASSPROP)
This command lists the mass properties for specified parts. If you select a single part, the Designer Mass Properties dialog box, Figure 14–27, appears. If you select more than one part, the dialog box in Figure 14–28 appears.

Transfer
This submenu contains the following commands:

Part Out (ADPARTOUT) saves selected part(s) into a separate .dwg file, which you name. Only Designer parts are saved, no drawing views.

Part In (ADPARTIN) inserts Designer parts into the current drawing. Only parts are inserted from the .dwg file; views created in the Drawing mode are not inserted.

SAT In (ADSATIN) reads in an .sat format file, which is an ACIS international data exchange file. Only ACIS solid bodies are read in. Wire bodies are ignored.

SAT Out (ADSATOUT) writes out a Designer file in an .sat format (ACIS) file. Only ACIS solid bodies are read in; wire bodies are ignored. You would use this command instead of ADPARTOUT if you plan to use the file in another program.

AutoSurf Out (ADASFCONV) converts Designer parts into a collection of AutoSurf surfaces. These surfaces could then be used with the AutoSurf program to create more complex surfaces.

Show Active (ADSHOWACT)
This command highlights the active part. You will use this when you have several parts on a drawing and you forget which is the active one.

Load Designer
Selecting this from the menu loads the Designer program.

Unload Designer
Selecting this from the menu unloads the Designer program.

Settings. . . (ADSETTINGS), Figure 14–38

This command activates the Designer Settings dialog box, Figure 14–38. When you pick Drawing Settings. . . , an additional Drawing Variables dialog box appears that allows you to make other settings affecting the drawing views. The default settings for all these variables are correct for most of the drawings you will be required to do. The First Angle setting found on the Drawing Variables dialog box places drawing views in an orientation that is different from what you are used to seeing. Use this setting if you are doing drawings for European customers who use First Angle Projection for most of their drawings. Consult any good engineering graphics text book for an explanation of projection methods.

FIGURE 14–38
Designer Settings Dialog Box

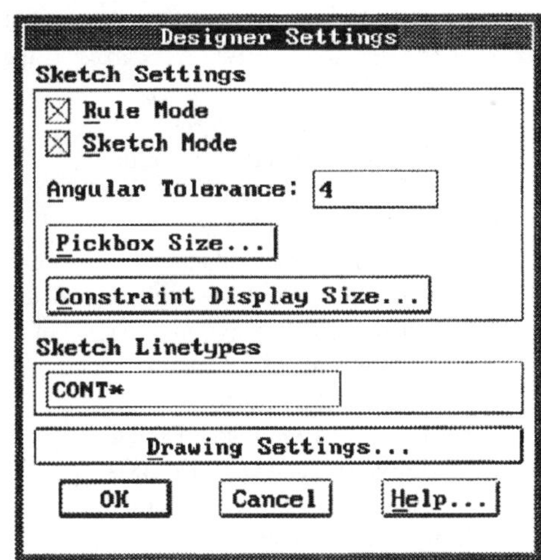

About Designer. . .

This item gives you copyright information about Designer.

Designer Help. . . , Figure 14–39

Get familiar with using Designer Help by picking Designer Help and then picking Help from the Designer Help dialog box. The Help on AutoCAD Help dialog box appears. Spend a few minutes learning how to use Help to get answers to questions you may encounter as you learn the Designer program.

FIGURE 14–39
Designer Help

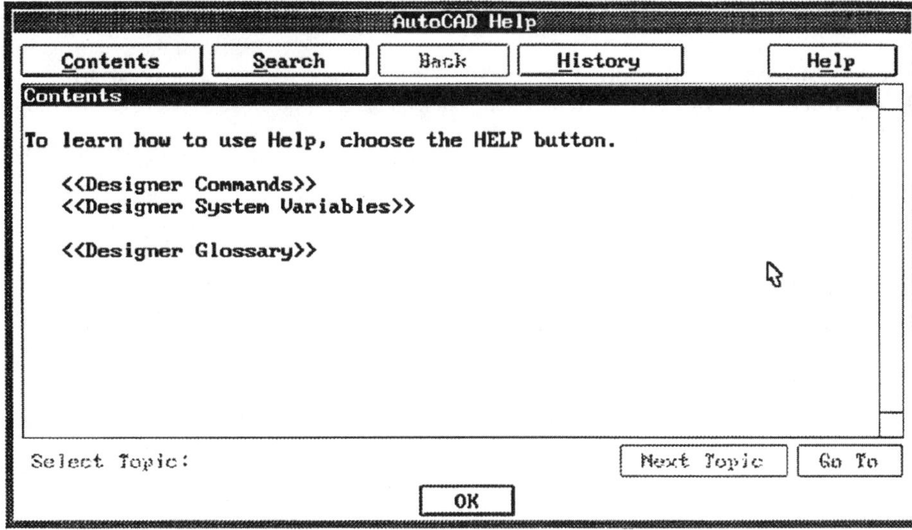

REVIEW QUESTIONS

Circle the correct answer.

1. AutoCAD Designer is part of the standard AutoCAD program.
   a. True b. False
2. Parametrics as it relates to Designer consists of:
   a. Dimensions of shape
   b. Dimensions and constraints
   c. Constraints only
   d. Dimensions only
   e. Material density
3. Which of the following is not an example of a Designer constraint?
   a. Concentric
   b. Colinear
   c. Horizontal
   d. Tangent
   e. Endpoint
4. The sketch plane is similar to which of the following AutoCAD commands?
   a. Mview:
   b. Dview:
   c. UCS:
   d. Vpoint:
   e. Vports:
5. Work planes are used to do which of the following?
   a. Act as the sketch plane
   b. Locate the sketch plane
   c. Locate work axes
   d. Locate the correct viewpoint
   e. Assign layers

6. The parametric work plane option that could be used to locate a work plane through two work axes in the centers of two holes is:
   a. On Edge/Axis and Tangent
   b. On Edge/Axis and Planar Parallel
   c. On Edge/Axis and On Edge/Axis
   d. On Edge/Axis and Planar Normal
   e. Tangent and Planar Parallel
7. The parametric work plane option that could be used to locate a work plane on a work axis in the center of a hole and parallel to the bottom plane of the part is:
   a. On Edge/Axis and Tangent
   b. On Edge/Axis and Planar Parallel
   c. On Edge/Axis and On Edge/Axis
   d. On Edge/Axis and Planar Normal
   e. Tangent and Planar Parallel
8. The parametric work plane option that could be used to locate a work plane on a work axis in the center of a hole and through the front edge of the bottom surface is:
   a. On Edge/Axis and Tangent
   b. On Edge/Axis and Planar Parallel
   c. On Edge/Axis and On Edge/Axis
   d. On Edge/Axis and Planar Normal
   e. Tangent and Planar Parallel
9. Which of the following is an option for a nonparametric work plane?
   a. Tangent and Planar Normal
   b. Sweep
   c. On 3 Vertices
   d. On UCS
   e. On Edge/Axis and Tangent
10. Which of the following is not a Termination option on the Designer Extrusion dialog box?
    a. Blind
    b. Mid Plane
    c. From Plane
    d. To Plane
    e. Through

Complete.

11. Describe the function of the ADSWEEP command.

    ____

    ____

12. List the three Operation options on the Designer Hole dialog box.

    __________ __________ __________

13. List four features through which a work axis may be created.

    ____

    ____

    ____

    ____

14. Describe the difference between parametric and reference dimensions.

    ____

    ____

15. Describe the function of a parent view.

    ____

    ____

    ____

    ____

16. List three types of views from which a cross-sectional view may be created.

    __________ __________ __________

17. List the command that creates a profile of a 2-D object that may then be extruded.

    ____

18. List the command that allows you to add a parametric dimension to a sketch.

    ____

19. List the command that creates a standard note for a selected hole in drawing.

    ____

20. List the option of the Part Viewing (ADPARTVIEW) command that is the same as the plan view of the world UCS.

    ____

15 Drawing Designer Solid Models

OBJECTIVES

After completing this chapter, you will be able to:

- □ Draw, dimension, and assign constraints to a single Designer solid model.
- □ Draw, dimension, and assign constraints to a four-piece assembly constructed with AutoCAD Designer.

INTRODUCTION

This chapter leads you step-by-step through the construction of two solid models: one a single part, the other a four-piece assembly. Each Designer command used to construct these parts is explained in detail as it is used. The location of each command on the pull-down menu is shown the first time the command is used. We will begin with the single part shown in Figure 15–1. When you have completed Exercise 15–1, your drawing will look like Figure 15–23.

EXERCISE 15–1
DRAWING A SOLID MODEL OF A SINGLE PART USING AUTOCAD DESIGNER COMMANDS

Set Up the Drawing

Step 1. On Your Own:

1. Turn on the computer, start AutoCAD Designer, and pick New. . . from the menu bar File menu. Name the drawing: 15-1 (your initials).
2. Make the following settings:

UNITS: Decimal; 3 digits to the right of the decimal point

LIMITS: Lower left corner: 0,0
Upper right corner: 8.5,11

GRID: .2

SNAP: .05

STYLE: STANDARD; FONT: SIMPLEX; HEIGHT: 0

Create the following layers:

LAYER NAME	COLOR	LINETYPE
Y	YELLOW	CONTINUOUS
R	RED	CONTINUOUS
G	GREEN	CONTINUOUS

Set layer G current.

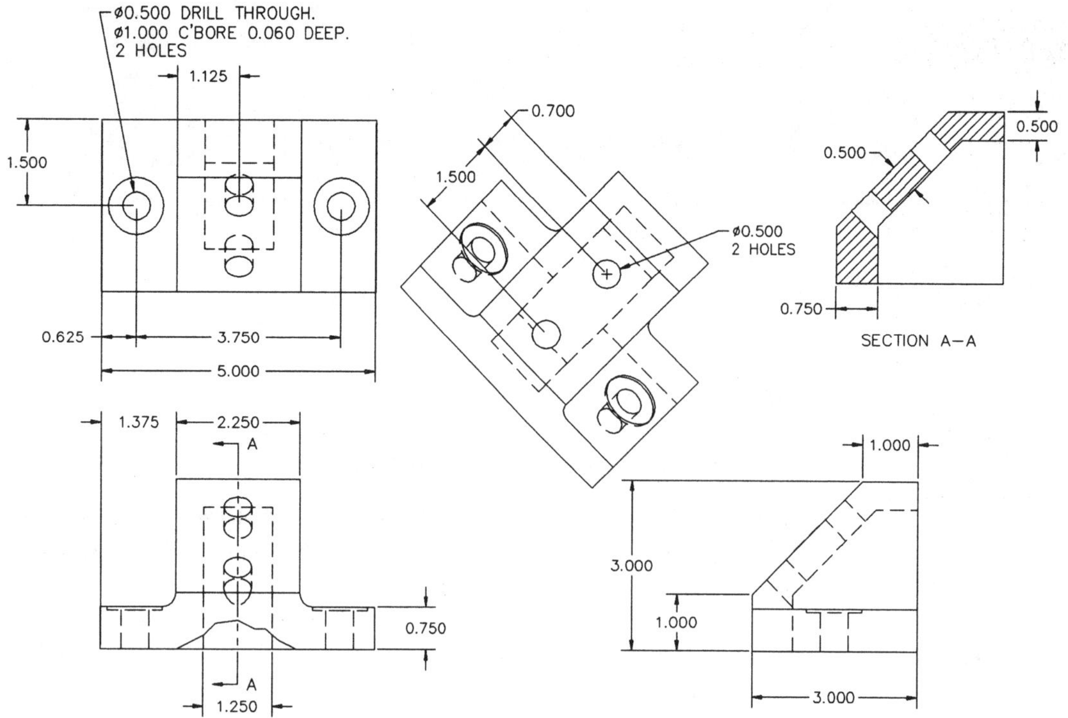

FIGURE 15–1
Dimensions for the Model

Create the Base.

Warning: Designer places sketch geometry and dimensions for all newly created features on the ADP_FRZ layer so they can be displayed later. Do not edit the contents of the ADP_FRZ layer by thawing it. This will permanently destroy or corrupt the model.

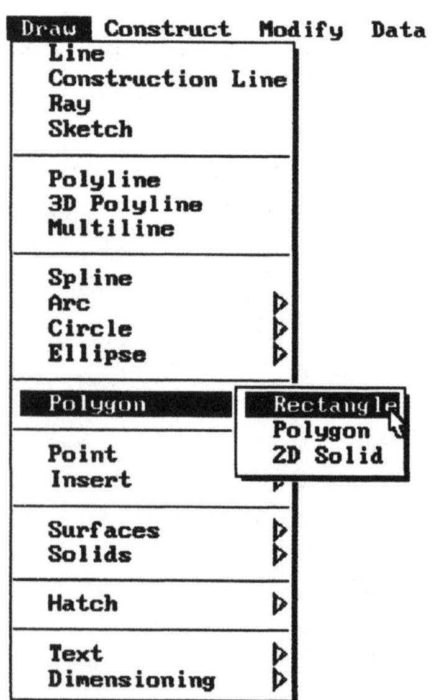

Step 2. Make a sketch, create a profile for the base, and dimension it. Although the sketch may be much less accurate than the drawing method used below, since you know how to draw accurately, it will be simpler to use accurate dimensions.

Prompt	**Response**
Command:	**Rectang:**
First corner:	*Type:* **1.5,5** ↵
Other corner:	*Type:* **@5,.75** ↵

Making a profile of the rectangle is the next step. Let's examine the ADPROFILE command before you use it.

ADPROFILE

This command creates an active sketch that can be used to construct solids using Extrude, Revolve, and Sweep. Profiles are created from 2-D geometry, model edges, sketch planes, work axes, and dimensions. The sketch for the profile must be closed. ADPROFILE automatically applies certain constraints to the sketch, such as vertical, horizontal, parallel, and tangent, and with ADSKMODE (sketch mode) on, lines that are almost vertical, horizontal, and parallel are assumed to be such. With ADSKMODE off, the sketch must be drawn precisely.

Step 3. Make the profile.

Prompt	**Response**
Command:	**Profile**
Select objects for sketch.	
Select objects:	**D1** (Figure 15–2)

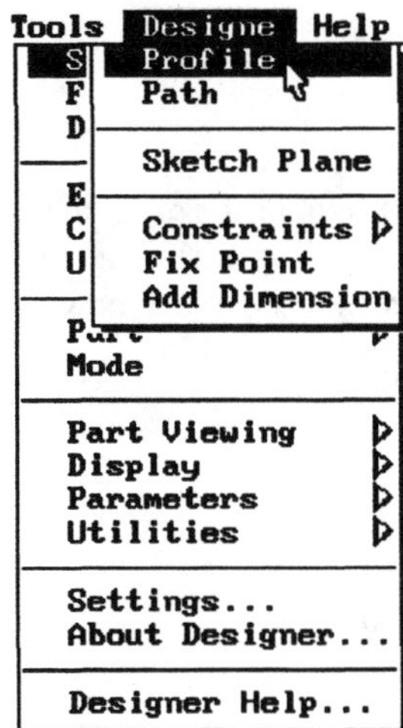

Select objects:
Solved under constrained sketch
requiring 2 dimensions/constraints. ↵

Now let's look at the ADPARDIM command.

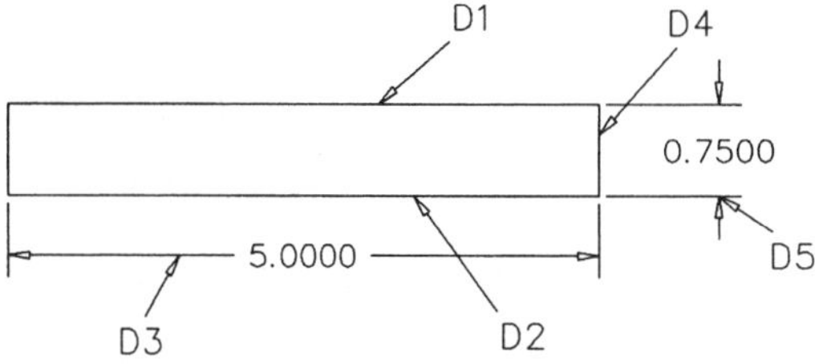

FIGURE 15–2
Dimensioning the Profile

ADPARDIM

ADPARDIM allows you to dimension the active sketch with values that control the creation of the part. For example, when you use this command, you apply a parametric dimension that can be changed when it is created or later if necessary. As the value of the dimension is changed the part itself changes to the new value (the ADUPDATE command must be used when changes have been made to an existing part). The following prompt appears when the dimension is placed:

Undo/Hor/Ver/Align/Par/Dimension value < >:

Undo
Eliminates the current dimension.
Hor
Changes the newly created dimension to a horizontal dimension.
Ver
Changes the newly created dimension to a vertical dimension.
Align
Changes the newly created dimension to an aligned dimension.
Par
Changes the newly created dimension to a parallel dimension.
Dimension value < >
Pressing ↵ accepts the dimension value shown in brackets.

Where you specify the placement of the dimension determines whether you have a horizontal, vertical, or aligned dimension. These placement rules will be examined when dimensions are added.

The sketch does not have to be fully constrained for you to proceed with the drawing, but since you will need these two dimensions later, let's add them now.

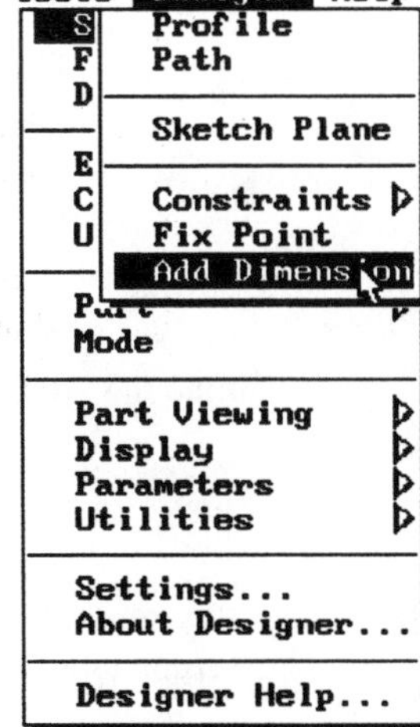

Step 4. Add parametric dimensions.

Prompt	Response
Command:	**Add Dimension**
Select first item:	**D2** (Figure 15–2)
Select second item or place dimension:	**D3**
Undo/Hor/Ver/Align/Par/Dimension value <5.0000>:	↵
Solved under constrained sketch requiring 1 dimension/constraint.	
Select first item:	**D4** (Figure 15–2)
Select second item or place dimension:	**D5**
Undo/Hor/Ver/Align/Par/Dimension value <0.7500>:	↵

Prompt	Response
Solved fully constrained sketch.	
Select first item:	↵

These dimensions carry the default setting of 4 places to the right of the decimal point. Let's say we need a setting of 3 places to the right of the decimal point. Changing the setting now will allow you to make all dimensions with 3-place decimals. Do that now.

Step 5. Change the dimensioning units to 3-place decimals.

Prompt	Response
Command:	*Type:* **DDIM** ↵
The Dimension Styles dialog box appears:	*Pick:* **Annotation. . .**
The Annotation dialog box appears:	*Pick:* **Units**
The Primary Units dialog box, Figure 15–3, appears:	Pick the Precision: slider bar and highlight 0.000 as shown.
	Pick OK on all three Dimension Styles dialog boxes.

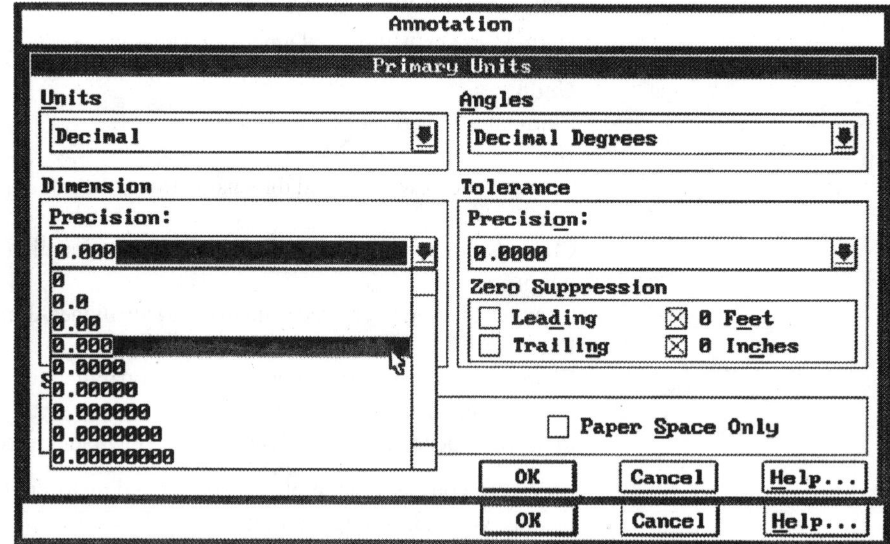

FIGURE 15–3
Primary Units Dialog Box

From this point forward all dimensions will be in 3-place decimals. Let's fix the two dimensions you already have that contain 4-place decimals by using the dimension command Update.

Prompt	Response
Command:	*Type:* **DIM** ↵
Dim:	*Type:* **UP** ↵
Select objects:	Pick the two dimensions containing 4-place decimals.

The next step is to extrude the profile. Before you do that, let's examine the ADEXTRUDE command.

ADEXTRUDE

ADEXTRUDE creates an extruded solid from the active sketch. When this command is activated, the Designer Extrusion dialog box, Figure 15–4, appears. The Termination, Operation, and Size options are described next:

FIGURE 15–4
Designer Extrusion Dialog Box

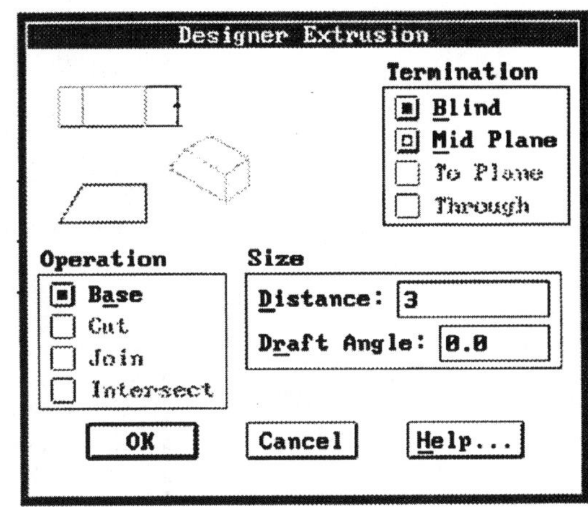

Termination

Blind

Extrudes the profile to a specified distance.

Mid Plane

Extrudes the profile equally in both directions, so that if you specify a size distance of 2″, the extrusion is formed 1″ in front and 1″ in back of the profile.

To Plane

Extrudes the profile to a specified planar surface or work plane.

Through

Cuts completely through the solid part. This option is available for cuts and intersections only.

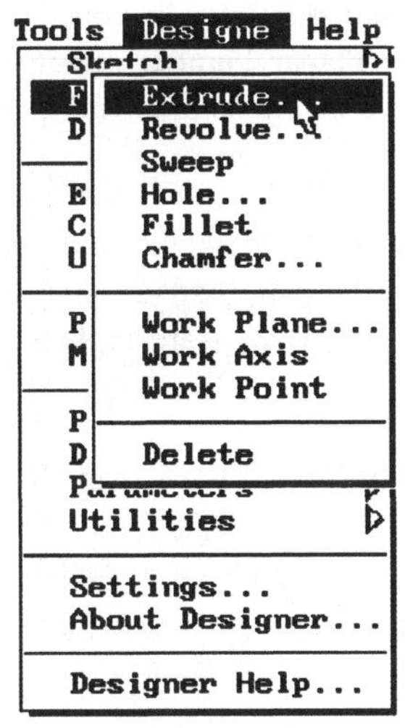

Operation

Base

Creates the first feature of a part.

Cut

Removes material from the active part; similar to Subtrac: in AutoCAD solids.

Join

Adds the extruded feature to the active part.

Intersect

Creates a new feature from the common volume of the existing part and the extruded profile.

Size

Distance

Specifies the distance the profile will be extruded.

Draft Angle

Specifies the slant angle of the profile as it is extruded. A negative draft angle creates a negative draft.

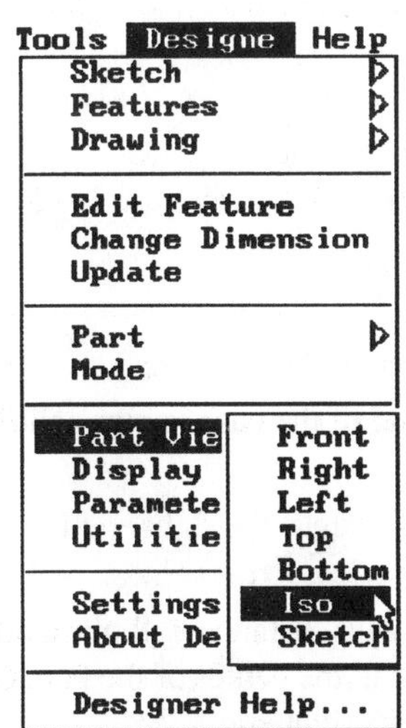

Step 6. Extrude the base.

Prompt	Response
Dim:	**Extrude. . .**
The Designer Extrusion dialog box, Figure 15–4, appears:	Change the Distance: value to 3 as shown. *Pick:* **OK**

Now let's view the part so you can see what you are doing.

Prompt	Response
Command:	**Part Viewing** **Iso**

Before you construct your first work plane, let's examine the ADWORKPLN command.

ADWORKPLN

ADWORKPLN creates a work plane on the active part. When you activate this command, the Designer Work Plane dialog box, Figure 15–5 appears. This dialog box is divided into three areas: Parametric, Non-Parametric, and Create Sketch Plane.

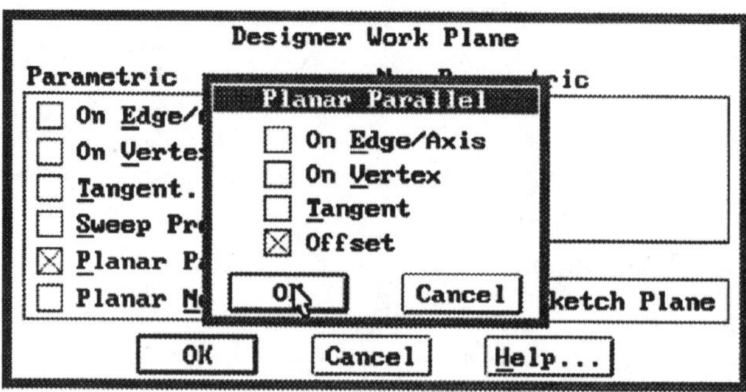

FIGURE 15–5
Designer Work Plane Dialog Box

Parametric
Parametric work planes are attached to edges, axes, vertices, and surfaces of a part so that when the geometry of the part changes, the location of the work plane changes with it.

When you select one of the options of the Parametric area a dialog box for that option appears. For example, when Planar Parallel is picked, the Planar Parallel dialog box appears. This allows you to combine options to specify the constraints of a work plane. Chapter 14 contains a complete description of these options.

Non-Parametric
Nonparametric work planes are in fixed positions with no links to the geometry of the part. Nonparametric work planes do not change position when the part changes its size or shape. The two types of nonparametric work planes—UCS and WCS—are explained in detail in Chapter 14.

Create Sketch Plane
The Create Sketch Plane area allows you to specify the newly created work plane as the sketch plane.

Create the Upright Part of the Model

Step 7. Construct a work plane.

Prompt	Response
Command:	**Work Plane**
The Designer Work Plane dialog box, Figure 15–5, appears:	*Pick:* **Planar Parallel** then **Offset** as shown (Figure 15–5).
	Pick: **OK** twice.
Xy/Yz/Zx/Ucs/<Select work plane or planar face>:	*Pick:* **D1** (Figure 15–6)
Next/<Accept>:	If the right end of the base is highlighted, *Press:* ↵.
	If not, type **N** ↵ until the right end is highlighted, then *Press:* ↵
Offset <1>:	*Type:* **2.5** ↵ (This distance will place the work plane in the center of the base parallel to its right end.)

FIGURE 15–6
Selecting the Planar Surface

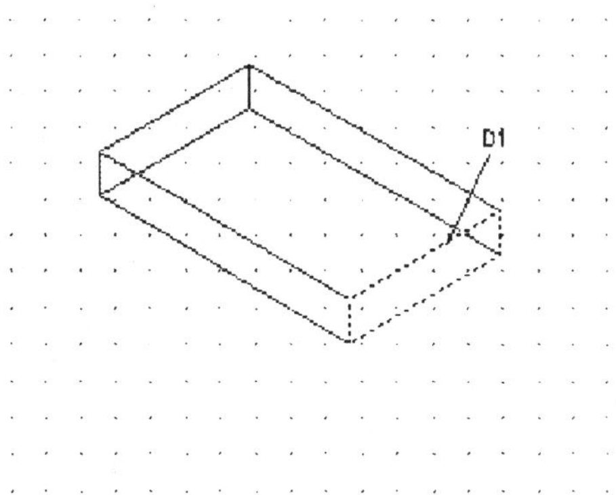

Flip/<Accept>:

If the work plane appears as shown in Figure 15–7,
Type: **F** ↵.

FIGURE 15–7
Flipping the Work Plane

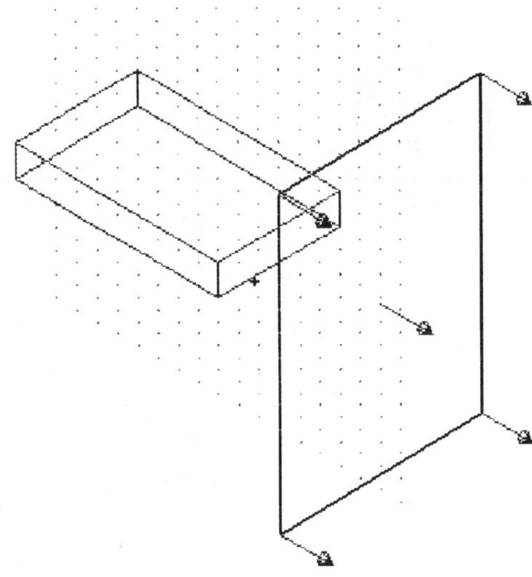

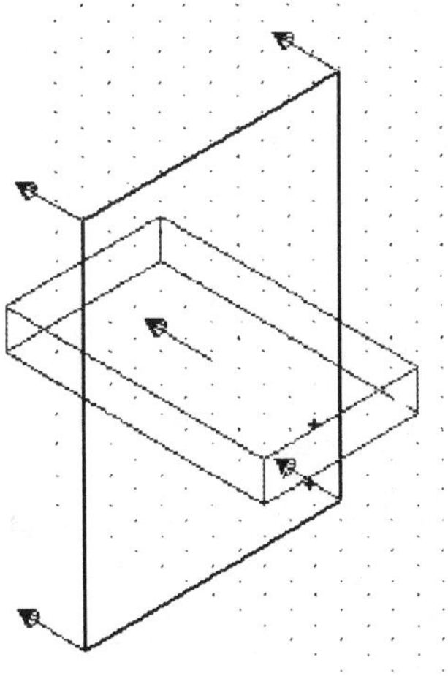

FIGURE 15–8
Accepting the Work Plane

Flip/<Accept>:

If the work plane appears as shown in Figure 15–8,
Press: ↵.

Before you make your first sketch plane, let's look at the ADSKPLN command.

ADSKPLN

This command sets the sketch plane on which the profile for the next feature of the part is drawn. You do not see the sketch plane, as you do work planes. There is only one sketch plane that is moved from surface to surface as new features on the part are created. The options of the Sketch Plane command are:

Xy/Yz/Zx/Ucs/<Select work plane or planar face>:

At this point you may type the first letter of any of the first four options to specify how you want the coordinates of the sketch oriented. You may also pick a work plane or any other surface as a sketch plane.

After the first option has been selected, the following prompt appears:

X/Y/Z/<Select work axis or straight edge>: You may now specify the X, Y, or Z axis by typing one of those letters, or you may select a work axis or a straight edge of a surface.

After you have selected the axis or straight edge, the UCSICON appears with the following prompt:

Rotate/<Accept>: You may now rotate the sketch plane if it is not in the correct orientation or accept the current orientation.

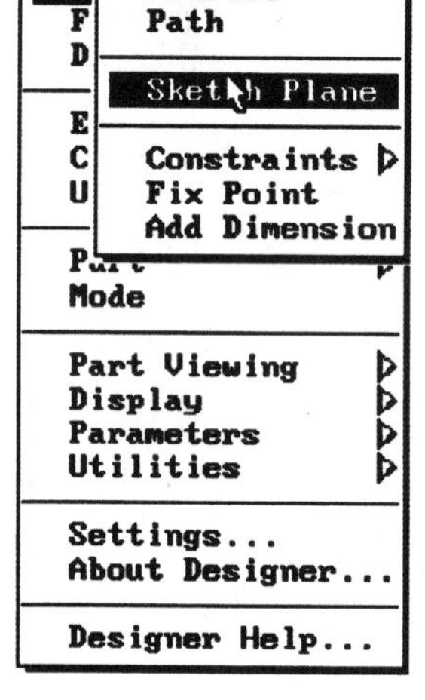

Step 8. Create the sketch plane.

Prompt	Response
Command:	**Sketch Plane**
Xy/Yz/Zx/Ucs/<Select work plane or planar face>:	**Pick the work plane.**
X/Y/Z/<Select work axis or straight edge>:	**D1** (Figure 15–9)
Rotate/<Accept>:	*Type:* **R** ↵ until the UCSICON is in the position shown in Figure 15–9, then *Press:* ↵.

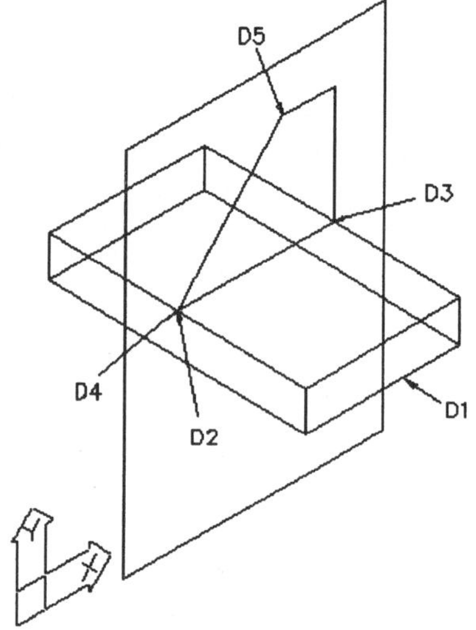

FIGURE 15–9
Making a Sketch of the Upright Part of the Model

Step 9. Draw the sketch.

Prompt	Response
Command:	*Type:* **PL** ↵
From Point:	**Osnap-MIDpoint, D2**
Arc/Close/Halfwidth/Length/Undo/Width/<Endpoint of line>:	**Osnap-MIDpoint, D3**
Arc/Close/Halfwidth/Length/Undo/Width/<Endpoint of line>:	*Type:* **@2.25<90** ↵
Arc/Close/Halfwidth/Length/Undo/Width/<Endpoint of line>:	*Type:* **@1<180** ↵
Arc/Close/Halfwidth/Length/Undo/Width/<Endpoint of line>:	↵

Prompt	Response
Command:	↵
From Point:	**Osnap-ENDpoint, D4**
Arc/Close/Halfwidth/Length/Undo/ Width/<Endpoint of line>:	*Type:* **@.25<90** ↵
Arc/Close/Halfwidth/Length/Undo/ Width/<Endpoint of line>:	**Osnap-ENDpoint, D5**
Arc/Close/Halfwidth/Length/Undo/ Width/<Endpoint of line>:	↵

Step 10. Make the profile.

Prompt	Response
Command:	**Profile**
Select objects:	Pick the two polylines you just drew.
Select objects:	
Solved under constrained sketch requiring 6 dimensions/constraints.	↵

Because this part will likely be changed, some dimensions should be added at this point so that the part will change predictably.

Step 11. Add necessary dimensions to the sketch.

Prompt	Response
Command:	**Add Dimension**
Select first item:	**D1** (Figure 15–10)
Select second item or place dimension:	**D2**
Specify dimension placement:	**D3**
Undo/Hor/Ver/Align/Par/Dimension value <1.0000>:	↵

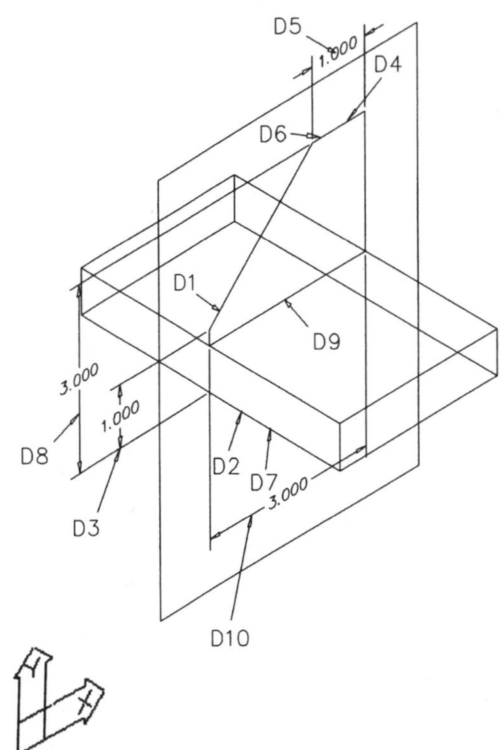

FIGURE 15–10
Adding Parametric Dimensions

Prompt	Response
Select first item:	**D4**
Select second item or place dimension:	**D5**
Undo/Hor/Ver/Align/Par/Dimension value <1.0000>:	↵
Select first item:	**D6**
Select second item or place dimension:	**D7**
Specify dimension placement:	**D8**
Undo/Hor/Ver/Align/Par/Dimension value <3.0000>:	↵
Select first item:	**D9**
Select second item or place dimension:	**D10**
Undo/Hor/Ver/Align/Par/Dimension value <3.0000>:	↵
Select first item:	↵

Step 12. Extrude the new sketch.

Prompt	Response
Command:	**Extrude. . .**
The Designer Extrusion dialog box, Figure 15–11, appears:	*Pick:* **Mid Plane** *Pick:* **Join** **Change distance to 2.25 as shown.** *Pick:* **OK**

FIGURE 15–11
Designer Extrusion Dialog Box

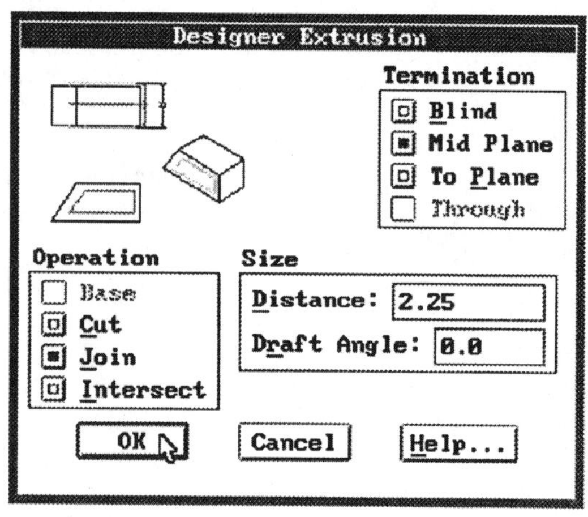

The shape shown in Figure 15–12 appears.

Create the Cavity

Step 13. Now that you still have a usable sketch plane, draw the shape of the cavity shown as hidden lines in Figure 15–1.

Prompt	Response
Command:	*Type:* **PL** ↵
From Point:	**Osnap-MIDpoint, D1** (Figure 15–12)
Arc/Close/Halfwidth/Length/Undo/ Width/<Endpoint of line>:	*Type:* **@2.25<180** ↵

FIGURE 15–12
The Extruded Shape and the New Sketch for the Cavity

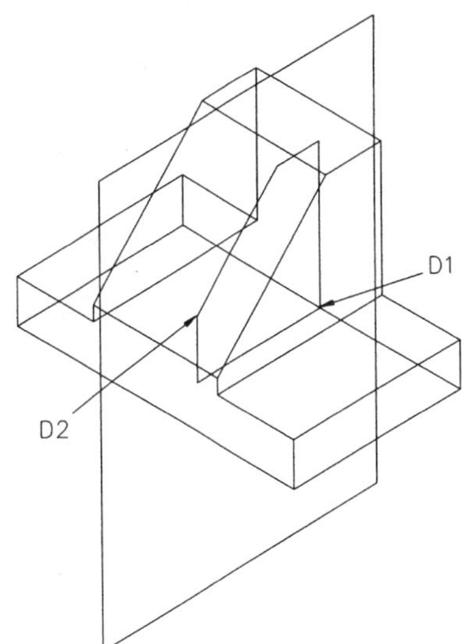

Arc/Close/Halfwidth/Length/Undo/ Width/<Endpoint of line>:	*Type:* **@1<90** ↵
Arc/Close/Halfwidth/Length/Undo/ Width/<Endpoint of line>:	↵
Command:	↵
From Point:	**Osnap-ENDpoint, D1**
Arc/Close/Halfwidth/Length/Undo/ Width/<Endpoint of line>:	*Type:* **@2.5<90** ↵
Arc/Close/Halfwidth/Length/Undo/ Width/<Endpoint of line>:	*Type:* **@.75<180** ↵
Arc/Close/Halfwidth/Length/Undo/ Width/<Endpoint of line>:	**Osnap-ENDpoint, D2**
Arc/Close/Halfwidth/Length/Undo/ Width/<Endpoint of line>:	↵

Step 14. Make a profile on the sketch.

Prompt	**Response**
Command:	**Profile**
Select objects:	Pick the two polylines you just drew.
Solved under constrained sketch requiring 6 dimensions/constraints.	

Because it is likely that this part will change, it is important to add dimensions and constraints that give you control over how the part will react when dimensions change. The wall thickness should remain the same no matter how the height of the part changes, and the bottom of the cavity should stay where the bottom of the part is; therefore, the following are needed:

A parallel constraint linking the cavity to the inclined surface
A collinear constraint linking the bottom of the cavity to the bottom of the part
Two parametric dimensions showing the wall thickness

The following explanation of the ADADDCON command is needed before you begin adding constraints:

ADADDCON

ADADDCON allows you to add constraints to the active profile or path. It works only on the active profile, but constraints, once assigned, remain with the sketch when it is no longer active. This command is used to add constraints between features that are not part of the active sketch and to clean up profiles that were so poorly sketched that Designer cannot make correct assumptions. The following prompt appears when the ADADDCON command is activated:

**Hor/Ver/PErp/PAr/Tan/CL/CN/PRoj/
Join/XValue/YValue/Radius/<exit>:**

To select any of the options, type the capitalized letter or letters of your choice and press ↵. The options **Horizontal, Vertical, Perpendicular, Parallel,** and **Tangent** are obvious constraints between entities.

Collinear (CL)
Determines that two lines or planes are on the same line.
Concentric (CN)
Makes the centers of two circles or arcs the same.
Project (PRoj)
Allows you to select the endpoint of a line or arc then project or extend it to another line or plane.
Join
Is used to close gaps in the profile of a sketch.
XValue
Allows you to assign the same X value to two circles.
YValue
Allows you to assign the same Y value to two circles.
Radius
Allows arcs and circles to have the same radius after you have dimensioned one or more radii for arcs or circles.

When you construct a profile or path, Designer numbers each entity in the sketch and assigns constraints in accordance with sketch rules. Use the ADSHOWCON command to see these numbers and the constraints. Each different type of constraint is assigned a letter, as follows:

Horizontal: H
Vertical: V
Perpendicular: L
Parallel: P
Tangent: T
Collinear: C
Concentric: N
Project: J
Join: No symbol
XValue: X
YValue: Y
Radius: R

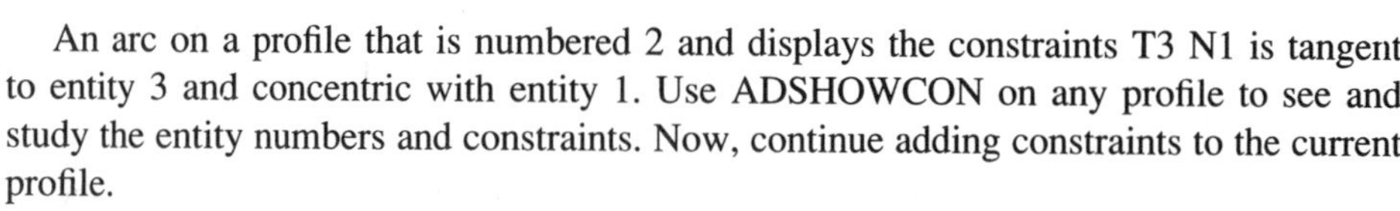

An arc on a profile that is numbered 2 and displays the constraints T3 N1 is tangent to entity 3 and concentric with entity 1. Use ADSHOWCON on any profile to see and study the entity numbers and constraints. Now, continue adding constraints to the current profile.

Step 15. Add necessary constraints.

Prompt	**Response**
Command:	**Constraint-Add (ADADDCON)**
Hor/Ver/PErp/PAr/Tan/CL/CN/PRoj/ Join/XValue/Yvalue/Radius/<exit>:	*Type:* **PA** ↵
Select first line:	**D1** (Figure 15–13)

FIGURE 15–13
Adding Dimensions and Constraints to the Cavity Profile

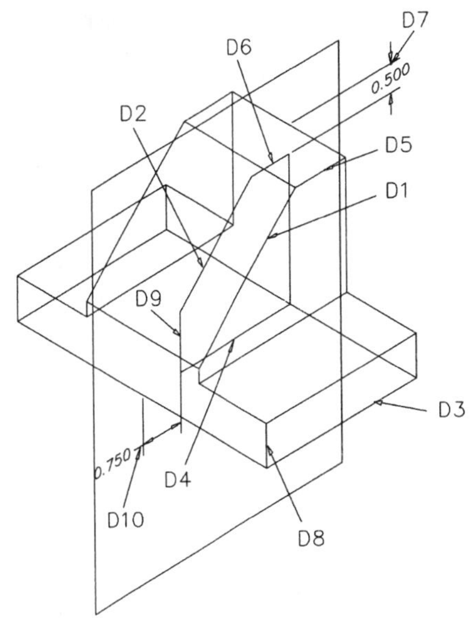

Select second line:	**D2**
Hor/Ver/PErp/PAr/Tan/CL/CN/PRoj/ Join/XValue/Yvalue/Radius/<exit>:	*Type:* **CL** ↵
Select first line:	**D3**
Select second line:	**D4**
Hor/Ver/PErp/PAr/Tan/CL/CN/PRoj/ Join/XValue/Yvalue/Radius/<exit>:	↵

Step 16. Add necessary dimensions.

Prompt	Response
Command:	**Add Dimension**
Select first item:	**D5**
Select second item or place dimension:	**D6**
Specify dimension placement:	**D7**
Undo/Hor/Ver/Align/Par/Dimension value <0.5000>:	↵
Select first item:	**D8**
Select second item or place dimension:	**D9**
Specify dimension placement:	**D10**
Undo/Hor/Ver/Align/Par/Dimension value <0.7500>:	↵
Select first item:	↵

Step 17. Extrude the cavity and cut it out of the part.

Prompt	Response
Command:	**Extrude. . .**
The Designer Extrusion dialog box, Figure 15–14, appears:	*Pick:* **Mid Plane** *Pick:* **Cut** **Change distance to 1.25 as shown.** *Pick:* **OK**

FIGURE 15–14
Designer Extrusion Dialog Box

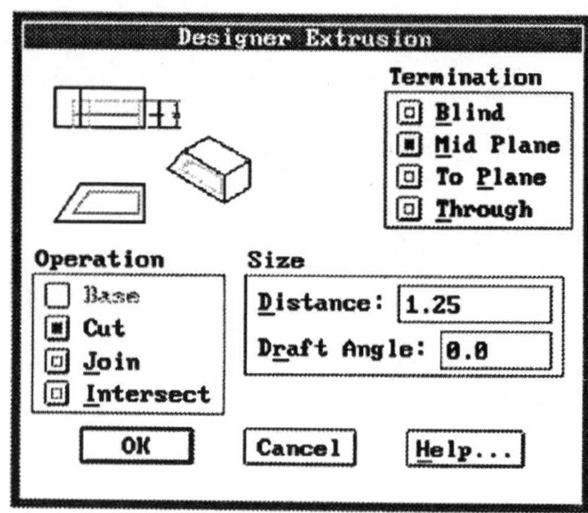

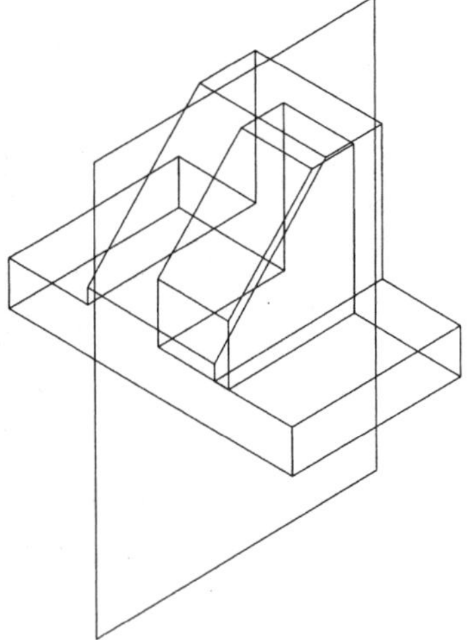

FIGURE 15–15
Cutting the Cavity

The shape shown in Figure 15–15 appears.

Step 18. Drill holes in the inclined front surface.

On Your Own: Because you will not need the work plane through the center of the part anymore, erase it.

Prompt	Response
Command:	**Sketch Plane**
Xy/Yz/Zx/Ucs/<Select work plane or planar face>:	*Pick:* **D1** (Figure 15–16)

FIGURE 15–16
Selecting the Inclined Surface As the Sketch Plane

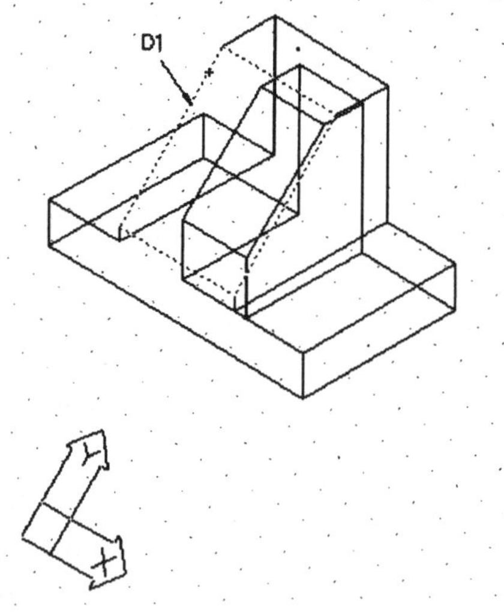

Prompt	Response
Next/<Accept>:	If the inclined surface of the part is highlighted, *Press:* ↵. If not, type **N** ↵ until the inclined surface is highlighted, then *Press:* ↵ to accept
X/Y/Z/<Select work axis or straight edge>:	**D1** (again)
Rotate/<Accept>:	*Type:* **R** ↵ to rotate the UCS until it appears as shown in Figure 15–16, then *Press:* ↵ to accept.

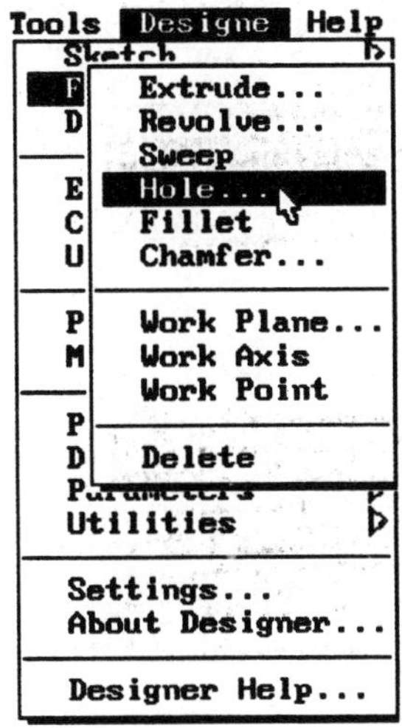

Command: **Hole**

The Designer Hole dialog box appears: *Pick:* **Drilled, 2 Edges, Through (Change the Drill Size Dia: to .5 if it isn't already as shown in Figure 15–17.)**

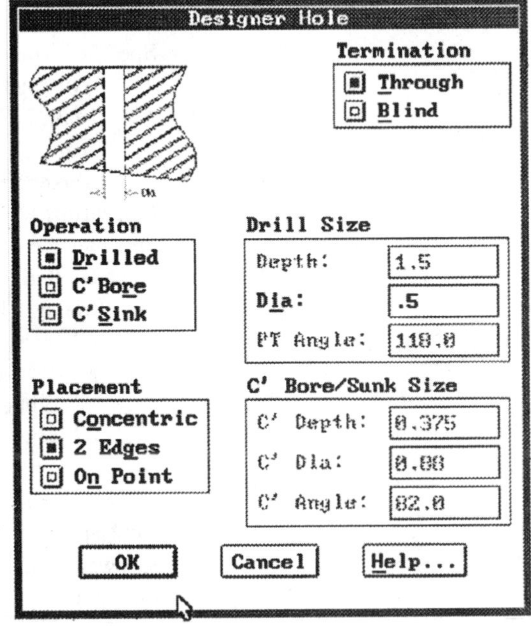

FIGURE 15–17
Designer Hole Dialog Box

Pick: **OK**

Select first edge: **D1** (Figure 15–18)

Select second edge: **D2**

Select hole location: **D3** (approximately as shown; the precise location will be determined by the dimensions you specify next.)

Distance from first edge <default>: *Type:* **1.125** ↵ (Get dimensions from Figure 15–1.)

Distance from second edge <default>: *Type:* **.7** ↵

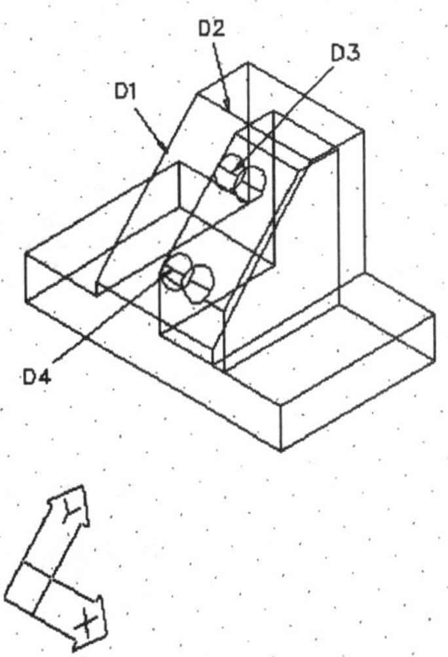

FIGURE 15–18
Drilling Holes in the Inclined Surface

Now that you have used the ADHOLE command, let's examine each part of the Designer Hole dialog box.

ADHOLE

This command activates the Designer Hole dialog box. There are five areas on this dialog box:

Termination
Specifies where the hole ends.

Through
Makes a hole from the selected surface through the entire part.

Blind
Makes a hole end at a specified depth from the selected surface.

Operation
Specifies the type of hole.

Drilled
Makes a hole with a specified diameter.

C'Bore
Makes a counterbored hole with a specified drill diameter, counterbore depth, and counterbore diameter.

C'Sink
Makes a hole of a specified drill diameter, countersink diameter, and countersink angle.

Drill Size
Allows you to specify the values for depth, diameter, and point angle of the drilled hole.

Placement
Gives you three methods for placing holes.

Concentric
Locates the hole in the center of a cylinder, cone, or torus.

2 Edges
Allows you to pick two edges and then locate the hole by specifying the distance from each edge.

On Point
Locates the hole on a selected work point with its axis perpendicular to the sketch plane of the work point.

C' Bore/Sunk Size
When you have selected a counterbore or countersink for the hole this area becomes active and allows you to specify the counterbore diameter and depth or the countersink diameter and angle.

Prompt	Response
Command:	↵
The Designer Hole dialog box appears:	*Pick:* **OK**
Select first edge:	**D1** {Figure 15–18 (again)}
Select second edge:	**D2** (again)
Select hole location:	**D4** (approximately as shown; the precise location will be determined by the dimensions you specify next.)
Distance from first edge <default>:	*Type:* **1.125** ↵
Distance from second edge <default>:	*Type:* **2.2** ↵ (.7 + 1.5 from Figure 15–1)

Complete the Drawing and Plot It

Step 19. Drill counterbored holes in the base.

Prompt	Response
Command:	**Sketch Plane**

Xy/Yz/Zx/Ucs/<Select work plane or planar face>:	*Pick:* **D1** (Figure 15–19)

FIGURE 15–19
Selecting the Sketch Plane for the Counterbored Holes

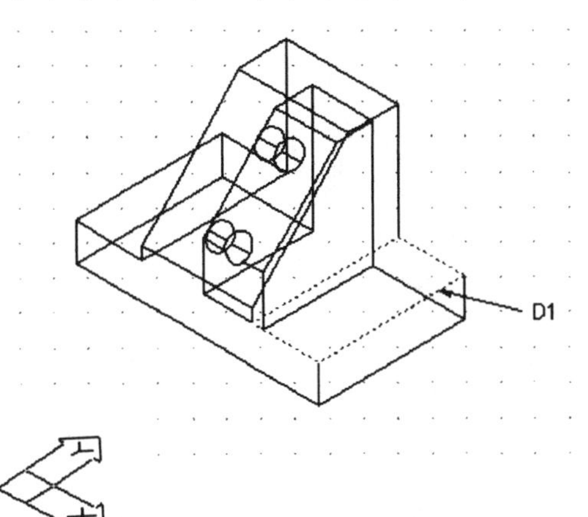

Next/<Accept>:	If the top surface of the base is highlighted, *Press:* ↵ If not, *Type:* **N** ↵ until the top surface is highlighted, then *Press:* ↵
X/Y/Z/<Select work axis or straight edge>:	**D1** (again)
Rotate/<Accept>:	Type: **R** ↵ to rotate the UCS until it appears as shown in Figure 15–19. *Press:* ↵
Command:	**Hole**
The Designer Hole dialog box appears:	*Pick:* **C'Bore, 2 Edges, Through (Leave the Drill Size Dia: at .5, change C' Depth: to 0.06, and C'Dia to 1 as shown in Figure 15–20.)** *Pick:* **OK**

FIGURE 15–20
Designer Hole Dialog Box

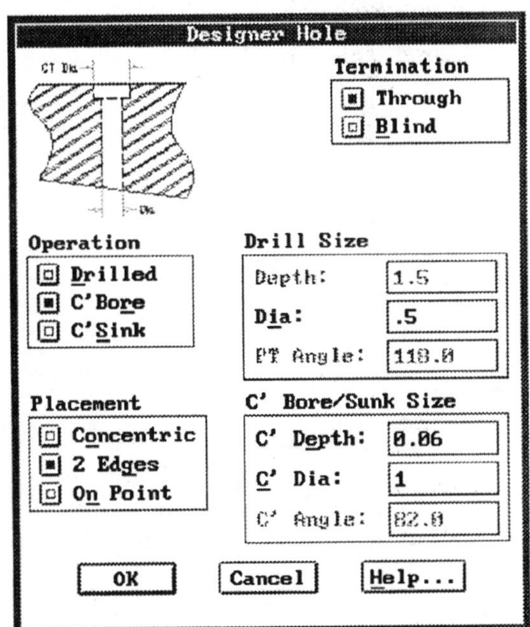

Prompt	Response
Select first edge:	**D1** (Figure 15–21)

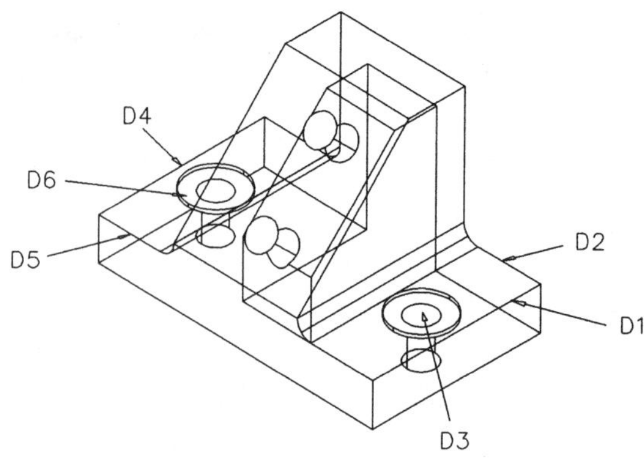

FIGURE 15–21
Drilling Counterbored Holes

Select second edge:	**D2**
Select hole location:	**D3** (approximately as shown; the precise location will be determined by the dimensions you specify next.)
Distance from first edge <default>:	*Type:* **.625** ↵ (Get dimensions from Figure 15–1.)
Distance from second edge <default>:	*Type:* **1.5** ↵
Command:	↵
The Designer Hole dialog box appears:	*Pick:* **OK**
Select first edge:	**D4** (Figure 15–21)
Select second edge:	**D5**
Select hole location:	**D6** (approximately as shown; the dimensions you specify next will determine the location.)
Distance from first edge <default>:	*Type:* **.625** ↵
Distance from second edge <default>:	*Type:* **1.5** ↵

The next step is to add fillets. Before you do that, take a minute to read the explanation of the ADFILLET command.

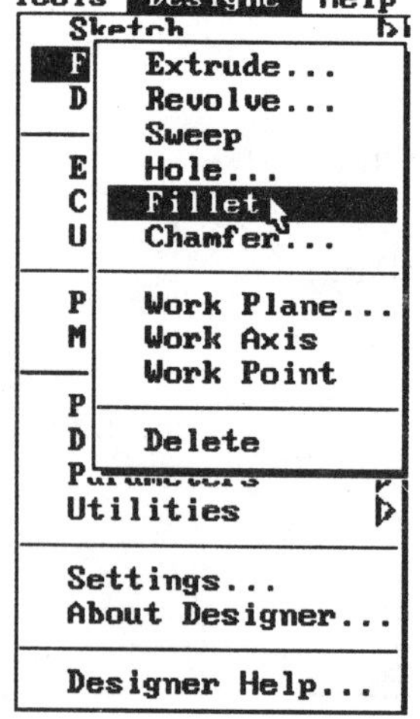

ADFILLET

The ADFILLET command allows you to add fillets (inside radii) or rounds (outside radii) on any selected edges. You first select the edge or edges you want to fillet and then specify the size of the radius.

Step 20. Add fillets.

Command:	**Fillet:** (If you type commands, use ADFILLET ↵. Do not use the AutoCAD Fillet: command.)
Select edge:	**D1** (Figure 15–22)
Select edge:	**D2**
Select edge:	↵
Fillet radius <0.5>:	*Type:* **.25** ↵

FIGURE 15–22
Adding Fillets

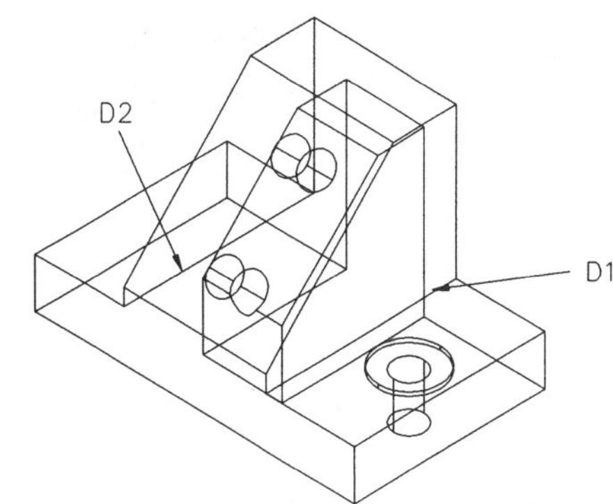

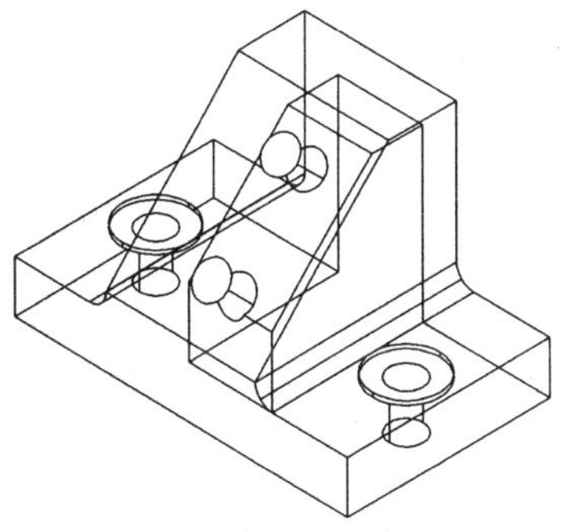

FIGURE 15–23
The Completed Model

The model is now complete as shown in Figure 15–23. You will use this model in Chapter 16 to make 2-D drawings that contain orthographic views with dimensions, sectional views, auxiliary views, and isometric views as shown in Figure 15–1. The model may also be prepared for rendering by using the ADMESH command and rendered with the AutoCAD Render: command.

Step 21. On Your Own:

1. Set UCS to View and place your name on the drawing in the lower right corner.
2. Plot the drawing at full scale (1 = 1) and center it on an 8.5″ × 11″ sheet.
3. Save the drawing in two places and exit AutoCAD.

The next exercise is an assembly containing four separate parts. It will involve several interesting problems that a single part does not.

EXERCISE 15–2 DRAWING A SOLID MODEL OF AN ASSEMBLY CONTAINING FOUR PARTS USING AUTOCAD DESIGNER COMMANDS

Set Up the Drawing

Step 1. On Your Own:

1. Turn on the computer, start AutoCAD Designer, and pick New. . . from the menu bar File menu. Name the drawing: 15-2 (your initials).
2. Make the following settings:

UNITS: Decimal; 3 digits to the right of the decimal point
LIMITS: Lower left corner: 0,0
Upper right corner: 8.5,11
GRID: .2
SNAP: .05
STYLE: STANDARD; FONT: SIMPLEX; HEIGHT: 0
Create the following layers:

LAYER NAME	COLOR	LINETYPE
Y	YELLOW	CONTINUOUS
R	RED	CONTINUOUS
G	GREEN	CONTINUOUS

Set layer G current.

Construct the Bushing

Step 2. Use the dimensions from Figure 15–24 to make a sketch for the bushing inside the larger hole in the housing.

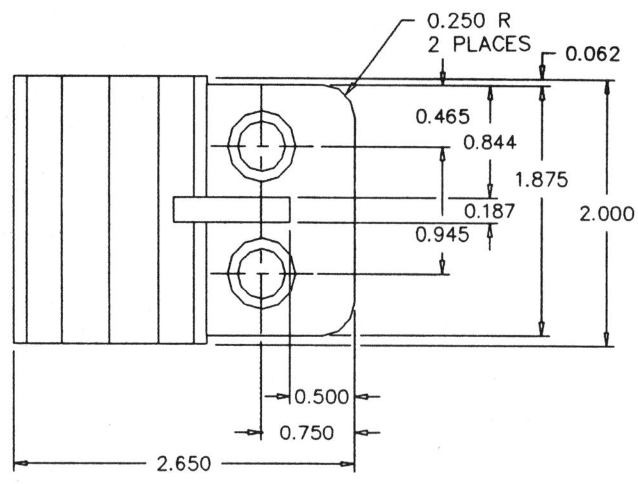

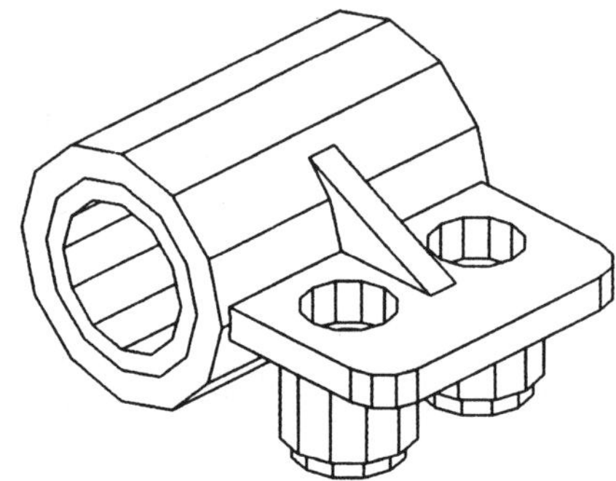

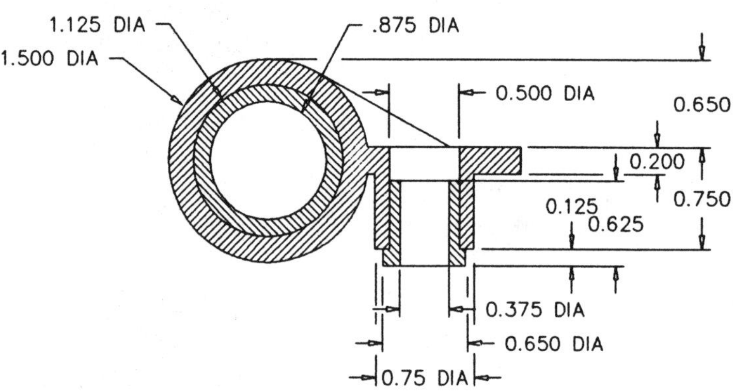

FIGURE 15–24
Dimensions for Exercise 15–2

Although the sketch may be much less accurate than the drawing method used next, since you know how to draw accurately, it will be simpler to use accurate dimensions.

Prompt	**Response**
Command:	*Type:* **C** ↵
CIRCLE 3P/2P/TTR/<Center Point>:	*Type:* **4.5,5** ↵ **(or pick a point near the center of the page, Figure 15–25)**
Diameter/<Radius>:	*Type:* **D** ↵
Diameter:	*Type:* **.875** ↵
Command:	↵
CIRCLE 3P/2P/TTR/<Center Point>:	*Type:* **4.5,5** ↵ **(or use Osnap-CENter and pick a point on the circumference of the existing circle)**
Diameter/<Radius>:	*Type:* **D** ↵
Diameter:	*Type:* **1.125** ↵

Step 3. Make a profile of the bushing.

Prompt	Response
Command:	**Profile**
Select objects:	**D1** (Figure 15–25)
Solved under constrained sketch requiring 1 dimensions/constraints.	

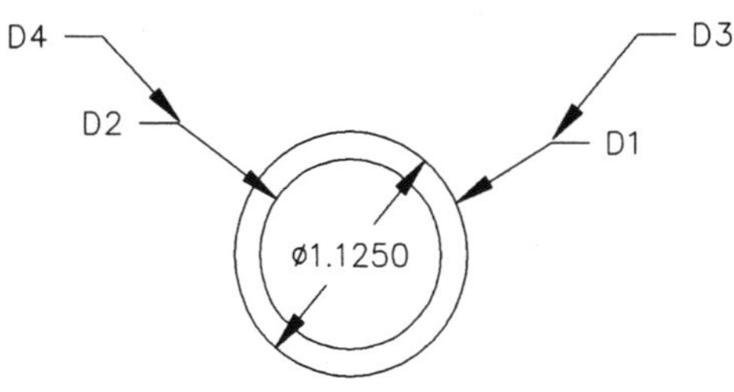

FIGURE 15–25
Constructing the Bushing

Step 4. Add dimensions to the bushing.

Prompt	Response
Command:	**Add Dimension**
Select first item:	**D1**
Select second item or place dimension:	**D3**
Undo/Hor/Ver/Align/Par/Dimension value <1.125>:	↵ (or *Type:* **1.125** ↵ if the default is not this value)
Select first item:	↵

Step 5. Extrude the sketch of the bushing.

Prompt	Response
Command:	**Extrude. . .**
The Designer Extrusion dialog box appears:	**Change Distance: to 2.**
	Pick: **OK**

Step 6. Make a profile for the hole in the bushing.

Prompt	Response
Command:	**Profile**
Select objects:	**D2** (Figure 15–25)
Solved under constrained sketch requiring 3 dimensions/constraints.	

Step 7. Add a dimension to the hole in the bushing.

Prompt	Response
Command:	**Add Dimension**
Select first item:	**D2**
Select second item or place dimension:	**D4**
Undo/Hor/Ver/Align/Par Dimension value <0.8750>:	↵ (Or *Type:* **.875** ↵ if the default is not this value.)
Select first item:	↵

Step 8. Add a concentric restraint to the two cylinders.

Prompt	Response
Command:	**Constraints** **Add**
Hor/Ver/PErp/PAr/Tan/CL/CN/PRoj/ Join/XValue/Yvalue/Radius/<eXit>:	*Type:* **CN** ↵
Select first circle or arc to be concentric:	**Pick the larger circle.**
Select second circle or arc to be concentric:	**Pick the smaller circle.**
Hor/Ver/PErp/PAr/Tan/CL/CN/PRoj/ Join/XValue/Yvalue/Radius/<eXit>:	↵

Step 9. Select an isometric view for the part.

Prompt	Response
Command:	**Part Viewing** **Iso**

Step 10. Extrude the hole in the bushing.

Prompt	Response
Command:	**Extrude. . .**
The Designer Extrusion dialog box appears:	**Change Distance: to 2 if it is not already.** **Change Operation to Cut if it is not already.** *Pick:* **OK**
Direction Flip/<Accept>:	If the direction is as shown in Figure 15–26, *Press:* ↵ to accept. (The cut operation may be done automatically so that the flip step is not necessary.) If the direction is not as shown in Figure 15–26, *Type:* **F** ↵, then *Press:* ↵.

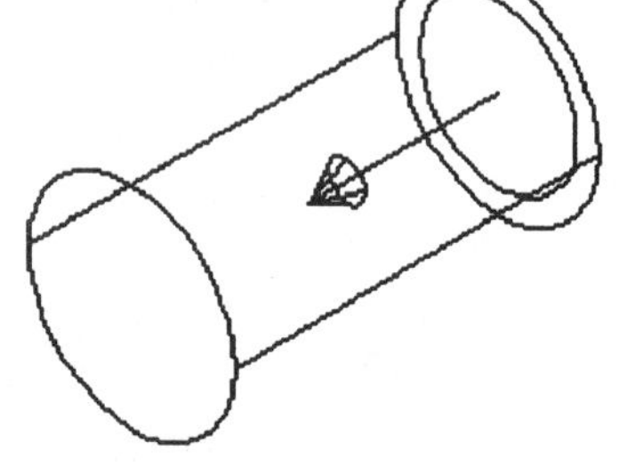

FIGURE 15–26
Extruding the Cut

Tools Designe Help
Sketch
Features
Drawing
Edit Feature
Change Dimension
Update
Par New
Mod Make Active
Part Viewing
Display
Parameters
Utilities
Settings...
About Designer...
Designer Help...

Construct the Cylindrical Part of the Housing

Step 11. Set layer R current.

Because the housing is not part of the bushing, you must activate a new part before you begin creating any new features. This is done with the ADNEWPART command.

ADNEWPART

This command starts a new part and makes it the active part. The sketch you draw after using the ADNEWPART command becomes the base feature for the new part. This command is unique to drawings containing more than one part.

Step 12. Activate a new part and draw a sketch for the cylindrical part of the housing.

Prompt	Response
Command:	**Part** **New**

Command:	*Type:* **C** ↵
CIRCLE 3P/2P/TTR/<Center Point>:	*Type:* **4.5,5** ↵ **(or use Osnap-CENter and pick a point on the circumference of the circle, D1, Figure 15–27.)**

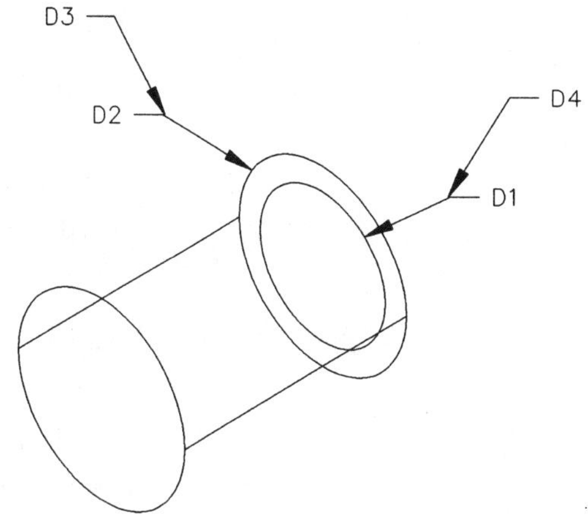

FIGURE 15–27
Constructing the Cylindrical Part of the Housing

Diameter/<Radius>:	*Type:* **D** ↵
Diameter:	*Type:* **1.125** ↵
Command:	↵
CIRCLE 3P/2P/TTR/<Center Point>:	*Type:* **4.5,5** ↵ **(Or use Osnap-CENter and pick a point on the circumference of the existing circle.)**
Diameter/<Radius>:	*Type:* **D** ↵
Diameter:	*Type:* **1.5** ↵

Step 13. On Your Own:

Turn layer G off.

Step 14. Make the profile.

Prompt	Response
Command:	**Profile**
Select objects:	**D2** (Figure 15–27)
Solved under constrained sketch requiring 1 dimensions/constraints.	

Step 15. Dimension the profile of the cylinder.

Prompt	Response
Command:	**Add Dimension**
Select first item:	**D2**
Select second item or place dimension:	**D3**
Undo/Hor/Ver/Align/Par/Dimension value <1.500>:	↵ (Or *Type:* **1.5** ↵ if the default is not this value.)
Select first item:	↵

Step 16. Extrude the profile of the cylinder.

Prompt	Response
Command:	**Extrude. . .**
The Designer Extrusion dialog box appears:	**Change Distance: to 2.** *Pick:* **OK**

Step 17. Make a profile for the hole in the cylinder.

Prompt	Response
Command:	**Profile**
Select objects:	**Pick the inner circle.**
Solved under constrained sketch requiring 3 dimensions/constraints.	

Step 18. Dimension the profile for the hole.

Prompt	Response
Command:	**Add Dimension**
Select first item:	**D1**
Select second item or place dimension:	**D4**
Undo/Hor/Ver/Align/Par/Dimension value <1.125>:	↵ (Or *Type:* **1.125** ↵ if the default is not this value.)
Select first item:	↵

Step 19. Add a concentric constraint.

Prompt	Response
Command:	**Constraints** **Add**
Hor/Ver/PErp/PAr/Tan/CL/CN/PRoj/Join/XValue/Yvalue/Radius/<eXit>:	*Type:* **CN** ↵
Select first circle or arc to be concentric:	**Pick the larger circle.**
Select second circle or arc to be concentric:	**Pick the smaller circle.**
Hor/Ver/PErp/PAr/Tan/CL/CN/PRoj/Join/XValue/Yvalue/Radius/<eXit>:	↵

Step 20. Extrude the hole.

Prompt	Response
Command:	**Extrude. . .**
The Designer Extrusion dialog box appears:	**Change Distance: to 2** if it is not already. **Change Operation to Cut** if it is not already. *Pick:* **OK** (The cut operation may be automatic. If so, skip the next command prompt.)
Direction Flip/<Accept>:	If the direction is as shown in Figure 15–28, *Press:* ↵ to accept.

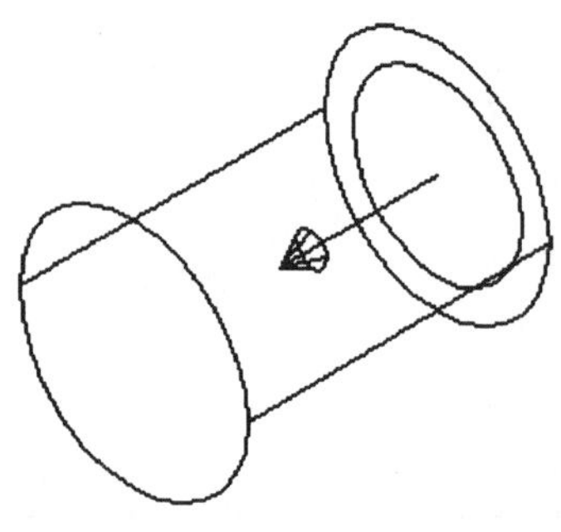

FIGURE 15–28
Extruding the Cut

If the direction is not as shown in Figure 15–28,
Type: **F** ↵, then
Press: ↵.

Add the Flange Containing the Two Holes

You need a sketch plane through the center of the cylinder. The easiest way to do that is to set up a UCS in the plane that you want, make a nonparametric work plane on it, and make that your sketch plane as follows:

Step 21. Locate the UCS.

Prompt	Response
Command:	*Type:* **UCS** ↵
Origin/ZAxis/3point/OBject?View/ X/Y/Z/Prev/Restore/Save/Del/?/ <World>:	*Type:* **3** ↵
Origin point <0,0,0>:	**Osnap-CENter, D1** (Figure 15–29)

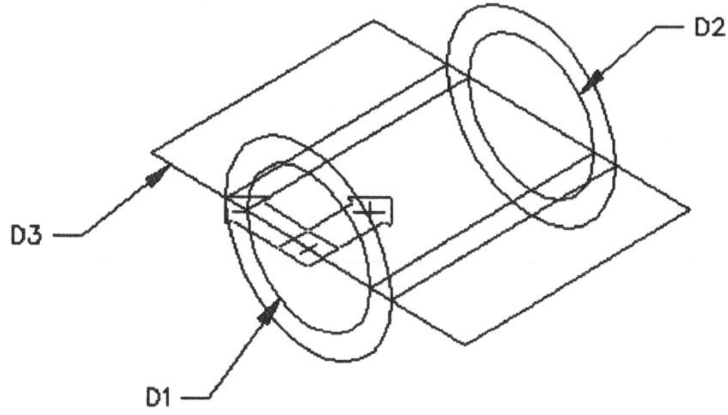

FIGURE 15–29
Constructing a Nonparametric Work Plane on a UCS

Prompt	Response
Point on positive portion of the X axis <1.000,0.000,0.000>:	**Osnap-CENter, D2**
Point on positive portion of the Y axis <default>:	**Turn ortho on and pick any point toward the upper left in line with the center of the first circle, D3.**

To make sure the origin is where you think it is, set UCSICON to Origin so that the icon moves to the selected origin as shown.

Step 22. Create the work plane.

Prompt	Response
Command:	**Work Plane**
The Designer Work Plane dialog box appears:	In the Non-Parametric area, *Pick:* **On UCS** *Pick:* **OK**

Step 23. Create the sketch plane.

Prompt	Response
Command:	**Sketch Plane**
Xy/Yz/Zx/Ucs/<Select work plane or planar face>:	**Pick the work plane you just constructed.** (You may not receive the next prompt. If so, skip it.)

Prompt	Response
X/Y/Z/<Select work axis or straight edge>:	*Type:* X ↵
Rotate/<Accept>:	If the UCS icon is in the position shown in Figure 15–29, *Press:* ↵ to accept. If the UCS icon is not in the correct position, *Type:* **R** ↵ until it is, then, *Press:* ↵

Step 24. Split the screen into two viewports so you can see what is happening as you draw, Figure 15–30.

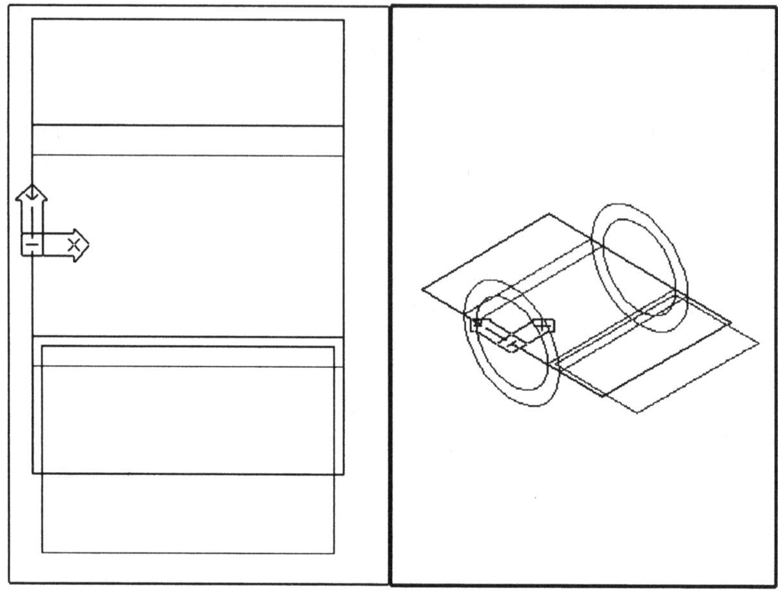

FIGURE 15–30
Two Viewports

Prompt	Response
Command:	**Vports:**
Save/Restore/Delete/Join/SIngle/?/2/3/4:	*Type:* **2** ↵
Horizontal/<Vertical>:	↵
Command:	**Pick the left viewport to make it the active one and *Type:* PLAN** ↵
<Current UCS>/Ucs/World:	↵

Step 25. Draw the sketch.

Command:	*Type:* **RECTANG** ↵
First corner:	*Type:* **.062,−.625** ↵
Other corner:	*Type:* **@1.875,−1.275** ↵

Notice that the dimensions for the flange were calculated so they intersect the cylinder .125″.

Prompt	Response
Command:	**Fillet:** (This is the AutoCAD Fillet: command, not ADFILLET.)
Polyline/Radius/Trim/<Select first object>:	*Type:* **R** ↵
Enter fillet radius <0.000>:	*Type:* **.25** ↵
Command:	↵

Polyline/Radius/Trim/<Select first object>:	**D1** (Figure 15–31)
Select second object:	**D2**
Command:	↵
Polyline/Radius/Trim/<Select first object>:	**D3**
Select second object:	**D4**

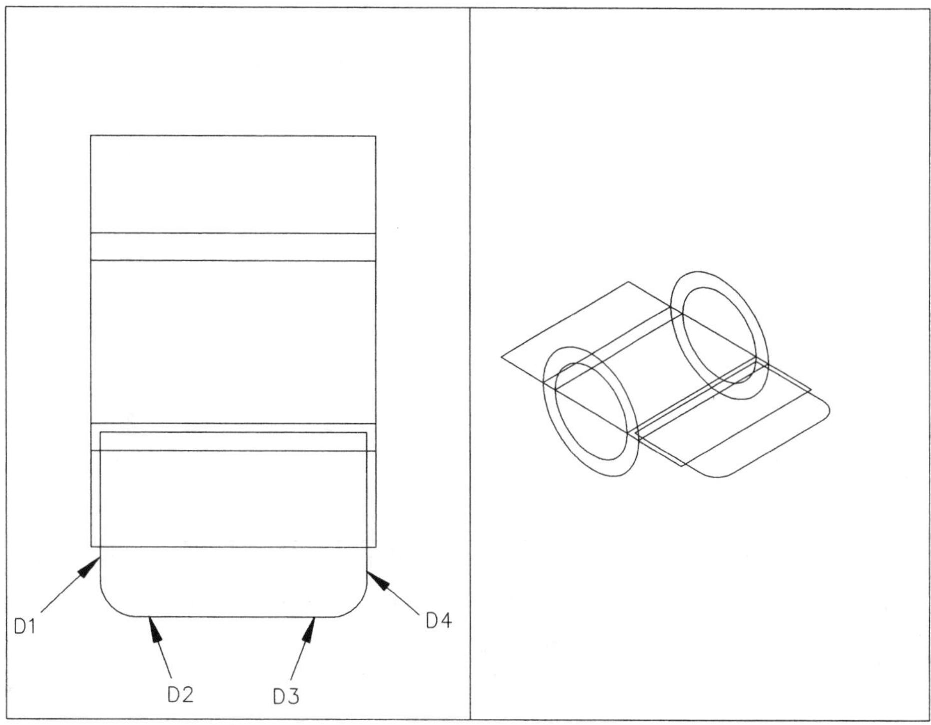

FIGURE 15–31
Making a Sketch for the Flange

Step 26. Make the profile.

Command:	**Profile**
Select objects:	**Pick the rectangle.**

Step 27. On Your Own:

Add the 1.875 dimension and the .250 radius as shown in Figure 15–32.

FIGURE 15–32
Adding Dimensions

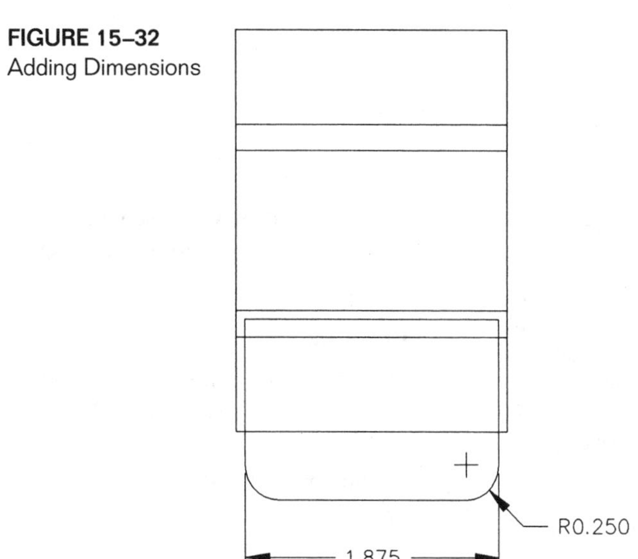

Step 28. Extrude the profile.

Command:	**Extrude. . .**
The Designer Extrusion dialog box, Figure 15–33, appears:	*Pick:* **Mid Plane** *Pick:* **Join** Change Distance: to .20. *Pick:* **OK**

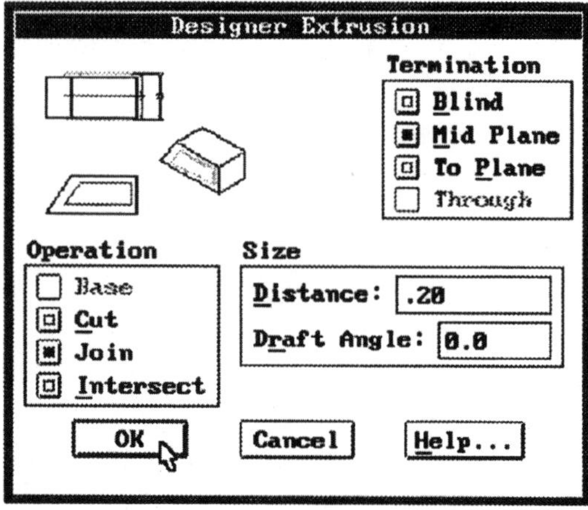

FIGURE 15–33
Designer Extrusion Dialog Box

Add the Two Cylinders That Are at Right Angles to the Flange

Step 29. Create the sketch plane.

Prompt	**Response**
Command:	**Sketch Plane**
Xy/Yz/Zx/Ucs/<Select work plane or planar face>:	**Pick the top surface of the flange you just constructed.** *Type:* **N** ↵ until the top surface of the flange is highlighted (Figure 15–34), then *Press:* ↵
X/Y/Z/<Select work axis or straight edge>:	*Type:* **X** ↵
Rotate/<Accept>:	If the UCS icon is in the position shown in Figure 15–34, *Press:* ↵ to accept. If the UCS icon is not in the correct position, *Type:* **R** ↵ until it is. Then *Press:* ↵

FIGURE 15–34
Highlighting the Top Surface of the Flange for Making It the Sketch Plane

Step 30. To make it easy to use the dimensions shown on Figure 15–24, move the UCS origin to the lower left corner of the flange.

Prompt	**Response**
Command:	*Type:* **UCS** ↵
Origin/ZAxis/3point/OBject?View/X/Y/Z/Prev/Restore/Save/Del/?/<World>:	*Type:* **O** ↵
Origin point <0,0,0>:	*Type:* **.X** ↵
of	**Osnap-ENDpoint**
of	**D1** (Figure 15–35)

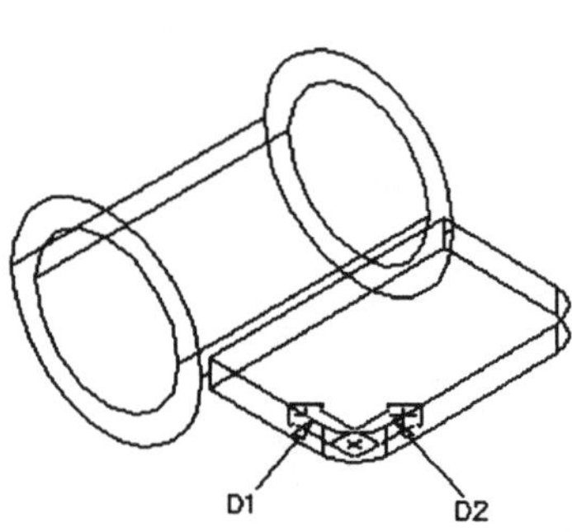

FIGURE 15–35
Moving the UCS Origin

(need YZ):	**Osnap-ENDpoint**
of	**D2**

Step 31. Draw sketches for the two cylinders.

Prompt	Response
Command:	*Type:* **C** ↵
3P/2P/TTR/<Center point>:	*Type:* **.465,.75** ↵
Diameter/<Radius>:	*Type:* **.375** ↵
Command:	*Type:* **CP** ↵
Select objects:	**Pick the circle.**
Select objects:	↵
<Base point or displacement>/Multiple:	**Pick any point.**
Second point of displacement:	*Type:* **@.945<0** ↵

Step 32. Make a profile of one of the cylinders.

Prompt	Response
Command:	**Profile**
Select objects:	**Pick one of the circles.**

Step 33. Extrude the profile.

Prompt	Response
Command:	**Extrude. . .**
The Designer Extrusion dialog box, Figure 15–36, appears:	*Pick:* **Blind** *Pick:* **Join** **Change Distance: to .75.** *Pick:* **OK**
Direction Flip/<Accept>:	*Type:* **F** ↵ to flip the arrow down if it is not already, then *Press:* ↵.

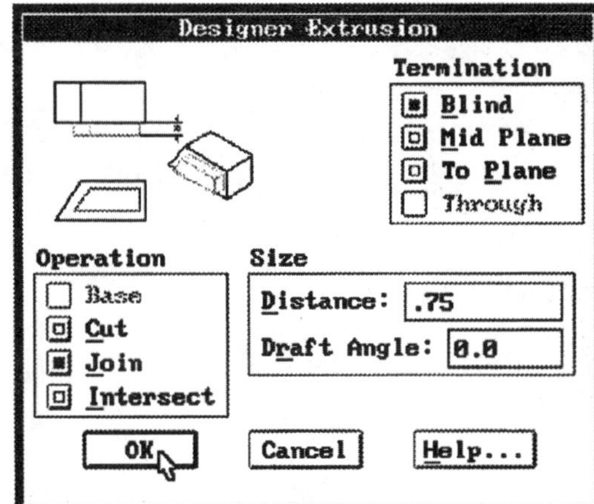

FIGURE 15–36
Designer Extrusion Dialog Box

Step 34. On Your Own:

Make a profile and extrude the other circle.

Drill Holes in the Flange

Step 35. Drill the first hole in the flange.

Prompt	Response
Command:	**Hole**

Prompt	Response
The Designer Hole dialog box, Figure 15–37, appears:	*Pick:* **Through** *Pick:* **Drilled** *Pick:* **2 Edges** **Change Dia: to .5 if it is not already.** *Pick:* **OK**

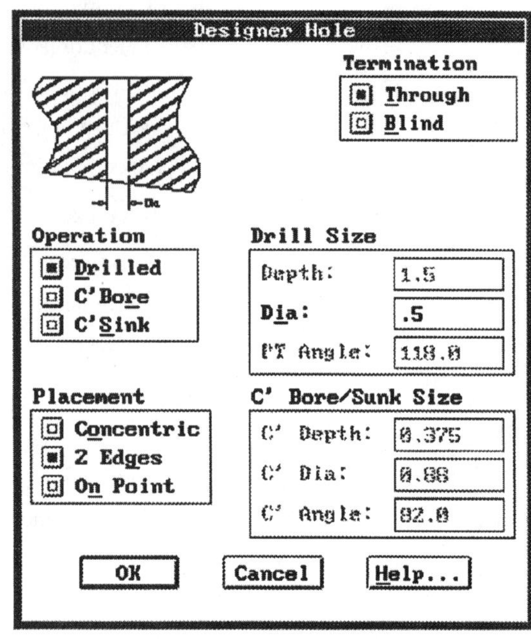

FIGURE 15–37
Designer Hole Dialog Box

Select first edge:	*Pick:* **D1** (Figure 15–38)
Select second edge:	**D2**
Select hole location:	*Pick:* **D3,** any point in the approximate location shown.
Distance from first edge <default>:	*Type:* **.465** ↵
Distance from second edge <default>:	*Type:* **.75** ↵

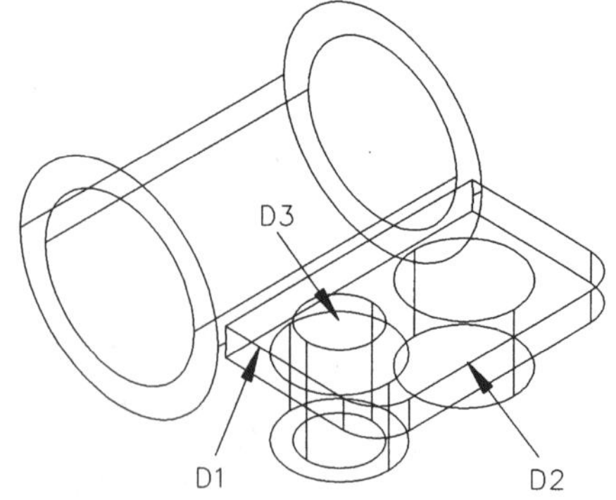

FIGURE 15–38
Drilling the First Hole in the Flange

Step 36. On Your Own:

Drill the second hole in the flange.

Add the Web

Step 37. Create a work plane.

Prompt	**Response**
Command:	**Work Plane**
The Designer Work Plane dialog box appears:	*Pick:* **Planar Parallel**
The Planar Parallel dialog box appears:	*Pick:* **Offset** *Pick:* **OK** *Pick:* **OK**
Xy/Yz/Zx/Ucs/<Select work plane or planar face>:	*Pick:* **D1** (Figure 15–39)

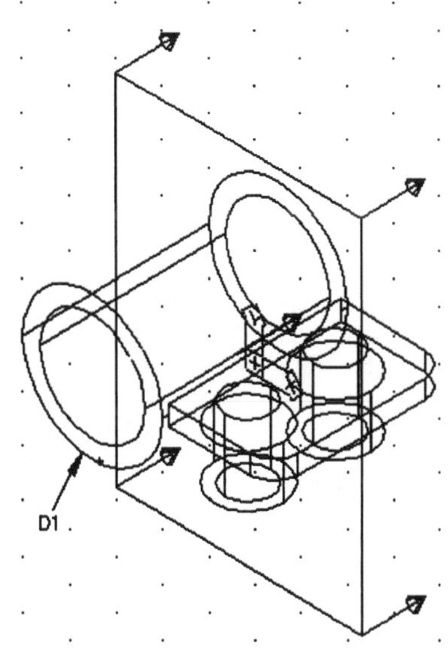

FIGURE 15–39
Constructing a Work Plane

Offset <1>:	↵ or Type: 1↵ if 1 is not the default. (This distance will place the work plane in the center of the cylinder parallel to its left end.)
Flip/<Accept>:	If the work plane appears as shown in Figure 15–39, *Press:* ↵. If not, *Type:* **F**↵, then *Press:* ↵.

Step 38. Make the work plane the sketch plane.

Prompt	**Response**
Command:	**Sketch Plane**
Xy/Yz/Zx/Ucs/<Select work plane or planar face>:	**Pick the work plane you just constructed.**
X/Y/Z/<Select work axis or straight edge>:	*Type:* **X** ↵
Rotate/<Accept>:	If the UCS icon is in the position shown in Figure 15–40, *Press:* ↵ to accept. If the UCS icon is not in the correct position, *Type:* **R** ↵ until it is. Then *Press:* ↵

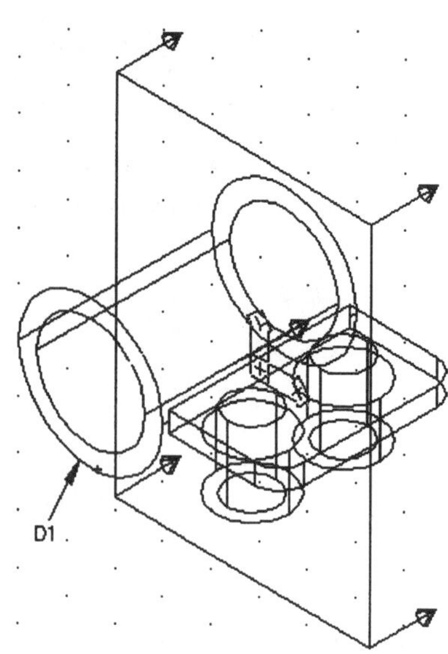

FIGURE 15–40
Accepting the UCS

Step 39. Select a plan view of the current UCS.

Prompt	Response
Command:	*Type:* **PLAN** ↵
<Current UCS>/Ucs/World:	↵

The view should appear as shown in Figure 15–41. If the UCS icon is not in the position shown in Figure 15–41, move it to that location.

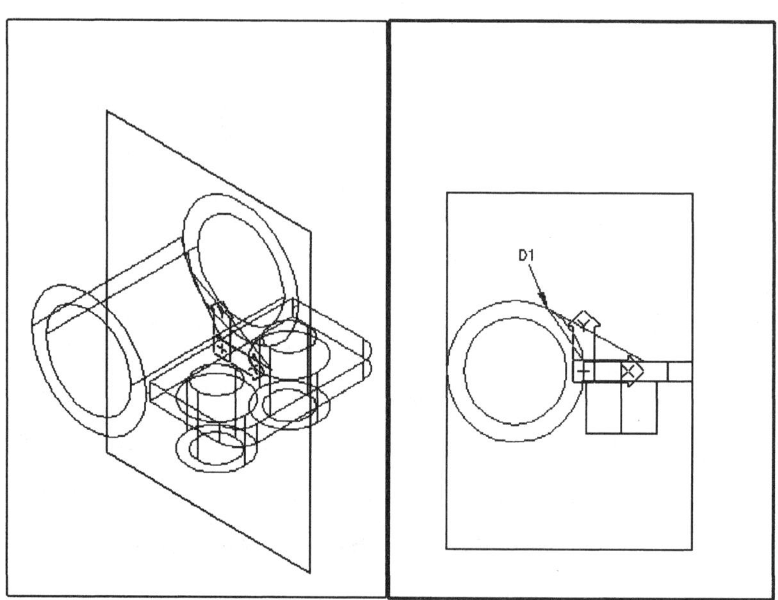

FIGURE 15–41
Constructing a Profile

Step 40. On Your Own:

Pick the left viewport and set it to the ISO view as shown in Figure 15–41.

Step 41. Make a sketch for the web.

Prompt	Response
Command:	*Type:* **PL** ↵
Arc/Close/Halfwidth/Length/Undo/ Width/<Endpoint of line>:	*Type:* **0,.1** ↵
Arc/Close/Halfwidth/Length/Undo/ Width/<Endpoint of line>:	*Type:* **@.65,0** ↵

Arc/Close/Halfwidth/Length/Undo/ Width/<Endpoint of line>:	**Osnap-TANgent**
to	**D1** (Figure 15–41)
Arc/Close/Halfwidth/Length/Undo/ Width/<Endpoint of line>:	*Type:* **C ↵**

Step 42. Make a profile of the web.

Prompt	Response
Command:	**Profile:**
Select objects:	**Pick the pline you just drew.** (If Designer will not make the profile for you, erase the pline and draw it again using the same dimensions.)

Step 43. Extrude the profile.

Prompt	Response
Command:	**Extrude. . .**
The Designer Extrusion dialog box, Figure 15–42, appears:	*Pick:* **Mid Plane** *Pick:* **Join** **Change Distance: to .187.** *Pick:* **OK**

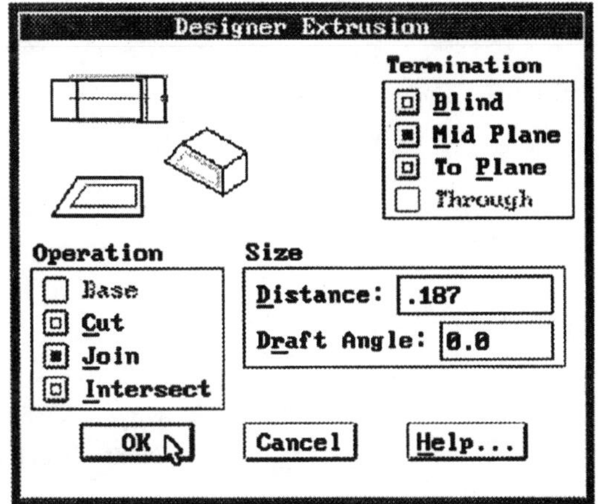

FIGURE 15–42
Designer Extrusion Dialog Box

The completed housing, Figure 15–43, appears as shown.

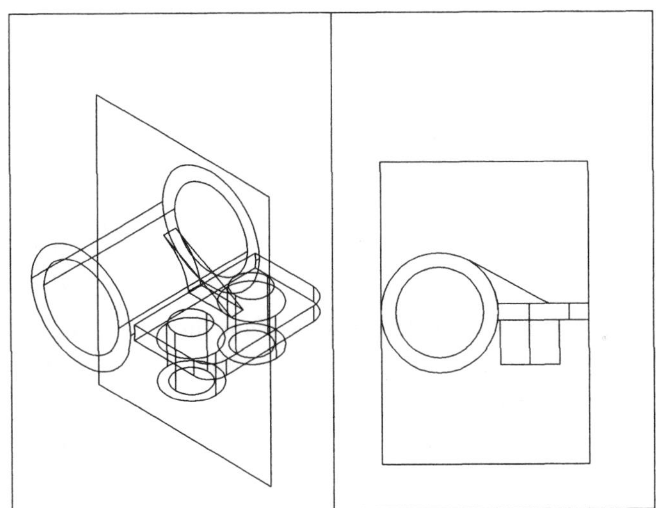

FIGURE 15–43
The Completed Housing

Step 44. On Your Own:

Before you proceed, erase all the work planes you have constructed because you will not need them again, and they will be in the way.

Construct Bushings for the Holes in the Flange

Step 45. On Your Own:

Set layer Y current.

Step 46. Create a work plane through the center of the right hole.

Prompt	Response
Command:	**Work Plane**
The Designer Work Plane dialog box appears:	*Pick:* **Planar Parallel** then **Offset**
	Pick: **OK** twice.
Xy/Yz/Zx/Ucs/<Select work plane or planar face>:	*Pick:* **D1** (Figure 15–44)

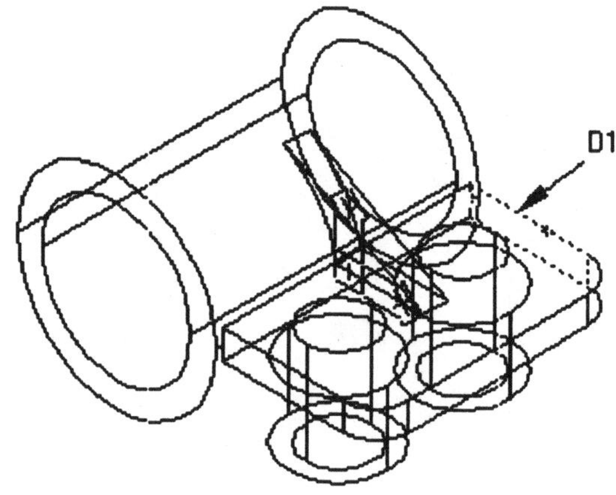

FIGURE 15–44
Picking the Right End of the Flange

Next/<Accept>:	If the right end of the flange is highlighted, *Press:* ↵.
	If it is not, *Type:* **N** ↵ until the right end is highlighted, then *Press:* ↵
Offset <1>:	*Type:* **.465** ↵ (This distance will place the work plane in the center of the right hole.)
Flip/<Accept>:	If the work plane appears as shown in Figure 15–45, *Press:* ↵. If not, *Type:* **F** ↵ until it does, then *Press:* ↵.

Step 47. Make the work plane the sketch plane.

Command:	**Sketch Plane**
Xy/Yz/Zx/Ucs/<Select work plane or planar face>:	**Pick the work plane you just constructed.**

FIGURE 15–45
Work Plane Through the Center of the Right Hole in the Flange

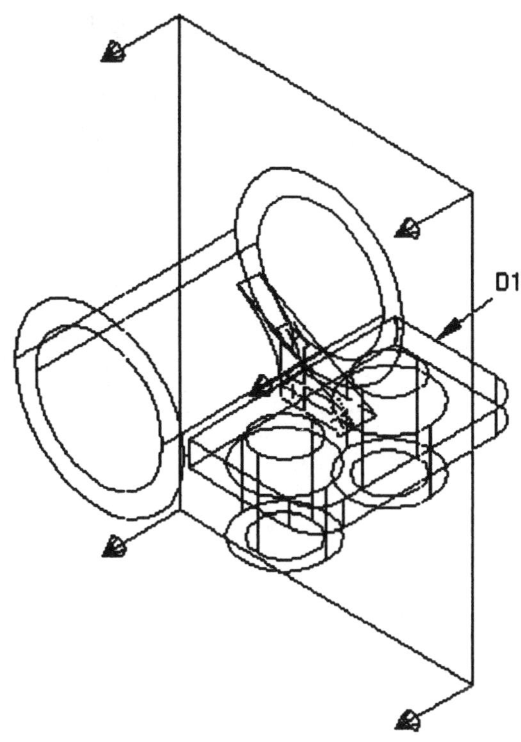

X/Y/Z/<Select work axis or straight edge>:	*Type:* **X** ↵
Rotate/<Accept>:	If the UCS icon is in the position shown in Figure 15–46, *Press:* ↵ to accept. If the UCS icon is not in the correct position, *Type:* **R** ↵ until it is, then *Press:* ↵.

FIGURE 15–46
UCS Icon Correctly Oriented

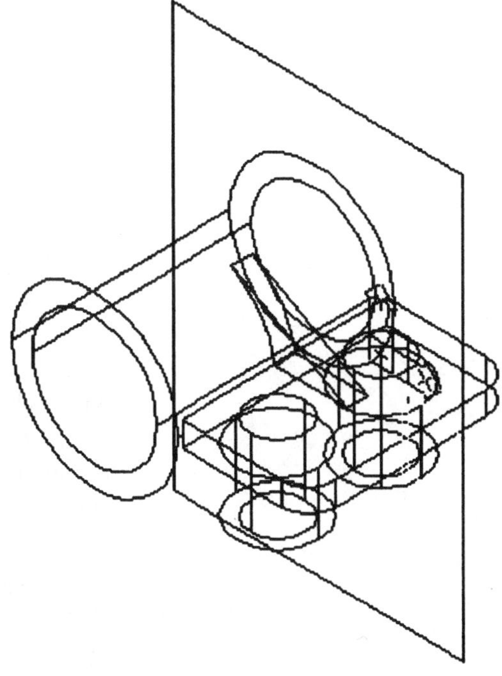

Step 48. Move the UCS to a location that will make it easy to calculate dimensions, in this case the center of the right hole in the flange.

Command:	*Type:* **UCS** ↵
Origin/ZAxis/3point/OBject?View/ X/Y/Z/Prev/Restore/Save/Del/?/ <World>:	*Type:* **O** ↵
Origin point <0,0,0>:	**Osnap-CENter**
of	**D1** (Figure 15–47)

FIGURE 15–47
Selecting a UCS Origin

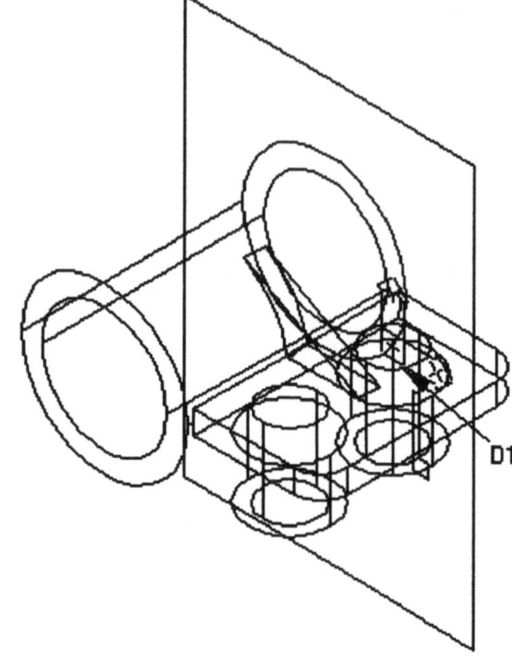

Step 49. Before you begin drawing the sketch, activate a new part.

Prompt	Response
Command:	**Part** **New**

Step 50. Draw the cross-sectional sketch of the bushing. The dimensions in the following sequence were taken from Figure 15–24.

Prompt	Response
Command:	*Type:* **PL** ↵
Arc/Close/Halfwidth/Length/Undo/ Width/<Endpoint of line>:	*Type:* **.25,−.25** ↵
Arc/Close/Halfwidth/Length/Undo/ Width/<Endpoint of line>:	*Type:* **@.0625<180** ↵
Arc/Close/Halfwidth/Length/Undo/ Width/<Endpoint of line>:	*Type:* **@.625<270** ↵
Arc/Close/Halfwidth/Length/Undo/ Width/<Endpoint of line>:	*Type:* **@.1375<0** ↵
Arc/Close/Halfwidth/Length/Undo/ Width/<Endpoint of line>:	*Type:* **@.125<90** ↵
Arc/Close/Halfwidth/Length/Undo/ Width/<Endpoint of line>:	*Type:* **@.075<180** ↵
Arc/Close/Halfwidth/Length/Undo/ Width/<Endpoint of line>:	*Type:* **C** ↵

Step 51. Draw a center line so you will have an axis around which to revolve the sketch after you have made the profile.

Prompt	Response
Command:	*Type:* **L** ↵
From point:	*Type:* **0,0** ↵
To point:	*Type:* **@1<270** ↵

Step 52. On Your Own:

Set layer Y current.

Step 53. Create the profile.

Prompt	Response
Command:	**Profile:**
Select objects:	**Pick the pline and the center line you just drew.**

Before you use the ADREVOLVE command for the first time, let's examine the command.

ADREVOLVE

This command activates the Designer Revolution dialog box. There are three areas on this dialog box:

Termination
Specifies how the revolution is ended.

By Angle
Revolves the profile to the specified angle.

Mid Plane
Revolves the profile equally in both directions. It ends at the specified overall angle.

To Plane
Allows you to specify a plane on the active part or a work plane to end the revolve operation.

Full
Revolves the profile 360°.

Operation
Allows you to select how the revolution is created.

Base
Creates the first feature on the part.

Cut
Cuts the revolved profile out of the part.

Join
Adds material to the active part.

Intersect
Creates a new feature from the common volume of the existing part and the revolved profile.

Size
Allows you to specify the angle of revolution.

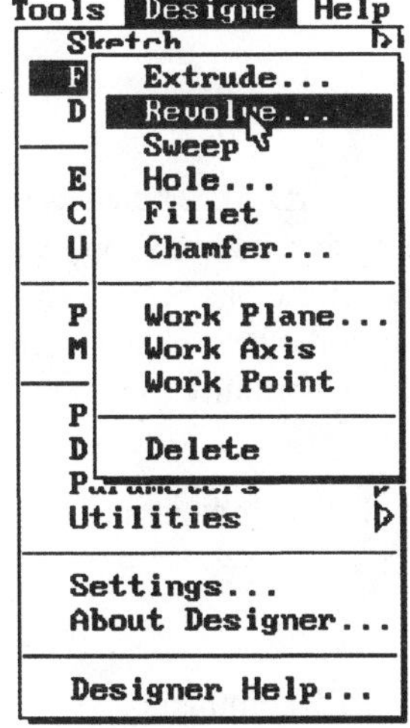

Step 54. Revolve the profile.

Prompt	Response
Command:	**Revolve. . .**
The Designer Revolution dialog box, Figure 15–48, appears:	*Pick:* **Full**
	Pick: **OK**

FIGURE 15–48
Designer Revolution Dialog Box

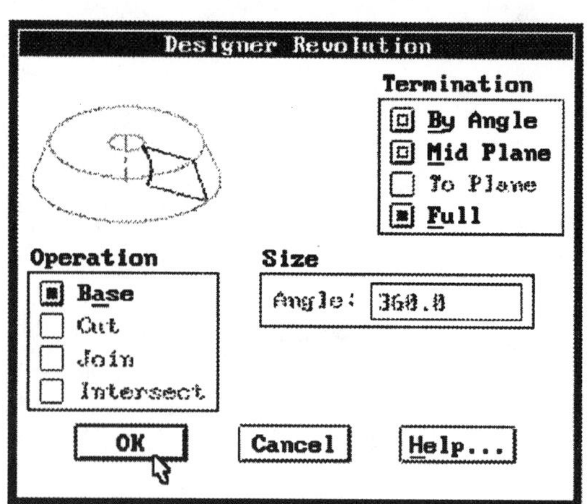

Prompt	Response
Select axis of revolution:	**Pick the center line.** (If you get an error message, undo back to the profile and zoom in closer, before you revolve the profile.)

The bushing is now complete.

Complete the Drawing and Plot It

Step 55. On Your Own:

1. Copy the bushing to the left hole in the flange, erase the work plane, and turn on the G layer so that the final assembly appears as shown in Figure 15–49.

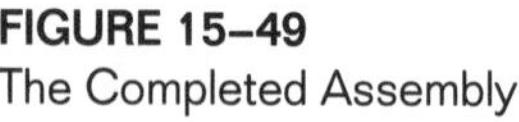
FIGURE 15–49
The Completed Assembly

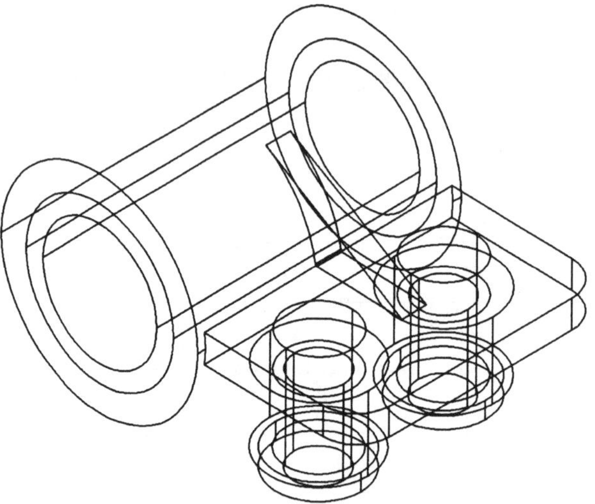

The model can now be meshed using ADMESH, and rendered. ADMESH creates surfaces on all outside edges so that Hide:, Shade:, Render, and other rendering commands work. The results are not always satisfactory, however, so no exercise has been prepared for rendering. The isometric drawing view automatically done in the next chapter offers much better results, as Figure 15–24 shows. You will have the opportunity to make 2-D views, including an isometric view of this model, in Chapter 16.

2. Set UCS to View and place your name on the drawing in the lower right corner.
3. Plot the drawing at full scale (1 = 1) and center it on an 8.5″ × 11″ sheet.
4. Save the drawing in two places and exit AutoCAD.

The last exercise in this chapter allows you to use the ADSWEEP command.

EXERCISE 15–3
DRAWING A SOLID MODEL OF AN OBJECT OF UNIFORM PROFILE ALONG A PATH USING THE AUTOCAD DESIGNER SWEEP COMMAND

Set Up the Drawing

Step 1. On Your Own:

1. Turn on the computer, start AutoCAD Designer, and pick New. . . from the menu bar File menu. Name the drawing: 15-3 (your initials).
2. Make the following settings:

UNITS: Decimal; 3 digits to the right of the decimal point

LIMITS: Lower left corner: 0,0
Upper right corner: 8.5,11

GRID: .2

SNAP: 0.5

STYLE: STANDARD; FONT: SIMPLEX; HEIGHT: 0

Create the following layers:

LAYER NAME	COLOR	LINETYPE
Y	YELLOW	CONTINUOUS
R	RED	CONTINUOUS
G	GREEN	CONTINUOUS

Set layer G current.

Before you begin this exercise, let's examine the ADSWEEP command.

ADSWEEP

The ADSWEEP command allows you to create a solid by extruding a profile along a path, Figure 15–50. You must have two sketches, one for the profile and one for the path. The ADSWEEP command has the following options:

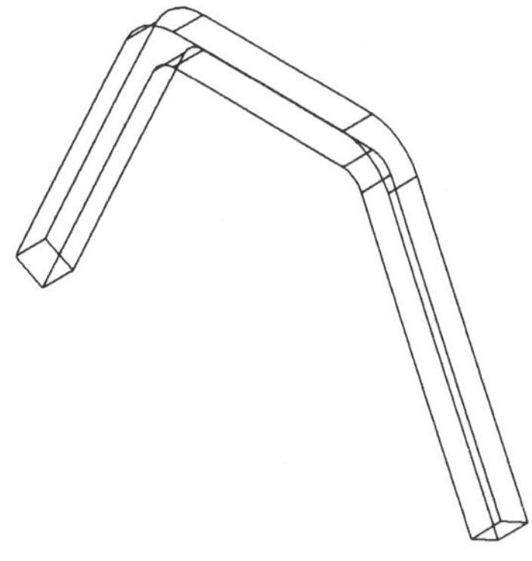

FIGURE 15–50
A Profile Swept Along a Path

Parallel
Creates a solid by extruding the profile parallel to the sketch plane.

Normal
Creates a solid by extruding the profile perpendicular to the sketch plane. If both the path and the profile contain only lines and polylines (no arcs or circles), you may specify a draft angle (a taper) of a positive or negative value.

If you are adding a feature to an existing part, Designer gives you these additional options:

Cut
Removes material from the existing active part.

Join
Adds material to the existing active part.

Intersect
Creates a new feature from the shared volume of the existing part and the sweep feature.

Make a Path for the Profile and Dimension It

This time make a sloppy sketch so you can see how Designer handles inaccurate sketches.

Step 2. On Your Own:

Make a sketch similar to Figure 15–51. Make it approximately 3-1/2″ high by 6″ at the bottom. Make the fillets about 1/2″.

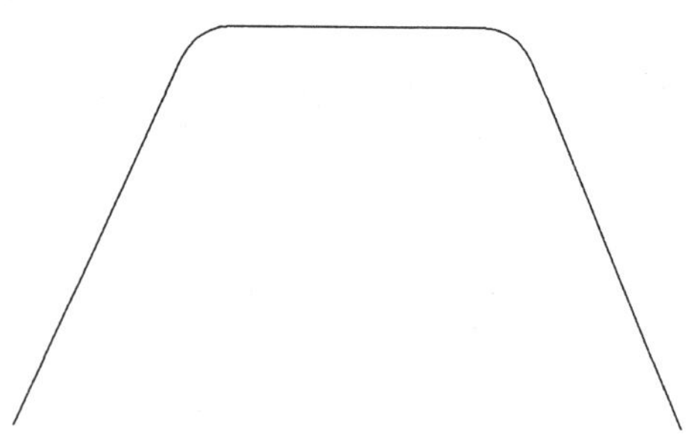

FIGURE 15–51
Making a Sketch

Step 3. Make the path.

Tools Designe Help
Profile
Path
Sketch Plane
Constraints
Fix Point
Add Dimension
Mode
Part Viewing
Display
Parameters
Utilities
Settings...
About Designer...
Designer Help...

Prompt	Response
Command:	**Path**
Select objects:	**Use a crossing window to select the entire sketch.**
Specify start point of path:	**Pick the left end of the path.**

Step 4. Create a work plane.

Prompt	Response
Command:	**Work Plane**
The Designer Work Plane dialog box appears:	*Pick:* **Sweep Profile** *Pick:* **OK**
Select an item in the path:	**Pick the left leg of the path.**

Step 5. Set the number of places to the right of the decimal point.

Prompt	Response
Command:	*Type:* **DIMDEC** ↵
New value for DIMDEC <4>:	*Type:* **3** ↵

Now, add dimensions.

Step 6. Add dimensions.

Prompt	Response
Command:	**Add Dimension**
Select first item:	**D1** (Figure 15–52)

FIGURE 15–52
Dimensioning the Sketch

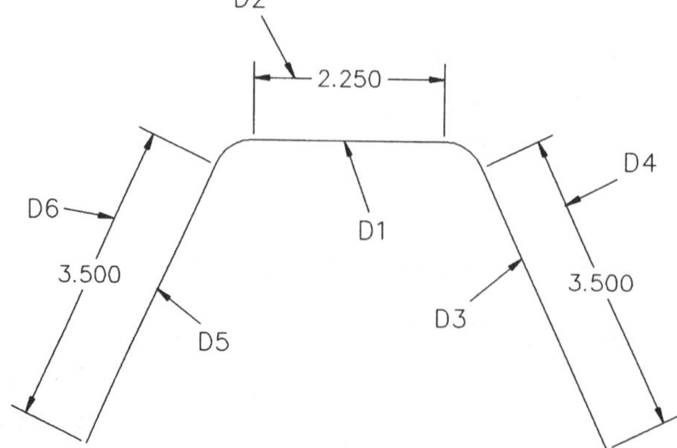

Select second item or place dimension:	**D2**
Undo/Hor/Ver/Align/Par/Dimension value <default>:	*Type:* **2.25** ↵
Select first item:	**D3**
Select second item or place dimension:	**D4**
Undo/Hor/Ver/Align/Par/Dimension value <default>:	*Type:* **3.5** ↵ (You may have to type: A ↵ to get an aligned dimension.)
Select first item:	**D5**
Select second item or place dimension:	**D6**
Undo/Hor/Ver/Align/Par/Dimension value <default>:	*Type:* **3.5** ↵ (You may have to type: A ↵ to get an aligned dimension.)
Select first item:	**D1** (Figure 15–53)

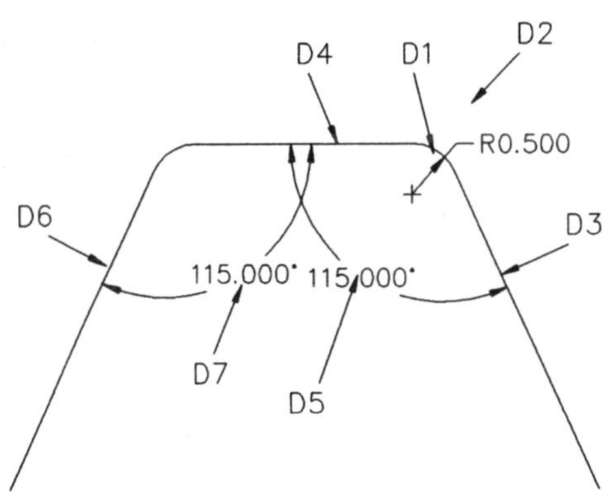

FIGURE 15–53
Dimensioning the Sketch

Select second item or place dimension:	**D2**
Undo/Hor/Ver/Align/Par/Dimension value <default>:	*Type:* **.5** ↵
Select first item:	**D3** (Pick near the MIDpoint of the lines to get an angular dimension.)
Select second item or place dimension:	**D4**
Specify dimension placement:	**D5**
Undo/Hor/Ver/Align/Par/Dimension value <default>:	*Type:* **115** ↵
Select first item:	**D4**
Select second item or place dimension:	**D6**
Specify dimension placement:	**D7**
Undo/Hor/Ver/Align/Par/Dimension value <default>:	*Type:* **115** ↵
Select first item:	↵

Make the Profile and Dimension It

Step 7. Create a work plane.

Prompt	**Response**
Command:	**Work Plane**

Prompt	Response
The Designer Work Plane dialog box appears:	*Pick:* **Sweep Profile** *Pick:* **OK**
Select an item in the path:	**Pick the left leg of the sketch.**

Step 8. Select an isometric view so you can see what is happening as you create your model.

Prompt	Response
Command:	**Part Viewing** **Iso**

Step 9. Make the work plane the sketch plane.

Prompt	Response
Command:	**Sketch Plane**
Xy/Yz/Zx/Ucs/<Select work plane or planar face>:	**Pick the work plane.**
Rotate/<Accept>:	*Type:* **R** ↵ until the UCS icon is in the position shown in Figure 15–54, then *Press:* ↵.

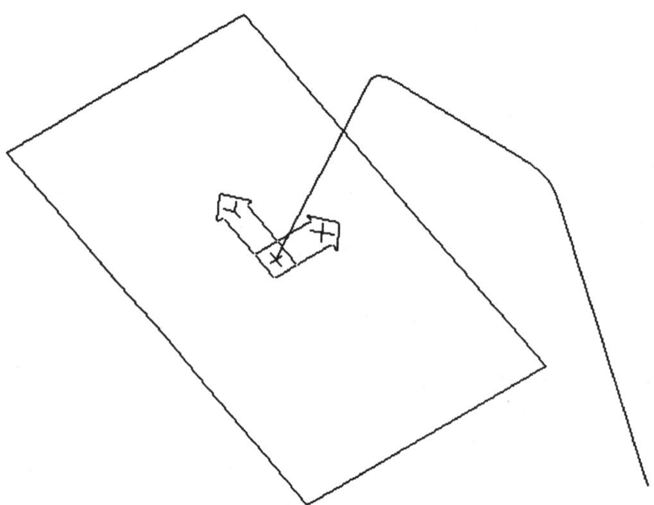

FIGURE 15–54
Rotating the UCS

Step 10. Make the sketch of the cross-sectional area.

Prompt	Response
Command:	**Polygon:**
Number of sides <4>:	↵
Edge/<Center of polygon>:	**Osnap-ENDpoint**
of	**D1** (Figure 15–55)
Inscribed in circle/Circumscribed about circle (I/C) <I>:	↵
Radius of circle:	*Type:* **.25** ↵

Step 11. Make a profile of the sketch.

Prompt	Response
Command:	**Profile**
Select objects:	**Pick the polygon.**

FIGURE 15–55
Making the Profile and Adding Dimensions

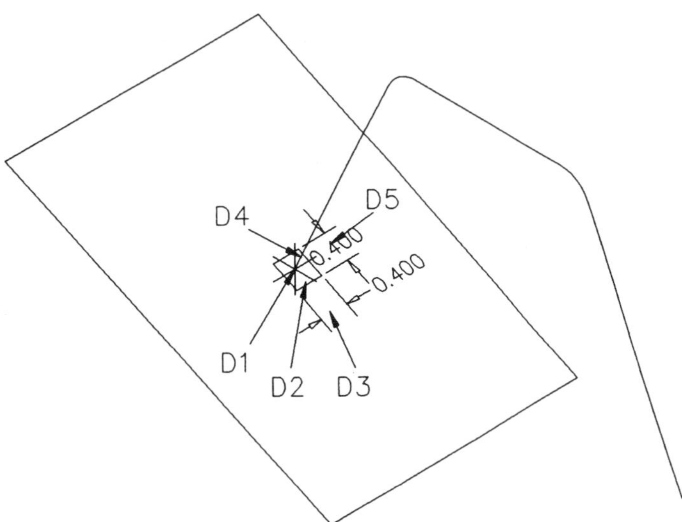

Step 12. Dimension the profile.

Prompt	Response
Command:	**Add Dimension**
Select first item:	**D2**
Select second item or place dimension:	**D3**
Undo/Hor/Ver/Align/Par/Dimension value <0.354>:	*Type:* **.4** ↵
Select first item:	**D4**
Select second item or place dimension:	**D5**
Undo/Hor/Ver/Align/Par/Dimension value <0.354>:	*Type:* **.4** ↵
Select first item:	↵

Sweep the Profile Along the Path

Step 13. Sweep the profile along the path.

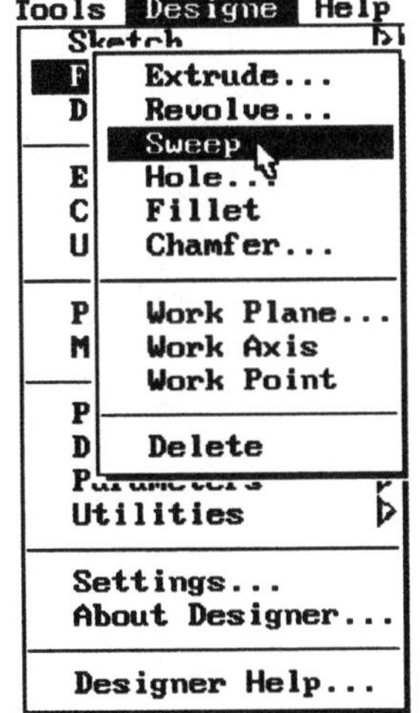

Prompt	Response
Command:	**Sweep**
Select sweep path:	**Pick the path.**
Select sweep cross-section profile:	**Pick the profile of the polygon.**
Parallel/<Normal>:	↵

The model appears as shown in Figure 15–56. Be aware that if a sweep is added to an existing part, it may be used to cut a hole the size of the sweep as well as to add material the size of the sweep.

Complete the Drawing

Step 14. On Your Own:

1. Set UCS to View and place your name on the drawing in the lower right corner.
2. Plot the drawing at full scale (1 = 1) and center it on an 8.5″ × 11″ sheet.
3. Save the drawing in two places and exit AutoCAD.

You have now created three models in Designer. In the next chapter you will make 2-D drawings automatically of the first two models. The drawings will include top, front, right side, sectional, isometric, and auxiliary views—all done quickly and with little additional notation required.

FIGURE 15-56
The Completed Sweep

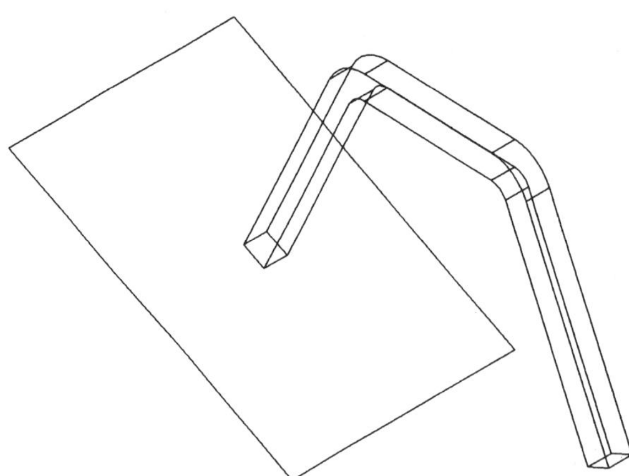

EXERCISES

15–1. Follow the instructions in this chapter to draw Figure 15–23. Your final drawing should look like that figure.

15–2. Follow the instructions in this chapter to draw Figure 15–49. Your final drawing should look like that figure.

15–3. Follow the instructions in this chapter to draw Figure 15–56. Your final drawing should look like that figure without the work plane.

15–4. Make a solid model from the dimensions shown in Figure 15–57. Set the Part Viewing option to Iso, set UCS to View, and place your name in the lower right corner using the SIMPLEX font .2 high. Show only the isometric view.

15–5. Make a solid model from the dimensions shown in Figure 15–58. Set the Part Viewing option to Iso, set UCS to View, and place your name in the lower right corner using the SIMPLEX font .2 high. Show only the isometric view.

15–6. Make a solid model from the dimensions shown in Figure 15–59. Set the Part Viewing option to Iso, set UCS to View, and place your name in the lower right corner using the SIMPLEX font .2 high. Show only the isometric view.

15–7. Make a solid model from the dimensions shown in Figure 15–60. Set the Part Viewing option to Iso, set UCS to View, and place your name in the lower right corner using the SIMPLEX font .2 high. Show only the isometric view.

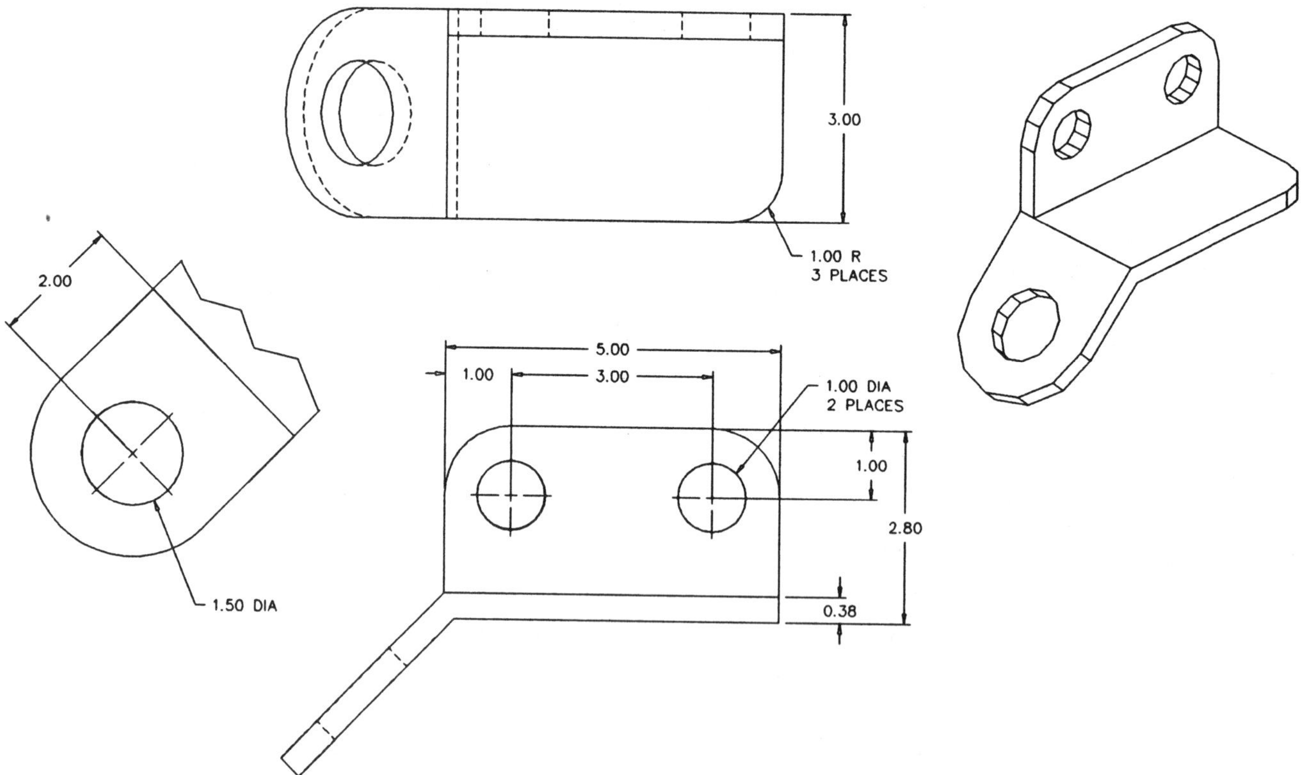

FIGURE 15-57
Exercise 15-4

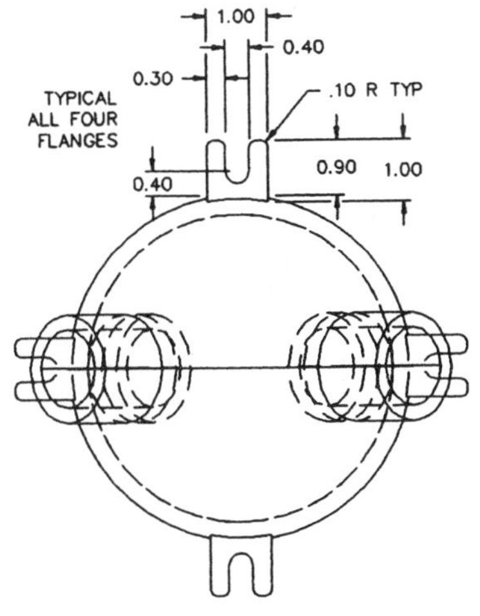

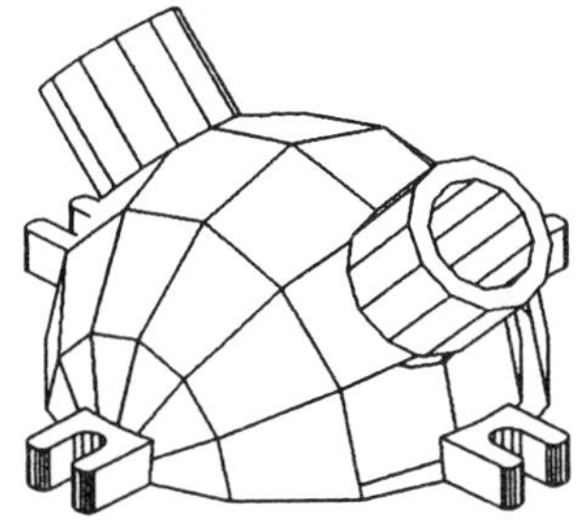

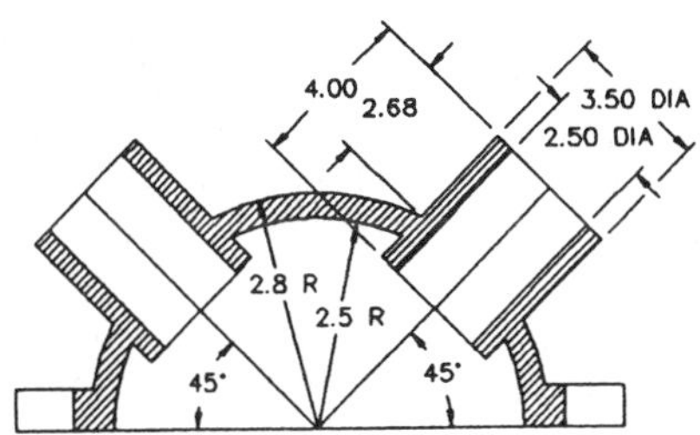

FIGURE 15–58
Exercise 15–5

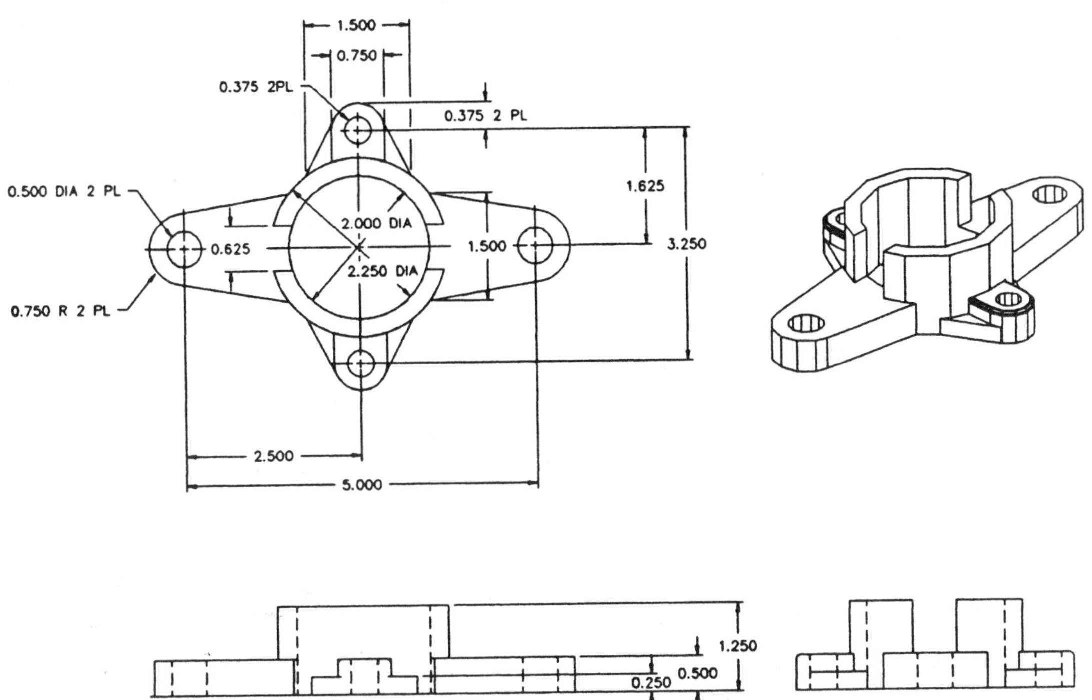

FIGURE 15–59
Exercise 15–6

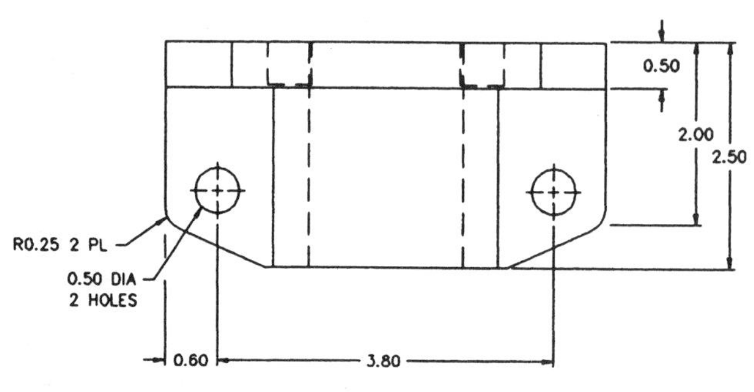

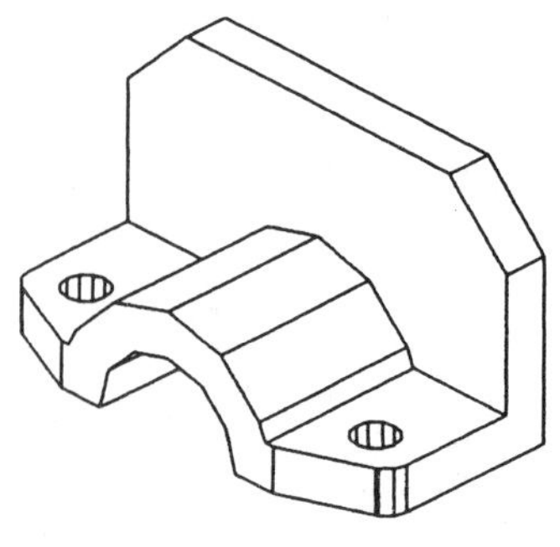

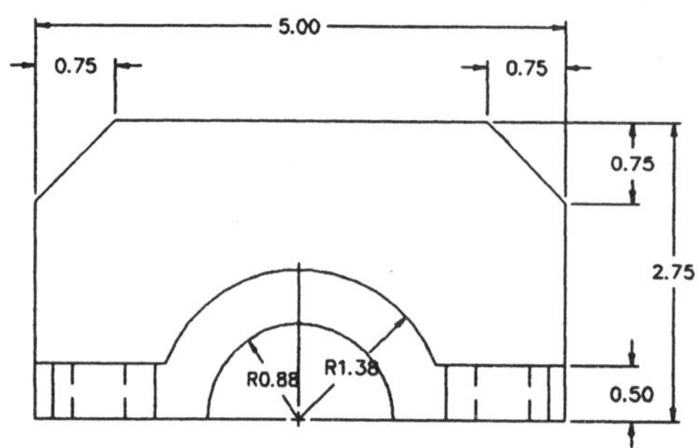

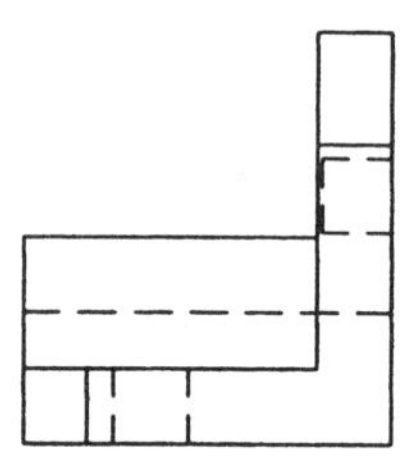

FIGURE 15–60
Exercise 15–7

15–8. Make a solid model from the dimensions shown in Figure 15–61. Set the Part Viewing option to Iso, set UCS to View, and place your name in the lower right corner using the SIMPLEX font .2 high. Show only the isometric view.

15–9. Make a solid model from the dimensions shown in Figure 15–62. Set the Part Viewing option to Iso, set UCS to View, and place your name in the lower right corner using the SIMPLEX font .2 high. Show only the isometric view.

15–10. Make a solid model by measuring the isometric view shown in Figure 15–63 and make your drawing twice that size. Set the Part Viewing option to Iso, set UCS to View, and place your name in the lower right corner using the SIMPLEX font .2 high. Show only the isometric view.

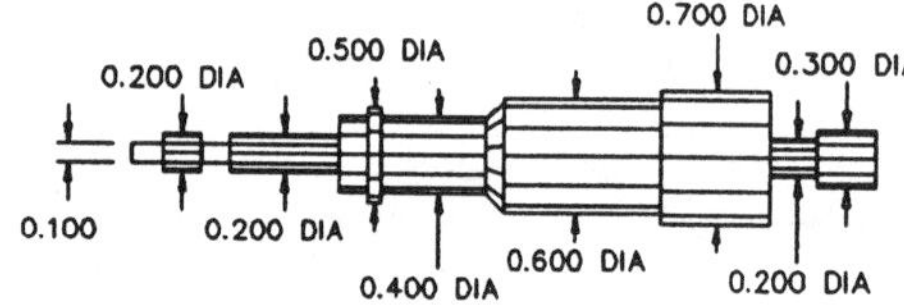

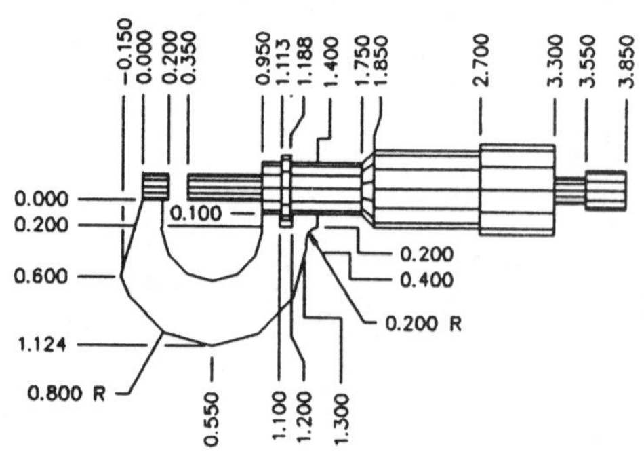

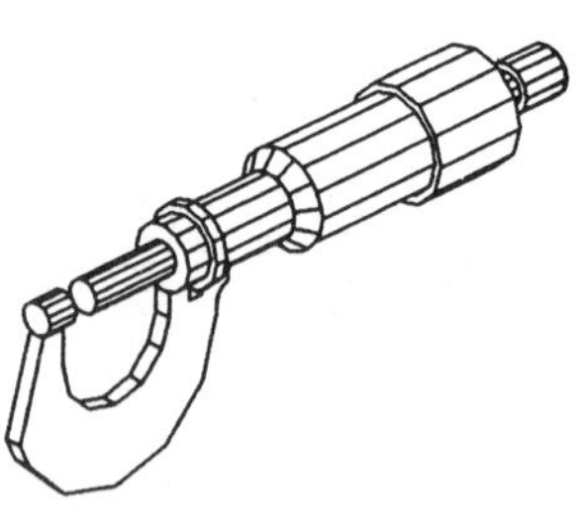

FIGURE 15–61
Exercise 15–8

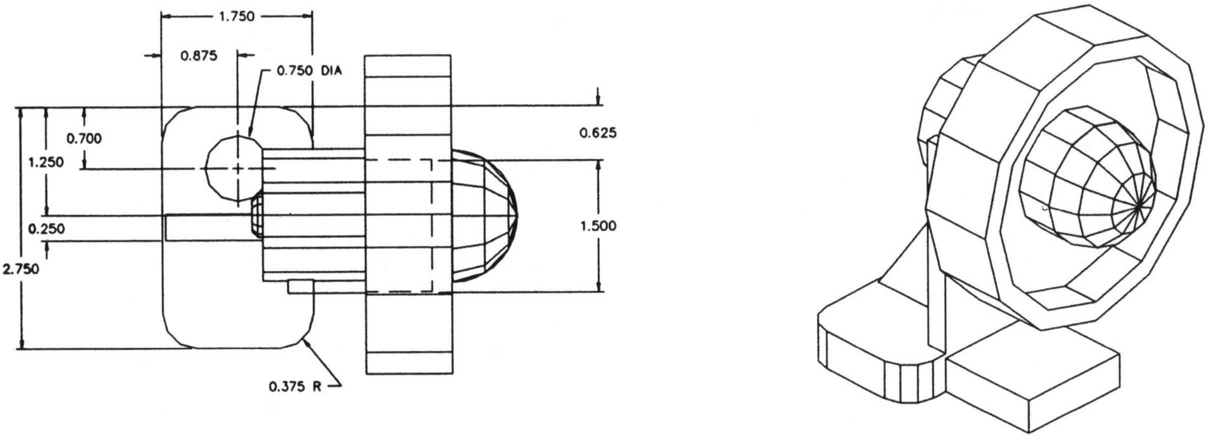

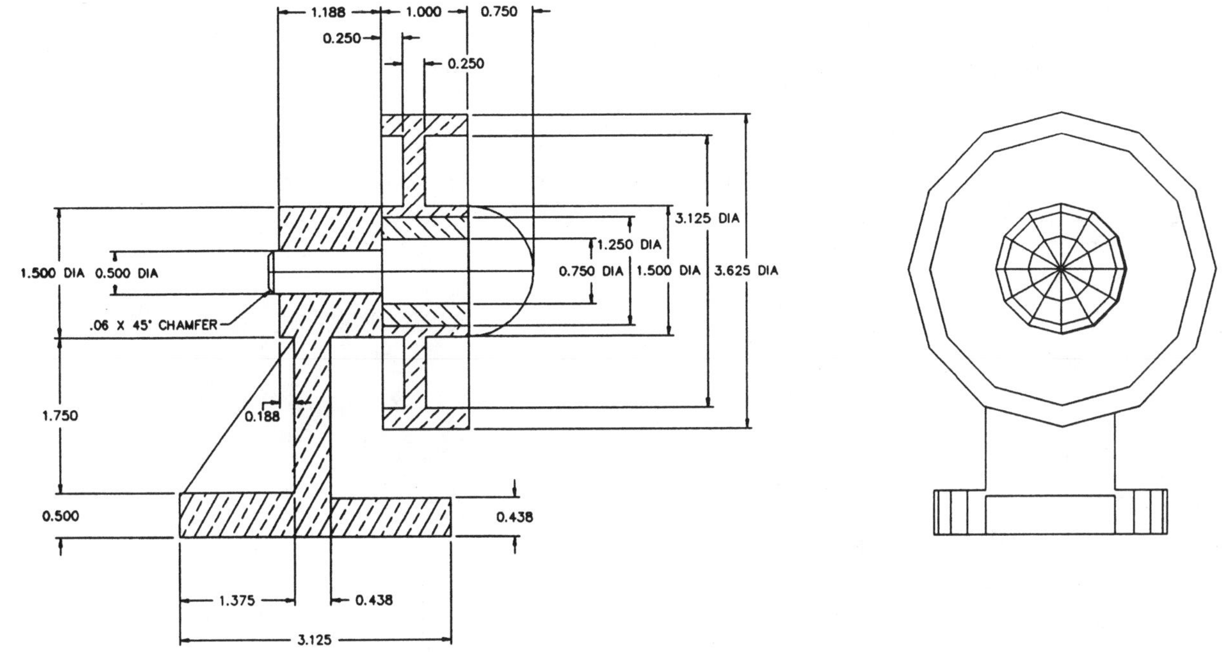

1.750
0.875
0.750 DIA
0.700
1.250
0.250
2.750
0.375 R
0.625
1.500

1.188
1.000
0.750
0.250
0.250
1.500 DIA
0.500 DIA
.06 X 45° CHAMFER
3.125 DIA
1.250 DIA
0.750 DIA
1.500 DIA
3.625 DIA
1.750
0.188
0.500
0.438
1.375
0.438
3.125

FIGURE 15–62
Exercise 15–9

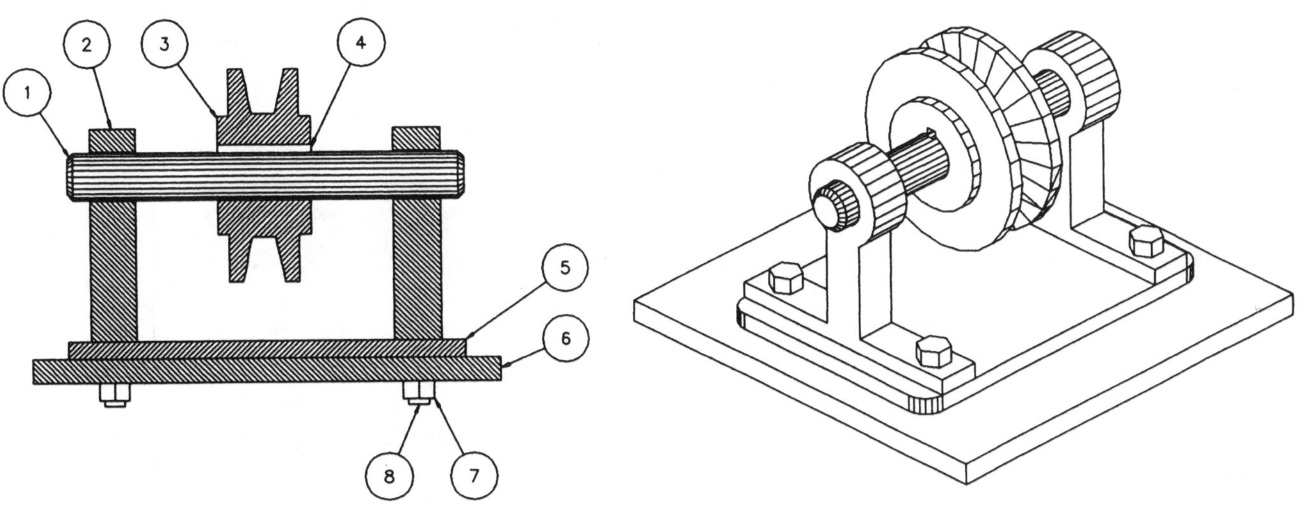

FIGURE 15–63
Exercise 15–10

REVIEW QUESTIONS

Circle the correct answer.

1. The ADPROFILE command does which of the following?
   a. Creates a profile from an open sketch
   b. Automatically adds constraints with ADSKMODE on
   c. Automatically adds dimensions to the profile
   d. Automatically extrudes the sketch
   e. Automatically revolves the sketch
2. The ADPARDIM command does which of the following?
   a. Allows you to add parametric dimensions
   b. Adds nonparametric dimensions
   c. Adds reference dimensions
   d. Automatically adds all necessary dimensions
   e. Automatically updates an existing part when a dimension is changed
3. All sketches must be fully constrained.
   a. True b. False
4. Which of the following sets the number of places to the right of the decimal?
   a. DIMUNITS d. DIMCEN
   b. DIMTXT e. DIMSCALE
   c. DIMDEC
5. The ADEXTRUDE command does which of the following?
   a. Extrudes a profile as a hole when Blind is selected
   b. Extrudes a profile equally in both directions when Through is selected
   c. Extrudes a profile equally in both directions when Mid Plane is selected
   d. Adds the extruded feature to the existing part when Intersect is selected
   e. Creates a new feature from the common volume of the existing part and the extruded profile when Join is selected
6. Which of the following Designer Viewing selections is the same as the plan view of the world UCS?
   a. Top d. Bottom
   b. Front e. Iso
   c. Right
7. The ADWORKPLN command does which of the following?
   a. Creates the sketch plane on any work plane
   b. Creates work axes
   c. Creates work points
   d. Creates parametric work planes
   e. Creates a profile
8. Nonparametric work planes are created with which of the following options?
   a. Planar Parallel d. On UCS
   b. Sweep e. Offset
   c. Planar Normal
9. The ADSKPLN command does which of the following?
   a. Creates parametric work planes
   b. Creates one or more sketch planes that can be active at the same time
   c. Sets one sketch plane on which a profile may be created
   d. Creates nonparametric work planes
   e. Creates work axes
10. Which of the following constraint options makes two surfaces lie in the same plane?
    a. Concentric d. Tangent
    b. Collinear e. Horizontal
    c. Parallel

Complete.

11. Describe the function of the ADADDCON command.

    ____

    ____

12. List the command and the options that must be selected to extrude a shape from a work plane located in the center of a part so that the shape is *cut* equally in both directions.

    ____

    ____

13. Describe what each of the following constraint options does and list the letter that Designer assigns to each option.

    Letter

    Concentric ______________________ ____

    Project ______________________ ____

    XValue ______________________ ____

    Radius ______________________ ____

14. Prepare the following Designer Hole dialog box to drill a .500-diameter hole through that is counterbored to a 1.000 diameter, .250 deep, located from two edges.

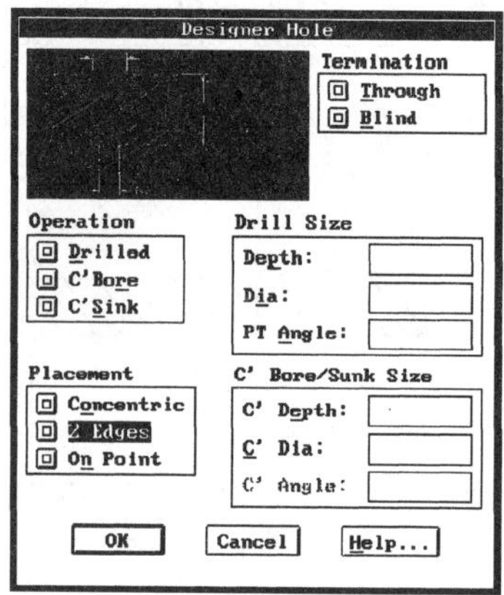

15. Prepare the following Designer Hole dialog box to drill a .375-diameter blind hole that is .625 deep located in the center of a cylinder.

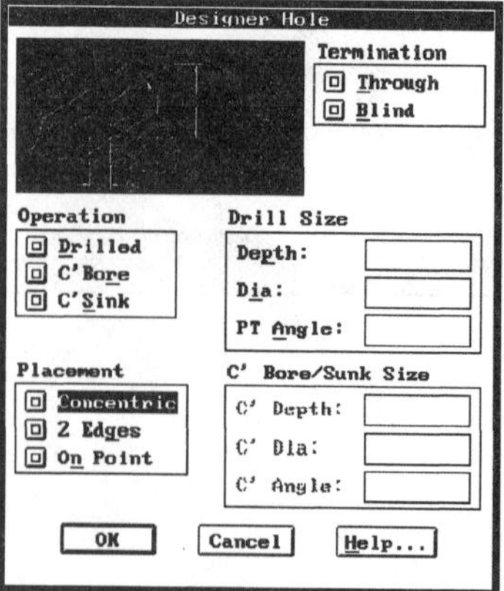

16. List three steps needed to make a .250-radius fillet on a single edge using the ADFILLET command.

Prompt	Response
Step 1. Command:	____________
Step 2. Select edge:	____________
Step 3. Fillet radius <0.250>:	____________

17. List the command that is unique to a multiple-part drawing that is not needed on a single-part drawing.

____

18. List the four options on the Planar Parallel dialog box.

____

____

____

____

19. List the four Operation options on the Designer Extrusion dialog box and explain how each one is used.

____

____

____

____

20. List the responses to the following prompts to make a sweep path and a work plane for the profile to be swept.

Prompt	Response
Step 1. Command:	____________
Step 2. Select objects:	____________
Step 3. Specify start point of path:	____________
Step 4. Command:	____________
Step 5. The Designer Work Plane dialog box appears:	____________
Step 6. Select an item in the path:	____________

16 Creating 2-D Drawings from Designer Solid Models

OBJECTIVES

When you have completed this chapter, you will be able to:

- □ Make 2-D orthographic and auxiliary external views from Designer solid models.
- □ Set variables to obtain hatch patterns on sectional views.
- □ Make 2-D sectional views from solid models.
- □ Insert a standard drawing format around 2-D drawings.
- □ Place reference dimensions and notes on 2-D detail drawings.
- □ Make isometric views of solid models.

INTRODUCTION

Now that you have constructed several Designer solid models, you have reached a point where your hard work will really pay off. Making 2-D manufacturing drawings from the solid model is automatic. Some dimensions, hole notes, and other notations must be added, but the painstaking drawing of 2-D views is done for you. Let's begin with the first drawing you did in Chapter 15.

EXERCISE 16–1 MAKING AN ORTHOGRAPHIC DETAIL DRAWING FROM A DESIGNER SOLID

Your final drawing will look similar to Figure 16–1.

Set Up the Drawing

Step 1. On Your Own:

1. Pick New. . . from the menu bar File menu. Name the drawing: 16-1 (your initials)=15-1 (your initials).
2. Make the following settings:

UNITS: Decimal; 3 digits to the right of the decimal point

LIMITS: Lower left coroner: 0,0
Upper right corner: 11,8.5

GRID: .2

SNAP: .05

STYLE: STANDARD; FONT: SIMPLEX; HEIGHT: 0

Create the following layers:

LAYER NAME	COLOR	LINETYPE
Y	YELLOW	CONTINUOUS
R	RED	CONTINUOUS
G	GREEN	CONTINUOUS

Set layer G current.

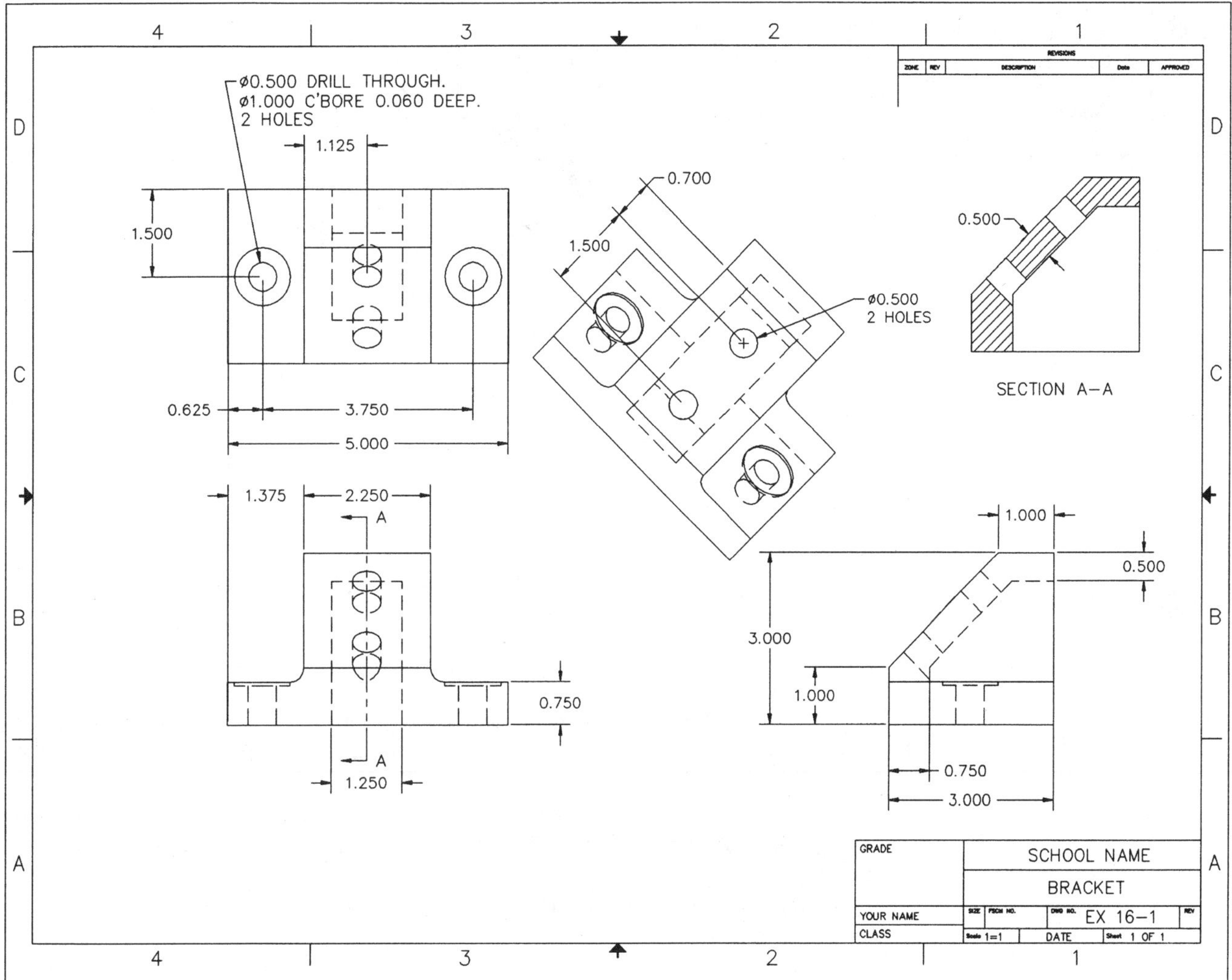

FIGURE 16–1
The Completed Drawing

3. Set UCS to World, erase your name, and Zoom: All so that your model appears as shown in Figure 16–2.

Before you use the ADVIEW command for the first time, let's examine it in detail.

ADVIEW

ADVIEW makes the standard engineering view types from a Designer solid model. As you specify which view you want Designer does the following:

1. Numbers each view as it is created. The first view you make is numbered 0, the second is 1, and so on.
2. Creates two layers for each view:

   ADV_#_HID for hidden lines
   ADV_#_VIS for visible or object lines

   For example, for the first view you make, Designer creates two layers: ADV_0_HID and ADV_0_VIS; the second view gets layers ADV_1_HID and ADV_1_VIS.

   WARNING: Do not change the contents of these layers. Your drawing can be permanently corrupted if you do so.

FIGURE 16–2
The Model With the World UCS

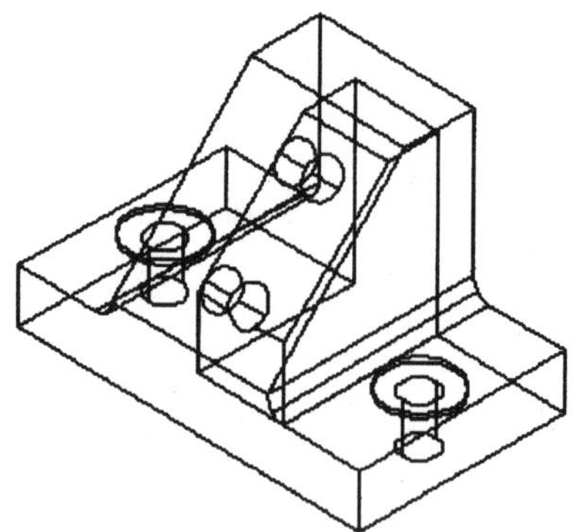

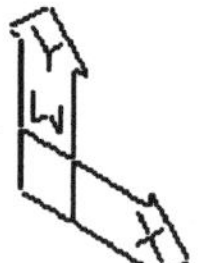

The view types that Designer makes are shown on the Designer Drawing View dialog box, Figure 16–3. All parts of this dialog box are described next.

Type

Base

Creates a view of the model based on the surfaces you select as the base view. In most cases you will choose to make the base view the front view.

Ortho

Creates an orthographic view at 90° to another view, often the base view. For example the top orthographic (2-D) view is created above the front view.

Aux

Creates an auxiliary view at 90° to a specified inclined surface on any of the standard orthographic views.

Iso

Creates an isometric view at a scale that is relative to the parent view. A parent view is the view from which another view is created.

FIGURE 16–3
Designer Drawing View Dialog Box for the Front View

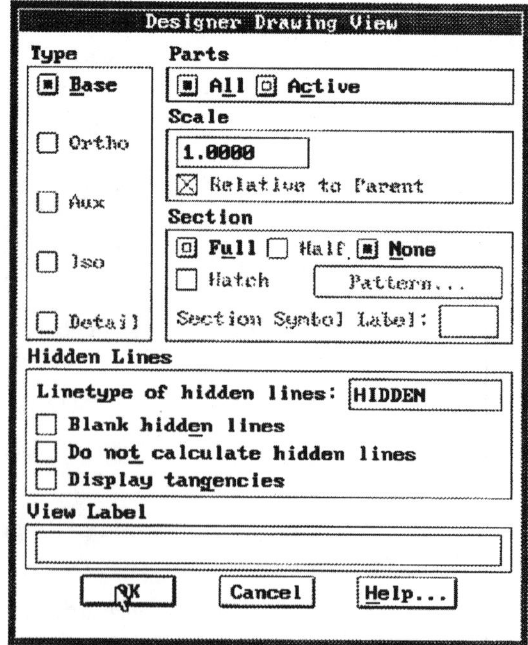

Detail

Creates a detail view at a scale relative to the parent view. Usually the detail view is enlarged to show small details.

Parts

Allows you to specify whether all the parts in a multiple-part drawing or just the active part is to be included in the view. This is particularly helpful when you are making a sectioned assembly drawing, as in Exercise 16–2.

Scale

Sets the scale for the isometric and detail views, allowing you to enlarge or reduce them relative to the parent view.

Section

Allows you to make cross-sectional views for base, orthographic, and auxiliary views.

Full

Makes a full sectional view across the part or parts.

Half

Makes a sectional view across half the part or parts.

None

Makes no sectional view.

Hatch

Places a hatch pattern on the view.

Pattern. . .

Displays the AutoCAD Hatch Option dialog box and allows you to select a hatch pattern or define a continuous line pattern of a specified spacing and angle.

Section Symbol Label:

Allows you to enter the letter you want to appear at the ends of the cutting plane line that is created on the work plane you specify for the sectional view.

Hidden Lines

Linetype of hidden lines:

Sets the linetype for hidden lines.

Blank hidden lines

This box is automatically checked for sectional and isometric views. You can remove the check so that hidden lines appear in the view you want to make. Usually the default is the correct selection.

Do not calculate hidden lines

Hidden lines are not generated.

Display tangencies

Allows you to change the display of tangent edges in the view.

View Label

Allows you to type a label that will appear on the view. Usually the standard views (top, front, right side, etc.) are not labeled; sectional views and detail views are often labeled.

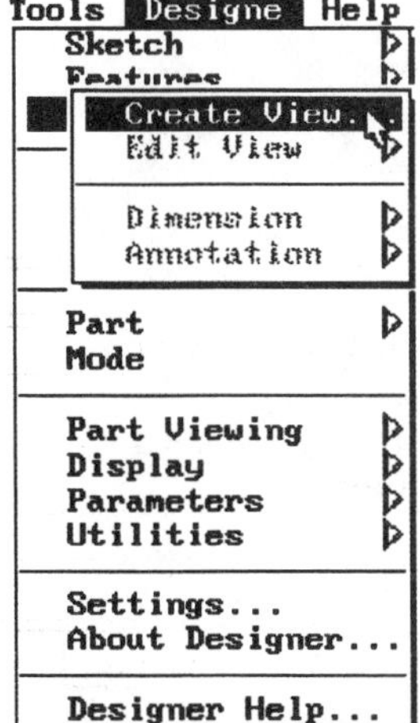

Create the Front View

Step 2. Use ADVIEW to make the front 2-D view.

Prompt	Response
Command:	**Drawing** **Create view. . .**
The Designer Drawing View dialog box, Figure 16–3, appears:	*Pick:* **OK** (if your dialog box is the same as Figure 16–3) (If it is not, change it to the settings in Figure 16–3, and *Pick:* **OK.**)
Xy/Yz/Zx/Ucs/<Select work plane or planar face>:	*Pick:* **D1** (Figure 16–4)

FIGURE 16–4
Highlighting the Front Surface

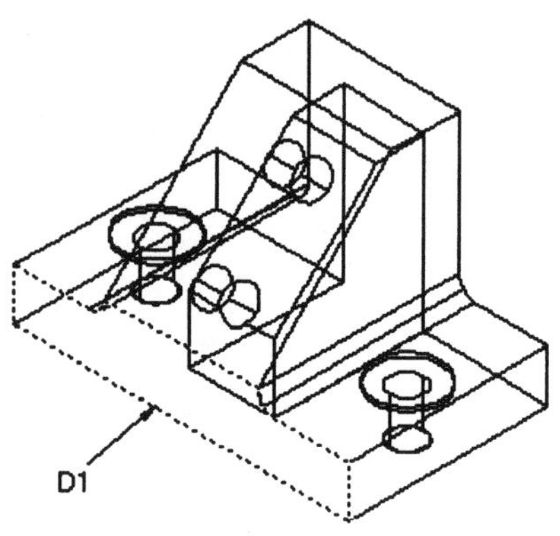

Prompt	Response
Next/<Accept>:	*Type:* **N** ↵ until the front surface is highlighted as shown in Figure 16–4, then *Press:* ↵ to accept.
X/Y/Z/<Select work axis or straight edge>:	*Pick:* **D1** (again)
Rotate/<Accept>:	*Type:* **R** ↵ until the UCS icon appears as shown in Figure 16–5, then *Press:* ↵ to accept.
View center:	*Type:* **4,3** ↵ (or pick a point in that approximate location)
View center: (Designer allows you to pick as many different locations as you want to change where the center of the view will be located.)	↵

Notice that you are now in paper space. If you look at the Layer Control dialog box, you will find a layer named ADD-VIEWS that is turned Off. That is the layer that contains the line surrounding the paper space viewport. If you ever need to erase a paper space viewport, turn this layer on, erase the viewport, and turn it off again. **Do not thaw or otherwise edit the ADP_FRZ layer.** Doing so will corrupt your model.

Before you create any more views, place a title block around the drawing, and move the view so it is arranged well in the field of the drawing. (The field of the drawing is the space inside the borders and title block.) The command used to do this is MV Setup.

FIGURE 16–5
Rotating the UCS to This Position

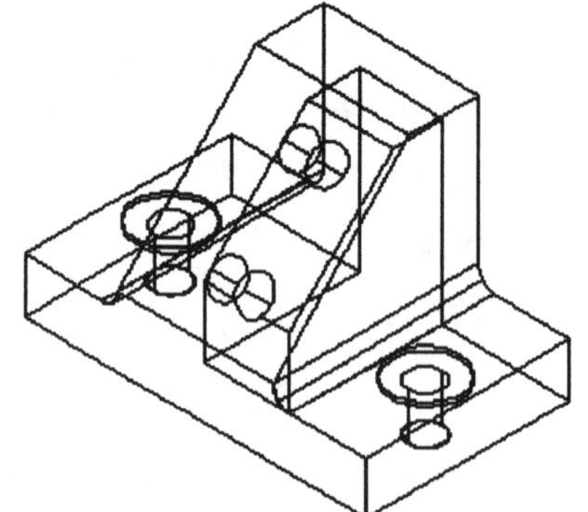

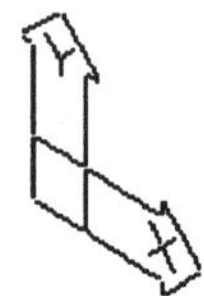

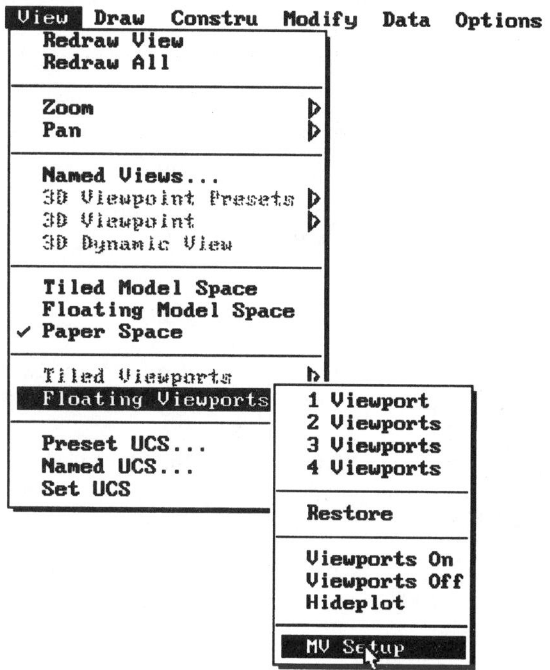

MV Setup

MV Setup has two different modes—one with Tilemod: on and one with Tilemod: off. When Tilemod: is on, MV Setup allows you to select drawing units, scale, and paper size. This is a holdover from early versions of AutoCAD and can be done better with other commands. You will have definite use for MV Setup with Tilemod: off. With Tilemod: off the following options are available to you:

Align
Allows you to align paper space views with each other.

Create
Allows you to make viewports in several different arrangements. This option is also used to delete viewports.

Scale viewports
Allows you to scale any one or all viewports to the same or different scales.

Options
Allows you to set layer, limits, units, and xrefs.

Title block
Allows you to insert any one of 13 different formats.

Undo
Acts like any other undo to undo the last command.

Insert a Title Block Around the Drawing

Step 3. Use MV Setup to place a title block around the drawing.

Prompt	Response
Command:	**MV Setup**
Align/Create/Scale viewports/Options/ Title block/Undo:	*Type:* **T** ↵
Delete objects/Origin/Undo/ <Insert title block>:	↵
Add/Delete/Redisplay/ <Number of entry to load>:	*Type:* **9** ↵ (to select an ANSI-C–size title block)

Prompt	Response
Create a drawing named ansi-c.dwg? <Y>:	↵
Align/Create/Scale viewports/Options/ Title block/Undo:	↵

Next, you will need to move the front view as described in Step 4. Let's examine ADMOVEVIEW before using it.

ADMOVEVIEW:

Tools Designer Help
Sketch
Features
Create View
Attributes
Delete
Move
Part
Mode
Part Viewing
Display
Parameters
Utilities
Settings...
About Designer...
Designer Help...

ADMOVEVIEW moves a view to anywhere on the drawing. You must be in drawing mode (paper space) for ADMOVEVIEW to work.

Step 4. Move the front view so it is better arranged in the format.

Prompt	Response
Command:	**Drawing** **Edit View** **Move**
Select view to move:	**Pick the view you just created.**
View location:	*Type:* **6.5,6** ↵ (Or pick a point in the approximate location shown in Figure 16–6.)
View location:	↵

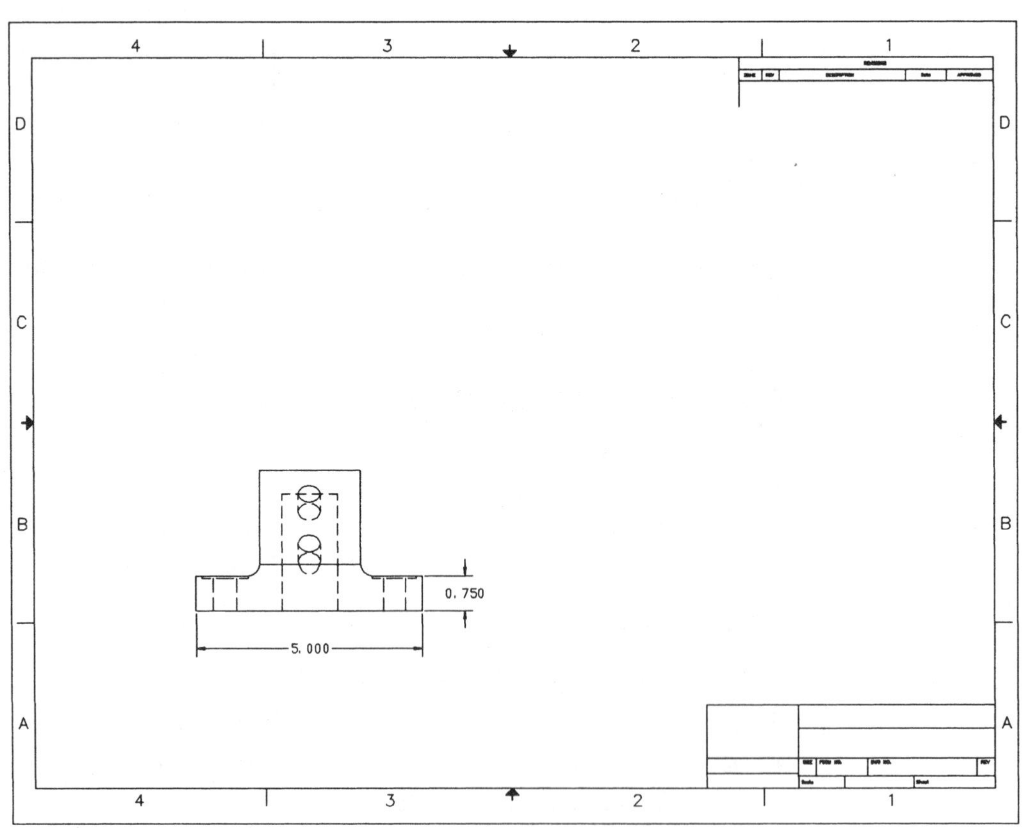

FIGURE 16–6
Inserting a Format and Moving the Front View

Create the Top View

Step 5. Make the top view.

Prompt	Response
Command:	**Drawing** **Create view**
The Designer Drawing View dialog box, Figure 16–7, appears:	*Pick:* **Ortho** *Pick:* **OK**

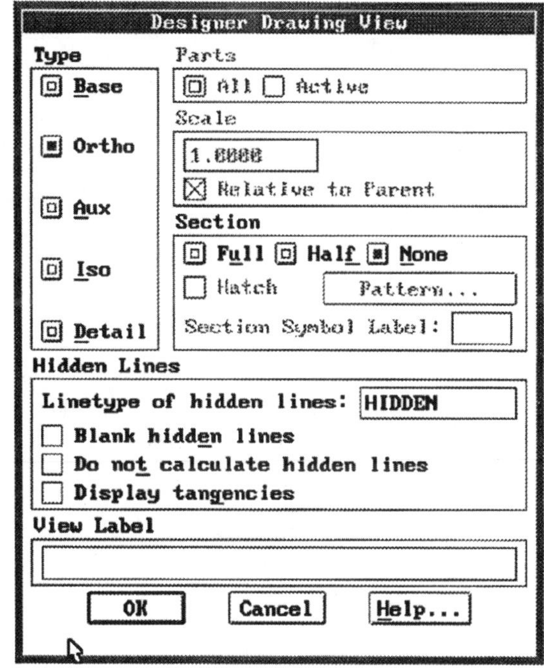

FIGURE 16–7
Designer Drawing View Dialog Box for the Top View

Select parent view:	**Pick the front view (the view you have already created).**
Location for orthographic view:	**Pick a point in the approximate location shown in Figure 16–8.**
Location for orthographic view:	↵

Create the Right Side View

Step 6. On Your Own:

1. Make the right side view.
2. Use ADVIEW to make the right side view in the approximate location shown in Figure 16–9.

Create Section A-A

Step 7. Make a sectional view, Figure 16–10.

Prompt	Response
Command:	**Create View**
The Designer Drawing View dialog box, Figure 16–11, appears:	*Pick:* **Full** (in the Section area) In the Section Symbol Label: text box *Type:* **A.**

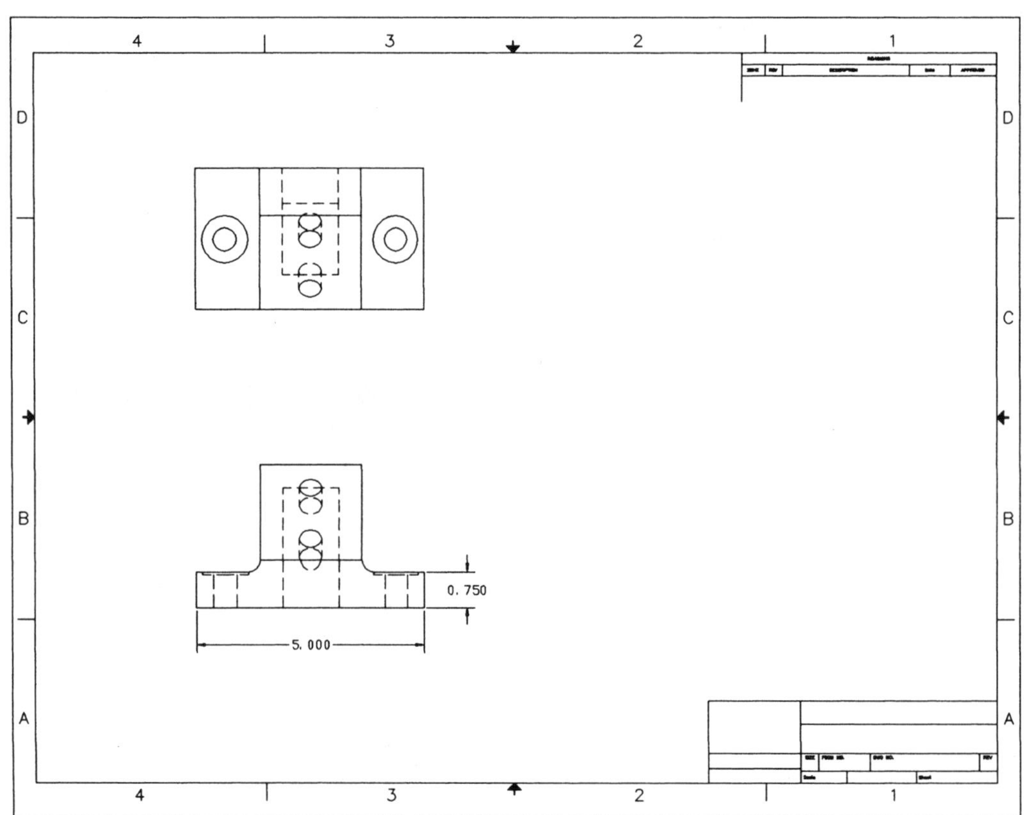

FIGURE 16–8
Making the Top View

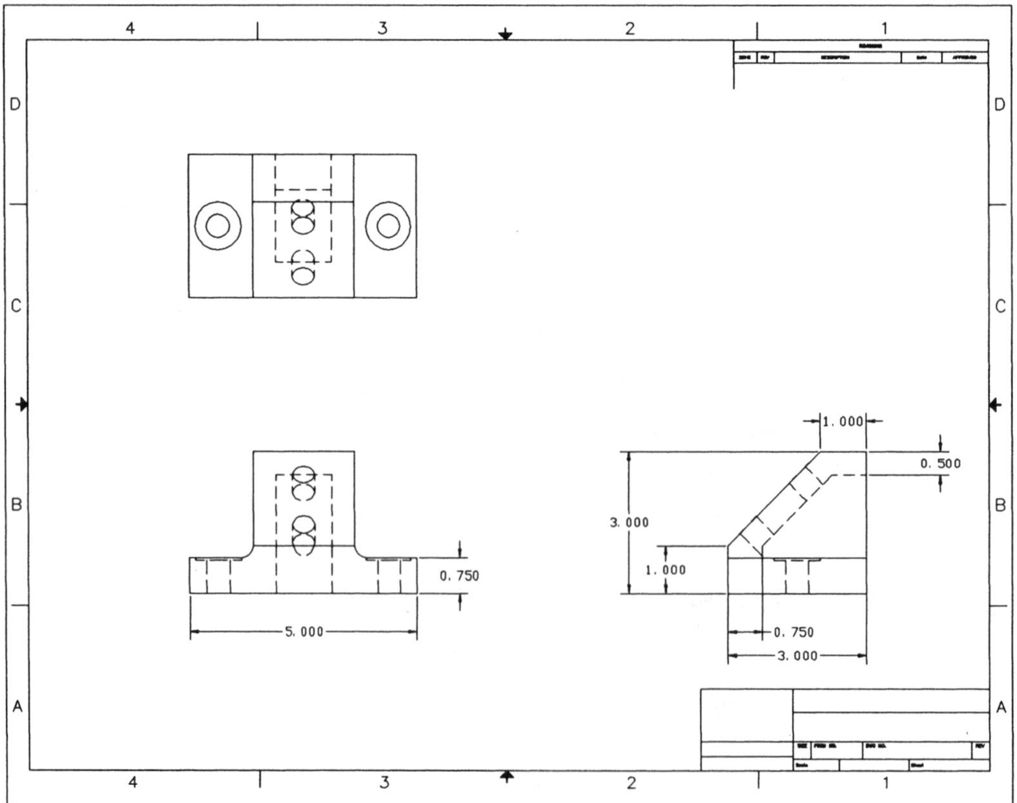

FIGURE 16–9
Making the Right Side View

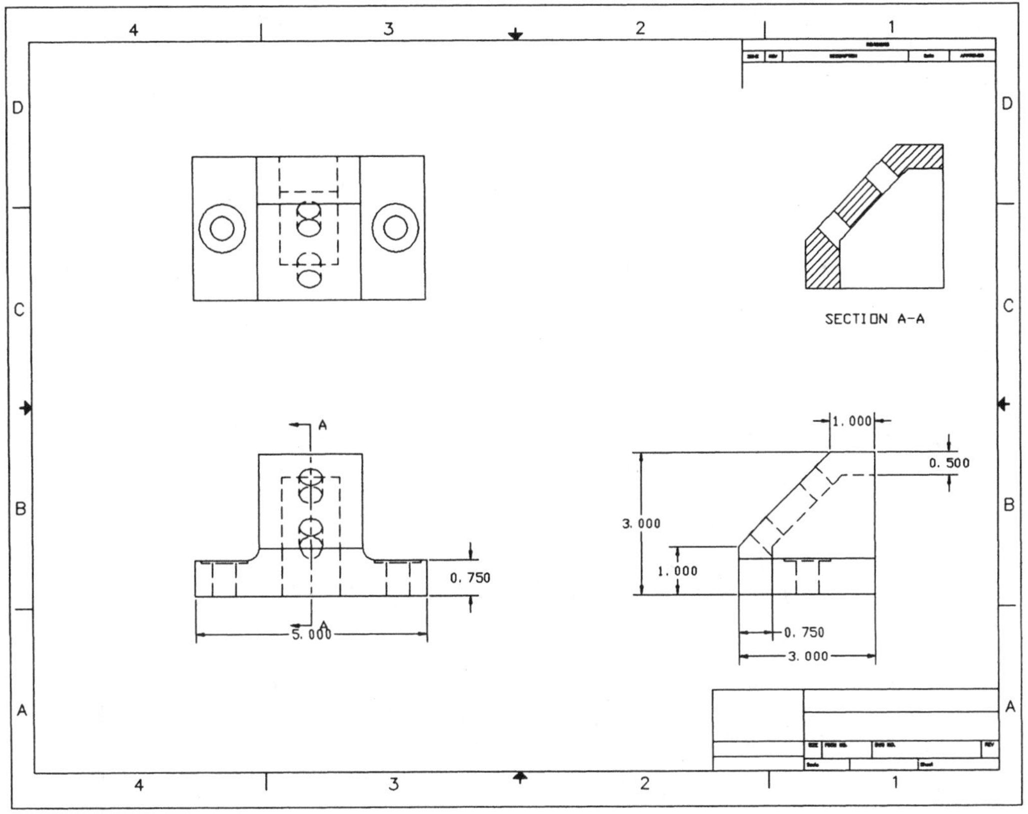

FIGURE 16–10
The Sectional View

FIGURE 16–11
Designer Drawing View Dialog Box for the Sectional View

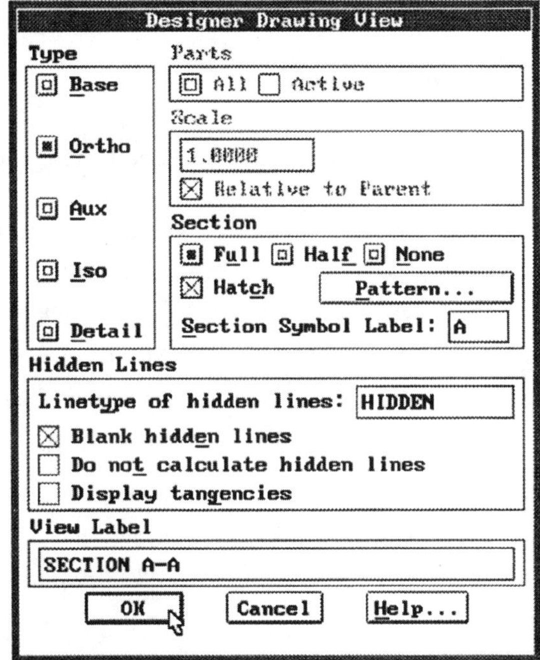

Prompt	Response
	In the View Label text box *Type:* **SECTION A-A.**
	Pick: **Hatch**
	Pick: **Pattern. . .**
The AutoCAD Hatch Options dialog box, Figure 16–12, appears:	If the Pattern. . . shows ANSI31, Scale: 1.0000, Angle: 0, *Pick:* **OK.** (If not, *Pick:* **Pattern. . .** and select ANSI31, Scale: 1.0000, Angle: 0, then *Pick:* **OK.**)

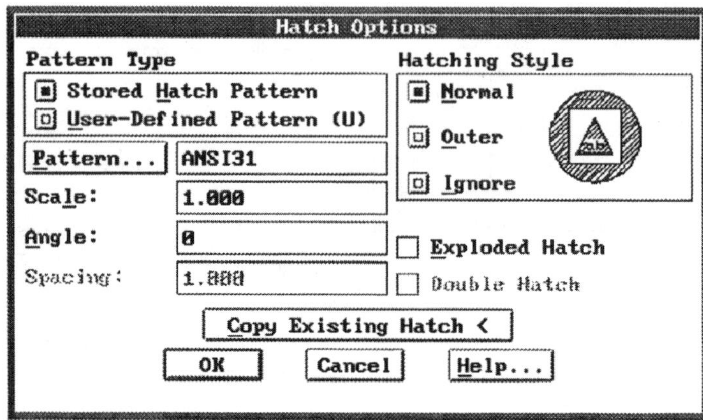

FIGURE 16–12
Hatch Options Dialog Box

Prompt	Response
The Designer Drawing View dialog box appears:	*Pick:* **OK**
Select parent view:	**Pick the front view.**
Location for orthographic view:	**Pick a point between the front and the right side views.** (You will have to move this view, so the location at this point is not critical.)
Location for orthographic view:	↵
Section through Point/<Work plane>:	↵
Select work plane in parent view for the section:	**D1** (Figure 16–13)

The drawing should appear as shown in Figure 16–14.

Step 8. On Your Own:

Turn on the ADD_VIEWS layer.

Step 9. Move the sectional view and its label, Figure 16–15.

Prompt	Response
Command:	*Type:* **M** ↵
Select objects:	**Pick any point on the outside edge of the viewport containing the sectional view.** Pick **the label, SECTION A-A.**
Select objects:	↵
Base point or displacement:	**Pick any point on the sectional viewport.**
Second point of displacement:	**Pick a point in the approximate location shown in Figure 16–15.**

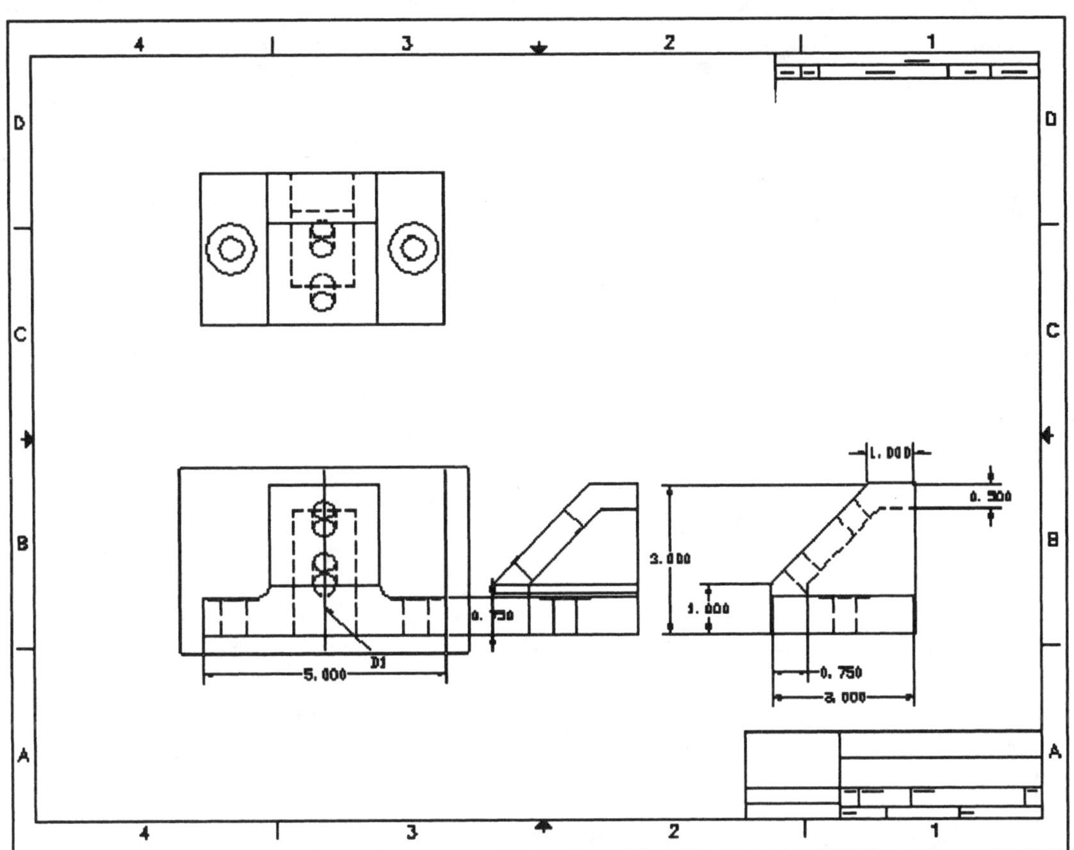

FIGURE 16–13
Picking the Work Plane in the Parent View

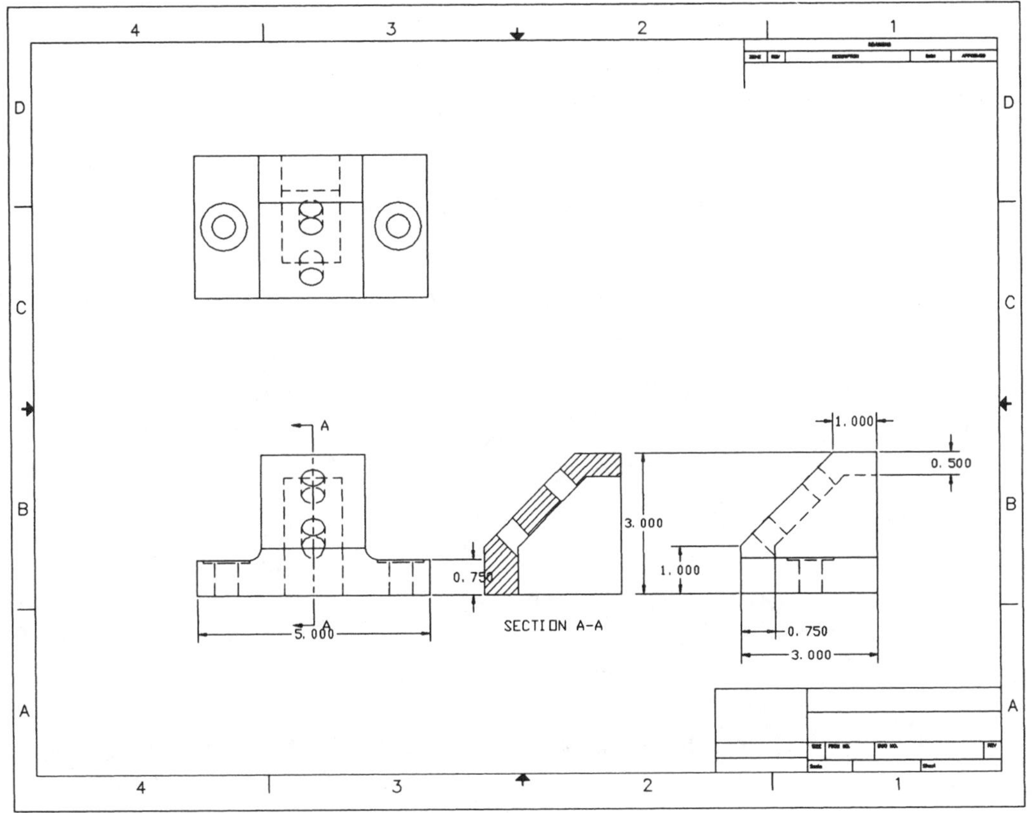

FIGURE 16–14
Making the Sectional View

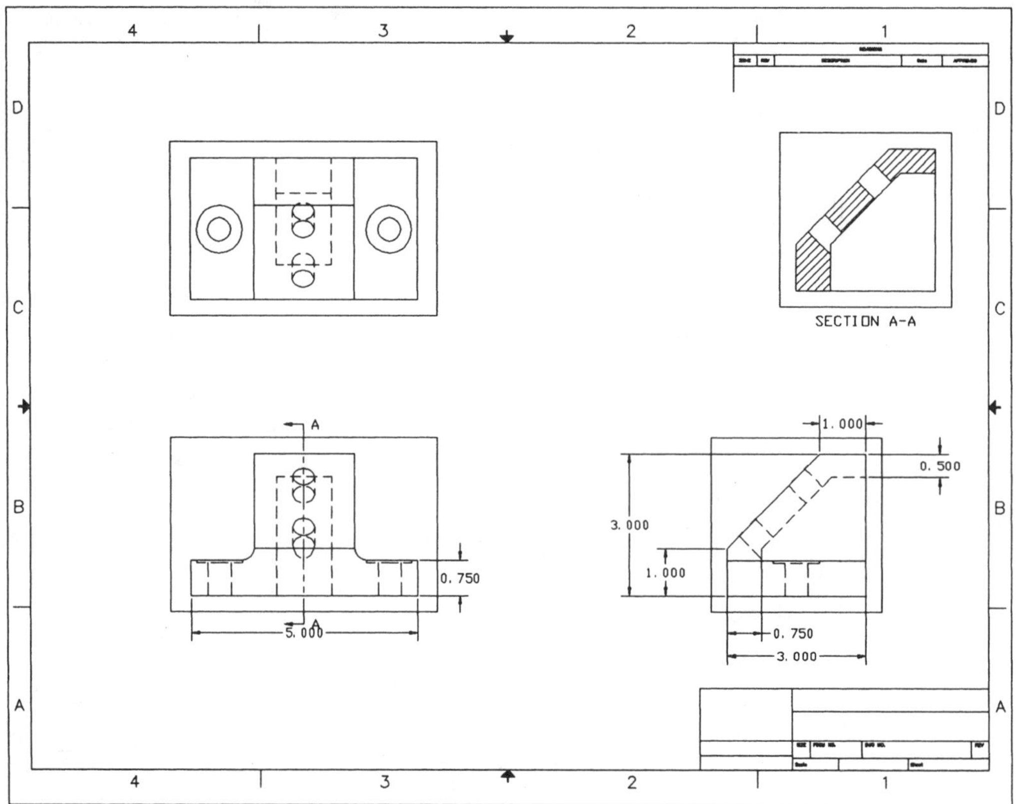

FIGURE 16–15
Moving the Sectional View and Its Label

Step 10. On Your Own:

Turn off the ADD_VIEWS layer.

Create an Auxiliary View

Step 11. Make an auxiliary view, Figure 16–16. (Auxiliary views are used to show the true shape of slanted surfaces so they may be properly dimensioned.)

Prompt	Response
Command:	**Drawing** **Create view**
The Designer Drawing View dialog box, Figure 16–17, appears:	*Pick:* **Aux** *Pick:* **None** (in the Section area) *Pick:* **OK**
Select a straight edge in the parent view:	**Pick the solid line on the inclined surface in the right side view.**
Select second point or <RETURN> to use the selected edge:	↵
Location for auxiliary view:	**Pick any point in the approximate location shown in Figure 16–16.**

Now, move a dimension from one view to another so you have the opportunity to use the ADMOVEDIM command.

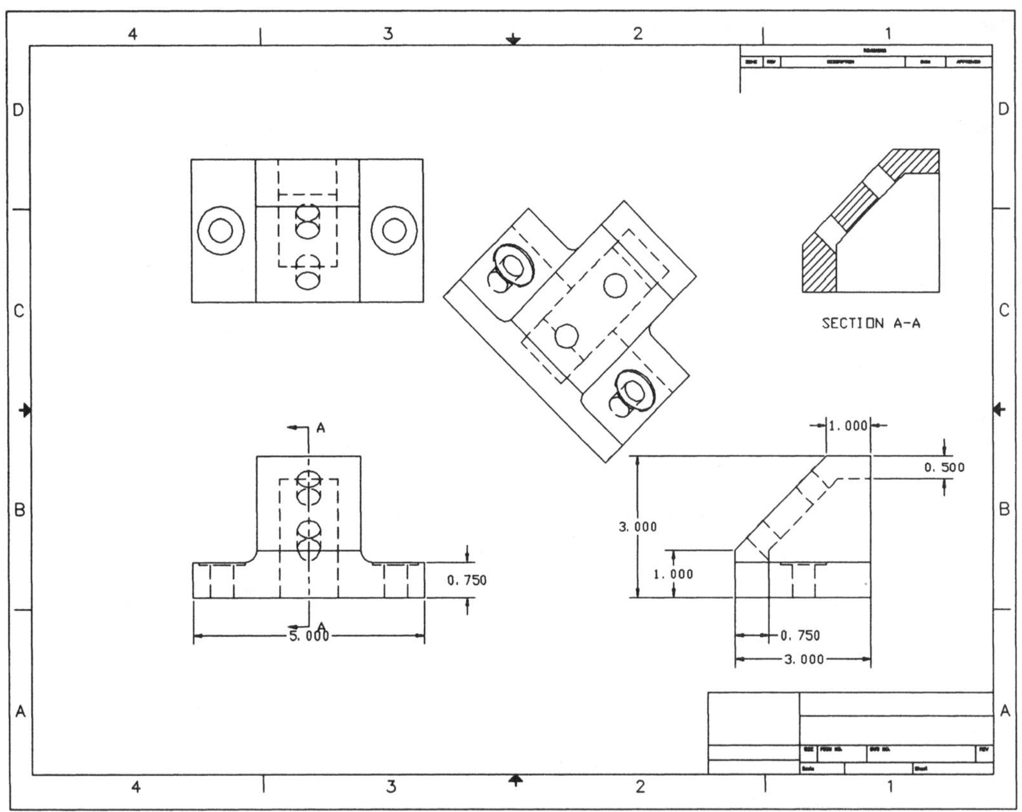

FIGURE 16–16
Making the Auxiliary View

FIGURE 16–17
Designer Drawing View Dialog Box for the Auxiliary View

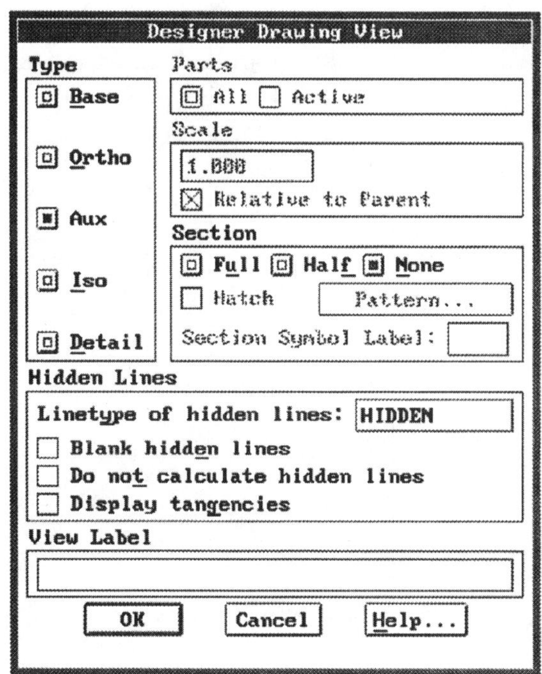

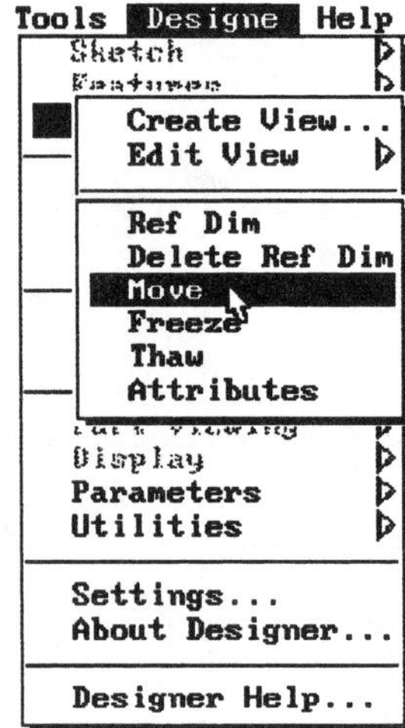

ADMOVEDIM

The ADMOVEDIM command allows you to move dimensions and still maintain their associativity to the drawing view geometry.

Modify Dimensions, Add Notes, and Plot the Drawing

Step 12. Move one dimension, Figure 16–18.

Prompt	Response
Command:	**Drawing** **Dimension** **Move**
Reattach/<Move>:	↵
Select dimension to move:	**Pick the 5.000 dimension on the front view.**
Select view to place dimension:	**Pick the top view.**
Location for dimension:	**Pick a location approximately ⅞″ from the front edge of the top view, Figure 16–18.**
Location for dimension:	↵

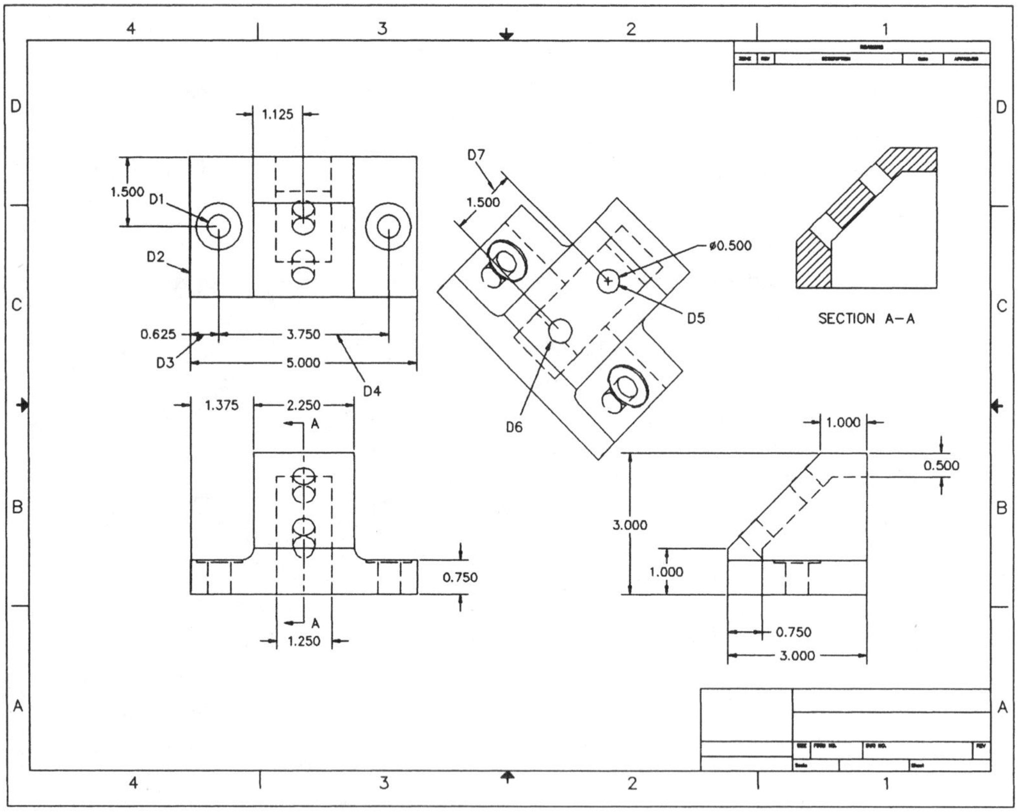

FIGURE 16–18
Adding Reference Dimensions

Before you add reference dimensions, let's look at the ADREFDIM command.

ADREFDIM

ADREFDIM allows you to create reference dimensions on drawing views to supplement or replace parametric dimensions that were used to create the model. Reference dimen-

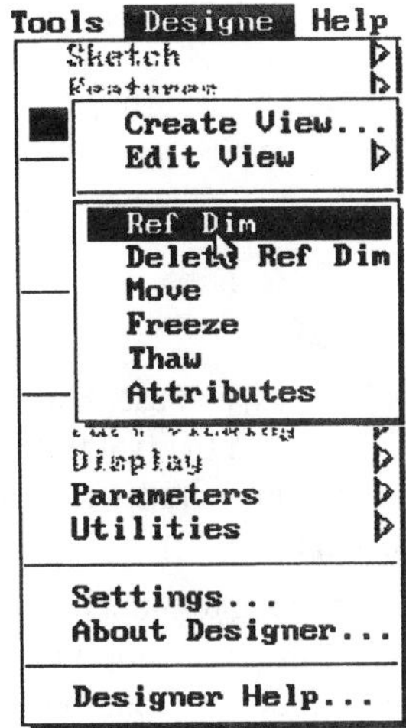

sions have no control over the geometry of the model. Changing a reference dimension does not change the size or location of a feature.

Step 13. Add reference dimensions, Figure 16–18.

Prompt	Response
Command:	**Drawing** **Dimension** **Ref Dim**
Select first item:	**Pick the hole on the left side of the top view. D1**
Select second item or place dimension:	**Pick the left edge of the top view. D2**
Specify dimension placement:	*Pick:* **D3**
Undo/Hor/Ver/Align/PAr/Ref/Basic/ PLacement point:	↵
Command:	↵
Select first item:	**Pick the hole on the left side of the top view.**
Select second item or place dimension:	**Pick the hole on the right side of the top view.**
Specify dimension placement:	*Pick:* **D4**
Undo/Hor/Ver/Align/PAr/Ref/Basic/ PLacement point:	↵
Select first item:	**Pick the upper hole on the auxiliary view. D5**
Select second item or place dimension:	**Pick the lower hole on the auxiliary view. D6**
Specify dimension placement:	*Pick:* **D7**
Undo/Hor/Ver/Align/PAr/Ref/Basic/ PLacement point:	*Type:* **A** ↵

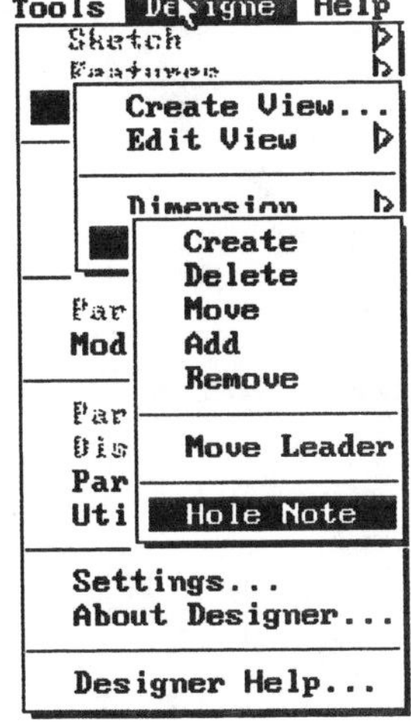

Step 14. On Your Own:

Add all other reference dimensions as shown in Figure 16–18.

Step 15. Add hole note, Figure 16–19.

Prompt	Response
Command:	**Drawing** **Annotation** **Hole Note**

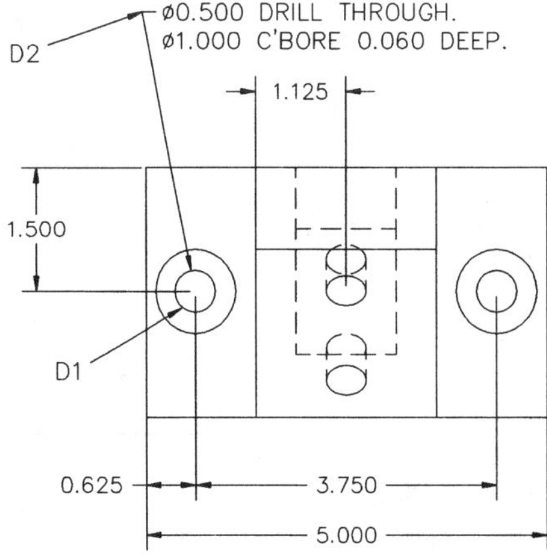

FIGURE 16–19
Adding a Hole Note

Prompt	Response
Select arc or circle of hole feature:	**D1** (Figure 16–19)
Location for hole note:	**D2**
Location for hole note:	↵

Step 16. On Your Own:

1. Complete dimensioning and clean up the drawing, Figure 16–20.
2. Use Dtext: to add additional text (2 HOLES) (.2 high) to hole notes, and use AutoCAD dimensioning to add the 0.700 dimension on the auxiliary view and the 0.500 dimension to SECTION A-A. (You may have to draw a construction line parallel to the extension line for the 1.500 dimension to get the 0.700 dimension to work.)
3. Although drawing convention suggests that you avoid dimensioning to hidden lines, it will be better to leave the 0.750 and the 0.500 dimensions on the right side view because they are parametric. You could show the 1.250 dimension on the front view as a cutaway feature as shown in Figure 15–1 if you choose to draw the break lines.
4. Complete the title block information, Figure 16–21. Use the SIMPLEX font .2 high for the larger type, .12 for the smaller type.

The drawing is now complete and should look similar to Figure 16–1.

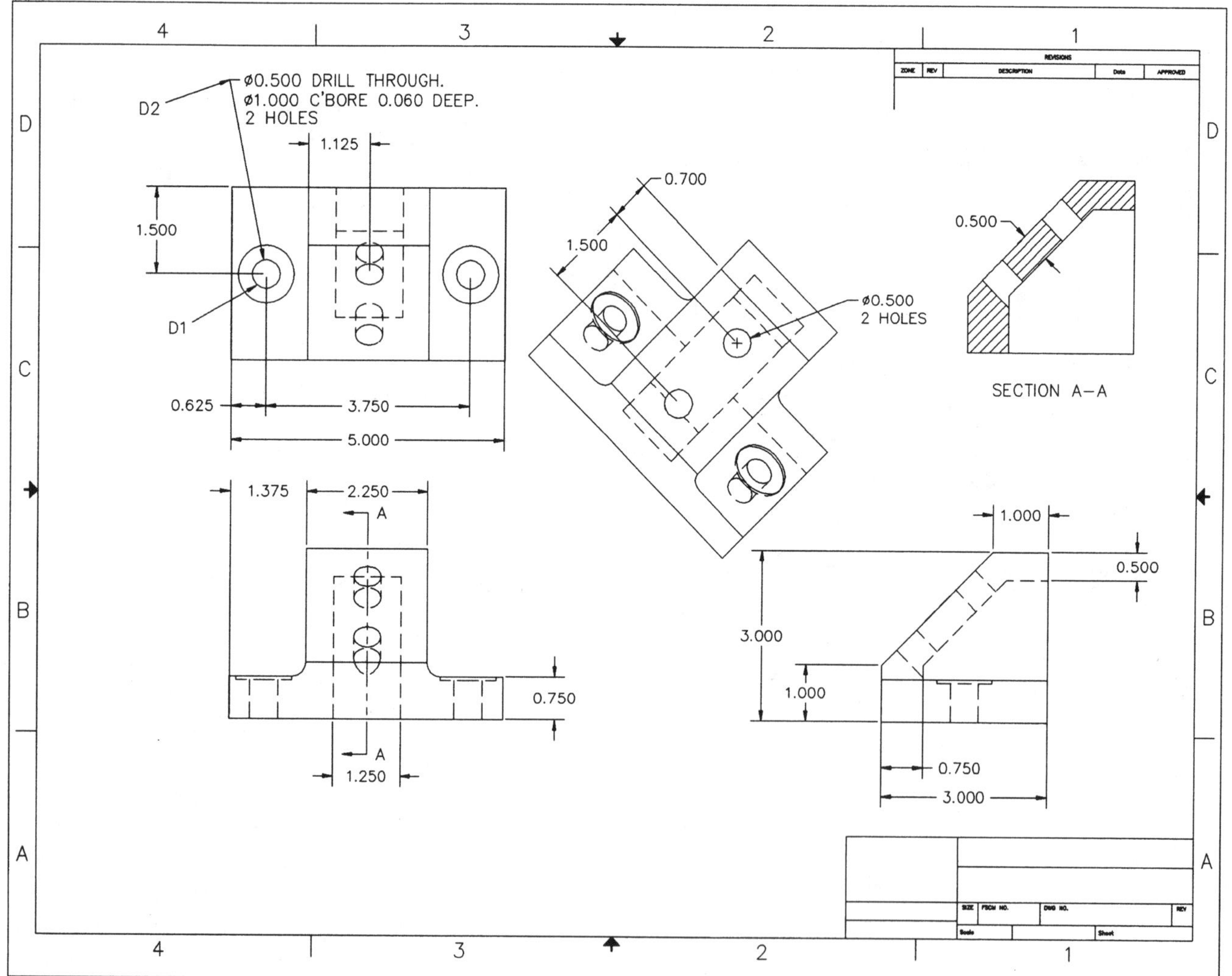

FIGURE 16–20
Adding Final Dimensions and Text to Notes

FIGURE 16–21
Completing the Title Block

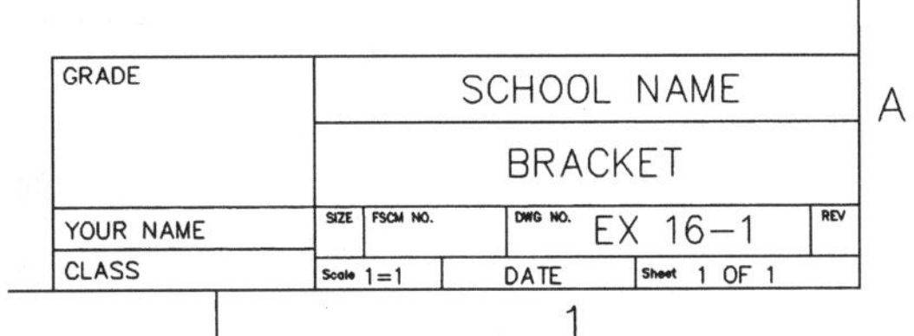

5. Plot the drawing at a scale of .375 = 1 on an 11″ × 8.5″ sheet.
6. Save the drawing in two places and exit Designer.

The next exercise gives you the experience of making an assembly drawing from a Designer assembly. The assembly drawing shows only overall dimensions and callouts that refer to a parts list that identifies the parts.

EXERCISE 16–2
MAKING AN ASSEMBLY DRAWING FROM A DESIGNER SOLID ASSEMBLY CONSISTING OF FOUR PARTS

Your final drawing will look similar to Figure 16–22.

Set Up the Drawing

Step 1. On Your Own:

1. Pick New. . . from the menu bar File menu. Name the drawing: 16-2 (your initials)=15-2 (your initials).

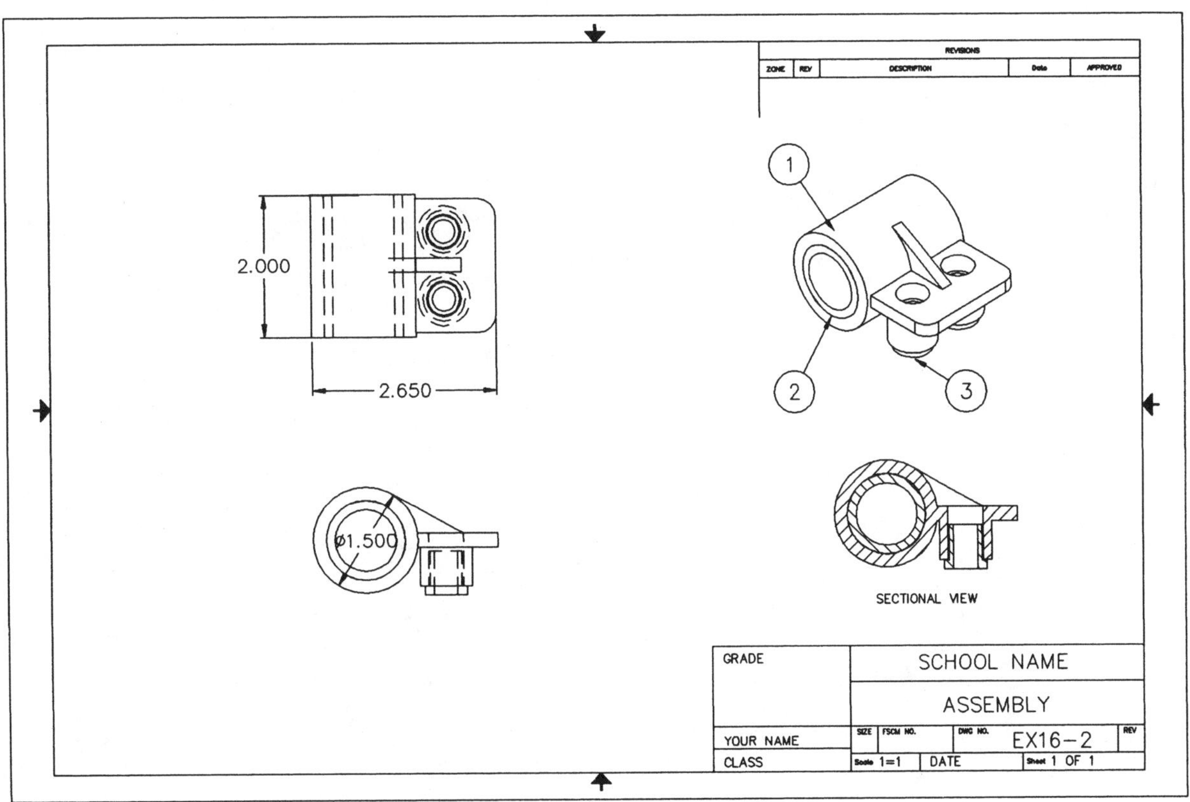

FIGURE 16–22
The Completed Assembly Drawing

2. Make the following settings:

UNITS: Decimal; 3 digits to the right of the decimal point
LIMITS: Lower left corner: 0,0
Upper right corner: 11,8.5
GRID: .2
SNAP: .05
STYLE: STANDARD; FONT: SIMPLEX; HEIGHT: 0
Create the following layers:

LAYER NAME	COLOR	LINETYPE
Y	YELLOW	CONTINUOUS
R	RED	CONTINUOUS
G	GREEN	CONTINUOUS

Set layer G current.

3. Set UCS to World, return to a single viewport, erase your name, and Zoom: All so that your model appears as shown in Figure 16–23.

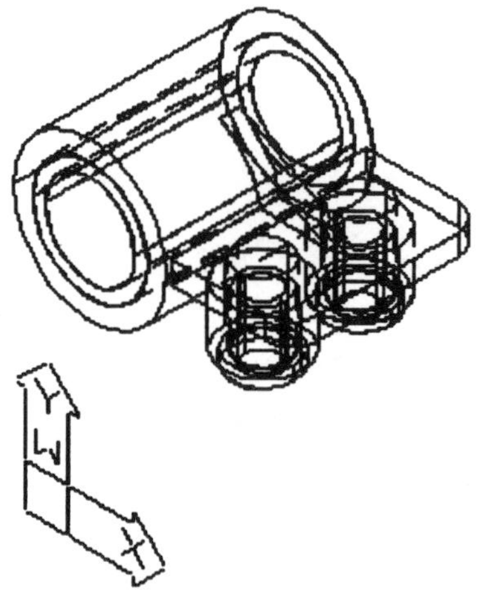

FIGURE 16–23
The Solid Model

Create the Front View of the Assembly

Step 2. Create the front view of the assembly drawing.

Prompt	Response
Command:	**Drawing** **Create view**
The Designer Drawing View dialog box, Figure 16–24, appears.	*Pick:* **OK** (if your dialog box is the same as Figure 16–24) (If not, change it to the settings in Figure 16–24, and *Pick:* **OK.**)

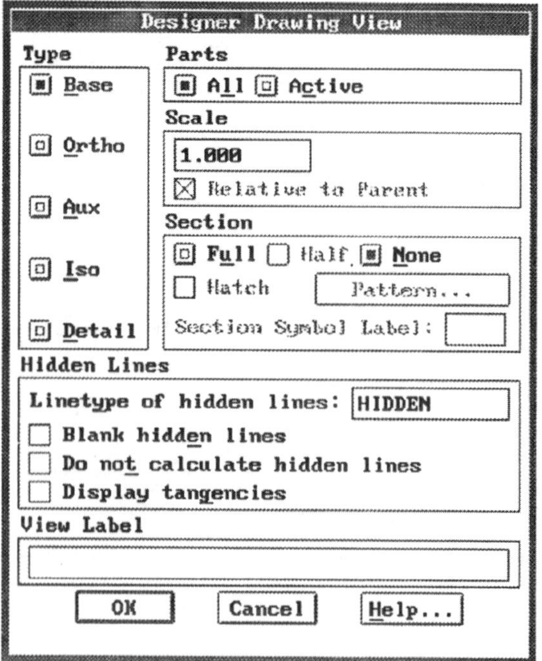

FIGURE 16–24
Designer Drawing View Dialog Box for the Front View

Note: If you get the message "Cannot pick inactive part. Use ADACTPART to activate part." *Select:* Part-Make Active (or *Type:* **ADACTPART ↵**) and pick the housing at the Select part: prompt. Then start this sequence over again.

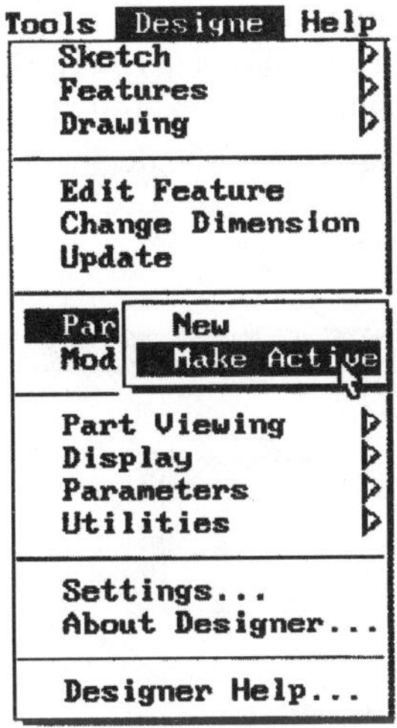

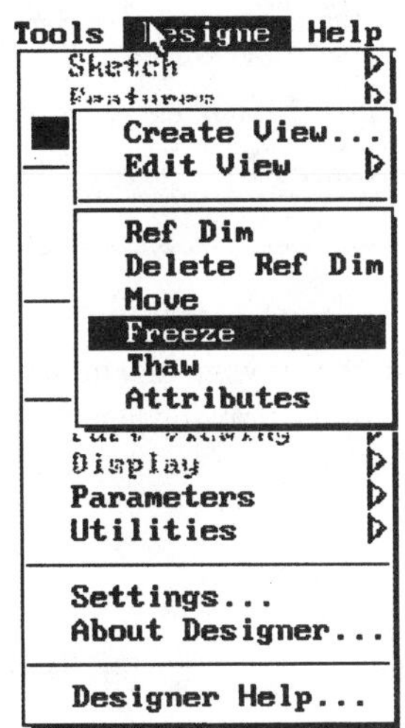

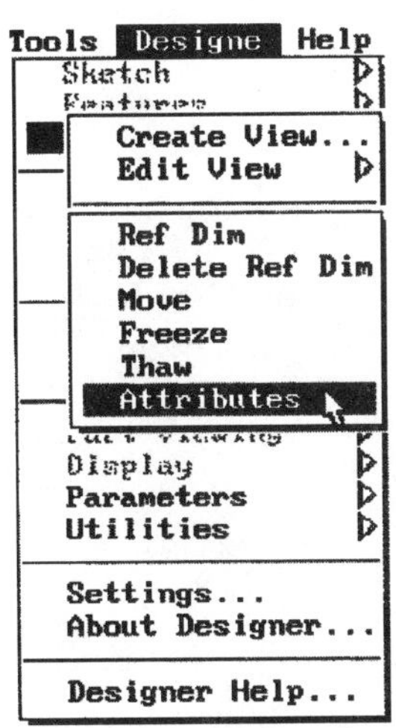

Xy/Yz/Zx/Ucs/<Select work plane or planar face>: *Pick:* **D1** (Figure 16–25)

Next/<Accept>: *Type:* **N** ↵ until the front surface is highlighted then *Press:* ↵ to accept.

X/Y/Z/<Select work axis or straight edge>: *Pick:* **D1** (again)

Rotate/<Accept>: *Type:* **R** ↵ until the UCS icon appears as shown in Figure 16–25, then *Press:* ↵ to accept.

View center: *Type:* **6,4.5** ↵

View center: ↵

The front view appears as shown in Figure 16–26.

(You may have more dimensions than the two shown here.) Only the 1.500 dimension is necessary for this drawing, but others will be needed if the part is to be changed later. Instead of erasing the extra dimensions, use ADFRZDIM to freeze them so they can be thawed later.

ADFRZDIM

The ADFRZDIM command hides selected dimensions on drawing views. The dimension remains frozen even if the drawing is updated. To thaw the dimension use ADTHAWDIM.

Command: **Drawing**
Dimension
Freeze

Freeze dimensions All/View/<Select>: ↵

Select dimension: **Pick all dimensions except the 1.5000 diameter.**

Select dimension: ↵

If your drawing shows dimensions with 4 places to the right of the decimal, as Figure 16–26 does, change to a 3-place decimal using the ADDIMATT command.

ADDDIMATT

The ADDDIMATT command allows you to change the dimension style of units, precision, text height, layer, tolerance, text placement (such as whether the dimension and arrows go inside the circle or outside), and tolerance of dimensions on drawing views. It also allows you to add a prefix or a suffix to the dimension.

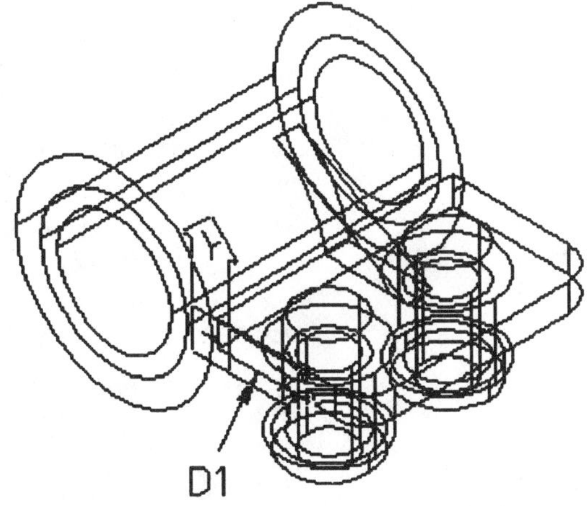

FIGURE 16–25
Selecting the Front

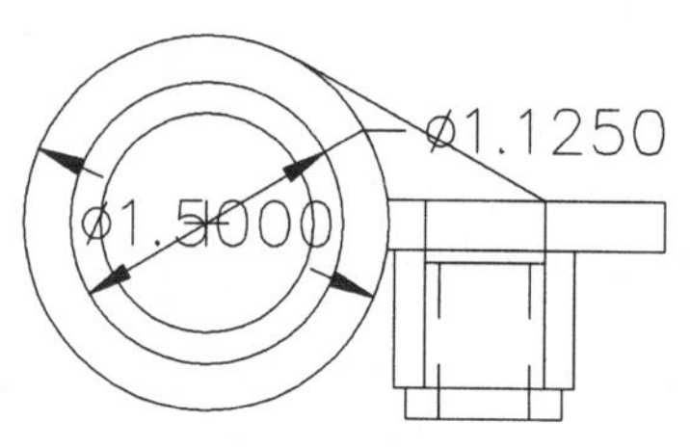

FIGURE 16–26
The Front View in Place

Prompt	Response
Command:	**Drawing** **Dimension** **Attributes**
Select dimension to edit:	**Pick the 1.5000 dimension.**
The Designer Dimension Options dialog box, Figure 16–27, appears:	**Pick the Precision: down arrow, and highlight 0.000 to set the units to 3 places to the right of the decimal.** *Pick:* **OK**

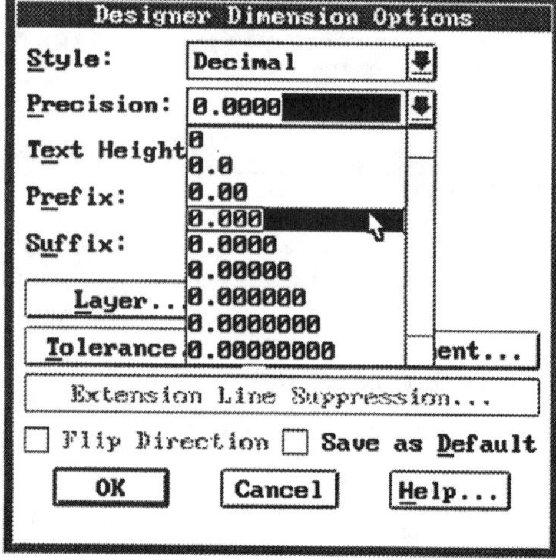

FIGURE 16–27
Designer Dimension Options Dialog Box

Before you create any more views, place a title block around the drawing and move the view so it is arranged well in the field of the drawing. (The field of the drawing is the space inside the borders and title block.)

Insert a Title Block Around the Drawing

Step 3. Use MVSETUP to place a title block around the drawing.

Prompt	Response
Command:	**MV Setup**
Align/Create/Scale viewports/Options/ Title block/Undo:	*Type:* **T** ↵
Delete objects/Origin/Undo/ <Insert title block>:	↵
Add/Delete/Redisplay/ <Number of entry to load>:	*Type:* **8** ↵ (to select an ANSI-B–size title block)
Create a drawing named ansi-b.dwg? <Y>:	↵
Align/Create/Scale viewports/Options/ Title block/Undo:	↵

Create the Top View of the Assembly

Step 4. Create the top view of the assembly drawing.

Prompt	Response
Command:	**Drawing** **Create View. . .**

The Designer Drawing View dialog box, Figure 16–28, appears:	*Pick:* **Ortho**
	Pick: **OK**

FIGURE 16–28
Designer Drawing View Dialog Box for the Top View

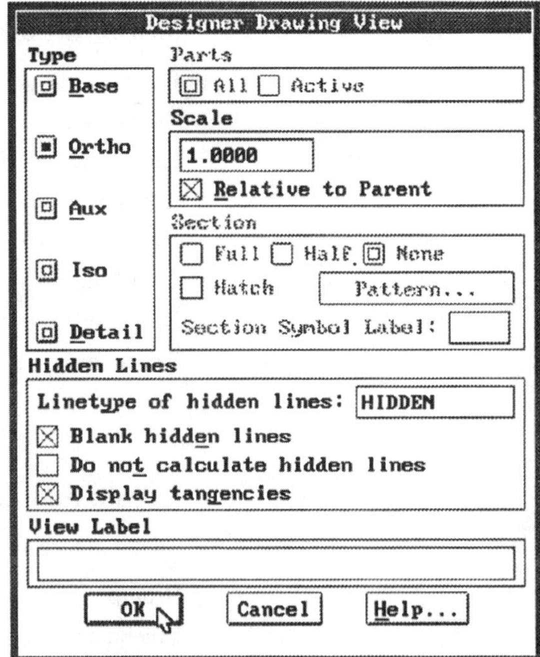

Select parent view:	**Pick the front view.**
Location for orthographic view:	**Pick the approximate location shown in Figure 16–29.**
Location for orthographic view:	↵

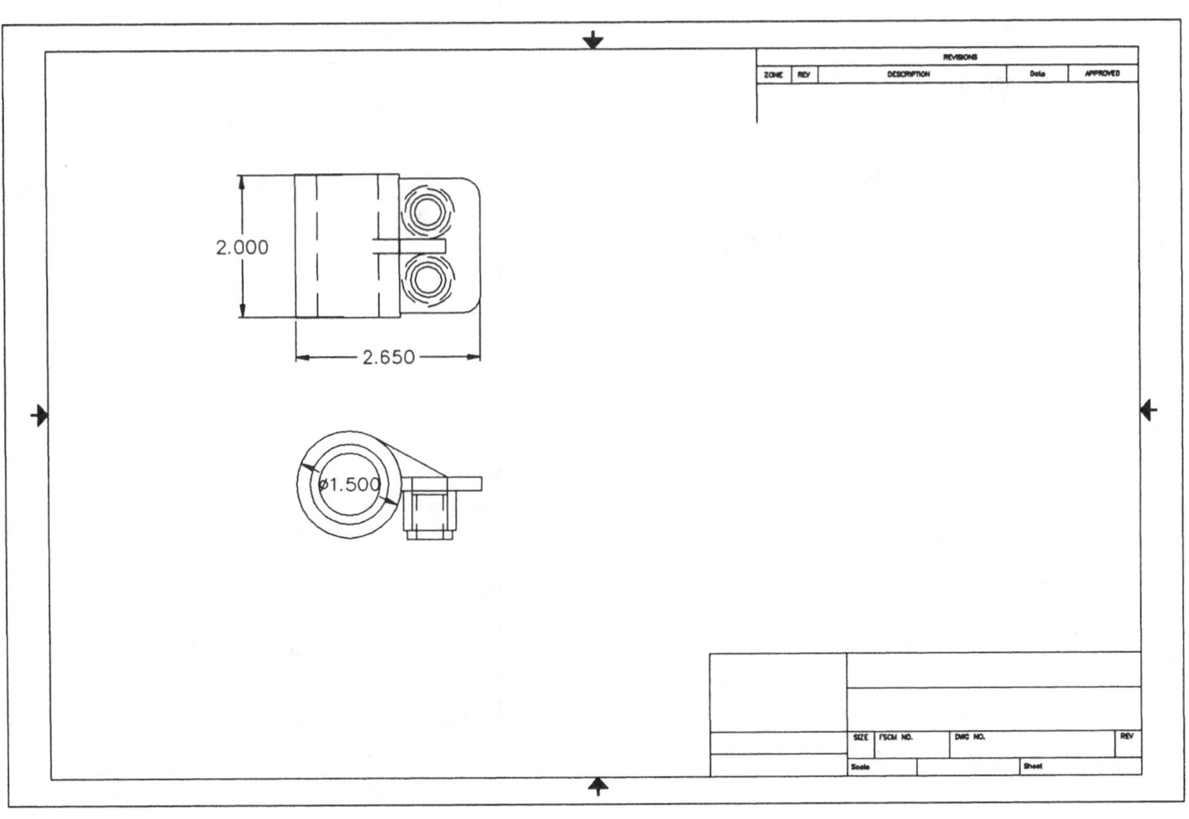

FIGURE 16–29
Creating the Top View

Step 5. On Your Own:

1. Use ADFRZDIM to freeze any unnecessary dimensions.
2. Use ADREFDIM to add the two dimensions showing the overall size of the assembly.

Step 6. Set DIMEXE=.06, and DIMDEC=3 and update dimensions if necessary.

Prompt	Response
Command:	*Type:* **DIMEXE** ↵
New value for DIMEXE <default>:	*Type:* **.06** ↵
Command:	*Type:* **DIMDEC** ↵
New value for DIMDEC <default>:	*Type:* **3** ↵
Command:	*Type:* **DIM** ↵
Dim:	*Type:* **UP** ↵
Select objects:	**Pick any dimensions that have long extension lines and dimensions with 4 places to the right of the decimal.**

Create an Isometric View of the Assembly

Step 7. Create an isometric view of the assembly drawing.

Prompt	Response
Command:	**Drawing** **Create View. . .**
The Designer Drawing View dialog box, Figure 16–30, appears:	*Pick:* **Iso**
(Notice that the Blank hidden lines box is checked. Only in very unusual cases do isometric drawings show hidden lines.)	*Pick:* **OK**
Select parent view:	**Pick the front view.**

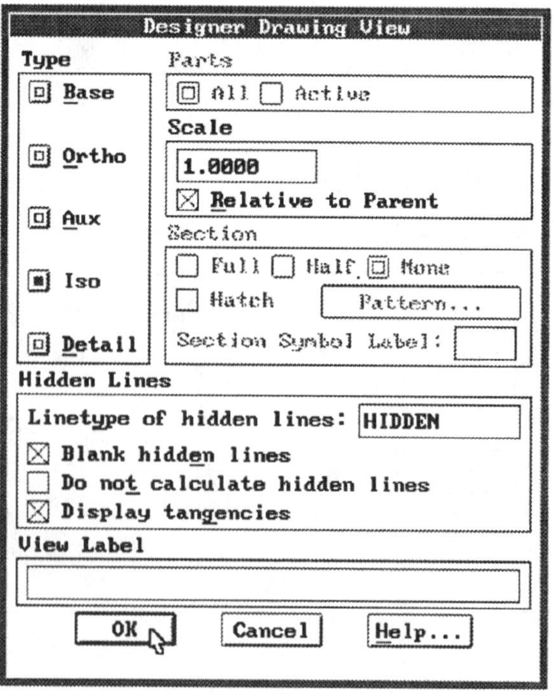

FIGURE 16–30
Designer Drawing View Dialog Box for the Isometric View

Location for isometric view:	**Pick the approximate location shown in Figure 16–31.**
Location for isometric view:	↵

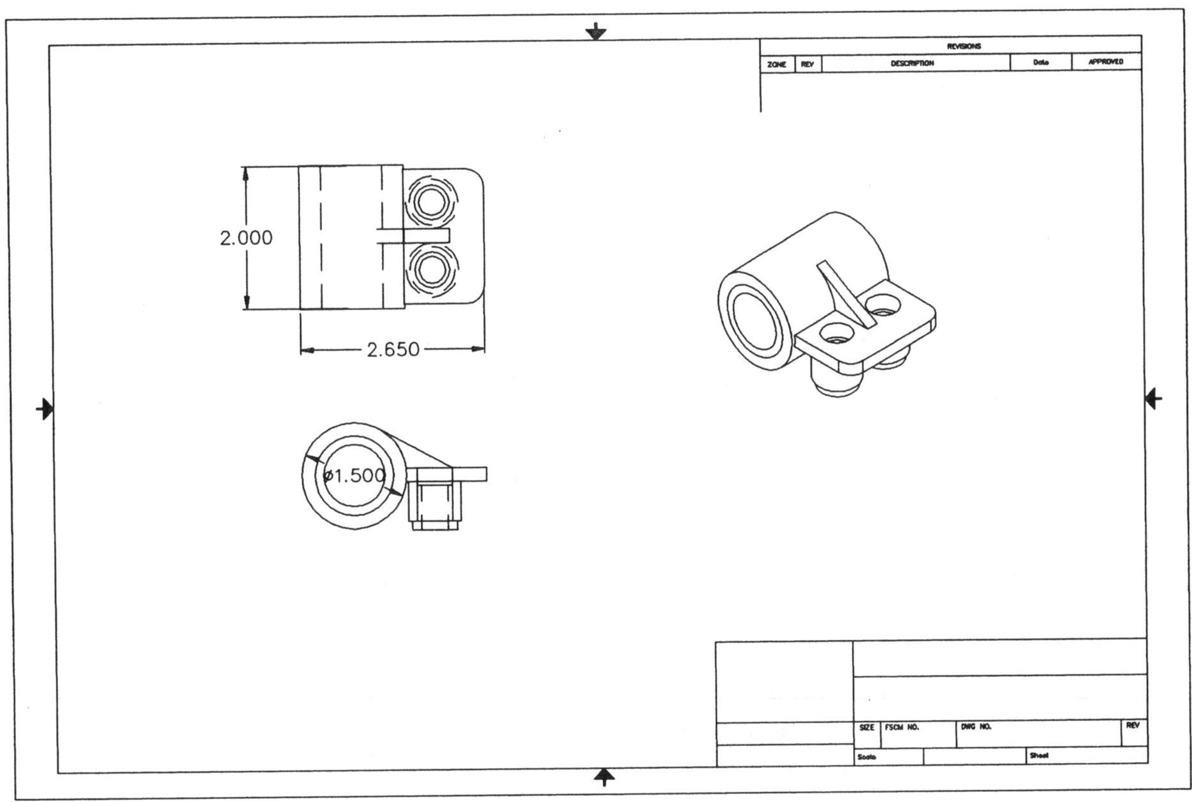

FIGURE 16–31
Creating the Isometric View

Read the description of ADANNOTE before proceeding.

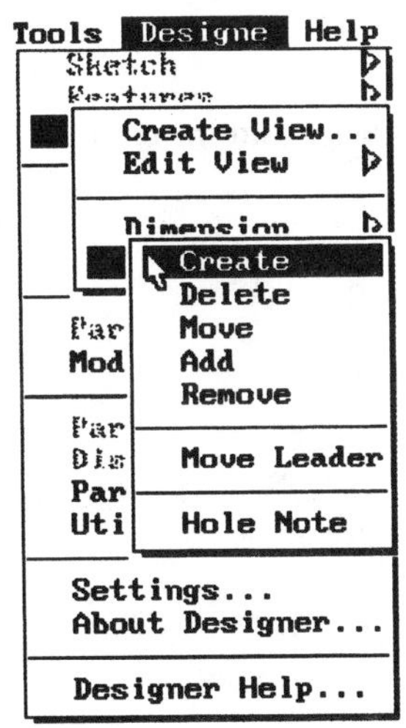

ADANNOTE

The ADANNOTE command allows you to create, delete, and move annotations on drawing views. You may also add items to or remove items from annotations. Annotations include balloons, index numbers, center lines, and finish symbols. You make the text and geometry with AutoCAD and use ADANNOTE to attach them parametrically to the drawing view.

Annotations move with the drawing when you use ADMOVEVIEW, and their locations are automatically updated when the geometry moves on the drawing.

Step 8. Add balloons and index numbers and use ADANNOTE to attach them to part edges.

Prompt	Response
Command:	*Type:* **C** ↵
3P/2P/TTR/<Center point>:	**D1** (Figure 16–32)
Diameter/<Radius>:	*Type:* **.25** ↵
Command:	*Type:* **CP** ↵
Select objects:	**Pick the circle you just drew.**
<Base point or displacement>/Multiple:	*Type:* **M** ↵
Base point:	**D1** (again)

FIGURE 16–32
Adding Balloons and Index Numbers

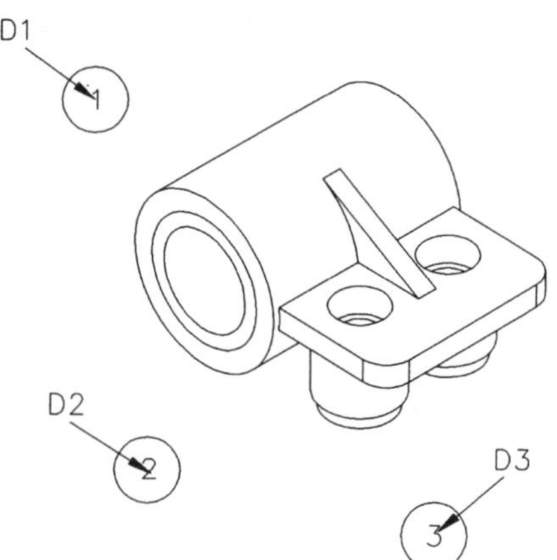

Prompt	Response
Second point of displacement:	**D2**
Second point of displacement:	**D3**
Second point of displacement:	↵
Command:	**Dtext:**
Justify/Style/<Start point>:	*Type:* **M** ↵
Middle point:	**Osnap-CENter**
of	*Pick:* any point on the circumference of the circle containing the number 1.
Height <default>:	*Type:* **.15** ↵
Rotation angle <0>:	↵
Text:	*Type:* **1** ↵
Text:	*Pick:* **D2**
Text:	*Type:* **2** ↵
Text:	*Pick:* **D3**
Text:	*Type:* **3** ↵
Command:	**Drawing** **Annotation** **Create**
Select objects:	**Pick the number 1 and the circle around it.**
Select objects:	↵
Locate point on view to attach annotation:	**D1** (Figure 16–33)

FIGURE 16–33
Attaching Annotations to the Parts

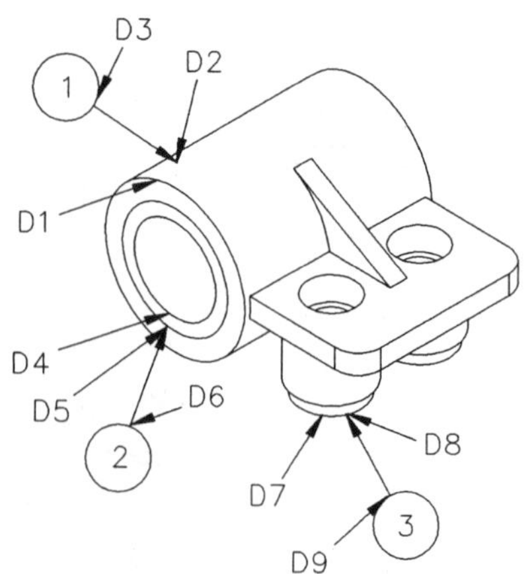

Leader startpoint:	**D2**
Leader endpoint:	**Osnap-PERpendicular**
to	**D3** (on the circumference of the circle)
Next leader vertex:	↵
Annotation containing 2 entities attached to view.	
Command:	↵
Create/Delete/Move/Add/<Remove>:	*Type:* **C** ↵
Select objects:	**Pick the number 2 and the circle around it.**
Locate point on view to attach annotation:	**D4** (Figure 16–33)
Leader startpoint:	**D5**
Leader endpoint:	**Osnap-PERpendicular**
to	**D6** (on the circumference of the circle)
Next leader vertex:	↵
Annotation containing 2 entities attached to view.	
Command:	↵
Create/Delete/Move/Add/<Remove>:	*Type:* **C** ↵
Select objects:	**Pick the number 3 and the circle around it.**
Locate point on view to attach annotation:	**D7** (Figure 16–33)
Leader startpoint:	**D8**
Leader endpoint:	**Osnap-PERpendicular**
to	**D9** (on the circumference of the circle)
Next leader vertex:	↵
Annotation containing 2 entities attached to view.	

Create a Sectional View of the Housing

To create the assembly section view shown in the lower right corner of Figure 16–22, you must create a work plane that becomes a cutting plane before you use ADVIEW.

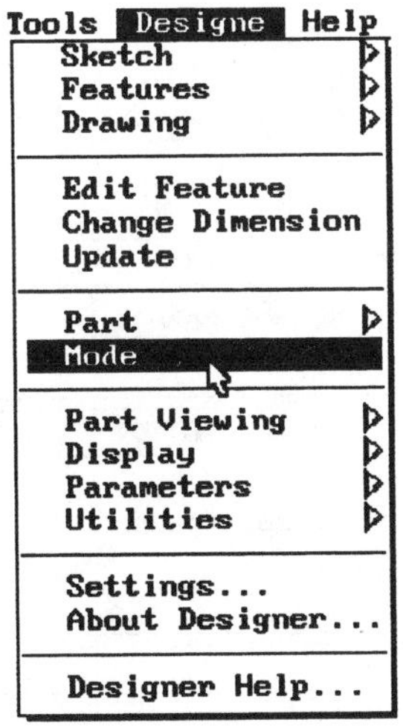

Tools Designe Help
Sketch ▷
Features ▷
Drawing ▷
Edit Feature
Change Dimension
Update
Part ▷
Mode
Part Viewing ▷
Display ▷
Parameters ▷
Utilities ▷
Settings...
About Designer...
Designer Help...

Step 9. Create a work plane.

Prompt	Response
Command:	**Mode**
Drawing/<Part>:	↵
Command:	**Work Plane. . .**
The Designer Work Plane dialog box appears:	*Pick:* **Planar Parallel**
The Planar Parallel dialog box appears:	*Pick:* **Offset** *Pick:* **OK**
The Designer Work Plane dialog box appears:	*Pick:* OK
Xy/Yz/Zx/Ucs/<Select work plane or planar face>:	*Pick:* **D1** (Figure 16–34)
Next/<Accept>:	*Type:* **N** ↵ until the front surface is highlighted as shown in Figure 16–34, then *Press:* ↵ to accept.

FIGURE 16–34
Selecting the Front Surface

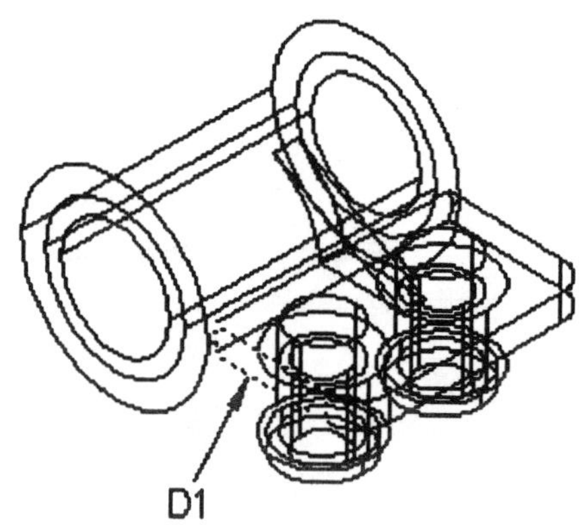

Prompt	Response
Offset <default>:	*Type:* **.465** ↵
Flip/<Accept>:	*Type:* **F** ↵ if the work plane does not go through the center of the left hole in the flange, then *Press:* ↵ to accept.

Step 10. Create the sectional view.

Prompt	Response
Command:	**Drawing** **Create view**
The Designer Drawing View dialog box, Figure 16–35, appears.	*Pick:* **Base** (if it is not already active) *Pick:* **Active** (so that only the active part will be cross hatched at the default angle for the selected hatch pattern) *Pick:* **Full** (in the Section area)

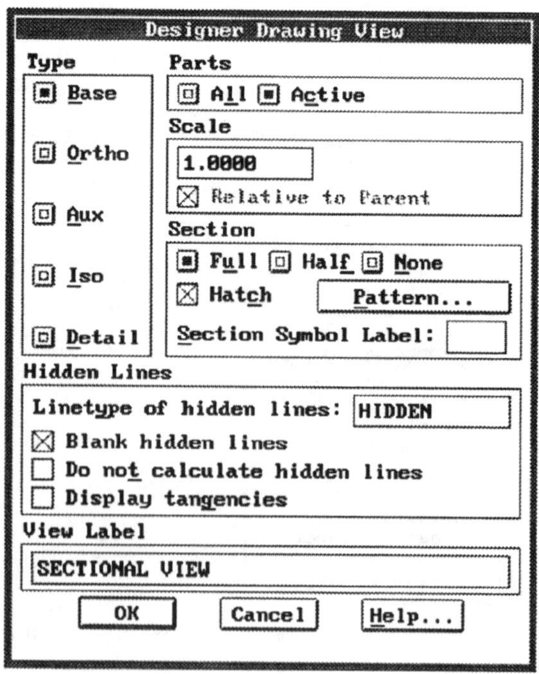

FIGURE 16–35
Designer Dialog Box for the Sectional View

Prompt	Response
	Pick: **Hatch**
	Pick: **Pattern. . .** (The Hatch Options dialog box should read ANSI31, Scale: 1.000, Angle: 0. If it does, *Pick:* **OK;** if not, select those values and *Pick:* **OK**
	Type: **SECTIONAL VIEW** (in the View Label text box)
	Pick: **OK** (if your dialog box is now the same as Figure 16–35) (If not, change it to the settings in Figure 16–35, and *Pick:* **OK.**)
Select work plane:	**Pick the work plane just constructed.**
X/Y/Z/<Select work axis or straight edge>:	*Pick:* **D1** (Figure 16–36)

FIGURE 16–36
The Correct UCS

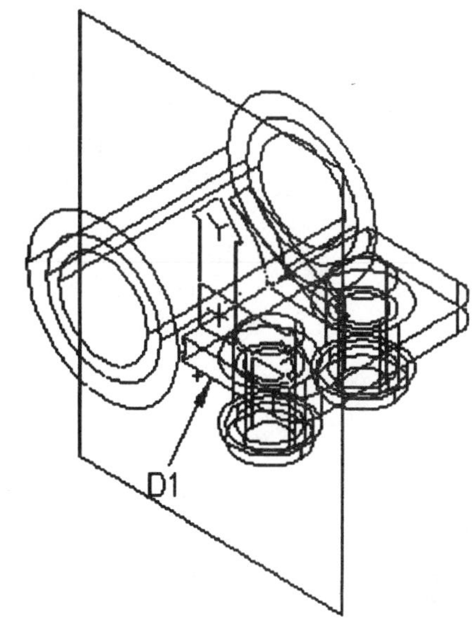

Prompt	Response
Rotate/<Accept>:	*Type:* **R** ↵ until the UCS icon appears as shown in Figure 16–36, then *Press:* ↵ to accept.
View center:	*Type:* **12.5,4.5** ↵
View center:	↵

The section front view of the active part appears as shown in Figure 16–37.

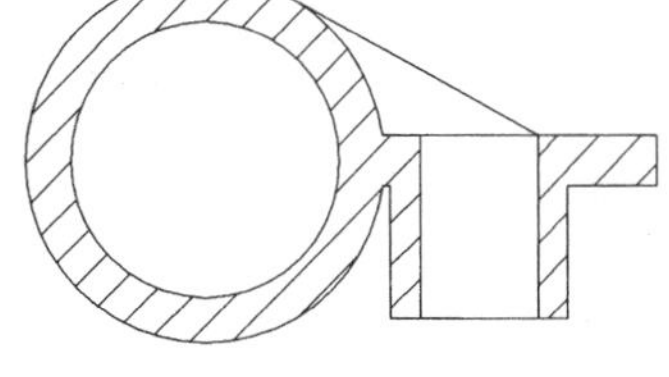
SECTIONAL VIEW

FIGURE 16–37
The Housing Front View in Section

Create a Sectional View of the Bushing inside the Circular Part of the Housing

Step 11. Return to the model and make the bushing the active part.

Prompt	Response
Command:	**Mode**
Drawing/<Part>:	↵

Prompt	Response
Command:	**Part** **Make Active**
Select part:	**Pick the bushing inside the circular part of the housing.**

Step 12. Create a work plane that will be the cutting plane for the next part of the section. (You cannot use the same work plane for another part.)

Prompt	Response
Command:	**Work Plane. . .**
The Designer Work Plane dialog box appears:	*Pick:* **Planar Parallel**
The Planar Parallel dialog box appears:	*Pick:* **Offset** *Pick:* **OK**
The Designer Work Plane dialog box appears:	*Pick:* **OK**
Xy/Yz/Zx/Ucs/<Select work plane or planar face>:	*Pick:* **D1** (Figure 16–38)

FIGURE 16–38
Picking the Planar Face

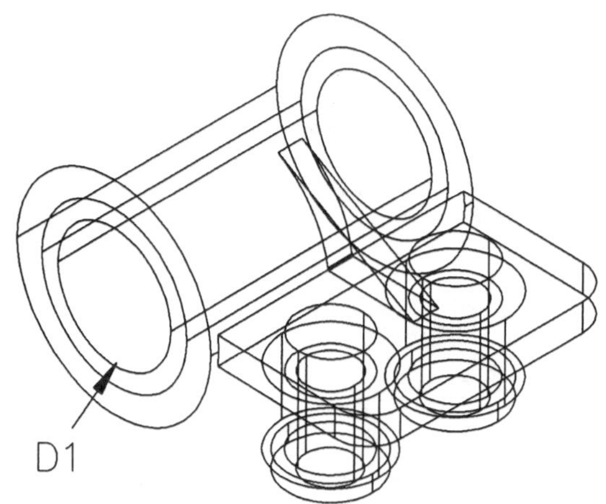

Prompt	Response
Offset <default>:	*Type:* **.527** ↵ (from the dimensions in Figure 15–24, 0.465 + 0.062 = .527)
Flip/<Accept>:	*Type:* **F** ↵ if the work plane does not go through the center of the left hole in the flange, then *Press:* ↵ to accept.

Step 13. Create the sectional view.

Prompt	Response
Command:	**Drawing** **Create view**
The Designer Drawing View dialog box, Figure 16–39, appears:	*Pick:* **Base** *Pick:* **Full** (in the Section area) *Pick:* **Hatch** Pick: **Pattern. . .**

FIGURE 16–39
Designer Drawing View Dialog Box for the Sectional View of the Large Bushing

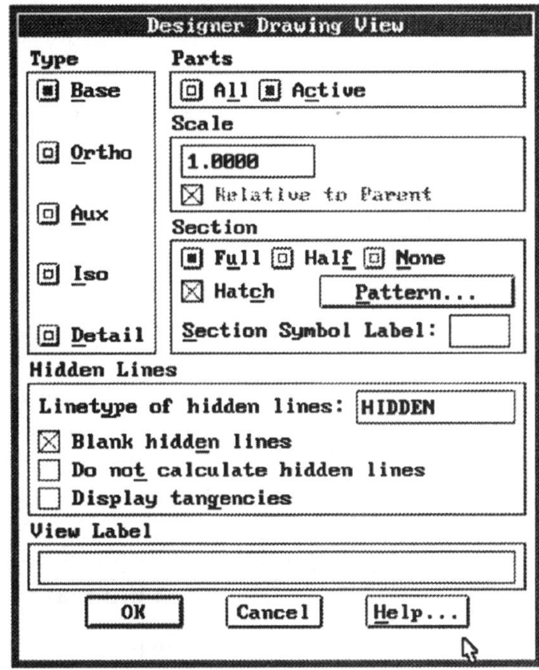

The Hatch Options dialog box appears:

Change Angle: to 90 as shown in Figure 16–40.
Pick: **OK**

FIGURE 16–40
Hatch Options Dialog Box

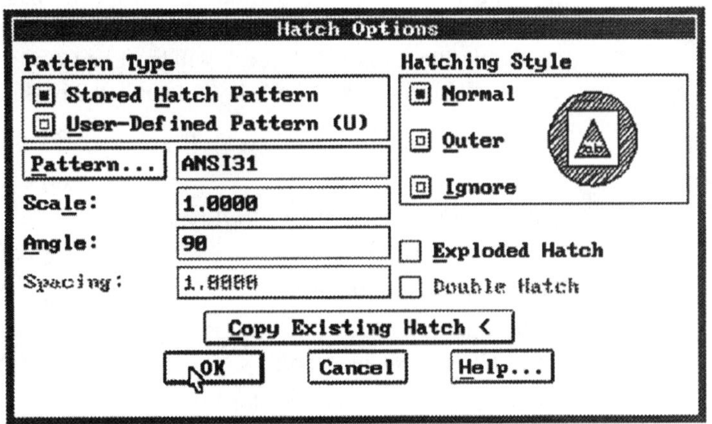

Prompt	Response
The Designer Drawing View dialog box appears:	If all parts of the dialog box are as shown in Figure 16–39, *Pick:* **OK.**
Select work plane:	**Pick the work plane just constructed.**
X/Y/Z/<Select work axis or straight edge>:	*Type:* **X** ↵
Rotate/<Accept>:	*Type:* **R** ↵ until the UCS icon appears as shown in Figure 16–41, then *Press:* ↵ to accept.
View center:	**Osnap-CENter**
of	**Pick any point on the circumference of the circular part of the housing.**
View center:	↵

FIGURE 16–41
The Correct UCS

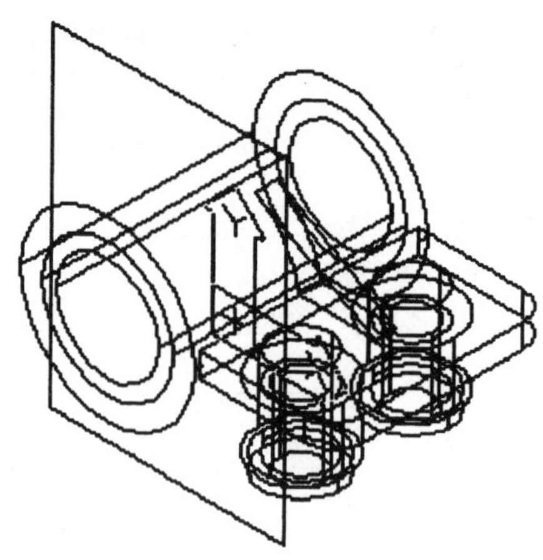

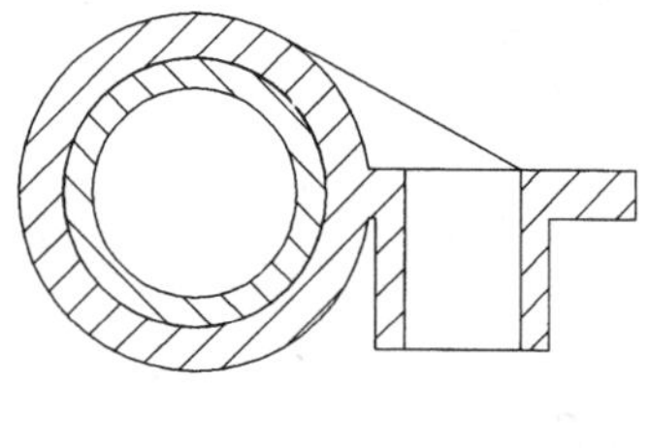

FIGURE 16–42
The Cylinder in Section

The section front view of the cylinder is now shown with cross hatch lines in the direction opposite the housing, Figure 16–42.

Create a Sectional View of One of the Smaller Bushings in the Flange

Step 14. Return to the model, turn off all but the Y layer, and make the smaller bushing the active part.

Prompt	Response
Command:	**Mode**
Drawing/<Part>:	↵

If you drew this assembly following the directions in Chapter 15, the bushing inside the housing flange is on layer Y. If you did not, use the Chprop: command to change the two smaller bushings to the Y layer. It will be easier to complete this part of the exercise if you turn off all layers except the Y layer so only the bushing is visible.

Prompt	Response
Command:	*Type:* **LA** ↵
?/Make/Set/New/ON/OFF/Color/Ltype/ Freeze/Thaw/LOck/Unlock:	*Type:* **OFF** ↵
Layer name(s) to turn Off:	*Type:* ***** ↵
Really want layer G (the CURRENT layer) off? <N>	*Type:* **Y** ↵
?/Make/Set/New/ON/OFF/Color/Ltype/ Freexe/Thaw/LOck/Unlock:	*Type:* **ON** ↵
Layer name(s) to turn ON:	*Type:* **Y**
?/Make/Set/New/ON/OFF/Color/Ltype/ Freexe/Thaw/LOck/Unlock:	↵
Command:	**Part** **Make Active**
Select part:	Pick the left bushing.

Step 15. Move the UCS to the center of the bushing and create a nonparametric work plane that will be the cutting plane for the next part of the section. (You cannot use the same work plane for another part.)

Prompt	Response
Command:	*Type:* **UCS** ↵
Origin/ZAxis/3point/OBject?View/ X/Y/Z/Prev/Restore/Save/Del/?/ World>:	*Type:* **O** ↵

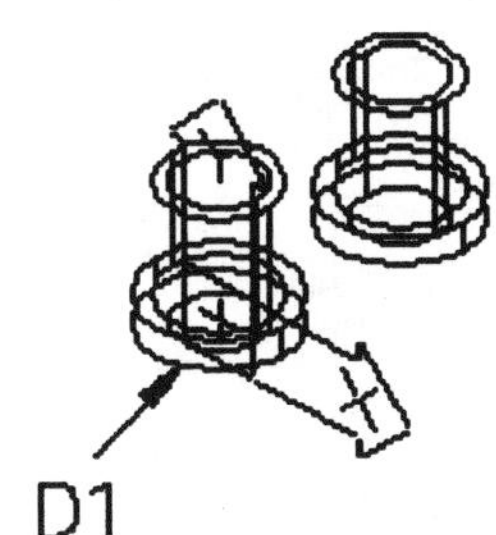

FIGURE 16–43
Moving the UCS Origin

Origin point <0,0,0>:	**Osnap-CENter**
of	**D1** (Figure 16–43)
Command:	**Work Plane. . .**
The Designer Work Plane dialog box appears:	*Pick:* **On UCS** *Pick:* **OK**

Step 16. On Your Own:

Turn on layer ADP_WORK so the work plane appears as shown in Figure 16–44 and Zoom in closely on the part so you can pick the work plane during the creation of the view.

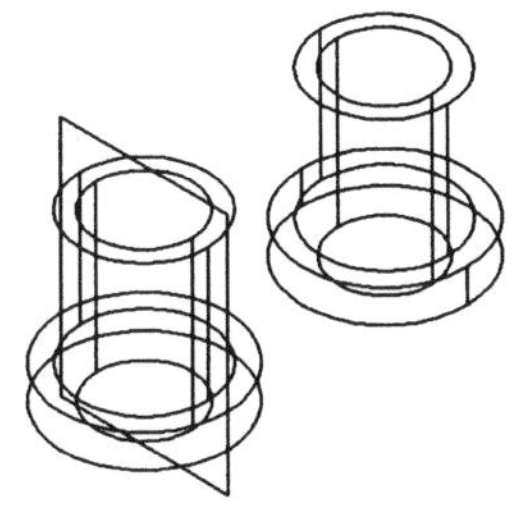

FIGURE 16–44
The Work Plane Appears

Step 17. Create the sectional view.

Prompt	Response
Command:	**Drawing** **Create view**
The Designer Drawing View dialog box, Figure 16–45, appears:	*Pick:* **Base** *Pick:* **Full** (in the Section area) *Pick:* **Hatch** *Pick:* **Pattern. . .**

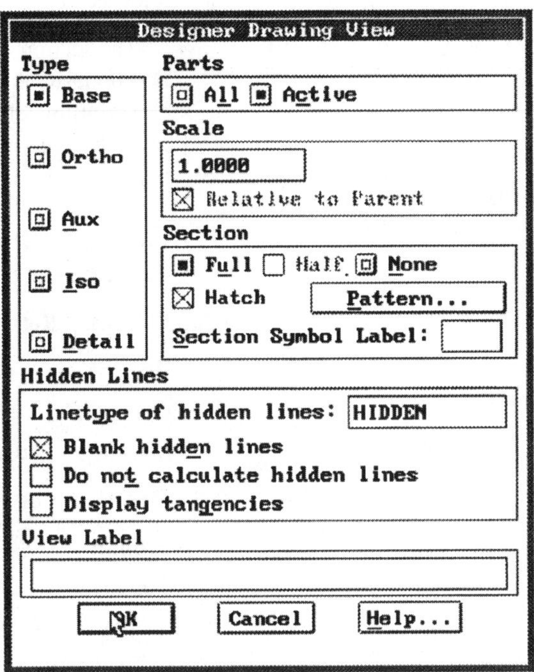

FIGURE 16–45
Designer Drawing View Dialog Box for the Sectional View of the Small Bushing

The Hatch Options dialog box appears:	**Change Angle: to 90 if it is not already.** *Pick:* **OK**
The Designer Drawing View dialog box appears:	If all parts of the dialog box are as shown in Figure 16–45, *Pick:* **OK**
Select work plane:	**Pick the front vertical edge of the work plane just constructed.**
Rotate/<Accept>:	*Type:* **R** ↵ until the UCS icon appears as shown in Figure 16–46, then *Press:* ↵ to accept.

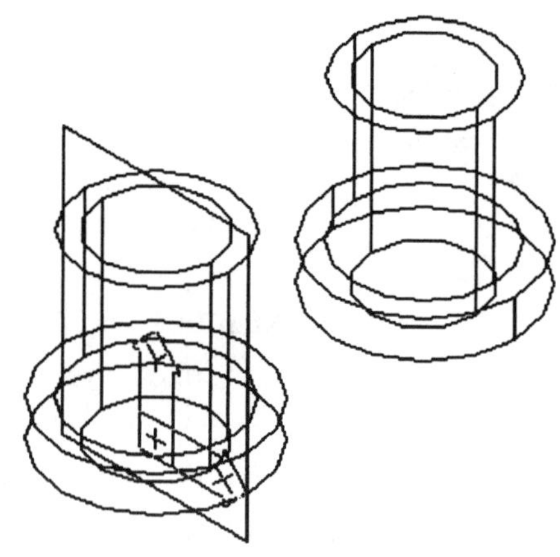

FIGURE 16–46
The Correct UCS

Prompt	Response
View center:	*Type:* **.X** ↵
of	**Osnap-MIDpoint**
of	**D1** (Figure 16–47)
(need YZ):	*Type:* **@.356<90** ↵
View center:	↵

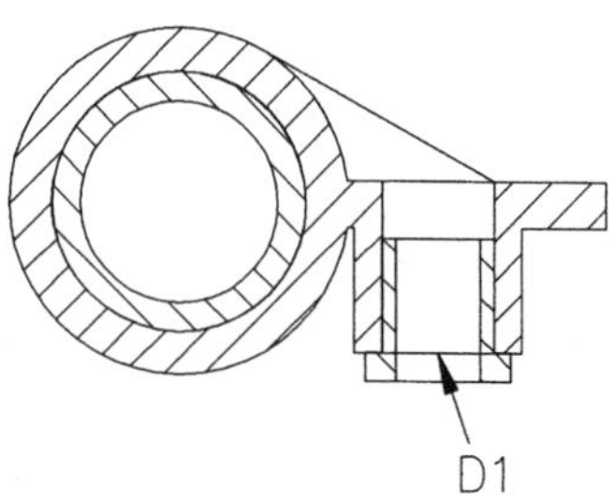

FIGURE 16–47
The Bushing in Section

The section front view of the bushing is now shown with cross hatch lines in the direction opposite the housing, Figure 16–47.

Unfortunately, there is a line crossing the bushing that should not be there. That is a line from the section view of the housing. It can be eliminated with a little maneuvering. Do that now.

Clean up the Drawing, Complete the Title Block, and Plot the Drawing

Step 18. Return to the drawing.

Prompt	Response
Command:	**Mode**
Drawing/<Part>:	↵

Step 19. Turn on all layers.

Prompt	Response
Command:	*Type:* **LA** ↵
?/Make/Set/New/ON/OFF/Color/Ltype/ Freeze/Thaw/LOck/Unlock:	*Type:* **ON** ↵
Layer name(s) to turn ON:	*Type:* ***** ↵
?/Make/Set/New/ON/OFF/Color/Ltype/ Freeze/Thaw/LOck/Unlock:	↵

Step 20. Select a plan view of the current UCS.

Prompt	Response
Command:	*Type:* **PLAN** ↵
<Current UCS>/Ucs/World:	↵

Step 21. Find out what layer the unnecessary line is on.

Prompt	Response
Command:	*Type:* **LIST** ↵

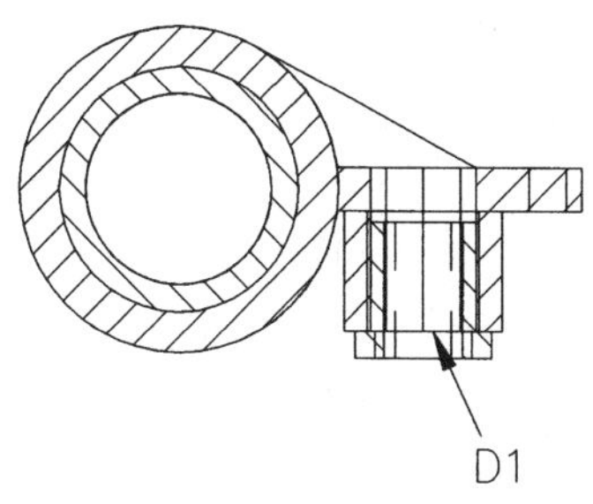

FIGURE 16–48
Listing the Layer of the Created View Outline

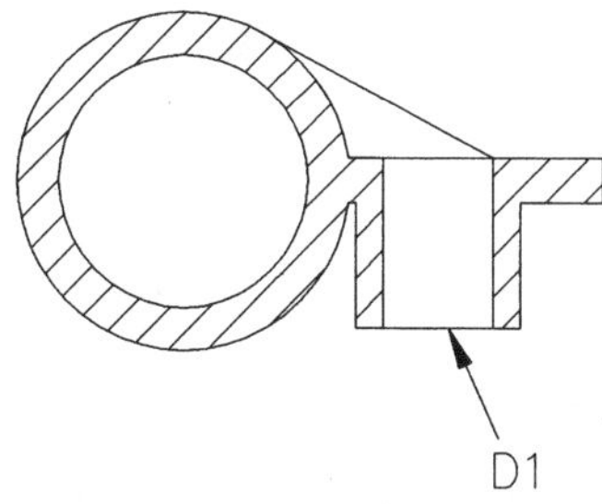

FIGURE 16–49
Exploding the View Outline and Erasing the Problem Line

Select objects:	*Pick:* **D1** (Figure 16–48)
Select objects:	↵

The listing will tell you what layer the problem line is on.

Step 22. On Your Own:

Turn off all layers but the one that the problem line is on. (Mine was ADV_4_VIS.)

Step 23. Eliminate the unnecessary line.

Prompt	**Response**
Command:	**Explode:**
Select objects:	**Pick any point on the view. D1 (Figure 16–49)**
Select objects:	↵
Command:	*Type:* **E** ↵
Select objects:	*Pick:* **D1** (again)
Command:	**Mode**
Part/<Drawing>:	↵

Step 24. On Your Own:

1. Turn on all layers except the ADD_VIEWS layer that shows the outline of each viewport.

   The assembly sectional view is now complete and correct, Figure 16–50.

2. Complete the title block information, Figure 16–51. Use the SIMPLEX font .2 high for the larger type, .12 for the smaller type.

   The drawing is now complete and should look similar to Figure 16–22.

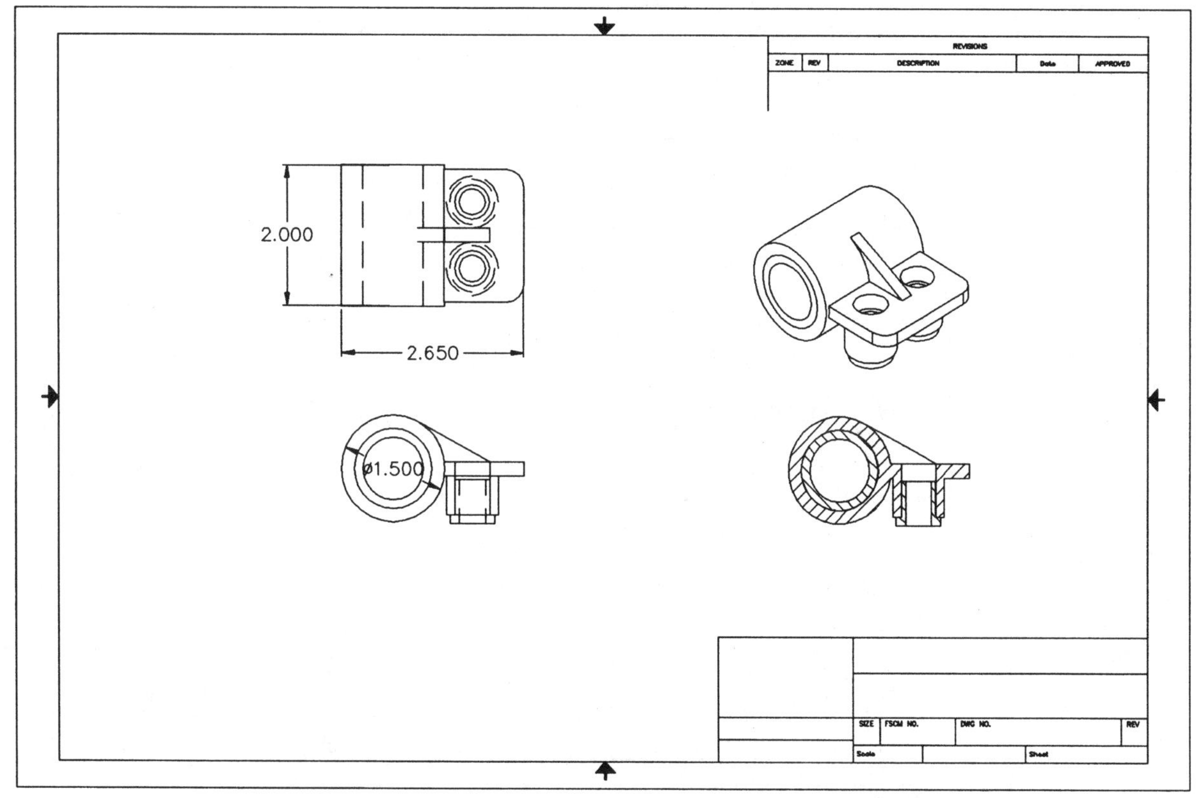

FIGURE 16–50
The Completed Sectional Assembly

FIGURE 16–51

GRADE	SCHOOL NAME			
	ASSEMBLY			
YOUR NAME	SIZE	FSCM NO.	DWG NO. EX16–2	REV
CLASS	Scale 1=1	DATE	Sheet 1 OF 1	

3. Plot the drawing full scale on an 11″ × 8.5″ sheet.
4. Save the drawing in two places and exit Designer.

Now that you know how to use ADVIEW and its associated commands to make 2-D drawings from solid models, test your skills on some of the following exercises.

EXERCISES

16–1. Follow the instructions in this chapter to draw Figure 16–1. Your final drawing should look like that figure.

16–2. Follow the instructions in this chapter to draw Figure 16–22. Your final drawing should look like that figure.

16–3. 1. If you have not made a solid model of Exercise 15–3, do so at this time.
2. Make 2-D drawings as shown in Figure 16–52.
3. Add a B-size format and complete the title block information as shown.
Your final drawing should look like Figure 16–52.
4. Plot the drawing at a scale of 1 = 1 on an 11″ × 17″ sheet.

16–4. 1. If you have not made a solid model of Exercise 15–4, do so at this time.
2. Make 2-D drawings as shown in Figure 16–53.
3. Add a C-size format and complete the title block information as shown.
Your final drawing should look like Figure 16–53.
4. Plot the drawing at a scale of 1 = 1 on a 17″ × 22″ sheet.

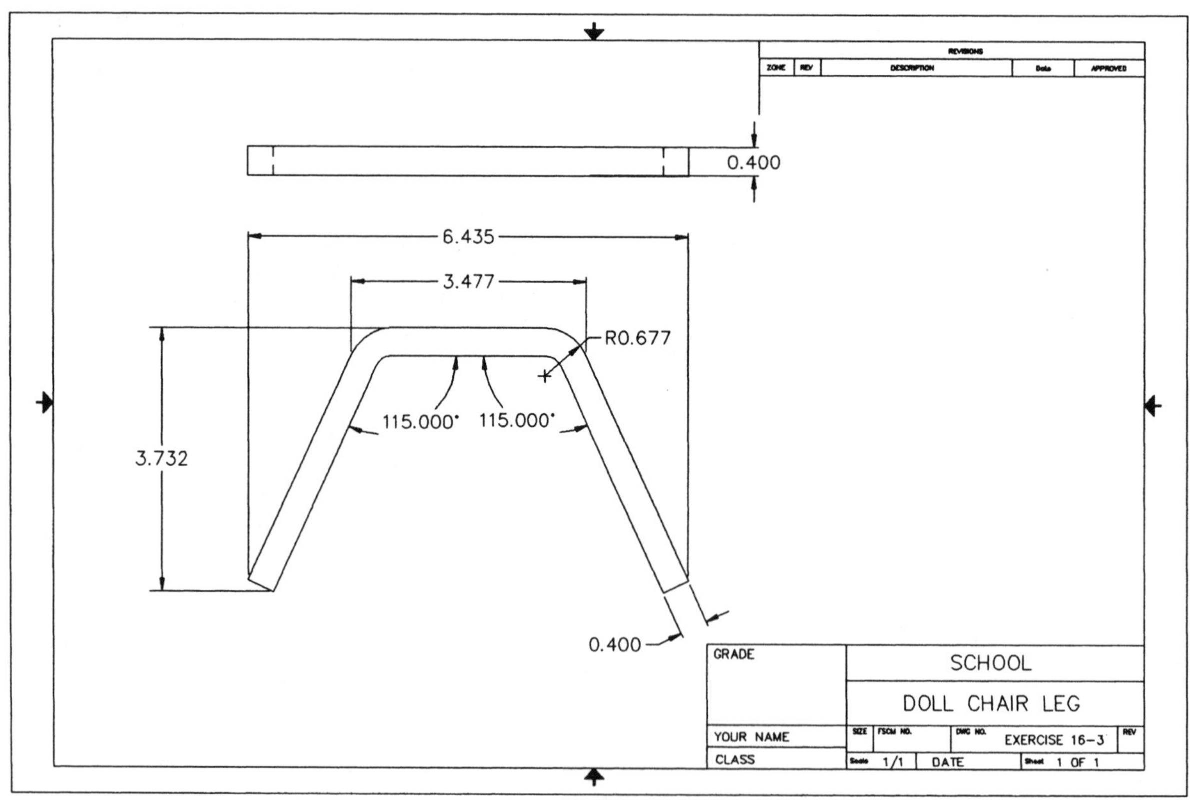

FIGURE 16–52
Exercise 16–3

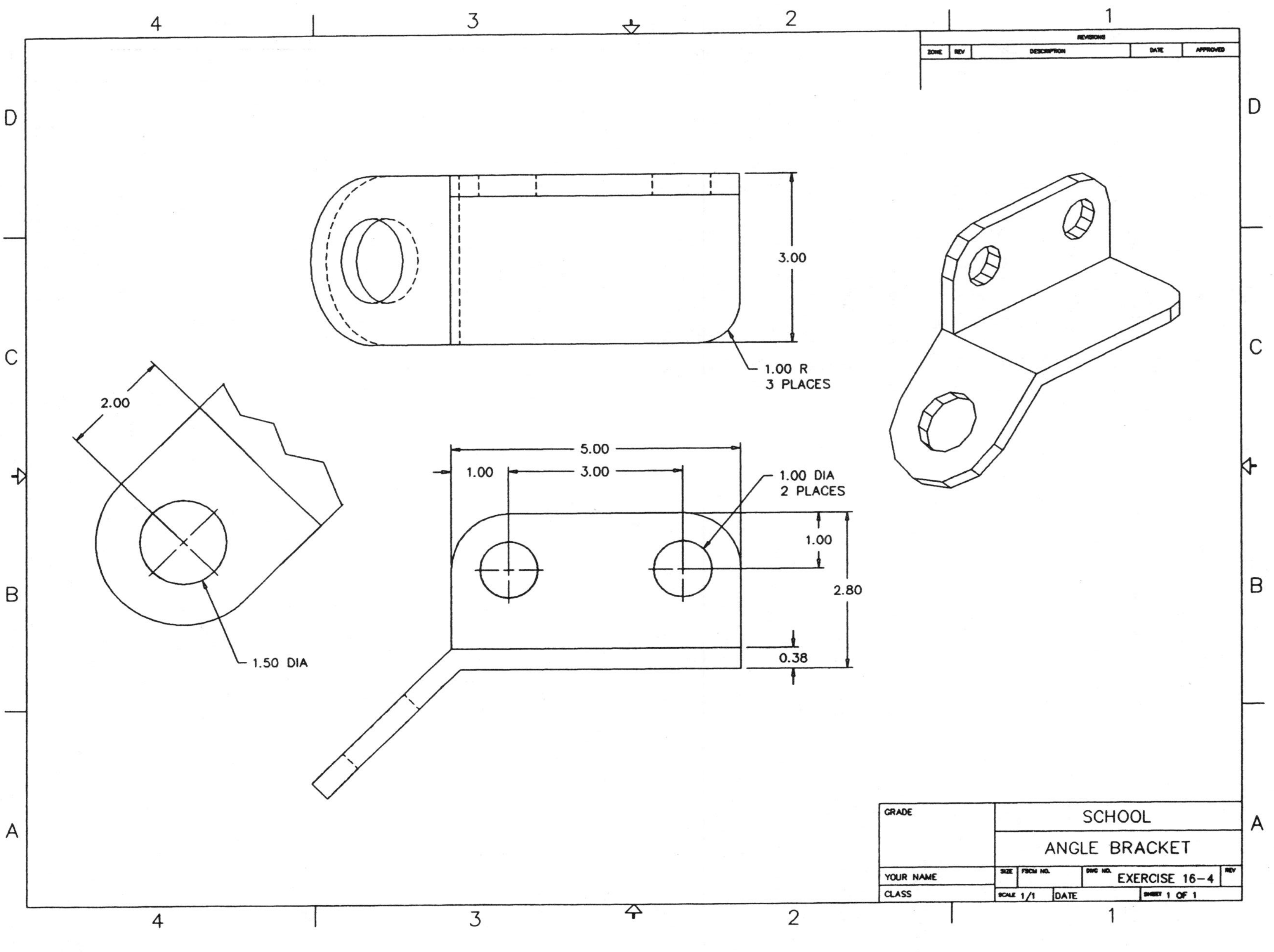

FIGURE 16–53
Exercise 16–4

16–5. 1. If you have not made a solid model of Exercise 15–5, do so at this time.
2. Make 2-D drawings as shown in Figure 16–54.
Notice that the drawing was reduced to half-scale before it was printed. You will have to turn on the ADD_VIEWS layer and use the scale command to reduce the drawing views before you add the format. Then, turn off layer ADD_VIEWS.
3. Add a B-size format and complete the title block information as shown.
Your final drawing should look like Figure 16–54.
4. Plot the drawing at a scale of .5 = 1 on an 11″ × 8.5″ sheet.

16–6. 1. If you have not made a solid model of Exercise 15–6, do so at this time.
2. Make 2-D drawings as shown in Figure 16–55.
Notice that the drawing was reduced to ¾ scale before it was printed. You will have to turn on the ADD_VIEWS layer and use the scale command to reduce the drawing views before you add the format. Then, turn off layer ADD_VIEWS.
3. Add a B-size format and complete the title block information as shown.
Your final drawing should look like Figure 16–55.
4. Plot the drawing at a scale of .5 = 1 on an 11″ × 8.5″ sheet.

16–7. 1. If you have not made a solid model of Exercise 15–7, do so at this time.
2. Make 2-D drawings as shown in Figure 16–56.
3. Add a C-size format and complete the title block information as shown.
Your final drawing should look like Figure 16–56.
4. Plot the drawing at a scale of 1 = 1 on a 17″ × 22″ sheet.

16–8. 1. If you have not made a solid model of Exercise 15–8, do so at this time.
2. Make 2-D drawings as shown in Figure 16–57.
3. Add a C-size format and complete the title block information as shown.
Your final drawing should look like Figure 16–57.
4. Plot the drawing at a scale of 1 = 1 on a 17″ × 22″ sheet.

16–9. 1. If you have not made a solid model of Exercise 15–9, do so at this time.
2. Make 2-D drawings as shown in Figure 16–58.
3. Add a C-size format and complete the title block information as you did for all other exercises.
Your final drawing should look like Figure 16–58.
4. Plot the drawing at a scale of .375 = 1 on an 11″ × 8.5″ sheet.

16–10. 1. If you have not made a solid model of Exercise 15–10, do so at this time.
2. Make 2-D drawings as shown in Figure 16–59.
3. Add a B-size format and complete the title block information as shown.
4. Add the parts list shown in the lower right corner and make sure the index numbers agree with the ballooned callouts.
Your final drawing should look like Figure 16–59.
5. Plot the drawing at a scale of .5 = 1 on an 11″ × 8.5″ sheet.

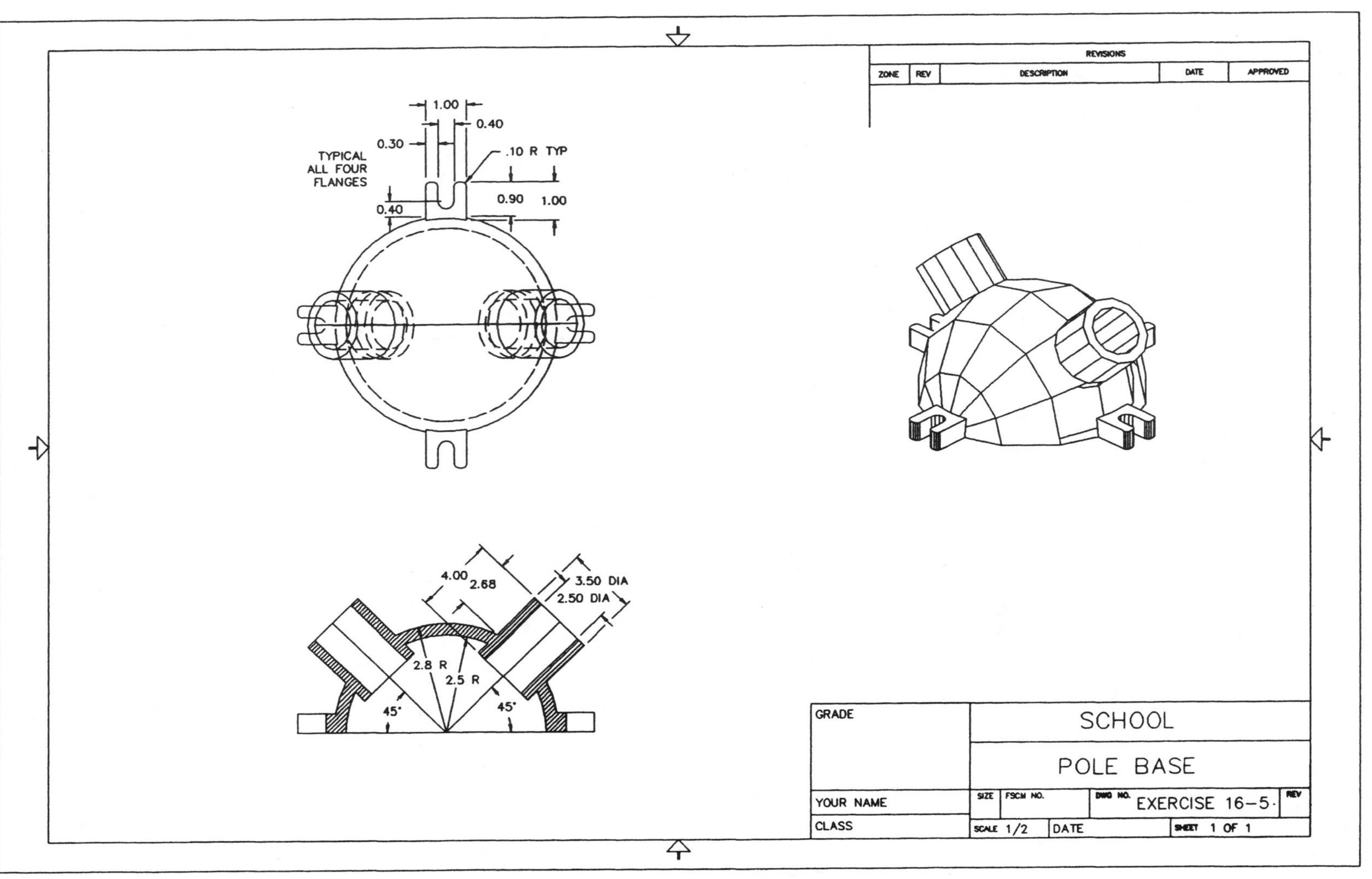

FIGURE 16–54
Exercise 16–5

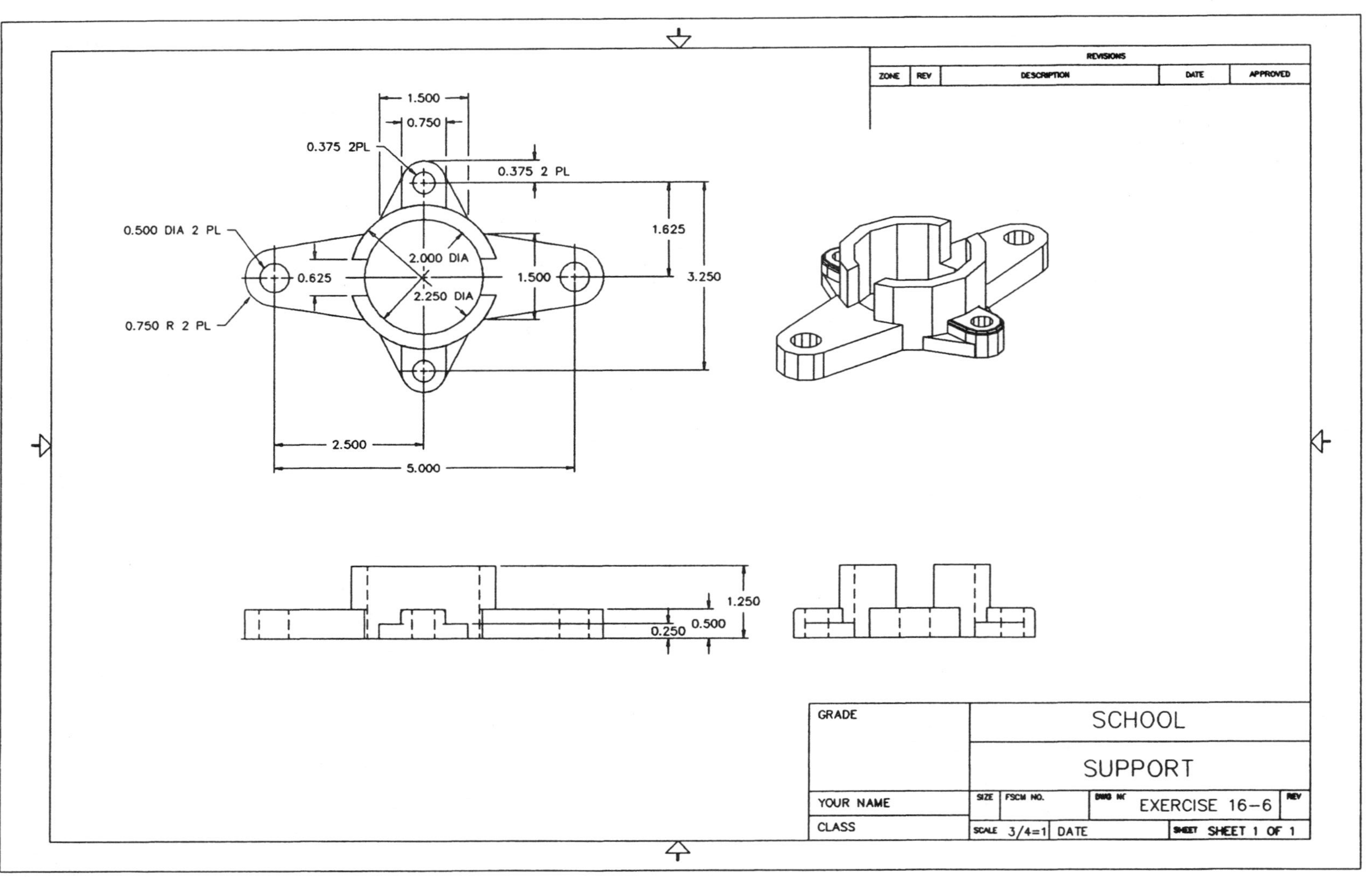

FIGURE 16–55
Exercise 16–6

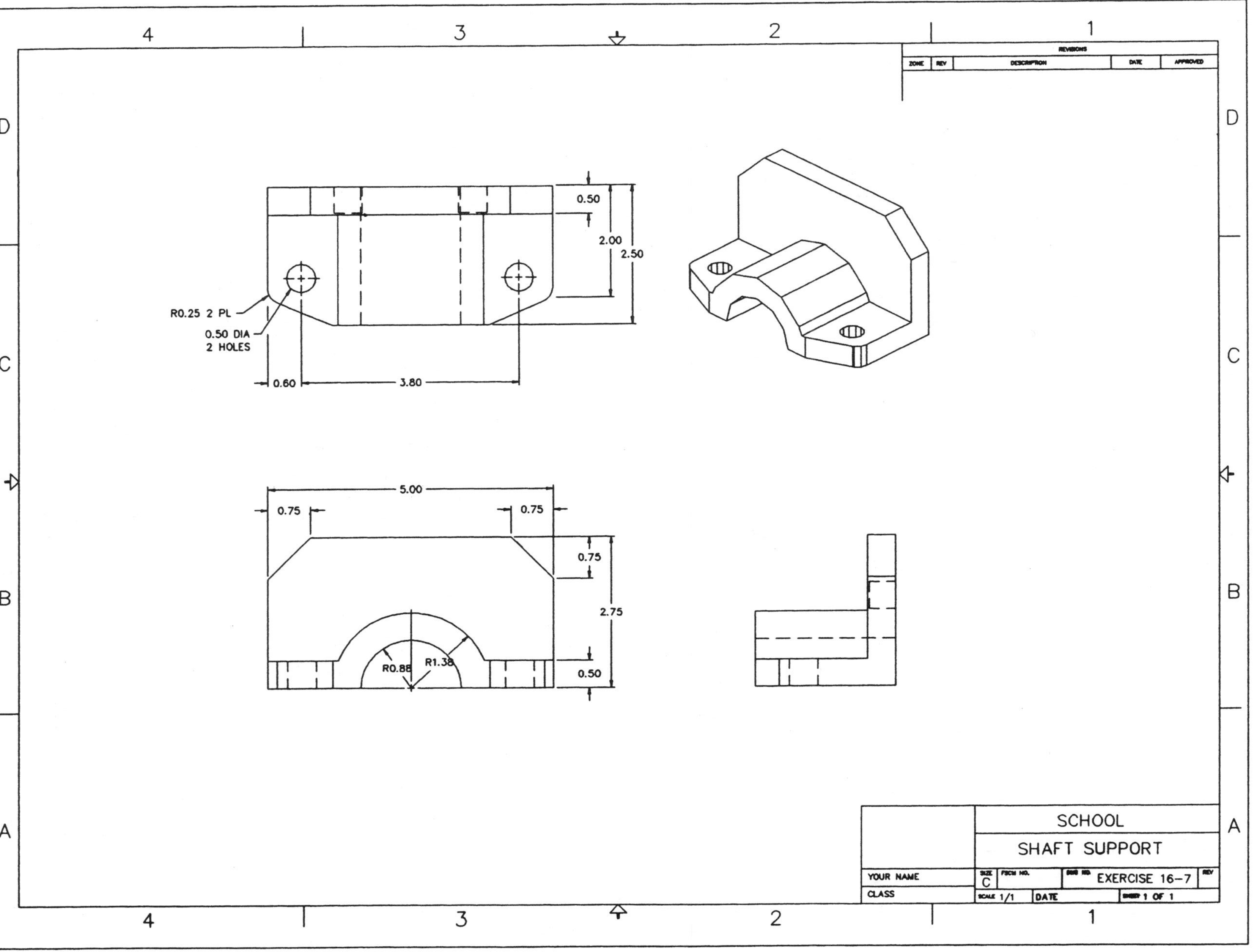

FIGURE 16–56
Exercise 16–7

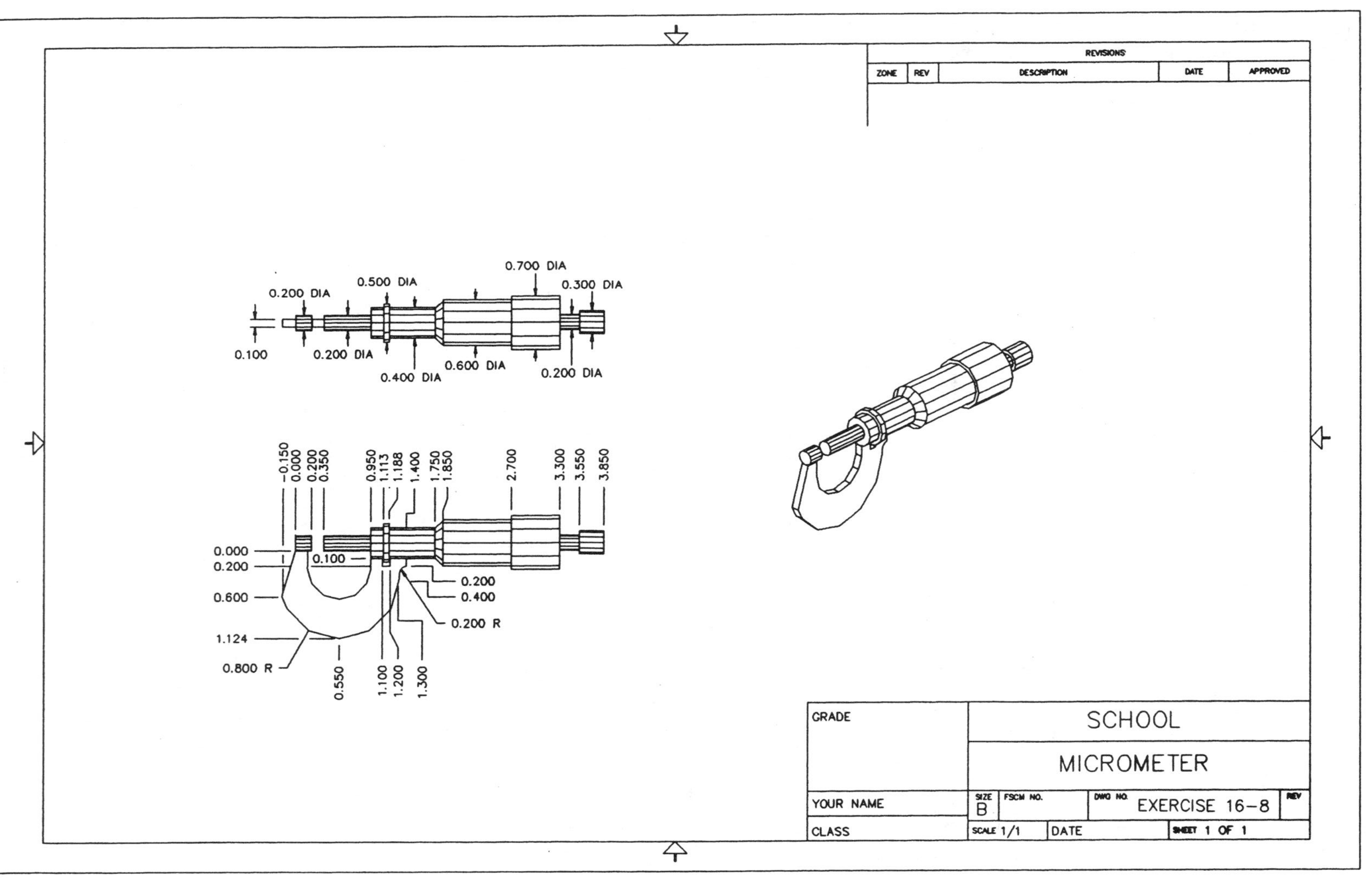

FIGURE 16–57
Exercise 16–8

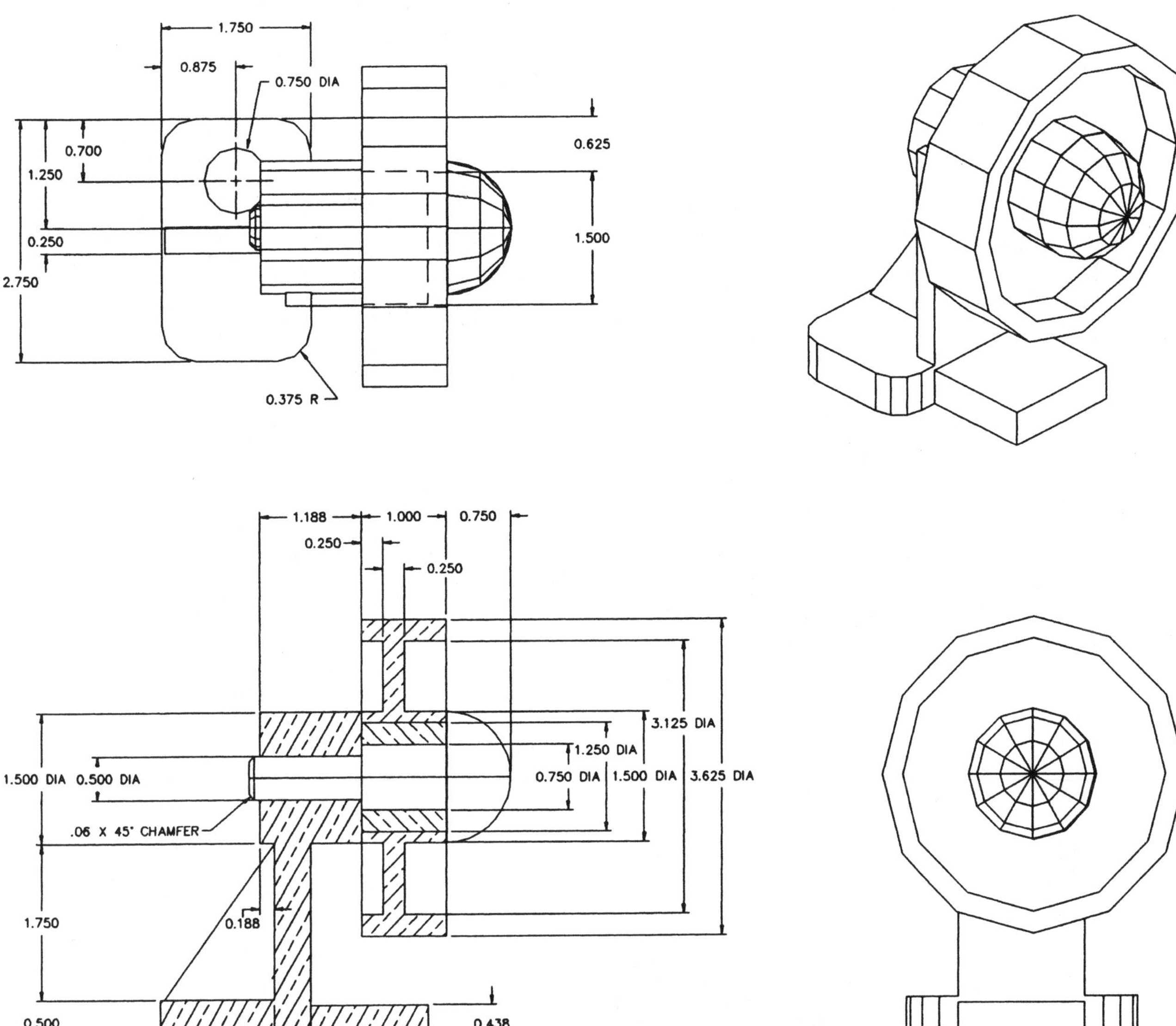

FIGURE 16–58
Exercise 16–9

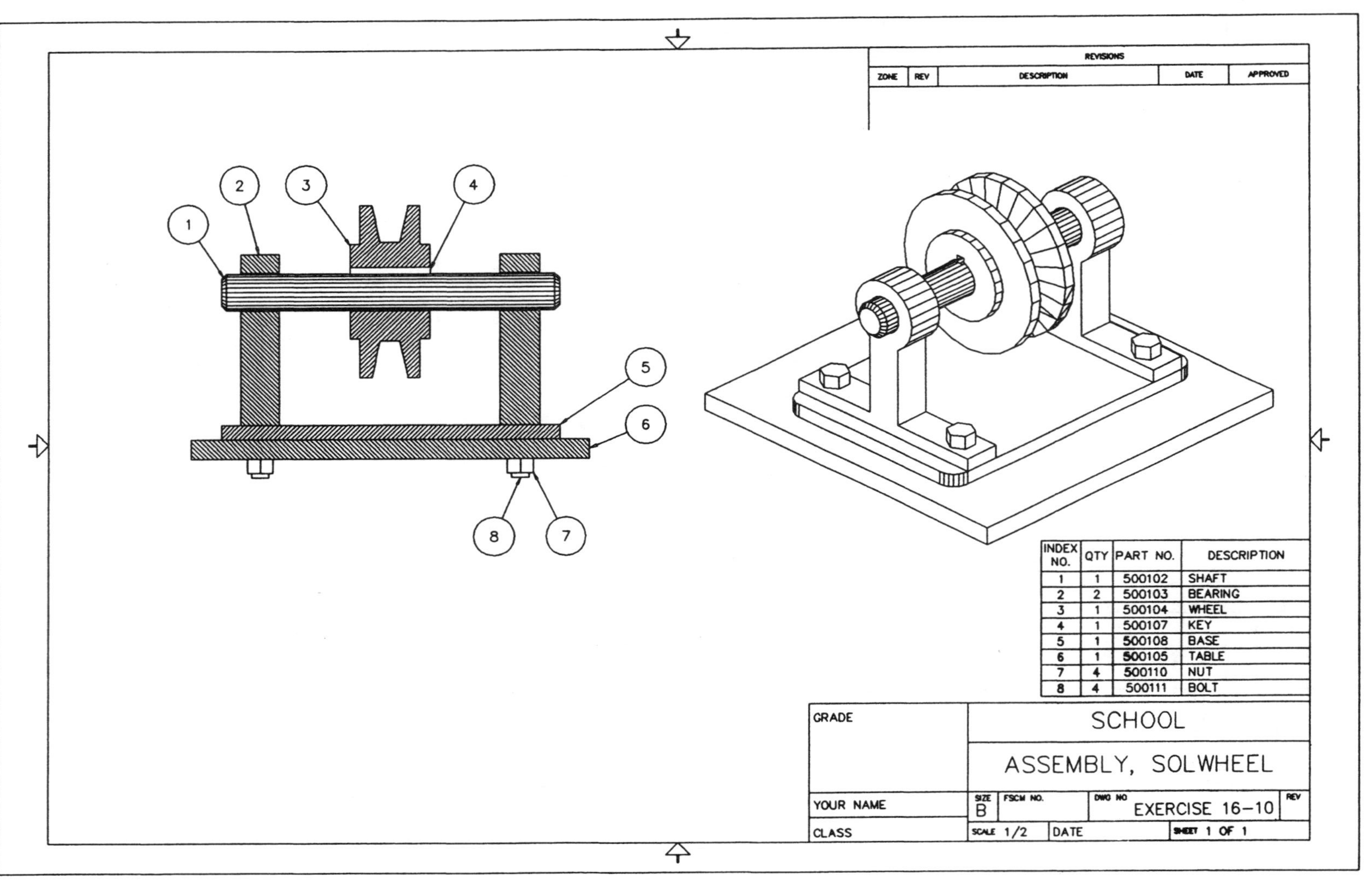

FIGURE 16–59
Exercise 16–10

REVIEW QUESTIONS

Circle the correct answer.

1. Which of the following layers does Designer create for visible geometry when ADVIEW is used the first time?
   a. ADV_0_HID d. ADV_1_OBJ
   b. ADV_0_VIS e. ADD_VIEWS
   c. ADD_0_VIS
2. Changing the linetype of the ADV_1_HID layer has little effect on the drawing.
   a. True b. False
3. The Detail option on the Designer Drawing View dialog box does which of the following?
   a. Makes a detail drawing including top, front, and right side views
   b. Enlarges a view to show small details
   c. Cleans up unnecessary dimensions and does not show them
   d. Creates a drawing with more detail than normal
   e. Can be used on assembly drawings only
4. If the Hatch option does not show an X in its check box, and a sectional view is created:
   a. The resulting view contains no cross hatch pattern.
   b. The resulting view contains the hatch pattern last used.
   c. The resulting view contains the default hatch pattern, ANSI31.
   d. The resulting view is created as an external view.
   e. No sectional view is created.
5. On which of the following would hidden lines *not* normally be shown?
   a. TOP d. DETAIL
   b. FRONT e. ISOMETRIC
   c. AUXILIARY
6. Which of the following layers contains the lines showing the boundaries of the viewports?
   a. ADV_#_VIS
   b. ADD_VIEWS
   c. ADV_#_HID
   d. The layer that was current when the views were created
   e. ADP_FRZ
7. If you want to move a single view, which of the following commands should be used?
   a. ADVIEW d. ADMODE
   b. ADUPDATE e. ADMOVEVIEW
   c. ADMOVELDR
8. When you created the front view, why did Designer repeat the prompt "View center"?
   a. So you may have two chances only to move the view center
   b. So you may place two copies of the view if you need to
   c. So you may have as many chances as you like to move the view center
   d. The prompt is not repeated
   e. Because the pick point was outside the drawing limits
9. Which of the following commands contains drawing formats that you may use on drawings in drawing mode?
   a. ADVIEW d. MVSETUP
   b. ADISOLINES e. There is no such command
   c. TILEMODE
10. When you activate ADVIEW to make a sectional view and you type an "A" in the Section Symbol Label: text box and then pick OK:
    a. No work plane or axis is needed to create the sectional view.
    b. A-A appears in the center of the cutting plane line.
    c. An "A" appears at each end of the cutting plane line.
    d. The sectional view is labeled "A-A".
    e. The sectional view is labeled "A".

Complete.

11. What is the purpose of an auxiliary view?

    ____

    ____
12. How does a reference dimension differ from a parametric dimension?

    ____

    ____

    ____
13. What is the purpose of the ADHOLENOTE command?

    ____

    ____
14. What is the purpose of the ADACTPART command?

    ____
15. Which command activates the Designer Dimension Options dialog box?

    ____
16. Which command freezes parametric dimensions on a drawing view?

    ____
17. Which command was used to attach the index numbers and balloons to individual parts on the isometric drawing?

    ____
18. Which numbered title block option on the MVSETUP command gives you an ANSI-C–size drawing?

    ____
19. What is the effect of editing the APP_FRZ layer?

    ____
20. List the layer on which Designer places hidden lines of the second view you have created on a drawing.

    ____

17 Editing Designer Solid Models

OBJECTIVES

When you have completed this chapter, you will be able to:

- □ Change the dimensions of Designer solid models and use the ADUPDATE command to change the size of the solid and its associated drawings.
- □ Add features to and delete features from a Designer solid model and use the ADUPDATE command to change the solid and its associated drawings.
- □ Move, freeze, thaw, delete, and change the value and the appearance of dimensions on drawings and use the ADUPDATE command to change the size of the solid.
- □ Use Designer commands to move, delete, scale, and change the display of drawing views.

INTRODUCTION

Now that you have constructed several Designer solid models, and made the 2-D manufacturing drawings from these models, let's see what happens when it becomes necessary to make changes to the model. Let's begin with the first drawing you did in Chapter 16.

EXERCISE 17–1
CHANGING THE SIZE OF FEATURES ON A DESIGNER SOLID

Your final drawing will look similar to Figure 17–1.

Set Up the Drawing

Step 1. On Your Own:

1. Pick New. . . from the menu bar file menu. Name the drawing: 17-1 (your initials) = 16-1 (your initials).
2. Make the following settings:

UNITS: Decimal; 3 digits to the right of the decimal point.

LIMITS: Lower left corner: 0,0
Upper right corner: 11,8.5

GRID: .2

SNAP: .05

STYLE: STANDARD; FONT: SIMPLEX; HEIGHT: 0

Create the following layers:

LAYER NAME	COLOR	LINETYPE
Y	YELLOW	CONTINUOUS
R	RED	CONTINUOUS
G	GREEN	CONTINUOUS

Set layer G current.

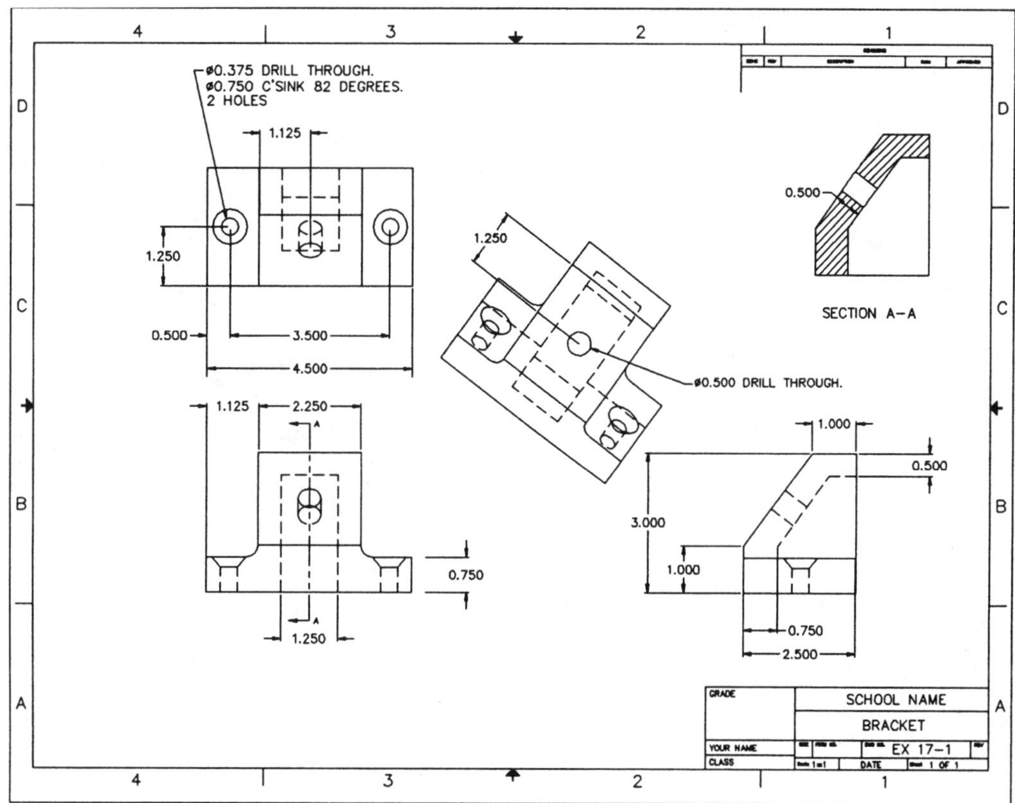

FIGURE 17–1
The Final Drawing

Before you use the ADEDITFEAT command for the first time, let's examine it in detail.

ADEDITFEAT

ADEDITFEAT works only in part mode. It allows you to display and change the dimension value for the active part. You may use equations for dimension values, as you can for the command ADMODDIM. ADEDITFEAT has two options:

Select Feature This is the default. It allows you to select a feature, display dimensions, and make any changes you choose.

Sketch The Sketch option allows you to select the feature and change the sketch of that feature. You can change dimensions and constraints, but you cannot change the geometry.

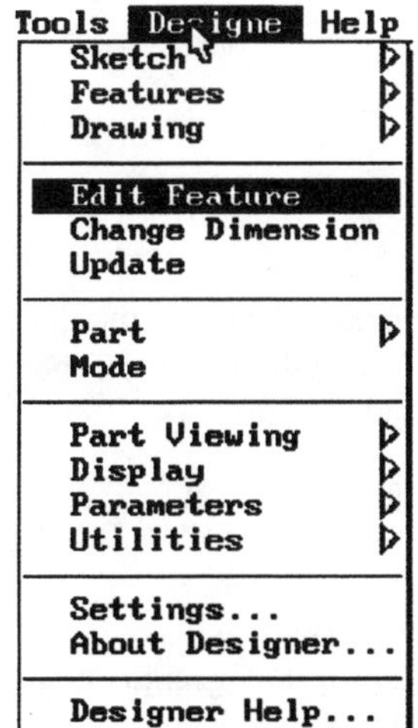

Edit the Part

Step 2. Change the size of the counterbored holes, and change them to countersunk holes.

Prompt	Response
Command:	**Mode**
Drawing/<Part>:	↵
The model, Figure 17–2, appears.	
Command:	**Edit Feature**
Sketch/<Select feature>:	↵
Select feature:	*Pick:* **D1** (the counterbored hole as shown in Figure 17–3) (If picking the counterbore does not work, pick the drilled hole.)

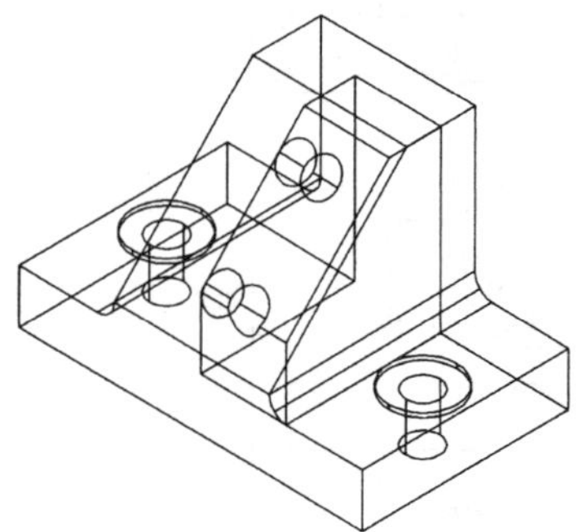

FIGURE 17–2
The Unchanged Model

Prompt	Response
Next/<Accept>:	
The Designer Hole dialog box, Figure 17–4 appears:	*Pick:* **C'Sink** **Change Dia: to .375 (in the Drill Size area).** **Change C'Dia: to .75.** *Pick:* **OK**

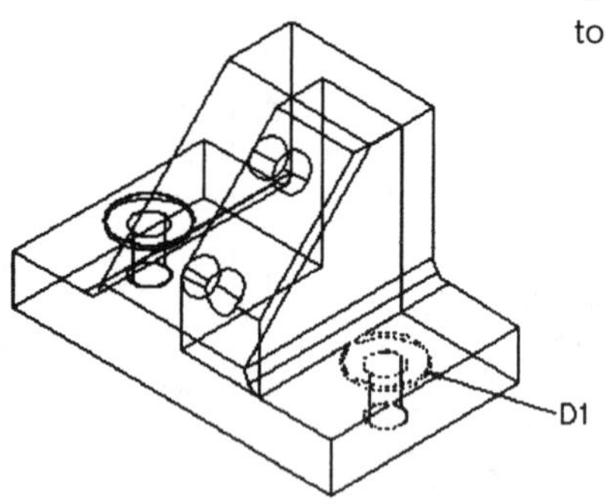

FIGURE 17–3
Picking the Counterbored Hole

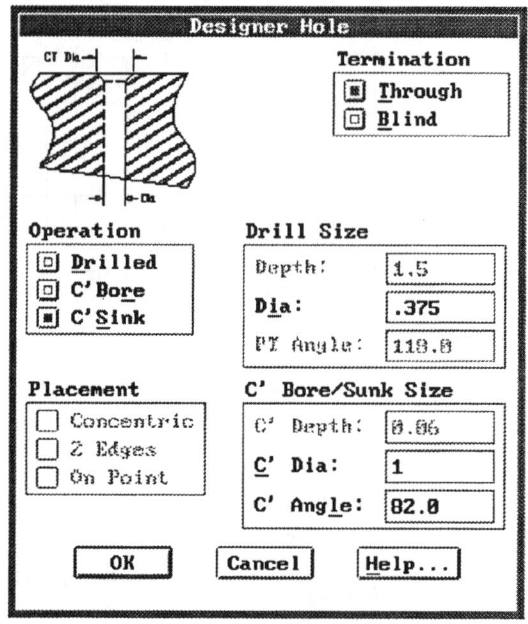

FIGURE 17–4
Designer Hole Dialog Box for Changing the Counterbored Hole to a Countersunk Hole

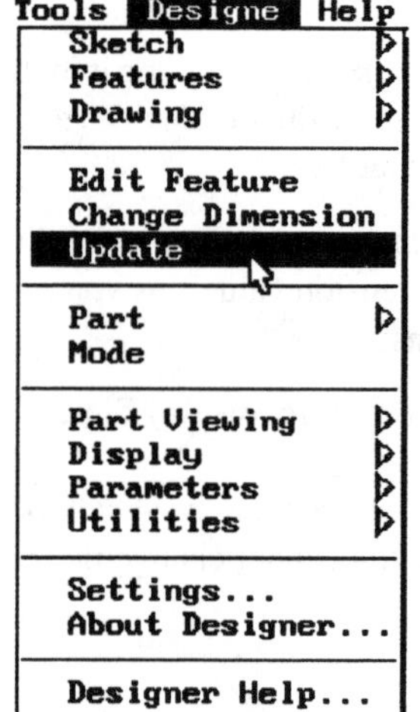

Select dimension to change:	**Pick the .625 dimension.**
New value for dimension <.625>:	*Type:* **.75** ↵
Select dimension to change:	↵

ADUPDATE

ADUPDATE regenerates the active part using the changed dimensions or sketches. ADUPDATE works in either part or drawing mode and updates both the part and the drawing views.

Prompt	Response
Command:	**Update**

The model appears as shown in Figure 17–5.

Step 3. On Your Own:

Change the other counterbored hole in the same manner, except change the distance from the left edge to the center of the hole from .625 to .5. (You will cut .25 off the right end of the part so that the holes will be the same distance from both edges.)

Step 4. Change some of the dimensions of the model base.

Prompt	Response
Command:	**Edit Feature**
Select feature:	**Pick any point on the outside of the bottom of the base.**

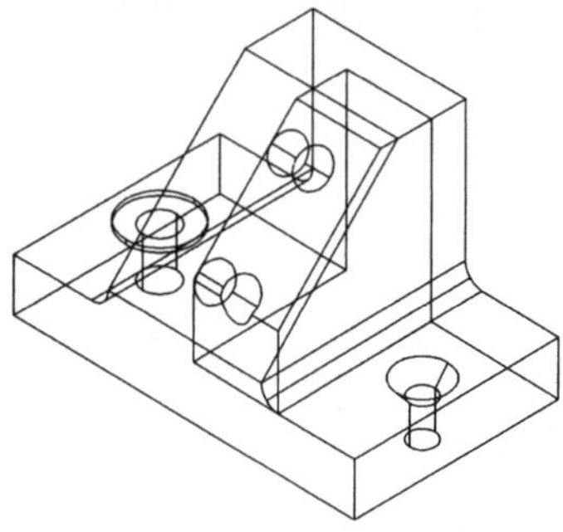

FIGURE 17–5
Changing the Counterbore to a Countersink

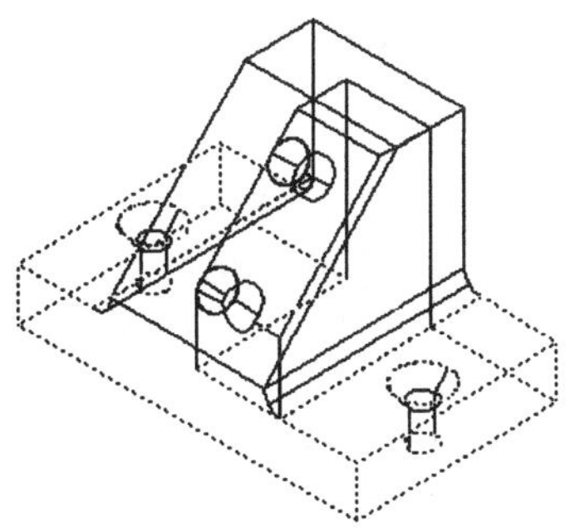

FIGURE 17–6
Highlighting the Feature Surface

Next/<Accept>:	*Type:* **N** ↵ until the model is highlighted as shown in Figure 17–6, then *Press:* ↵.
Select dimension to change:	**Pick the 3.000 dimension.**
New value for dimension <3.0>:	*Type:* **2.5** ↵
Select dimension to change:	**Pick the 5.000 dimension.**
New value for dimension <5.000>:	*Type:* **4.5** ↵
Select dimension to change:	↵
Command:	**Update**

The model changes as shown in Figure 17–7.

The upper part of the model has not changed as anticipated, and it is no longer centered in the base. You can change the 3.000 depth dimension on the upper part to 2.5 also, but centering the upper part of the model in the base cannot be done with the existing set of dimensions. Therefore, you will have to undo the most recent change and take a different approach. This happens often, so check each change carefully so you do not waste time by having to undo more than is necessary.

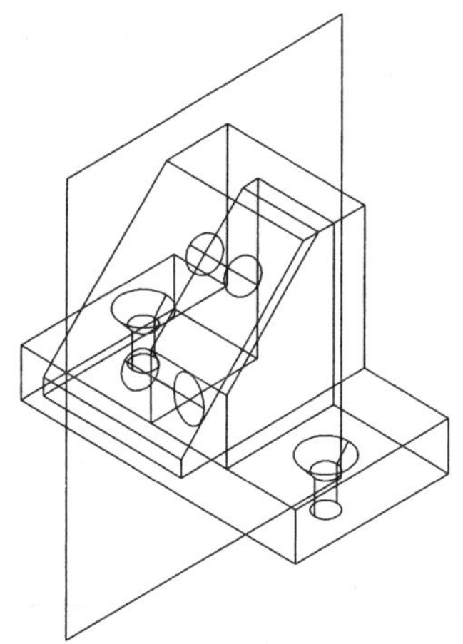

FIGURE 17–7
Changing the Base

Prompt	Response
Command:	*Type:* **U** ↵
Command:	*Type:* **U** ↵

Now, change the 3.000 dimension again, but leave the 5.000 dimension alone. You will have to take another approach to that change. Change the 3.000 depth dimension on the upper part of the model before you update the part.

Prompt	Response
Command:	**Edit Feature**
Select feature:	**Pick any point on the outside of the bottom of the base.**

Note: If you cannot pick the base, start over again with Step 1.

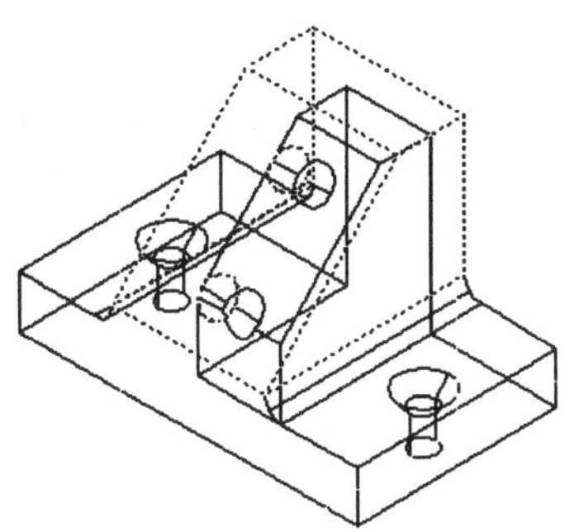

FIGURE 17–8
Highlighting the Upper Part of the Model

Prompt	Response
Next/<Accept>:	*Type:* **N** ↵ until the model is highlighted as shown in Figure 17–6, then *Press:* ↵.
Select dimension to change:	**Pick the 3.000 dimension.**
New value for dimension <3.0>:	*Type:* **2.5** ↵
Select dimension to change:	↵
Command:	**Edit Feature**
Sketch/<Select feature>:	**Pick the outside vertical edge of the upright part of the model near its center.**
Next/<Accept>:	*Type:* **N** ↵ until the model is highlighted as shown in Figure 17–8, then *Press:* ↵.
Select dimension to change:	**Pick the 3.000 depth dimension (not the vertical one).**
New value for dimension <3.000>:	*Type:* **2.5** ↵
Select dimension to change:	↵
Command:	**Update**

The part appears as shown in Figure 17–9.

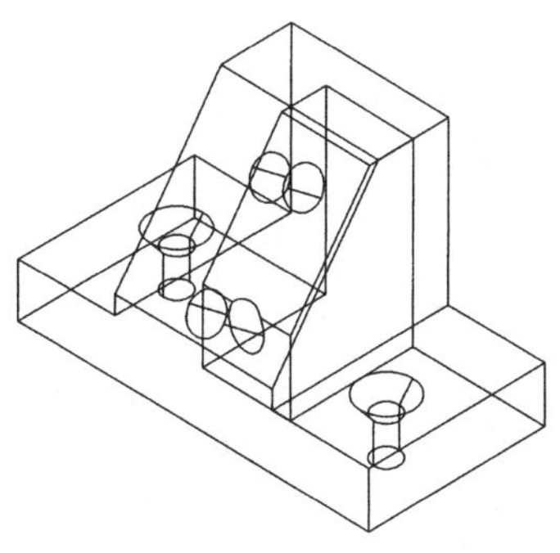

FIGURE 17–9
The Changed Model

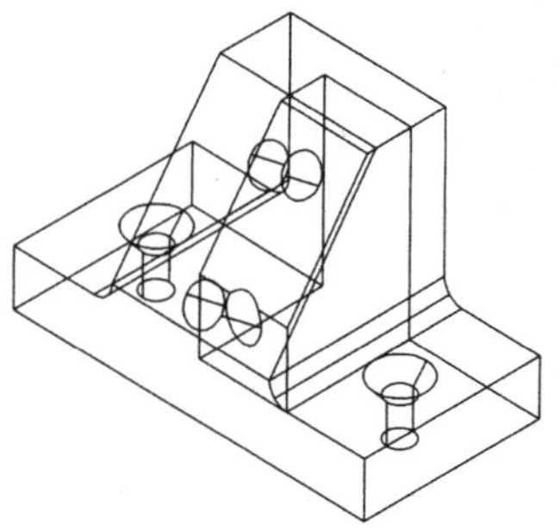

FIGURE 17–10
Centering Holes and Replacing Fillets

Notice that the countersunk holes are now not centered in the model, and the fillets may or may not have disappeared.

Step 5. On Your Own:

1. Move the countersunk holes so they are centered on the depth of the base (1.25 is the correct dimension). Use Edit Feature, pick the hole, pick OK on the Hole dialog box, pick the depth dimension, and change it to 1.25.
2. Add .25 radius fillets if necessary on both sides of the upright piece where it meets the base, as shown in Figure 17–10.

Now fix the 5.000 length of the base. When you tried to change it to 4.500 before, the entire .500 difference came off the left end. The reason for that is that the fix point of your sketch is at the left end. One solution is to take half of the .500 (.250) off the left end and then extrude a cut to take .250 off the right end. It would seem that moving the fix point of the sketch to the right end should allow you to take the other half off the right end, and updated versions of the software may allow you to do that. Such is not the case with this version, so extruding the .25 cut is a solution that works.

Note: You may be thinking that you would rather move the fix point of the sketch to the midpoint of the base so that half of the .500 would come off each end. You cannot use Osnap on the profile. Any pick on the profile is automatically to the endpoint of the line or the center of a circle or arc on the profile.

Step 6. Change the length of the base by shortening one end.

Prompt	Response
Command:	**Edit Feature**
Sketch/<Select feature>:	**Pick any point on the base.** *Type:* **N** ↵ until the base is highlighted as shown in Figure 17–11, then *Press:* ↵.
Select dimension to change:	**Pick the 5.000 dimension.**
New value for dimension <5.000>:	*Type:* **4.75** ↵
Select dimension to change:	↵
Command:	**Update**

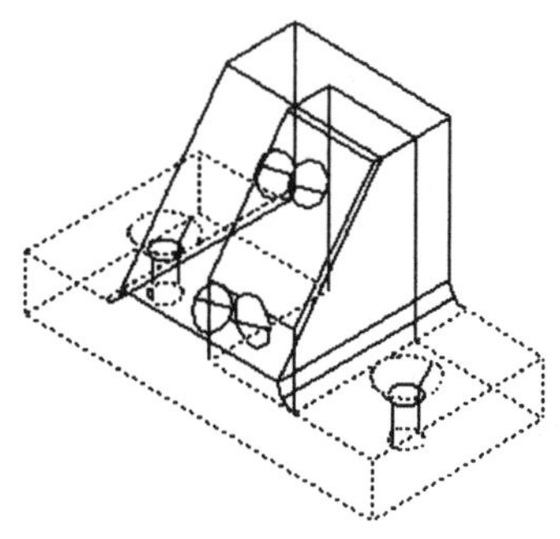

FIGURE 17–11
Highlighting the Base

Oops, the fillets disappeared again. The lesson to be learned from this is that fillets are deleted when any dimension on a feature to which the fillet is attached is changed. You may replace them now or wait until the base is modified with the extruded cut.

Shorten the Other End of the Base

Step 7. Create the sketch plane.

Prompt	Response
Command:	**Sketch Plane**
Xy/Yz/Zx/Ucs/<Select work plane or planar face>:	Pick the base.
	Type: **N** ↵ until the front surface of the base is highlighted as shown in Figure 17–12, then *Press:* ↵.
X/Y/Z/<Select work axis or straight edge>:	*Type:* **X** ↵
Rotate/<Accept>:	If the UCS icon is in the position shown in Figure 17–13, *Press:* ↵ to accept.
	If the UCS icon is not in the correct position, *Type:* **R** ↵ until it is, then *Press:* ↵.

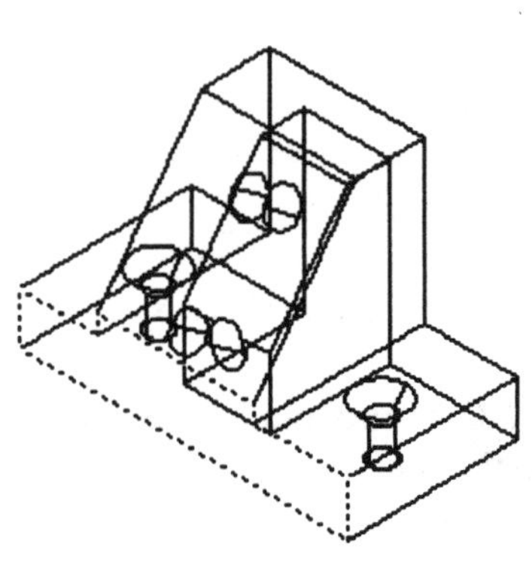

FIGURE 17–12
Highlighting the Front Surface

FIGURE 17–13
The Correct UCS Icon

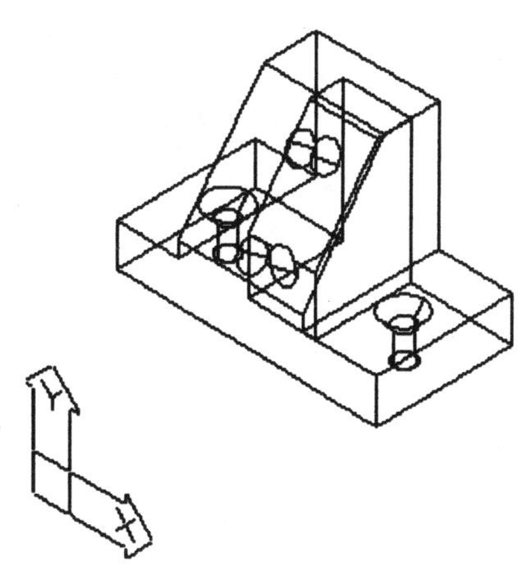

Step 8. Select the plan view of the current UCS.

Prompt	Response
Command:	*Type:* **PLAN** ↵
<Current UCS>/Ucs/World:	↵

Step 9. Make the sketch.

Prompt	Response
Command:	**Rectang:**
First corner:	With snap on, *Pick:* **D1** (Figure 17–14).
Other corner:	*Type:* **@−.25,−.75** ↵

FIGURE 17–14
Drawing the Rectangle

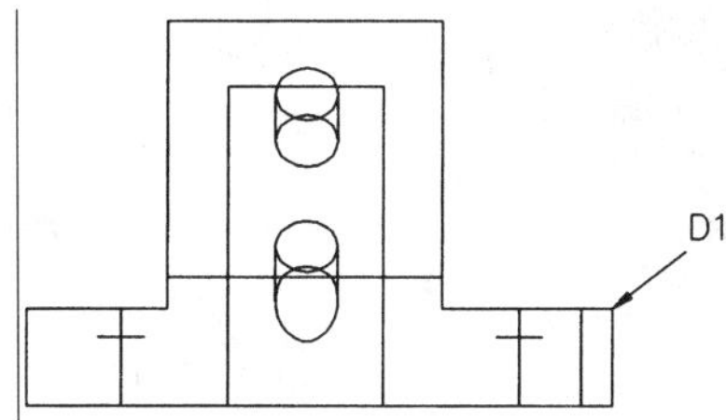

Step 10. Select an isometric view.

Prompt	Response
Command:	**Part Viewing** **Iso**

Step 11. Make the profile.

Prompt	Response
Command:	**Profile**
Select objects:	**Pick the rectangle**
Select objects:	↵

Step 12. Extrude the profile.

Prompt	Response
Command:	**Extrude. . .**
The Designer Extrusion dialog box, Figure 17–15, appears:	**Change Distance: to 3.0 as shown. When the dialog box is like Figure 17–15,** *Pick:* **OK.**

FIGURE 17–15
Designer Extrusion Dialog Box for the .25 Cut

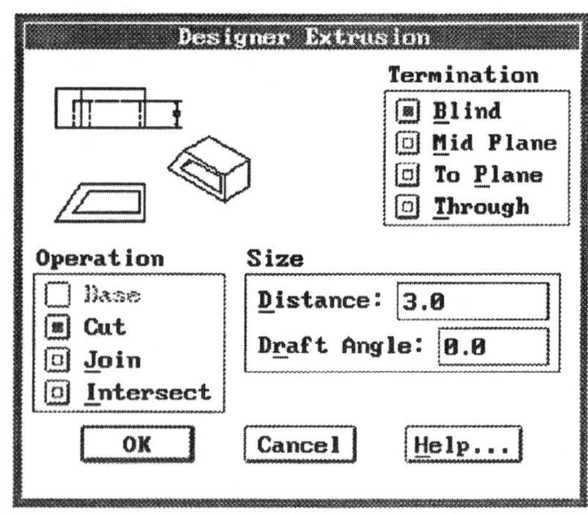

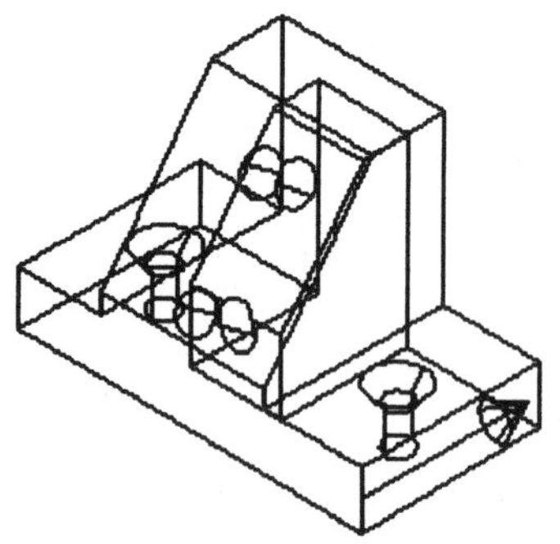

FIGURE 17–16
Accepting the Extrusion Direction

Prompt	Response
Direction Flip/<Accept>:	*Type:* **F** ↵ if the arrow is not pointing in the direction shown in Figure 17–16. When the arrow is pointing as shown, *Press:* ↵.

Step 13. On Your Own:

Replace the .25 fillets on each side of the upper part of the model where it meets the base if you have not already done so.

Edit Other Parts of the Model

Step 14. Use ADDELFEAT to delete one of the holes in the inclined surface, then move the other hole so it is centered in the inclined surface.

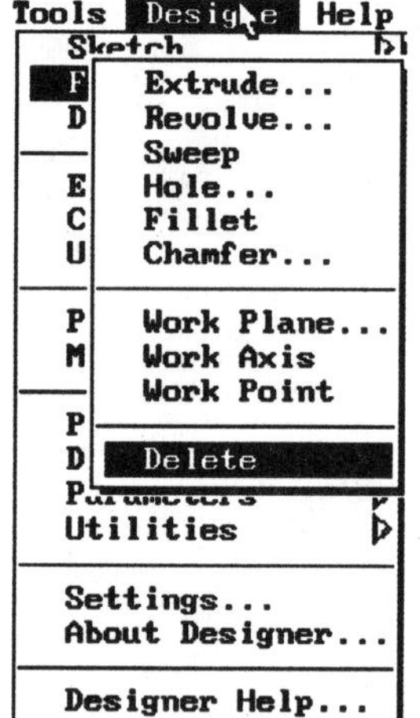

ADDELFEAT

ADDELFEAT deletes features on the active part but does not delete the part itself. You may use the Erase: command to delete entire parts.

Prompt	Response
Command:	**Delete**
Select feature to delete:	**Pick the bottom hole in the inclined surface, Figure 17–17.**
Next/<Accept>:	↵
Delete feature No/<Yes>:	↵
Command:	*Type:* **DIST** ↵
First point:	**Osnap-ENDpoint**
of	**Pick the upper left corner of the inclined surface.**
Second point:	**Osnap-ENDpoint**
of	**Pick the lower left corner of the inclined surface.**

Distance = 2.500

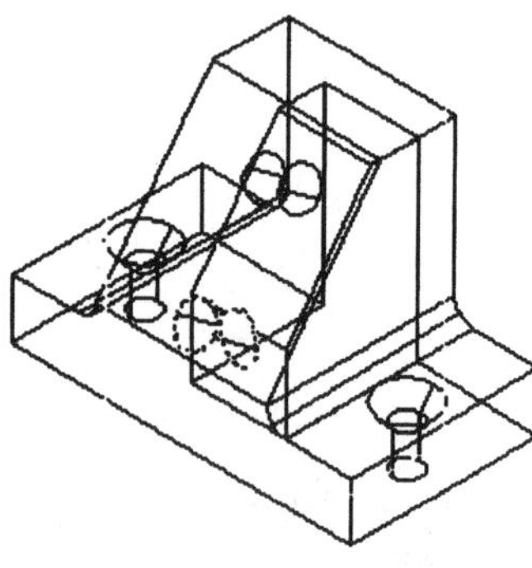

FIGURE 17–17
Deleting the Lower Hole

Now that you know the length of the inclined surface, you know that half of that distance will center the hole in this surface.

Prompt	Response
Command:	**Edit Feature**

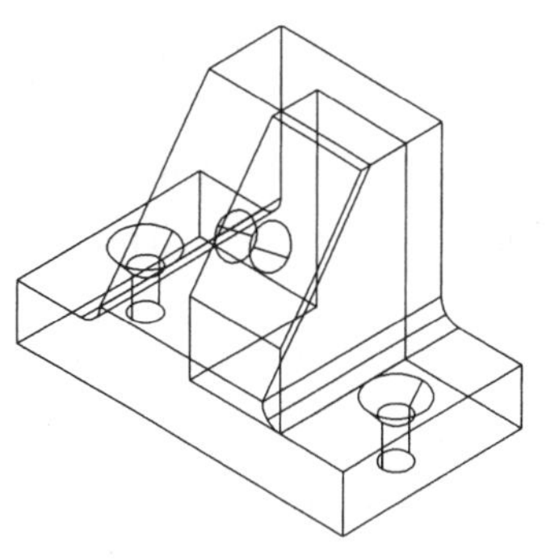

FIGURE 17–18
The Changed Model

Sketch/<Select feature>:	**Pick the remaining hole in the inclined surface.**
Next/<Accept>:	↵
The Designer Hole dialog box appears:	*Pick:* **OK**
Select dimension to change:	**Pick the 0.700 dimension.**
New value for dimension <.7>:	*Type:* **1.25** ↵
Select dimension to change:	↵
Command:	**Update**

The model appears as shown in Figure 17–18.

Now let's see what has happened to the 2-D drawings and what you will have to do to fix them.

Step 15. On Your Own:

Change the mode to drawing Figure 17–19.

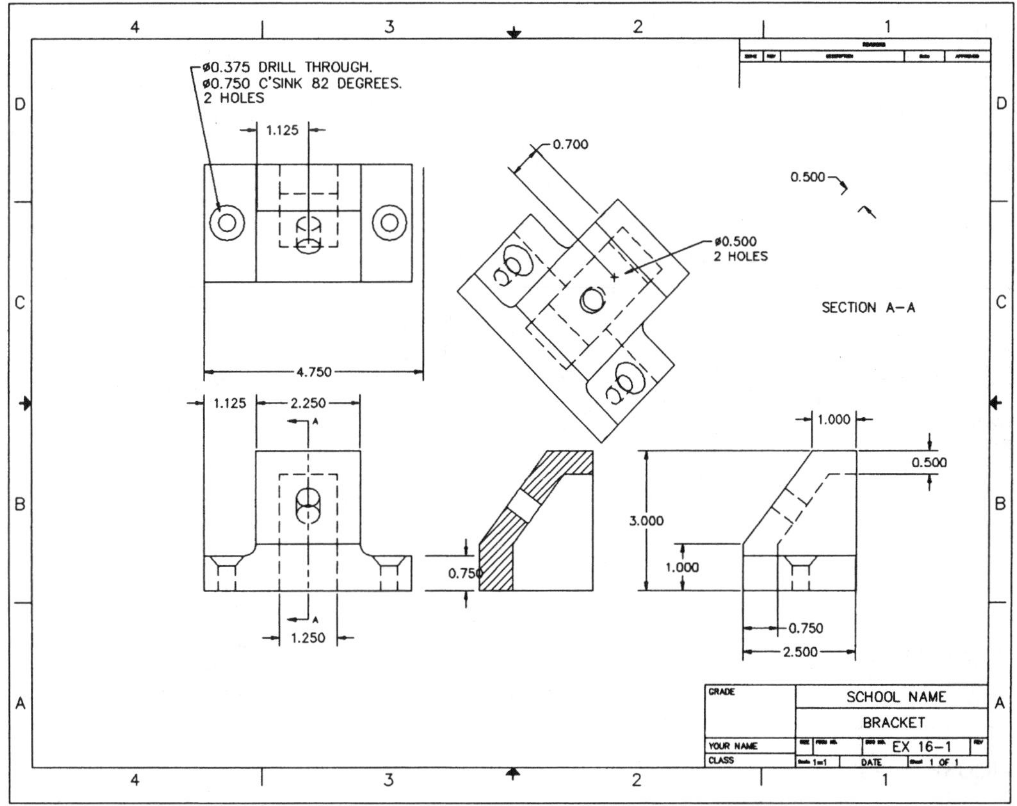

FIGURE 17–19
Returning to Drawing Mode

Correct the 2-D Drawing

Your drawing may not need exactly the same corrections as this one, but similar problems will exist and must be solved. You need to change this drawing as follows:

Move Section A-A back to the upper right corner.
Replace the auxiliary view with a new one. This one is now incorrect because the angle of the inclined plane changed.
Replace reference dimensions that located the centers of the counterbored holes.
Change the 4.750 dimension to 4.500 and its extension line.

Let's take these in order.

Step 16. On Your Own:

1. Turn on the ADD_VIEWS layer.
2. Erase the auxiliary view viewport, the text, and anything else associated with it.
3. Move the viewport containing Section A-A back to the upper right corner and redo the 0.500 reference dimension.
4. Use Create View to make a new auxiliary view and add reference dimensions. When Designer prompts you to "Select a straight edge in the parent view", be sure to pick the inclined edge in the right side view. Use Hole Note to replace the dimension on the hole. You may have to draw a construction line from the center of the hole perpendicular to the edge of the upper part of the model and use AutoCAD aligned dimensioning to get the 1.250 dimension.
5. Replace the reference dimensions in the top view as shown in Figure 17–20.

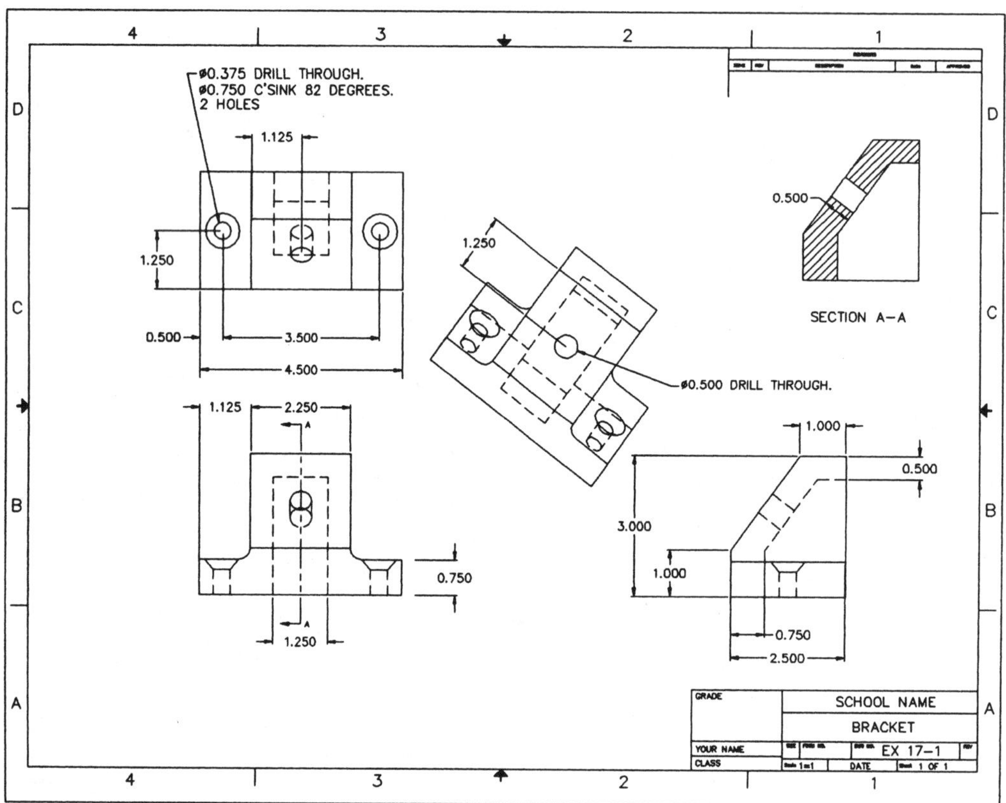

FIGURE 17–20
The Corrected Drawing

6. Use Delete Ref Dim to delete the 4.750 dimension on the top view.
7. Use Redraw to refresh the screen.
8. Use Drawing-Dimension-Attributes (ADDIMATT) to suppress the left extension line of the .500 dimension on the top view.
9. Use Drawing-Dimension-Ref Dim (ADREFDIM) to add the 4.500 dimension in the top view.
10. Change the Drawing Number to EX 17-1.
11. Plot the drawing at ⅜ scale (.375 = 1), X Origin 1, Y Origin 1, Plot Rotation 90, on an 11″ × 8.5″ sheet.
12. Save the drawing in two places and exit AutoCAD.

Now, use the assembly drawing from Chapter 16 to change the appearance of views.

EXERCISE 17–2
CHANGING THE APPEARANCE OF VIEWS ON A DESIGNER DRAWING

Your final drawing will look similar to Figure 17–21.

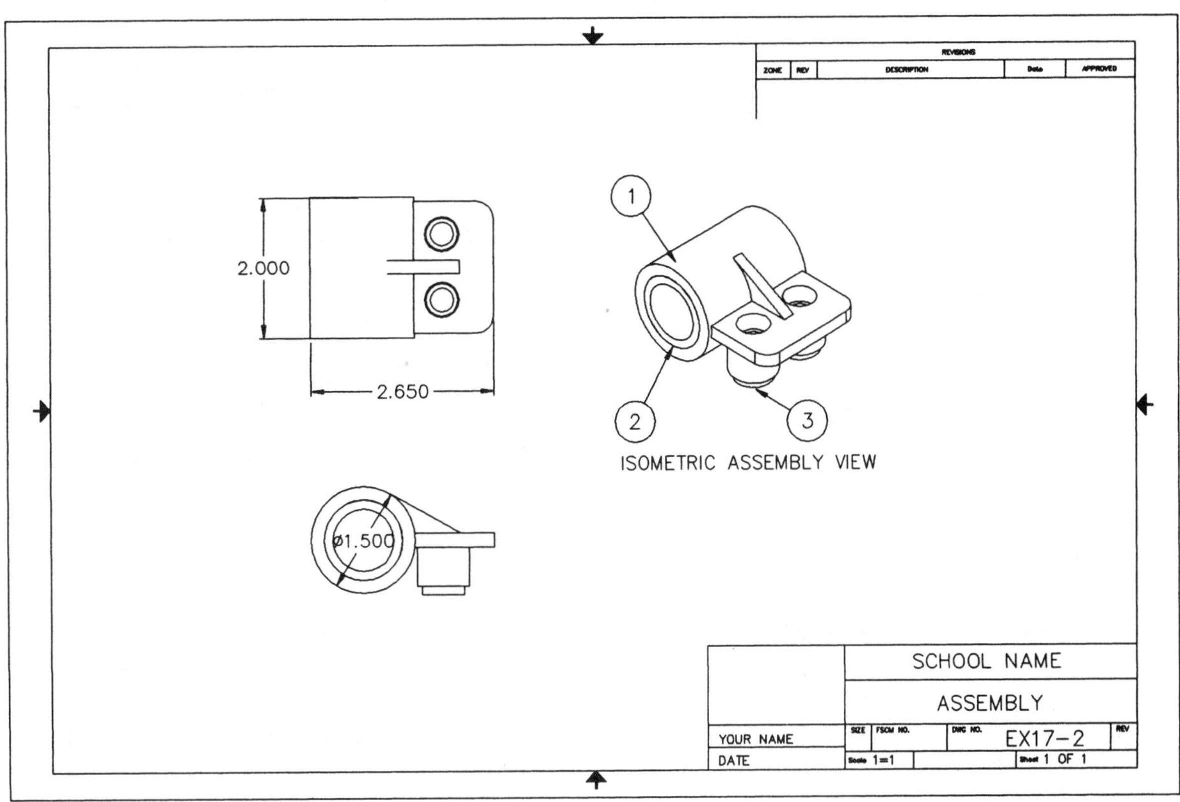

FIGURE 17–21
The Corrected Views

Set Up the Drawing

Step 1. On Your Own:

Pick New. . . from the menu bar File menu. Name the drawing: 17-2 (your initials) = 16-2 (your initials).

Before you use the ADEDITVIEW command for the first time, read the following description.

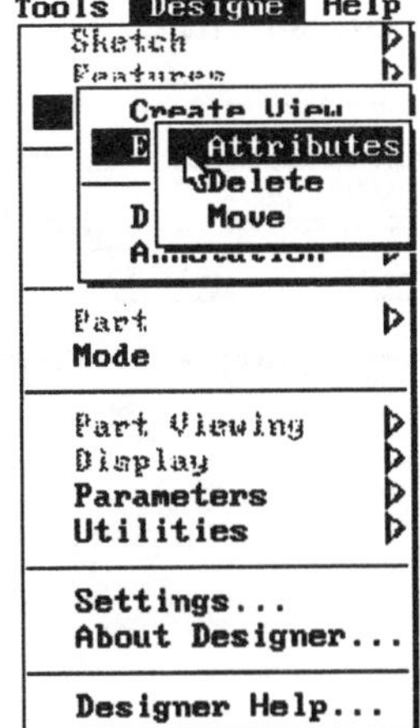

ADEDITVIEW

ADEDITVIEW allows you to change the scale, hidden line display, and View Label of a selected view.

Edit the Drawing Views and Plot the Drawing

Step 2. Change top and front views so that hidden lines are no longer shown, and add a view label to the isometric view.

Prompt	Response
Command:	**Drawing** **Edit View** **Attributes**

Prompt	Response
Select view:	**Pick the center of the front view.**
The Base Drawing View Attributes dialog box appears:	**Pick: The Blank hidden lines box so an X appears as shown in Figure 17–22.** *Pick:* **OK**

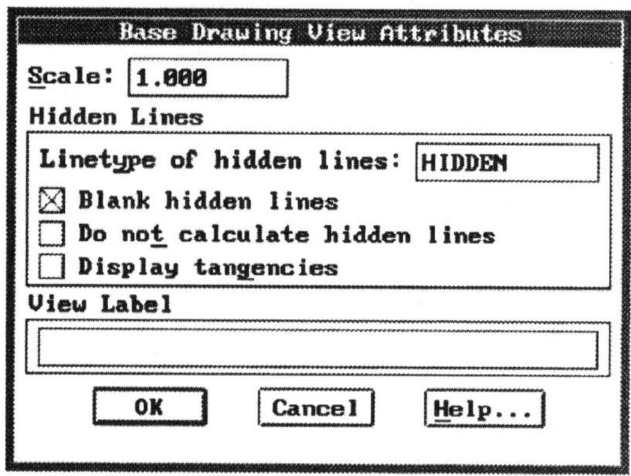

FIGURE 17–22
Base Drawing View Attributes Box

Prompt	Response
The front view appears with hidden lines removed.	
Command:	↵
Select view:	**Pick the center of the isometric view.**
The Isometric Drawing View Attributes dialog box appears:	*Type:* **ISOMETRIC ASSEMBLY VIEW** (in the View Label text box, Figure 17–23). *Pick:* **OK**

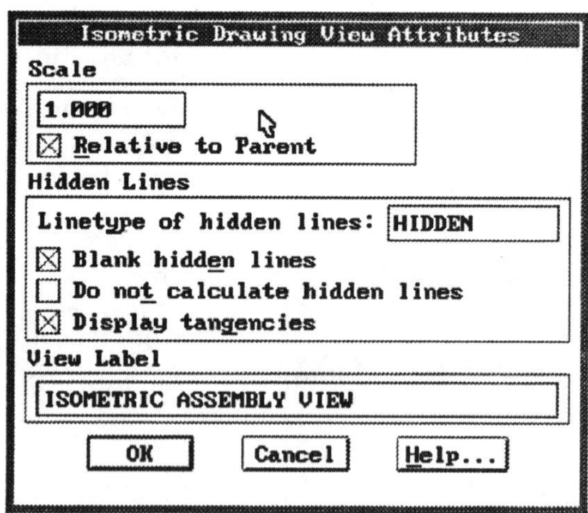

FIGURE 17–23
Isometric Drawing View Attributes Dialog Box

Step 3. On Your Own:

1. Use ADEDITVIEW to blank hidden lines in the top view.
2. Change the Drawing Number to EX17-2.

The final drawing appears as shown in Figure 17–24.

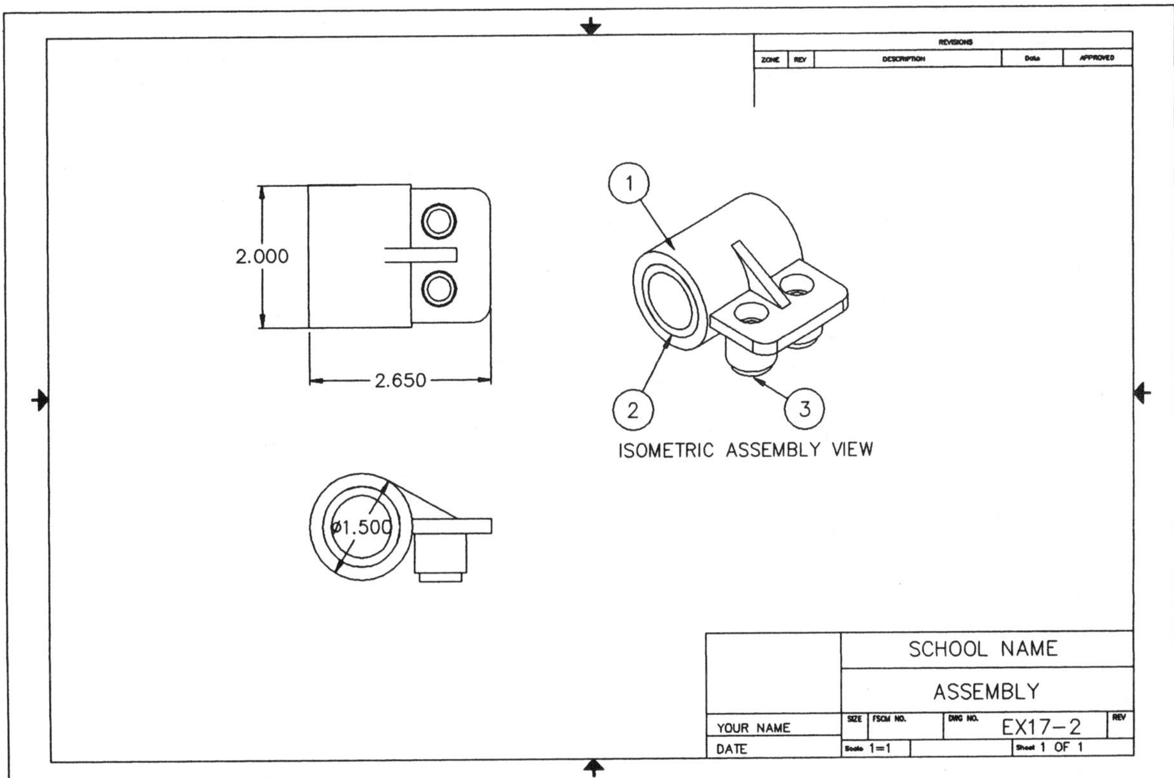

FIGURE 17–24
The Final Drawing

3. Plot the drawing at ½ scale (.5 = 1) on an 11″ × 8.5″ sheet.
4. Save the drawing in two places and exit AutoCAD.

Now, change the model by making changes to parametric dimensions on the drawing and see them reflected in the model and on all views of the drawing. Use the model created in Exercise 17–1.

EXERCISE 17–3
CHANGING PARAMETRIC DIMENSIONS ON THE DRAWING TO UPDATE THE MODEL AND ALL VIEWS OF THE DRAWING

Your final drawing will look similar to Figure 17–25.

Set Up the Drawing

Step 1. On Your Own:

1. Pick New. . . from the menu bar File menu. Name the drawing: 17-3 (your initials) = 17-1 (your initials).
2. Use the ADMODDIM command to change two dimensions on the drawing, and update the model so that the part is changed to the new dimensions.

   Before you use the ADMODDIM command for the first time, let's examine it.

ADMODDIM

This command allows you to change a dimension value on the active sketch or on the drawing. It works only on parametric dimensions. Use ADUPDATE to update the model

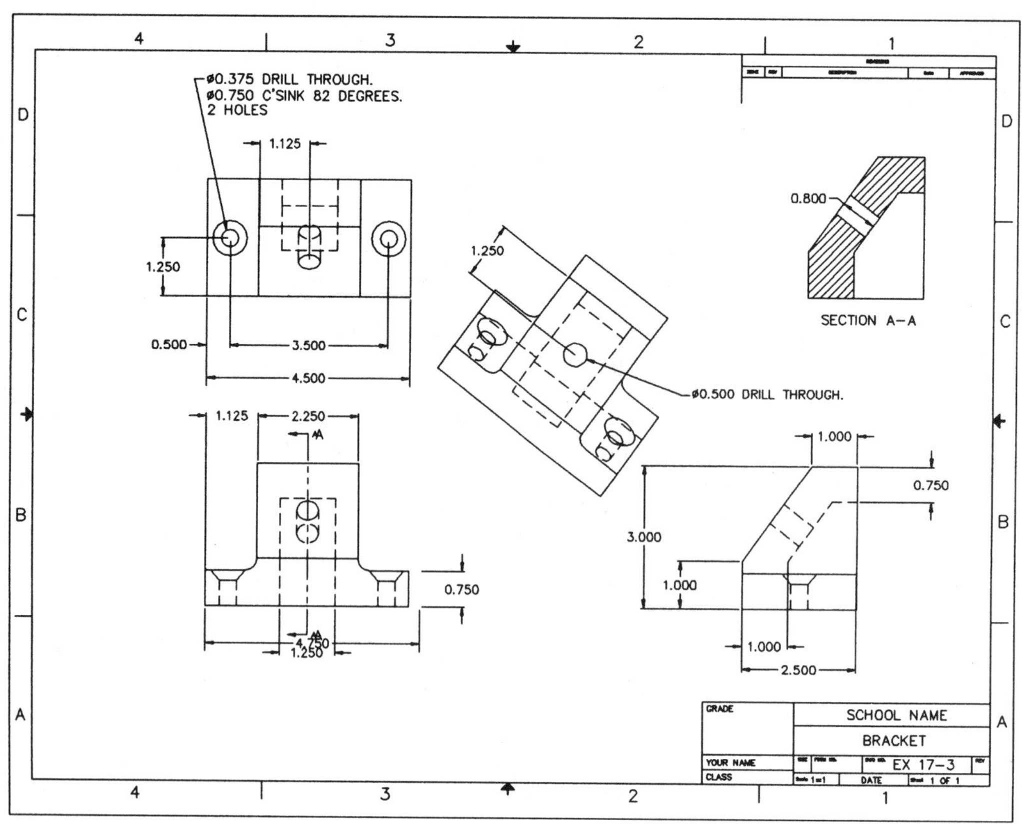

FIGURE 17–25
The Final Drawing

and the drawing views when you are changing the model or the drawing. The update is automatic when you are working on a sketch.

Modify and Add Dimensions and Plot the Drawing

Prompt	**Response**
Command:	**Change Dimension**
Select dimension to change:	*Pick:* **D1** (the 0.750 dimension) (Figure 17–26)
New value for dimension <0.750>:	*Type:* **1** ↵
Select dimension to change:	*Pick:* **D2** (the 0.500 dimension)

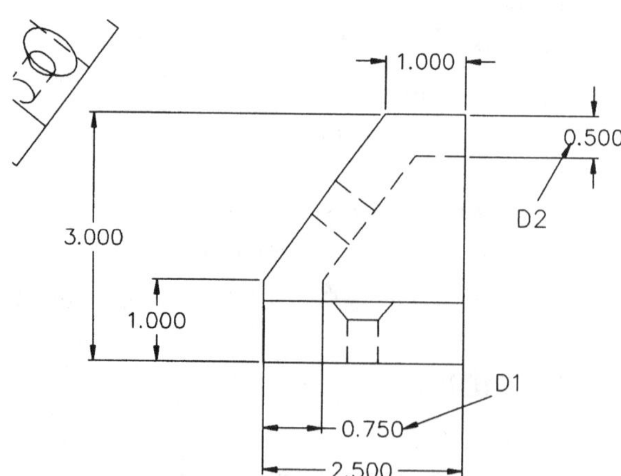

FIGURE 17–26
Changing Parametric Dimensions

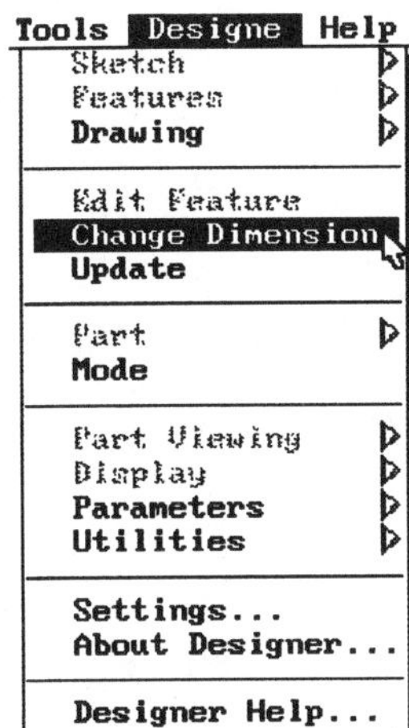

New value for dimension <0.500>:

Select dimension to change: *Type:* **.75** ↵

Select dimension to change: ↵

Command: **Update**

The drawing appears as shown in Figure 17–27.

Step 2. On Your Own:

1. Add a reference dimension to the sectional view.
2. Erase the old reference dimension.
3. Turn on the ADD_VIEWS layer.
4. Move the sectional view and the new reference dimension to the upper right corner, as shown in Figure 17–28.
5. Turn off the ADD_VIEWS layer.
6. Change the drawing number to EX17-3.
7. Plot the drawing at ½ scale (.5 = 1) on an 11″ × 8.5″ sheet.
8. Save the drawing in two places and exit AutoCAD.

Other Editing Considerations

Update Failures

Update failures occur when dimensions or constraints make the sketch impossible to solve. Designer will highlight the problem area and give you the opportunity to change dimensions or constraints in that area using ADEDITFEAT and try to update again.

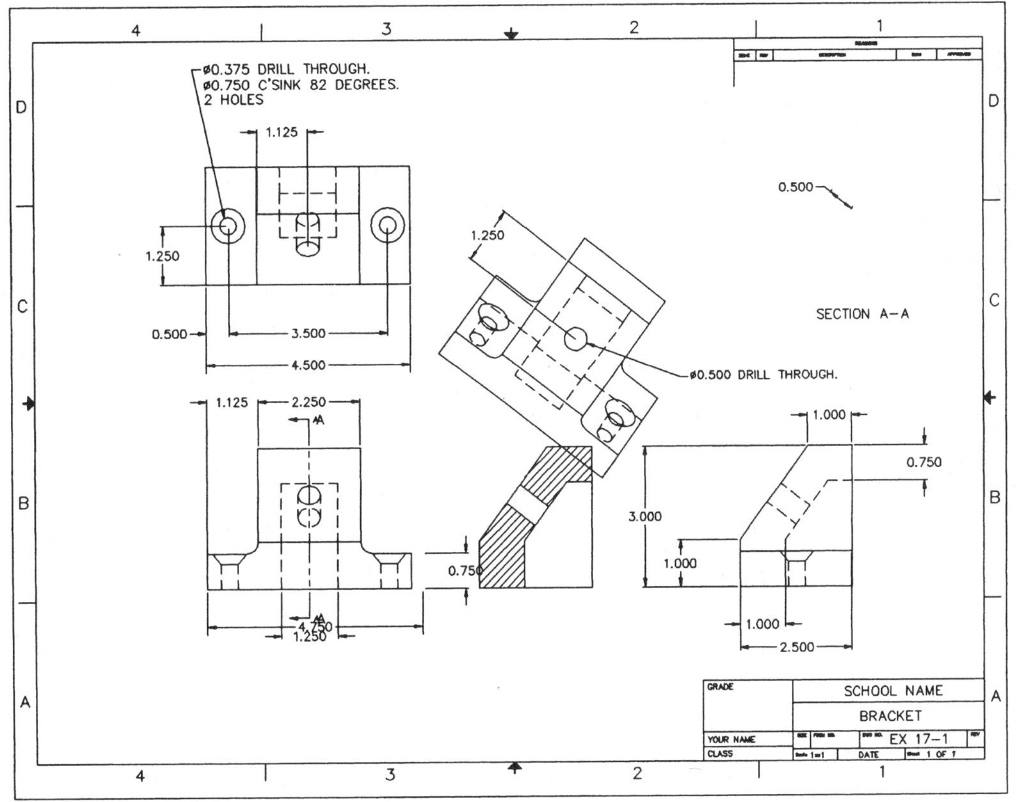

FIGURE 17–27
The Updated Drawing

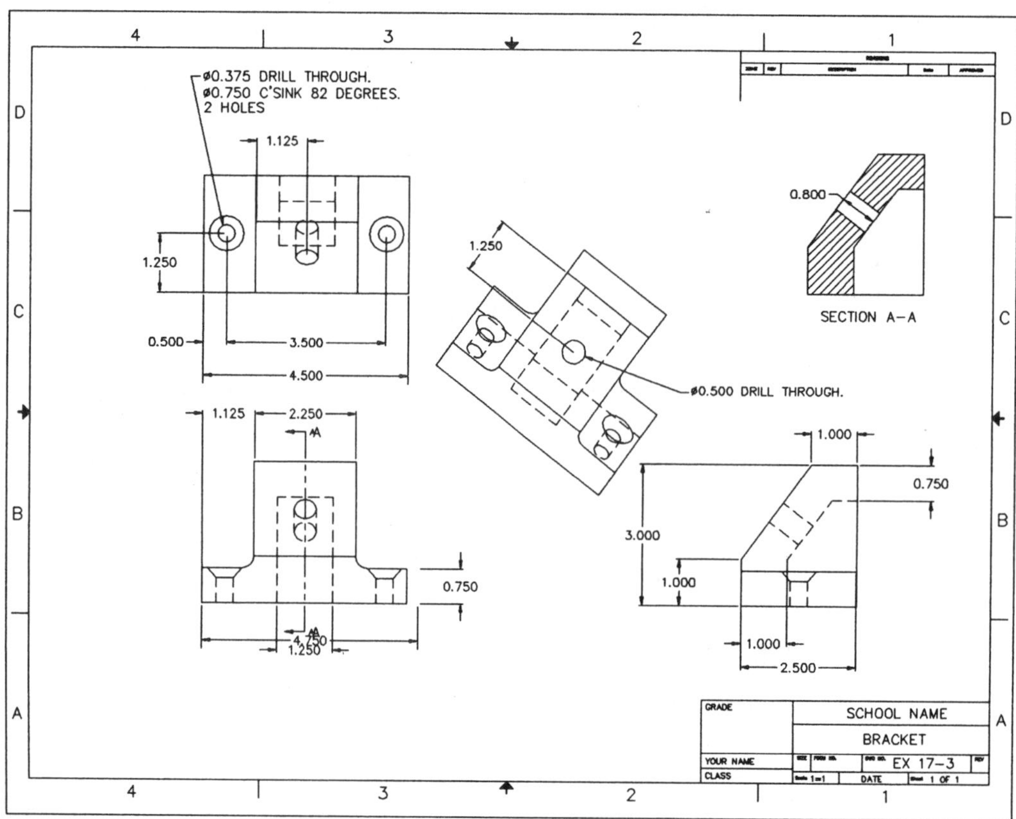

FIGURE 17–28
The Final Corrected Drawing

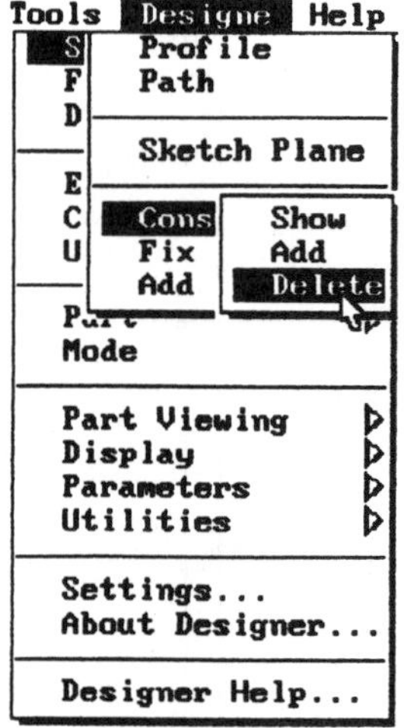

Overconstrained Sketches

Designer will not solve overconstrained sketches. An *overconstrained* sketch has two or more dimensions or constraints for the same item—for example, a vertical line that has both a vertical constraint and a 90° angle dimension. To delete dimensions use the Erase: command. To delete constraints use the ADDELCON command.

Making Copies of Parts

When you make a copy of a part using Copy:, Block:, Wblock:, or Insert:, the parametric information is lost. Do not use these commands to make copies of a solid if you want to maintain the parametric relationships on the copy. Use the command ADPARTOUT instead of Copy:, Block:, or Wblock: to make the copy. Use ADPARTIN instead of Insert: to bring the copy into the drawing.

ADPARTOUT

ADPARTOUT allows you to name the part and specify an insertion point and gives it the .DWG extension. This command writes out the solid part only; no drawings are included. ADPARTOUT works only in part mode.

ADPARTIN

ADPARTIN allows you to select any Designer solid by name, specify an insertion point, and bring it into the current drawing. This command reads in the solid part only; no drawings are included. ADPARTIN works only in part mode.

Reducing File Size

Often the file size of a drawing becomes very large even though features have not been added. This is caused by the retention of unreferenced blocks that are used by the program as the drawing is created. To delete these blocks, use the following procedure:

Start AutoCAD without loading Designer. (If Designer is located automatically use the Utilities command Unload Designer.)

Open the drawing you want to reduce in size.

Type PURGE ↵, then type B ↵ to select the blocks option, and type Y for "Yes you want to Purge the block".

Save the purged drawing so that it overwrites the original one.

You may have a large number of blocks on any particular drawing. The drawing shown in Figure 17–1 had over 200 unreferenced blocks. Drawing file size was reduced from 570,000 bytes to 170,000 bytes after the Purge: command was used.

You may also reduce the file size by making base features of any part you do not want to edit. The command ADMAKEBASE reduces the size of the part, often dramatically. Use Make Base, for example, when you are making an assembly drawing and positioning parts but not editing them.

Do Not Use Fractions for Entering Dimensions

Although Designer recognizes fractions and often interprets them correctly, ADUPDATE sometimes experiences an error as a result of a fractional dimension. You can have fractional values on the drawing by setting the fractional option on the Units: command, but you must enter decimal values at all Designer prompts.

EXERCISES

17–1. Follow the instructions in this chapter to draw Figure 17–1. Your final drawing should look like that figure.

17–2. Follow the instructions in this chapter to draw Figure 17–21. Your final drawing should look like that figure.

17–3. Follow the instructions in this chapter to draw Figure 17–28. Your final drawing should look like that figure.

17–4. Make the following changes to Exercise 16–4, Figure 16–53:

1. Change the 1.50 dia hole to 1.25 dia.
2. Change the 1.00 dia holes to .75 dia.
3. Change the 2.800 dimension to 3.250.
4. Change the 1.00 R to .75 R, 3 places.

Use the ADUPDATE command to update all views of the model and the model itself.

Your final drawing should look like Figure 16–53 with the preceding changes.

Plot the drawing at ½ scale (.5 = 1), X Origin 1, Y Origin 1, and Plot Rotation 90 on an 11″ × 8.5″ sheet.

17–5. Make the following changes to Exercise 16–5, Figure 16–54:

1. Change the 2.8 radius in the front sectional view to 3.0.
2. Change the 2.5 radius to 2.7.
3. Change the 3.50 diameter to 3.75 diameter.
4. Change the 2.50 diameter to 2.75 diameter.

Use the ADUPDATE command to update all views of the model and the model itself.

Your final drawing should look like Figure 16–54 with the preceding changes.

Plot the drawing at ½ scale (.5 = 1), X Origin 1, Y Origin 1, and Plot Rotation 90 on an 11″ × 8.5″ sheet.

17–6. Make the following changes to Exercise 16–6, Figure 16–55:

1. Change the 0.500 diameter hole in the top view to .625 diameter, 2 places.
2. Change the 2.000 diameter to 1.750 diameter.
3. Delete the 0.375 diameter hole, 2 places.
4. Change the 2.500 dimension to 2.250.
5. Change the 5.000 dimension to 4.500.

Use the ADUPDATE command to update all views of the model and the model itself.

Your final drawing should look like Figure 16–55 with the preceding changes.

Plot the drawing at ½ scale (.5 = 1), X Origin 1, Y Origin 1, and Plot Rotation 90 on an 11″ × 8.5″ sheet.

17–7. Make the following changes to Exercise 16–7, Figure 16–56:

1. Change the 0.50 diameter holes in the top view to .375 diameter, 2 places.
2. Change the 0.88 radius in the front view to 0.75.
3. Change the 1.38 radius in the front view to 1.50.
4. Change the 2.75 dimension in the front view to 3.00.

Use the ADUPDATE command to update all views of the model and the model itself.

Your final drawing should look like Figure 16–56 with the preceding changes.

Plot the drawing at ½ scale (.5 = 1), X Origin 1, Y Origin 1, and Plot Rotation 90 on an 11″ × 8.5″ sheet.

17–8. Make the following changes to Exercise 16–8, Figure 16–57:

1. Change the 0.600 diameter in the top view to 0.700 diameter.
2. Change the 0.700 diameter in the top view to 0.800 diameter.
3. Change the 3.550 dimension in the front view to 3.750.

4. Change the 3.850 dimension in the front view to 4.200.

Use the ADUPDATE command to update all views of the model and the model itself.

Your final drawing should look like Figure 16–57 with the preceding changes.

Plot the drawing at ½ scale (.5 = 1), X Origin 1, Y Origin 1, and Plot Rotation 90 on an 11″ × 8.5″ sheet.

17–9. Make the following changes to Exercise 16–9, Figure 16–58:

1. Change the 1.250 dimension in the top view to 1.500.
2. Change the 2.750 dimension in the top view to 3.250.
3. Delete the 0.750 diameter hole.
4. Change the 3.625 diameter in the front sectional view to 3.750.
5. Change the 1.750 dimension in the front sectional view to 2.500.

Use the ADUPDATE command to update all views of the model and the model itself.

Your final drawing should look like Figure 16–58 with the preceding changes.

Plot the drawing at ½ scale (.5 = 1), X Origin 1, Y Origin 1, and Plot Rotation 90 on an 11″ × 8.5″ sheet.

17–10. Make the following changes to Exercise 16–10, Figure 16–59:

1. Delete the four bolts and nuts and any holes associated with them.
2. Make a .500 radius on all four corners of item 6, the table.

Use the ADUPDATE command to update all views of the model and the model itself.

Your final drawing should look like Figure 16–59 with the preceding changes.

Plot the drawing at ½ scale (.5 = 1), X Origin 1, Y Origin 1, and Plot Rotation 90 on an 11″ × 8.5″ sheet.

REVIEW QUESTIONS

Circle the correct answer.

1. Which of the following is an option for the ADEDITFEAT command?
   a. Xy
   b. Yz
   c. Ucs
   d. Select work plane or planar face
   e. Sketch
2. The ADMODE command has only two modes, Part or Drawing.
   a. True b. False
3. When you activate the ADEDITFEAT command and select a hole which of the following is true?
   a. The hole is deleted.
   b. The Designer Hole dialog box appears, and you may change the hole to a counterbore from a countersink.
   c. The Designer Hole dialog box does not appear, and you are prompted to change the present diameter.
   d. The Designer Hole dialog box appears with the location dimensions and the hole diameter, any one of which may be changed.
   e. The hole is changed to the default diameter.
4. ADUPDATE works only in Part mode.
   a. True b. False
5. If you activate ADEDITFEAT and pick the part, but the feature you want to change is not highlighted, which is the correct response?
   a. Press ESC, then ↵, and pick another point on the part.
   b. Pick another point on the part.
   c. Press Ctrl-C and start over.
   d. *Type:* **N** ↵ until the feature you want is highlighted.
   e. Type: **U** ↵
6. What is the purpose of the Plan: command?
   a. To give you a plan view of the current UCS
   b. To give you a plan or top view of the part
   c. Allows you to view the part in an isometric view
   d. Gives you top, front, and right side drawing views automatically
   e. Is part of the MV Setup command
7. If the extrusion direction is incorrect after you pick OK on the Designer Extrusion dialog box, which is the correct response?
   a. Press ESC, then ↵, and pick another point on the part.
   b. *Type:* **F** ↵
   c. *Type:* **N** ↵
   d. Press Ctrl-C and start over.
   e. *Type:* **U** ↵
8. Which of the following is used to delete a hole on the active part?
   a. ADDELFEAT
   b. ADEDITFEAT
   c. ADUPDATE
   d. ADDELHOLE
   e. ADHOLE
9. Which of the following layers contains the lines defining the boundaries of the viewports in drawing mode?
   a. ADP_WORK
   b. ADP_FRZ
   c. ADV_1_VIS
   d. ADD_DIMS
   e. ADD_VIEWS
10. Which of the following is used to suppress an extension line on a reference dimension?
    a. ADREFDIM
    b. ADDIMATT
    c. ADDDELFEAT
    d. ADEDITVIEW
    e. ADDIM

Complete.

11. Which command is used to change the scale of a selected view?

    ____

12. Which command is used to blank hidden lines in a selected view?

    ____

13. Which command is used to change parametric dimensions?

    ____

14. Which command is used to delete features on the active part?

    ____

15. Which command must be used to copy parts with parametric features?

____

16. Which command must be used to insert parametric parts into the current drawing?

____

17. What happens if the Wblock: command is used to copy a parametric part?

____

18. Which command can be used to reduce the file size of a drawing?

____

19. Which command can be used to delete a constraint on an overconstrained sketch?

____

20. Which command can be used to make a base feature of a part you do not want to edit?

____

Index

A

B

C

D

T

U

V

W

Z